Handbook of Research Methods in Tourism

Quantitative and Qualitative Approaches

Edited by

Larry Dwyer

University of New South Wales, Australia

Alison Gill

Simon Fraser University, Canada

Neelu Seetaram

Bournemouth University, UK

Edward Elgar
Cheltenham, UK • Northampton, MA, USA

Published by
Edward Elgar Publishing Limited
The Lypiatts
15 Lansdown Road
Cheltenham
Glos GL50 2JA
UK

Edward Elgar Publishing, Inc.
William Pratt House
9 Dewey Court
Northampton
Massachusetts 01060
USA

A catalogue record for this book
is available from the British Library

Library of Congress Control Number: 2012935315

ISBN 978 1 78100 128 8 (cased)

Typeset by Servis Filmsetting Ltd, Stockport, Cheshire
Printed and bound by MPG Books Group, UK

Contents

Contributors

Kathleen M. Adams is Professor of Anthropology at Loyola University Chicago and Adjunct Curator at the Field Museum of Natural History. Her book, *Art as Politics: Recrafting Identities, Tourism and Power in Tana Toraja, Indonesia* (2006), received the 2009 Alpha Sigma Nu National Book Award. She also co-edited *Home and Hegemony: Domestic Work and Identity Politics in South and Southeast Asia* (2000) and *Everyday Life in Southeast Asia* (2011). Her articles on tourism and ethnic identity, travel and nation-building, cultural representations and politics of arts appear in *Annals of Tourism Research, Tourist Studies, American Ethnologist, Museum Anthropology* and other journals.

Ehsan Ahmed is an associate lecturer in the School of Marketing, Australian School of Business at the University of New South Wales. His research is based on inter-organizational relationships and networks. He has a particular interest in how the relationships between tourism stakeholders influence their behaviour and business decisions. Ehsan is currently researching his PhD at the University of New South Wales. In his thesis, Ehsan uses quantitative network analysis to examine how the relationships among tourism stakeholders influence socially responsible business practices such as saving energy, contributing to the local community and keeping a long-term balance between economic gain and non-economic stewardship.

Alexandros Apostolakis is a senior lecturer at the Department of Economics, University of Portsmouth. The research interests of Dr Apostolakis focus on the economics of tourism, economics of culture and cultural resources, database analysis, the analysis of discrete choice experiments, marketing and management of tourism and tourism businesses and the economics of defence. Dr Apostolakis has published in leading academic journals and has conducted extensive advisory work. He has also been a reviewer for several international journals such as the *Annals of Tourism Research, Tourism Management, Journal of Environmental Management, Oxford Economic Papers* and *Tourism Economics.*

Shuang Cang is a senior lecturer in statistics and quantitative analysis at the School of Tourism, Bournemouth University (UK). She gained her PhD from the University of Abertay Dundee (UK), MSc with distinction from King's College London (UK) and BSc with first class from Heilongjiang University (China). She has expertise and wide experience in data mining, artificial intelligence, pattern recognition and multivariate statistics. Her tourism-related research interests cover tourism demand forecasting model, tourist impact studies and tourism segmentation. She has served as a reviewer for tourism journals including the *Annals of Tourism Research* and *Tourism Management.*

Carl Cater is a lecturer in tourism at Aberystwyth University, Wales. His research centres on the experiential turn in tourism and the subsequent growth of special interest sectors, particularly adventure tourism and ecotourism. He has undertaken field research, supervision and teaching worldwide. He is a fellow of the Royal Geographical Society, a qualified pilot, diver, lifesaver, mountain and tropical forest leader, and maintains an interest in both the practice and pursuit of sustainable outdoor tourism activity. He has written over 20 papers and book chapters, is co-author (with Dr Erlet Cater) of *Marine Ecotourism: Between the Devil and the Deep Blue Sea* (CABI, 2007), and is an editorial board member of *Tourism Geographies, Journal of Ecotourism* and *Tourism in Marine Environments*.

Sarath Divisekera is an Associate Professor in Economics at Victoria University, Melbourne, Australia. Sarath has a Bachelor of Economics (First-Class Honors), a Masters in Development Economics and a PhD in the economics of travel and tourism. His recent research is mainly in the areas of tourism demand modelling and consumption analysis, tourism policy and taxation, and tourism and climate change. He has authored over 50 peer-reviewed articles and monographs, and has published in most top-tier tourism journals. He is the recipient of the Vice Chancellor's Citation Award for Excellence in Research (2008) and the Faculty of Business and Law Staff Research Award (2011). He was a visiting Professor at the National Centre for Tourism Policy Studies at Limerick University, Ireland, and FH JOANNEUM University of Applied Sciences, Austria. Sarath is an appointed member of the editorial board of *Tourism Economics*.

Dianne Dredge is an associate professor in the School of Tourism and Hospitality Management, Southern Cross University, Australia. She has 20 years experience as a tourism and environmental planner in Queensland, New South Wales, Canada, Mexico and China. Her work has included conceptual design and site analyses of large-scale integrated resort proposals; integration of tourism in strategic and local area plans; comparative analyses of competitive destinations; studies into the re-imaging of destinations in crisis; and assessment of the environmental impacts of tourism. She has also been involved in tourism capacity-building activities in local governments and tourism organizations, including stakeholder audits and community consultation. Dianne's current research is in local government tourism management, place-based planning and management of tourism destinations, capacity building in tourism organizations and tourism planning and policy.

Larry Dwyer, PhD, is Professor of Travel and Tourism Economics in the Australian School of Business at the University of New South Wales. Larry publishes widely in the areas of tourism economics, management and policy, and has been awarded numerous research grants to contribute to tourism knowledge. Larry is President of the International Academy for Study of Tourism, President of the International Association for Tourism Economics and a member of the International Advisory Board of the Business Enterprises for Sustainable Tourism Education Network (BESTEN). He is an appointed member of the editorial boards of 21 international tourism journals.

Eric W. Foemmel, PhD, is an independent researcher and writer living in California. Dr Foemmel is a graduate of the Recreation, Park and Tourism Management Department at Pennsylvania State University with a doctoral minor in anthropology. His primary interest is the study of the American tattoo culture, and he has conducted ethnographic research at Venice Beach and Traditional Ink in Los Angeles, California, to explore the intrinsic motivations behind tattooing and its impact on social norms. He has also collected the oral life histories of venerated tattooers who have heavily influenced the American tattoo industry. Dr Foemmel has also established a research and publishing company, Uptown Research, LLC.

Liz Fredline is a senior lecturer in the Department of Tourism, Leisure, Hotel and Sport Management at Griffith University, Queensland, Australia. She gained her doctorate at Griffith University. Her main area of research interest is the impacts of tourism and events on host communities. She is also interested in quantitative research design and analysis.

Alison Gill, PhD, is a professor at Simon Fraser University in Vancouver, British Columbia, Canada, where she holds a joint appointment in the Department of Geography and the School of Resource and Environmental Management. Alison has published extensively on issues of tourism and the transformation of place. For many years her research has focused on aspects of growth and change associated with tourism in mountain resort communities. She serves on a number of editorial boards for both geography and tourism journals and is a Fellow of the International Academy for the Study of Tourism.

Ulrike Gretzel is Associate Professor for Marketing at the Institute for Innovation in Business and Social Research, University of Wollongong, and Director of the Laboratory for Intelligent Systems in Tourism (LIST). She received her PhD in communications from the University of Illinois at Urbana-Champaign. Her research focuses on persuasion in human–technology interaction, experience design, use of technology for interpretation, adoption and use of social media, interorganizational information systems and other issues related to the development and use of intelligent systems in tourism. She uses qualitative and quantitative research methods and has a particular interest in network analysis and text mining.

Rob Hales is a lecturer in the Department of Tourism, Leisure, Hotel and Sport Management, Griffith University, Australia. His research interests focus on social science issues in a range of contexts that include sustainable tourism, ecotourism, outdoor recreation, social movement studies and indigenous studies. His current research interest is a community-based project aiming to understand urban and peri-urban Indigenous Peoples' vulnerability and adaptive capacity to climate change. The central theme running through all his research projects is an emphasis on social and environmental justice issues. His background in environmental science, eco- and adventure guiding as well as outdoor environmental education informs his research and teaching.

Gayle R. Jennings, PhD, is the Director of Research, Imagine Consulting Group International. Her research agenda focuses on practical and applied research for business and industry, research training and education, qualitative methodologies, and quality tourism experiences. Gayle is also Adjunct Professor of Tourism Management, Department of Tourism, Leisure, Hotel and Sport Management, Griffith University, Gold Coast Campus. She has sole authored and edited a number of books, written book chapters and journal articles across a range of topics relating to theoretical paradigms that inform research processes, education, waterbased tourism and quality tourism experiences.

Olga Junek is a lecturer in tourism and events management at Victoria University, Melbourne. Her lengthy overseas work experience in education and tourism has given her a broad international perspective, which permeates her teaching and her research interests. She teaches and researches in a number of tourism and events-related areas, including event and tourism education, internationalization of the curriculum and the well-being of international students. She is currently undertaking her PhD in the area of international students and their leisure and travel behaviour.

Heather Kennedy-Eden is a PhD candidate in the Institute for Innovation in Business and Social Research at the University of Wollongong and a research assistant in the Laboratory for Intelligent Systems in Tourism (LIST). She has 15-years experience working in the tourism industry, specifically event management, hotel operations, environment interpretation and the travel industry. Her research focuses on the influence of smart phones on family bonding and family vacation, adoption and use of social media, technology adoption in event management and other areas related to technology use in tourism and involves qualitative as well as quantitative research methods.

Les Killion is Associate Professor in Tourism at Central Queensland University, Australia, where he has served as Head of School of Marketing and Tourism. He has undertaken research consultancies for regional tourism authorities and destination marketing organizations in New South Wales and Central Queensland. His research interests, founded primarily on qualitative approaches and paradigms, are in the areas of tourism policy, impacts assessment, marketing and development and events management.

Gerard Kyle is a professor within the Department of Recreation, Park and Tourism Sciences at Texas A&M University. His research is informed by theory rooted in environmental/conservation psychology and explores humans' interactions and response to nature and wildland areas. This work primarily relies on survey research methods and multivariate modelling tools to construct models of human behaviour in varied contexts. Applications have examined an array of human dimensions-related issues within the United States and Australia related to wildfire management, coastal and inland fisheries management, climate change, invasive species and other threats to parks and protected areas. His peer-reviewed articles have been published in the *Journal of Environmental Psychology, Environment & Behavior, Society & Natural Resources* and *Leisure Sciences*.

Jenny (Jiyeon) Lee is a lecturer of School of Marketing at the University of New South Wales, Sydney, Australia. She received her doctoral degree in Recreation, Park, and Tourism Sciences from the Texas A&M University. Her research interest lies in tourism marketing, focusing on place meaning/attachment, tourist behaviours and psychology and structural equation modelling. Her research has spanned a wide domain to address managerial and marketing issues, both the public (i.e., park services) and private sectors (i.e., travel agencies, festivals/events, and destination marketing organizations). Her work is published in *Journal of Travel Research*, *Journal of Travel and Tourism Marketing*, and *Journal of Park and Recreation Administration*.

Zheng Lei is a lecturer in the Department of Air Transport at Cranfield University, UK. He received his doctorate from Surrey University. His main research interests are aviation policy, business strategy and regional competitiveness. He is a specialist in panel data analysis and has also served as a reviewer for several international journals such as *Annals of Tourism Research*. He is Assistant Editor of the *Journal of Air Transport Studies*.

Gang Li is a senior lecturer in economics in the School of Hospitality and Tourism Management at the University of Surrey in the UK, where he also received his PhD in 2004. Before then, he studied economics and statistics in China. Dr Li's research interests include econometric modelling and forecasting of tourism demand and quantitative studies of tourist behaviour. His research is published in leading tourism and forecasting journals such as *Annals of Tourism Research*, *Tourism Management*, *Journal of Travel Research* and *International Journal of Forecasting*. He is a co-author of the book *The Advanced Econometrics of Tourism Demand* (2009).

Tiffany Low is a researcher based at the Institute for Tourism Research at the University of Bedfordshire. She completed double degrees in Business and Hotel Management with a specialism in financial economics. She is currently undertaking research for a PhD examining how customers value ethical consumption in the hotel sector. Tiffany has worked as a research assistant at universities in Australia and has experience project managing research projects funded under the Commonwealth Government's Australian Research Council; one involving the conceptualization and measurement of derived customer value in relation to the timeshare industry; and the second in relation to the needs of customers and employees following service failures.

Nancy Gard McGehee is an associate professor and J. Willard and Alice S. Marriott Junior Faculty Fellow of Hospitality in the Hospitality and Tourism Management Department at Virginia Tech, Blacksburg, VA, USA. She is a sociologist whose primary research interests fall under the socio-cultural impacts of tourism development. Nancy has explored this in a number of contexts, including tourism-related entrepreneurship, the role of tourism in the cultivation of various forms of community capital, and volunteer tourism. While she has conducted research using a wide range of methods, Nancy's passion lies in qualitative research, as it allows for a more critical and interpretive perspective.

Clive Morley is Professor of Quantitative Analysis and Deputy Head (Learning and Teaching) in the Graduate School of Business and Law at RMIT, where he teaches in the MBA. His expertise lies in the areas of applied quantitative data analysis, tourism economics, forecasting and strategic analysis techniques. He has published a series of papers in leading journals on the theory and practice of tourism demand modelling and on the impacts of global airline alliances on tourism. Other research has considered the entrepreneurial climate in Australia, the (mis)use of performance indicators in Australian call centres, the career progression of women in accounting, Australian football attendances and why business academics remain in academia.

Andreas Papatheodorou is Associate Professor in Industrial and Spatial Economics with Emphasis on Tourism at the School of Business Administration, University of the Aegean, Greece. He is also an external examiner at Cranfield University. He received his doctorate from the University of Oxford and commenced his academic career at the

University of Surrey, UK. His research interests are related to competition, competitiveness and regional development in tourism with focus on air transport. He is also the Editor-in-Chief of the *Journal of Air Transport Studies* and a resource editor for *Annals of Tourism Research*.

Grace Bo Peng graduated from the School of Economics, Xiamen University, with a Bachelor degree in finance and law. She was an exchange student with Feng Chia University in Taiwan for one semester during her undergraduate study and joined the School of Hotel and Tourism Management at the Hong Kong Polytechnic University as an MPhil student in August 2010. Her MPhil research topic is 'A meta-analysis of international tourism demand elasticities and forecasting accuracy'.

Sylvain Petit is an assistant professor at the Faculté de Droit, d'Economie et de Gestion, University of Valenciennes et Hainaut-Cambrésis (France) where he teaches international trade, econometrics and history of economics. He is the manager of the Mobility and Sustainable Development branch for the laboratory of the Institut de Développement et de Prospective (Institute of Development and Prospects) at University of Valenciennes. He is an executive member of the board of the International Association for Tourism Economics (IATE). He obtained his PhD from the University of Lille I. With co-authors Dr J-J. Nowak and Dr M. Sahli, he was awarded best paper prize at the 3rd conference of IATE in 2011. His research areas are tourism economics, international trade and applied econometrics.

Tien Duc Pham, PhD, is a lecturer at the School of Tourism, Queensland University. He has a strong background in impact analysis using the CGE modelling technique in general, and has applied the technique to tourism research in recent years. He has been heavily involved in the production of tourism satellite account at the state and sub-state levels of the Australian Economy. Dr Pham has been awarded several research grants from Sustainable Tourism Cooperative Research Centre, Australia. He also provides consultancy advice on tourism issues to Australian government departments.

Clemente Polo is Professor of Economics at the Universidad Autónoma de Barcelona since 1992. He obtained his BA in economics at the Universidad Complutense de Madrid in 1972 and his PhD at the Universidad Autónoma de Barcelona in 1984. He served as economic adviser to the President of Spain from 1990 until 1993. He has taught at other Spanish universities. His research has focused on the study of the effects of fiscal policies, tourism shocks and public capital accumulation using input–output, SAM, CGE and econometric models. His work has been published in prestigious international and national journals and books.

Nuno F. Ribeiro, PhD, is a Research Associate with the Indigenous Peoples' Health Research Centre in Saskatchewan, Canada. Dr Ribeiro's research interests are primarily related to the comparative study of culture and behaviour within tourism and leisure contexts, with parallel interests in the development and application of innovative research methodologies. Dr Ribeiro's educational background is in tourism planning and development and cultural anthropology and he holds graduate degrees from the Pennsylvania State University in University Park, United States in tourism management and anthropology. He has been awarded several research grants, keeps an active research and publication agenda, and has presented in numerous scholarly conferences and symposia.

Jaume Rosselló gained his PhD in economics and business at the University of the Balearic Islands (Spain) in 2001. He is Associate Professor at the Department of Applied Economics and Associate Researcher at the Economic Research Center, and teaches microeconomics and tourism economics at the same university. He is director of the Master in Tourism and Environmental Economics. His main research interests include tourism demand modelling, environmental economics and climate change. In 2009 he was awarded with the honour of 'Emerging Scholar of Distinction' from the International Academy for the Study of Tourism.

Carla Almeida Santos is an associate professor and Director of Graduate Studies in the Department of Recreation, Sport and Tourism at the University of Illinois. Her research programme is focused on the examination of communicative practices as a means of addressing the socio-political and cultural impact of tourism on the world's people and cultures. She currently serves on the editorial boards of *Annals of Tourism Research*, *Journal of Travel Research*, *Journal of Hospitality and Tourism Management* and *Tourism, Culture and Communication*.

Neelu Seetaram is a lecturer in tourism development and impacts at Bournemouth University, UK. She is a member of the editorial board of the *Journal of Travel Research* and co-editor of a special issue of the *Journal Tourism Economics*. She is an executive member of the Board of the International Association for Tourism Economics (IATE) and a member of the German Aviation Research Society. She obtained her PhD at Monash University (Australia) and recipient of the Hamburg Airport prize for best PhD paper in 2009. Neelu has an MSc in economics and econometrics from Nottingham University, UK, and a BSc (Hons) in economics from the University of Mauritius. Her research interests are focused on the areas of tourism and airline economics, demand modeling and economic impact studies.

Changsup Shim is a PhD candidate in the Department of Recreation, Sport and Tourism at the University of Illinois. He completed a master's degree in urban and regional planning at the Seoul National University in South Korea and has been involved in multiple tourism research projects. His research is focused on the impact of globalization, commercialism and urban development on the concept of place and local identity. He approaches this issue through tourism and leisure phenomena that take place in contemporary metropolitan areas. His research interests include: urban tourism, cultural sustainability, authenticity, urban regeneration and postmodernism.

Haiyan Song is Chair Professor of Tourism and Associate Dean of the School of Hotel and Tourism Management at the Hong Kong Polytechnic University. His research interests include tourism demand modelling and forecasting, tourist impact assessment, tourism supply chain management and tourist satisfaction studies. He has published widely in such journals as *Annals of Tourism Research*, *Tourism Management*, and *Journal of Travel Research*. Haiyan is a Fellow and First Vice President of the International Academy for the Study of Tourism.

Svetlana Stepchenkova, PhD, is an assistant professor at the Department of Tourism, Recreation and Sport Management at the University of Florida and an associate director of the Eric Friedheim Tourism Institute. Her research interests include destination management, marketing and branding, with a focus on quantitative assessment of destination image using qualitative data. Svetlana studies the influence of media messages on image formation, and destination image as a factor in explaining destination choice. Svetlana is also interested in applications of information technologies in travel and tourism, particularly virtual travel communities, destination websites and user-generated content as a means of obtaining a competitive advantage in destination marketing and management.

Dallen J. Timothy is Professor of Community Resources and Development and Senior Sustainability Scientist at Arizona State University. He is also Visiting Professor of Heritage Tourism at the University of Sunderland (UK) and Adjunct Professor of Geography at Indiana University. Professor Timothy is the editor of the *Journal of Heritage Tourism* and serves on the editorial boards of 11 international journals. His tourism-related research interests include intangible heritage, religious tourism, visual images, responsible tourism, geopolitics, supranational and globalization, and developing region dynamics. He currently has ongoing research projects in Israel/Palestine, Western Europe, Central America, Mexico and South Asia.

Lindsay W. Turner is Professor of Econometrics in the School of International Business at Victoria University, Australia. He is also a professorial research fellow at the Central University of Finance and Economics, Beijing and Senior Research Fellow in the Institute of the Chinese Economy, Peking University, Beijing. Lindsay is an internationally recognized researcher and a specialist in tourism forecasting and tourism economics. He is author of the *Pacific Asia Travel Association (PATA) Forecasts* published annually. Lindsay is a Fellow of the International Academy for the Study of Tourism and the International Association of Scientific Experts in Tourism, special advisor on the editorial board of the journal *Tourism Economics*, editorial board member of the *Journal of Travel Research* and the *China Tourism Research Journal*.

Elisabeth Valle is Doctor Assistant at the Department of Applied Economics at the University of the Balearic Islands (UIB). She has a Bachelor's Degree in economics from UIB (1998), and in 2004 she got her PhD from the same university with the thesis 'Multisectorial models applied to the Balearic economy', a project awarded with the II International Prize of Tourist Studies Gabriel Escarrer 2005. Her research is focused on input–output tables, systems of social accounting and general equilibrium models.

Chau Vu is a senior lecturer in the Faculty of Business and Law, School of Accounting and Finance at Victoria University, Melbourne. Her research interests include tourism economics and forecasting, applied quantitative data analysis and financial econometrics. She has published in journals such as the *Journal of Tourism Research*, *Tourism and Hospitality Research* and *Tourism Economics*.

Stephen F. Witt is Emeritus Professor (Tourism Forecasting) in the Faculty of Business, Economics and Law at the University of Surrey, UK, and a consultant to the Pacific Asia Travel Association (PATA) based in Bangkok, Thailand. His main research interests are econometric modelling of international tourism demand and assessment of the accuracy of different forecasting methods within the tourism context. He has published 150 journal articles and book chapters as well as 30 books. The latter include: *The Tourism Marketing and Management Handbook*; *The Management of International Tourism*; *Modeling and Forecasting Demand in Tourism*; *The Advanced Econometrics of Tourism Demand*; *Tourism Forecasts for Europe 2001–2005*; and *Asia Pacific Tourism Forecasts 2011–2013*.

Preface

The chapters in this book address the most important established and emerging qualitative and quantitative research methods in tourism. There are many books on research methods, including research methods in tourism. The question thus arises: why another book? Our response to this question is that we are not aware of any book that structures the material on research methods in the way that the authors have done for this book. Each chapter is structured to provide detailed overview of the nature of the research method, its use in tourism, its advantages and limitations and future directions for research.

The process began with a determination of the major research methods that are used by tourism researchers, quantitative, qualitative and mixed. While we believe that we have selected the major research methods in current use, we are aware that some readers will be disappointed that one or other research method has not been included. To this we must plead that any book such as this has limitations on length. While we acknowledge that the book does not address all research methods used by tourism researchers, the content does capture the methods that are most used at the present time.

The next step was to invite authors to contribute to the book. All are active researchers in tourism and all have international standing in the discipline. All have published works that use the technique that they write about. The 42 authors are based in 30 universities in eight countries giving the book a truly international perspective. A biography for each contributor is given at the beginning of the book.

An important element of the book is that all of the authors were required to structure their chapter in the same way.

1. Nature of the technique and its evolution
2. Background and types of problems that the technique is designed to handle
3. Applications of the technique to tourism, including discussion of studies that have used the technique and their findings
4. Advantages and limitations of technique conceptually and for policy formulation
5. Further developments and applications of the technique in tourism research

We believe that this structure makes the contents of each chapter much more informative to the reader, providing a comprehensive discussion of the technique itself as well as its application in tourism and related contexts. We are confident that the imposed structure will result in the individual contributions making an important contribution to tourism studies, ensuring that each will be highly informative and widely referenced in the literature. The chapters are constructed in a way that they provide a detailed overview of the different techniques irrespective of their tourism applications. In this way the volume should appeal to social scientists in general and not just to researchers in tourism. We would like to take this opportunity to thank each of the contributors for the professional way that they approached their tasks and for the high quality of their contributions.

PART I

QUANTITATIVE RESEARCH METHODS

In the last two decades the application of quantitative techniques in the study of the tourism phenomenon has gained momentum. This can be traced back to several factors. The most prominent is perhaps the fact that, as the reliance of destinations on tourism has grown and the industry expanded globally, more resources have been devoted to the collection of quantitative data and the maintenance of tourism data sets. This may have encouraged researchers interested in quantitative data analysis to give higher priority to the tourism industry in their research agenda. At the same time stakeholders in the industry, including destination managers and local and federal governments, keen to make more informed decisions, by devising better policies and evaluating existing ones are paying more attention to results from quantitative research. Consequently, the application of quantitative methods in tourism data analysis has become more pronounced in academic and non-academic research enriching the literature.

Ideally, this section would have addressed all the various quantitative techniques used in tourism research. However, limited by space and time, the contributions in this section of the book do not address the full range of quantitative research methods in tourism. They do, however, cover the most important ones used by tourism researchers. This introduction does not do justice to the detailed arguments and comprehensive treatment of the issues that comprise the content of the different contributions. It is intended, hopefully, to 'whet the reader's appetite' for the much more detailed discussion in each chapter.

As highlighted by Gang Li in Chapter 1, **Statistical testing techniques** are key in quantitative tourism research. A statistical hypothesis test is a method of making decisions using data, whether from a controlled experiment or an observational study (not controlled). In statistics, a result is called statistically significant if it is unlikely to have occurred by chance alone, according to a pre-determined threshold probability, the significance level. Given different assumptions concerning the distribution of the population, statistical techniques can be broadly divided into parametric and non-parametric groups. Both parametric and non-parametric tests have their advantages as well as limitations. Tourism researchers are interested in examining the behavioural characteristics of consumers in a variety of tourism contexts, such as tourists' perception of destination images, travel motivation, behavioural intention, perceived service performance and satisfaction. In addition, some researchers are interested in the perceptions, attitudes and behaviours of residents in tourist destinations. Statistical testing is regularly performed

1

in these tourism studies in order to obtain robust findings and conclusions. Li argues that, in general, parametric tests are more popular than their non-parametric alternatives in tourist behaviour studies, mainly because they are relatively more robust and capable of handling complicated research designs. By introducing more and more newly developed, robust, non-parametric techniques into future tourism research, he claims that the accuracy and reliability of research findings can be further improved.

As Jaume Rosselló indicates in Chapter 2, **Regression analysis** includes many techniques for modeling and analysing several variables, when the focus is on the relationship between a dependent variable and one or more independent variables. Regression analysis, which is being increasingly used in both demand and supply side analyses in tourism, helps one understand how the typical value of the dependent variable changes when any one of the independent variables is varied, while the other independent variables are held fixed. When a causal relationship between a 'dependent variable' and one or more 'independent variables' is hypothesized, regression analysis comes to the fore as a technique for use in circumstances where a particular phenomenon is controlled and determined by certain factors, and the aim is to try to explain and quantify variations in the dependent variable through variations in the independent ones. Most commonly, regression analysis estimates the conditional expectation of the dependent variable given the independent variables – that is, the average value of the dependent variable when the independent variables are held fixed. Less commonly, the focus is on a quantile, or other location parameter of the conditional distribution of the dependent variable given the independent variables. In all cases, the estimation target is a function of the independent variables called the *regression function*. In regression analysis, it is also of interest to characterize the variation of the dependent variable around the regression function, which can be described by a probability distribution. As Rosselló emphasizes, however, correlation does not imply causation. This is because a spurious relationship is always possible between variables where some degree of covariance can be found.

In Chapter 3, Cang and Seetaram provide an exposé of **Time series analysis** as applied in the tourism context. They first discuss the properties of time series data, such as stationarity, seasonality and existence of structural breaks in the data. These properties are important as they provide information on how the data behave under different circumstances. For example, the effect of a shock, such as a terrorist attack on tourists, will have a permanent effect on a destination if the data on international arrivals is non-stationary. These properties also assist the researchers in their choice of modelling techniques. The basis for time series modelling is that the current data is dependent on their historical values. The aim of time series modelling is to predict the future values of the data with as low margin of error as possible.

Following this, the authors discuss model selection to predict future trends in the data set, as well as estimation techniques. The review of literature on time series techniques shows that newer models are better at prediction but there is no single class of models which dominates in terms of accuracy in forecasting.

This argument is further expanded by Grace Bo Peng, Haiyan Song and Stephen Witt in **Demand Modeling and Forecasting**, the topic of Chapter 4. Tourism demand is normally measured by either tourist arrivals in a destination, tourists' expenditure when they visit a destination or tourist nights stayed in the destination. The variables that have been generally accepted as the main determinants of international tourism demand comprise potential tourists' income levels, the relative price of tourism products in the origin and destination countries, substitute prices of tourism products in alternative foreign destinations, transportation cost, population of origin country, exchange rates, marketing expenditure by the destination in the origin country and one-off events (which can have a positive or negative effect). Quantitative forecasting methods organize past tourism demand information by mathematical rules and there are three main subcategories: time series models, econometric approaches and artificial intelligence methods. Within these categories there are numerous different approaches as outlined by the authors. Peng, Song and Witt note that past empirical findings show that no single forecasting method is superior to others in all situations. The forecasting performance of the models varies considerably depending on the forecast error measure, the forecasting horizon, data frequency, destination–origin country pairs and the competitors included in a comparison. An ongoing objective of tourism forecasting is therefore to find optimal forecasting models according to the data characteristics. Future research directions identified by the authors include use of meta analysis to synthesize the research findings of the previous studies over the past four to five decades with a view to generalizing the research findings based on the characteristics of the data used in the tourism forecasting literature. The authors also recommend a forecasting competition based on a wide range of forecasting methods used in the past literature with the involvement of the experts who have published extensively using the quantitative methods highlighted above. In conclusion, the integration of judgmental (qualitative) forecasts and quantitative forecasts would also be a useful direction for future research as this research topic has been relatively scarce in the tourism context.

In Chapter 5, Jiyeon (Jenny) Lee and Gerard Kyle discuss **Structural equation modeling**, a statistical technique for testing and estimating causal relations using a combination of statistical data and qualitative causal assumptions. Structural equation models (SEM) combine both multiple regression and factor analysis (see Chapter 10). Structural equation models go beyond ordinary regression models to incorporate multiple independent and dependent variables as well as latent constructs that cluster the observed variables they are hypothesized to represent. They also provide a way to test a specified set of relationships among observed and latent variables as a whole, and allow theory testing even when experiments are not possible. As a result, these methods have become ubiquitous in all the social and behavioural sciences. Factor analysis, path analysis and regression all represent special cases of SEM. With an advance of statistical software with graphical user interfaces, several 'user-friendly' SEM programs have become accessible to tourism researchers. Of these, the most widely used programs are LISREL (Linear Structural Relationships), AMOS (Analysis of Moment Structures), EQS (Equations), Mplus, and PLS (Partial Least Squares). In tourism research, the technique has primarily been limited to: (1) the use of confirmatory (and sometimes combined with exploratory) factor analysis to determine scale structure, psychometric properties, and for scale purification; (2) testing causal relationships among latent (and sometimes manifest) variables; and (3) testing for measurement and structural model invariance across select groups. Lee and Kyle identify several advantages of SEM over other analytical methodologies for hypothesis testing. Given the analysis can be applied to both non-experimental and experimental data, it provides researchers with modeling flexibility; an array of analytical capabilities (i.e., multi-group invariance testing); and the ability to account for measurement error. Limitations of SEM are also highlighted including that SEM requires a priori specifications, which implies that model development and modification should be directed by theory and empirical evidence making it inappropriate for exploratory research where the measurement structure is not well defined or where guiding theory and empirical evidence underlying patterns of construct relationships is not well established. Another limitation of the use of SEM and the use of the maximum likelihood estimation is associated with its inherent assumption of multivariate normality and asymptotic theory that requires large sample sizes. Further developments within SEM are identified and discussed by the authors to determine their significance for tourism research.

Clive Morley discusses **Discrete choice analysis and experimental design** in Chapter 6. Choice modelling attempts to model the decision process of an individual or segment in a particular context. Choice modelling is regarded as an accurate and general purpose tool available for making probabilistic predictions about certain human decision-making behaviour. The methods of discrete choice analysis are sometimes referred to as 'random utility' methods (as the underlying econometric theory uses a random utility specification) or 'limited dependent variable' analysis (the dependent variable in the model is categorical). Logit, multinomial logit and probit models are particular cases of discrete choice analysis.

Tourists make many decisions in determining their trip, and many of these decisions are intrinsically categorical, multinomial (many options are available) and unordered. Discrete choice theory provides an appropriate and sophisticated framework for analysis of the data at the level of individuals' evoked responses, and one that has been proven to work well in practice. The obvious applications of discrete choice methods are in demand modelling, and especially in assessing the impact of potentially explanatory variables on demand. This then gives useful results for marketing, forecasting, planning and policy evaluation and development, and other decision making by operators. For example, the technique has been used to estimate visitors' willingness to pay for attractions and substitution rates, that is the rate at which people will trade off less of one attribute for more of another attribute, for a particular destination. Other applications range widely from analysing various price effects on demand for a single destination from one through wider investigations of demand across combinations of origins and destinations (and types of destinations), to particular tourism preferences. Morley provides many different examples of the use of this attractive and valuable technique.

Overall the combination of experimental design, stated preference data and discrete choice models form a powerful body of techniques for analysis of tourism demand. The potential explanatory variables used are driven by the purpose of the investigation, and vary widely in the reported studies The more sophisticated choice models derived from discrete choice theory quantify the impact of variables for detailed policy analysis, strategic market planning and economic analysis.

As indicated by Neelu Seetaram and Sylvain Petit in Chapter 7, **Panel data analysis** is an increasingly popular form of longitudinal data analysis among social and behavioural science researchers. A panel is a cross section or group of people who are surveyed periodically over a given time span. Panel data analysis is a method of studying a particular subject within multiple sites, periodically observed over a defined time frame. Panel analysis has enabled researchers to undertake longitudinal analyses in a wide variety of fields in the social sciences. With repeated observations of enough cross sections, panel analysis permits the researcher to study the dynamics of change with short time series. Panel data analysis endows regression analysis with both a spatial and temporal dimension. The spatial dimension pertains to a set of cross-sectional units of observation. These could be countries, states, counties, firms, commodities, groups of people or even individuals. The temporal dimension pertains to periodic observations of a set of variables characterizing these cross-sectional units over a particular time span.

Seetaram and Petit divide the empirical literature based on the panel data methods and applied to the tourism sector, into two broad areas. The first concerns the determinants of tourism demand. The study of international tourism arrivals and receipts is a vibrant area of research and it cannot be confined to gravity models due to factors such as seasonality, cultural links or time constraints which are particular to the consumption of tourism products. The second area consists mainly of analysis of the link between tourism and economic growth. Since, several destinations have simultaneously experienced economic development and expansion of their tourism sector. While panel data techniques are powerful, and generally yield reliable estimates, they nevertheless suffer from some weaknesses. Estimations can be complex and data requirements are fairly large, especially for dynamic panel models. The main limitation, however, is that the panel data survey design is inevitably subject to problems related to attrition. The latter drawback, however, does not seem to have affected tourism research as the existing studies are based on secondary data or 'macro' data where the occurrence is either easier to deal with or less frequent. It is expected that future research may be based on survey data when researchers seek to find answers to the behaviour of tourists using micro-level data. Seetaram and Petit conclude that the use of panel data modelling techniques is becoming more common in the analysis of tourism data. In less than a decade, the literature has progressed from the development of standard static fixed effect and random effect models to the more sophisticated dynamic panel data cointegration models. So far, the application of this technique has been restricted to tourism demand studies and others which have explored the relationship between the expansion of tourism sectors and economic growth or international trade. It can be extended to other topics of research within the tourism context, including supply side studies.

In Chapter 8, Sarath Divisekera reviews the specification and applications of **The almost ideal demand system** (AIDS). Since its introduction in 1980 as a technique to analyse consumer behaviour, AIDS has become an essential aspect of demand theory and has been widely used in numerous empirical studies. The attraction of AIDS is that it gives an arbitrary first-order approximation to any demand system; it satisfies the axioms of choice; it aggregates perfectly without invoking the assumption of parallel linear Engel curves; and it has a functional form which is consistent with known household budget data. As Divisekera states, the AIDS model has been the principal and most widely used established demand system employed by researchers in the tourism field. The available empirical studies may be broadly classified into two categories: destination choice or demand for tourist destinations; and studies that seek to analyse the demand for tourism goods and services. The former group of studies attempts to evaluate the effects of incomes and prices as determinants of tourism demand for different destinations including domestic destinations. This has been the central focus of most of the early empirical studies of tourism demand. The latter group of studies investigates those aspects of tourism demands that focus on the demand for destination-specific tourism goods and services. More specifically, they attempt to analyse tourists' consumption behaviour or allocations of tourists' spending among various goods and services at the destinations they visited. Most attention among researchers in recent times appears to be on keeping up with the changing econometric methodology, rather than on improving the modelling process. For example, few studies have attempted to incorporate the cost of transport into modelling international tourism demand. Similarly, most studies continue to use the CPI (adjusted for exchange rates) as a proxy for tourism prices. This is a major drawback, as this grossly overestimates or underestimates the real cost of tourism goods and services. Thus, there is a need to develop appropriate tourism price indices as inputs for demand model estimation. Future studies need to concentrate on improving databases and developing reasonable price measures that capture both the costs of travel and tourism goods which are the key determinants of tourism demands.

Hedonic price analysis (HPA) is the topic of Chapter 9. Andreas Papatheodorou, Zheng Lei and Alexandros Apostolakis note that while pricing is a strategic choice for all firms, pricing decisions are often complex. From a managerial perspective, it is critically important to understand the consumer perceptions of each of the attributes associated with the characteristics that a customer is willing to make an extra payment for and those which are irrelevant in the determination of consumer choices and preferences.

HPA, an economic valuation technique based on revealed preferences, has its origin in Lancaster's (1971) theory of consumer demand, wherein consumer products are regarded as essentially bundles of 'separable' characteristics – such as comfort, convenience and reliability – that can be assessed accurately by value-conscious consumers. The theory of HPA was formally formulated by Rosen using a conventional utility-maximizing approach to derive implicit attribute prices for multi-attribute goods under conditions of perfect competition. The value that consumers attach to the characteristics is reflected in the price of the differentiated product. Thus, HPA is used to estimate economic values for attributes or product characteristics that directly affect prices for tourism products and services in the marketplace.

HPA aims to disentangle the impact of the various attributes on implicit prices where positive attributes are expected to boost the overall price and have a positive effect on individual utility levels. Correspondingly, negative attributes exert downward pressure on the price and have a negative effect on utility levels. Seen in this way, appropriate pricing not only generates revenue for a company to survive but can also be used as a communicator, as a bargaining tool and a competitive weapon. The consumer can use price as a means of comparing products, judging relative value for money or product quality. Hence, this technique is particularly useful for managerial decision making and evaluating individual preferences. HPA makes it easier to discern which characteristics are valued by consumers and to what extent, providing useful insight for the strategy to be followed in terms of market positioning, pricing and branding.

The authors argue that the methodological reliance of the technique on Lancaster's characteristics approach, make hedonic price analysis particularly adept to the study of a multi-attribute and multi-value sector such as the tourism industry. HPA establishes surrogate markets to place a premium to the effect of non-market based attributes on the tourism product or service on offer. Regression techniques are then used to estimate the implicit price for each attribute with the parameter of the hedonic price function revealing the marginal value consumers place on each of the individual attributes that comprise tourism experiences. The recent convergence of tourism and non-market environmental resources (illustrated through the increasing popularity of the sustainability concept in tourism operations, environmentally friendly tourism practices and ecotourism resources) necessitates the need for an evaluation approach that would allow estimation of the associated value placed by consumers/tourists on these non-market based characteristics of the tourism product or service on offer. Again, HPA is well suited to accommodate this need. The technique is based on the construction of surrogate markets to evaluate the effect of each product or service attribute on implicit prices consumers/tourists are willing to pay. In this respect, and despite some caveats, HPA offers a valid alternative method of examining demand patterns compared to other (market-based) methods.

As stated by Lindsay Turner and Chau Vu in Chapter 10, **Factor analysis** is a complex methodology that provides an objective way of determining latent (hidden) concepts within social data. *Principal Component Analysis (PCA)* is the most common use of factor analysis because it is descriptive, providing significant insight into the latent structure of data that can often be used for further analysis, for example in structural equation modelling (SEM). *Confirmatory Factor Analysis (CFA)* is used to determine whether a particular set of hypotheses defining the number and type of factors applies to particular data. The hypotheses require specific theoretical definition presumably justified by previous research, or theoretical construction such as a conceptual framework or definition from PCA. At the very least the factors must be named in advance on the basis of theory, and possibly the variables defining these names at least suggested. As such, CFA is potentially more powerful in deriving conclusions to research problems. The method analyses only the variance in the correlation matrix that is shared (common) with other (not necessarily all) variables. Consequently, the number of factors extracted may be less than the number of variables, which in research terms is more parsimonious in defining the original data set as founded on underlying structure. The problem lies in determining the shared variance (covariance) in the first place.

Factor analysis is an important tool for analysing tourism data, and potentially solving tourism-related problems. It is fundamental to a wide variety of problems encountered in tourism because, as a social science, there is significant requirement to measure unstructured concepts, as opposed to structured items with readily measurable attributes. In tourism the concepts requiring measurement relate to social systems involving values, attitudes, motivations, risks, satisfaction and beliefs. Turner and Vu highlight many examples of factor analysis used in tourism research, but argue that more needs to be done developing hypothetical structures from previous studies and confirming constant relationships in future research. In order to aid this process there needs to be agreement and understanding of the basic elements from analyses that are to be reported, what statistics and survey elements should be clearly evident, and what standards of interpretation are required. They conclude that factor analysis will continue as a major tourism research tool but there is room for improvement in the use of the technique to raise the standard of research analysis and consequent findings.

Chapter 11 addresses **Cluster analysis**. Clustering is the task of assigning a set of objects into groups (called clusters) so that the objects in the same cluster are more similar (in some sense or another) to each other than to those in other clusters. As Liz

Fredline indicates, cluster analysis is a family of multivariate techniques useful for analysing cases based on their scores on a range of measured variables. Essentially the technique identifies cases with a comparable pattern of responses that can be regarded, for the purposes of the analysis, as similar. In so doing a large number of individual cases are summarized into a smaller, more manageable number of clusters. The outcome of a successful cluster analysis is a small number of highly homogeneous clusters that are substantially different to each. Cluster membership can then be used as a variable for further analysis aimed at understanding the clusters and the bases on which they were formed. It is useful in any situation where the researcher wants to identify groups of cases that are similar to each other but different from other groups, that is, segmentation of the population. This segmentation can be based on any variables that are regarded as important for discriminating between groups and could include simple demographic characteristics or psychographic characteristics such as attitudes, perceptions, and motivations. Fredline emphasizes that cluster analysis is an 'interdependence' rather than a 'dependence' technique. This means that it does not aim to assess the relationship between independent and dependent variables; rather it is focussed on the underlying structure of variables and the usefulness of this structure in categorizing cases. Interpretation of the results of cluster analysis must be based on researcher knowledge and experience, as well as the logic of the solution and the extent to which clusters demonstrate high internal homogeneity and high external heterogeneity.

As Fredline notes, the two most common applications of cluster analysis in tourism are market segmentation and segmentation of host community attitudes or perceptions toward tourism. Market segmentation analysis allows tourism researchers and operators to identify important sub-groups of the total market which have different needs and wants, including travel motivations and therefore to modify their product to specifically target selected markets or alternatively to attempt to meet the differing needs of all segments. Segmentation of the host community is associated with research into perceptions of the impact of different types of tourism developments and entertainment options and the holding of special events. The assessment of how residents of a host community feel about tourism has seen numerous applications of cluster analysis with the aim of understanding the impacts of tourism on host communities.

Fredline argues that the main advantage of cluster analysis is that it provides an effective and meaningful reduction of data. All tourism customers have slightly different needs and wants but it is impossible to treat them all as individuals. For this reason it has been common practice to either assume they all have the same needs or to segment them based on geographic or demographic variables. Cluster analysis provides a better segmentation approach that allows groups to be defined by their needs and therefore identifies groups who can be targeted in a similar way because they are genuinely similar. One of the major disadvantages of the technique in terms of its application is that the solution is not definitive. That is, there is no single correct solution, all possible cluster solutions are correct, it is just that some do not explain the data in a manner that is as easy to interpret and use.

As discussed by Clemente Polo and Elisabeth Valle in Chapter 12, **Input–output and SAM models** are tools that economists have used for many decades to measure sectoral interdependencies, compare the economic structure of economies, quantify production impacts, measure structural and productivity changes, study the effects of redistribution policies, calculate the energy content of commodities, estimate CO_2 emissions, etc.

The input–output (IO) model is a simple linear model first proposed by Leontief to determine production quantities and prices in a set up where commodities are produced with commodities. IO models (or approaches inspired by it), incorporating multiplier analysis, have been used since the 1960s to quantify the impact of international tourism in large, medium and small national economies as well as in regions, counties, cities and recreational areas worldwide. The typical study included the completion of two surveys: one directed at local businesses to determine their cost structure and the other to incoming tourists to estimate their expenditures. The size of multipliers depends on three factors: the importance of import leakages, the value-added coefficients of tourism oriented sectors and the strength of linkages between tourism-oriented sectors and other sectors. Many of the tourism studies undertaken provide other useful pieces of information on the economies studied of great interest for policy makers: backward linkages of tourism sectors; the relative importance of tourism with respect to other exports; government revenues derived from tourism; imports required to satisfy tourists' demands and multipliers for different tourist services (accommodation types, non-real estate renting, food, entertainment, car renting, etc.) and different tourists' types (residents and non-residents classified by origin or trip motivation). Some studies have also estimated the production, value-added and employment shares accounted for tourists' demand and measure the weight of tourism under alternative assumptions on final demand. IO models have been extensively criticized, however, because of their restrictive assumptions and disregard for capacity restrictions that lead to exaggerated economic impacts.

As Polo and Valle indicate, the extension of the IO table and Leontief's open model into a social accounting matrix (SAM) and SAM model, respectively, was a quite natural development. A SAM may include accounts for industries, commodities, institutional sectors (households, non-profit institutions, corporate sector, public administrations and foreign sectors), capital (savings–investment) and as many auxiliary accounts as needed. Polo and Valle argue that SAM models have two main advantages over IO models. First, the household(s) and capital (savings–investment) accounts are balanced and the 'induced' effects caused by income generation (consumption and savings–investment) can be analysed in a more consistent way than in extended IO models. Second, SAM models can analyse the distributive consequences of injections, a subject that has no room in the IO models. There are disadvantages too. On the one hand, SAM models require a SAM and only a few statistical offices that routinely elaborate IO tables for national or regional economies also compile SAMs.

SAM models have been employed to study tourism impacts in national, regional and small economies during the last two decades. Since expenditure coefficients are ratios of SAM flows to column totals, the only requirements to estimate tourism impacts with a SAM model are a SAM of the economy studied and a vector of tourists' impacts. The fact that many national statistical offices in developed economies publish IO tables along with national accounts but only a few of them elaborate SAMs has hampered its use in tourism studies. For many developing countries, SAMs have been assembled to explore the links between growth, inequality and employment, and the associations between poverty and savings and investment levels, balance of payments, production and distribution. SAMs constructed for these purposes can be employed to quantify the role of tourism in the economy and its impact on all endogenous accounts including households. While the extension of fix coefficients beyond the production sphere is even more questionable than in the IO model, SAM models are conceptually more satisfactory than IO models since the households and capital accounts are balanced. The authors' conclude that 'all things equal' SAM models are preferable to IO models. Overall, the results of IO and SAM models can be viewed as a particular case of more general models and it is not a coincidence that the SAM framework is also known as fix-price multiplier analysis. Simulation results from IO and SAM models should always be interpreted with caution.

Polo and Valle conclude with some observations on the importance of IO and SAM models to the development of tourism satellite accounts and estimates of energy consumption and the environmental impacts of tourism. They see a continuing role for these approaches in tourism research.

CGE modeling is the topic of Chapter 13 by Larry Dwyer and Tien Duc Pham. Computable general equilibrium (CGE) models are simulations that combine the abstract Walrasian general equilibrium structure, formalized by Arrow, Debreu and Hahn, with realistic economic data to solve numerically for the levels of supply, demand and price that support equilibrium across a specified set of markets. CGE modeling involves a mathematical specification of simultaneous relationships within the economy. Many features can be built into this framework, to tailor it to the different conditions that characterize alternative real world circumstances. In this way, the framework provides a widely encompassing means of evaluating the effects of policy changes and exogenous shocks on resource allocation and can also permit assessment of the distributional effects of such changes. CGE models treat an economy as a whole, allowing for feedback effects of one sector on another. They represent the economy as a system of flows of goods and services between sectors.

A CGE model is a versatile structure, which can easily be adapted to the special features of any economy, to the questions that are asked, and to the data which are available. Its assumptions can easily be changed so that the results of a simulation can be interpreted, for instance, as describing a short-term equilibrium, or a medium-run equilibrium. The majority of CGE models can be separated into two broad categories, *comparative static* and *dynamic.* For policy analysis, results from such a model are often interpreted as showing the reaction of the economy in some future period to some external shock or policy change that the adjustment path is not known. *Dynamic CGE* models explicitly trace each variable through time, often at annual intervals so that the adjustment path of the economy can be examined.

CGE models are now increasingly used in tourism economics analysis and policy formulation. CGE models are well suited to tourism analysis and policy, given their multi-sectoral basis. In contrast to partial equilibrium approaches, CGE models can take account of the interrelationships between tourism, other sectors in the domestic economy and foreign producers and consumers. CGE modeling can be tailored to alternative conditions, such as flexible or fixed prices, alternative exchange rate regimes, differences in the degree of mobility of factors of production and different types of competition. CGE models can be used to quantify the effects of actual policies, such as changes in taxation, subsidies or government borrowing, as well as predicting the effects of a range of alternative policies or exogenous expenditure shocks. They can be used to estimate the impacts of changes in tourism expenditure under a range of alternative macroeconomic scenarios; tailoring them to alternative conditions such as flexible or fixed prices, various exchange rate regimes, differences in the degree of mobility of factors of production, different government fiscal policy stances and different types of competition. CGE models are helpful to tourism policy makers who seek to use them to provide guidance about a wide variety of 'What if?' questions, arising from a wide range of domestic or international expenditure shocks or alternative policy scenarios.

Despite its growing importance in tourism research, CGE modeling can be applied to a much broader set of policy issues than at present. One agenda for future research in this area should be to extend the analysis to different tourism destinations, and to include detailed analyses of the appropriate behavioural characteristics of the economic agents that are included in model specification and of the government policy settings that determine the context for their behaviour. This could include the effects of foreign direct investment in tourism, tourism productivity and competitiveness, fiscal policies for tourism, policies within wider international groupings such as the European Union, ASEAN and so on, policies for transportation, the environment and related externalities, including the impacts of climate change on tourism. CGE tourism modeling provides a versatile and effective means of examining the wide range of scenarios that can occur.

Cost–benefit analysis (CBA) is discussed in Chapter 14 by Larry Dwyer. Foreshadowed by Dupuit in the nineteenth century, CBA is the primary technique used for the economic appraisal of actions or proposals in terms of economic efficiency. A CBA provides an estimate of the worth of a proposal relative to an accompanying estimate of what would happen in its absence. CBA is a systematic process for identifying and assessing all costs and benefits of a proposal in monetary terms, as they are expected to occur through the life of a project. CBA is concerned with measuring, the change in all sources of economic welfare, whether occurring in markets or as implicit values. Future costs and benefits are discounted relative to present costs and benefits in a net present value sum. The policy or project is deemed to be socially acceptable if the sum of the benefits to society (including private and social benefits) exceeds the sum of the costs to society (including private and social costs).

In CBA, 'value' or 'benefit' is measured by willingness to pay (WTP) or willingness to accept (WTA). Formally using the compensating variations principle, the net social benefit is the maximum net amount that residents would be willing to pay for the proposal and be just as well off with the proposal as without it. Using the equivalent variations principle, the net social benefit is the minimum amount that the community would be willing to accept as compensation for not having the proposal. The social costs of a project are measured in terms of opportunity costs – that is, the value of the marginal benefits foregone from the same resources in alternative uses. Using these two valuation principles (for benefits and costs) the analyst can determine whether the value of consumption gained is greater than the value of consumption that it given up. The net benefit is the sum of all welfare benefits less costs. Maximizing net welfare is the standard policy objective implicit or explicit in cost–benefit studies. By quantifying the net benefits of projects, programmes and policies in a standard manner, CBA improves the information base for public sector decision making, thereby assisting in the assessment of relative priorities.

As the most comprehensive of the economic appraisal techniques, CBA is particularly important in the context of evaluating tourism policy, programmes, regulations, projects and developments. Specific examples might include regional or local tourism plans; rezoning of land for tourism purposes; and major tourism developments such as the creation of tourism shopping precincts, airport development, resorts and hotels, nature reserves and sporting facilities. As such projects generally have relatively wide economic, environmental and social implications for a community that are not captured in the basic financial analysis undertaken by project proponents. CBA is especially appropriate to tourism because there is often a clear trade off between economic benefits and social costs of some programme, policy, project, investment or proposal. Tourism proposals that might be economically beneficial may be rejected because of their adverse environmental and/or social impacts.

Dwyer argues that there is substantial scope for greater use of CBA in tourism contexts, including assessment of special events. CBA picks up a whole range of benefits and costs due to non priced effects arising from the absence of markets for some goods and services affected which would not be included in economic impact analysis. CBA is not without its challenges as the discussion by Dwyer highlights. Each type of limitation is being addressed in the research literature and CBA remains the primary technique for informing policy makers of the net benefits of different strategies to achieve objectives associated with 'the public good'.

1 Statistical testing techniques
Gang Li

INTRODUCTION

Statistical testing is one of the key tasks in quantitative tourism research. It is based on inferential statistics, which "based on probability theory and logic, are used to make inferences about the characteristics of a population from the characteristics of a random sample drawn from the population" (Grimm, 1993, p. 123). Statistical testing has been used for research purposes since the early 1700s (Huberty, 1993). Over the past 300 years of the development of statistical testing, four early twentieth-century statisticians, namely R.A. Fisher, J. Neyman, E.S. Pearson and K. Pearson, made the most significant contribution toward formalizing the concept (McLean and Ernest, 1998). Most of the current statistical testing techniques are still based on the same logic they developed.

Specifically, the pioneers developed two different approaches to statistical testing: Fisher's *significance testing* approach and Neyman–Pearson's *hypothesis testing* approach. The former involves a single (null) hypothesis with a strength-of-evidence statistic p value, while the latter involves both a null hypothesis (H_0) and an alternative hypothesis (H_1) and specifies a fixed level of the probability at which the test statistic should be rejected. The significance testing approach does not typically consider the region of rejection or Type I and Type II errors (to be explained below), whilst the hypothesis testing approach does not consider the extent of support (i.e., the p value). The hypothesis testing approach is most often discussed in statistical methods for behavioral sciences. Although the two approaches are based on different philosophical beliefs, they share the same basic foundation: probability. Statistical testing is not deterministic, but probabilistic. In more recent development of statistical testing, Huberty (1987) proposed a hybrid approach which used hypothesis testing notions in designing the study and then used significance testing as a basis for making statistical inferences. An advantage of this hybrid approach is to take account of the two types of potential inferential decision errors and an alternative hypothesis characterization of interest (Huberty, 1987).

Statistical testing techniques, as with many other quantitative research methods, are commonly applied in tourism research, particularly in relation to tourist behavior. Based on general consumer behavior models such as the Andreasen (1965) model, the Nicosia (1966) model and the Howard and Sheth (1969) model, tourism researchers are interested in examining the behavioral characteristics of consumers in a variety of tourism contexts, such as tourists' perception of destination images, travel motivation, behavioral intention, perceived service performance, and satisfaction. In addition, some researchers are interested in the perceptions, attitudes, and behaviors of residents in tourist destinations. Statistical testing is regularly performed in these tourism studies in order to obtain robust findings and conclusions.

The rest of this chapter will introduce some commonly used statistical testing techniques in quantitative tourism studies. Given different assumptions concerning the distribution of the population, these statistical techniques can be broadly divided into parametric and non-parametric groups. Parametric techniques, such as the *t*-test, are based on the assumption that the sampled populations have approximately normal distribution with equal variances, while nonparametric tests, sometimes called distribution-free statistics, such as the χ^2 test, require less stringent assumptions about the nature of the probability distributions of the populations. Another important reason for using non-parametric tests is that they allow for the analysis of categorical and ranked data, such as the relationships between people's holiday preference rankings and their demographic characteristics including gender, age, educational background, marital status, and so on.

PROCEDURES OF STATISTICAL TESTING

Most statistical tests follow the same logical sequence. Following Neyman–Pearson's hypothesis testing approach, the procedural steps for a statistical test are: (1) to formulate the null and alternative hypothesis; (2) to determine a significance level and rejection region; (3) to specify the test statistic and referent (null) distribution; (4) to calculate the test statistic value; and (5) to choose between the null and alternative hypothesis. The steps will be explained briefly before individual tests are introduced.

Hypothesis Formulation

A common feature of statistical testing techniques is the concept of the *null hypothesis*. It usually proposes no difference between two observed values or no relationship between two variables. The *alternative hypothesis*, on the other hand, proposes a significant difference or relationship. It is usually the alternative hypothesis that is directly related to the research question which a researcher is interested in. Hypothesis formation is based on a relevant theoretical framework and is related to a deductive research approach (Veal, 2006).

The alternative hypothesis can be formulated with or without a predetermined direction, depending on the prior knowledge about the research question. If the null hypothesis states that there is no statistical difference between observed values A and B, then the alternative hypothesis can be A ≠ B, A > B or A < B. Clearly A ≠ B includes the possibility of both directions of A > B and A < B, and is related to a two-tailed test, while A > B or A < B relates to a one-tailed test. In another case, if the null hypothesis states that there is no relationship between variables X and Y, the alternative hypothesis may refer to either a positive or negative relationship (i.e., a one-tailed test) or both (i.e., a two-tailed test). For example, Mok (1990) investigated a research question: whether destination advertising increased tourist flows based on one-tailed hypothesis testing, because the alternative hypothesis referred to only a positive relationship between destination advertising and tourist flows. One-tailed and two-tailed tests are further related to the definition of the rejection region of a hypothesis test.

Table 1.1   Consequences of decisions in hypothesis testing

Decision	True state of nature	
	H_0 is true	H_1 is true
Accept H_0 and reject H_1	Right decision (probability = $1 - \alpha$)	Type II error (probability = β)
Reject H_0 and accept H_1	Type error (probability = α)	Right decision (probability = $1 - \beta$)

Significance Level and Rejection Region

To reject the null hypothesis, a statistical standard needs to be established as the basis. The level of significance is the minimum acceptable probability that a value actually comes from the population (Waters, 2001). If a 5 percent significance level is chosen, the null hypothesis is rejected only when there is a probability of less than 5 percent that the value comes from the hypothesized population. This implies that the probability of rejecting the null hypothesis is 5 percent, when it is actually true. This error is called a *type I error*, and its probability is always equal to the level of significance, designated by "α". Thus the probability of accepting a true null hypothesis is $(1 - \alpha)$.

In contrast to a type I error, the error of accepting a false null hypothesis is called a *type II error*, and its probability is denoted "β". Therefore, the probability of rejecting a false null hypothesis is $(1 - \beta)$, which is called the power of the test. The probability of a type II error is often difficult to determine precisely. It depends on the actual alternate value of the population mean when the null hypothesis is false. When the test statistic does not fall in the rejection area, instead of concluding with the acceptance of H_0, it is usually preferable to state that *there is insufficient sample evidence to reject the null hypothesis at the significance level of* α (McClave et al., 1998). Table 1.1 summarizes four possible consequences of a hypothesis-testing decision.

As mentioned above, the rejection region is related to the formation of the alternative hypothesis or, in other words, whether a one-tailed or two-tailed test is to be adopted. Figure 1.1 illustrates the relationship between the type of a hypothesis test and the rejection region.

Test Statistic and Reference Distribution

The test statistic is the value, based on a sample, used to determine whether the null hypothesis should be rejected or not (Kazmier and Pohl, 1987). For instance, the value of a sample mean can be used as the test statistic for the hypothesized value of the population mean. The general practice is to transform a sample statistic into a value on the appropriate standard distribution and then use this transformed value as the test statistics. Given that the sample distribution of the mean can be assumed to follow normal distribution, the sample mean can be transformed into a z value: $z = \overline{X} - \mu_0/\sigma_{\overline{X}}$, where $\overline{X}$ is the sample mean, μ_0 is the population mean value specified in the null hypothesis, $\sigma_{\overline{X}}$ is the standard error of the mean, assuming the population's standard deviation σ is known.

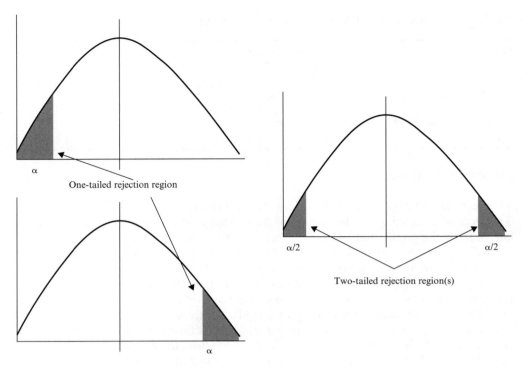

Figure 1.1   Rejection regions for one- and two-tailed tests

Once the test statistic is determined, the critical value(s) can be established. A critical value defines the rejection region at the designated level of significance. Given a normal distribution, critical values are typically specified in terms of z values, and they also depend on whether one-tailed or two tailed tests are used. The frequently used critical values of z are listed in Table 1.2. The test statistic will then be calculated and compared to the critical values in order to decide whether the null hypothesis will be rejected or not.

Table 1.2   Critical values of z at different levels of significance

Level of significance	One-tailed test	Two-tailed test
10%	1.28 or −1.28	±1.645
5%	1.645 or −1.645	±1.96
1%	2.33 or −2.33	±2.58

P-values

As discussed earlier, Fisher's *significance testing* approach is concerned with a strength-of-evidence statistic p value instead of the rejection region, and Huberty (1987) recom-

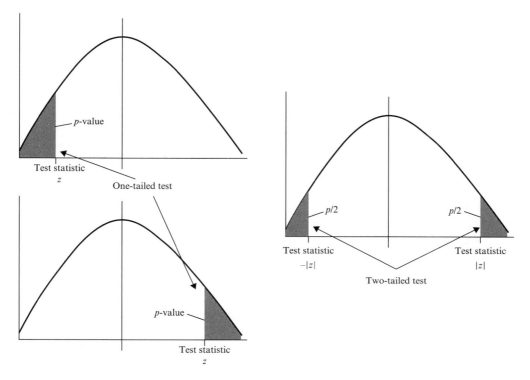

Source: Adapted from Marusteri and Bacarea (2010, p. 28).

Figure 1.2   P-values for one-tailed and two-tailed tests

mended both should be considered in his proposed hybrid approach. Therefore, it is worth introducing the p value here. The p-value is the probability associated with the occurrence of the test statistic, given that the null hypothesis is true (Kazmier and Pohl, 1987). For example, in a one-tailed test where $H_1 : \mu < \mu_0$, the computed test statistic is $z = -2.50$. Therefore, the p-value $= P(z \leq -2.50)$. If the alternative hypothesis is $H_1 : \mu > \mu_0$ and $z = 2.50$, then the p-value $= P(z \geq 2.50)$. As seen in Figure 1.2, the p-values in these two cases of one-tailed tests are the areas under the standard normal curve to the left of $z = -2.50$ and to the right of $z = 2.50$, respectively. Referring to the standard normal probability distribution table (where the z score of 2.5 corresponds to a probability value of 0.4938, i.e., the area between 0 and 2.5), we can observe that p-value $= 0.5 - 0.4938 = 0.0062$. In the case of a two-tailed test, the p-value includes the areas in both directions (see Figure 1.2). In other words, the p-value is doubled as in one-tailed tests: p-value $= 0.0062 \times 2 = 0.0124$. Following the p-value approach of hypothesis testing, the calculated p-value is compared to the level of significance in order to decide to reject or not reject the null hypothesis. If the p-value $< \alpha$, then the null hypothesis is rejected. In the above example, if $\alpha = 0.05$ is selected, then the null hypothesis is rejected in both one-tailed and two-tailed tests.

PARAMETRIC TESTS

There are a number of parametric tests for hypothesis testing. In tourism research, t-tests, correlation tests, and the analyses of variance and covariance are applied most often and are thus introduced here. To apply a parametric test some general assumptions need to be met: (1) the scores obtained from the population are based on random sampling; (2) the population from which a sample is taken follows normal distribution; (3) the scores in a sample are independent of each other; (4) samples are taken from populations of equal variances, i.e., the variability of scores for each of the groups is similar. It is also called homogeneity of variance (Pallant, 2005). With regard to the normal distribution assumption, Gravetter and Wallnau (2000, p. 302) and Stevens (1996, p. 242) argue that most of these statistical tests are reasonably robust with large sample sizes (above 30 observations in each of the groups to be analysed). In these cases, violation of normality should not cause major problems. In comparison, homogeneity of variance is more important and needs to be tested before conducting a t-test or analysis of variance.

T-tests of Hypotheses About Population Means

In tourism research the population standard deviation (σ) is usually unknown or the sample size is relatively small. In these cases, the standard normal distribution and z-scores cannot be used to make inference about population means. Instead, the t-distribution should be adopted and t-scores need to be calculated. The t-distribution has a similar shape as the normal distribution but with heavier tails, which means it is more prone to producing values that fall far from its mean score. The t-score is calculated as $t_{(n-1)} = (\overline{X} - \mu_0/s_x)/\sqrt{n}$, where $\overline{X}$ and s_x are the sample mean and standard deviation respectively, μ_0 is the hypothesized population mean value, n is the sample size, and $(n - 1)$ is the degrees of freedom of the t- distribution.

There are two types of t-tests: the independent samples t-test and the paired samples t-test. The former is used to compare the mean scores of two different groups of people or conditions (e.g., the mean scores of perceived performance evaluated by male and female guests), while the latter is for comparing the mean scores for the same group of people on two different occasions (e.g., the mean scores of expectation and perceived performance of a hotel's services, evaluated by the same group of hotel guests). Hence the independent t-test involves a continuous variable (usually measured on an interval or ratio scale) such as the perceived performance of hotel services and a categorical variable with two categories being concerned, such as gender. A paired t-test requires both variables to be on interval or ratio scales (continuous), such as service expectation and service performance.

The test statistic for an independent samples t-test is:

$$t = \frac{(\overline{x}_1 - \overline{x}_2) - (\mu_1 - \mu_2)}{\sqrt{\dfrac{s_1^2}{n_1} + \dfrac{s_2^2}{n_2}}} \tag{1.1}$$

where $\overline{x}_1$ and $\overline{x}_2$ are the mean scores of two independent samples, μ_1 and μ_2 are the hypothesized mean values of the two populations and the null hypothesis is usually H_0: $\mu_1 = \mu_2$, s_1 and

s_2 are standard deviations of the two samples, and n_1 and n_2 are the sample sizes. If the equal variance assumption holds, then $s_1 = s_2 = \sqrt{[(n_1 - 1)s_1^2 + (n_2 - 1)s_2^2]/(n_1 + n_2 - 2)}$. In this case, the degrees of freedom of the test are $(n_1 + n_2 - 2)$. However, if the equal variance assumption does not hold, the degrees of freedom are more complicated and can be calculated by the following formulae:

$$\frac{(s_1^2/n_1 + s_2^2/n_2)^2}{(s_1^2/n_1)^2/(n_1 - 1) + (s_2^2/n_2)^2/(n_2 - 1)} \tag{1.2}$$

For a paired samples t-test, the test statistic is given by:

$$t_{n-1} = \frac{\bar{d}}{\sqrt{\dfrac{\sum d^2 - n\bar{d}^2}{n(n - 1)}}} \tag{1.3}$$

where d is the difference between each pair of values of two variables in the paired sample, $\bar{d}$ is the mean difference, and n is the sample size. The degrees of freedom of this test are $(n - 1)$. The paired samples t-test has an additional assumption that the difference between the paired scores (d) follows normal distribution. However, with a sample size above 30, violation of this assumption is unlikely to cause serious problems (Pallant, 2005).

Wang et al. (2005) used an independent-samples t-test to analyse the effects of residents' employment status and income on their attitudes towards tourism development and tourism impacts. They found that high-income residents had significantly more positive attitudes towards socio-cultural impacts of tourism ($t = 2.213$, $p = 0.028$) and residents who worked in (or residents whose relatives worked in) the tourism industry rated the economic benefits of tourism development significantly higher ($t = 1.999$, $p = 0.047$). Li et al. (2009) used a paired-samples t-test to investigate the impact of online information searches on tourists' destination image development. By comparing a group of participants' perceived image of China before and after an online information search, they found the participants' overall image and affective image about China experienced significant and positive changes after an online search, while the cognitive image remained the same.

Correlation Analysis

Correlation analysis examines the strength of association between two variables by calculating a correlation coefficient. The Pearson product–moment correlation is the most commonly used parametric method for correlation analysis. It analyses the association between two continuous variables (measured on an interval or ratio scale), such as service quality and tourist satisfaction, or perceived destination image and visit intention. Based on a sample to estimate the population correlation, Pearson's correlation coefficient (r) can be computed as follows:

$$r = \frac{N_p(\sum XY) - (\sum X)(\sum Y)}{\sqrt{[N_P(\sum X^2) - (\sum X)^2][N_P(\sum Y^2) - (\sum Y)^2]}} \tag{1.4}$$

where X and Y are two continuous variables and N_p is the number of pairs of observations. A correlation coefficient ranges from -1 to 1, suggesting a perfect negative relationship to a perfect positive relationship. The higher the coefficient's absolute value, the stronger the association between the two variables. Although there is no agreement on the cut-off values of r for different levels of association, it is generally accepted that $|r| < 0.3$ would suggest the relationship is weak (or small), and $|r| > 0.7$ would imply a strong (or large) association between the two variables (see, for example, Grimm, 1993, p. 377).

The correlation coefficient r computed based on a sample is an estimator of the population correlation coefficient ρ. An r score only shows the level of association between two variables, but it does not suggest whether this relationship is statistically significant or not. Therefore, a statistical test of the significance of the correlation needs to be carried out. The appropriate test is based on the t distribution, which is a transformation of sampling distributions of r of differing sample sizes. The test statistic t is written as:

$$t = r\sqrt{\frac{N_p - 2}{1 - r^2}} \tag{1.5}$$

where the degrees of freedom equal $N_p - 2$. Depending on the specification of the alternative hypothesis, either $H_1:\rho \neq 0$ or $H_1:\rho > 0$ (or $H_1:\rho < 0$), a two-tailed or one-tailed t-test will be used, respectively. If the direction of the association between two variables is clear, for example, prices are most likely to have a negative association with tourism demand, a one-tailed t-test should be used instead of a two-tailed one.

In addition to finding out whether there is a significant relationship between variables X and Y, researchers may also want to know if the strength of this relationship is significantly different between groups. To test statistical significance of the difference between correlation coefficients, the r values computed from different groups need to be converted into z scores and the observed value of z (z_{obs}) as a test statistic must be calculated following the formulae below:

$$z_{obs} = \frac{z_1 - z_2}{\sqrt{\dfrac{1}{N_1 - 3} + \dfrac{1}{N_2 - 3}}} \tag{1.6}$$

where z_1 and z_2 are converted z scores from r values in relation to groups 1 and 2, respectively; and N_1 and N_2 are the numbers of observations in the two groups. The calculated z_{obs} will be compared with critical values of z (see Table 1.2) to decide if the correlation coefficients are statistically significantly different.

In an example of testing the relationship between destination image and travel intention, if it is suspected that the tourists' past visit experience (Z, measured by a continuous variable: the number of past visits) is likely to be related to both their perceived destination image (X) and their travel intention (Y). In this case, the computed Pearson's correlation coefficient between the perceived destination image and travel intention without controlling the influence of tourists' past visit experience, may be inflated. Therefore, a more accurate correlation analysis should control the effect of other variables that may be associated with both variables concerned. This is called *partial correlation analysis*.

It follows the same concept of the aforementioned Pearson correlation analysis, but the computation of the partial correlation coefficient ($r_{XY \cdot Z}$) is revised as follows:

$$r_{XY \cdot Z} = \frac{r_{XY} - (r_{XZ})(r_{YZ})}{\sqrt{(1 - r_{XZ}^2)(1 - r_{YZ}^2)}} \tag{1.7}$$

where r_{XY}, r_{XZ} and r_{YZ} are Pearson correlation coefficients between any two of the three variables.

It should be noted that the Pearson correction and partial correlation tests only detect linear relationships between variables. A low and non-significant Pearson correlation coefficient between variables X and Y does not necessarily mean there is no association between them. A non-linear relationship may still exist. It is necessary to plot each subject's X and Y scores on a graph (i.e., to draw a scatter plot) and visually examine the shape of the plot to decide whether a linear correlation analysis is appropriate. Moreover, the above correction analysis aims to detect linear association between X and Y, but not a causal relationship. So a significant correlation coefficient between X and Y does not necessarily mean that either X causes Y or Y causes X. Hence the result of a correlation test should be interpreted with caution. In addition, the calculated correlation coefficient is sensitive to outliers, especially in small samples. A misleading r will be derived from such a sample. Therefore, it is necessary to detect and remove outliers before running a correlation test.

Li and Petrick (2008) used Pearson's product–moment correlation test to detect the relationships between consumers' attitudinal loyalty and each of its three antecedents: satisfaction, quality of alternatives, and brand investment in the context of cruising. They found that the cruise passengers' attitudinal loyalty to a cruise line's brand was weakened by the quality of alternative options ($r = -0.22$) but strengthened by their satisfaction with the brand and investment in it ($r = 0.720$ and 0.601, respectively). In another study, Snepenger et al. (2004) employed Pearson's correlation analysis to examine whether different tourism places had shared, independent, or divergent normative meanings. The results suggested Downtown and Yellowstone shared many meanings ($r > 0$, $p < 0.05$), but Downtown had very different meanings from big-box stores ($r < 0$, $p < 0.05$).

Analysis of Variance and Covariance

Analysis of variance (ANOVA) can be regarded as an extension of the independent samples t-test. It compares means of more than two groups at a time. Assuming there are g groups of subjects in a sample and we are comparing their mean scores of a continuous variable (e.g., comparing destination satisfaction levels of tourists from g countries of origin), the null and alternative hypotheses are: $H_0 : \mu_1 = \mu_2 = \ldots = \mu_g$, H_1: the means of the g groups are not all equal. In the above example, $\mu_1, \mu_2, \ldots, \mu_g$ are the population mean values of destination satisfaction of tourists from these g countries. ANOVA draws inferences about population means by analysing sample variances. There are two sources of variability in scores (i.e., variance): the variation *between* the groups and the variation *within* each of the groups. The test statistic of ANOVA is an F ratio which represents the variance between the groups divided by the variance with the groups and is defined as:

$$F = \frac{\textit{between-group variance}}{\textit{within-group variance}} =$$

$$\frac{\left[\dfrac{(\sum X_1)^2}{n_1} + \dfrac{(\sum X_2)^2}{n_2} + \ldots + \dfrac{(\sum X_g)^2}{n_g} - \dfrac{(\sum X)^2}{N}\right] \Big/ (g-1)}{\left\{\sum X^2 - \left[\dfrac{(\sum X_1)^2}{n_1} + \dfrac{(\sum X_2)^2}{n_2} + \ldots + \dfrac{(\sum X_g)^2}{n_g} - \dfrac{(\sum X)^2}{N}\right]\right\} \Big/ (N-g)} \tag{1.8}$$

where $\sum X_g$ is the sum of scores in Group g, n_g is the number of subjects in Group g, $\sum X$ is the sum of all the scores in the study, N is the total number of subjects in the study and $\sum X^2$ is the sum of all squared scores in the study. The F-statistic follows the F-distribution with $(g-1, N-g)$ degrees of freedom under the null hypothesis.

A significant F-value means the null hypothesis is rejected, indicating that at least two of the population means are not equal. However, a significant F-value does not show which means are significantly different from one another. To find this out, pairwise comparisons among all the means need to be controlled carefully and carried out with the Type I error. This analysis is called a *post-hoc test*, such as Tukey's honestly significant different (HSD) test (Tukey, 1953[1984]) and modified Bonferroni procedures (Olejnik et al., 1997). Due to space constraints, any discussion of these tests is beyond the scope of this chapter.

The above explanation of ANOVA refers to one factor (or independent variable) that separates a sample into a few groups (e.g., nationalities of tourists at a destination) and one continuous variable (i.e., dependent variable, such as destination satisfaction). This ANOVA is called *one-way between-groups ANOVA*. One-way ANOVA can also be applied to the same subjects under different conditions. This is referred to as a *repeated-measures ANOVA* or a within-subjects design. Often researchers are interested in investigating the individual or joint effect of two independent variables on one dependent variable, such as comparing destination satisfaction levels across tourists' nationalities and age groups. This analysis is called *two-way between-groups ANOVA*. It involves testing the effects of each of the two independent variables (i.e., the main effects) and the effect of the interaction between the two independent variables, all on the dependent variable concerned. All of these three tests are based on F-tests, as with a one-way ANOVA.

In both one-way and two-way ANOVA analyses above, only one independent variable is concerned. In some research situations, however, researchers are interested in comparing groups on a range of related dependent variables such as comparing, across tourists of different nationalities, their satisfaction with four dimensions of destination attributes: services, prices, infrastructure, and environment. This analysis is called a *multivariate analysis of variance* (or MANOVA), which is an extension of the ANOVA: it includes more than one related dependent variable. As with ANOVA, there are one-way and two-way MANOVA, depending on the number of independent variables being considered.

In comparison to running a series of ANOVAs, it is more effective and robust to run only one MANOVA. This is because to run a number of ANOVAs separately increases the risk of an "inflated Type I error" (Tabachnik and Fidell, 2007), while MANOVA takes this risk into consideration. Moreover, MANOVA takes the intercorrelations between the dependent variables into account, which can only be achieved if these dependent variables are considered together in one test. MANOVA has two additional assumptions in relation to multiple dependent variables. First, the significant test is based on multivariate normal distribution; in other words, any linear combination of the dependent variables should be distributed normally. Second, the matrices of the covariances, i.e., the variance shared between any two dependent variables, have to be equal across all levels of the independent variable(s). The test is reasonably robust to modest violations of the multivariate normality assumption as long as a minimum sample size of 20 is ensured for each sub-group that the whole sample is divided into by the independent variable(s) (Tabachnik and Fidell, 2007).

The latest development of multivariate analysis is to test the effects of one or two independent variables on one or more dependent variables while controlling for an additional continuous variable, which is called a covariate and believed to have some influence on the dependent variable(s) (Pallant, 2005). This type of analysis is called *analysis of covariance* or ANCOVA. By controlling the effect of the covariate, ANCOVA increases the power of the *F*-test, so that it is more likely to detect differences among groups. For example, tourists' past visit experiences may affect their destination satisfaction evaluation. Therefore, to control the effect of this factor (measured by the number of past visits to the destination), it is easier to find satisfaction differences across tourists of different nationalities, different age groups, and so on. By introducing a covariate into one-way ANOVA, two-way ANOVA, and MANOVA, one-way ANCOVA, two-way ANCOVA, and MANCOVA can be exercised, respectively.

Various analyses of variance can be seen in tourism research. For instance, Simpson and Siguaw (2008) applied one-way ANOVA to the investigation of the effects of tourist type on place satisfaction, identity salience and place promotion. The results were all statistically significant ($F > 18$, $p < 0.001$ for all). In subsequent post-hoc tests, the authors found that winter tourists were more likely to be satisfied with the place and to promote it via positive word-of-mouth recommendation than any other tourist segment. Rewtrakunphaiboon and Oppewal (2008) adopted two-way ANOVA to study the impact of destination image (more favorable and less favorable) and information format (destination name as a package heading, price as a package heading, and destination name only) on the intention to visit a destination. They found that destinations with a more favorable image received a significantly higher intention to visit rating than destinations with a less favorable image, while the difference between information format conditions was not significant. The results were that the interaction between image and format did not have a significant effect on the intention to visit either. At a more advanced level of statistical testing, Tsaur and Wang (2009) employed a two-way between-groups MANOVA to detect the effects of the tip-collection strategy (tipping by participants and tip included) and the type of service guarantee (none, attribute-specific, and full satisfaction) on consumer evaluations of a group package tour, in terms of expected service quality, financial risk, performance risk, and willingness to buy. This study found significant main effects of both independent variables, but no significant interaction effect between them. Subsequently, a number of one-way between-groups ANOVAs were performed on each of the dependent variables, followed by post-hoc tests.

NON-PARAMETRIC STATISTICAL TESTS

The above parametric statistical tests have some stringent assumptions and normally require large sample sizes. If the assumptions cannot be met, or the sample size is too small (less than 20), or the data are measured on normal (categorical) or ordinal (ranked) scales, non-parametric statistical tests should be considered. A number of non-parametric tests have been developed to respond to their parametric counterparts. Given the space constraints, this chapter focuses on the most often used techniques in tourism studies. Explanation of other non-parametric techniques is available from Gibbons and Chakraborti (2003).

Chi-square Tests

There are two types of chi-square test: for one-way designs and for two-way designs. In one-way designs, the chi-square test is the categorical counterpart of a one-way ANOVA with two or more groups. It is concerned with the frequency distribution of a nominal variable and used with a sample to make an inference about the frequency distribution of the population. It is also called the *goodness-of-fit test*. It requires a specification of the population frequency distribution (i.e., expected frequencies) as the null hypothesis and the alternative hypothesis states that the population distribution of frequencies does not follow an expected manner. The goodness-of-fit test is used to statistically determine if the observed frequencies obtained from a sample are significantly different from the expected frequencies. For example, it is expected that the percentages of male and female tourists in a holiday resort are equal, but the observed gender distribution of tourists in a given period may deviate slightly from this balance. The goodness-of-fit test can be used to find out whether the deviation is statically significant. The chi-square statistic (χ^2) is computed as:

$$\chi^2 = \sum \frac{(f_o - f_e)^2}{f_e} \qquad (1.9)$$

where f_o and f_e are observed and expected frequencies, respectively. The degrees of freedom of the goodness-of-fit test are the number of groups, minus one. The test is based on the χ^2 distribution. As the degrees of freedom increase, the χ^2 distribution approximates the shape of a normal distribution, but all χ^2 values are positive. The critical values become larger as the degrees of freedom increase.

The chi-square test can also be used in two-way designs, to detect whether there is a relationship between two categorical variables or if they are independent, so this chi-square test is called the *chi-square test for independence*. For example, researchers may want to know if the employment status of residents in a tourist destination (i.e., working in a tourism sector or not) is related to their opinion on a new tourism policy (i.e., in favor of the new policy or not). The null hypothesis of the chi-square test for independence states that the two categorical variables are independent (or have no relationship) and the alternative hypothesis states that these two variables are related. Based on the presentation of this two-way design in a frequency or cross-tabulation table, the chi-square test for independence examines whether the frequency distribution for one categorical variable is different, depending on the classification of the other categorical variables (Grimm, 1993, p. 442). The test statistic (χ^2) is computed using the same formulae as with the one-way design, while the expected frequency for each cell of the cross-tabulation table has to be calculated in advance, based on the relevant observed frequencies, following the formulae below:

$$f_e = \frac{f_c f_r}{N} \tag{1.10}$$

where f_e refers to the expected frequency of a cell in the cross-tabulation table, f_c and f_r are the totaled frequencies for the relevant column and row of this cell, respectively, and N is the total number of subjects. The degrees of freedom of this chi-square test are: $df = (C - 1)(R - 1)$, where C and R are the numbers of columns and rows respectively, i.e., the number of categories of these two categorical variables. This test requires the expected frequency for any cell to be a minimum of 5, i.e., $f_e \geq 5$. In a 2×2 design (i.e., $C = R = 2$), violation of this assumption means a different test; Fisher's exact probability test, should be considered instead (Pallant, 2005).

Compared with the applications of parametric statistical testing techniques, the applications of their non-parametric alternatives are much fewer. The variety of non-parametric techniques being applied in tourism research is relatively limited. Li (2010) applied the chi-square test for independence in his study of the association of loyalty (low and high categories) and brand size (small, medium, and big). This study found that attitudinal loyalty and brand size were marginally related ($\chi^2 = 5.894$, $p = 0.052$), but market size did affect respondents' behavioral loyalty significantly ($\chi^2 = 35.174, p < 0.001$).

Other Non-parametric Tests

Chi-square tests are useful when handling nominal variables, but often a study design involves measurement at the ordinal level, such as levels of education, income and involvement in some activities (never, seldom, sometimes, often and always). On other occasions, some variables originally designed to be measured at interval scales fail to meet one or more assumptions for parametric tests. A number of other non-parametric tests have been developed to meet research needs where the conditions of using parametric alternatives are not met. Table 1.3 summarizes these tests, along with their parametric counterparts.

Table 1.3 Summary of non-parametric tests and their parametric alternative

Non-parametric test	Parametric alternative
Wilcoxon signed-rank test	Paired-samples t-test
Mann–Whitney test	Independent-samples t-test
Kruskal–Wallis test	One-way between-groups ANOVA
Friedman test	One-way repeated-measures ANOVA
Spearman rank test	Pearson's product–moment correlation

The Wilcoxon signed-rank test is used for two repeated measures at different times or conditions, and is the non-parametric alternative to the repeated measures, or paired samples *t*-test. Instead of comparing means, the Wilcoxon test converts scores to ranks and compares them between Treatments 1 and 2 (or at Times 1 and 2). The null hypothesis states that there is no treatment effect. The test statistic *T* is found by comparing the sum of positive ranks (i.e., in favor of Treatment 1) and the sum of negative ranks (i.e., in favor of Treatment 2). *T* is the smaller sum of the two. The degrees of freedom of this test are the number of pairs in the two treatments.

The Mann–Whitney test is the non-parametric alternative to the independent-samples *t*-test. As with the Wilcoxon signed-rank test, the Mann–Whitney *U* test compares and converts scores to ranks and evaluates whether the ranks for the two groups are significantly different. The test statistic is *U*, which can be calculated directly, if the number of scores is small, by counting the number of X_1 less than X_2 and the number of X_2 less than X_1. *U* equals the smaller of the two numbers. When the number of scores is a bit larger, *U* can be calculated by using the following formulae:

$$U_i = n_1 n_2 + \frac{n_i(n_i + 1)}{2} - R_i \qquad (1.11)$$

where n_1 and n_2 are the numbers of scores in group 1 and group 2, R_i is the sum of ranks for group *i* (*i*=1 or 2), *U*=smaller of U_1 and U_2, and the degrees of freedom are (n_1, n_2).

When the sample size is large (above 50 pairs for the Wilcoxon signed-rank test or above 20 in either group for the Mann–Whitney *U* test), the sampling distributions of *T* and *U* approximate a normal distribution. The *T* and *U* values can then be transformed to *z* scores and compared to the desired critical value of *z* to decide whether the null hypothesis is rejected or not.

The Kruskal–Wallis test is the non-parametric alternative to the one-way between-groups ANOVA. The test statistic *H* can be calculated by:

$$H = \left[\frac{12}{N(N + 1)} \sum_{i=1}^{k} \frac{R_i^2}{n_i} \right] - 3(N + 1) \qquad (1.12)$$

where *k* is the number of independent groups, n_i is the number of observations in group *i*, *N* is the total number of observations, and R_i is the sum of the ranks in group *i*.

Wang and Pfister (2008) applied the Mann–Whitney *U* test and Kruskal–Wallis test to the analysis of the effects of gender, Civil Club membership, educational levels, and length of residence on residents' perception of each of the personal benefits from tourism. The reason for choosing these tests instead of the independent-sample *t*-test and one-way ANOVA was because of violation of the normality assumption. Significant test results indicated that female residents were more likely to perceive that they had obtained benefits from downtown revitalization and tourism activities with arts and cultural features than male residents were.

The Friedman test is the non-parametric alternative to the one-way repeated measures ANOVA. The test statistic F_r is calculated as follows:

$$F_r = \left[\frac{12}{Nk(k+1)} \sum_{i=1}^{k} R_i^2 \right] - 3N(k+1) \tag{1.13}$$

where N, k and R_i are defined in the same way as in the Kruskal-Wallis H test.

When the null hypothesis is true, in large samples the sampling distributions of H and F_r are closely approximated by the chi-squared distribution, with the degrees of freedom equal to $k - 1$.

In a study comparing different methodologies of measuring service quality in a tour operating context, Hudson et al. (2004) ranked the ratings of 13 dimensions of service quality based on each of the four methodologies. The Friedman test was then applied to the four ranked variables (each with 13 ranked observations) to determine if there were any statistically significant differences between the four approaches to measuring service quality. The result was not statistically significant. To substantiate the finding, each methodology was individually compared with the other three, using the Wilcoxon signed-ranks test. Once again, no statistically significant difference was found.

The Spearman's rank order correlation is the non-parametric equivalent of the Pearson's product-moment correlation. The correlation coefficient (r_s) can be calculated by the following formula, which can be derived from the formula for the Pearson's correlation coefficient by using the ranks as the values of X and Y.

$$r_s = 1 - \frac{6 \sum d^2}{n(n^2 - 1)} \tag{1.14}$$

where $d = X - Y$ for each pair of ranks and n is the number of paired observations. Given that $n \geq 10$, the test for significance of r_s can be carried out in the same way as for the Pearson correlation coefficient. That is, the test statistic is based on the Student's t-distribution, with the degrees of freedom equal to $(n - 2)$ and the test statistic is:

$$t = \frac{r_s}{\sum (1 - r_s^2)/(n - 2)} \tag{1.15}$$

Horneman et al. (2002) used the Spearman rank correlation coefficient to examine the association of senior travelers' holiday preference rankings and some demographic variables such as income and education across six market segments. The results suggested that respondents with more formal educations tended to prefer pioneer-type holidays. Senior travelers with less formal education preferred 'Aussie-type holidays' emphasizing the natural environment and appealing to travelers who are active, adventurous, group/family oriented, outward directed, older, cautious spenders.

ADVANTAGES, LIMITATIONS, AND FURTHER DEVELOPMENTS

As discussed above, both parametric and non-parametric tests have their advantages as well as limitations. Parametric tests have stringent assumptions and normally require large sample sizes. If these conditions are met, parametric tests tend to be more powerful than their non-parametric counterparts, because parametric tests make more use of the information available in the collected data. Parametric tests are based on measurement at the interval level, while non-parametric tests use the ordinal information only. In some cases where assumptions of parametric tests are not met, original measures at the interval level have to be converted to ranks, by which a certain amount of information in the original data is sacrificed. So non-parametric tests are less powerful and sometimes they fail to detect a real statistical difference. Moreover, parametric statistical tests are more flexible and can handle a range of complex situations (such as one-way ANCOVA, two-way ANCOVA, and MANCOVA), while the situations non-parametric tests can deal with are much more limited.

However, non-parametric tests have advantages in certain situations where parametric alternatives are unsuitable or unavailable, such as hypothesis testing associated with categorical variables. In addition, some non-parametric tests can handle samples made up of observations from different populations without making seemly unrealistic assumptions (Siegel and Castellan, 1988).

Often researchers face less straightforward situations for making a choice between parametric and non-parametric tests, for instance, when scores deviate from normality to some extent. Should the researcher use non-parametric techniques or still apply the more powerful parametric tests? Although there is no clear-cut rule for the choice, some rules of thumb have been recommended. For example, according to Leech and Onwuegbuzie (2002), the standardized skewness and kurtosis coefficients of the scores lying within ±2 can be regarded as no serious departure from normality. In such cases, most parametric tests are reasonably robust and can still be applied. Standardized skewness and kurtosis coefficients beyond the ±3 range indicate serious deviation from normality and therefore non-parametric tests are more appropriate.

To overcome the limitations of traditional non-parametric statistical techniques, particularly the lack of power and robustness, further developments have been seen. *Robust statistics* is in the process of developing into a new subspecialty of its own. Several new, more robust non-parametric methods have been developed which seek to control the Type I error rate at their nominal levels and also maintain adequate statistical power, even when data are non-normal and heteroskedastic (Wilcox, 2005). The developments in new techniques such as bootstrapping contribute to the further development of non-parametric statistical techniques. Bootstrapping is a computer-intensive re-sampling technique which creates a new sampling distribution based on original observations, when the assumption of a theoretical distribution is violated. The bootstrapped distribution is then used to compute *p*-values and test hypotheses (Erceg-Hurn and Mirosevich, 2008). Techniques from other statistical branches have also been incorporated into non-parametric tests, such as the non-parametric Bayesian approach (see, for example, Ghosal and Roy, 2009). Meanwhile, some developments also take place in the field of parametric statistics, such as the study of outliers. With parallel developments in both parametric and non-parametric statistics, their distinctions are narrowed and the differences are bridged.

The above new developments have been rarely seen in the tourism literature. Future quantitative tourism studies should consider these more advanced techniques to enhance the power of statistical testing and robustness of empirical findings.

CONCLUSIONS

This chapter discussed the foundations of statistical testing, followed by a number of parametric and non-parametric statistical techniques and their applications in tourism research. In general, parametric tests are more popular than their non-parametric alternatives in tourist behavior studies, mainly because they are relatively more robust and capable of handling complicated research designs. By introducing more and more newly developed, robust, non-parametric techniques into future tourism research, the accuracy and reliability of research findings can be further improved. It should be noted that statistical significance does not necessarily mean theoretical significance. On the other hand, statistical non-significance does not necessarily indicate theoretical non-significance. Therefore caution should be exercised when interpreting a result of statistical testing.

REFERENCES

Andreasen, A.R. (1965), 'Attitudes and consumer behavior: a decision model', in L. Preston (ed.), *New Research in Marketing*, Berkeley: Institute for Business and Economic Research, University of California, pp. 1–16.

Erceg-Hurn, D.M. and V.M. Mirosevich (2008), 'Modern robust statistical methods: an easy way to maximize the accuracy and power of your research', *American Psychologist*, **63** (7), 591–601.

Ghosal, S. and A. Roy (2009), 'Bayesian nonparametric approach to multiple testing', in N.S. Narasimha Sastry, T.S.S.R.K. Rao, M. Delampady and B. Rajeev (eds), *Perspectives in Mathematical Sciences I: Probability and Statistics*, Singapore: World Scientific Publishing, pp. 139–164.

Gibbons, J.D. and S. Chakraborti (2003), *Nonparametric Statistical Inference: Fourth Edition, Revised and Expanded*, New York: Marcel Dekker.

Gravetter, F.J. and L.B. Wallnau (2000), *Statistics for the Behavioral Sciences*, 5th edition, Belmont, CA: Wadsworth.

Grimm, L.G. (1993), *Statistical Applications for the Behavioral Sciences*, New York: John Wiley & Sons.

Horneman, L., R.W. Carter, S. Wei and H. Ruys (2002), 'Profiling the senior traveler: an Australian perspective', *Journal of Travel Research*, **41** (1), 23–37.

Howard, J.A. and J.N. Sheth (1969), *The Theory of Buyer Behavior*, New York: John Wiley.

Huberty, C.J. (1987), 'On statistical testing', *Educational Research*, **16** (8), 4–9.

Huberty, C.J. (1993), 'Historical origins of statistical testing practices: the treatment of Fisher versus Neyman-Pearson views in textbooks', *The Journal of Experimental Education*, **61** (4), 317–333.

Hudson, S., P. Hudson and G.A. Miller (2004), 'The measurement of service quality in the tour operating sector: a methodological comparison', *Journal of Travel Research*, **42** (3), 305–312.

Kazmier, L.J. and N.F. Pohl (1987), *Basic Statistics for Business and Economics*, 2nd edition, Singapore: McGraw-Hill.

Leech, N.L. and A.J. Onwuegbuzie (2002), 'A call for greater use of nonparametric statistics', paper presented at the Annual Meeting of the Mid-South Educational Research Association. Retrieved from http://www.eric.ed.gov/ERICWebPortal/contentdelivery/servlet/ERICServlet?accnoED471346.

Li, X. (2010), 'Loyalty regardless of brands? Examining three nonperformance effects on brand loyalty in a tourism context', *Journal of Travel Research*, **49** (3), 323–336.

Li, X. and J.F. Petrick (2008), 'Examining the antecedents of brand loyalty from an investment model perspective', *Journal of Travel Research*, **47** (1), 25–34.

Li, X., B. Pan, L. Zhang and W.W. Smith (2009), 'The effect of online information search on image development: insights from a mixed-methods study', *Journal of Travel Research*, **48** (1), 45–57.

McClave, J.T., P.G. Benson and T. Sincich (1998), *Statistic for Business and Economics*, 7th edition, London: Prentice Hall.

McLean, J.E. and J.M. Ernest (1998), 'The role of statistical significance testing in educational research', *Research in the Schools*, **5** (2), 15–22.

Marusteri, M. and V. Bacarea (2010), 'Comparing groups for statistical differences: how to choose the right statistical test?', *Biochemia Medica*, **20** (1), 15–32.

Mok, H.M.K. (1990), 'A quasi-experimental measure of the effectiveness of destinational advertising: some evidence from Hawaii', *Journal of Travel Research*, **29** (1), 30–34.

Nicosia, F.M. (1966), *Consumer Decision Processes: Marketing and Advertising Implications*, Englewood Cliffs, NJ: Prentice-Hall.

Olejnik, S., J. Li, S. Supattathum and C.J. Huberty (1997), 'Multiple testing and statistical power with modified Bonferroni procedures', *Journal of Educational and Behavioral Statistics*, **22** (4), 389–406.

Pallant, J. (2005), *SPSS Survival Manual*, 2nd edition, Maidenhead, UK: Open University Press.

Rewtrakunphaiboon, W. and H. Oppewal (2008), 'Effects of package holiday information presentation on destination choice', *Journal of Travel Research*, **47** (2), 127–136.

Siegel, S. and N.J. Castellan Jr. (1988), *Nonparametric Statistics for the Behavioral Sciences*, New York: McGraw–Hill.

Simpson, P.M. and J.A. Siguaw (2008), 'Destination word of mouth: the role of traveler type, residents, and identity salience', *Journal of Travel Research*, **47** (2), 167–182.

Snepenger, D., L. Murphy, M. Snepenger and W. Anderson (2004), 'Normative meanings of experiences for a spectrum of tourism places', *Journal of Travel Research*, **43** (2), 108–117.

Stevens, J. (1996), *Applied Multivariate Statistics for the Social Sciences*, 3rd edition, Mahway, NJ: Lawrence Erlbaum.

Tabachnik, B.G. and L.S. Fidell (2007), *Using Multivariate Statistics*, Boston, MA: Allyn & Bacon.

Tsaur, S.-H. and C.-H. Wang (2009), 'Tip-collection strategies, service guarantees, and consumer evaluations of group package tours', *Journal of Travel Research*, **47** (4), 523–534.

Tukey, J.W. (1953[1984]), 'The problem of multiple comparisons', in H.I. Braun (ed.), *The Collected Works of John W. Tukey, Volume VIII Multiple comparisons: 1948–1983*, New York: Chapman & Hall, pp. 1–300.

Veal, A.J. (2006), *Research Methods for Leisure and Tourism: A Practical Guide*, 3rd edition, Harlow, UK: Prentice Hall.

Wang, Y.A. and R.E. Pfister (2008), 'Residents' attitudes toward tourism and perceived personal benefits in a rural community', *Journal of Travel Research*, **47** (1), 84–93.

Wang, Y., G. Li and X. Bai (2005), 'A residential survey on urban tourism impacts in Harbin', *China Tourism Research*, **1** (1), 116–129.

Waters, D. (2001), *Quantitative Methods for Business*, 4th edition, Harlow, UK: Prentice Hall.

Wilcox, R.R. (2005), *Introduction to Robust Estimation and Hypothesis Testing*, 2nd edition, San Diego, CA: Academic Press.

2 Regression analysis
Jaume Rosselló

INTRODUCTION

Qualitative and quantitative research methods have often both been classed as useful and legitimate by social researchers. However, during recent decades, quantitative methods have come to prevail in the social sciences, and tourism research is not an exception. The main role of quantitative research has typically been reduced to helping generate and pose hypotheses that can then be tested using mathematical research methods. Nowadays, many tourism journals reflect this bias in favor of quantitative methods, and it can be seen that the purpose of qualitative research is usually to provide information for developing further quantitative research (Lewis et al., 1995).

Within the social sciences and some natural sciences, statistics are the most widely used branch of mathematics in quantitative research when hypotheses have to be tested. Statistical methods are extensively used in fields such as economics, social sciences, and biology. Quantitative research using statistical methods starts with the collection of data, based on a certain hypothesis or theory. For instance, quantitative opinion surveys are widely used in tourism, where statistics are commonly reported, such as the proportion of respondents agreeing with a certain stance. In these opinion surveys, the respondents are asked a set of structured questions and their responses are then tabulated. On other occasions, researchers compile and compare different statistics in order to identify some kind of correlation. In this case, when a causal relationship between a "dependent variable" and one or more "independent variables" is hypothesized (and must be tested), regression analysis comes to the fore as a technique for use in circumstances where a particular phenomenon is controlled and determined by certain factors, and the aim is to try to explain and quantify variations in the dependent variable through variations in the independent ones. In tourism, researchers might measure and study the relationship between the demand (measurable in terms of the number of tourists, length of stay, etc.) and other key variables, such as price, income, marketing expenditure, etc. One fundamental principle in quantitative research should nonetheless be highlighted: that correlation does not imply causation. This is because a spurious relationship is always possible between variables where some degree of covariance can be found. Thus associations can be carefully examined between any combination of continuous and categorical variables, using statistical methods.

Because regression analysis estimates how the value of the dependent variable changes when any one of the independent variables is modified (while the other independent variables are held fixed), the said technique can be used in two main frameworks. The first focuses on exploring the nature of the relationship between the dependent variable and one (or more) independent variable(s) in order to analyse expected reactions in the dependent variable, caused by induced changes in the independent one. The second concentrates on how to predict and forecast the independent variable. Using the example of the relationship between tourism demand and prices, income, and other determining variables, in the first case the interest appeal of a research study might be to quantify the effect of an economic crisis or the effect of a tourist tax on tourism demand. In the second case, the interest appeal might be the expected number of tourist arrivals next year at a particular destination.

Since initial applications, numerous techniques for carrying out regression analysis have been developed. With most simple methods, such as linear regressions and ordinary least square regressions, the regression function is defined in terms of a finite set of unknown parameters, estimated from a collected data set. In fact, the performance of a regression analysis will depend on the nature of the data-generating process and how it relates to the regression approach that is used. Since the true nature of the data-generating process is unknown, regression analysis depends to some extent on making assumptions about this process. Although these assumptions are sometimes testable if a large amount of data is available, the validity of the results will be conditional upon the validity of these assumptions. Hence knowledge of the background technique is as important as knowledge of implicit assumptions, so that any biases and shortcomings in the application of the regression analysis are taken into account.

The rest of the chapter is organized as follows: the next section outlines the basic foundations of the technique and gives an intuitive overview of it; then its main applications in tourism research are reviewed; the limitations of regression analysis are considered; and the final section contains the main conclusions.

BACKGROUND TO THE TECHNIQUE

Simple Regressions

Let us assume that the number of vacation days abroad is determined by a single attribute: personal income. At the outset of any regression study, a hypothesis is formulated about the relationship between the variables under analysis: in this case, vacation days and earnings. According to economic theory (and common experience), tourists in the higher income bracket tend to make more trips abroad. Thus the hypothesis can be posed that higher income levels (the independent variable) lead to more vacations days abroad (the dependent variable). The problem can be expressed analytically as:

$$E(Y/X) = f(X, \beta) \tag{2.1}$$

where $E(Y/X)$ represents the expected value of dependent variable Y (vacation days abroad in our case), conditional upon independent variable X (one single independent variable in the case of a simple regression); f is a mathematical function that must be specified; and β are unknown parameters defining the mathematical function f to be estimated.

To illustrate the problem, let us suppose that a data set containing the number of vacation days abroad (Y) and personal income (X) for various individuals (i) is available, and let us plot this information for all the individuals in the sample using a two-dimensional

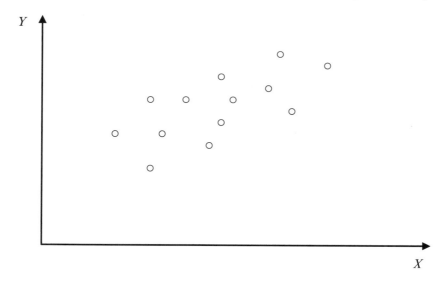

Y

X

Figure 2.1 X–Y plot

diagram, conventionally termed a "scatter" diagram, where each point on it represents an individual from the sample (Figure 2.1).

Figure 2.1 suggests that higher values of X tend to yield higher values of Y, although the relationship is not perfect. (It seems that knowledge of X does not suffice for an entirely accurate prediction of Y.) In other words, the effect of income on vacation days appears to differ across individuals, or else factors other than income influence vacation days. Although omitted variables can lead to a bias problem (as pointed out later), the general assumption is that vacation days are determined by earnings and by an aggregation of omitted factors named "noise".

At this point, one of the simplest options is the assumption of linearity between the variables; that is, each additional amount of income adds the same amount to vacation days.[1] Then the hypothetical relationship between vacation days and income may be written as:

$$Y = \beta_0 + \beta_1 X + \varepsilon \qquad (2.2)$$

where, β_0 represents the constant term (that can be interpreted as the number of vacation days with zero income); β_1 the effect of an additional unit of income; and ε the "noise" term reflecting other factors that influence earnings. The task of a regression analysis is to produce an estimate of unobservable parameters β_0 and β_1, based upon information contained in the data set and upon some assumptions about the characteristics of ε.

A simple regression analysis can be illustrated graphically thanks to the problem's two dimensions. Thus if the noise term (ε) is ignored, Equation 2.2 becomes a line with an "intercept" of β_0 on the vertical axis and a "slope" of β_1 (Figure 2.2), and so it could be said that the task of estimating β_0 and β_1 is equivalent to the task of estimating where this line is located.

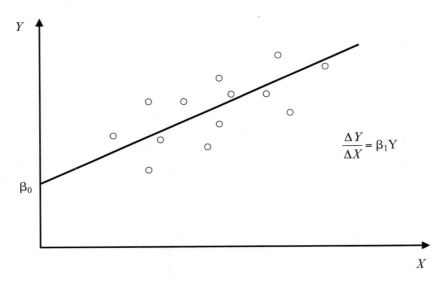

Figure 2.2   X–Y plot with regression line

In order to estimate this line, it is useful to define the *estimated error* for each observation as the vertical distance between the value of Y along the estimated line $\hat{Y}_i = \beta_0 + \beta_1 X_i$ (where $\hat{Y}_i$ is a generated observation i of Y by plugging the actual value of X_i into the equation). Thus estimated errors for each observation i may be calculated as follows:

$$\varepsilon_i = \hat{Y}_i - Y_i \qquad (2.3)$$

It is important to note that for each possible line that might be estimated, this will lead to a different set of estimated errors. Thus in the most simple usual context, regression analysis then chooses from among all possible lines by selecting the one for which the sum of the squares of the estimated errors is at a minimum. This is termed the minimum sum of squared errors or Ordinary Least Squares (OLS) criterion. The virtues of the OLS criterion reside in the fact that it is very easy to use computationally and it has attractive statistical properties under plausible noise term assumptions, as discussed later.

Multiple Regression

The number of vacation days abroad clearly seems to be affected by a variety of factors in addition to personal income. A multiple regression is a procedure that generalizes a simple regression by separately incorporating additional factors into the analysis. Because the effect of each of these additional factors is estimated, it is valuable because it quantifies the impact of various simultaneous influences on a single dependent variable. Furthermore, multiple regressions are often indispensable, even when we are interested in examining the effect of one of the independent variables, given the problem of the bias caused by omitted variables in a simple regression.

Let us now assume that the number of vacation days abroad (Y) is determined by two attributes: personal income (X_1) and the exchange rate (X_2). If a linear effect between the exchange rate and vacation days is assumed, the modified model may be written as:

$$Y = \beta_0 + \beta_1 X_1 + \beta_2 X_2 + \varepsilon \tag{2.4}$$

where β_2 represents the effect of an additional unit on the exchange rate.

The task of estimating parameters β_0, β_1, and β_2 is conceptually identical to the earlier task of estimating just β_0 and β_1. The difference is that it is no longer a question of choosing a line on a two-dimensional diagram. For Equation (2.4), regression analysis will select a plane so that the sum of the squared errors is at a minimum. However, for a more general multiple regression with more than two explanatory variables, the vision of the problem that a graph allows is lost, although the estimation procedures remain the same. Analytically, if it is assumed that the dependent variable (Y) is determined by n attributes ($X_1, X_2, \ldots, X_n$), then the general model may be written as:

$$Y = \beta_0 + \beta_1 X_1 + \beta_2 X_2 + \cdots + \beta_n X_n + \varepsilon \tag{2.5}$$

where β_0 is the constant term that indicates the estimated value of Y when all the explanatory variables are 0 ($X_1 = X_2 = \ldots = X_n = 0$), and $\beta_1, \beta_2, \ldots, \beta_n$ is the vector of parameters to be estimated, indicating the effect of an additional unit of each of the independent variables ($X_1, X_2, \ldots, X_n$) on Y when the rest of the independent variables remain constant. As in the case of a simple regression, the OLS criterion is an attractive option because it is easy to compute and also due to its attractive statistical properties, as discussed in continuation.

Essential Assumptions and Statistical Properties

The assumptions and statistical properties that are required in regression analysis are dependent on the noise term ε being considered a random variable, drawn by nature from some probability distribution. It thus becomes clear that the estimates of β_1, β_2, $\ldots$, β_n will also be random variables, because estimates generated by the minimum OLS criterion (OLS estimator)[2] will depend upon the particular value of ε, drawn by nature for each observation in the data set. Likewise, because there is a probability distribution from which each ε_i is drawn, there must also be a probability distribution from which each parameter estimate is drawn, with the distribution of the latter being a function of the distributions of the former. The attraction of the statistical properties of a regression all reside in the relationship between the probability distribution of the parameter estimates and the true values of those parameters. Thus if the mean of that probability distribution is equal to the true value of the parameter we are trying to estimate, the estimator is *unbiased*.

An estimator is termed *consistent* if it takes advantage of additional data to generate more accurate estimates. In other words, a consistent estimator yields estimates that converge on the true value of the underlying parameter as the sample size gets larger. Thus the probability distribution of the estimate of any parameter will have a lower variance as the sample size increases, and in the limit (infinite sample size), the estimate will equal the true value. At this point it should be noted that a lower variance in the probability distribution of the estimator is clearly desirable, because it reduces the probability of an estimate that differs greatly from the true value of the underlying parameter. In comparing different unbiased estimators, the one with the lowest variance is termed *efficient* or best.

The OLS estimator is characterized as being unbiased, consistent, and efficient under certain assumptions. First, if the noise term for each observation, ε_i, is drawn from a distribution that has a zero mean, the sum of squared errors criterion generates estimates that are unbiased and consistent. Thus for each observation in the sample, a noise term is drawn by nature from a different probability distribution. As long as each of these distributions has a zero mean, the minimum OLS criterion is unbiased and consistent. This assumption is sufficient to ensure that each of the explanatory variables in the model is uncorrelated with the expected value of the noise term.

Second, if the distributions from which the noise terms are drawn for each observation have the same variance, and the noise terms are statistically independent from each other, then the sum of squared errors criterion gives the most efficient estimates available from any linear estimator. Additionally, it should be highlighted that, if this second assumption is violated, the OLS criterion will remain unbiased and consistent, and it is possible to decrease the variance of the estimator by considering what is known about the noise term. The statistical procedures for dealing with this sort of problem go beyond the scope of this chapter.[3] However, when regression analysis in tourism literature is considered in the next section, an outline will be given of some cases of special interest in the field of tourism analysis.

APPLICATIONS OF REGRESSION ANALYSIS TO TOURISM

Tourism Demand Modeling and Forecasting

One field of research in academic tourism literature where regression analysis has been used as a central research tool is tourism demand modeling and forecasting (Song and Li, 2008). Frechtling (1996) argues that tourism products and the tourist industry have different characteristics from other products or sectors as reasons why the determinants of tourism demand must be identified for forecasting purposes, more than in any other activity. These reasons include the fact that tourism products cannot be stored, and so any unused supply cannot be kept for a later date when there is a higher demand. Neither is it possible to separate the production process from consumption. This interaction between consumers and producers means that goods and services must be offered when there is a demand. At the same time, it must be remembered that tourist satisfaction is largely dependent on complementary services. For example, destination loyalty or the repeat visitation rate are not only dependent on tourism accommodation facilities, but, more specifically, on all the other goods and services consumed by tourists directly or indirectly during their stay. Likewise, tourism demand is extremely sensitive to natural disasters and socio-political problems, such as wars, terrorist attacks, or natural disasters. Finally, we must also add the need for long-term investment into facilities and infrastructure able to meet the expectations of future demands.

The literature highlights the existence of two big groups of quantitative methods of determining and forecasting tourism demand: univariate and causal models (Witt and Witt, 1995). Univariate models, used primarily for the purposes of forecasting, are based on the assumption that forecasts can be made without including factors that determine the level of the variable. Thus the only information that they require is the past evolution of the variable to be forecasted. Within the regression analysis context, a simple example of a univariate model can be represented by the autoregressive model

$$Y_t = \beta_0 + \beta_1 Y_{t-1} + \beta_2 Y_{t-2} + \cdots + \beta_n Y_{t-n} + u_t \qquad (2.6)$$

where it is important to note that observations of tourism demand (Y) refer to time periods t (years, quarters, months, etc) and that the explanatory variables are, in fact, the lags of the same dependent variable. Different options have been proposed for variables capable of capturing the concept of tourism demand, with the number of tourists being the most common choice followed by tourist expenditures (Crouch, 1994).

Whatever the case, in regression analyses that use time series data, autocorrelation of the errors is a frequent problem, violating the OLS assumption that the error terms are uncorrelated. (This is why the error term is denoted by u_t instead of ε_t.) While it does not bias the OLS coefficient estimates, standard errors tend to be underestimated when the autocorrelations of the errors at low lags are positive. Autocorrelation of the errors, which themselves are unobserved, can generally be detected, because it produces auto-correlation in the observable residuals, and different alternatives have been proposed to overcome this problem (Box et al., 1994).

Although an autoregressive model is a basic univariate model, the complexity of this set of models (including the most illustrative problem of autocorrelation using time series data) depends on the number of mathematical operations and implicit assumptions that are involved. Methods such as Box–Jenkins, which are relatively complex given the high number of estimations that are required, offer no computational problems nowadays, thanks to the numerous econometric programs that are available. In the tourism demand literature, forecasts obtained with more complex models normally use forecasts generated by simple univariate models to demonstrate (or reject) their superiority (Kulendran and Witt, 2001; Lim and McAleer, 2001; Rosselló, 2001; Smeral and Wëger, 2005).

Within the univariate context, an alternative group of models can be included that considers time (instead of the lagged independent variable) as the only variable in determining tourism demand. Witt and Witt (1991) propose ten different functional forms that try to explain the growth in tourism demand. Witt and Witt (1995) introduced the use of the Gompertz curve for forecasting, based on the evolutionary stage of the tourism product in the lifecycle. Later, Chan (1993), Chu (1998a, 1998b, 2004) and Wong (1997a) focused on the strong seasonal component and proposed the use of the sinusoid function for forecasting.

When a causal framework is considered in tourism demand, a simple example of a regression model can be represented by the following equation:

$$Y_t = \beta_0 + \beta_1 X_{1t} + \beta_2 X_{2t} + \cdots + \beta_n X_{nt} + u_t \qquad (2.7)$$

It should be noted that again the variables included in the regression analysis show t as a subscript, denoting the time dependence of the observations included in the model both for the dependent (Y) and independent variables ($X_1, X_2, \ldots, X_n$), as well as an error term (u_t) often characterized by a high level of autocorrelation. Although the economic underpinnings of Equation (2.6) were described in Morley (1992) and Sakai (1988), the first estimation of these models can be found in Gerakis (1965), Gray (1966) and Laber (1969). In fact, empirical applications developed during the 1970s and the '80s did not vary very much from these initial applications, despite the theoretical difficulties involved in aggregating individual tourism demands (Morley, 1995) and the neglected treatment of the u_t term and use of diagnostic tests (Crouch, 1994; Lim, 1997a).

The set of independent variables ($X_1, X_2, \ldots, X_n$) can include consumers' approximate income, generally measured by using available family income or the per capita GDP (Archer, 1980; Deng and Athanasopoulos, 2011; Gray, 1982; Harrop, 1973; Kulendran and Divisekera, 2007); the price of the destination, usually specified as the ratio between the consumer price indexes of the destination and country of origin, given the difficulty in finding statistical series of tourism prices (Jung and Fujii, 1976; Kulendran and Divisekera, 2007; Kwack, 1972; Rosensweig, 1988); the cost of transport from the issuing country to the destination (Brida and Risso, 2009; Martin and Witt, 1988); the nominal (or real) exchange rate between the origin country and the destination (Brida and Risso, 2009; Kulendran and Divisekera, 2007; Tremblay, 1989; Truett and Truett, 1987); the price of substitute and/or complementary destinations, usually defined in the form of an index, based on the weighted average of the prices of other destinations that compete for the same market as the destination under consideration (Divisekera, 2003; Uysal and Crompton, 1985; Witt and Martin, 1987, advertising or the cost of promotion; and other types of variables such as a change in preferences (Barry and O'Hagan, 1972; Crouch et al., 1992; Kulendran and Divisekera, 2007), the capital invested in infrastructure, which defines both the tourist industry's quality and capacity (Carey, 1989; Geyikdagi, 1995, Khadaroo and Seetanah, 2007), the stock of immigrants at the home country (Seetaram and Dwyer, 2009) or at the destination (Dwyer et al., 2010; Seetaram, 2012), and even meteorological variables (Barry and O'Hagan, 1972).

No definitive conclusions can be reached from different meta-analyses of the results of tourism demand modeling made before the '90s (Crouch 1994, 1996; Lim 1997b, 1999) with regard to the value of the parameters of those variables most often used in specifications. What does stand out is the infrequency with which econometric tests are used to examine the basic hypotheses of the linear regression model, together with the absence of serial correlation, homoscedasticity, the linear functional form, the normality of the error term, and the exogeneity of the independent variables (Lim, 1997a).

Possibly, this is why since the 1990s studies have tried to improve on specifications. Wong (1997b), for example, analyses the statistical properties of series of tourist arrivals from different countries, demonstrating an absence of stationarity in most cases. The solution to this problem involves the use of cointegration analysis, which was not widely applied to aggregate estimation models and tourism demand forecasting until the 1990s, with some of the most representative studies being made by Bonham and Gangnes (1996), Dritsakis (2004), Kulendran (1996), Kulendran and King (1997), Lathiras and Syriopoulos (1998) and Syriopoulos (1995).

Within the causal model category, demand systems or tourist expenditure systems should also be mentioned. These have centered their attention on the problem of consumers faced with a choice of market goods and services. The formulation of simultaneous equation systems seeks to avoid the biases that occur with uni-equation models, when consumer decisions regarding tourism services are considered in isolation from all other consumer goods. The first applications of this methodology can be found in Kliman (1981), Taplin (1980) and Van Soest and Kooreman (1987). However, the appearance of an article by Deaton and Muellbauer (1980) lent greater weight by laying the foundations of consumer behavior theory, leading to the adoption of the methodology and its application to tourism demand in Divisekera (2003), Fujii et al. (1985), Pyo et al. (1991), and Sakai (1988). In O'Hagan and Harrison (1984), Smeral (1988), or Syriopoulos and Sinclair (1993), the model is extended to include the second-stage selection of one of a choice of destinations, so that the following third stage would correspond to the allocation of spending on goods and services at each destination. During the last decade, simultaneous equation systems have centered on an analysis of time series properties within the said system (Cortés-Jiménez et al. 2009; De Mello and Fortuna, 2005; Durbarry and Sinclair, 2003; Li et al., 2004; Li et al., 2006; Mangion et al, 2005).

Nonetheless, together with aggregate models, thanks to recent developments in the field of microeconometrics, models with microdata have been gaining ground. Since the earliest applications by Morley (1992), Rugg (1973), and Witt (1982), based on discrete choice models, random utility models have been used as a tool to estimate the parameters that determine a certain choice of destination (Morley 1994a and 1994b). In reference to regression analysis, the main problem that these models have to solve is the nature of the dependent variable, which could be binomial (entailing making or not making a specific choice, and so it can only take 0 or 1), multinomial (entailing making a choice from a particular set), count data (observations can take only non-negative integer values), etc. Different applications have attempted to tackle problems of various kinds. One of the main goals within this new framework is the number of dependent variables (dependent on the aim of the study) that may influence such decisions (Correia et al., 2007; Eugenio-Martin and Campos-Soria, 2010; Huybers, 2005; Nicolau and Más, 2005; Pestana et al., 2008; Thrane, 2008).

Supply-oriented, Policy, and Environmental Analyses and Other Issues

Given that regression analysis is a research tool capable of finding a statistical relationship between an objective (dependent) variable and a set of causal factors (independent variables), it is not surprising that its use in tourism research has not been limited to tourism demand analysis. In analyses of the supply, the first issue that comes to mind is modeling the tourist supply function (Borooah, 1999), including, for instance, the number of hotel beds as a dependent variable and other factors, such as previous demand indicators, quality, or exchange rates, as independent ones. However, it should be noted that the huge complexity of defining the tourism supply product, a lack of supply-related data at most destinations and difficulty in identifying the different components that make up the tourism product have led analyses of the supply and the use of regression analysis to center on some specific issues.

One of the most interesting of these applications is the hedonic pricing model, where an explanation of how prices are formed from different key characteristics is proposed.

Using regression analysis as a reference, the price of a package holiday or overnight stays at a hotel are used as the dependent variable, explained by a set of explanatory variables, such as the destination's location, number of nights' stay, hotel category, characteristics of the services offered by the hotels, etc. Some applications of the hedonic regression method in tourism can be found in Clewer et al. (1992), Espinet et al. (2003), Haroutunian and Pashardes (2005), Mangion et al. (2005), Papatheodorou (2002), Rambonilaza (2006), Rigall-i-Torrent and Fluvià (2007), Sinclair et al. (1990), and Thrane (2005). Estimating the hedonic price function econometrically allows percentage price differences among destinations to be derived, together with the marginal value of an additional unit of a certain characteristic.

Davies and Downward (1996) centered their attention on the amount of sales, using a sample of UK hotel companies during the period 1989–93. Using regression analysis, variations in benefits in relation to sales were explained as a function of lagged market share variables, the cyclical evolution of the unemployment rate and a concentration index. Skill at capturing a marked segment, with a longer season by hotels, is analysed in Capó et al. (2007), where the number of months the hotel stays open is explained through a set of supply factors, using a sample of Balearic hotels. In this case, because of the integer and limited nature of the independent variable (number of months), an ordered logit was used as the estimation procedure. The problem of seasonality and its determinants is also studied in Rosselló et al. (2004), where the economic determinants of seasonal patterns are analysed from a demand perspective using the Gini coefficient as the dependent variable.

Regression analysis has not only focused on revenues and benefits from tourism. The environmental effects of tourism have generated debate on a new concept – sustainable tourism – which has been the object of growing attention by governments, international organizations, academic institutions, and individual researchers. A good reflection of the interest that this issue has aroused is the abundance of literature mainly motivated by an analysis of factors that can help to achieve sustainable tourism levels. Most natural resources related to tourism are characterized by the impossibility of their exclusion, so the role of prices as an indicator of scarcity or as a motivating factor in the behavior of economic agents disappears. The result is the deterioration and over-exploitation of the environment. That is why it is necessary to convert the importance that the environment represents in social wellbeing into monetary units and then to internalize the externalities generated by tourism, thereby achieving a sustainable model of tourism development.

Valuation methodologies can be classified by differentiating those that produce a direct monetary valuation and those that produce an indirect one. The first group includes the contingent valuation method and bidding games, while the second involves the travel cost and hedonic pricing methods.[4] Both groups, especially the second, require a regression analysis for different purposes. Contingent valuation involves asking people directly (or indirectly) for an economic valuation of an environmental (or non-market) good or service. Some examples of its application include Asafu-Adjaye and Tapsuwan (2008) for scuba diving; Dutta et al. (2007) for heritage tourism; Greiner and Rolfe (2004) for natural areas; Lee and Han (2002) for national parks, and Rulleau et al. (2011) for recreational values. The usefulness of regression analysis in contingent valuation techniques lies mainly (but not exclusively) in the quantification of the payment decision.

The travel cost method, which is suited to estimating the user value of a natural resource when it is mainly visited for recreational purposes, has been used to assess the value of destinations specializing in nature or ecotourism and natural areas or resources located at destinations where the main motivation for the trip is a visit to a natural area or contact with the natural environment (Herath and Kennedy, 2004; Loomis and Keske, 2009; Maille and Mendelsohn, 1993; Riera, 2000; Wang at al. 2009). In this case, regression analysis can be used in the estimation of the demand for visits to a certain destination.

Once environmental issues have been evaluated, policy measures must be considered and applied. Although a wide range of instruments can be found in the literature on policies for the protection of the environment, the internalization of externalities and management of public services most commonly analysed through regression analysis are market-based instruments. Thus a possible extension of demand studies that consider prices to be a determining factor in tourism is an analysis of taxes (Aguiló et al., 2005; Blair et al., 1987; Bonham et al., 1991; Palmer et al., 2007). When a unit tax is levied on tourism accommodation, the tax burden falls on buyers and sellers, depending on supply and demand elasticities. Generally speaking, levying an *ad-valorem* tax on accommodation will reduce occupancy rates by raising prices. The price rise for consumers, divided by the reduction in the producer price, is more or less equal to the ratio between the supply and demand elasticities. The higher the elasticity of supply compared with the elasticity of demand, the higher the tax burden on the buyers. In cases where there is an infinite elasticity of supply or zero demand, the tax burden falls exclusively on buyers.

LIMITATIONS OF REGRESSION ANALYSIS

Since the true form of the data-generating process is generally not known, regression analysis often depends to some extent on making assumptions about this process. Two common mistakes are (1) to reach the conclusion that there is a strong link between two variables, while the influence of another perhaps more important one may not have been estimated and (2) not to take into account the fact that relations between the different explained and explanatory variables can be circular (X explains Y and Y explains X).

Other limitations that should be highlighted are sometimes (but not always) testable if a large amount of data is available and they are linked to the assumptions of the regression analysis. First, as is evident in the name multiple linear regression, it is assumed that the relationship between variables is linear. As a general rule, it is prudent to look always at bivariate scatterplots of the variables under analysis. If curvature in the relationships is evident, it is possible to consider either transforming the variables or explicitly allowing for non-linear components. In practice, the assumption of linearity is difficult to confirm and more complex functional forms require a large amount of data that is not always available. Second, in reference to the normal distribution of the residuals, even though most tests are quite robust with regard to violations of this assumption, it is always a good idea, before drawing final conclusions, to review the distributions of the major variables of interest. The recommendation here is to depict histograms for the residuals, as well as normal probability plots, in order to inspect the distribution of the residual values.

Additional limitations concerning the amount of explanatory variables to be used and the necessary number of observations should also be mentioned. Although one can be seduced by including as many predictor variables as possible (and usually at least a few of them will come out significant), it is important to be aware that the confidence intervals are not 100 percent, so it is possible (a low probability, but higher when an additional number of independent variables is included) to find a statistical relationship when, in fact, there is no relationship between the variables. This problem is compounded when, in addition, the number of observations is relatively low. Some authors recommend that, as a general rule, one should have at least 10 to 20 times as many observations as one has variables, otherwise parameter estimations are probably very unstable and unlikely to be replicated if the study were conducted again.

The multicollinearity problem should also be highlighted here. Multicollinearity can appear when two or more predictor variables in a multiple regression model are highly correlated and, as a result, the coefficient estimates may change erratically in response to small changes in the model or the data. Multicollinearity does not reduce the predictive power or reliability of the model as a whole, at least within the sample data itself. However, it can affect calculations regarding individual predictors. A high degree of multicollinearity can also cause computer software packages to be unable to perform the matrix inversion that is required for computing the regression coefficients, or it may make the results of that inversion inaccurate.

Even though most multiple regression assumptions cannot be tested explicitly, major violations can be detected and they should be dealt with appropriately. Error analysis and test diagnostics can be used to detect particular problems and, in the end, to validate results obtained through regression analysis. However, the statistical procedures for dealing with this sort of problem go beyond the scope of this chapter.

CONCLUSIONS

Regression analysis has become a popular statistical instrument in tourism for the investigation of relationships between variables. The investigator looks to determine the causal effect of one or more variable upon another; for instance, the effect of a price increase or income decrease on tourism demand. To explore such issues, the investigator collects data for the variables of interest and uses regression analysis to estimate the quantitative effect of the causal variables on the dependent variable. Additionally the degree of confidence of the true relationship being close to the estimated one (known as statistical significance) is also usually assessed in order to make the exercise more credible.

Regression techniques have long been central to the field of econometrics and increasingly they have become important to tourism researchers as well. In this chapter, an overview of the technique has been given in order to show how regression analysis works, what it assumes, and what the most typical limitations are, using different examples from tourism literature. It has been shown that regression analysis has mainly focused on determining tourism demand, both in order to forecast and quantify the relationship between its determinants. However, its use in tourism research has not been limited to demand analysis. Other tourism research issues such as tourism supply, analyses of policy measures, valuation techniques applied to environmental tourism issues, and, in general, any study aimed at quantifying the relationship between a dependent variable and a set of causal factors have benefited and can benefit in the future from regression analysis.

The major conceptual limitation of all regression techniques is that you can only discover relationships, but never be sure about underlying causal mechanisms. Nonetheless, as a bare minimum, regression analysis helps establish the existence of connections that call for closer investigation.

NOTES

1. Although the linearity assumption is common in regression studies, it is by no means essential to the application of the technique, and it can easily be relaxed when the researcher has reason to suppose a priori that the relationship in question is non-linear. For instance, the popular relationship $Y = aX^b$ (a and b being parameters to be estimated) can be transformed into the linear relationship $\ln Y = \ln a + b \log X$. In this context, b can be interpreted directly as the elasticity between Y and X.
2. Please note that other alternative criteria for generating parameter estimates would also be considered as estimators, such as minimizing the sum of the absolute values of errors.
3. Numerous manuals deal with the issue of regression analysis. Some of the most popular among economists are Greene (2006) and Gujarati and Porter (2009).
4. The hedonic price model is discussed in Chapter 9 of this volume.

REFERENCES

Aguiló, E., A. Riera and J. Rosselló (2005), 'The short-term price effect of a tourist tax on the demand for tourism through a dynamic demand model', *Tourism Management*, **26** (3), 359–365.

Archer, B.H. (1980), 'Forecasting demand: quantitative and intuitive techniques', *International Journal of Tourism Management*, **1** (1), 5–12.

Asafu-Adjaye, J. and S. Tapsuwan (2008), 'A contingent valuation study of scuba diving benefits: case study in Mu Ko Similan Marine National Park, Thailand', *Tourism Management*, **29** (6), 1122–1130.

Barry, K. and J. O'Hagan (1972), 'An econometric study of British tourist expenditure in Ireland', *Economic and Social Review*, **3** (2), 143–161.

Blair, A.R., F. Giarrantini and H. Spiro (1987), 'Incidence of the amusement tax', *National Tax Journal*, **40** (1), 61–69.

Bonham, C.S. and B. Gangnes (1996), 'Interevention analysis with cointegrated time series: the case of Hawaii hotel room tax', *Applied Economics*, **28**, 1281–1293.

Bonham, C.S, E. Fujiii, E. Im and J. Mak (1991), 'The impact of the hotel tax room: an interrupted time series approach', *National Tax Journal*, **45** (4), 433–441.

Borooah, V. (1999), 'The supply of hotel rooms in Queensland, Australia', *Annals of Tourism Research*, **26**, 985–1003.

Box, G.E.P., G.M. Jenkins and G.C. Reinsel (1994), *Time Series Analysis: Forecasting and Control*, Upper Saddle River, NJ: Prentice-Hall.

Brida, J.G. and W.A. Risso (2009), 'A dynamic panel data study of the German demand for tourism in South Tyrol', *Tourism and Hospitality Research*, **9** (4), 305–313.

Capó, J., A. Riera and J. Rosselló (2007), 'Accommodation determinants of seasonal patterns', *Annals of Tourism Research*, **34** (2), 422–436.

Carey, K. (1989), 'Tourism development in LDCs: hotel capacity expansion with reference to Barbados', *World Development*, **17** (1), 59–67.

Chan, Y.M. (1993), 'Forecasting tourism: a sine wave time series regression approach', *Journal of Travel Research*, **32** (2), 58–60.

Chu, F.L. (1998a), 'Forecasting tourist arrivals: nonlinear sine wave or ARIMA?', *Journal of Travel Research*, **36** (3), 79–84.

Chu, F.L. (1998b), 'Forecasting tourism: a combined approach', *Tourism Management*, **19** (6), 515–520.

Chu, F.L. (2004), 'Forecasting tourism demand: a cubic polynomial approach', *Tourism Management*, **25** (2), 209–218.

Clewer, A., A. Pack and M.T. Sinclair (1992), 'Price competitiveness and inclusive tourim holidays in European cities', in P. Johnson and B. Thomas (eds) *Choice and Demand in Tourism*, London: Mansell, pp. 123–144.

Correia, A., C.M. Santos and C.P. Barros (2007), 'Tourism in Latin America. a choice analysis', *Annals of Tourism Research*, **34** (3), 610–629.

Cortés-Jiménez, I., R. Durbarry and M. Pulina (2009), 'Estimation of outbound Italian tourism demand: a monthly dynamic EC-LAIDS model', *Tourism Economics*, **15** (3), 547–565.

Crouch, G.I. (1994), 'A meta-analysis of tourism demand', *Annals of Tourism Research*, **22** (1), 103–118.

Crouch, G.I. (1996), 'Demand elasticities in international marketing. a meta-analytical application to tourism', *Journal of Business Research*, **36**, 117–136.

Crouch, G.I., L. Schultz and J. Valerio (1992), 'Marketing international tourism to Australia: a regression analysis', *Tourism Management*, **13** (2), 196–208.

Davies, B. and D. Downward (1996), 'The structure, conduct, performance paradigm as applied to the UK hotel industry', *Tourism Economics*, **2** (2), 151–158.

De Mello, M.M. and N. Fortuna (2005), 'Testing alternative dynamic systems for modelling tourism demand', *Tourism Economics*, **11**, 517–537.

Deaton, A. and J. Muellbauer (1980), *Economics and Consumer Behaviour*, New York: Cambridge University Press.

Deng, M. and G. Athanasopoulos (2011), 'Modelling Australian domestic and international inbound travel: a spatial and temporal approach', *Tourism Management*, **32**, 1075–1084.

Divisekera, S. (2003), 'A model of demand for international tourism', *Annals of Tourism Research*, **30** (1), 31–49.

Dritsakis, N. (2004), 'Cointegration analysis of German and British tourism demand for Greece', *Tourism Management*, **25** (1), 111–119.

Durbarry, R. and M.T. Sinclair (2003), 'Market shares analysis: the case of French tourism demand', *Annals of Tourism Research*, **30**, 927–941.

Dutta, M., S. Banerjee and Z. Husain (2007), 'Untapped demand for heritage: a contingent valuation study of Prinsep Ghat, Calcutta', *Tourism Management*, **28**, 83–95.

Dwyer L., P. Forsyth, B. King and N. Seetaram (2010), 'Migration related determinants of Australian inbound and outbound tourism flows', report submitted to Sustainable Tourism Cooperative Research Centre (STCRC), Australia.

Espinet, J.M., M. Saez, G. Coenders and M. Fluvià (2003), 'Effect on prices of the attributes of holiday hotels: a hedonic prices approach', *Tourism Economics*, **9** (2), 165–177.

Eugenio-Martin, J.L. and J.A. Campos-Soria (2010), 'Climate in the region of origin and destination choice in outbound tourism demand', *Tourism Management*, **31**, 744–753.

Frechtling, D.C. (1996), *Practical Tourism Forecasting*, London: Butteworth-Heinemann.

Fujii, E.T., M. Khaled and J. Mak (1985), 'An almost ideal demand system for visitor expenditures', *Journal of Transport Economics and Policy*, May, 161–171.

Gerakis, A.S. (1965), 'Effects of exchange-rate devaluations and revaluations on receipts from tourism', *International Monetary Fund Staff Papers*, **12** (3), 365–84.

Geyikdagi, N.V. (1995), 'Investments in tourism development and the demand for travel', *Rivista Internazionale di Scienze Economiche e Commerciali*, **42** (5), 391–403.

Gray, H.P. (1966), 'The demand for international travel by the United States and Canada', *International Economic Review*, **7** (1), 83–92.

Gray, H.P. (1982), 'The contributions of economics to tourism', *Annals of Tourism Research*, **9** (1), 105–25.

Greene, W. (2006), *Econometric Analysis*. Ventura, CA: Academic Internet Publishers.

Greiner, R. and J. Rolfe (2004), 'Estimating consumer surplus and elasticity of demand of tourist visitation to a region in North Queensland using contingent valuation', *Tourism Economics*, **10** (3), 317–328.

Gujarati, D.N. and D.C. Porter (2009), *Basic Econometrics*, New York: McGraw-Hill.

Haroutunian, S. and P. Pashardes (2005) 'Using brochure information for the hedonic analysis of holiday packages', *Tourism Economics*, **11** (1), 69–84.

Harrop, J. (1973), 'On the economics of the tourist boom', *Bulletin of Economic Research*, (May), 55–72.

Herath, G. and J. Kennedy (2004), 'Estimating the economic value of Mount Buffalo National Park with the Travel Cost and Contingent Valuation Models', *Tourism Economics*, **10** (1), 63–78.

Huybers, T. (2005), 'Destination choice modelling: what's in a name?', *Tourism Economics*, **11** (3), 329–350.

Jung, J.M. and E.T. Fujii (1976), 'The price elasticity of demand for air travel: some new evidence', *Journal of Transport Economics and Policy*, **10** (3), 257–262.

Khadaroo, J. and B. Seetanah (2007), 'Transport infrastructure and tourism development', *Annals of Tourism Research*, **34**, 1021–1032.

Kliman, M.L. (1981), 'A quantitative analysis of Canadian overseas tourism', *Transportation Research A*, **15** (6), 487–497.

Kulendran, N. (1996), 'Modelling quarterly tourist flows to Australia using cointegration analysis', *Tourism Economics*, **2** (3), 203–222.

Kulendran, N. and S. Divisekera (2007), 'Measuring the economic impact of Australian tourism marketing expenditure', *Tourism Economics*, **13**, 261–274.

Kulendran, N. and M.L. King (1997), 'Forecasting international quarterly tourists flows using error-correction and time-series models', *International Journal of Forecasting*, **13**, 319–327.

Kulendran, N. and S.F. Witt (2001), 'Cointegration versus least squares regression', *Annals of Tourism Research*, **28** (2), 291–311.

Kwack, S.Y. (1972), 'Effects of income and prices on travel spending abroad 1960 III–1967 IV', *International Economic Review*, **13** (2), 245–256.

Laber, G. (1969), 'Determinants of international travel between Canada and the United States', *Geographical Analysis*, **1** (4), 329–336.

Lathiras, P. and C. Siriopoulos (1998), 'The demand for tourism to Greece: a cointegration approach', *Tourism Economics*, **4** (2), 171–185.

Lee, C.K. and S. Han (2002), 'Estimating the use and preservation values of national parks' tourism resources using a contingent valuation method', *Tourism Management*, **23** (5), 531–540.

Lewis, R.C., R.E. Chambers and Il. E. Chacko (1995), *Marketing: Leadership in Hospitality*, New York: Van Nostrand Reinhold.

Li, G., H. Song and S.F. Witt (2004), 'Modeling tourism demand: a dynamic linear AIDS approach', *Journal of Travel Research*, **43**, 141–150.

Li, G., H. Song and S.F. Witt (2006), 'Time varying parameter and fixed parameter linear AIDS: an application to tourism demand forecasting', *International Journal of Forecasting*, **22**, 57–71.

Lim, C. (1997a), 'An econometric classification and review of international tourism models', *Tourism Economics*, **3** (1), 69–82.

Lim, C. (1997b), 'Review of international tourism demand models', *Annals of Tourism Research*, **24** (4), 835–849.

Lim, C. (1999), 'A meta-analytic review of international tourism demand', *Journal of Travel Research*, **37** (3), 273–289.

Lim, C. and M. McAleer (2001), 'Forecasting tourism arrivals', *Annals of Tourism Research*, **28** (4), 965–977.

Loomis, J. and C. Keske (2009), 'The economic value of novel means of ascending high mountain peaks: a travel cost demand model of Pikes Peak cog railway riders, automobile users and hikers', *Tourism Economics*, **15** (2), 426–436.

Maille, R. and R. Mendelsohn (1993), 'Valuing ecotourism in Madagascar', *Journal of Environmental Management*, **38**, 213–218.

Mangion, M.L., R. Durbarry and M.T. Sinclair (2005), 'Tourism competitiveness: price and quality', *Tourism Economics*, **11**, 45–68.

Martin, C.A. and S.F. Witt (1988), 'Substitute prices in models of tourism demand', *Annals of Tourism Research*, **15** (2), 255–268.

Morley, C.L. (1992), 'A microeconomic theory of international tourism demand', *Annals of Tourism Research*, **19**, 250–267.

Morley, C.L. (1994a), 'Discrete choice analysis of the impact of tourism prices', *Journal of Travel Research*, **33** (2), 8–14.

Morley, C.L. (1994b), 'Experimental destination choice analysis', *Annals of Tourism Research*, **21** (4), 780–791.

Morley, C.L. (1995), 'Tourism demand: characteristics, segmentation and aggregation', *Tourism Economics*, **1** (4), 315–328.

Nicolau, J.L. and F.J. Más (2005), 'Stochastic modeling. A three-stage tourist choice process', *Annals of Tourism Research*, **32** (1), 49–69.

O'Hagan, J.W. and M.J. Harrison (1984), 'Market shares of US tourist expenditure in Europe: an econometric analysis', *Applied Economics*, **16**, 919–931.

Palmer, T., A. Riera and J. Rosselló (2007), 'Taxing tourism: the case of rental cars in Mallorca', *Tourism Management*, **28** (1), 271–279.

Papatheodorou, A. (2002), 'Exploring competitiveness in Mediterranean resorts', *Tourism Economics*, **8** (2), 133–150.

Pestana, C., R. Butler and A. Correia (2008), 'Heterogeneity in destination choice. Tourism in Africa', *Journal of Travel Research*, **47** (2), 235–246.

Pyo, S.S., M. Uysal and R.W. Mclellan (1991), 'A linear expenditure model for tourism demand', *Annals of Tourism Research*, **18** (3), 443–454.

Rambonilaza, M. (2006), 'Labelling and differentiation strategy in the recreational housing rental market of rural destinations: the French case', *Tourism Economics*, **12** (3), 347–359.

Riera, A. (2000), 'Mass tourism and the demand for protected natural areas: a travel cost approach', *Journal of Environmental Economics and Management*, **39**, 97–116.

Rigall-i-Torrent, R. and M. Fluvià (2007), 'Public goods in tourism municipalities: formal analysis, empirical evidence and implications for sustainable development', *Tourism Economics*, **13** (3), 361–378.

Rosensweig, J.A. (1988), 'Elasticities of substitution in Caribbean tourism', *Journal of Development Economics*, **29** (1), 89–100.

Rosselló, J. (2001), 'Forecasting turning points in international tourist arrivals in the Balearic Islands', *Tourism Economics*, **7** (4), 365–380.

Rosselló, J., A. Riera and A. Sansó (2004), 'The economic determinants of seasonal patterns', *Annals of Tourism Research*, **31** (3), 697–711.

Rugg, D. (1973), 'The choice of journey destination: a theoretical and empirical analysis', *Review of Economics and Statistics*, **55** (1), 64–72.

Rulleau, B., J. Dehez and P. Point (2011), 'Recreational value, user heterogeneity and site characteristics in contingent valuation', *Tourism Management*, doi:10.1016/j.tourman.2011.03.002.

Sakai, M.Y. (1988), 'A micro-analysis of business travel demand', *Applied Economics*, **20**, 1481–1495.

Seetaram, N. (2012), 'Estimating demand elasticities for Australia's international outbound tourism', *Tourism Economics*, (in press).

Seetaram, N. and L. Dwyer (2009), 'Immigration and tourism demand in Australia: a panel data approach', *ANATOLIA: An International Journal of Tourism and Hospitality Research*, **20** (1), 212–222.

Sinclair, M.T., A. Clewer and A. Pack (1990), 'Hedonic prices and the marketing of package holidays: the case of tourism resorts in Malaga', in G.J. Ashworth and B. Goodall (eds) *Marketing of Tourism Places*, London: Routledge, pp. 85–103.

Smeral, E. (1988), 'Tourism demand, economic theory and econometrics: an integrated approach', *Journal of Travel Research*, **26**, 38–43.

Smeral, E. and M. Wëger (2005), 'Does complexity matter? Methods for improving forecasting accuracy in tourism: the case of Austria', *Journal of Travel Research*, **44** (1), 100–110.

Song, H. and G. Li (2008), 'Tourism demand modeling and forecasting: a review of recent research', *Tourism Management*, **29**, 203–220.

Syriopoulos, T.C. (1995), 'A dynamic model of demand for Mediterranean tourism', *International Review of Applied Economics*, **9** (3), 318–336.

Syriopoulos, T.C. and M.T. Sinclair (1993), 'An econometric study of tourism demand: the AIDS model of US and European tourism in Mediterranean countries', *Applied Economics*, **25**, 1541–1552.

Taplin, J.H.E. (1980), 'A coherence approach to estimates of price elasticities in the vacation travel market', *Journal of Transport Economics and Policy*, May, 19–35.

Thrane, C. (2005), 'Hedonic price models and sun-and-beach package tours: the Norwegian case', *Journal of Travel Research*, **43** (3), 302–308.

Thrane, C. (2008), 'The determinants of students' destination choice for their summer vacation trip', *Scandinavian Journal of Hospitality and Tourism*, **8** (4), 333–348.

Tremblay, D. (1989), 'Pooling international tourism in Western Europe', *Annals of Tourism Research*, **16** (4), 477–491.

Truett, D.B. and L.J. Truett (1987), 'The response of tourism to international economic conditions: Greece, Mexico, and Spain', *The Journal of Developing Areas*, **21** (2), 177–190.

Uysal, M. and J.L. Crompton (1985), 'An overview of approaches used to forecast tourism demand', *Journal of Travel Research*, **23**, 7–15.

Van Soest, A. and P. Kooreman (1987), 'A micro-econometric analysis of vacation behaviour', *Journal of Econometrics*, **2**, 215–226.

Wang, E., Z. Li, B.B. Little and Y. Yang (2009), 'The economic impact of tourism in Xinghai Park, China: a travel cost value analysis using count data regression models', *Tourism Economics*, **15** (2), 413–425.

Witt, S.F. (1982), 'A binary choice model of foreign holiday demand', *Journal of Economic Studies*, **10** (1), 46–59.

Witt, S.F. and C.A. Martin (1987), 'Deriving a relative price index for inclusion in international tourism demand estimation models: comment', *Journal of Travel Research*, **25** (3), 23–30.

Witt, S.F. and C.A. Witt (1991), 'Tourism forecasting: error magnitude, direction of change error, and trend change error', *Journal of Travel Research*, **30** (2), 26–33.

Witt, S.F. and C.A. Witt (1995), 'Forecasting tourism demand: a review of empirical research', *International Journal of Forecasting*, **11** (3), 447–475.

Wong, K. (1997a), 'The relevance of business cycles in forecasting international tourist arrivals', *Tourism Management*, **18** (8), 581–586.

Wong, K. (1997b), 'An investigation of the time series behaviour of international tourist arrivals', *Tourism Economics*, **3** (2), 185–200.

3 Time series analysis
Shuang Cang and Neelu Seetaram

INTRODUCTION

'A time series typically consists of a set of observations made on a variable y, taken at equally spaced internals over time' (Harvey, 1993, p. 1). The study of time series data is normally performed on two levels. Time series analysis comprises methods for extracting meaningful statistics and identifying key characteristics of the data. Time series modelling is performed in order to predict the future behaviour of y using historical data. The basis of time series modelling is that movement in y is explained solely by its past values or by its 'position in relation [to] time' (Harvey, 1993). Since time series models only require historical observations of a variable, it is less costly in terms of data collection and model estimation (Song and Li, 2008).

In tourism research, both time series analysis and time series modelling have received great attention in the past three decades, perhaps due to the availability of relevant time series data. Common types of tourism time series are tourist arrivals, departures, expenditure levels, number of nights spent at a destination, price of hotel room, airfare, tourism contribution to the GDP and so on. These time series are mostly available on a monthly, quarterly and/or yearly basis. Frechtling (1996, 2001) highlighted five patterns in tourism time series: stationarity, seasonality, linear trend, non-linear trend and stepped series. The identification of these patterns can be an end in itself as seen by several studies which have attempted to describe the characteristics of tourism data for a number of destinations. On the other hand, prior information on key features on the data set in use, assists researchers when choosing an appropriate method for developing and estimating time series and regression models.

As mentioned above, the main purpose of time series modelling is for forecasting. This is done to equip stakeholders with relevant information that would assist them in their decision-making processes and in order to devise relevant tourism-related policies for the industry. However, according to Frechtling (1996, 2001), the time series non-causal approach is limited by the lack of explanatory variables and it is best used for short- to medium-term forecasting because it is assumed that the factors related to seasonality, trend and cycle are slow to change and can be extrapolated in the short term (Cheong and Turner, 2005).

The aim of this chapter is to review the application of time series analysis and modelling in the tourism literature. Note that there exists a vast number of such techniques which have been employed to analyse tourism data. It is beyond the scope of this chapter to discuss all. This chapter instead focuses on the most widely applied methods within the tourism context. It is made up of three distinct sections. In the first section the characteristics of time series data are discussed. The second section concentrates on the 'classic' time series modelling techniques. The last section discusses directions for new research and focuses on approaches which are fairly recent such as neural networks models which may be expected to become more extensively utilized by tourism researchers in the near future.

TIMES SERIES CHARACTERISTICS OF TOURISM DATA SETS

Stationarity

> A stochastic process is said to be stationary if its mean and variance are constant over time and the value of its covariance between the two time periods depends only on the distance or gap or lag between the two time periods and not the actual time at which the covariance is computed. (Gujarati and Porter, 2009, p. 741)

Generally researchers seek to know the stationarity status of variables for two reasons. First, they are keen to verify that their regression results are valid and not spurious. According to Granger and Newbold (1974), the rule of thumb for suspecting spurious results is an R^2 which is higher than the Durbin Watson statistic. Second, they wish to know whether the effect of external shocks on the variable will be temporary or permanent. The mathematical formulae for mean, variance and covariance are defined as follows: mean, $E(y_t) = \eta$; variance, $Var(y_t) = E(y_t - \eta)^2 = \sigma^2$; covariance, $E[(y_t - \mu)(y_{t+k} - \mu)] = \lambda_k$ (η is the expected value of mean, variance is a measure of how far a set of variables (y_t) is spread out and covariance is a measure of how much two random variables change together).

A stationary process is one where the mean, variance and covariance of y_{t+k} is the same as the covariance of y_t, they are time invariant and the process is said to be mean reverting. A purely random or white noise process has zero mean, constant variance and is serially uncorrelated. On the other hand, a series which has a time varying mean, variance, or both, is nonstationary. An example of a nonstationary process is a random walk. There are two types of random walks: random walks with drifts and random walks without drifts. If

$$y_t = y_{t-1} + e_t \tag{3.1}$$

where e_t is a white noise error term (mean is zero and variance is constant) then the series is said to be a random walk without a drift. As t increases, so does the variance while the mean remains constant. In this case, the effect of random shocks in the data is said to be persistent. The random walk series is said to have infinite memory as the effect of shocks does not die out. Take the case of tourist arrivals at a destination. If a random shock occurs, for example, a terrorist attack, the outbreak of an epidemic or a natural disaster, the number of arrivals will not revert back to its original mean if the time series of arrivals follow a random walk. The shock will have a permanent effect on the number of arrivals at the destination.

A random walk with a drift is given by the equation below:

$$y_t = \mu + y_{t-1} + e_t \tag{3.2}$$

μ is the drift parameter. The variance and mean are dependent on time. A random walk series without drift can be made stationary by taking the first difference. This type of series is also referred to as a difference stationary series or a series containing unit root or integrated of order 1. They are said to have a stochastic trend that is the slow long-run evolution of the time series cannot be predicted (Gujarati and Porter, 2009). On the other hand, when y_t is a function of time, the series can be made stationary by subtracting the mean of y_t from y_t, in which case the series is referred to as a trend stationary series. The process of removing the influence of time from y_t is called detrending. A random walk with a drift and a time trend is given below

$$y_t = \beta_1 + \beta_2 t + y_{t-1} + e_t \tag{3.3}$$

Time series which need to be differenced 'd' number of times before they turn stationary are said to be integrated of the order (d) or $y_t \sim I(d)$. Several tests have been developed in order to test for stationarity of time series data. The two most popular tests used in the tourism literature are the augmented Dickey–Fuller (ADF) (Dickey and Fuller, 1979) which is the extension of the Dickey–Fuller (DF) and the Phillips–Perron (PP) (Phillips and Perron, 1988). These tests use the existence of a unit root as the null hypothesis. Dickey–Fuller (DF) tests whether a unit root is present in an autoregressive model. It is named after the statisticians D.A. Dickey and W.A. Fuller, who developed the test in 1979. DF test involves fitting the regression model:

$$y_t = \mu + \vartheta y_{t-1} + e_t \tag{3.4}$$

where

$$e_t \sim N(0, \sigma^2)$$

and y_t is the variable of interest, t is the time index, ϑ is a coefficient and e_t is the error term. The hypotheses to be tested are as follows:

H_0: $\vartheta = 1$
H_1: $|\vartheta| < 1$

If H_0 is rejected, the process is stationary, otherwise it is non-stationary. An augmented Dickey–Fuller (ADF) test removes all the structural effects (autocorrelation) in the time series and then tests using the same procedure.

In the PP test, the null hypothesis is that a time series is integrated of order 1. The PP test addresses the issue that the process generating data for y_t might have a higher order of autocorrelation than is admitted in the test equation, making y_{t-1} endogenous and thus invalidating the Dickey–Fuller (DF) *t*-test. Whilst the ADF addresses this issue by introducing lags of Δy_t as regressors in the test equation, the Phillips–Perron test makes a non-parametric correction to the *t*-test statistic. The test is robust with respect to unspecified autocorrelation and heteroskedasticity in the disturbance process of the test equation. Table 3.1 summarizes the different forms of unit root tests and the type of time series data for which they are relevant.

Table 3.1   Summaries of ADF and PP tests under H_0: $\vartheta = 0$ and H_1: $\vartheta = 1$ hypotheses

TYPE	Equation	Condition
ADF	$\Delta y_t = \vartheta y_{t-1} + \sum_{i=1}^{\rho} \alpha_i \Delta y_{t-i} + e_t$ $e_t \sim N(0, \sigma^2)$	When the time series doesn't have a trend and is potentially slow turning around zero
ADF	$\Delta y_t = \alpha_0 + \vartheta y_{t-1} + \sum_{i=1}^{\rho} \alpha_i \Delta y_{t-i} + e_t$	When the time series does not have a trend and is potentially slow turning around a non-zero value
ADF	$\Delta y_t = \gamma t + \alpha_0 + \vartheta y_{t-1} + \sum_{i=1}^{\rho} \alpha_i \Delta y_{t-i} + e_t$	When the time series has a trend in it (either up or down) and is potentially slow turning around a trend line you would draw through the data
PP	$\Delta y_t = \vartheta y_{t-1} + e_t$	Autoregressive
PP	$\Delta y_t = \mu + \vartheta y_{t-1} + e_t$	Autoregressive with drift
PP	$\Delta y_t = \mu + \gamma t + \vartheta y_{t-1} + e_t$	Trend stationary

When performing these tests it is crucial to select the correct number of augmenting lags (ρ). The number of lags is determined by minimizing the Schwartz Bayesian information criterion or minimizing the Akaike information criterion or lags are dropped until the last lag is statistically insignificant. The Dickey–Fuller *t*-statistic does not follow a standard *t*-distribution as the sampling distribution of this test statistic is skewed to the left with a long, left-hand-tail. The test statistic is $t = \hat{\vartheta} / SE(\hat{\vartheta})$, where $\hat{\vartheta}$ and $SE(\hat{\vartheta})$ are the estimated coefficient on y_{t-1} and its standard error from the ordinary least square regression.

Unit root testing can be the sole focus of a study or a prerequisite for regression analysis among researchers who wish to avoid reporting data that lack statistical robustness. Testing for unit root has become fairly common in tourism demand modelling. This practice started in the mid-1990s. Gonzáles and Moralez (1995) were among the first to check for unit roots using tourism data. They found the presence of unit root on annual tourism expenditure in Spain. Note that since they also utilised a monthly series: January 1979 to December 1993, they performed seasonal unit root tests. These tests are discussed in the next section. Song and Witt (2000), use PP and ADF to pretest their data set for unit root before specifying a demand model for outbound tourism from the UK to Austria, Belgium, France, Germany, Italy, the Netherlands, Greece, Spain, the Irish Republic, Switzerland, the United States and rest of the world. They found number of holidays and income to be I(1) (integrated of order 1) while mixed results were obtained for relative prices. Prior to model specification, Lim and McAleer (2002) conducted the individual ADF tests for the logarithms of arrivals from Hong Kong and Singapore to Australia. These two series were found to be trend stationary. While studying tourist arrivals to South Korea, Song and Witt (2003) used the ADF and Perron (1989) tests to show that the number of arrivals from Germany, Japan, UK and the United States, income of the host countries, respective exchange rate and relevant airfares to South Korea were I(1).

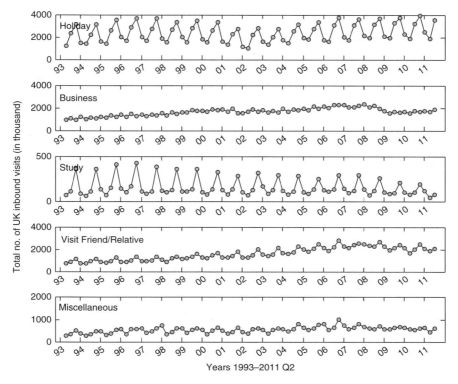

Source: Compiled from 'International Passenger Survey' UK National Statistics available at http://www. statistics.gov.uk.

Figure 3.1 UK inbound tourism demand (quarterly data)

Unit Roots with Seasonality

It is a fact that seasonality is one of the most salient characteristics of the tourism industry. Seasonality has been described as 'a temporal imbalance in the phenomena of tourism, and may be expressed in terms of dimensions of such elements as number of visitors, expenditure of visitors, traffic on highways and other forms of transportation, employment and admission to attractions' (Butler, 1994, p. 332). In other words since most destinations have peak and off-peak seasons, consumption in the tourism industry display a predictable and regular pattern which recur every year. It occurs for two reasons: natural factors, such as climate, and institutional, such as school holidays (Butler, 2001). The effect of seasonality is seen in monthly or quarterly data. Figure 3.1 shows international arrivals to the UK (UK inbound) for four categories of visitors.

The data clearly shows that arrivals for holiday and study purposes are subject to a high degree of seasonality, with the third quarter representing the peak time. The pattern is repeated from 1993 to 2010. On the other hand, arrivals for business purposes do not display any such patterns. Seasonality is identifiable in the more frequent

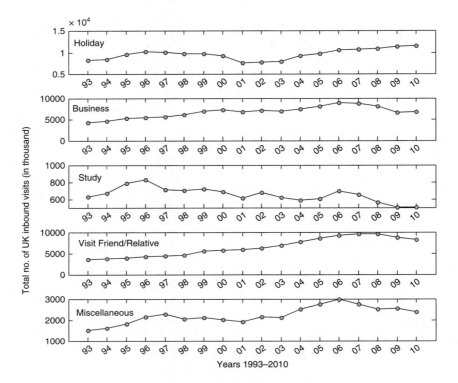

Source: Compiled from 'International Passenger Survey' UK National Statistics available at http://www.statistics.gov.uk.

Figure 3.2   UK inbound tourism demand (yearly data)

intervals, for example, monthly and quarterly data but this is lost in annual data. This is illustrated in Figure 3.2 where seasonality has been removed by aggregating the data.

When data display seasonal patterns, the type of unit roots present is different too. They can be quarterly, semi annual or annual and the relevant differencing strategy is required to achieve stationarity (Song et al., 2009). The most commonly used test is the Hylleberg, Engle, Granger and Yoo (1990) also known as HEGY. Below is the standard HEGY regression applicable to quarterly data.

$$\Delta_4 y_t = \sum_{i=1}^{4} \pi_i y_{it-1} + e_t \qquad (3.5)$$

(where π_i ($i = 1, 2, 3, 4$) are the coefficients)

Acceptance of the null hypothesis implies that the series contain seasonal unit root while rejecting H_0 implies that the series is stationary. If all of the values of π are not simultaneously equal to zero, the interpretation of the test results changes. If only $\pi_1 = 0$ then the series has normal unit root; if $\pi_2 = 0$ then the series has semi-annual root and if

$\pi_3 = \pi_4 = 0$, then an annual units root is present (Song et al., 2009). The HEGY test may be adjusted for a constant and a seasonal deterministic trend as given below

$$\Delta_4 y_t = \pi_0 + \sum_{i=1}^{4} \pi_i y_{it-1} + e_t$$

$$\Delta_4 y_t = + \sum_{i=1}^{4} \pi_i y_{it-1} + \sum_{i=1}^{4} b_i Q_{it-1} + e_t$$

(3.6)

where Q_i represents seasonal dummies. These tests have been widely applied in the tourism context. Some examples are Alleyne (2006), Kulendran and King (1997), Kulendran and Wong (2005) and Lim and McAleer (2002). Lim and McAleer (2002) found tourist arrivals have unit roots at zero and semi-annual frequencies, but no annual unit roots. They used data of quarterly tourist arrivals from Malaysia to Australia from 1975 to 1996. Kulendran and King (1997) applied HEGY to test for seasonal and non-seasonal unit roots in the log of tourist arrivals to Australia from Japan, New Zealand, the UK and the United States. The test was also applied to the log of quarterly income and the log of relevant price variables. The results of the HEGY tests suggest that quarterly tourist arrivals from the United States and New Zealand had unit roots at zero and biannual frequencies. The series for the UK had one non-seasonal unit root. The Japanese series had unit roots at the zero frequency and one seasonal frequency and all income, price and airfare series had one non-seasonal unit root. Kulendran and Wong (2005) applied the HEGY technique to 19 series including quarterly international to Australia from 1975(1) to 1998(4) from ten markets and quarterly departures from the UK to nine destinations. Alleyne (2006) tested for seasonal unit root in tourist arrivals to Jamaica using six tourist arrival series, from 1968(1) to 2001(3). He concluded that pretesting for seasonal unit roots improves forecasting of arrivals to Jamaica.

Unit Root with Structural Breaks

Time series can contain structural breaks. Structural breaks occur when there is a change in one of the parameters (the trend coefficient, mean or variance) of a data-generating process (Hansen, 2001). The breaks are caused by shocks which are applied to the series. Shocks can be positive or negative. Examples of positive shocks are the hosting of special events such as the Olympic Games, and negative shocks that have affected the tourism industry are the 9/11 terrorist attacks, outbreak of epidemics, war and peaks in the price of crude oil. The effect of these shocks on the data series can be can be permanent or temporary. 'Permanent' in this context means that in a given sample of data, the change resulting from a shock will still be in effect at the end of the data sample (Perron, 2005). Thus, if the series contain a unit root, a shock will permanently change its growth path while, if it is found to be trend-stationary shocks will have only temporary effects and the series will eventually revert back to its original trend. The presence of structural breaks may bias the results of standard unit root tests. A unit root test which allows for structural breaks in the data was proposed by Perron (1989). This was an exogenous test for structural breaks since the date of the break is estimated using a priori information. More recent tests devised are endogenous, where the break point in the data is determined by the tests.

One commonly used test in the literature is that of Zivot and Andrews (1992). This test allows for a one-time break in the trend and/or intercept of a time series. The aim of the Zivot–Andrews test is to see if a structural break exists in a time series, by testing the null hypothesis of a unit root against the alternative of (trend) stationarity with structural change at some unknown point. According to Byrne and Perman (2006) and Perron (2005), however, the weakness of the Zivot–Andrews test is that under the null hypothesis, structural breaks are not allowed, which creates a bias towards rejecting the null hypothesis of a unit root process in favour of the alternative. Another weakness of the Zivot–Andrews test is the inability to deal with more than one structural break in a series. Other tests for structural break in the data include those of Lee and Strazicich (2003, 2004) and Lumsdaine and Papell (1997).

Whiltshire (2009) performed a Zivot–Andrews test of the annual time series on Australian international passenger flow from 1956 to 2008. The test identified a break in 1974 which corresponded to the first oil crisis. The effect of the break on the data is illustrated in Figure 3.3.

Narayan (2005) performs the Zivot–Andrews (1992) and Lumsdaine–Papell (1997), and finds that the Rabuka's military coups only had a temporary effect on tourist expenditure in Fiji. In their study of the tourism industry of Bali, Smyth et al. (2009) demonstrate that the effects of the recent terrorist acts on the growth path of tourist arrivals from major markets are only transitory and that as a consequence Bali's tourism sector is sustainable in the long run.

Njegovan (2006) quantified the effect of exogenous shocks on annual passenger numbers to Australia, Canada, Germany, the US and the UK using the Zivot–Andrews (1992) test. The evidence for the UK, Germany and Australia indicates that the series are trend-stationary containing one structural break in both the trend and intercept in 1977. The authors conclude that the structural break is most likely a result of the OPEC oil crises in the 1970s. His analysis of more recent demand shocks suggests that they had only temporary effects on annual passenger growth.

Using the Zivot–Andrews (1992) and Lumsdaine–Papell (1997) unit root tests, Lee and Chien (2008) analysed Taiwanese data on the real GDP, tourism development and real international value of the Taiwanese currency. Their aim was to investigate whether regime changes have broken down the stability of the long-run relationships between tourism development and real GDP in Taiwan from 1959 to 2003. They conclude that the variables are subject to structural breaks which corresponded to actual incidents related to the politics economy and tourism which occurred in Taiwan.

Cointegration Test and ECM

If two or more variables are non-stationary but integrated of the same order i.e., $x \sim$ I(d) and $y \sim$ I(d) there may exist linear combinations of these variables which are stationary. Then there is a long-run relationship that prevents them from drifting away from each other and they are said to be cointegrated. The idea of variables which are non-stationary but cointegrated is credited to Granger (1981) and further developed in Granger and Weiss (1983) and Engle and Granger (1987). These authors revolutionized the way non-stationary data are perceived and introduced methods for modelling data which ensures that regression results from non-stationary data are statistically

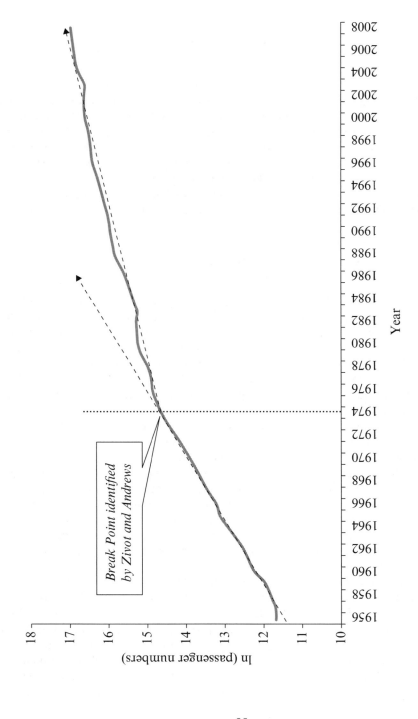

Source: Whiltshire (2009).

Figure 3.3 Australian international passenger numbers with trend line and structural break

sound. One of the most widely applied tests is Engle and Granger (1987). Consider the following model

$$y_t = \alpha_1 + \alpha_2 x_t + u_t \qquad (3.7)$$

where $x \sim I(d)$ and $y \sim I(d)$.

Estimating Equation (3.7) will give spurious results unless y_t and x_t are cointegrated. The first step to detect cointegration is to estimate the equation to obtain u_t. The second step is to test for the stationarity of u_t using the ADF statistics. If u_t is found to be stationary then y_t and x_t are cointegrated and the equation can be expressed in the form or an error correction model. The vector $(\alpha_1\ \alpha_2)$ is referred to as the cointegration vector. According to Engle and Granger (1987), α_1 and α_2 will be consistent and efficient. α_2 is the long-run coefficient. This relationship can be modelled into an error correction. Error correction is defined by Engle and Granger as 'a proportion of the disequilibrium from one period is corrected in the next period' (Engle and Granger, 1987, p. 254).

$$\Delta y_t = \sum_{i=0}^{\rho} \beta_i \Delta x_{t-i} + \sum_{j=1}^{\rho} \phi \Delta y_{it-j} + \lambda \hat{u}_{t-1} + e_t \qquad (3.8)$$

The ECM is estimated to obtain the short term coefficients. This technique is referred to as the Engle and Granger (1987) two step method. Since the standard errors of the parameters of the second regression are the true standard errors, the model may be used for forecasting purposes (Song et al., 2009). An advantage of ECM is that since regressors in the model are almost orthogonal, the problem of multicollinearity can be avoided (Song et al., 2009; Syriopoulos, 1995). This method is, however, not without flaws. According to Song and Witt (2000), the Engle and Granger method does not prove that the relationships among the cointegrated variables are long term and the robustness of estimations from small samples is not always achieved. Futhermore, problems arise in identifying individual structural relationships.

In their modelling of outbound tourism from UK, Song and Witt (2000) applied ADF and PP tests for the 12 long-run regressions and found that in every case except France, the null hypothesis of no cointegration is rejected at least at the 10 per cent level of significance. They used the Engle–Granger (1997) technique to specify the long-run relationship between departures from UK and income and relative prices. Furthermore, the authors perform *ex-post* forecasts over a period of 6 years, on four different model specifications and show that their ECM model outperforms the remaining three in predicting UK outbound tourism.

The aim of the study Kulendran and Wilson (2000) was to identify the economic variables that are important in influencing business trips to Australia from four of its major trading partners. Quarterly data from 1982(1) to 1996(4) were used. The HEGY method was applied to examine the time series properties of the dependent and independent variables: business travel, origin country real income, openness to trade, real imports, relative price and holiday travel. The Full Information Maximum Likelihood technique was used to estimate the long-run relationship between business travel and its determinants. The authors concluded that the importance of the economic variables varied from country to country, although overall openness to trade and origin country real income were important variables explaining business travel.

Kulendran and Witt (2001) study business travel to Australia from Japan, New Zealand, the United Kingdom and the United States. They utilize quarterly data for the period 1982(1)–96(4). Real gross domestic product, trade openness and real exchange rate were amongst the variables included in their model. After having tested for unit root and finding that the majority of the variables have unit roots at zero frequency, Johansen's (1988) and Johansen and Juselius (1990) tests for cointegration were applied. The results suggest that there is one significant long-run relationship for Japan, and there are four for New Zealand and two for both the United Kingdom and the United States.

Lim and McAleer (2002) developed demand models to explain tourism arrivals to Australia from Hong Kong and Singapore. Incomes in Hong Kong and Singapore, tourism prices in Australia, and transportation costs and exchange rates between the two countries and Australia were used to explain the number of arrivals to Australia. Quarterly data from 1975(1) to 1996(4) were used for Hong Kong and 1980(4)–96(4) for Singapore. After performing an ADF test for unit roots and Johansen's maximum likelihood procedure for cointegration to estimate the number of cointegrating vectors, the authors developed ECM models to explain tourism demand.

Narayan (2004) examined the short- and long-run relationships between visitor arrivals in Fiji, real disposable incomes and relative hotel and substitute prices for the period 1970–2000, using cointegration techniques and error correction models. A generalized Dickey–Fuller type regression was used to test the significance of lagged levels of the variables under consideration in a conditional unrestricted ECM. The results of this study suggest that rises in income in the main markets of Fiji had a positive impact on arrivals while relative hotel and substitute prices have negative impacts on visitor arrivals.

Algieri (2006) examined the determinants of and their relevant impact on tourism revenues in Russia over the period 1993(12) to 2002(10). Variations in income, exchange rates and prices, as well as unpredicted events such as relevant political changes were identified as the relevant factors affecting demand. A cointegration analysis is performed and the results suggested a robust and significant long-run cointegration relationship between Russian tourism receipts, world GDP, real exchange rates and prices of air transport.

Webber (2001) used the Johansen (1988) and the Engle and Granger (1987) methods to test for the long-run demand for Australian outbound leisure using quarterly data from 1983(1) to 1997(4) for nine major tourism destinations. It was found that variances in the exchange rate are significant determinants of long-run tourism demand. Real disposable income and substitute prices have inelastic long-run effects on tourism, while the long-run relative price elasticity tends to differ widely across destinations.

TIME SERIES MODELLING

This section expands further on the different types of time series models available to tourism researchers. There are two main types of modelling in time series analysis. The first is the classic time series model. Here the naïve model may be considered as one of the most basic. The degree of complexity rises greatly as researchers move to modelling techniques such as the moving average (MA), autoregressive (AR), autoregressive moving average (ARMA), autoregressive integrated moving average (ARIMA) and seasonal ARIMA (SARIMA), exponential smoothing (ES) and Winters' multiplicative ES, basic structural modelling (BSM) and generalized autoregressive conditional heteroskedasticity (GARCH). These modelling techniques have been widely applied in the tourism literature. Often studies develop several models which are estimated and results compared. The aim is to find the best model that fits the data and outperforms the rest in terms of accuracy in forecasting. From the review of literature provided by Coshall and Charlesworth (2011), it is apparent that one class of forecasting models does not consistently dominate the other in terms of predictive accuracy. Their performance depends on the data set in use, for example, destination origin pairs and the frequency of data. The effectiveness of the different models is also conditional on the forecasting horizon and the technique used to assess their accuracy (Coshall and Charlesworth, 2011). Since several techniques are applied in a given study, this section will first explain the different 'classic' techniques before providing their application to the tourism literature. The preferred estimation technique is often the Box–Jenkins Method.

The second type of modelling technique using time series data is based on artificial intelligence (AI), especially neural network (NN) techniques. Given that they are fairly new in the tourism context, their application in the tourism literature is not as widespread as the 'classic' models. The common NN techniques that are applied in the tourism context are the multi-layer perceptron neural networks (MLPNN) and support vector regression neural networks (SVRNN).

'Classic' Time Series Model

Naïve models: naïve 1 and naïve 2
The naïve 1 model simply states that the future forecasts are equal to the recent available value. For example, the naïve 1 model operates on the assumption that there is no change and that the number of visitors at time t, $\hat{y}_t$, is the same as the value at time $t - 4$, denoted by y_{t-4} and is described as $\hat{y}_t = y_{t-4}$. The naïve 2 model operates on the assumption that the number of visitors at time t, is subject to a constant growth, $\hat{y}_t$ is equal to the value at time $t - 4$ times by a modification factor which includes the influence of the y_{t-8} (long-range value) and the naïve 2 formula is $\hat{y}_t = y_{t-4}\{1 + (y_{t-4} - y_{t-8}) / y_{t-8}\}$. The naïve 1 and 2 are frequently used as benchmarks for assessing predictive accuracy in tourism forecasting exercises (Coshall and Charlesworth, 2001).

Moving average and autoregressive moving average (ARMA)
As a means to improve on the naïve model, the patterns and trends of a time series can be extrapolated using a moving average (MA) or smoothing model. A moving average is taken to estimate the local mean which is used for forecasting. This method is to 'smooth' out peaks in the original series. An MA model is where y_t, at time t, is equal to a constant (α_0) plus a moving average of current year and past year errors is given below.

$$y_t = a_0 + a_t + \beta_1 a_{t-1} \tag{3.9}$$

This series is an MA(1) since it includes one lag of the error term. A more general Ma(q) series take the form of

$$y_t = a_t + \beta_1 a_{t-1} + \beta_2 a_{t-2} + \ldots + \beta_p a_{t-p} \tag{3.10}$$

where a_t is white noise with zero mean and variance. The equation above can be rewritten in terms of the backward shift operator B

$$y_t = (1 + \beta_1 B + \beta_2 B^2 + \ldots + \beta_q B^q) a_t = \Phi_q(B) a_t \tag{3.11}$$

where $Ba_t = a_{t-1}$. An autoregressive also known as vector autoregressive series, is a multivariate series where the dependent variable is related to its past values. An autoregressive series of order p, also referred to as an AR(p) or VAR(p) series can be written in the form of:

$$y_t = \beta_1 y_{t-1} + \beta_2 y_{t-2} + \ldots + \beta_p y_{t-p} + a_t = \Theta_p(B) y_t \tag{3.12}$$

where at is white noise and B is a backward shift operator. A mixed series is one which combines autoregressive and moving average terms and is known as an ARMA (Box and Jenkins, 1970).

$$y_t = \beta_1 y_{t-1} + \beta_2 y_{t-2} + \ldots + \beta_p y_{t-p} + a_t = (1 + \beta_1 B + \beta_2 B^2 + \ldots + \beta_q B^q) a_t \quad (3.13)$$

or

$$\Theta_p(B) y_t = \Phi_q(B) a_t$$

An ARMA (p, q) contains p autoregressive and q moving average terms. The process is stationary when the roots of θ all exceed unity in absolute value. The process is invertible when the roots of Φ all exceed unity in absolute value.

Univariate autoregressive integrated moving average (ARIMA) and seasonal ARIMA (SARIMA)

Note that the AR(p) model is the special case ARMA(p, 0) and the MA(q) model is the special case ARMA(0, q). If y $\sim$ I(d) and then ARMA is applied to it. The resulting model is an autoregressive integrated moving average (ARIMA) (p,d,q). ARIMA models can also be used to model seasonality. This type of models are called seasonal autoregressive integrated moving average model or SARIMA ARIMA(p,d,q)(P,D,Q)$_s$ (Box and Jenkins, 1970), which is presented as follows:

$$\phi_p(B)\Phi_P(B^s)\left[(1 - B)^d (1 - B^s)^D y_t - \mu\right] = \theta_q(B)\Theta_Q(B^s) a_t \tag{3.14}$$

where B is a backward shift operator with $By_t = y_{t-1}$ and $Ba_t = a_{t-1}$, y_t is the value to be forecasted and a_t is the residual at time period t, μ is overall mean of series which is a constant. $\phi_p(B) = 1 - \varphi_1 B - \varphi_2 B^2 - \ldots - \varphi_p B^p$ is a non-seasonal AR of order p, $\theta_q(B) = 1 - \vartheta_1 B - \vartheta_2 B^2 - \ldots - \vartheta_q B^q$ is a non-seasonal MA of order q, $\Phi_P(B^s) = 1 - \Phi_1 B^s - \Phi_2 B^{s2} - \ldots - \Phi_P B^{sP}$ is a seasonal AR of order P, $\Theta_Q(B^s) = 1 - \Theta_1 B^s - \Theta_2 B^{s2} - \ldots - \Theta_Q B^{sQ}$ is a seasonal MA polynomial of order Q. y_t as in the above equation of ARIMA(p,d,q) $(P,D,Q)_s$, is the forecasting value and $s = 4$ if it is quarterly data and $s = 12$ if it is monthly data. The ARIMA(p,d,q) is as follows, where $s = 0$, $P = D = Q = 0$ in SARIMA.

$$\phi_p(B)\,[(1 - B)^d y_t - \mu] = \theta_q(B) a_t \qquad (3.15)$$

According to Song and Li (2008), ARIMA models dominate the literature on tourism time series. They have been applied to over two-thirds of post-2000 studies of tourism demand that have employed time series forecasting techniques (Song and Li, 2008).

Exponential smoothing (ES)
Exponential smoothing models have been shown to generate accurate forecasts of tourism demand; furthermore, when seasonality is a pertinent factor, the existence of unit roots is not an issue in their application (Lim and McAleer, 2002). These methods use weighted values of past observations to generate forecasts. The weights decline exponentially over time, since the most recent data are considered to be more influential on forecasts than are older observations. The simple (one parameter) exponential smoothing model has limited application to tourism forecasting, since it requires no trend or seasonality to be present in the time series. The use of an algorithm to remove noise from a data set in order to highlight important patterns is referred to as data smoothing. In exponential smoothing more recent data are given more weight by assigning exponentially decreasing weight to observations as they get older.

It can be shown that most ES models such as simple ES, Holt's ES, Brown's ES, damped-trend ES, simple seasonal ES, and Winters' additive ES are all special cases of the ARIMA model. In fact, simple ES is equivalent to an ARIMA (0, 1, 1), Holt's ES is equivalent to an ARIMA (0, 2, 2), Brown's ES is equivalent to an ARIMA (0, 2, 2) with restriction among MA parameters, damped-trend ES is equivalent to an ARIMA (1, 1, 2), simple seasonal ES is equivalent to an ARIMA (0, 1, (1, s, s + 1))(0, 1, 0) with restrictions among MA parameters, and Winters' additive ES is equivalent to an ARIMA (0, 1, s + 1)(0, 1, 0) with restrictions among MA parameters.

Winters' multiplicative ES
The Winters' multiplicative exponential smoothing (WMES) (Douglas et al., 1990) considers the effects of seasonality to be multiplicative, which is, growing (or decreasing) over time.

$$\hat{y}_t = T_t \times S_t \times L_t + \varepsilon_t \qquad (3.16)$$

where $\hat{y}_t$ is the forecasting at time t, T_t represents the trend component, S_t represents the seasonality, L_t is the long term cycles and ε_t is the error. The WMES method constructs three statistically related series used to make the actual forecast: the smoothed data series, the seasonal index and the trend series. This method requires at least 2 years of back data to calculate forecasting values. It is calculated by solving the following three 'updating formulas' (Equations (3.17)–(3.19)).

$$L_t = \alpha \frac{y_t}{S_{t-s}} + (1 - \alpha)\{L_{t-1} + T_{t-1}\} \qquad (3.17)$$

$$T_t = \gamma\{L_t - L_{t-1}\} + (1 - \gamma)T_{t-1} \qquad (3.18)$$

$$S_t = \delta\left\{\frac{y_t}{L_t}\right\} + (1 - \delta)S_{t-s} \qquad (3.19)$$

$$\hat{y}_{t+k} = \{L_t + kT_t\}S_{t+k-s} \qquad (3.20)$$

where s is a number of periods per year, k is the period ahead forecasting. α, γ and δ represent three smoothing constants with values between 0 and 1. Equation (3.20) can be used in the forecasting.

Box–Jenkins method

The Box and Jenkins' (1970) method for forecasting autoregressive integrated moving average (ARIMA) has become widely used in many fields for time series analysis including tourism demand forecasting. This is a three-step iterative procedure used in forecasting. In order to specify the model, the data is tested for stationarity and presence of seasonality is identified. Data is first differenced to achieve stationarity, if necessary and appropriate values of p and q are fitted to the model. In the second step the model is estimated. In the third step, diagnostic tests are performed to verify how well the model fit the data and whether the residuals are white noise. If the results are not satisfactory, the process is repeated from step 1.

Lim and McAleer (2002) applied various Box–Jenkins autoregressive integrated moving average (ARIMA) models which they estimate using quarterly data from 1975(1) to 1989(4) on tourist arrivals to tourist arrivals to Australia from Hong Kong, Malaysia and Singapore. The best-fit model was used to perform post-sample forecasts for the period 1990(1) to 1996(4). They concluded that while the ARIMA model for Hong Kong was effective in forecasting arrivals, it was not as accurate as the model for Singapore.

In an analysis of tourist arrivals to Durban, South Africa, from the United States, Burger et al. (2001) considered a variety of techniques. These were naïve, MA, decomposition, single ES, ARIMA, multiple regression and two non traditional methods, genetic regression and neural networks. The authors used data from 1992 to 1998 to compare actual and the predicted number of visitors, given by each model. They found that the neural network method performed the best.

Papatheodorou and Song (2005) studied tourism flows for the period 1960 to 2000 for the six major World Tourism Organization regions and the world. The results of the ADF test suggested that all the series were I(1). ARIMA models were estimated using the Box–Jenkins technique to forecast international tourism arrivals, international tourism receipt and real per capita international tourism receipt. They concluded that performance differed dramatically among the regions, with sharp fluctuations. Some regions were even expected to experience negative tourism growth in real and per capita terms.

The aim of the study performed by Wong et al. (2007) was to assess the relative effectiveness of techniques as compared to combined techniques in forecasting exercises. The study is based on data on demand for Hong Kong tourism from its top ten markets: mainland China, Taiwan, Japan, the United States, Macau, South Korea, Singapore, the UK, Australia and the Philippines. Quarterly data from 1984(1) to 2004(2) were utilized. The data period 1984(1) to 1999(2) was used to estimate the individual forecasting models and the subsequent period for forecasting evaluation. The forecasts are derived from four different forecasting models: the ARIMA model, the autoregressive distributed lag model, the ECM and the vector autoregressive model.

The HEGY test was used to test for seasonal unit roots and it shows that all the variables have non-seasonal unit roots. Tourist arrivals from Macau, the United States, Singapore and the Philippines have annual seasonal unit roots while the series of tourist arrivals from the UK has both annual and semi-annual seasonal unit roots. For the GDP variables, one semi-annual seasonal unit root is found in the Taiwan series. In addition, two seasonal unit roots were identified in the China, Macau, Korea, the UK and the Philippines series. The Engle and Granger two-stage approach was used to specify the ECM and the seasonal ARIMA based on the standard Box–Jenkins method. The authors concluded that although the combined forecasts do not always outperform the best single model forecasts, there is sufficient evidence to suggest that forecast combination can considerably reduce the risk of forecasting failure. More recent studies have reached similar conclusions.

Cang and Hemmington (2010) studied inbound tourism expenditure in the UK disaggregated by purpose of visit: holiday, business, study, visit friends or relatives (VFR) and miscellaneous. Data were modelled using ARIMA and WMES. The naïve 2 forecasting model was used as a benchmark to compare with the ARIMA and WMES models. This study demonstrated that the ARIMA model outperforms the WMES model, but it is not statistically superior to the WMES model. The ARIMA and WMES models are both statistically superior to the naïve 2 model for this UK inbound expenditure data set. The ARIMA model forecasted a higher increasing trend for expenditure for the business travel, whereas the WMES model forecasted a higher increasing trend for expenditure for the miscellaneous group. The authors recommended combining values from the ARIMA and the WMES models to use as forecasting values for business and miscellaneous purposes.

Coshall and Charlesworth (2011) used four models to forecast UK outbound tourism to Europe. They were univariate volatility models, exponential smoothing models, a regression-based approach and the naïve 2 model. The data used were seasonally unadjusted quarterly UK outbound tourism numbers by air to the 18 most popular destinations in Europe in 2006. Each of the models was considered individually and in combination in terms of forecasting demand for international tourism. The authors concluded that the models generated accurate predictions of tourism flows, but they were most effective when combined with other models.

Brida and Risso (2011) explored the SARIMA technique to forecast tourism demand by using monthly time series of the overnight stays in South Tyrol (Italy) from January 1950 to December 2005. The authors tested for seasonal unit roots using HEGY to find that the variables of interest are seasonally stationary. A Dickey–Fuller (ADF) test was used to examine the null hypothesis of a stochastic trend (or a unit root). The presence of a unit root in the logarithm of overnight stays in South Tyrol was detected, making it necessary to first difference the series. The seasonal ARIMA method was developed from the standard model of Box and Jenkins (1970). The forecasting performance was assessed using a SARIMA (2,1,2)(0,1,1) and data for January 2006 to December 2008.

Generalized autoregressive conditional heteroskedasticity (GARCH)
Auto-regressive conditional heteroskedasticity (ARCH) (Engle, 1982) are commonly used in modelling financial time series that exhibit time-varying volatility clustering, i.e., periods of swings followed by periods of relative calm. Time series also often exhibit volatility clustering or persistence. In volatility clustering, large changes tend to follow large changes, and small changes tend to follow small changes. The changes from one period to the next are typically of unpredictable sign. Large disturbances, positive or negative, become part of the information set used to construct the variance forecast of the next period's disturbance.

In the ARCH(q) model, the error term split into a stochastic term z_t and a time-dependent standard deviation σ_t characterizing the typical size of the term, the error term is presented as follows:

$$\varepsilon_t = \sigma_t z_t \tag{3.21}$$

where z_t is a random variable drawn from a Gaussian distribution centred at 0 with standard deviation equal to 1. $z_t \sim N(0, 1)$ and $\sigma_t^2 = \alpha_0 + \Sigma_{i=1}^{q}\alpha_i\varepsilon_{t-i}^2$, where $\alpha_0 > 0$ and $\alpha_i > 0$ and $\Sigma_{i=1}^{q}\alpha_i < 1$. An ARCH($q$) model can be estimated using Ordinary Least Squares. A methodology to test for the lag length of ARCH errors using the Lagrange multiplier test was proposed by Engle (1982). In that case, the GARCH(p, q) model, where p is the order of the GARCH terms σ^2 and q is the order of the ARCH terms ε^2, is given by

$$\sigma_t^2 = \alpha_0 + \sum_{i=1}^{q}\alpha_i\varepsilon_{t-i}^2 + \sum_{i=1}^{p}\beta_i\sigma_{t-i}^2 \tag{3.22}$$

where $\alpha_0 > 0$ and $\alpha_i > 0$ and $\Sigma_{i=1}^{q}\alpha_i < 1$ and $\beta_i > 0$ and $\Sigma_{i=1}^{q}\beta_i < 1$

The GARCH modelling technique and its variations have applied in the study of tourism demand. For example, Shareef and McAleer (2005) modelled the volatility in monthly international tourist arrivals and the growth rate of monthly tourist arrivals for six small island tourist economies using GARCH(1,1). Chan et al. (2005) examined the volatility of the logarithm of the monthly tourist arrivals from Japan, New Zealand, the UK and the United States to Australia between 1975 and 2000 using this technique.

LIMITATIONS AND FUTURE DIRECTIONS

The most important limitations of time series analysis are that it supposes that data are either stationary or can be made stationary by simple transformations and that data can be accurately represented in a linear form (Rodrigues et al., 2010). However, in a complex world data often have structures which are non linear and chaotic (Rodrigues et al., 2010). This makes it difficult for typical time series models to fit the data with an adequate level of accuracy and, thereby, reduces the effectiveness of the model in forecasting. AI techniques such as artificial neural networks (ANN) can overcome this problem since a feature of ANN is nonlinear mapping from inputs to outputs. ANN can extract meaningful patterns from data to represents relevant information and has been proposed as a suitable alternative to classic time series methods. ANN is a computing technique that processes information in a similar manner to the human brain (Law, 2000).

According to Rodrigues et al. (2010, p. 619), the 'ability to learn through examples and to generalize the learned information is one of the most attractive characteristics of the ANN'. Due to its capacity for modelling complex non-linear relationships among data, the ANN can be used successfully in solving time series forecasting problems. Furthermore, Song and Li (2008, p. 413) stipulate that '[t]he main advantage of AI techniques is that it does not require any preliminary or additional information about data such as distribution and probability' and that 'the unique features of ANNs, such as the ability to adapt to imperfect data, nonlinearity, and arbiter function mapping, make this method a useful alternative to the classical (statistic) regression forecasting models'. AI has grown rapidly as a field of research across a variety of disciplines in recent years (Song and Li, 2008). ANNs 'have three fundamental features – parallel processing, distributed memory and adaptability – that provide them with a series of advantages compared to other processing systems, such as robustness and a tolerance to error and noise' (Palmer et al. 2006, p. 782). According to Song and Li (2008) empirical evidence shows that ANNs generally outperform the classical time-series and multiple regression models in tourism forecasting.

Multi-layer Perceptron Neural Networks (MLPNN)

The MLPNN is a feed forward neutral network with a single-layer and proper number of hidden units can be used to closely approximate the true relationship among the variables. MLPNN is especially useful when this true relationship is unknown or non-linear. MLPNN is based on a linear combination of the input variables which is transformed by a nonlinear activation function, thus a linear combination of the outputs of these activation functions is constructed for the final outputs $\hat{y}_i$. In MLPNN, the training data is considered as a set of pairs $(X^{(1)}, y^{(1)}), \ldots, (X^{(i)}, y^{(i)}), \ldots, (X^{(N)}, y^{(N)})$, where $X^{(i)} \subset R^m$ denotes the input space and has a corresponding actual target value $y^{(i)} \subset R$ for $i = 1, 2, \ldots, N$, where N corresponds to the size of the data set. Vector $X^{(i)}$ has m dimensions and normally uses the historical tourism demand observations as inputs which is $X^{(i)} = \{x_1^{(i)}, x_2^{(i)}, x_3^{(i)}, \ldots, x_m^{(i)}\} = \{y_{t-1}, y_{t-2}, \ldots, y_{t-m}\}^m \subset R^m$, where $t = m + 1, m + 2, \ldots, N$ and $i = t - m$, the actual target value $y^{(i)} = y_t \subset R$ at time t. For example, $X^{(1)} = \{y_4\, y_3\, y_2\, y_1\}$, $X^{(2)} = \{y_5\, y_4\, y_3\, y_2\}$ and corresponding target values $y^{(1)} = y_5$, $y^{(2)} = y_6$ if setting $m = 4$.

For inputs dimension M vector with H hidden units of neural networks, the output $\hat{y}_i$ of the neural networks can be written as

$$\hat{y}_t = \sum_{k=1}^{H} w_k^{(2)} g\left(\sum_{j=1}^{M} w_{kj}^{(1)} x_j^{(i)} \right) \tag{3.23}$$

where $x_j^{(i)}$ is the input value at time t, g is a nonlinear activation function. The common logistic sigmoid activation function $g(x) = 1/(1 + \exp(-x))$ is used in general. The parameters H and the weights $w_{kj}^{(1)}$, $w_k^{(2)}$ need to be determined by minimizing the error of output of combination model $\hat{y}_t^C$ and the actual true target output y as following formula using the training data set. Sometimes, the validation data set (apart from the training data set) is used to determine the parameters weights and number of hidden units H in the models in order to overcome the over training problem (Christopher, 1995).

$$E(W) = \tfrac{1}{2}\sum_{i=1}^{N} \{\hat{y}_i^C - y_i\}^2 = \tfrac{1}{2}\sum_{i=1}^{N} \left\{ \sum_{k=1}^{H} w_k^{(2)}g\left(\sum_{j=1}^{M} w_{kj}^{(1)}x_j^{(i)}\right) - y_i\right\}^2 \qquad (3.24)$$

Minimizing the error function $E(W)$ by initial W (which might for instance be chosen at random) and then update the weight vector by moving a small distance η (learning rate parameter) in W-space in the direction in which $E(W)$ decreases most rapidly (the direction of $-\nabla_W E$). By iterating this process using the equation below, eventually the weight W vector will converge to a point at which E is minimized. This point of the W value is the final value that is used in $\hat{y}_t = \Sigma_{k=1}^{H} w_k^{(2)}g(\Sigma_{j=1}^{M} w_{kj}^{(1)}x_j^{(i)})$.

$$W^{new} = W^{old} - \eta\frac{\partial E}{\partial W} \qquad (3.25)$$

Support Vector Regression Neural Networks (SVRNN)

The foundations of support vector regression neural networks (SVRNN) were first developed by Vapnik (Vapnik, 1995; Vapnik et al., 1996). Contrary to other methods that seek to minimize the forecasting error term, the basis of the SVMs is to allow an insensitive error range to avoid over- or the under-fitting (Pai and Hong 2005). In SVRNN, the training data which is used to construct a forecasting model is a subset of the whole available data and is considered as a set of pairs $(X^{(1)}, y^{(1)}), \ldots, (X^{(i)}, y^{(i)}), \ldots, (X^{(N)}, y^{(N)})$, where $X^{(i)} \subset R^m$ denotes the input space (m is the width or dimension of the inputs) and has a corresponding actual target value $y^{(i)} \subset R$ for $i = 1, 2, \ldots, N$, where N corresponds to the size of the data set. Vector $X^{(i)}$ with m dimension and actual target value $y^{(i)}$ are inputs and outputs, respectively. For this study, the historical tourism demand observations at time t, $X^{(i)} = \{y_{t-1}\,y_{t-2}, \ldots, y_{t-m}\}^m \subset R^m$ and $t = m + 1, m + 2, \ldots, N$ and $i = t - m$. Here we set the actual target value $y^{(i)} = y_t \subset R$ at time t. For example, $X^{(1)} = \{y_4\,y_3\,y_2\,y_1\}$, $X^{(2)} = \{y_5\,y_4\,y_3\,y_2\}$ and corresponding target values $y^{(1)} = y_5$, $y^{(2)} = y_6$ if $m = 4$.

The idea of the regression problem is to determine a function that can predict future values accurately. The generic support vector regression (SVR) estimating function, the forecasting model, has the following general form:

$$\hat{y}^{(i)} = f(X) = (W \cdot \Phi(X)) + b \qquad (3.26)$$

where X has the form $X^{(i)}$, $W \subset R^m$, $b \subset R$ are the best weights and base to be determined using the training data set (subset of the whole data set which is used to build the forecasting model), and Φ denotes a nonlinear transformation from R^m to a high dimensional space. The weight vector W can be written in terms of data points as:

$$W = \sum_{i=1}^{N} (\alpha_i - \alpha_i^*)\Phi(X^{(i)}) \qquad (3.27)$$

where α_i, α_i^* are the quadratic problem Lagrange multipliers and the ε-insensitive loss function is the most widely used cost function (Müller et al. 1997). The ε-insensitive loss function function is in the form:

$$\Gamma(f(X) - y) = \begin{cases} |f(X) - y| - \varepsilon, & for \ |f(x) - y| \geq \varepsilon \\ 0 & otherwise \end{cases} \quad (3.28)$$

By solving the quadratic optimization problem in Equation (3.29), the ε-insensitive loss function can be minimized:

$$\frac{1}{2} \sum_{i,j=1}^{N} (\alpha_i^* - \alpha_i)(\alpha_j^* - \alpha_j) \Phi(X^{(i)}) \cdot \Phi(X^{(j)}) - \sum_{i=1}^{N} \alpha_i^* (y^{(i)} - \varepsilon) - \alpha_i(y^{(i)} + \varepsilon) \quad (3.29)$$

subject to

$$\sum_{i=1}^{N} (\alpha_i - \alpha_i^*) = 0, \quad \alpha_i, \alpha_i^* \in [0, C]$$

By substituting Equation (3.27) into Equation (3.26), the generic forecasting SVRNN model can be rewritten as follows:

$$\hat{y}^{(i)} = f(X) = \sum_{i=1}^{N} (\alpha_i - \alpha_i^*)(\Phi(X^{(i)}) \cdot \Phi(X)) + b = \sum_{i=1}^{N} (\alpha_i - \alpha_i^*) K(X^{(i)}, X) + b \quad (3.30)$$

In this equation, the dot product can be replaced with function $K(X^{(i)}, X)$, known as the kernel. The Gaussian and linear functions are commonly used as the kernel function in SVR and are $K(X^{(i)}, X) = \exp\{-\gamma|X - X^{(i)}|^2\}$ (γ is constant) and $K(X^{(i)}, X) = X^{(i)T}X$, respectively. Kernel functions enable dot product to be performed in high-dimensional feature space using low-dimensional space data inputs without knowing the transformation Φ. For example, if the data set is quarterly tourism data, thus the previous one year (inputs width $m = 4$), a year and a quarter ($m = 5$) up to the previous two years ($m = 8$), etc. can be used as inputs, respectively. For simplicity, the Gaussian with $\sigma = 1$ is often used.

Although the first applications of the ANN technique can be traced back to the mid to late 1990s, see for example, Pattie and Snyder (1996) and Law and Au (1999), it is not until the 2000s that this technique started gaining momentum within the tourism context. Pattie and Snyder (1996) used a back-propagation neural network model with two hidden layers to forecast monthly overnight stays in US national park systems. Law and Au (1999) presented a feed-forward neural network with six input and one output nodes to forecast arrivals in Hong Kong. Cho (2003) found that the Elman's neural network model performs well in forecasting arrivals in Hong Kong from six countries.

Law (2000) studied tourism arrivals from 1966 to 1996 from Taiwan to Hong Kong using several forecasting methods including back propagation ANN and a feed forward ANN. Data from 1966 to 1991 were used for training the ANN process with data for subsequent years used for forecasting purposes. The other methods used were multiple regression, naïve, MA and Holt's ES. His results indicate that the back propagation

ANN causal model outperforms regression models, time series models and feed-forward networks with an exceptionally high level of accuracy.

Cheong and Turner (2005) analysed tourism arrivals to Singapore from Australia, China, India, Japan, the UK and the United States using quarterly data. Data on total arrivals for holiday and business were utilized. The aim of this study was to compare the forecasting accuracy of the basic structural method (BSM) and the neural network method. The authors also modelled their data using the naïve and Holt Winters' methods for base comparisons. The results confirmed that the BSM remains a highly accurate method and that correctly structured neural models can outperform BSM and the simpler methods in the short term, and can also use short data series. They concluded that their findings make neural methods a significant area for future research.

Palmer et al. (2006) apply the MLPNN technique to forecast tourism expenditure in the Balearic Islands using quarterly data from 1986 to 2000. They show that data do not need to be detrended or deseasonalized when MLPNN is applied and that the latter technique outperforms classic time series methods in forecasting accuracy. Other studies which have shown the pre-eminence of the ANN method over other classic statistical techniques are Burger et al. (2001), Cang (2011), Law (1998), Law and Au (1999) and Pattie and Snyder (1996).

The SVRNN method was applied by Cang (2011), in a study of UK inbound tourism from the world for five purposes: holiday, business, study, VFR and miscellaneous. Quarterly data from 1993(1) to 2007(4) were used. The paper investigates nine individual models, including five support vector regression neural networks with different dimension of inputs from 4 to 8, naïve 1, naïve 2, SARIMA, and WMES. The author states that since the five SVRNN models with different inputs have different time series structures, they should be treated as five different time series. Combinations of forecasting techniques were also considered. This paper proposed a non-linear combination method using MLPNN. The empirical results show that the proposed nonlinear MLPNN combination model is robust, powerful and can provide better performance at predicting arrivals than linear combination models.

The ANN method is not without criticism, ANN is a complex model compared to 'classic' time series and the 'good' models dependent on the choice of the parameters. This means that the determination of the parameters in the model is crucial. However, one of advantages of ANN is that it can cope with any complex nonlinear inputs and outputs mapping. Thus, the decision regarding the choice of whether to use classic time series or ANN type models depend on the pattern of the data and the level of accuracy required. Generally speaking, it is better to use simple time series models rather than complex time series model if there is an almost regular pattern and the level of accuracy is not a major issue. Otherwise, ANN is a very good alternative.

CONCLUSION

The aim of this chapter is to provide a review of time series techniques as applied in the tourism context. This is achieved by explaining each of the most commonly used methods and illustrating their application by providing relevant reviews of the literature. It is seen that these techniques have mostly been applied to study tourism demand for different origins and destination pairs. The chapter highlights the fact that, broadly speaking, the studies which have used these techniques can be categorized into two groups. The first seeks to solely identify the characteristics of time series data and verify whether the series contained unit roots, structural breaks or seasonality. The second, after having defined the features of the data, uses these as a means for selecting models and estimation techniques. The ultimate goal of the latter group is to predict future trends in the data set.

As pointed out by Song and Li (2008) and Coshall and Charlesworth (2011), newer models are better at prediction but there is not one single class of models which dominates in terms of accuracy in forecasting. The performance of the models depends on the data set in use (Coshall and Charlesworth, 2011). ANN models have been suggested as a suitable alternative to the class time series models. In fact, authors such as Burger et al. (2001), Palmer at al. (2006) and Cang (2011) have shown that the neural network models are better at prediction. There is, however, some consensus in the literature that a higher level of accuracy is achieved by combining models for example in Cang (2011), Coshall and Charlesworth (2011) and Wong et al. (2007). It is expected that future researchers may choose to use combined techniques more frequently.

REFERENCES

Algieri, B. (2006), 'An econometric estimation of the demand for tourism: the case of Russia', *Tourism Economics*, **12** (1), 5–20.

Alleyne, D. (2006), 'Can seasonal unit root testing improve the forecasting accuracy of tourist arrivals?', *Tourism Economics*, **12** (1), 45–64.

Box, G. and G. Jenkins (1970), *Time Series Analysis: Forecasting and Control*, San Francisco, CA: Holden-Day.

Brida, J.G. and W.A. Risso (2011), 'Tourism demand forecasting with SARIMA models: the Case of South Tyrol', *Tourism Economics*, **17** (1), 209–221.

Burger, C.J.S.C., M. Dohnal, M. Kathrada and R. Law (2001), 'A practitioner's guide to time-series methods for tourism demand forecasting: a case study of Durban, South Africa', *Tourism Management*, **22**, 403–409.

Butler, R.W. (1994), 'Seasonality in tourism: issues and problems', in A.V. Seaton (ed.) *Tourism: State of the Art*, Chichester, UK: Wiley, pp. 332–339.

Butler, R.W. (2001), 'Seasonality in tourism: issues and implications', in T. Baum and S. Lundtorp (eds), *Seasonality in Tourism*, Advances in Tourism Research Series, Amsterdam: Elsevier, pp. 5–21.

Byrne, J.P. and R. Perman (2006), 'Unit roots and structural breaks: a survey of the literature', Working Papers 2006_10, University of Glasgow, UK.

Cang, S. (2011), 'A non-linear tourism demand forecast combination model', *Tourism Economics*, **17** (1), 5–20.

Cang, S. and N. Hemmington (2010), 'Forecasting UK inbound expenditure by different purposes of visit', *Journal of Hospitality and Tourism Research*, **34** (3), 294–309.

Chan F., C. Lim and M. McAleer (2005), 'Modelling multivariate international tourism demand and volatility', *Tourism Management*, **26**, 459–471.

Cheong, K.S. and L.W. Turner (2005), 'Neural network forecasting of tourism demand', *Tourism Economics*, **11** (3), 301–328.

Cho, V. (2003), 'A comparison of three different approaches to tourist arrival forecasting', *Tourism° Management*, **24**, 323–330.

Christopher, M.B. (1995), *Neural Networks for Pattern Recognition*, Oxford: Oxford University Press.

Coshall, J.T. and R. Charlesworth (2011), 'A management orientated approach to combination forecasting of tourism demand', *Tourism Management*, **32**, 759–769.

Dickey, D.A. and W.A. Fuller (1979), 'Distribution of the estimators for autoregressive time series with a unit root', *Journal of the American Statistical Association*, **74**, 427–431.

Douglas C.M., A.J. Lynwood and S.G. John (1990), *Forecasting and Time Series Analysis*, 2nd edition, Columbus, OH: McGraw-Hill, Inc.

Engle, R.F. (1982), 'Autoregressive conditional heteroscedasticity with estimates of the variance of United Kingdom inflation', *Econometrica*, **50**, 987–1007.

Engle, R.F. and C.W.J. Granger (1987), 'Co-integration and error-correction: representation, estimation, and testing', *Econometrica*, **55**, 251–276.

Frechtling, D.C. (1996), *Practical Tourism Forecasting*, Oxford: Butterworth-Heinemann.

Frechtling, D.C. (2001), *Forecasting Tourism Demand*, Oxford: Butterworth-Heinemann.

González Pilar and Paz Moralez (1995), 'An analysis of the international tourism demand in Spain', *International Journal of Forecasting*, **11**, 233–251.

Granger, C.W.J. (1981), 'Some properties of time series data and their use in econometric model specification', *Journal of Econometrics*, **16**, 121–130.

Granger, C.W.J. and P. Newbold (1974), 'Spurious regressions in econometrics', **2** (2), 111–120.

Granger, C.W.J. and A.A. Weiss (1983), *Time Series Analysis of Error-correction Models*, New York: Academic Press.

Gujarati, D.N. and D.C. Porter (2009), *Basic Econometrics*, 5th edition, New York: McGraw Hill.

Hansen, B.E. (2001), 'The new econometrics of structural change: dating breaks in U.S. labour productivity', *Journal of Economic Perspectives*, **4**, 117–128.

Harvey, A.C. (1993), *Time Series Models*, 2nd edition, London: Harvester Wheatsheaf.

Hylleberg, S., R.F. Engle, C.W.J. Granger and B.S. Yoo (1990), 'Seasonal integration and cointegration', *Journal of Econometrics*, **44**, 215–238.

Johansen, S. (1988), 'Statistical analysis of cointegration vectors', *Journal of Economic Dynamics and Control*, **12**, 231–254.

Johansen, S. and K. Juselius (1990), 'Maximum likelihood estimation and inference on cointegration with applications to the demand of money', *Oxford Bulletin of Economics and Statistics*, **52**, 169–210.

Kulendran, N. and M.L. King (1997), 'Forecasting international quarterly tourist flows using error correction and time series models', *International Journal of Forecasting*, **13**, 319–327.

Kulendran, N. and K. Wilson (2000), 'Modelling business tourism', *Tourism Economics*, **6** (1), 47–59.

Kulendran, N. and S.F. Witt (2001), 'Cointegration versus least squares regression', *Annals of Tourism Research*, **28**, 291–311.

Kulendran, N. and S.F. Witt (2003), 'Forecasting the demand for international business tourism', *Journal of Travel Research*, **41**, 265–271.

Kulendran, N. and K.F. Wong (2005), 'Modeling seasonality in tourism forecasting', *Journal of Travel Research*, **44**, 163.

Law, R. (1998), 'Room occupancy rate forecasting: a neural network approach', *International Journal of Contemporary Hospitality Management*, **10** (6), 234–239.

Law, R. (2000), 'Back-propagation learning in improving the accuracy of neural network-based tourism demand forecasting', *Tourism Management*, **21**, 331–340.

Law, R. and N. Au (1999), 'A neural network model to forecast Japanese demand for travel to Hong Kong', *Tourism Management*, **20** (1), 89–97.

Lee, C.C. and M.-S. Chien (2008), 'Structural breaks, tourism development, and economic growth: evidence from Taiwan', *Mathematics and Computers in Simulation*, **77** (4), 358–368.

Lee, J. and M.C. Strazicich (2003), 'Minimum LM unit root test with two structural breaks', *Review of Economics and Statistics*, **63**, 1082–1089.

Lee, J. and M.C. Strazicich (2004), 'Minimum LM unit root test with one structural break', Working Paper, Department of Economics, Appalachian State University.

Lim, C. and M. McAleer (2002), 'Time series forecasts of international travel demand for Australia', *Tourism Management*, **23**, 389–396.

Lumsdaine, R.L. and D.H. Papell (1997), 'Multiple trend breaks and the unit root hypothesis', *Review of Economics and Statistics*, **79** (2), 212–218.

Müller, K.R., A. Smola, G. Rätsch, B. Schölkopf, J. Kohlmorgen and V. Vapnik (1997), 'Predicting time series with support vector machines', Artificial Neural Networks–ICANN'97, 999–1004.

Narayan, P.K. (2004), 'Fiji's tourism demand: the ARDL approach to cointegration', *Tourism Economics*, **10** (2), 193–206.

Narayan, P.K. (2005), 'The structure of tourist expenditure in Fiji: evidence from unit root structural break tests', *Applied Economics*, **37** (10), 1157–1161.

Njegovan, N. (2006), 'Are shocks to air passenger traffic transitory or permanent?', *Journal of Transport Economics and Policy*, **40** (2), 315–328.

Pai, P.F. and W.C. Hong (2005), 'An improved neural networks model in forecasting arrivals', *Annals of Tourism Research*, **32** (4), 1138–1141.

Palmer, A., J.J. Montaño and A. Sesé (2006), 'Designing an artificial neural network for forecasting tourism time series', *Tourism Management*, **27**, 781–790.

Papatheodorou, A. and H. Song (2005), 'International tourism forecasts: time-series analysis of world and regional data', *Tourism Economics*, **11** (1), 11–23.

Pattie, D.C. and J. Snyder (1996), 'Using a neural network to forecast visitor behavior', *Annals of Tourism Research*, **23** (1), 151–164.
Perron, P. (1989), 'The Great Crash, the oil price shock and the unit root hypothesis', *Econometrica*, **57**, 1361–1401.
Perron, P. (2005), 'Dealing with structural breaks', *Palgrave Handbook of Econometrics, Vol. 1: Econometric Theory*. New York: Palgrave Macmillan.
Phillips, P.C.B. and P. Perron (1988), 'Testing for a unit root in time series regression', *Biometrika*, **75**, 335–346.
Rodrigues, L.J., P.S.G. de Mattos Neto, J. Albuquerque, S. Bocanegra and T.A.E. Ferreira (eds) (2010), 'Forecasting chaotic and non-linear time series with artificial intelligence and statistical measures', in *Modelling Simulation and Optimization*, available at http://www.intechopen.com/articles/show/title/forecasting-chaotic-and-non-linear-time-series-with-artificial-intelligence-and-statistical-measures.
Shareef, R. and M. McAleer (2005), 'Modelling international tourism demand and volatility in small island tourism economies', *International Journal of Tourism Research*, **7**, 313–333.
Smyth, R., I. Nielsen and V. Mishra (2009), '"I've been to Bali too" (and I will be going back): are terrorist shocks to Bali's tourist arrivals permanent or transitory?', *Applied Economics*, **41** (11), 1367–1378.
Song, H. and G. Li (2008), 'Tourism demanding modelling and forecasting: a review of recent research', *Tourism Management*, **29**, 203–220.
Song, H. and S.F. Witt (2000), *Tourism Demand Modelling and Forecasting: Modern Econometric Approaches*, Advances in Tourism Research Series, Oxford: Pergamon.
Song, H. and S.F. Witt (2003), 'Tourism forecasting: the general-to-specific approach', *Journal of Travel Research*, **42**, 65–74.
Song, H., S.F. Witt and G. Li (2009), *The Advanced Econometrics of Tourism Demand*, London: Routledge.
Syriopoulos, T. (1995), 'A dynamic model of demand for Mediterranean tourism', *International Review of Applied Economics*, **9**, 318–336.
Vapnik, V. (1995), *The Nature of Statistical Learning Theory*, New York: Springer.
Vapnik, V., S. Golowich and A. Smola (1996), 'Support vector machine for function approximation regression estimation, and signal processing', *Advances in Neural Information Processing Systems*, **9**, 281–287.
Webber, A. (2001), 'Exchange rate volatility and cointegration in tourism demand', *Journal of Travel Research*, **39**, 398–405.
Whiltshire, T. (2009), 'A time-series analysis of Australian international passenger numbers', thesis submitted to Monash University Australia, unpublished.
Wong, K.K.F., H. Song, S.F. Witt and C.D. Wu (2007), 'Tourism forecasting: to combine or not to combine?', *Tourism Management*, **28**, 1068–1078.
Zivot, E. and D.W.K. Andrews (1992), 'Further evidence on the great crash, the oil-price shock, and the unit-root hypothesis', *Journal of Business and Economic Statistics*, **10** (3), 251–270.

4 Demand modeling and forecasting

Grace Bo Peng, Haiyan Song and Stephen F. Witt

NATURE OF TOURISM DEMAND MODELING AND FORECASTING

Tourism demand forecasting methods can be divided into two categories: qualitative and quantitative methods. Quantitative forecasting methods organize past tourism demand information by mathematical rules and there are three main subcategories: time series models, econometric approaches, and artificial intelligence methods. According to the complexities of the models and estimation techniques, the time series forecasting methods can be subdivided into basic and advanced time series models. Based on their temporal structure, econometric models can be grouped into two categories: static and dynamic models.

Tourism demand is normally measured by either tourist arrivals in a destination, tourists' expenditure when they visit a destination, or tourist nights stayed in the destination. The variables that have been generally accepted as the main determinants of international tourism demand comprise potential tourists' income levels, the relative price of tourism products in the origin and destination countries, substitute prices of tourism products in alternative foreign destinations, transportation cost, population of origin country, exchange rates, marketing expenditure by the destination in the origin country, and one-off events (which can have a positive or negative effect). For a detailed review of tourism demand measures and their determinants, see, for example, Martin and Witt (1987, 1988); Song and Li (2008); Song et al. (2009); Witt and Martin (1987b); and Witt and Witt (1992, 1995).

BASIC TIME SERIES METHODS

Time series forecasting methods (see Tables 4.1 and 4.2) are also called extrapolative methods, and only use past data on the series to be forecast in extrapolating the future. These models attempt to identify the patterns in the time series that cause the shifts in the forecast variable. The advantage of time series models is that they are relatively simple to estimate, requiring no more than one data series. Time series models may be separated into two categories: basic time series models and advanced time series models. The basic time series models include the naïve, simple moving average, and single exponential smoothing models. The advanced time series models include the double exponential smoothing, autoregressive moving average, and basic structural time series models.

The *Naïve 1 (No Change) Model* is the simplest forecasting model, which assumes that the forecast value for this period (t) is equal to the actual value in the last period ($t - 1$). The naïve 1 model has often been shown to generate the most accurate one-year-ahead forecasts in comparison with other more sophisticated forecasting models (Martin and

Table 4.1   Basic time series models

Method	Equation
Naïve 1	$F_t = A_{t-1}$
Naïve 2	$F_t = A_{t-1}*[1 + (A_{t-1} - A_{t-2})/A_{t-2}]$
Simple moving average	$F_t = (A_{t-1} + A_{t-2} + A_{t-3} + \ldots A_{t-n})/n$
Single exponential smoothing	$F_t = \alpha A_{t-1} + (1 - \alpha)F_{t-1}$

Note: F_t = forecast at time t; A_{t-1} = actual value at time $t - 1$; n = number of lags in the moving average process; α = smoothing constant $(0 < \alpha < 1)$.

Table 4.2   Advanced time series models

Method	Equation
Brown's	$Y_t = \alpha A_{t-1} + (1 - \alpha)Y_{t-1}$ $Y'_t = \alpha Y_{t-1} + (1 - \alpha)Y'_{t-1}$ $C_t = Y_t + (Y_t - Y'_t)$ $T_t = [(1 - \alpha)/\alpha]*(Y_t - Y'_t)$ $F_{t+n} = C_t + n*T_t$
Holt's	$L_t = \alpha A_t + (1 - \alpha)(L_{t-1} + b_{t-1})$ $b_t = \beta(L_t - L_{t-1}) + (1 - \beta)b_{t-1}$ $F_{t+n} = L_t + n*b_t$
Holt–Winters	$L_t = \alpha(A_t - sn_{t-h}) + (1 - \alpha)(L_{t-1} + b_{t-1})$ $b_t = \beta(L_t - L_{t-1}) + (1 - \beta)b_{t-1}$ $sn_t = \gamma(A_t - L_t) + (1 - \gamma)sn_{t-h}$ $F_{t+n} = L_t + n*b_t + sn_{t+n-h}$
Box–Jenkins	$A_t = d + a_1A_{t-1} + a_2A_{t-2} + \ldots + a_pA_{t-p} - b_1e_{t-1} - b_2e_{t-2} - \ldots - b_qe_{t-q}$
Basic structural time series	$F_t = \mu_t + \gamma_t + \psi_t + \varepsilon_t$

Note: F_t = forecast value at time t; A_t = actual value at time t; Y_t = SES series at time t; Y'_t = DES series at time t; C_t = the intercept; T_t = the slope coefficient; n = the number of forecasting periods; L_t = smoothed value at time t; b_t = trend estimate at time t; sn_t = seasonal variation at time t; d = constant; e = error term; α, β, γ are smoothing constants which are between 0 and 1; μ_t, γ_t, ψ_t, ε_t denote the trend, seasonal, cyclical and irregular components, respectively.

Witt, 1989; Witt and Witt, 1995; Witt et al., 1994). However, the performance of the no change model declines when dealing with sudden structural change and longer term forecasting (Chan et al., 1999; Witt et al., 1994).

The *Naïve 2 (Constant Change) Model* is a widely used simple time series forecasting model when a continuous trend is present in the data. The forecast value for period t is obtained by multiplying the demand in period $(t - 1)$ by the growth rate between the previous period $(t - 2)$ and the current period $(t - 1)$. Chan et al. (1999) used the Gulf War as an example of a sudden shock and found that the naïve 2 model performed best compared with the ARIMA, exponential smoothing and quadratic trend curve models in dealing with unstable data.

Since naïve models often yield better results than econometric models (Martin and Witt, 1989; Witt and Witt, 1995), many researchers use the naïve models as benchmarks for forecasting evaluations (Song et al., 2003a (Denmark); Turner and Witt, 2001(New Zealand); Veloce, 2004 (Canada)).

The *Simple Moving Average (SMA) Model* allows the past values of a variable to determine the forecast values with equal weights assigned to the past values. The number of observations included in the model determines the responsiveness of the model and it is clear that the more lagged values included in the SMA model, the smoother the forecasts become. If a time series shows wide variations around a trend, including more observations in the SMA model, will allow the model to pick up the trend better. However, the main limitation of the SMA model is that it gives equal weight to all the lagged observations, which may not be realistic as the more recent values are likely to have a bigger impact on the current value of the time series. Therefore, the SMA method normally generates more accurate forecasts if the time series is less volatile (Frechtling, 1996; Makridakis et al., 1998). Systematic errors may occur when the SMA model deals with a time series that has a linear trend. To overcome this problem, the double moving average method can be used to further smooth the series (Hu et al., 2004; Lim and McAleer, 2008).

The *Single Exponential Smoothing (SES) Model* is used to forecast a time series when there is no trend or seasonal pattern. In a SES model, the forecast for period t is equal to the forecast for period $(t - 1)$ plus a smoothing constant multiplied by the forecasting error incurred in period $(t - 1)$. The smoothing constant must be between zero and one, and is set by the forecaster, and the smaller the smoothing constant, the more weight the method gives to the previous forecast value (Witt and Witt, 1992). Witt et al. (1992) showed that the SES model generates forecasts with lower error magnitudes than the no change model for domestic tourism demand, which is generally less volatile than international tourism demand.

ADVANCED TIME SERIES METHODS

Brown's Double Exponential Smoothing (DES) Model was developed to deal with time series that have a linear trend over time, either increasing or decreasing. When there is no trend, this technique reduces to SES. Geurts and Ibrahim (1975) first applied Brown's model to forecast tourist arrivals in Hawaii and suggested that it is cheaper and easier than the Box–Jenkins approach for use in forecasting tourism demand. Sheldon (2008) found that the DES and naïve 1 models also performed well in forecasting international tourism expenditures. However, the disadvantage of the DES model is that it does not track non-linear trends well and often fails in picking up structural breaks in the time series (Frechtling, 1996).

Holt's Double Exponential Smoothing Model allows the trend and slope to be smoothed using different smoothing constants. Since Brown's method only uses one constant, the estimated trend is very sensitive to random impacts, whereas Holt's method is more flexible in selecting the smoothing constants (Makridakis et al., 1998). However, according to Chen et al. (2008), Brown's method outperformed Holt's method based on the mean absolute percentage error (MAPE) in forecasting tourist arrivals to US national parks.

Holt–Winters Triple Exponential Smoothing Model adds seasonal variations to Holt's model, and is appropriate when a time series has a linear trend with an additive seasonal pattern. Since the Holt–Winters model captures both the seasonal pattern and trend of the time series, it usually outperforms other exponential smoothing methods (Lim and McAleer, 2001). Grubb and Mason (2001) showed that the Holt–Winters method with damped trend greatly improved long-run forecasting accuracy compared with the Box–Jenkins and basic structural models in the case of UK air passenger series.

The *Box–Jenkins Model* is the most frequently used advanced time series approach in tourism demand forecasting. It is considered to be a relatively sophisticated technique with the autoregressive moving average (ARMA) process as its basic form. Box–Jenkins forecasting models are identified by examining the behavior of the autocorrelation function (AF) and partial autocorrelation function (PAF) of a stationary time series. Stationarity of the time series is essential for the implementation of the classical Box–Jenkins model. A stationary series refers to a series that has a constant mean and variance. If a time series is nonstationary, it should be differenced until it becomes stationary. When the dth differences of a time series has an ARMA representation, the time series can be written as an autoregressive integrated moving average (ARIMA) model. The AF can help determine the number of times that the series needs to be differenced.

Both the autoregressive (AR) and moving average (MA) models are useful forms of the Box–Jenkins model, and the AF and PAF are used to determine whether the time series is an AR, MA, or ARMA process. When the PAF drops off to 0 after lag p, it indicates that it is an AR (p) process while if AF drops off to 0 after lag q, it means that the time series follows a MA (q) process (Chen et al., 2008).

The advantage of the Box–Jenkins method is not only that these models can track the behavior of a diverse range of time series, but also that they have fewer parameters to be estimated in the final model than the multivariate regression approach. Such statistics as the Akaike information criterion (AIC), Akaike final prediction error (AFPE), and Bayesian information criterion (BIC) are used to add mathematical rigor to the judgment process of identifying an appropriate ARMA or ARIMA model (De Gooijer and Hyndman, 2006). Since seasonality is an important feature in most tourism series, seasonal ARIMA (SARIMA) has gained popularity in recent years. Some key studies using this approach include Goh and Law's (2002) study of Hong Kong tourism demand and Kulendran and Witt's (2003b) analysis of international business tourism in Australia.

To improve the explanatory power of the ARMA or ARIMA models, some researchers have included causal variables in the model, which are known as the ARMAX or ARIMAX models. The causal ARMAX models, on average, outperformed both the purely extrapolative models and simple econometric models in terms of forecasting accuracy, as they are developed by incorporating both the short-run dynamics as well as the long-run cointegration relationships between the dependent and causal variables (Akal, 2004; Cho, 2001).

The *Basic Structural Time Series Model (BSM)* is constructed by decomposing a time series into its trend, seasonal, cycle, and irregular components. A stochastic trend captures changing consumer tastes in tourism demand, whereas stochastic seasonality allows for variations in the seasonal pattern. The irregular component represents the transitory variations in tourism demand which are not explained by the other components. The trend, seasonal, and cyclical components can be modeled in various ways. Greenidge (2001) successfully applied the BSM to forecasting tourist arrivals to Barbados. Explanatory variables can be included into the BSM to form a multivariate structural time series model (STSM) (Gonzalez and Moral, 1995). However, according to Turner and Witt (2001) and Kulendran and Witt (2003b), no evidence has emerged to suggest that the inclusion of explanatory variables improves the forecasting accuracy of the BSM. Therefore, for practitioners who are only interested in forecasting, the BSM should be sufficient (Kim and Moosa, 2005).

ECONOMETRIC MODELS

Although time series approaches are useful tools for tourism demand forecasting, a major limitation of these models is that the construction of the models is not based on any economic theory that underlies tourists' decision-making processes. Therefore, not only can they not be used to analyse tourists' behavior, but also they are incapable of assisting policy makers in evaluating the effectiveness of the strategies and policies that have been implemented in tourism development. Econometric models are superior to time series approaches from this perspective (Song et al., 2009).

Table 4.3   Static econometric models

Method	Equation
Traditional regression	$Y = \alpha + \sum_i \beta_i x_i + \varepsilon_i$
Gravity model	$Y = G\dfrac{P_i P_j}{D^2}$
Static LAIDS	$w_i = \alpha_i + \sum_j \gamma_{ij} \log p_j + b_i \log\left(\dfrac{x}{P^*}\right) + \sum_k \varphi_{ik} dum_k + \varepsilon_i$
	$\log P^* = \sum_i w_i \log p_i$

Note: Y = forecasts of tourism demand; x_i = explanatory variables; P_j = population of region j; D = the distance from region i to j; w_i = budget share of the ith good, p_j = price of the jth good; x = total expenditure on all goods in the system; P^* = aggregate price index; dum_k = dummy variables; ε_i = disturbance term; α= constant ; β_i, G, α_i, γ_{ij}, b_i, φ_{ik} are the parameters to be estimated.

Static Econometric Models (see Table 4.3) refer to those models that include the current values of explanatory variables, but do not include lagged dependent or explanatory variables. The main objective of static econometric models is to explore the factors that affect tourism demand. The traditional regression approach, gravity models, and the static almost ideal demand system (AIDS) are examples of static econometric models.

The *Traditional Regression Approach* generally uses ordinary least squares (OLS) as the estimation procedure. This approach follows six main steps: (1) formulate hypotheses based on demand theory; (2) identify the model's functional form; (3) collect data; (4) estimate the model; (5) test hypotheses; and (6) generate forecasts or evaluate the policies (Song et al., 2009).

The advantages of the static regression approach are: (1) it explicitly addresses the causal relationships between the demand for tourism and its influencing factors; (2) it is useful for the assessment of political and business plans; (3) it provides several statistics to measure the accuracy and validity of the model and improve it based upon these statistics (Frechtling, 1996). However, there are a number of limitations. The first limitation of the static regression model is that tourism demand data tend to be trended (nonstationary), and a regression model which contains such nonstationary series tends to generate a spurious relationship between the dependent and independent variables and this invalidates the diagnostic statistics of the model. The second limitation of the static econometric model is that it cannot take dynamic changes in tourists' behavior into consideration when the model is estimated, which is rather restrictive and unnecessary. The third limitation relates to the uncertainty involved in deriving the final model for forecasting, as it is highly likely that different researchers armed with the same data set may come up with completely different models. This is because no clear procedure can be followed in terms of the model specification (Song et al., 2009). There are many examples of the use of the traditional regression approach in the tourism forecasting literature; see for example, Martin and Witt (1989), Witt and Martin (1987a) and Witt and Witt (1990).

The *Gravity Model (GraM)* examines the effects of such variables as distance and population size on tourism demand. It assumes that the attractiveness between two countries/regions is an inverse function of the square of their distance and is proportional to the product of their populations. The gravity model has been widely used in international trade research. Guo (2007) developed the gravity model to analyse the determinants of inbound tourism demand in China, and Khadaroo and Seetanah (2008) used this approach to investigate the role of transportation infrastructure on tourism flow. However, the reliability of gravity models is questionable for their lack of a strong theoretical underpinning, which leads to the ad hoc choice of the explanatory variables (Che, 2004; Witt, 1980).

The *Static Linear Almost Ideal Demand System (LAIDS)* was originally introduced by Deaton and Muellbauer (1980). It is a system of equations method, which is concerned with long-run consumer behavior. In the static AIDS model, the budget share for good *i*, which is the dependent variable, is related to the logarithms of prices and total real expenditures. Since single equation models fail to estimate adequately the effect of a change in tourism prices in a specific destination on the demand for traveling to other destinations (substitution effect), the system of equations model was introduced to overcome this limitation. The AIDS model is the most popular among a number of system of equations methods, because it gives an arbitrary first-order approximation to any demand function; and it has a functional form which complies with known household budget data (Deaton and Muellbauer, 1980). It also has a flexible functional form which does not impose any a priori restrictions on the elasticities of demand, that is, any good and service in the system can be either an inferior or a normal good (Fujii et al., 1985). Past empirical studies have shown that the static AIDS model has been a popular technique for analysing the market share of tourism demand, and also provides a range of information about the sensitivity of tourism demand to price and expenditure changes (De Mello et al., 2002; Han et al., 2006; Papatheodorou, 1999; Syriopoulos and Sinclair, 1993).

The static LAIDS, however, focuses on the long-run solution of the model that assumes that consumers behave in the same manner over time and ignores the short-run dynamics of the demand system. In reality, consumer behavior varies over time due to change in tastes, adjustment costs, imperfect information, incorrect expectations, and misinterpreted real price changes (Song et al., 2009).

Although static econometric models have advantages in exploring and interpreting the elasticities of the explanatory variables, they still do not perform well in forecasting tourism demand, as they do not consider the long run cointegration relationships and short run dynamics in the estimation of the models (Song et al., 2009). The poor performance of the static models may partly be due to the fact that they omit the "word-of-mouth" effect. They ignore the dynamics of the demand system and assume that tourism demand is not affected by previous values of the economic variables. Furthermore, the stationarity properties of the variables are not considered in static models. As a result, spurious regression is very likely to occur (Li, 2010).

Dynamic Econometric Models. The adoption of advanced econometric techniques, such as the vector autoregressive (VAR) models, time varying parameter (TVP) models and error correction models have much improved the forecasting performance of econometric models. The dynamic models capture the "word-of-mouth" effect and the inclusion of the causal variables increases the models' explanatory power.

The *Autoregressive Distributed Lag Model (ADLM)* is a dynamic econometric model, which involves a general functional form containing both the current and lagged values of the variables. Stepwise reduction, which is also known as the general-to-specific approach, is applied to estimate the ADLM. This process continues until all the criteria are satisfied, including a high R^2 value, statistically significant coefficients of the explanatory variables, and lack of autocorrelation and heteroskedasticity in the error term (Song and Witt, 2003).

The model selection process in the ADLM involves the following steps. First, a general demand model with a large number of explanatory variables, including the lagged dependent and independent variables, is constructed as a general ADLM; second, the *t*, F, and Wald statistics are used to test the various restrictions, in order to achieve a simple but statistically significant specification; third, the normal diagnostic tests are carried out to examine whether the final model is statistically acceptable; and in the last step, the final model is used for policy evaluation and forecasting (Song et al., 2009). The main criteria for selecting an ADLM include: consistent with economic theory, data coherency, parsimony, encompassing, parameter constancy and exogeneity (Thomas, 1993).

The general-to-specific methodology overcomes the disadvantages of the specific-to-general method, which tends to end up with a highly complicated final model involving too many variables, which may still not be able to capture the dynamic characteristics of the demand model and leads to poor forecasting performance. Furthermore, the ADLM does not necessarily need a priori knowledge about the integration properties of the variables, and provides robust estimation of the model parameters even in small samples (Narayan, 2004).

With different restrictions imposed on the parameters, an ADLM can be written into different econometric models, such as the static model, the autoregressive model, the growth rate model (Witt and Witt, 1992), the leading indicator model (Turner et al., 1997; Kulendran and Witt, 2003a), the partial adjustment model (Song et al., 2003b), the common factor model (Lee et al., 1996), the finite distributed lag model and the dead start model (Song et al., 2003b) (see Table 4.4). These models have been widely used in tourism forecasting in recent years, however, their performance has varied under different conditions.

The general-to-specific methodology has been popular in tourism demand analysis, and has been used to explore the determinants of tourism demand in specific destinations such as Australia (Kulendran and Divisekera, 2007), Asia (Song and Lin, 2010), Korea (Song and Witt, 2003), Denmark (Song et al., 2003a), Europe (Smeral, 2010), and Latin America (Vanegas, 2008). Meanwhile, it has been proven to perform well in forecasting turning points (Nadal, 2001). However, one of the possible problems with this method is that the structure of the selected final model relies too much on the data used, even though economic theory plays an important role in the initial form of the general model (Song and Witt, 2003).

The *Error Correction Model (ECM)* expresses the current value of the dependent variable as a linear function of past values of the dependent variable, current and past values of the explanatory variables and the previous values of the error term from the cointegration relationships (Kulendran and Witt, 2001). The general form of the ECM can be written as:

$$\Delta y = (\text{current and lagged } \Delta x_{jt}s, \text{ lagged } \Delta y_t s) - (1 - \phi_1)\left[y_{t-1} - \sum_{j=1}^{k}\xi_j x_{jt-1}\right] + \varepsilon_t \quad (4.1)$$

The ECM (1, 1) takes the form

$$\Delta y_t = \beta_0 \Delta x_t - (1 - \phi_1)[y_{t-1} - k_0 - k_1 x_{t-1}] + \varepsilon_t \quad (4.2)$$

where $k_0 = \alpha / (1 - \phi_1), k_1 = (\beta_0 + \beta_1) / (1 - \phi_1)$, β_0 is the impact parameter, $(1 - \phi_1)$ is the feedback effect, k_0 and k_1 are the long-run response coefficients.

Cointegration (CI) describes the relationship between a pair of nonstationary economic variables, who share a common stochastic trend, that is, if two or more time series are

Table 4.4   Variations of ADLM

Model	Equation
Unrestricted ADLM	$y_t = \alpha + \sum_{j=1}^{k}\sum_{i=0}^{p}\beta_{ji}x_{jt-i} + \sum_{i=1}^{p}\phi_i y_{t-i} + \varepsilon_t$
Static	$y_t = \alpha + \sum_{j=1}^{k}\beta_j x_{jt} + \varepsilon_t$
Autoregressive (AR)	$y_t = \alpha + \sum_{i=1}^{p}\phi_i y_{t-i} + \varepsilon_t$
Growth rate	$\Delta y_t = \alpha + \sum_{j=1}^{k}\beta_j \Delta x_{jt} + \varepsilon_t$
Leading indicator	$y_t = \alpha + \sum_{j=1}^{k}\sum_{i=1}^{p}\beta_{ji}x_{jt-i} + \varepsilon_t$
Partial adjustment	$y_t = \alpha + \sum_{j=1}^{k}\beta_j x_{jt} + \sum_{i=1}^{p}\phi_i y_{t-i} + \varepsilon_t$
Common factor	$y_t = \alpha + \sum_{j=1}^{k}\beta_j x_{jt} + \varepsilon_t$ $\varepsilon_t = \sum_{i=1}^{p}\beta_i \varepsilon_{t-i} + \mu_i$
Finite distributed lag	$y_t = \alpha + \sum_{j=0}^{k}\sum_{i=0}^{p}\beta_j x_{jt-i} + \varepsilon_t$
Dead start	$y_t = \alpha + \sum_{j=1}^{k}\sum_{i=1}^{p}\beta_j x_{jt-i} + \sum_{i=1}^{p}\phi_i y_{t-i} + \varepsilon_t$

Note: y_t = tourism demand; x_t = explanatory variables; k = number of explanatory variables; p = lag length; α = constant; ε_t and μ_i = error terms; β_{ji} and ϕ_i are the parameters to be estimated.

Source: Adapted from Song et al., 2009, p. 48.

individually integrated, but some linear combination of them has a lower order of integration, the series are said to be cointegrated. Unit roots tests are used to examine the CI relationship between the two series (Song et al., 2009). If the two variables are cointegrated, a regression model that relates the two variables to each other would not generate spurious relationships.

The ECM and CI are a bi-directional transformation which is often called the "Granger Representation Theorem" (Engle and Granger, 1987). The ECM and CI model are useful when both long run equilibrium and short run disequilibrium relationships are of interest. For example, Choyakh (2008), Daniel and Ramos (2002), Dritsakis (2004), and Halicioglu (2010) used the ECM and CI model to examine the demand for tourism in Tunisia, Portugal, Greece, and Turkey, respectively.

The ECM has the following advantages: (1) it overcomes the spurious regression problem by differencing the variables and it also avoids the problems of the growth rate model, where only differenced data are used; (2) it is another form of the ADLM, which fits in well with the general-to-specific methodology; (3) it reduces the problem of data mining during estimation (Song et al., 2009).

In their studies on the demand for Canadian and Tunisian tourism, Veloce (2004) and Querfelli (2008) found that ECMs provide more precise forecasts than time series models when a differenced demand variable is concerned. Kulendran and Witt (2001) also demonstrated that the ECM and CI models are more accurate than the traditional econometric models in forecasting tourism demand from the UK to Germany, Greece, the Netherlands, Portugal, Spain, and the United States.

Three main estimation methods are used to estimate ECMs: the Engle–Granger two stage (EG2S), the Wickens–Breusch (WB) and the ADLM procedures. However, these methods show different levels of performance when different forecasting horizons are considered. Wickens and Breusch (1988) suggested that in the case of the EG2S approach, the estimation bias in the first stage may be carried over to the second stage when the sample size is small.

The *VAR Model* was developed by Sims (1980), and here the variables are modeled purely as dynamic processes, except for the deterministic variables such as trend, intercept and dummy variables. In the VAR model, each variable is a linear function of the lagged values of all variables in the system. The VAR model treats all the variables as endogenous, and does not rely on the assumption that all the explanatory variables need to be exogenous as in the case of the single equation models. The general VAR (p) model can be written as:

$$Y_t = \sum_{i=1}^{p} A_i Y_{t-i} + BZ_t + U_t \qquad (4.3)$$

where, Y_t is a k vector of variables included in the system; Z_t is a vector of deterministic variables; U_t is a vector of regression errors that are assumed to be contemporaneously correlated but not autocorrelated; A_i and B are matrices of parameters to be estimated.

A general VAR model, also called the unrestricted VAR model, is the standard form of the VAR model. In the unrestricted model, lag lengths for each variable are identical and every variable in the system is included in each equation. In a mixed VAR model, different lag lengths are specified for each variable in each equation. A likelihood ratio test, the Akaike Information Criterion (AIC) and Schwarz Bayesian Criterion (SBC) are usually suggested to determine the optimal lag length (Song et al., 2009). Wong et al. (2006) found that the Bayesian VAR model that combines *priors* with sample information, overcomes the problem of overfitting and improves the forecasting performance of the VAR models when forecasting the demand for Hong Kong tourism.

The VAR models have proved to be capable of producing accurate medium- to long-term tourism forecasts. In a study of the demand for Macau tourism, Song and Witt (2006) concluded that the VAR technique was found to be superior to the traditional regression approach for the following two reasons. First, the VAR models do not require an implicit theoretical framework in the construction and estimation of the models.

Second, the forecasts are easy to generate using VAR, as it does not require generating forecasts of the explanatory variables first in order to generate the forecasts of the dependent variable. Therefore, it is easier from this aspect to produce tourism demand forecasts using VAR models than other econometric models. Although the VAR technique has been widely and successfully used in macroeconomic forecasting, little effort have been made to apply this method in tourism forecasting.

The *Time Varying Parameter Model* takes the possibility of parameter changes over time into consideration in the modeling exercise. The TVP model overcomes the structural instability problem caused by external shocks. According to Song and Witt (2000), the TVP model can simulate different types of external shocks to the tourism demand system, including policy and regime shifts, economic reforms and political uncertainties. Besides, the TVP model performs well in capturing external influences that are gradual and diffuse in nature, such as changes in consumer tastes and other social and psychological changes of the consumers (Song and Wong, 2003). The TVP model can be written in a state space form:

$$y_t = \beta_t x_t + \mu_t$$

$$\beta_t = \phi\beta_{t-1} + R_t e_t \qquad (4.4)$$

where y_t is tourism demand, x_t is a row vector of k explanatory variables, β_t is the column vector of k state variables, ϕ is a $k \times k$ matrix, R_t is a $k \times g$ matrix, μ_t is a residual with zero mean and constant covariance, and e_t is a $g \times 1$ vector of serially uncorrelated residuals with zero mean and constant covariance (Song et al., 2009).

The TVP method incorporates structural changes in forecasting and puts more weight on the most recent data in estimating the demand model in order to improve forecasting accuracy. The TVP model can be estimated using an efficient recursive algorithm called the Kalman filter. This method is increasingly used in tourism demand analysis (for example, Riddington, 1999; Song and Witt, 2000; Song and Wong, 2003; Wu, 2010). According to Song et al. (2009), based on their examination of tourist arrivals in the UK and United States, the TVP model generated the most accurate short-run forecasts, which is consistent with previous studies on forecasting tourism demand (Song and Wong, 2003; Song et al., 1998). In their study of the demand for Denmark tourism, Witt et al., (2003) stated that the TVP model performs consistently well for 1-year-ahead forecasting for the various forecasting error criteria selected.

The *Dynamic AIDS Model* is the error correction form of the AIDS model. It incorporates a short-run adjustment mechanism, which is written as:

$$\Delta w_i = \delta_i \Delta w_{it-1} + \sum_j r_{ij} \Delta \log p_j + b_i \Delta \log\left(\frac{x}{P*}\right) + \lambda_i \mu_{it-1} \qquad (4.5)$$

where, μ_{it-1} is the EC term, which measures the feedback effect and is estimated from the corresponding CI equation (Li et al., 2004).

Durbarry and Sinclair (2003) first applied the EC-AIDS approach to a tourism demand analysis of tourist expenditure in France, but they failed to include any short-run independent variables due to insignificant coefficients. Li et al. (2004) used the EC-AIDS model to evaluate the international tourism competitiveness of five Western European countries and found that the dynamic linear AIDS model performed better than the static linear AIDS model. De Mello and Fortuna (2005) studied the demand for European tourism by UK residents and found that the dynamic AIDS model is a data-coherent and theoretically consistent model, which provided robust estimates and reliable forecasts.

ARTIFICIAL INTELLIGENCE METHODS

Besides the time series and econometric forecasting methods, techniques such as the artificial intelligence (AI) model have emerged in the tourism demand forecasting literature. AI is the study and design of intelligent agents, which is a system that perceives its environment and takes actions that maximize its chances of success. AI techniques have rapidly developed within various research areas. According to Wang (2004), the AI forecasting methods, including neural networks, rough sets theory, fuzzy time series theory, grey theory, genetic algorithms, and expert systems, tend to perform better than traditional forecasting methods. Applications of AI techniques in tourism demand analysis include the following studies: Uysal and Roubi (1999) studied Canadian tourists' expenditures in the United States; Law and Au (1999) forecast the demand for Hong Kong tourism by the Japanese; Cho (2003) analysed tourist arrivals in Hong Kong; and Wang (2004) examined the trend of tourist arrivals in Taiwan from Hong Kong.

Not requiring preliminary information or additional data are the main advantages of AI methods, while the lack of a theoretical underpinning and the inability to interpret demand from an economic perspective are the limitations of these techniques (Song and Li, 2008). These limitations restrict the practical application of AI methods in tourism demand analysis.

The *Artificial Neural Network (ANN) Model*, also called *Neural Network (NN) Model*, is the most widely used AI model in tourism demand forecasting. ANN is a computational model that is inspired by the structure of biological neural networks. A typical ANN consists of a number of simple processing elements called neurons, nodes, or units. ANN is an adaptive system that changes its structure based on external or internal information that flows through the network during the learning phase. A typical architecture of ANN models includes one input layer, one or two hidden layers and one output layer (Simpson, 1989). The input layer of the ANN models comprises the explanatory variables, and the output layer denotes the dependent variable, i.e., tourism demand. In the hidden layers, the core part of the ANN model, different weights are given to each explanatory variable as well as the dependent variable. The computing process is repeated until a set of optimal weights is obtained. Each node y_i in the hidden layer can be expressed as:

$$y_i = \frac{1}{1 + e^{-f_i}}$$

$$f_j = \sum_{i=1}^{2} x_i w_{ji} \qquad (4.6)$$

And the final node Y of the output layer is obtained from:

$$Y = \sum_{j=1}^{3} y_j w_j \qquad (4.7)$$

where, w is the weight of interconnection and x is the input variable.

The ANN model was first applied in tourism demand forecasting in the late 1990s and incorporated some improvements in the post-2000 literature. Kim et al. (2003) studied the senior tourist market of Western Australia. Palmer et al. (2006) forecast tourists' expenditure in the Balearic Islands of Spain. ANNs are useful for non-linear threshold functions, which overcomes a restriction of multiple regression analysis. In forecasting the demand for US and Hong Kong tourism, Cho (2003) and Uysal and Roubi (1999) separately showed that ANNs generally outperformed the classical time series and multiple regression models. Moreover, the ANN model can easily be updated and it performs fairly well in one-year-ahead forecasting due to the repetitions of expected similar seasonal patterns (see for example, Burger et al., 2001 in the case of forecasting the demand for Durban tourism).

However, the limitations of the model cannot be ignored. First, the learning process of the hidden layers needs a large amount of data; second, the impact of explanatory variables on tourism demand cannot be generated from the model; third, the elasticities of tourism demand cannot be calculated from ANN models (Wu, 2010).

The *Rough Sets Approach* was first used to forecast the demand for hotel rooms in Hong Kong by Law and Au (1998). This model is generated from the rough sets theory and based on data mining techniques to discover the knowledge. The advantages of the rough sets approach are that: (1) it can model the decision processes underlying the data in both numeric and non-numeric forms, which makes it a useful classification and pattern recognition technique; and (2) it can generate comprehensive decision rules that are useful for practitioners (Au and Law, 2002; Goh and Law, 2003). The only assumption of this approach is that the values of the attributes can be categorized.

The rough sets approach pays much attention to such categorical variables as demographic features and psychographic variables, and forecasts tourism demand levels as high or low instead of exact values. It analyses tourism demand from a microperspective, which is viewed as a complementary tool to econometric forecasting models (Goh et al., 2008; Song and Li, 2008).

The *Support Vector Regression (SVR)* mechanism is a novel learning machine based on statistical learning theory and adheres to the principle of structural risk minimization seeking to minimize an upper bound of the generalization error rather than minimize the training error, which is the principle of ANN. It is an alternative technique which can be used to solve classification, nonlinear regression and forecasting problems by introducing a loss function.

Chen and Wang (2007) incorporated the *Genetic Algorithm (GA)* technique into support vector regression to form a GA-SVR model to improve forecasting accuracy. GA is a heuristic search algorithm that mimics natural evolution. This method is routinely used to generate useful solutions to optimization and search problems. Using GA, Chen and Wang (2007) forecast tourist arrivals to China, and compared the forecasting performance between the GA-SVR, *Back Propagation Neural Network* (*BPNN*, the most popular ANN model) and ARIMA techniques. The results suggested that the GA-SVR model generated more accurate forecasts than both the BPNN and ARIMA models.

The *Fuzzy Time Series Method* is used to forecast a process with linguistic value observations and deals with the first order difference of the time series. The main assumption of the fuzzy time series model is that the variation of this year is related to the variation of the previous year and follows the trend of recent years. Therefore, if the actual variation is considerably different from recent trends, the forecasting error is likely to be large (Yu and Schwartz, 2006). Human judgments should be involved in the fuzzy time series model when a decision about two parameters needs to be made. The first parameter is the number of grades which describes the extent of variation and the second is the window basis size referring to the number of previous observations used to generate the prediction (Yu and Schwartz, 2006). Wang (2004) confirmed that the fuzzy time series technique is considered to be an appropriate tool for forecasting short-term tourism demand in Hong Kong by Taiwanese tourists. However, one of the foremost disadvantages is that it can hardly adapt to the shocks of the special events (Wang and Hsu, 2008).

Grey Theory is a generic theory that deals with systems with poor, incomplete, and uncertain information. The grey model reduces randomness by using the *accumulated generating operation* where an exponential function is fitted based on a differential equation to estimate the future trend (Yu and Schwartz, 2006). The advantage of the grey model is that it can be constructed based on very short time series. It even can be fitted with as few as four observations (Chiang et al., 1998). The limitations of the grey model are that the data used must be taken at equal intervals and in consecutive order (Lin et al., 2001).

FORECASTING PERFORMANCE

Ex post and *ex-ante* forecasting are two different forecasting concepts. As Figure 4.1 shows, the data are available from period 1 to *N*, forecasts from time *n* to *N* are called *ex post* forecasts, and forecasts after time *N* are called *ex-ante* forecasts. In practice, only the accuracy of *ex-post* forecasts can be evaluated by actual data. In terms of the *ex-ante* forecasts, which are more important for practitioners, the explanatory variables have to be forecast first before the *ex-ante* forecasts can be produced (Song et al., 2009).

Measures of Forecasting Accuracy

A number of forecasting evaluation criteria are available and these include forecasting accuracy, time costs, money costs, and the complexity of the model. Among these criteria, researchers are more concerned about the forecasting accuracy of the models, as forecasting accuracy is crucial to decision making by tourism practitioners and

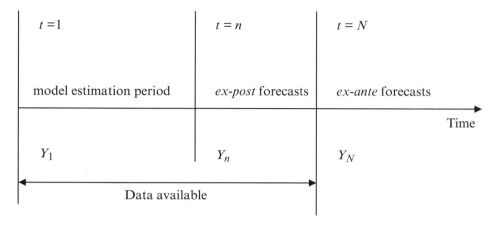

Figure 4.1 Time horizons of forecasts

Table 4.5 Error magnitude measures

Measure	Equation
Mean absolute percentage error (MAPE)	$MAPE = \dfrac{1}{n}\sum_{t=1}^{n}\dfrac{\lvert Y_t - \hat{Y}_t\rvert}{Y_t}$
Root mean square percentage error (RMSPE)	$RMSPE = \sqrt{\dfrac{1}{n}\sum_{t=1}^{n}\left(\dfrac{Y_t - \hat{Y}_t}{Y_t}\right)^2}$
Mean absolute error (MAE)	$MAE = \dfrac{1}{n}\sum_{t=1}^{n}\lvert Y_t - \hat{Y}_t\rvert$

Note: n denotes the length of forecasting horizon; Y_t is the actual value of the dependent variable; $\hat{Y}$ is the forecast value of the dependent variable.

policy makers. In practice, the most widely used method to measure forecasting accuracy is error magnitude (see Table 4.5), which includes the mean absolute percentage error (MAPE), root mean square percentage error (RMSPE) and mean absolute error (MAE).

Besides the above commonly used error magnitude measures, some other statistical measures can also be used to assess the performance of the forecasting models, such as Theil's U statistic, which is used to compare the performance between other forecasting models and the naive no change model, the acceptable output percentage and the normalized correlation coefficient, which are often used in measuring the forecasting accuracy of ANN models (Law and Au, 1999); and the unbiasedness test, which is used to test forecasting consistency (Witt et al., 2003) (see Table 4.6).

Another forecasting measure suggested by Witt and Witt (1991) is directional change,

Table 4.6   Other forecasting assessment measures

Measures	Equation
Theil's U statistic	$$U = \sqrt{\dfrac{\sum\limits_{i=1}^{n}(\Delta Y_{t+n} - \Delta \hat{Y}_{t+n})^2}{\sum\limits_{i=1}^{n}(\Delta \hat{Y}_{t+n})^2}}$$
Acceptable output percentage	$$Z = \dfrac{\sum\limits_{i=1}^{n} t_i}{n} \times 100\% \text{ for } \begin{cases} t_i = 1 & \text{if } \dfrac{|Y_i - \hat{Y}_i|}{Y_i} \leq 5\% \\ t_i = 0 & \text{otherwise} \end{cases}$$
Normalized correlation coefficient	$$r = \dfrac{\sum\limits_{i=1}^{n}(Y_i \times \hat{Y}_i)}{\sqrt{\sum\limits_{i=1}^{n} Y_i^2 \times \sum\limits_{i=1}^{n} \hat{Y}_i^2}}$$
Unbiasedness test	$Y_{t+h} = \beta_0 + \beta_1 \hat{Y}_{t+h} + u_{t+h}$ $H_0 : \beta_0 = 0, \beta_1 = 1$

Note: Y_t is the actual value of the dependent variable; $\hat{Y}_t$ is the forecast value of the dependent variable; and n is the length of the forecasting horizon.

which assesses the probability of correctly forecasting directional change. Turning point accuracy measures and trend measures are particular subsets of directional change error measures (Witt and Witt, 1991, 1995). According to Henriksson and Merton (1981), the probabilities of directionally correct forecasts can be written as:

$$p_1 = prob(\Delta \hat{Q}_t \Delta Q_t > 0 | \Delta Q_t < 0)$$

$$p_2 = prob(\Delta \hat{Q}_t \Delta Q_t > 0 | \Delta Q_t \geq 0) \tag{4.8}$$

where p_1 is the probability of a directionally correct forecast on the condition that tourism demand falls at time t, and p_2 is the probability of a directionally correct forecast conditional on no fall in tourism demand at time t. Suppose that n_1 is the number of observations for a decrease in tourism demand, n_2 is the number of observations for no decrease in tourism demand, m_1 is the number of correct forecasts given a fall in tourism demand, and m_2 is the number of incorrect forecasts given no fall in tourism demand. Then the estimated value of $p_1 + p_2$ is $\hat{p}_1 + \hat{p}_2 = m_1 / n_1 + (n_2 - m_2) / n_2$. For a forecasting model which generates rational forecasts, the condition $p_1 + p_2 \geq 1$ must hold; otherwise the naïve no-change model is preferred (Witt et al., 2003). The directional change error measures have been used in many other areas, but few efforts have been made to use the tests to evaluate tourism demand forecasting models (except, for example, Witt and Witt, 1989, 1991; Witt et al., 2003).

FUTURE RESEARCH DIRECTIONS

Past empirical findings show that no single forecasting method is superior to others in all situations. The forecasting performance of the models varies considerably depending on the forecast error measure, the forecasting horizon, data frequency, destination–origin country pairs, and the competitors included in a comparison. An ever-growing interest in tourism forecasting is, therefore, to find optimal forecasting models according to the data characteristics. Based on this interest, the future research directions in tourism forecasting include the following. First, carry out a comprehensive review of the existing studies using such methods as meta-analysis to synthesize the research findings of the previous studies over the past four to five decades with a view to generalizing the research findings based on the characteristics of the data used in the tourism forecasting literature. Second, another way of generalizing the research findings is to carry out a forecasting competition based on a wide range of forecasting methods used in the past literature with the involvement of the experts who have published extensively using the quantitative methods highlighted above. Third, the integration of judgmental (qualitative) forecasts and quantitative forecasts would also be a useful direction for future research as this research topic has been relatively scarce in the tourism context.

ACKNOWLEDGEMENTS

The authors would like to acknowledge the financial support of The Hong Kong Polytechnic University (Grant No: G-U743).

REFERENCES

Akal, M. (2004), 'Forecasting Turkey's tourism revenues by ARMAX Model', *Tourism Management*, **25** (5), 565–580.

Au, N. and R. Law (2002), 'Categorical classification of tourism dining', *Annals of Tourism Research*, **29** (3), 819–833.

Burger, C.J.S.C., M. Dohnal, M. Kathrada and R. Law (2001), 'A practitioner's guide to time-series methods for tourism demand forecasting: a case study of Durban, South Africa', *Tourism Management*, **22** (4): 403–409.

Chan, Y., T. Hui and E. Yuen (1999), 'Modeling the impact of sudden environmental changes on visitor arrival forecasts: the case of the Gulf War', *Journal of Travel Research*, **37** (4), 391–394.

Che, Y.B. (2004), 'An approach to modeling regional tourist attraction', *Resource Development & Market*, **20** (3), 163–165.

Chen, K. and C. Wang (2007), 'Support vector regression with genetic algorithms in forecasting tourism demand', *Tourism Management*, **28** (1), 215–226.

Chen R.J.C., P. Bloomfield and F.W. Cubbage (2008), 'Comparing forecasting models in tourism', *Journal of Hospitality & Tourism Research*, **32** (1), 3–21.

Chiang J.S., P.L. Wu, S.D. Chiang, T.J. Chang, S.T. Chang and K.L. Wen (1998), *Introduction of Grey Theory*, Taiwan: Gao-Li.

Cho, V. (2001), 'Tourism forecasting and its relationship with leading economic indicators', *Journal of Hospitality and Tourism Research*, **25** (4), 399–420.

Cho, V. (2003), 'A comparison of three different approaches to tourist arrival forecasting', *Tourism Management*, **24** (3), 323–330.

Choyakh, H. (2008), 'A model of tourism demand for Tunisia: inclusion of the tourism investment variable', *Tourism Economics*, **14** (4), 819–838.

Daniel, A.C.M. and F.F.R. Ramos (2002), 'Modelling inbound international tourism demand to Portugal', *International Journal of Tourism Research*, **4** (3), 193–209.

De Gooijer, J.G. and R.J. Hyndman (2006), '25 years of time series forecasting', *International Journal of Forecasting*, **22** (3), 443–473.

De Mello, M.M., A. Pack and M.T. Sinclair (2002), 'A system of equations model of UK tourism demand in neighbouring countries', *Applied Economics*, **34** (4), 509–521.

De Mello, M.M. and N. Fortuna (2005), 'Testing alternative dynamic system for modelling tourism demand', *Tourism Economics*, **11** (4), 517–537.

Deaton, A. and J. Muellbauer (1980), 'An almost ideal demand system', *The American Economic Review*, **70** (3), 312–326.

Dritsakis, N. (2004), 'Cointegration analysis of German and British tourism demand for Greece', *Tourism Management*, **25** (1), 111–119.

Durbarry, R. and M.T. Sinclair (2003), 'Market shares analysis: the case of French tourism demand', *Annals of Tourism Research*, **30** (4), 927–941.

Engle, R.F. and C.W.J. Granger (1987), 'Co-integration and error correction: representation, estimation, and testing', *Econometrica*, **55** (2), 251–276.

Frechtling, D.C. (1996), *Practical Tourism Forecasting*, Oxford: Butterworth-Heinemann.

Fujii, E.T., M. Khaled and J. Mak (1985), 'An almost ideal demand system for visitor expenditures', *Journal of Transport Economics and Policy*, **19** (2), 161–171.

Geurts, M.D. and I.B. Ibrahim (1975), 'Comparing the Box–Jenkins approach with the exponentially smoothed forecasting model application to Hawaii tourists', *Journal of Marketing Research*, **12** (2), 182–188.

Goh, C. and R. Law (2002), 'Modeling and forecasting tourism demand for arrivals with stochastic nonstationary seasonality and intervention', *Tourism Management*, **23** (5), 499–510.

Goh, C. and R. Law (2003), 'Incorporating the rough sets theory into travel demand analysis', *Tourism Management*, **24** (5), 511–517.

Goh, C., R. Law and H.M.K. Mok (2008), 'Analyzing and forecasting tourism demand: a rough sets approach', *Journal of Travel Research*, **46** (3), 327–338.

Gonzalez, P. and P. Moral (1995), 'An analysis of the international tourism demand in Spain', *International Journal of Forecasting*, **11** (2), 233–251.

Greenidge, K. (2001), 'Forecasting tourism demand: an STM approach', *Annals of Tourism Research*, **28** (1), 98–112.

Grubb, H. and A. Mason (2001), 'Long lead-time forecasting of UK air passengers by Holt-Winters methods with damped trend', *International Journal of Forecasting*, **17** (1), 71–82.

Guo, W. (2007), 'Inbound tourism: an empirical research based on gravity model of international trade', *Tourism Tribune*, **22** (3), 30–34.

Halicioglu, F. (2010), 'An econometric analysis of the aggregate outbound tourism demand of Turkey', *Tourism Economics*, **16** (1), 83–97.

Han, Z., R. Durbarry and M.T. Sinclair (2006), 'Modelling US tourism demand for European destinations', *Tourism Management*, **27** (1), 1–10.

Henriksson, R.D. and R.C. Merton (1981), 'On market timing and investment performance. II. Statistical procedures for evaluating forecasting skills', *The Journal of Business*, **54** (4), 513–533.

Hu, C., M. Chen and S.C. McChain (2004), 'Forecasting in short-term planning and management for a casino buffet restaurant', *Journal of Travel & Tourism Marketing*, **16** (2), 79–98.

Khadaroo, J. and B. Seetanah (2008), 'The role of transport infrastructure in international tourism development: a gravity model approach', *Tourism Management*, **29** (5), 831–840.

Kim, J., S. Wei and H. Ruys (2003), 'Segmenting the market of West Australian senior tourists using an artificial neural network', *Tourism Management*, **24** (1), 25–34.

Kim, J.H. and I.A. Moosa (2005), 'Forecasting international tourist flows to Australia: a comparison between the direct and indirect methods', *Tourism Management*, **26** (1), 69–78.

Kulendran, N. and S. Divisekera (2007), 'Measuring the economic impact of Australian tourism marketing expenditure', *Tourism Economics*, **13** (2), 261–274.

Kulendran, N. and S.F. Witt (2001), 'Cointegration versus least squares regression', *Annals of Tourism Research*, **28** (2), 291–311.

Kulendran, N. and S.F. Witt (2003a), 'Leading indicator tourism forecasts', *Tourism Management*, **24** (5), 503–510.

Kulendran, N. and S.F. Witt (2003b), 'Forecasting the demand for international business tourism', *Journal of Travel Research*, **41**, 265–271.

Law, R. and N. Au (1998), 'A rough set approach to hotel expenditure decision rules induction', *Journal of Hospitality & Tourism Research*, **22** (4), 359–375.

Law, R. and N. Au (1999), 'A neural network model to forecast Japanese demand for travel to Hong Kong', *Tourism Management*, **20**, 89–97.

Lee, C.K., T. Var and T.W. Blaine (1996), 'Determinants of inbound tourism expenditure', *Annals of Tourism Research*, **23** (3), 527–542.

Li, G. (2010), 'Tourism demand modelling and forecasting: a review of literature related to Greater China', *Journal of China Tourism Research*, **5** (1), 2–40.

Li, G., H. Song and S.F. Witt (2004), 'Modelling tourism demand: a dynamic linear AIDS approach', *Journal of Travel Research*, **43** (2), 141–150.

Lim, C. and M. McAleer (2001), 'Forecasting tourist arrivals', *Annals of Tourism Research*, **28** (4), 965–977.

Lim, C. and M. McAleer (2008), 'Analysing seasonal changes in New Zealand's largest inbound market', *Tourism Recreation Research*, **33** (1), 83–91.

Lin, C.B., S.F. Su and Y.T. Hsu (2001), 'High-precision forecast using grey models', *International Journal of Systems Science*, **32** (5), 609–619.

Makridakis, S., S.C. Wheelwright and R.J. Hyndman (1998), *Forecasting: Methods and Applications*, 3rd edition, New York: John Wiley.

Martin, C.A. and S.F. Witt (1987), 'Tourism demand forecasting models: choice of appropriate variable to represent tourists' cost of living', *Tourism Management*, **8** (3), 233–246.

Martin, C.A. and S.F. Witt (1988), 'Substitute prices in models of tourism demand', *Annals of Tourism Research*, **15** (2), 255–268.

Martin, C.A. and S.F. Witt (1989), 'Forecasting tourism demand: a comparison of the accuracy of several quantitative methods', *International Journal of Forecasting*, **5** (1), 7–19.

Nadal, J.R. (2001), 'Forecasting turning points in international visitor arrivals in the Balearic Islands', *Tourism Economics*, **7** (4), 365–380.

Narayan, P.K. (2004), 'Fiji's tourism demand: the ARDL approach to cointegration', *Tourism Economics*, **10** (2), 193–206.

Palmer, A., J.J. Montano and A. Sese (2006), 'Designing an artificial neural network for forecasting tourism time series', *Tourism Management*, **27** (5), 781–790.

Papatheodorou, A. (1999), 'The demand for international tourism in the Mediterranean region', *Applied Economics*, **31** (5), 619–630.

Querfelli, C. (2008), 'Co-integration analysis of quarterly European tourism demand in Tunisia', *Tourism Management*, **29** (1), 127–137.

Riddington, G. (1999), 'Forecasting ski demand: comparing learning curve and varying parameter coefficient approaches', *Journal of Forecasting*, **18**, 205–214.

Sheldon, P.J. (2008), 'Forecasting tourism: expenditures versus arrivals', *Journal of Travel Research*, **32** (1), 13–20.

Simpson, P.K. (1989), *Artificial Neural Systems: Foundations, Paradigms, Applications, and Implementations*, Elmsford, NY: Pergamon.

Sims, C.A. (1980), 'Macroeconomics and reality', *Econometrica*, **48** (1), 1–48.

Smeral, E. (2010), 'Impacts of the world recession and economic crisis on tourism: forecasts and potential risks', *Journal of Travel Research*, **49** (1), 31–38.

Song, H. and G. Li (2008), 'Tourism demand modelling and forecasting: a review of recent research', *Tourism Management*, **29** (2), 203–220.

Song, H. and S. Lin (2010), 'Impacts of the financial and economic crisis on tourism in Asia', *Journal of Travel Research*, **49** (1), 16–30.

Song, H. and S.F. Witt (2000), *Tourism Demand Modelling and Forecasting: Modern Econometric Approaches*, Oxford: Pergamon.

Song, H. and S.F. Witt (2003), 'Tourism forecasting: the general-to-specific approach', *Journal of Travel Research*, **42** (1), 65–74.

Song, H. and S.F. Witt (2006), 'Forecasting international tourist flows to Macau', *Tourism Management*, **27** (2), 214–224.

Song, H. and K.K.F. Wong (2003), 'Tourism demand modelling: a time-varying parameter approach', *Journal of Travel Research*, **42** (1), 57–64.

Song, H., P. Romilly and X. Liu (1998), 'The UK consumption function and structural instability: improving forecasting performance using a time varying parameter approach', *Applied Economics*, **30** (7), 975–983.

Song, H., S.F. Witt and T.C. Jensen (2003a), 'Tourism forecasting: accuracy of alternative econometric models', *International Journal of Forecasting*, **19** (1), 123–141.

Song, H., S.F. Witt and G. Li (2003b), 'Modelling and forecasting the demand for Thai tourism', *Tourism Economics*, **9** (4), 363–387.

Song, H., S.F. Witt and G. Li (2009), *The Advanced Econometrics of Tourism Demand*, New York: Routledge.

Syriopoulos, T.C. and M.T. Sinclair (1993), 'An econometric study of tourism demand: the AIDS model of US and European tourism in Mediterranean countries', *Applied Economics*, **25** (12), 1541–1552.

Thomas, R.L. (1993), *Introductory Econometrics: Theory and Applications*, London: Longman.

Turner, L.W. and S.F. Witt (2001), 'Forecasting tourism using univariate and multivariate structural time series models', *Tourism Economics*, **7** (2), 135–147.

Turner, L.W., N. Kulendran and H. Fernando (1997), 'Univariate modelling using periodic and non-periodic analysis: inbound tourism to Japan, Australia and New Zealand compared', *Tourism Economics*, **3** (1), 39–56.

Uysal, M. and M.S.E. Roubi (1999), 'Artificial neural networks versus multiple regression in tourism demand analysis', *Journal of Travel Research*, **38** (2), 111–118.

Vanegas, Sr M. (2008), 'Tourism demand response by residents of Latin American countries', *International Journal of Tourism Research*, **11** (1), 17–29.

Veloce, W. (2004), 'Forecasting inbound Canadian tourism: an evaluation of error corrections model forecasts', *Tourism Economics*, **10** (3), 262–280.

Wang, C. (2004), 'Predicting tourism demand using fuzzy time series and hybrid grey theory', *Tourism Management*, **25** (3), 367–374.

Wang, C. and L. Hsu (2008), 'Constructing and applying an improved fuzzy time series model: taking the tourism industry for example', *Expert Systems with Applications*, **34** (4), 2732–2738.

Wickens, M.R. and T.S. Breusch (1988), 'Dynamic specification, the long-run and the estimation of transformed regression models', *The Economic Journal*, **98**, 189–205.

Witt, C.A. and S.F. Witt (1989), 'Measures of forecasting accuracy: turning point error versus size of error', *Tourism Management*, **10** (3), 255–260.

Witt, C.A. and S.F. Witt (1990), 'Appraising an econometric forecasting model', *Journal of Travel Research*, **18** (3), 30–34.

Witt, S.F (1980), 'An abstract mode–abstract (destination) node model of foreign holiday demand', *Applied Economics*, **12** (2), 163–180.

Witt, S.F. and C.A. Martin (1987a), 'Econometrics models for forecasting international tourism demand', *Journal of Travel Research*, **25** (3), 23–30.

Witt, S.F. and C.A. Martin (1987b), 'International tourism demand models: inclusion of marketing variables', *Tourism Management*, **8** (1), 33–40.

Witt, S.F. and C.A. Witt (1991), 'Tourism forecasting: error magnitude, direction of change error, and trend change error', *Journal of Travel Research*, **30** (2), 26–33.

Witt, S.F. and C.A. Witt (1992), *Modeling and Forecasting Demand in Tourism*, London: Academic Press Ltd.

Witt, S.F. and C.A. Witt (1995), 'Forecasting tourism demand: a review of empirical research', *International Journal of Forecasting*, **11** (3), 447–475.

Witt, S.F., G.D. Newbould and A.J. Watkins (1992), 'Forecasting domestic tourism demand: application to Las Vegas arrivals data', *Journal of Travel Research*, **31** (1), 36–41.

Witt, S.F., H. Song and P. Louvieris (2003), 'Statistical testing in forecasting model selection', *Journal of Travel Research*, **42** (2), 151–158.

Witt, S.F., C.A. Witt and N. Wilson (1994), 'Forecasting international tourist flows', *Annals of Tourism Research*, **21** (3), 612–628.

Wong, K.K.F., H. Song and K.S. Chon (2006), 'Bayesian models for tourism demand forecasting', *Tourism Management*, **27** (5), 773–780.

Wu, C. (2010), 'Econometric analysis of tourist expenditures', PhD Thesis, The Hong Kong Polytechnic University.

Yu, G. and Z. Schwartz (2006), 'Forecasting short time-series tourism demand with artificial intelligence models', *Journal of Travel Research*, **45** (2), 194–203.

5 Structural equation modeling
Jenny (Jiyeon) Lee and Gerard Kyle

NATURE OF STRUCTURAL EQUATION MODELING AND ITS EVOLUTION

Structural equation modeling (SEM) is a tool for analysing multivariate data that has been long known in social sciences to be especially appropriate for theory testing (e.g., Bagozzi, 1980). It is also referred to as covariance structure analysis or covariance structure modeling. Structural equation models go beyond ordinary regression models to incorporate multiple independent and dependent variables as well as latent constructs that cluster the observed variables they are hypothesized to represent. They also provide a way to test a specified set of relationships among observed and latent variables as a whole, and allow theory testing even when experiments are not possible. As a result, these methods have become ubiquitous in all the social and behavioral sciences (e.g., MacCallum and Austin, 2000).

With the advance of statistical software with graphical user interfaces, several "user-friendly" SEM programs have become accessible to tourism researchers (Kline, 2005). Of these, the most widely used programs are LISREL (Linear Structural Relationships), AMOS (Analysis of Moment Structures), EQS (Equations), Mplus, and PLS (Partial Least Squares). Each has idiosyncrasies and requirements for conducting analysis. These programs enable users to either choose to write code in syntax or use a graphical editor to generate the output by simply drawing the model. Over the past decade, these programs have also developed in conjunction with a plethora of introductory texts that provide insight on specific concepts, applications, and programming (e.g., LISREL (Byrne, 1998; Jöreskog and Sörbom, 2004), AMOS (Arbuckle, 2009), EQS (Bentler, 2003), Mplus (Muthén and Muthén, 1998–2010), PLS (Chin, 2001; Haenlein and Kaplan, 2004)). Field-specific publications are also appearing in the tourism literature (e.g., Reisinger and Turner, 1999).

BACKGROUND AND TYPES OF PROBLEMS ADDRESSED

Structural equation modeling combines both multiple regression and factor analysis (Hair et al., 1998). It simultaneously tests an entire system of variables in a hypothesized model to determine the degree to which the pattern of hypothesized relationships is congruent with that observed in the data. In particular, it is has been shown to be especially useful for testing theory where the constructs of interest are difficult to operationalize using single indicators (Fornell and Larcker, 1981).

Testing latent variable structural models in most tourism studies involves a two-step process (Anderson and Gerbing, 1988): (1) an examination of a measurement model (Models A, B, and C below); and (2) the examination of a structural model (Models D and E; Bollen, 1989; Byrne, 1998). First, measurement models can be examined through confirmatory factor analysis (CFA). Testing the measurement model effectively tests hypotheses related to anticipated factor structures. In this procedure, construct validity (i.e., convergent and discriminant validity) can be verified by assessing the extent to which the observed measures or manifest variables adequately represent each latent construct. Alternately, testing of the structural model examines hypothesized relationships among the latent constructs. This further provides insight on the predictive validity of the latent constructs. Some researchers have also followed a four-step approach which involves sequential testing of four nested models[1] (Hayduk and Glaser, 2000; Mulaik and Millsap, 2000): (1) a factor model (i.e., the least restricted model), (2) a confirmatory factor model (i.e., covariances among the factors), (3) a structural equation model (i.e., specification of direct effects among the factors), and (4) a more constrained model (i.e., additional constraints on the SEM model). It is intended to test nested models, thus pinpointing problems within the SEM model such as conceptual inadequacy or measurement misspecification (see Hayduk and Glaser (2000) for further discussion on the use of the four-step procedure and its limitations).

STEPS IN PERFORMING SEM ANALYSIS

Model Specification

When SEM is used as a confirmatory technique, the model must be specified correctly, based on the type of model the researcher is attempting to confirm. When building the model, the researcher uses two different kinds of variables, namely exogenous and endogenous variables. The distinction between these two types of variables is whether the variable regresses on another variable. As in regression, the dependent variable (DV) regresses on the independent variable (IV), meaning that the DV is being predicted by the IV. In SEM terminology, endogenous variables regress onto exogenous variables. Exogenous variables can be recognized in a graphical version of the model as the variables sending out arrowheads (see models depicted in Figure 5.1a–e), denoting which variable it is predicting. A variable that regresses on another variable is always an endogenous variable, even if this same variable is also used as a variable to be regressed upon. Endogenous variables are recognized as the receivers of an arrowhead in the model. For example, in Model A (Figure 5.1a), the manifest indicators (X_1 through X_4) are predicted by the latent exogenous construct (ξ_1). Alternately, in Model D (Figure 5.1d), the dependent latent construct (η_1) is an exogenous variable within the measurement part of the model (predicting Y_1 through Y_4), but is an endogenous variable within the structural part of the model given that it is being predicted by ξ_1.

When testing SEM models, often a set of plausible models are tested each reflecting variants of guiding theory or theories. Not only must the researcher account for the theoretical reasons for building the model, but the researcher must also take into account the number of data points (i.e., observed measures or manifest indicators) and the number of parameters that the model must estimate to identify the model. An identified model is a model where a specific parameter value uniquely identifies the model, and no other equivalent formulation can be given by a different parameter value (Bollen, 1989). The parameter is the value of interest (all single-headed arrows in Figure 5.1a–e), which might be a regression coefficient between the exogenous and the endogenous variable or the factor loading (regression coefficient between an indicator and its factor). If there are fewer data points (i.e., manifest indicators) than the number of estimated parameters, the resulting model is "unidentified", since there are too few reference points to account for all the variance in the model. The solution is to ensure enough data points have been collected or constrain parameters within the model (or both).

Estimation of Free Parameters

Parameter estimation is accomplished by comparing the actual covariance matrix (symbolized as S) representing the observed relationships between variables and the estimated covariance matrix (symbolized as Σ) of the best fitting model (Brown, 2006). This is obtained through numerical maximization of a fit criterion as provided by maximum

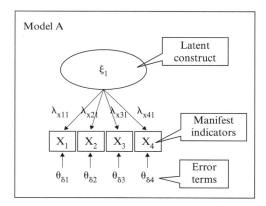

(a) Single factor first order measurement model

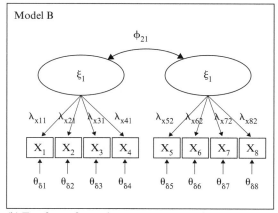

(b) Two factor first order measurement model

Figure 5.1   Measurement and structural models

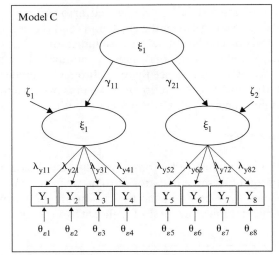

(c) Second order measurement model

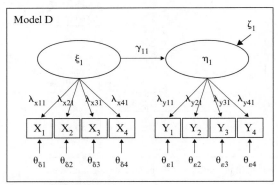

(d) Structural model

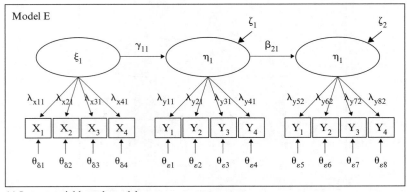

(e) Latent variable path model

Figure 5.1   (continued)

likelihood estimation (default in most SEM programs), weighted least squares, or asymptotically distribution-free methods. This is often accomplished by using a specialized SEM software.

Assessment of Fit

Assessment of fit is a basic task in SEM modeling; forming the basis for accepting or rejecting hypotheses and more often accepting one competing model over another. The output of SEM programs includes matrices of the estimated relationships between variables in the model. Assessment of fit essentially calculates how similar the predicted data (reflected in the structure of the hypothesized model) are to matrices containing the relationships in the actual data. Formal statistical tests and fit indices have been developed for these purposes. Individual parameters of the model can also be examined within the estimated model in order to see how well the proposed model fits the driving theory.

As with all statistical hypothesis tests, SEM model tests are based on the assumption that the correct and complete relevant data have been modeled. In the SEM literature, discussion of fit has led to a variety of different recommendations on the precise application of the various fit indices and hypothesis tests. Measures of fit differ in several ways. Traditional approaches to modeling start from a null hypothesis, rewarding more parsimonious models (i.e., those with fewer free parameters), to others such as the Akaike information criterion (AIC) that focuses on how little the fitted values deviate from a saturated model (i.e., how well they reproduce the measured values), taking into account the number of free parameters used. Because different measures of fit capture different elements of the fit of the model, it is appropriate to report a selection of different fit measures.

Some of the more commonly used measures of fit include:

- Chi-square (χ^2): A fundamental measure of fit used in the calculation of many other fit measures. Conceptually, it is a function of the sample size and the difference between the observed covariance matrix and the model covariance matrix. Chi-square, however, is seldom used in applied research as a sole index of model fit owing to its sensitivity to sample size (Brown, 2006).
- Akaike information criterion (AIC; Akaike, 1987): A test of relative model fit. The preferred model is the one with the lowest AIC value.
- Root mean square error of approximation (RMSEA; Steiger and Lind, 1980): Takes into account the error of approximation in the population and asks the question, "How well would the model, with unknown but optimally chosen parameter values, fit the population covariance matrix if it were available?" (Browne and Cudeck, 1993, pp. 137–138). Good models are considered to have a RMSEA values of 0.05 or less, acceptable models 0.08 or less, bad models of 0.1 or higher considered unacceptable (Browne and Cudeck, 1993).
- Standardized root mean residual (SRMR): The SRMR is a popular absolute fit indicator, meaning that it does not take into account other aspects such as fit in relation to more restricted solutions. A value of less than 0.08 is generally acceptable (Hu and Bentler, 1999).

- Comparative fit index (CFI; Bentler, 1990): In examining baseline comparisons, the CFI depends, in large part, on the average size of the correlations in the data. If the average correlation between variables is not high, then the CFI will not be very high. The CFI also rewards model parsimony. Values range from 0 to 1 with values closer to 1 indicating good model fit (Hu and Bentler, 1999).
- Non-normed fit index (NNFI): Also referred to as the Tucker–Lewis Index, the NNFI is similar to the NFI. However, the index is lower and hence the model is regarded as less acceptable if the model is complex. According to Marsh et al. (1988), the NNFI is relatively independent of sample size. The NNFI is usually lower than is the GFI but over 0.95 is considered acceptable (e.g., Hu and Bentler, 1999).
- Parsimonious normed fit index (PNFI; Mulaik et al., 1989): The PNFI takes into account model complexity in its assessment of model fit. There are now rigid rules for interpreting PNFI values although the closer their value is to 1, the stronger (and more parsimonious) the model.

With regard to which indices should be reported, it is not necessary or realistic to include every index from the program output given that they may contain redundant information. Given the plethora of fit indices, it becomes a temptation to choose those fit indices that indicate the best fit. This should be avoided as it is essentially "sweeping important information under the carpet." In a review by McDonald and Ho (2002), it was found that the most commonly reported fit indices are the CFI, GFI, NFI, and the NNFI. When deciding what indices to report, going by what is most frequently used is not necessarily good practice as some of these statistics (such as the GFI) are often relied on purely for historical reasons, rather than for their sophistication. While there are no "golden rules" for assessment of model fit, reporting a variety of indices is necessary (Crowley and Fan, 1997) because different indices reflect different aspects of model fit. Although the chi-square model has many problems associated with it, it is still essential that this statistic, along with its degrees of freedom and associated *p*-value, be reported (Hayduk et al., 2007; Kline, 2005). Threshold levels have been assessed by Hu and Bentler (1999), who suggested a two-index presentation format. This includes reporting the SRMR with the NNFI, the RMSEA, or the CFI. Alternately, Kline (2005) advocates the use of the chi-square test, the RMSEA, the CFI, and the SRMR. Based on these authors' guidelines, most support can be found for reporting the chi-square statistic, its degrees of freedom, and *p*-value, the RMSEA and its associated confidence interval, the SRMR, the CFI, and one parsimony fit index such as the PNFI. These indices have been chosen over other indices as they have been found to be the most insensitive to sample size, model misspecification, and parameter estimates.

Model Modification

A hypothesized model may need to be modified in order to improve its fit to the data, thereby estimating the most likely relationships between variables. Many programs provide modification indices (or Lagrange multiplier indices) which report the improvement in fit resulting from estimating additional parameters within the model. It is important to note, however, that post-hoc model modifications reflect departures from the initial theory and hypotheses guiding model construction. As such, they must be acknowledged accordingly and justified on conceptual or theoretical grounds. In the absence of substantive justification, post-hoc model modification can reflect a troublesome reaction to anomalies within the researcher's data that is unlikely replicable. Consequently, post-hoc modifications to theoretically derived models ought to be considered with caution.

Sample Size

Where the proposed SEM is the basis for a research hypothesis, ad-hoc rules of thumb requiring the choosing of ten observations per indicator in setting a lower bound for the adequacy of sample sizes have been widely used since their original articulation by Nunnally (1967). Being linear in model constructs, these are easy to compute, but have been found to result in sample sizes that are too small. Complexities which increased information demands in structural model estimation increase with the number of potential combinations of latent variables; while the information supplied for estimation increases with the number of measured parameters times the number of observations in the sample size – both are non-linear. Sample size in SEM can be computed through two methods: the first as a function of the ratio of indicator variables to latent variables, and the second as a function of minimum effect, power and significance. Software and methods for computing both have been developed by Westland (2010).

Interpretation and Communication

Following the establishment of a model adequately fitting the data, the researcher then moves to the interpretation of model parameters so that claims about the constructs can be made. Caution should always be taken when making claims of causality even when experimentation or time-ordered studies have been done. The term "causal model" must be understood to mean "a model that conveys causal assumptions", not necessarily a model that produces validated causal conclusions. Collecting data at multiple time points and using an experimental or quasi-experimental design can help rule out certain rival hypotheses but even a randomized experiment cannot rule out all such threats to causal inference. Good fit by a model consistent with one causal hypothesis invariably entails equally good fit by another model consistent with an opposing causal hypothesis. No research design, no matter how clever, can help distinguish such rival hypotheses, save for interventional experiments. As in any science, subsequent replication and perhaps modification will proceed from the initial finding.

APPLICATIONS IN TOURISM RESEARCH

Structural equation modelling has become one of the most commonly used data analysis techniques among tourism researchers over the past two decades. In a review of the 1790 articles published in the major 12 tourism and hospitality journals, Palmer et al. (2005) found that the number of articles using SEM had increased from 6 in 1998 to 21 in 2002. As of August 2011, our review of the three major tourism journals (i.e., *Annals of Tourism*

Research, Tourism Management, and *Journal of Travel Research*) identified over 300 published articles where the authors had chosen SEM as their analytical tool for scale development and the investigation of the causal structures among constructs. In tourism research, the technique has primarily been limited to: (1) the use of confirmatory (and sometimes combined with exploratory) factor analysis to determine scale structure, psychometric properties, and for scale purification; (2) testing causal relationships among latent (and sometimes manifest) variables; and (3) testing for measurement and structural model invariance across groups. Applications presented in this section provide specific examples of how selected tourism publications address research questions using SEM.

CONFIRMATORY FACTOR ANALYSIS

Testing First-order CFA Models

Confirmatory factor analysis has been used in tourism research to develop and refine multi-item measures of latent constructs. Most tourism researchers informally test hypotheses about the direct relations between a theoretical latent construct and its observed variable in first-order CFA models. These analyses evaluate the extent to which the observed measures in a hypothesized model derived from past evidence and theory adequately represent their underlying constructs. Tourism researchers have also used CFA to cross-validate factorial structures across study contexts and populations. It further allows for assessing the validity of a measurement scale of latent constructs (i.e., convergent and discriminant validity). This procedure usually precedes an examination of the fit of structural relationships (Anderson and Gerbing, 1988).

Tourism researchers have examined the plausibility of multidimensional structures for a number of constructs. These include constraints (Hung and Petrick, 2010), novelty (Petrick, 2002), perceived service quality (Albacete-Sáez et al., 2007; Vogt and Fesenmaier, 1995), leisure tourists' involvement, post-visit evaluation and behaviors (Gursoy and Gavcar, 2003; William and Soutar, 2009), and local residents' attitudes toward and perceptions of gaming as a tourism development strategy (Chen and Hsu, 2001; Kang et al., 1996). Some studies (e.g., Albacete-Sáez et al., 2007; Chen and Hsu, 2001; Hung and Petrick, 2010; Kang et al., 1996) have employed exploratory factor analysis (EFA) on selected scales that have little or no history of use in the tourism contexts to first explore the underlying structure of a construct of interest. Using CFA, they then confirm construct validity of the multidimensional scale emerging from EFA. For example, Hung and Petrick (2010) first developed and validated a measurement scale for constraints to cruising among 897 online panel members. Following Churchill's (1979) scale development guidelines, their measures were developed by first conducting an extensive review of the literature and interviews with prospective cruise passengers. After pre-testing the emerging scale, the authors used EFA of the pilot data for scale purification. The final scale emerging from the EFA was then validated in CFA using an online panel. They observed a four-dimensional structure within constraints to cruising, including intrapersonal, interpersonal, structural, and not an option.

Similarly, Albacete-Sáez et al. (2007) examined the service quality dimensions derived from EFA within the context of Spanish rural accommodations using CFA. They found that the overall fit of a five-dimensional service quality model was considered most adequate (i.e., personnel response, complementary offer, tourist relations, tangible elements, and empathy). In addition, Chen and Hsu (2001) and Kang et al. (1996) have confirmed the validity of the attitude scale derived from the EFA. The former study indicated that five dimensions of residents' perceptions of the riverboat gaming effects (i.e., free of crime, economic effects, community image, community activities, and public services) were valid, with each dimension having different effects on support for gaming legalization and future casino expansion. The latter study examined the validity of the two models (i.e., the a priori model and the model derived from EFA) conceptualizing resident perceptions of limited-stake casino development across tourism communities. The CFA results indicated that a unidimensional model (i.e., evaluation) was applicable to both the gambling and non-gambling town data whereas the two-factor model (i.e., attitudes and benefits) was applicable only to non-gambling town data.

Alternately, other researchers have primarily used CFA to test scales with an established structure in varied tourism contexts (e.g., Gursoy and Gavcar, 2003; Petrick, 2002; Vogt and Fesenmaier, 1995; William and Soutar, 2009). Using an existing novelty scale, Petrick (2002) investigated its reliability and validity using CFA in a golf vacation context. His results indicated that the four dimensions of novelty (i.e., thrill, change from routine, boredom-alleviation, and surprise) are valid and reliable when used with golf vacationers. Vogt and Fesenmaier (1995) further refined Parasuraman et al.'s (1988) SERVQUAL scale by evaluating the factorial structure of service quality between tourists and retailers in a tourism destination. While the four-dimension service quality model (i.e., reliability, responsiveness, assurance, and access) was found to be valid for both groups, its factor structure was different between tourists and retailers. In a similar fashion, William and Soutar (2009) verified the construct validity of five dimensional values (i.e., functional, emotional, social, novelty value, and value for money), satisfaction, and behavioral intentions in an adventure tourism context. Gursoy and Gavcar (2003) also examined the applicability of the consumer involvement profile (CIP) among European leisure tourists. Their study supported the multidimensional nature of tourists' involvement but revealed a different factor structure (i.e., interest/pleasure, risk probability, and risk importance) in studies with consumer goods and studies in other recreation, leisure and tourism contexts.

Testing Hierarchical CFA Models

Some tourism studies have tested the hierarchical relations between constructs in CFA models (see Model C in Figure 5.1c). In much the same way, first order measurement models are developed around the hypothesis that first order latent factors account for the variation within their manifest indicators, in hierarchical measurement models, higher-order factors are hypothesized to account for the variation in lower-order factors. In other words, higher-order factors are measured indirectly through the indicators of the lower-order factors because they have no manifest variables (Kline, 2005).

Several examples of analyses of hierarchical measurement models in tourism are provided in the literature. These includes the studies by First, Funk and Bruun (2007), who analysed the second-order model of sport tourists' motives; Konecnik and Gartner (2007), who tested a destination customer-based brand equity (CBBETD) higher-order

CFA model; and Caro and García (2008), who analysed the third-order model of service quality for the travel agency industry.

First, Funk and Bruun (2007) tested a measurement model of a six first-order latent variables relevant to sport tourist's motives (i.e., running involvement, strength of motivation, attitude toward the hosting destination, learning interest, cultural experience, and cultural learning) and their respective observed variables. They then examined the hierarchical CFA model specifying that (1) socio-psychological motivation in the second-order factors loaded on the first three first-order factors (i.e., involvement, motivation strength, and attitude), (2) culture-education motivation loaded on the last three factors (i.e., attitude, learning interest, and cultural experience), and (3) cultural learning predicted cultural experience. Various fit indices suggested that a second-order five-factor structure of travel motives most appropriately described a running event's participants who traveled internationally. Konecnik and Gartner (2007) also examined a higher-order CFA model of customer-based brand equity for a tourism destination (CBBETD) using telephone interviews with potential tourists from different countries. In their study, four first-order factors (i.e., awareness, destination image, quality, and loyalty) were reported to be sub-dimensions of a single higher-order factor of CBBETD. Last, Caro and García (2008) postulated a third-order structure for a conceptualization of travel agency service quality. In their measurement model, seven first order factors were considered sub-dimensions of three second order factors which were hypothesized to load onto a single third-order factor of "travel agency service quality".

Testing Structural Models

Another common use of SEM in tourism research involves the investigation of structural relations between and/or among latent constructs and their dimensions. A broad variety of models grounded in theory and empirical research have been tested using path analysis (see Models D and E in Figure 5.1d–e) across various study contexts and populations. The simultaneous testing of structural models among groups has also recently gained interest in the literature. Specifically, the procedure is used to assess whether certain paths in a specified causal structure are equivalent across populations. The discussion that follows reviews some of these applications beginning with work modeling associations among single-item measures, latent and variables measures, and concluding with multiple-group applications.

Testing Path Models Using Single-item Measures

As an alternative approach to multiple regression analysis, tourism researchers have used path analysis (PA) to simultaneously test direct and indirect relationships among the latent constructs and, in some instances, single-indicator models. Regardless of the approach, when testing path models, researchers typically aim to understand: (1) which independent variables (IVs) predict the hypothesized dependent variables (DVs), (2) how well a combination of IVs predict hypothesized DVs and account for their variance, and (3) the nature of each IV's influence on the DVs (i.e., effect valence).

For example, in a study of 169 countries' competitiveness, Mazanec et al. (2007) used a Competitiveness Monitor (CM) scale proposed by the World Travel and Tourism

Council (WTTC). They found that both social and cultural indicators of the eight measures explained destination competitiveness effectively. Similarly, Vargas-Sánchez et al. (2011) examined the effectiveness of several hypothesized antecedents of residents' attitudes toward tourism development in a Spanish province. They observed that residents' attitude was positively, although weakly, predicted by satisfaction with public services, their perception of personal benefits, and tourists' behavior. They also found that attitude was negatively influenced by the density of tourists within the destination (i.e., perceived crowding) and level of perceived tourism development. In another study employing single-item measures, Um et al. (2006) examined tourists' revisit intentions to Hong Kong. They found that perceived attractiveness of the destination, rather than overall satisfaction, was a stronger predictor of their respondents' revisit intentions. Likewise, Oh and Hsu (2001) adopted the theory of reasoned action (Fishbein and Azjen, 1975) to develop a model of gambling behavior among gamblers in Iowa. Their results indicated that gamblers' future participation in gambling had a direct, positive relationship with past behaviors and their behavioral intentions for future participation. Last, Beerli and Martín (2004) employed PA to examine the differences in the determinants of the image of a Spanish island among first-time and repeat tourists. Using the factor scores emerging from an EFA, they hypothesized a path model specifying the relationships among motivations, tourist experience, and perceived image. They reported that both models for first-time and repeat tourists showed an acceptable fit to the data. They further reported that tourist motivations related to relaxation, knowledge and past travel experience influenced the image of the sun-based destination for both groups.

Testing Path Models Using Latent Variables

It is more common in tourism research implementing SEM to test structural models with latent variables measured using multiple indicators. Typically, structural models are tested following the establishment of valid and reliable measurement models through the use of CFA (Byrne, 1998). Much of this work has been driven by a desire to understand: (1) *resident support for tourism development* (Dyer et al., 2007; Gursoy and Kendall, 2006; Gursoy and Rutherford, 2004; Gursoy et al., 2002; Kang et al., 2008; Lindberg and Johnson, 1997; Nicholas et al., 2009; Nunkoo and Ramkissoon, 2011; Yoon et al., 2001); and (2) *tourist behavior* (Bigné et al., 2001; Bigné et al., 2005a; Bigné et al., 2005b; Bigné Alcañiz et al., 2009; Connell and Meyer, 2009; del Bosque and San Martín, 2008; Denstadli and Jacobsen, 2011; Feng and Morrison, 2007; Gross and Brown, 2008; Han et al., 2010; Huang et al., 2010; Huang and Hsu, 2009; Hwang et al., 2005; Kaplanidou and Vogt, 2006; Kim et al., 2011; Kolar and Žabkar, 2010; Lee et al., 2005; Lee et al., 2007a; Lee et al., 2008; Martín-Ruiz et al., 2010; Nadeau et al., 2008; Qu and Lee, 2011; Reisinger and Turner, 2002; Sparks, 2007; Stokburger-Sauer, 2011; Wang and Fesenmaier, 2004; Wu et al., 2008; Yoon and Uysal, 2005; Yuan and Jang, 2008; Yuksel et al., 2010; Žabkar et al., 2010). These studies have employed multiple indicators of various constructs to better capture the latent phenomena. With multiple indicators, researchers are better able to assess constructs of interest. The breadth of this work has illustrated that factors influencing tourist behavior vary along multiple dimensions.

In particular, work has shown that tourists' intention to revisit specific destinations is positively influenced by facets of (1) destination image (Bigné et al., 2001; Bigné

Alcañiz et al., 2009; del Bosque and San Martín, 2008; Lee et al., 2008); (2) the attributes depicted through website design (Kaplanidou and Vogt, 2006); (3) satisfaction stemming from previous visits (Bigné et al., 2001; Bigné et al., 2005; Connell and Meyer, 2009; del Bosque and San Martín, 2008; Denstadli and Jacobsen, 2011; Huang and Hsu, 2009; Lee et al., 2005; Martín-Ruiz et al., 2010; Nadeau et al., 2008; Yoon and Uysal, 2005; Yuan and Jang, 2008; Yuksel et al., 2010; Žabkar et al., 2010) and perceived perform-ance quality (Baker and Crompton, 2000; Bigné et al., 2001; Žabkar et al., 2010); (4) the emotions elicited through travel experience (Bigné et al., 2005); and (5) attitude toward destination revisit (Huang and Hsu, 2009; Sparks, 2007); (6) awareness of the destination and its attributes (Stokburger-Sauer, 2011; Yuan and Jang, 2008); and (7) travel motiva-tions (Kolar and Žabkar, 2010; Yoon and Uysal, 2005).

The testing of path models in SEM also provides insight on the effects of hypothesized processes reflected in path models. These models typically reflect "causal sequences" derived from theory. Structural equation models speak directly to the tenability of these models and the associated theory. While they do not establish "causality", they do provide insight on the tenability of the theory or theories from which they are derived. For example, several studies have explored the mediating effect of satisfaction on the relationship between the perceived quality and behavioral intentions in the context of cultural festivals (Baker and Crompton, 2000; Lee, S. et al., 2007b; Yuan and Jang, 2008). In these investigations, the provision of service quality and its impact on visi-tors' intention to return is best understood through the effect of satisfaction. Baker and Crompton (2000) found that satisfaction mediated the effect of quality on behavioral intentions when they measured quality as the performance of the service attributes within a community festival context. Alternately, when operationalizing quality as a discrepancy measure (i.e., perceptions-minus-expectations), satisfaction was an insignifi-cant mediator of the quality–behavioral intentions relationship.

Multi-group Invariance Testing

Another application of SEM involves the testing of both the measurement and structural model simultaneously among specified groups – referred to as multigroup invariance testing. Testing of the measurement model using the multigroup procedure involves testing hypotheses relating to equivalence among groups in terms of: (1) the factor structure, pattern of factor loadings, and factor variances/covariances; (2) the pattern of structural relations among constructs across populations; (3) the constructs' latent means; and (4) the cross-validation of an instrument to establish its psychometric prop-erties across contexts and populations.

Briefly, multigroup analysis tests the null hypothesis that covariance structures across groups are equivalent (Byrne, 1998). Rejection of the null hypothesis suggests inequal-ity among the groups. Subsequent procedures directed at identifying the source of the inequality involve testing a series of increasingly restrictive hypotheses that imposes equality constraints on sets of parameters beginning with elements of the measurement model and continuing through the model's structural parameters.

Researchers using this procedure have typically explored the moderating effect of selected variables. These have included analyses of gender (Okazaki and Hirose, 2009), tourist knowledge (Wong and Yeh, 2009), place attachment (Chung et al., 2011), and distance to tourist attractions (Jurowski and Gursoy, 2004). For example, Okazaki and Hirose (2009) simultaneously tested a path model among men and women relating Japanese consumers' media use in searching for travel information. While they observed no variation between the groups with regard to the linear relationships tested in their path model, they did observe variation among men and women in terms of the latent means for satisfaction with, attitude toward, and the habitual usage of mobile internet. Women were found to be generally more positive about the technology compared to their male counterparts. Using tourists who had taken an overseas group package tour, Wong and Yeh (2009) also tested the invariance of a structural model to assess whether tourist knowledge moderated the relationship between risk perception and hesitation in travel decision making. In their analyses, they defined their two groups in terms of "tourist knowledge" (i.e., low/high). They observed that, for the high knowledge group, a higher level of knowledge decreased their level of risk perception and tendency to baulk at purchasing a vacation.

Cross-validation of Structural Models

Another application of SEM in tourism involves the cross-validation of hypothesized models. The strength of this approach lies in its ability to test relationships across populations and contexts and further support or reject hypotheses grounded in specific theory. Common in tourism research is the use of cross-sectional data. A limitation of this form of data, however, is its ability to affirm or disconfirm theory and generalize to broader populations. Testing among multiple (sub)populations provides a more rigorous test of theory and strengthens the external validity of related findings.

The most common approach in tourism research involves model development using a target sample and cross-validating using a second sample. The procedure investigates whether a specified model that has established validity in one context is replicable in another independent context. One less stringent approach adopted by tourism researchers has been to randomly split the sample into two groups. The first group is used to establish the structure of the model in question and the second group is then used to validate the emergent model. This split-half approach was employed by Oh et al. (2009), who hypothesized that three service performance phases (i.e., sales, pre-event, and event) would influence meeting planners' overall satisfaction. Their initial model was validated using the second sample offering strong support for their hypotheses.

Furthermore, tourism studies have performed comparative model testing to evaluate the acceptability of hypothesized models. Some have compared the fit of the proposed model with alternative nested models by imposing increasingly restrictive equality constraints (e.g., Kim and Littrell, 1999). The main goal of this particular procedure is to find a parsimonious model. In a study examining the superiority of three nested models relating to predictors of souvenir purchase intentions, Kim and Littrell (1999) demonstrated that a model where tourist attitudes, shaped through certain tourism experiences (i.e., recreational and ethnic tourism) and their associated values positively influenced tourist souvenir purchase intentions and provided a significantly better fit to the data compared to the other two models. Other researchers have compared fit indices and parameter estimates of two or more non-nested competing models in order to obtain a superior model (Bigné et al., 2005a; Boo et al., 2009; Lee and Back, 2008). For instance,

Bigné et al. (2005a) tested two non-nested models explaining how visitors' cognitive evaluation of a theme park experience (i.e., disconfirmation) and their emotions influence their satisfaction and revisit intentions. Selected fit indices allowed them to determine model superiority and conclude the importance of emotions in response to a visit as opposed to the role of pre-visit emotional states. Similarly, Lee and Back (2008) compared the explanatory power of the three non-nested models to better understand association meeting attendees' participation intentions. Their three competing models were derived from the theory of reasoned action (TRA), theory of planned behavior (TPB), and empirical evidence (meeting participation model, MPM). Their findings illustrated that the superiority of the MPM over other competing models.

Test for a Latent Growth Model

As an extension of a structural regression model testing, the analysis of a latent growth model (LGM) in SEM involves estimation of models with mean structures in addition to sample covariances for longitudinal data. Specifically, it can be applied to repeated measures data to estimate change in individual differences over time instead of treating differences in the growth trajectories of individual cases as error variance (Kline, 2005).

Latent growth modeling is analysed in the two-step procedure in order to single out potential sources of poor model fit (see Kline, 2005, pp. 272–287). The first step involves the analysis of the baseline model that evaluates its change using the repeated measures variables. The baseline model is structured such that: (1) each time measurement is an indicator of two latent growth factors (i.e., initial status and linear change); (2) these factors covary; (3) the exogenous factors are directly influenced by a mean structure; and (4) the measurement errors of the indicators covary. In model construction, the loadings of all indicators on the initial status factor are fixed to 1.0 while loadings on the linear change factor are fixed to be constant to correspond to measurement occasions. Given an acceptable change model, the subsequent procedure adds predictors to the baseline model predicting change over time.

The study by Assaker et al. (2011) provides one of the few examples of testing LGM in SEM within the tourism literature. They investigated the effects of novelty seeking, destination image and overall satisfaction levels on revisit intentions to sun, sea, and sand destinations over four occasions using 450 European tourists. Their findings illustrated that satisfaction positively influenced immediate revisit intentions and that its effect on intention decreases over time. It was also found that a higher level of novelty seeking diminished immediate revisit intentions but increased future revisits.

ADVANTAGES AND LIMITATIONS OF STRUCTURAL EQUATION MODELING

Advantages of SEM

Structural equation modeling has several advantages over other analytical methodologies for hypothesis testing. Given that the analysis can be applied to both non-experimental and experimental data, it provides researchers with (1) modeling flexibility; (2) an array of analytical capabilities (i.e., multi-group invariance testing); and (3) the ability to account for measurement error.

First, as noted earlier, CFA is used as a precursor to testing the structural model that specifies relationships among latent constructs (Brown, 2006). Because the CFA model is specified a priori, it assists researchers with obtaining a parsimonious model by offering guidance on decisions relating to the number of factors, the pattern of factor loadings, and the relationships among error variances. The acceptability of the specified model is assessed by evaluating the overall goodness of fit, statistical significance, and strength of parameter estimates. It is also a powerful technique for assessing construct validity of the measurement scale.

Another advantage of SEM is the ability to unveil complicated construct relationships. It enables researchers to test all variables of a hypothesized model simultaneously (Byrne, 1998). Because it estimates a series of multiple regression equations in a single comprehensive method, it increases explanatory power for model testing. For example, in a study testing a consumer commitment model in an e-commerce travel context, Nusair and Hua (2010) found that SEM revealed a greater number of statistically significant relationships in the model compared to those in ordinary least squares (OLS) regression analyses. They concluded that SEM is more effective than multiple regression analyses for determining the superiority of theoretically derived models.

Furthermore, SEM is a powerful analytical tool for evaluating the equivalence of measurement and structural model across population subgroups (Brown, 2006). It allows for detecting the potential source of group differences in the factor solution and latent causal structure (e.g., the number of factors, patterns of factor loadings, presence of error covariances, and the means of the latent dimensions). Particularly, measurement invariance tests can be used in scale development, as it evaluates the generalizability of an instrument measuring specified constructs among different groups.

Last, SEM more effectively accounts for measurement error in the estimation process (Hair et al., 1998). Unlike SEM, OLS approaches assume that all of the observed indicators measure the phenomena of interest perfectly without error (Brown, 2006). Consequently, it is a bold assumption that estimates derived from OLS methods are immune from measurement error. This assumption is rarely applicable to quantitative tourism research, which relies heavily on survey methods to measure variables. Traditional methods (i.e., ANOVA and MANOVA) that assume equal and independent error variances are also inadequate for repeated measures data (Kline, 2005). In this regard, to many tourism researchers, it is more appealing to estimate the relationships among variables while adjusting for measurement error.

Limitations of SEM

SEM requires a priori specifications, which implies that model development and modification should be directed by theory and empirical evidence (Kline, 2005). Therefore, this technique is inappropriate for exploratory research where the measurement structure is not well defined or where guiding theory and empirical evidence underlying patterns of construct relationships is not well-established (Brannick, 1995; Hurley et al., 1997). In such cases, alternative techniques for data analysis such as EFA and regression analysis may be considered (Hurley et al., 1997). Due to the confirmatory nature in SEM, post-hoc model fitting is further restricted without providing appropriate theoretical, conceptual or empirical justification. Modification of an initially hypothesized model solely based on model fit and misspecification information is considered exploratory in nature, which should be avoided in SEM.

Another limitation of the use of SEM and the use of the maximum likelihood estimation is associated with its inherent assumption of multivariate normality and asymptotic theory that requires sufficient sample sizes (Tomarken and Waller, 2005). Structural equation modeling is considered a valuable technique for testing hypotheses that imply causality in the non-experimental contexts. Yet, it has been underutilized in studies using experimental designs where it is common practice to randomly assign participants to treatments and directly manipulate independent variables, which has the potential to violate the multivariate normality assumptions. The inclusion of categorical variables denoting group status in experimental designs could also raise some concerns about the normality. Most SEM software, however, will enable researchers to address some issues of categorical or ordinal measurement through the use of polychoric or polyserial (and accompanying asymptotic) covariance matrices along with the weighted least squares estimator.

Finally, as indicated earlier, most applications of SEM require large samples. Although there is little consensus among researchers on precise sample size requirements, consideration ought to include the complexity of the model and the type of estimation algorithm (Kline, 2005). A small sample size increases the likelihood of encountering a technical problem in the analysis (e.g., bias of parameter estimates, inadmissible estimates, Heywood cases) and the limited statistical power (Tomarken and Waller, 2005). Generally, larger sample sizes produce smaller standard errors, narrower confidence intervals and, ultimately, more reliable parameter estimates.

FURTHER DEVELOPMENTS WITHIN SEM

In this final section, we discuss potential applications of SEM that have received little attention in the tourism literature. These applications have the potential to both increase the scientific rigor of tourism research and address a broader range of research questions.

Formative Versus Reflective Measurement

Most tourism researchers that have employed SEM have used multi-item measures of their latent constructs. When testing their measurement model, they assume that their indicators have been drawn from a hypothetical pool of items and that the addition or deletion of items has little bearing of the meanings of their latent construct. The covariation among items can also be accounted for through the latent construct. That is, they have all been developed with a narrow definition of a specific construct in mind. This approach yields a clean factor solution with all items loading strongly on their hypothesized construct and weakly on other constructs in the model. These measures are referred to as reflective indicators. These assumptions, however, have recently been questioned in the consumer and business management literature where researchers' indicators are often developed to capture the subtleties of a specific service or business contexts (for review, see Bollen and Lennox, 1991; Diamantopoulos and Winklhofer, 2001; Jarvis et al., 2003). For example, measures of service quality are often developed to capture the breadth of factors that underlie quality for the specific service type. Consequently, attribute indicators might not necessarily covary with one another even though they have been developed to reflect the same latent concept. Importantly, however, the removal of any specific item from the hypothesized construct may have the potential to drastically alter the meaning of that construct. These types of indicators are referred to as formative measures.

The reviews by the authors cited above outline guidelines for distinguishing formative from reflective indicators and the procedures for testing these models within SEM. For tourism researchers, it is imperative that these distinctions be understood and established a priori. Model misspecification has important implications for Type I error (e.g., concluding a statistically significant relationship when, in fact, it does not exist) and Type II error (e.g., concluding a statistically non-significant relationship when, in fact, it does exist) and, ultimately, study conclusions (Jarvis et al., 2003). Researchers should note, however, that the issue of formative measurement remains a hot topic within the SEM literature. Concerns over construct validity, reliability, and model identification remain problematic (for discussion, see Cenfetelli and Bassellier, 2009; Diamantopoulos and Siguaw, 2006). While simulation and testing in applied contexts is helping to resolve these issues and allay concern, there remain skeptics (Bagozzi, 2007; Howell et al., 2007; Wilcox et al., 2008).

Moderator Effects

One direction for future inquiry is to test hypotheses relating to interaction effects among latent variables. While invariance testing allows for the examination of nominal or ordinal indicator moderation, it does not test for the effect of interactions among latent variables (e.g., Okazaki and Hirose, 2009). Their limited use is likely associated with the potential problems and complexities of specifying and estimating SEM models with latent variable interactions (Tomarken and Waller, 2005). Some advantages over multiple regression analyses (i.e., correction of bias estimates and power adjustment, Tomarken and Waller, 2005) and the recent refinement of the technique (e.g., Kline and Moosbrugger, 2000) will likely lead to more extensive use of SEM in testing for interactions in tourism research.

Latent Growth Models

Most recently, latent growth modeling for the analysis of repeated measures data has become a viable alternative to repeated measures ANOVA (Kline, 2005). As highlighted by Tomarken and Waller (2005), there are various advantages associated with LGM: (1) the flexibility of modeling random effects and residuals; (2) the ability to comparatively evaluate growth functions and detect changes in more complex causal models; (3) the capacity to specify time-varying covariates; (4) a better ability to analyse multiple levels of hierarchically structured data and the multivariate change patterns across multiple measures; and (5) a stronger statistical method for treating missing data. These benefits are relevant for tourism researchers who utilize longitudinal or other repeated measures data (e.g., Assaker et al., 2011) although its potential has not fully explored in the existing literature. Owing to the benefits outlined above, it is likely that LGM testing using SEM will grow within the tourism literature not only for evaluating the developmental trajectory of constructs over time, but also for analysing multilevel models with clustered data structures in which repeated observations are nested within individuals.

NOTE

1. *Nested models* refer to two or more models that are structurally the same but differ in the number of freely estimated or constrained parameters (Brown, 2006). When the models are nested, direct statistical comparison between the models is possible. It is particularly useful to obtain a parsimonious model by trimming or building models (Kline, 2005).

REFERENCES

Akaike, H. (1987), 'Factor analysis and AIC', *Psychometrika*, **52**, 317–332.

Albacete-Sáez, C., M. Fuentes- Fuentes and F. Lloréns-Montes (2007), 'Service quality measurement in rural accommodation', *Annals of Tourism Research*, **34** (1), 45–65.

Anderson, J.C. and D.W. Gerbing (1988), 'Structural equation modeling in practice: a review and recommended two step approach', *Psychological Bulletin*, **103** (3), 453–460.

Arbuckle, J. (2009), *AMOS 18 User's Guide*, Crawfordville, FL: AMOS Development Corporation.

Assaker, G., V. Vinzi and P. O'Connor (2011), 'Examining the effect of novelty seeking, satisfaction, and destination image on tourists' return pattern: a two factor, non-linear latent growth model', *Tourism Management*, **32** (4), 890–901.

Bagozzi, R. (1980), 'Performance and satisfaction in an industrial sales force: an examination of their antecedents and simultaneity', *Journal of Marketing*, **44** (2), 65–77.

Bagozzi, R. (2007), 'On the meaning of formative measurement and how it differs from reflective measurement: comment on Howell, Breivik, and Wilcox', *Psychological Methods*, **12** (2), 229–237.

Baker, D. and J. Crompton (2000), 'Quality, satisfaction and behavioral intentions', *Annals of Tourism Research*, **27** (3), 785–804.

Beerli, A. and J.D. Martín (2004), 'Tourists' characteristics and the perceived image of tourist destinations: a quantitative analysis – a case study of Lanzarote, Spain', *Tourism Management*, **25** (5), 623–636.

Bentler, P. (1990), 'Comparative fit indexes in structural models', *Psychological Bulletin*, **107** (2), 238–246.

Bentler, P. (2003), *EQS 6.1 for Windows* [Computer Software], Encino, CA: Multivariate Software.

Bigné Alcañiz, E., I. Sánchez García and S. Sanz Blas (2009), 'The functional–psychological continuum in the cognitive image of a destination: a confirmatory analysis', *Tourism Management*, **30** (5), 715–723.

Bigné, J., L. Andreu and J. Gnoth (2005a), 'The theme park experience: an analysis of pleasure, arousal and satisfaction', *Tourism Management*, **26** (2), 833–844.

Bigné, J., L. Andreu, I. Küster and A. Blesa (2005b), 'Quality market orientation: tourist agencies' perceived effects', *Annals of Tourism Research*, **32** (4), 1022–1038.

Bigné, J., M. Sánchez and J. Sánchez (2001), 'Tourism image, evaluation variables and after purchase behaviour: inter-relationship', *Tourism Management*, **22** (6), 607–616.

Bollen, K. (1989), *Structural Equations with Latent Variables*. New York: Wiley.

Bollen, K. and R. Lennox (1991), 'Conventional wisdom on measurement: a structural equation perspective', *Psychological Bulletin*, **110** (2), 305–314.

Boo, S., J. Busser and S. Baloglu (2009), 'A model of customer-based brand equity and its application to multiple destinations', *Tourism Management*, **30** (2), 219–231.

Brannick, M.T. (1995), 'Critical comments on applying covariance structure modeling', *Journal of Organizational Behavior*, **16** (3), 201–213.

Brown, T.A. (2006), *Confirmatory Factor Analysis for Applied Research*. New York: The Guilford Press.

Browne, M. and R. Cudeck (1993), 'Alternative ways of assessing model fit', in K.A. Bollen and J.S. Long (eds), *Testing Structural Equation Models*, Newbury Park, CA: Sage, pp. 136–162.

Byrne, B.M. (1998), *Structural Equation Modeling with LISREL, PRELIS, and SIMPLIS: Basic Concepts, Applications, and Programming*, Mahwah, NJ: Lawrence Erlbaum Associates, Inc.

Caro, M.L. and M.J. García (2008), 'Developing a multidimensional and hierarchical service quality model for the travel agency industry', *Tourism Management*, **29** (4), 706–720.

Cenfetelli, R.T. and G. Bassellier (2009), 'Interpretation of formative measurement in information systems research', *MIS Quarterly*, **33** (4), 689–707.

Chen, J.S. and C. Hsu (2001), 'Developing and validating a riverboat gaming impact scale', *Annals of Tourism Research*, **27** (2), 459–476.

Chin, W.W. (2001), *PLS-Graph User's Guide* (Version 3.0), Houston, TX: Soft Modeling.

Chung, J., G. Kyle, J. Petrick and J. Absher (2011), 'Fairness of prices, user fee policy and willingness to pay among visitors to a national forest', *Tourism Management*, **32** (5), 1038–1046.

Churchill, G.A. (1979), 'A paradigm for developing better measures of marketing constructs', *Journal of Marketing Research*, **16** (1), 64–73.

Connell, J. and D. Meyer (2009), 'Balamory revisited: an evaluation of the screen tourism destination–tourist nexus', *Tourism Management*, **30** (2), 194–207.

Crowley, S. and X. Fan (1997), 'Structural equation modeling: basic concepts and applications in personality assessment research', *Journal of Personality Assessment*, **68** (3), 508–531.

del Bosque, I. and H. San Martín (2008), 'Tourist satisfaction: a cognitive-affective model', *Annals of Tourism Research*, **35** (2), 551–573.

Denstadli, J. and J. Jacobsen (2011), 'The long and winding roads: perceived quality of scenic tourism routes', *Tourism Management*, **32** (4), 780–789.

Diamantopoulos, A. and J.A. Siguaw (2006), 'Formative versus reflective indicators in organizational measure development: a comparison and empirical illustration', *British Journal of Management*, **17** (4), 263–282.

Diamantopoulos, A. and H.M. Winklhofer (2001), 'Index construction with formative indicators: an alternative to scale development', *Journal of Marketing Research*, **38** (2), 269–277.

Dyer, P., D. Gursoy, B. Sharma and J. Carter (2007), 'Structural modeling of resident perceptions of tourism and associated development on the Sunshine Coast, Australia', *Tourism Management*, **28** (2), 409–422.

Feng, R. and A. Morrison (2007), 'Quality and value network: marketing travel clubs', *Annals of Tourism Research*, **34** (3), 588–609.

Fishbein, M. and I. Azjen (1975), *Belief, Attitude, Intention, and Behavior: An Introduction to Theory and Research*, Reading, MA: Addison-Wesley.

Fornell, C. and D.F. Larcker (1981), 'Evaluating structural equation models with unobserved variables and measurement error', *Journal of Marketing Research*, **18** (1), 39–50.

Funk, D. and T. Bruun (2007), 'The role of socio-psychological and culture-education motives in marketing international sport tourism: a cross-cultural perspective', *Tourism Management*, **28** (3), 806–819.

Gross, M. and G. Brown (2008), 'An empirical structural model of tourists and places: progressing involvement and place attachment into tourism', *Tourism Management*, **29** (6), 1141–1151.

Gursoy, D. and E. Gavcar (2003), 'International leisure tourists' involvement profile', *Annals of Tourism Research*, **30** (4), 906–926.

Gursoy, D. and K. Kendall (2006), 'Hosting mega events: modeling locals' support', *Annals of Tourism Research*, **33** (3), 603–623.

Gursoy, D. and D. Rutherford (2004), 'Host attitudes toward tourism: an improved structural model', *Annals of Tourism Research*, **31** (3), 495–516.

Gursoy, D., C. Jurowski and M. Uysal (2002), 'Resident attitudes: a structural modeling approach', *Annals of Tourism Research*, **29** (1), 79–105.

Haenlein, M. and A.M. Kaplan (2004), 'A beginner's guide to partial least squares analysis', *Understanding Statistics*, **3** (4), 283–297.

Hair, J.F., R.E. Anderson, R.L. Tatham and W.C. Black (1998), *Multivariate Data Analysis*, 5th edition, Upper Saddle River, NJ: Prentice Hall.

Han, H., L. Hsu and C. Sheu (2010), 'Application of the theory of planned behavior to green hotel choice: testing the effect of environmental friendly activities', *Tourism Management*, **31** (3), 325–334.

Hayduk, L. and D. Glaser (2000), 'Jiving the four-step, waltzing around factor analysis, and other serious fun', *Structural Equation Modeling*, **7** (1), 1–35.

Hayduk, L., G. Cummings, K. Boadu, H. Pazderka-Robinson and S. Boulianne (2007), 'Testing! testing! one, two three: testing the theory in structural equation models!', *Personality and Individual Differences*, **42** (2), 841–850.

Howell, R.D., E. Breivik and J.B. Wilcox (2007), 'Reconsidering formative measurement', *Psychological Methods*, **12** (2), 205–218.

Hu, L. and P. Bentler (1999), 'Cutoff criteria for fit indexes in covariance structure analysis: conventional criteria versus new alternatives', *Structural Equation Modeling*, **6** (1), 1–55.

Huang, C., C. Chou and P. Lin (2010), 'Involvement theory in constructing bloggers' intention to purchase travel products', *Tourism Management*, **31** (4), 513–526.

Huang, S. and C. Hsu (2009), 'Effects of travel motivation, past experience, perceived constraint, and attitude on revisit intention', *Journal of Travel Research*, **48** (1), 29–44.

Hung, K. and J.F. Petrick (2010), 'Developing a measurement scale for constraints to cruising', *Annals of Tourism Research*, **37** (1), 206–228.

Hurley, A.E., T.A. Scandura, C.A. Schriesheim, M.T. Brannick, A. Seers, R.J. Vandenberg and L.J. Williams (1997), 'Exploratory and confirmatory factor analysis: guidelines, issues, and alternatives', *Journal of Organizational Behavior*, **18** (6), 667–683.

Hwang, S., C. Lee and H. Chen (2005), 'The relationship among tourists' involvement, place attachment and interpretation satisfaction in Taiwan's national parks', *Tourism Management*, **26** (2), 143–156.

Jarvis, C.B., S.B. MacKenzie and P.M. Podsakoff (2003), 'A critical review of construct indicators and measurement model misspecification in marketing and consumer research', *Journal of Consumer Research*, **30** (2), 199–218.

Jöreskog, K. and D. Sörbom (2004), *LISREL 8.7 for Windows* [Computer Software]. Lincolnwood, IL: Scientific Software International.

Jurowski, C. and D. Gursoy (2004), 'Distance effects on residents' attitudes toward tourism', *Annals of Tourism Research*, **31** (2), 296–312.

Kang, S., C. Lee, Y. Yoon and P. Long (2008), 'Resident perception of the impact of limited-stakes community-based casino gaming in mature gaming communities', *Tourism Management*, **29** (4), 681–694.

Kang, S., P. Long and R. Perdue (1996), 'Resident attitudes toward legal gambling', *Annals of Tourism Research*, **23** (1), 71–85.

Kaplanidou, K. and C. Vogt (2006), 'A structural analysis of destination travel intentions as a function of Web site features', *Journal of Travel Research*, **45** (2), 204–216.

Kim, M., N. Chung and C. Lee (2011), 'The effect of perceived trust on electronic commerce: shopping online for tourism products and services in South Korea', *Tourism Management*, **32** (2), 256–265.

Kim, S. and M.A. Littrell (1999), 'Predicting souvenir purchase intentions', *Journal of Travel Research*, **38** (2), 153–162.

Kline, A. and H. Moosbrugger (2000), 'Maximum likelihood estimation of latent interaction effects with the LMS method', *Psychometrika*, **65** (4), 457–474.

Kline, R. (2005), *Principles and Practice of Structural Equation Modeling*, 2nd edition, New York: The Guilford Press.

Ko, D. and W. Stewart (2002), 'A structural equation model of residents' attitudes for tourism development', *Tourism Management*, **23** (5), 521–530.

Kolar, T. and V. Žabkar (2010), 'A consumer-based model of authenticity: an oxymoron or the foundation of cultural heritage marketing?', *Tourism Management*, **31** (5), 652–664.

Konecnik, M. and W. Gartner (2007), 'Customer-based brand equity for a destination', *Annals of Tourism Research*, **34** (2), 400–421.

Lee, C., Y. Lee and B. Lee (2005), 'Korea's destination image formed by the 2002 World Cup', *Annals of Tourism Research*, **32** (4), 839–858.

Lee, C., Y. Yoon and S. Lee (2007a), 'Investigating the relationships among perceived value, satisfaction, and recommendations: the case of the Korean DMZ', *Tourism Management*, **28** (1), 204–214.

Lee, M. and K. Back (2008), 'Association meeting participation: a test of competing models', *Journal of Travel Research*, **46** (3), 300–310.

Lee, S., J. Petrick and J. Crompton (2007b), 'The roles of quality and intermediary constructs in determining festival attendees' behavioral intention', *Journal of Travel Research*, **45** (4), 402–412.

Lee, S., D. Scott and H. Kim (2008), 'Celebrity fan involvement and destination perceptions', *Annals of Tourism Research*, **35** (3), 809–832.

Lindberg, K. and R. Johnson (1997), 'Modeling resident attitudes toward tourism', *Annals of Tourism Research*, **24** (2), 402–424.

MacCallum, R.C. and J.T. Austin (2000), 'Applications of structural equation modeling in psychological research', *Annual Review of Psychology*, **51**, 201–226.

McDonald, R. and M. Ho (2002), 'Principles and practice in reporting structural equation analyses', *Psychological Methods*, **7** (1), 64–82.

Marsh, H., J. Balla and R. McDonald (1988), 'Goodness-of-fit indexes in confirmatory factor analysis: the effect of sample size', *Psychological Bulletin*, **103** (3), 391–410.

Martín-Ruiz, D., M. Castellanos-Verdugo and Á. Oviedo-García (2010), 'A visitors' evaluation index for a visit to an archaeological site', *Tourism Management*, **31** (5), 590–596.

Mazanec, J., K. Wöber and A. Zins (2007), 'Tourism destination competitiveness: from definition to explanation?', *Journal of Travel Research*, **46** (1), 86–95.

Mulaik, S. and R. Millsap (2000), 'Doing the four-step right', *Structural Equation Modeling*, **7** (1), 36–73.

Mulaik, S., L. James, J. Van Alstine, N. Bennett, S. Lind and C. Stillwell (1989), 'Evaluation of goodness-of-fit indices for structural equation models', *Psychological Bulletin*, **105** (3), 430–455.

Muthén, L. and B. Muthén (1998–2010), *Mplus User's Guide*, 6th edition, Los Angeles: Muthén & Muthén.

Nadeau, J., L. Heslop, N. O'Reilly and P. Luk (2008), 'Destination in a country image context', *Annals of Tourism Research*, **35** (1), 84–106.

Nicholas, L., B. Thapa and Y. Ko (2009), 'Residents' perspectives of a world heritage site: the Pitons management area, St. Lucia', *Annals of Tourism Research*, **36** (3), 390–412.

Nunkoo, R. and H. Ramkissoon (2011), 'Developing a community support model for tourism', *Annals of Tourism Research*, **38** (3), 964–988.

Nunnally, J.C. (1967), *Psychometric Theory*. New York: McGraw-Hill.

Nusair, K. and N. Hua (2010), 'Comparative assessment of structural equation modeling and multiple regression research methodologies: e-commerce context', *Tourism Management*, **31** (3), 314–324.

Oh, H. and C. Hsu (2001), 'Volitional degrees of gambling behaviors', *Annals of Tourism Research*, **28** (3), 618–637.

Oh, H., H. Kim and K. Hong (2009), 'A dynamic perspective of meeting planners' satisfaction: toward conceptualization of critical relevancy', *Tourism Management*, **30** (4), 471–482.

Okazaki, S. and M. Hirose (2009), 'Does gender affect media choice in travel information search? On the use of mobile Internet', *Tourism Management*, **30** (6), 794–804.

Palmer, A.L., A. Sesé and J.J. Montaño (2005), 'Tourism and statistics: bibliometric study 1998–2002', *Annals of Tourism Research*, **32** (1), 167–178.

Parasuraman, A., V.A. Zeithaml and L.L. Berry (1988), 'SERVQUAL: a multiple-item scale for measuring consumer perceptions of service quality', *Journal of Retailing*, **64** (1), 14–40.

Petrick, J.F. (2002), 'An examination of gold vacationers' novelty', *Annals of Tourism Research*, **29** (2), 384–400.

Qu, H. and H. Lee (2011), 'Travelers' social identification and membership behaviors in online travel community', *Tourism Management*, **32** (6), 1262–1270.

Reisinger, Y. and L. Turner (1999), 'Structural equation modeling with LISREL: application in tourism', *Tourism Management*, **20** (1), 71–88.

Reisinger, Y. and L. Turner (2002), 'Cultural differences between Asian tourist markets and Australian hosts: Part 2', *Journal of Travel Research*, **40** (4), 374–384.

Sparks, B. (2007), 'Planning a wine tourism vacation? Factors that help to predict tourist behavioural intentions', *Tourism Management*, **28** (5), 1180–1192.

Steiger, J.H. and J.C. Lind (1980), 'Statistically-based tests for the number of common factors', paper presented at the annual Spring Meeting of the Psychometric Society, Iowa City, IA.

Stokburger-Sauer, N. (2011), 'The relevance of visitors' nation brand embeddedness and personality congruence for nation brand identification, visit intentions and advocacy', *Tourism Management*, **32** (6), 1282–1289.

Tomarken, A.J. and N.G. Waller (2005), 'Structural equation modeling: strengths, limitations, and misconceptions', *Annual Review of Clinical Psychology*, **1**, 31–65.

Um, S., K. Chon and Y. Ro (2006), 'Antecedents of revisit intention', *Annals of Tourism Research*, **33** (4), 1141–1158.

Vargas-Sánchez, A., N. Porras-Bueno and M. Plaza-mejía (2011), 'Explaining residents' attitudes to tourism: is a universal model possible?', *Annals of Tourism Research*, **38** (2), 460–480.

Vogt, C.A. and D. Fesenmaier (1995), 'Tourists and retailers' perceptions of services', *Annals of Tourism Research*, **22** (4), 763–780.

Wang, Y. and D. Fesenmaier (2004), 'Towards understanding members' general participation in and active contribution to an online travel community', *Tourism Management*, **25** (6), 709–722.

Westland, J. (2010), 'Lower bounds on sample size in structural equation modeling', *Electronic Commerce Research and Applications*, **9** (6), 476–487.

Wilcox, B.J., R.D. Howell and E. Breivik (2008), 'Questions about formative measurement', *Journal of Business Research*, **61** (12), 1219–1228.

William, P. and G. Soutar (2009), 'Value, satisfaction and behavioral intentions in an adventure tourism context', *Annals of Tourism Research*, **36** (3), 413–438.

Wong, J. and C. Yeh (2009), 'Tourist hesitation in destination decision making', *Annals of Tourism Research*, **36** (1), 6–23.

Wu, S., P. Wei and J. Chen (2008), 'Influential factors and relational structure of Internet banner advertising in the tourism industry', *Tourism Management*, **29** (2), 221–236.

Yoon, Y., D. Gursoy and J. Chen (2001), 'Validating a tourism development theory with structural equation modeling', *Tourism Management*, **22** (4), 363–372.

Yoon, Y. and M. Uysal (2005), 'An examination of the effects of motivation and satisfaction on destination loyalty: a structural model', *Tourism Management*, **26** (1), 45–56.

Yuan, J. and S. Jang (2008), 'The effects of quality and satisfaction on awareness and behavioral intentions: exploring the role of a wine festival', *Journal of Travel Research*, **46** (3), 279–288.

Yuksel, A., F. Yuksel and Y. Bilim (2010), 'Destination attachment: effects on customer satisfaction and cognitive, affective and conative loyalty', *Tourism Management*, **31** (2), 274–284.

Žabkar, V., M. Brenčič and T. Dmitrović (2010), 'Modelling perceived quality, visitor satisfaction and behavioural intentions at the destination level', *Tourism Management*, **31** (4), 537–546.

6 Discrete choice analysis and experimental design
Clive Morley

NATURE OF THE TECHNIQUE AND ITS EVOLUTION

Tourists make many decisions in determining their trip, and many of these decisions are intrinsically categorical, multinomial (many options are available) and unordered. For example, the choice of destination, of hotel, whether a particular attraction is visited or not, the mode of travel. Discrete choice theory provides an appropriate and sophisticated framework for analysis of the data at the level of individuals' evoked responses, and one that has been proven to work well in practice.

Forecasting for some strategic policy and marketing analysis purposes using aggregate level demand models can be problematical. For example, a special fare offer may not be reflected in the typical fare used in the model and the effects of changes in hotel room rates may be very imperfectly analysed through the medium of CPI changes (which is how tourism prices are usually measured in such models). Policy analysis can require the use of variables that are more directly related to those the potential tourist considers in making their choices. The methodology to model choices at the individual level is theoretically established (McFadden, 1984; Manski and McFadden, 1981; Hensher et al., 1988) and was successfully applied in areas such as transport economics and marketing (for example, Hensher and Johnson, 1981) before being readily applied to tourism demand and policy analysis (Louviere and Timmermans, 1990). Early tourism applications include Witt (1980, 1983) and Sheldon and Mak (1987).

The methods of discrete choice analysis are sometimes referred to as 'random utility' methods (as the underlying econometric theory uses a random utility specification) or 'limited dependent variable' analysis (the dependent variable in the model is categorical). In a marketing context the term 'conjoint analysis' is used for very similar methods. Logit, multinomial logit and probit models are particular cases of discrete choice analysis.

In the simplest application, the dependent variable is binary (takes the values 0 or 1) denoting whether or not the particular alternative of interest was chosen. The explanatory variables can include various characteristics of the individual choosing and of the options. For example, a sample of tourists in Seville could be asked if they had visited a flamenco show, and this choice related to characteristics such as their age, gender, income, origin and the price of the show. It is inappropriate to use ordinary least squares (OLS) regression (for example, the dependent variable is not continuous, the errors are not homogeneous, the errors and explanatory variables are not independent). The binomial response theory can be readily extended to the more general multinomial case (McFadden, 1984) with more choice options (but still a finite number of mutually exclusive options). Extending to more alternatives to choose from is not enough to satisfy the fundamental requirements for OLS regression.

The most basic and common model, the binary logit model, comes from assuming independent, identically distributed random errors with an extreme value type 1 distribution, which makes estimation straightforward. See the next section for details of what this involves. It is also common to further assume the usual linear function of explanatory variables. The upshot of these assumptions is that the probability that the particular alternative is chosen by a particular individual can be written as:

$$P_i = \exp[\beta' X_i]/(1 + \exp[\beta' X_i]) \tag{6.1}$$

where X_i are the explanatory variables and β is a vector of coefficients (to be estimated) From this can be derived the expression:

$$\ln[P_i/(1 - P_i)] = \beta' X_i \tag{6.2}$$

The log of the odds ratio, the left hand side of this last equation, is known as a 'logit' and is a source of the name for this model.

Extending the dependent variable to encompass a choice from m alternatives gives the multinomial logit (MNL) model:

$$P_i = \exp[\beta' X_i]/(\Sigma \exp[\beta' X_j]). \tag{6.3}$$

$$= 1/(\Sigma \exp[\beta' X_j - \beta' X_i])$$

with the sum being over all m alternatives, indexed by j (the latter form shows that values of variables common to all alternatives are irrelevant).

The logit and MNL models are readily estimated with generally accessible statistical modelling software. To understand the consequences of the assumptions made in arriving at these simple (but powerful and useful) models, and extensions of them, requires a further outline of the underlying theory, as in the following section.

The data used in discrete choice analysis is at the level of individuals and includes variables for the choice made, characteristics of the alternatives and the individual and perhaps of the choice sets (which alternatives are available to choose from, if these vary, as they can be made to do in experimental conditions). The choices made are observable reflections of the preferences underlying them, so preferences can be analysed with this methodology. The data can derive from choices actually made and observed, such as whether or not a tourist visited France on their last trip abroad (this is known as revealed preference data) or from experiments in which respondents are presented with various alternatives and asked to express their choice from them (stated preference data). For example, stated preferences could be from a survey of potential tourists in Birmingham who are asked to choose between trips to Madrid, Paris and Brussels, with each destination having either a cheap or expensive air fare given. Typically revealed preference data has a single choice value per respondent, whilst in stated preference experiments respondents as potential tourists may be asked to choose a number of times in different circumstances (that is, consider various scenarios in which the alternatives presented to choose from, and/or their attributes, are varied). Respondents are usually asked to do this four or more times, with different sets of defined alternatives (choice sets). So in the Birmingham example the potential tourists might be asked to choose from Madrid with an expensive air fare, Paris with an expensive air fare and Brussels with a cheap air fare (choice set A), then to choose from Madrid with a cheap air fare, Paris with an expensive air fare and Brussels with a cheap air fare (choice set B), etc. Discrete choice analysis, with models like the MNL outlined above (and those discussed below), is used to analyse both revealed preference and stated preference data.

BACKGROUND AND TYPES OF PROBLEMS THE TECHNIQUES ARE DESIGNED TO HANDLE

Discrete Choice Analysis

The microeconomic theory of tourism demand (Morley, 1992) derives from a Lancasterian consumer theory in which the utility (or attractiveness) of a good (here alternative) is a function of characteristics of the good. For clarity, we will henceforth use the case of a choice of destination for a tourist visit, although the concepts just as readily apply to other types of choices. An individual's direct utility function is a function of characteristics of the destinations available to the individual and quantities of other goods and services that they might consume. Maximizing this utility subject to the constraints of their money budget and time available yields the indirect utility function V_{rj}, for individual r and destination j. The indirect utility is a function of characteristics of the individual (e.g., income, the time they have available and demographic attributes – the latter possibly as proxies for taste variables), and characteristics of the tourist destination (e.g., the fare, the transit time, attributes of the destination, the cost per day of staying) and prices of other goods and services. Let X_{rj} denote the vector of these exogenous variables.

Tour j is preferred to tour k if $V_{rj} > V_{rk}$, and that tour J is chosen for which $V_{rJ} = \max_j \{V_{rj}\}$. This includes the possibility (say, $j = 0$) that no tour is chosen.

In the random utility formulation $V_{rj} = v(X_{rj}, \varepsilon_{rj})$ the utilities cannot be completely characterized in terms of the observable, systematic part represented by the variables in X_{rj} and so a random, unobserved element ε_{rj} is incorporated. A common functional form $v(.)$ for the utilities is assumed to enable estimation to be operationally tractable. As in aggregated modelling it is usual to assume a linear additive random term:

$$V_{rj} = V_{rj}^* + \varepsilon_{rj} \tag{6.4}$$

The probability a particular destination (say $j = 1$) is chosen, the conditional distribution of the response given the exogenous variables, is:

$$P_r(1) = P[V_{r1} = \max_j \{V_{rj}\}]$$

$$= P[V_{rj}^* + \varepsilon_{rj} < V_{r1}^* + \varepsilon_{r1}] \text{ for all } j \neq 1 \tag{6.5}$$

This requires solution of an m dimensional integral (where m is the number of destinations to be chosen from). Until recently this was not feasible and standard practice has been to introduce simplifying assumptions, which will be followed here for the moment (although see later in the chapter for consideration of ways and means of testing the validity of these assumptions and of estimating without making them).

If the random components are assumed to be independent, identically distributed with cumulative density function $F(\varepsilon|X_{rj})$, then

$$P_r(1) = \Pi_j P[\varepsilon_{rj} < V_{r1}^* + \varepsilon_{r1} - V_{rj}^*]$$

$$= \int F'(x \mid X_{rj})\Pi_{j \neq 1} F[x + V_{r1}^* - V_{rj}^*]dx \tag{6.6}$$

where F' is the probability density function (the derivative of F with respect to x) and the integral is over all values of the error (x from $-\infty$ to $+\infty$).

This expression for P_r in terms of the error distribution emphasizes its dependence on the indirect utility function V_{rj}^*, particularly V_{r1}^*, and the convoluted form of relationship to the distribution F. For the expression to be tractable for estimation it is common to either adopt a distributional form for F that results in an estimable expression for P_r or to cut through the complexity of P_r as a function of F and assume a distributional form for P_r. The logit and probit models are widely used. The logit model derives straightforwardly from Equation (6.6). If F is taken as the Weibull extreme value distribution (also called the extreme value type I and the Gumbel distribution), then it follows that:

$$P_r(1) = \exp(V_{r1}^*) / \Sigma_j \exp(V_{rj}^*) \tag{6.7}$$

Alternatively, for the probit model P_r is expressed directly as

$$P_r(1) = \Phi(V_{r1}^*) \tag{6.8}$$

where Φ is the cumulative distribution function of the standard normal distribution (the assumption of independent, identically distributed errors is unnecessary here).

The more straightforward linear probability model:

$$P_r(1) = V_{r1}^* \tag{6.9}$$

is not attractive as it does not confine the probability P_r to the interval [0,1] and restrictions to ensure it does so can be difficult to enforce.

A linearity assumption, $V_{rj}^* = \beta'X_{rj}$ for a vector of coefficients β, is usual, (this gives Equation (6.3) for the MNL), although more general forms, such as second order (quadratic), interaction or translog approximations, can be readily used.

Unless there are extreme values of exogenous variables or observed choice frequencies close to zero or one in the data, there will be little empirical difference between the logit and probit models.

Brau (2008) used a MNL model to investigate the preferences of tourists visiting Sardinia (Italy) for stays with various proximities to the beach, risk of crowding, availability of services, cost and environmental variables. He was able to derive 'implicit prices' or willingness to pay values for differences in crowding, level of services, etc. On the other hand, Chaminuka et al. (2011) applied a probit model to Kruger National Park (South Africa) visitors' choices in terms of accommodation inside or outside the park, price and various ecotourism possibilities. Their results showed that certain ecotourism features were more attractive than others and that there was a willingness to pay more than expected for them.

A strong consequence of the independent and identically distributed errors assumptions of the logit (and MNL) model is what is called the independence from irrelevant alternatives (IIA) property. The IIA property means that the ratio $P_r(i)/P_r(j)$ depends only on the utilities of choices i and j, and not on any other alternatives (readily seen by substituting (6.7) in both terms of the ratio and cancelling out the sum terms). This means that a change in the utility of one alternative (such as an improvement in the attractiveness of a particular destination or a change in the taxes paid at a destination) will have a proportionately equal impact on the probability of choosing all the other alternatives (i.e., equality of the cross-elasticities of the probabilities of choosing alternatives with respect to the explanatory variables). This is not always plausible. The classic example is from the situation of the choice of mode of travel between an origin and a destination, where the traveller can choose between a bus (which happens to be blue), a car and a train. If a new bus service is introduced into the choice (this one is red, but otherwise very similar to the blue bus) then the new, red bus service would expect to draw patronage disproportionately from the blue bus, contrary to the IIA property. IIA implies that parameters of the model defined on a subset of the full choice set can be unbiasedly estimated from data on the subset. So a useful consequence of the IIA property is that estimates are valid (consistent) even if some important alternatives are not included in the choice set.

As these restrictions are not usually theoretically plausible it is important to test for the IIA property and this should be a standard part of the analysis of MNL models (not all empirical studies have recognised this). The Hausman and McFadden (1984) test is a useful one, based on the fact that, if the IIA property assumption is valid then parameter estimates from choice data over the full choice sets are, except for sampling error, equal to parameter estimates from conditional choice data over choice sets restricted to a subset of the full set of alternatives. Non-rejection of the IIA property can be taken as strong support of the MNL model used in an analysis. Despite the stringency of the IIA assumption empirical results often show that it is not a serious concern. But it can be, Chaminuka et al. (2011) used a probit model because the logit model failed an IIA test.

Experimental Design

Revealed preference data has the advantage of representing actual decisions made whereas stated preference data is of hypothetical decisions. But this means that revealed preferences are constrained to pre-existing conditions; stated preferences allow possibilities to consider extensions and hypothetical conditions, important in policy and planning studies. Revealed preference data will be deficient in information on non-chosen alternatives and so estimating the specific effects of the explanatory variables is limited. In stated preference studies the researcher designs the characteristics considered by the subjects, determining and manipulating them to facilitate estimation of the variables' effects on choice outcomes. In doing so statistical principles of experimental design are very important for efficiency and efficacy, to ensure the desired effects are well estimated within sample size limitations. For example, in an analysis of destination hotel prices (set at, say, high and low levels) and air fares (set at high, medium and low levels) on choice of destination, it is advisable to balance the experiment so that the high and low level fares are equally above and below the medium, and to define the choice sets so that each hotel price level is presented in combination with each air fare level in the options.

The key to experiments is that the researcher deliberately controls and manipulates (pre-sets) the values of the independent (explanatory) variables and measures the response value of the dependent variable. This enables much stronger inferences about causality than are possible with observational data (wherein the dependent variable is measured in response to naturally seen variations in the independent variables). The issues with observational data are that the independent variables are not controlled, the response values may be (in full or part) due to other variables not measured in the data, and often multicollinearity of observed variables is present. Further, the validity of the statistical tests and inferences usually assumes that the independent variables values are fixed; this means that the p-values, significance and critical values from regression and the like analyses as they are usually done in tourism (and many other economic) studies are more a conventional guide rather than the accurate probability statements they purport to be. The statistical inference from experimental data is more soundly based. On the other hand, when done on human subjects, experiments suffer from concerns about their artificiality (as in the difference between revealed and stated preferences) and that it is not always practical or ethical to vary the values of some variables in ways the experimenter may want. For example, including questions on illegal activities (such as drug taking, which may be important for some tourists).

Vital to the validity of experimental data is randomization. Whilst the combinations of values of the independent variables are set by the experimenter, the particular subjects assigned to respond to those values need to be chosen at random. This is essential both to provide a probabilistic basis for the statistical inference, and to randomize out the effect of any unaccounted for variables.

Discrete choice experiments rely heavily on the use of factorial designs (these are so called because the independent variables in experiments are commonly called 'factors'). Factorial designs enable large gains in efficiency, i.e., smaller sample sizes than would otherwise be needed. Essentially, the efficiency gains come about by analysing multiple variables' effects on the dependent variable in one designed experiment, on one set of data, designed so that each variable can be analysed on the whole data but independently of the other variables.

A full factorial design enables the effects of all variables, and all their interactions, to be estimated and tested. Interactions are when the effect of one variable is contingent on the value of another variable (so that the variables are not independent and additive in their effect on the response). In most (but not all) discrete choice experiments a fractional factorial design is used. In fractional factorial designs certain interactions are assumed to be negligible, so do not need to be included in the model, estimated or tested for. These assumed zero interactions are pre-specified by the experimenter and then determine the design. By dropping them from consideration, a smaller size of experiment, in terms of the number of combinations of variable values set, can be determined. This can be important in tourism discrete choice experiments, as otherwise the number of options respondents have to choose from can be too large to be reasonable. For example, in Albaladejo-Pina and Díaz-Delfa's (2009) study of tourist preferences for rural house stays in a region of Spain, the variables included type of building (four types), location (town or orchard or mountain or village), number of bedrooms, price (four levels) and ten other variables (each of two levels). There are hundreds of thousands of combinations of the levels, and hence alternatives, which need to be drastically reduced to get reasonable choice sets for presentation to respondents.

Fractional factorial designs are most useful when there are a relatively large number of explanatory variables to be investigated and the aim is to economically consider the effects of them all, at the expense of some ambiguity around interaction effects, as contrasted with a more in-depth analysis of a few variables in a scientific experiment seeking to establish cause and effect (Cox, 1958, p. 258). They are thus appropriate for the types of economic studies they have been used in tourism research (as in the studies referenced in this chapter).

In the application of these designs in tourism, nearly all published studies are designed to allow only estimation and testing of the 'main effects' of the variables; that is all interactions, or occasionally all but a very few interactions, are assumed negligible (an exception is Morley (1994b)). This is due to a combination of the number of variables (factors) it is wanted to include in the design, the number of levels (values) of these variables, and the number of times a respondent can be asked to make a choice before data quality degrades. This latter number is often held to be quite small (most reported studies keep it to a single digit: Morley (1994b) in his study of three price variables impacts on the choice of Sydney as a destination of Malaysian tourists uses 12), but Hensher et al. (2001) in an analysis of the choices of airline and ticket class for flight between Australia and New Zealand argue that, and provide some evidence for, 16 being reasonable and 32 quite feasible.

The issue of which interactions are confounded and assumed negligible in assessing main effects is not always made clear in the published reports of such experiments, although it would be useful to readers and users of such research if this was spelt out. For example, Lindberg et al. (1999) in their exploration of the trade-offs Danish residents are prepared to make in tourism's impacts on them appear to use a 1/16 fraction of a 4^4 experiment, which would necessitate some two factor interactions being confounded with some main effects, but which are not clarified in the paper.

Fractional designs can be designed to ensure that each alternative occurs equally often, and equally often with each other alternative, in the data. This enables each variable's effect to be estimated independently of other variables. It is recommended practice to always include a base option in every choice set presented to respondents. In the model, dummy variables can indicate the presence or not of an alternative in a particular choice set, so referring back to a common base is useful. The base alternative should be one that is likely to be relatively unpopular, to avoid it dominating the choices and hence the data not having sufficient frequencies for the other alternatives for efficient estimation, whilst at the same time it is helpful if it is meaningful as a reference point.

APPLICATIONS TO TOURISM

The obvious applications of discrete choice methods are in demand modelling, and especially in assessing the impact of potentially explanatory variables on demand. This then gives useful results for marketing, forecasting, planning and policy evaluation and development, and other decision making by operators. For example, the technique has been used to estimate visitors' willingness to pay for attractions and substitution rates, that is the rate at which people will trade-off less of one attribute for more of another attribute, for a particular destination (e.g., Sardinia; Brau, 2008) or attraction (e.g., Yanchep caves; Tapsuwan, 2010). Other applications range widely from analysing various price effects on demand for a single destination from one origin (e.g., demand for Sydney from Kuala Lumpur in Morley, 1994b) through wider investigations of demand across combinations of origins and destinations (and types of destinations), to ecotourism preferences (Chaminuka et al.'s 2011 study of Kruger National Park visitors). The potential explanatory variables used are driven by the purpose of the investigation, and vary widely in the reported studies. The papers in the tourism literature cited in this chapter provide many different examples of the use of this attractive and valuable technique.

Revealed preference data modelling is more usual in marketing (Baltas and Doyle, 2001), but in tourism applications stated preference data from choice experiments is more common. Revealed preference analyses in tourism are not unknown, for example Eymann and Ronning (1997) who analysed tourists' choice of destination (at a regional level), Nicolau and Más (2006) who considered the moderating role motivations played in the impacts of price and distance on destination choices, and Nicolau (2010) in an analysis of how cultural interest moderates price impacts on destination choice. The not uncommon practice in analyses of revealed preference data of dropping from the analysis infrequent visitors and less popular alternatives, due to problems in estimation on sparse and incomplete data, will induce a bias in the results.

One common aspect of the reporting of results is worth noting. The standard R^2 measure from regression is not applicable in the discrete choice case and the pseudo-R^2 measures used are less intuitively informative. It is not difficult for a model to be a significant improvement on a null model, in log-likelihood terms. It would be good practice to report on the fitness of the model in terms of the (in-sample) percentages of predicted choices made correctly by the model (for each actual choice category). At present this is not common practice, but it is recommended statistically.

ADVANTAGES AND LIMITATIONS OF THE TECHNIQUES

Econometric modelling using time series data is not always able to estimate effectively the independent effects of variables. Taking prices as an example, the observed price series are jointly determined by underlying variables such as taxation, inflation, costs of inputs and wages and there is therefore strong multicollinearity amongst price series. In discrete choice experiments the data comes from a designed experiment, which allows variations in conditions and scenarios of interest to the researcher to be put to the respondents, even if these do not, cannot or have not been seen in reality. The responses (choices) to these pre-determined conditions are recorded, allowing estimation of effects not able to be estimated in other ways. For example the components of the tourist price variables can be made to vary independently in the experimental design, and hence their independent effects discerned, although in observed reality they are highly correlated. Additionally, analysis of actual measured demand at a certain combination of prices reveals little about the demand that could be expected at the time with a different combination of prices. Experimental data on individuals' responses to price variations can be collected from an experiment designed to circumvent these problems.

Another advantageous feature of discrete choice methods is that they utilize micro-level data on individuals, rather than aggregated demand numbers. They give data on, and hence enable modelling of, the actual decision-making processes of potential tourists. As a result a much more realistic demand model can be estimated, with independent variables such as actual age, income and race of individuals, and both actual hotel prices and CPI (e.g., Morley, 1994b) – one closer to the actual decisions around travelling or not, the choice of destination, etc., and closer to the actual decision-making process.

It is usual in tourism demand analysis to rely on data derived from direct observation and measurement of actual tourism behaviour or, at one remove, from surveys asking about tourism behaviour. There are obvious strong reasons for basing models of demand on data of this type. However, there are serious deficiencies in analysis of observational data for addressing certain types of questions. Analysis is restricted to variable ranges found to have existed in the past. Parameter estimates are conditional on these ranges and extrapolation to new conditions is of uncertain validity. For example, the impacts of very low air fares, well below previous air fares, could not be estimated prior to some airlines offering such fares, or the impact of a major new attraction on a destination's attractiveness prior to it opening. Further it is not uncommon to find that some variables of interest do not vary, or vary only minimally, over the revealed data period, so that the impact of these variables cannot be reliably estimated. As noted, multicollinearity amongst important variables is frequently found and this also calls into question the reliability of estimation of model parameters.

Surveys of tourists at their destinations provide useful data for tourism planning. Survey data has advantages such as its being available, often from large samples and generally reliable, and it measures what tourists actually do. However, surveys and experiments at destinations, and all observational data of demand, suffer from a selection bias as the information is conditional on the tourist choosing the destination and those tourists who chose other destinations, plus those individuals who chose not to tour, are excluded. The samples of respondents cannot be representative of potential travellers to the destination, as those who might have chosen the destination under some circumstances, but did not under the existing circumstances, are excluded from the sample. The decision-making processes of those individuals excluded are important for demand and policy analysis. For such purposes, it is therefore necessary to go a step back and gather data on potential tourists in their origins.

Stated preference methods allow the researcher to focus on the individual's decision-making process directly, putting questions in a behavioural context of choice. The context is a simulated one in which the alternatives presented are pre-determined by the experimental design, but within that the question is put in a behavioural form such as 'which would you choose, given these options?', for example, which specific airline would you choose to go on holiday to Japan from options defined by fare, quality of food, leg room and limousine pickup service availability. This form concentrates on discrete choice as simulating the actual decision-making process of the potential tourist. For this reason, and because the task facing the respondent is easier and better understood, it is to be expected that choice data will give better results than ranking or preference ratings data (Hensher et al., 1988; Louviere, 1988). The alternatives presented in the simulations are designed by the researcher and respondents are asked to state their choice from a number of sets of alternatives. The researcher can control the alternatives presented for consideration, tailoring them to address the issues important to the particular research objectives and ensuring variables range over a suitable field. Multiple observations are gained from each respondent, and with appropriate design an experiment can be framed to obtain data in an efficient manner.

The major potential deficiency of stated choice data is that respondents are stating what they would do in certain simulated, somewhat artificial conditions, and this is perhaps not the same as what they actually do, or would do, in reality. There is evidence, from other contexts, of bias in such data, which makes absolute demand estimation problematical. However, as long as respondents can reasonably evaluate the alternatives proffered for their choice the relative utility weights which are the focus of the stated choice models can be estimated without bias. Stated choice data can be used to frame useful models which can be straightforwardly rescaled using observational data to estimate actual demand levels (Kroes and Sheldon, 1988). Discrete choice experiments have been found to give good predictions and fits to actual market shares (Louviere, 1988; Louviere and Woodworth, 1983) in areas such as modelling modal choices (e.g., for long distance inter-city travel: Koppelman and Sethi, 2005), and consumer goods brand choice (such studies abound, see as a starting point references in Baltas and Doyle, 2001).

The experimental design uses strict control over institutional rules to reduce the error in testing well defined hypotheses framed in terms of the variables. The sample can be randomly chosen from a defined population which fixes the external environment and enables statistical inference from the sample to the population. Further inference from the population sampled to other populations may be hazarded on the less scientific, but not uncommon, basis of analogy between populations. In an appropriately designed experiment, respondent individuals can be placed in choice contexts which satisfy orthogonality of the factors and allow independent estimation of parameters for the factor variables. To achieve these desirable features for the analysis it is necessary to carefully design and conduct the experiment, in contrast to the lesser emphasis on design considerations in observational studies.

A powerful property of logit (and probit) models is that they have been found to be quite robust to misspecification of the error distribution, and to the omission of explanatory variables that are uncorrelated with the included explanatory variables (Cramer, 2007). In the latter case the estimated coefficients of the model may be biased by such a misspecification, but the effects of the variables on the dependent variable (e.g., the odds ratio) are not.

Many of the limitations of these choice models are being addressed in more complex models made possible in recent times due to advances in computing power. These are discussed in the following section.

FURTHER DEVELOPMENTS AND APPLICATIONS

The restrictive nature of the IIA property of the MNL model has led to efforts to develop models that relax the distributional assumptions that give rise to it. The most straightforward of these is the nested multinomial logit (NMNL) model. In this model, the choice is structured as a hierarchical, multi-stage process with similar alternatives grouped together and a choice amongst groups preceding the choice within the chosen group. The distributional assumptions and IIA property now only need to hold within each group, not across choices in different groups. This is readily extended to more than two stages (groups within groups). It does not require that the actual decision process is multi-staged, just that it is modelled that way to allow for correlations within groups. But the grouping of alternatives needs to be pre-determined by the analyst, and both the grouping and the ordering of the nesting can affect the results. For example, in an exercise modelling tourists' destination choices, classing destinations into (say) Europe or Asia, and then into adventure- or sun-based, will give different results to doing the adventure- or sun-based classification first and then the Europe or Asia grouping, even if the final sets of destinations are the same (Nevo, 2000). As the example suggests, this is not always a satisfactory feature as a hierarchy of classifications is often not obvious. Bresnahan et al. (1997) have put forward a technique that may alleviate this problem.

Further extensions of the MNL model allow alternatives to be, to various extents, in more than one group of the NMNL model (called 'generalized nested multinomial logit' in Koppelman and Sethi, 2005). The heteroskedastic MNL model relaxes the identically distributed errors assumption to allow for differences in the variances of the errors. Koppelman and Sethi (2005) have proposed a generalization of the MNL model that allows for heterogeneous errors, heterogeneous covariances also and flexibility in elasticities of substitution between alternatives (i.e., relaxing the IIA restriction as in nested logit models). This results in a version of the MNL (called the heterogeneous generalized nested logit model: HGNL) that allows for the variance–covariance matrix of the errors to be quite general (not restricted to independent or constant variances) but which is still computationally feasible without resort to numerical integration.

Alternatively, the multinomial probit model allows for the heterogeneity of the HGNL model in a conceptually simpler and more appealing manner (normally distributed errors with a general variance–covariance matrix), but at the price of computational difficulties. The probit model has generally been confined in practice to analysing binary choices, due to the problems of computing multinomial probit models (without the independence assumption, Equation (6.6) involves $m - 1$ integrals, where m is the number of alternatives). Recent simulation based methods can be used to approximate the complex integrals involved and open up the possibility of such models being tractable (Weeks, 1997). These techniques can relax the independence and homogeneity restrictions. Chaminuka et al.'s (2011) study of ecotourism in the Kruger National Park is a recent example with three alternatives (a status quo alternative of the current offering, plus two ecotourism alternatives defined in terms of accommodation location, price and availability, or not, of visits to craft markets and village tours). Larger MNP models are still difficult to implement, but are becoming possible.

Variations across individuals in preferences are most readily addressed by including in the models variables for individuals' characteristics (such as income, age, gender, previous visits) as main effects and in interaction with alternatives measures variables. The random coefficients (or mixed MNL) model allows the parameters (coefficients in β) to vary across individuals, to allow for differences in tastes. Again, this has become recently estimable in practice with simulation-based (numerical integration) methods (McFadden and Train, 2000; Nevo, 2000). Random coefficients models can be a good approximation to any discrete choice random utility model (McFadden and Train, 2000), hence they are becoming a popular applied technique. It has been noted that controlling for variation across individuals generally increases the observed impact of the other variables (Baltas and Doyle, 2001).

Rather than using the individual level data directly, an alternative approach is to model the observed frequencies of the choices, which requires using Weighted Least Squares (or, the arguably more efficient Feasible Generalised Least Squares – see an advanced econometrics text such as Greene, 2003). Morley (1994a) is a tourism application of this approach, which analysed the impacts of price components on Malaysians' choice of international destination for a holiday. Nevo (2000) expounds on random coefficients logit models estimated on frequencies (market share) data.

Further developments can be expected in the joint modelling of both discrete and continuous variables, such as the choice of destination and time spent there, or the modelling of spending at a resort (which is zero if the resort is not chosen, but has a range of positive values if it is chosen). Alegre et al. (2011) in their study of the length of stay of tourists in the Balearic Islands have made a start in this direction with a binary logit model for the choice coupled with a Poisson distributed length of stay. The multinomial tobit model can be applied and the simulation-based techniques of likely value in the MNP case are just as likely to be of value here. The multinomial tobit has not yet been applied in tourism, but there is room for it to be considered.

Later developments in modelling techniques have increased in complexity and the estimation and use of these models' results is more difficult. Such models may also be less robust than the simple, tried and tested forms. These trade-offs are yet to be determined.

The conduct of the choice experiments can be advanced through the use of streaming video and other information technology. The choices can be presented in more realistic, dynamic, visual and tailored ways than the static listing of attributes that has to date been the norm (Verma and Plaschka, 2003) who report that they have 'extensively used web-based technologies (with hyperlinked pictures or written illustrations, brand logos, and audio and video files) to realistically illustrate choice scenarios' (Verma and Plaschka, 2003, p. 160) although this raises further potential issues of extraneous variables in the presentation affecting the results.

Overall the combination of experimental design, stated preference data and discrete choice models form a powerful body of techniques for analysis of tourism demand. Often general descriptive results, such as the significance of particular explanatory variables and differences between segments of tourists defined by demographic variables, are apparent from simple data analysis using contingency tables and aggregate level logit modelling. This is because a lot of analytic power comes from the experimental protocols and design. The more sophisticated choice models derived from discrete choice theory quantify the impact of variables for detailed policy analysis, strategic market planning and economic analysis.

REFERENCES

Albaladejo-Pina, I.P. and M.T. Díaz-Delfa (2009), 'Tourist preferences for rural house stays: evidence from discrete choice modelling in Spain', *Tourism Management*, **30**, 805–811.

Alegre, J., S. Mateo and L. Pou (2011), 'A latent class approach to tourists' length of stay', *Tourism Management*, **32**, 555–563.

Baltas, G. and P. Doyle (2001), 'Random utility models in marketing research: a survey', *Journal of Business Research*, **51**, 115–125.

Brau, R. (2008), 'Demand-driven sustainable tourism? A choice modelling analysis', *Tourism Economics*, **14**, 691–708.

Bresnahan, T., S. Stern and M. Trajtenberg (1997), 'Market segmentation and the sources of rents from innovation: personal computers in the late 1980s', *RAND Journal of Economics*, **28**, S17–S44.

Chaminuka, P., R.A. Groenveld, A.O. Sleomane and E.C van Ierland (2011), 'Tourist preferences for ecotourism in rural communities adjacent to Kruger National park: a choice experiment approach', *Tourism Management*, doi:10.1016/j.tourman.2011.02.016.

Cox, D.R. (1958), *Planning of Experiments*, New York: Wiley.

Cramer, J.S. (2007), 'Robustness of logit analysis: unobserved heterogeneity and mis-specified disturbances', *Oxford Bulletin of Economics and Statistics*, **69**, 545–555.

Eymann, A. and G. Ronning (1997), 'Microeconomic models of tourists' destination choice', *Regional Science and Urban Economics*, **27**, 735–761.

Greene, W.H. (2003), *Econometric Analysis*, 5th edition, New Jersey: Prentice Hall.

Hausman, J. and D. McFadden (1984), 'Specification tests for the multinomial logit model', *Econometrica*, **52**, 1219–1240.

Hensher, D.A., P.O. Barnard and P.T. Truong (1988), 'The role of stated preference methods in studies of travel choice', *Journal of Transport Economics and Policy*, **22**, 45–58.

Hensher, D.A. and L.W. Johnson (1981), *Applied Discrete Choice Modelling*, London and New York: Halstead Press.

Hensher, D.A., P.R. Stopher and J.J. Louviere (2001), 'An exploratory analysis of the effect of numbers of choice sets in designed choice experiments: an airline choice application', *Journal of Air Transport Management*, **7**, 373–379.

Koppelman, F.S. and V. Sethi (2005), 'Incorporating variance and covariance heterogeneity in the Generalized Nested Logit model: an application to modelling long distance travel choice behaviour', *Transportation Research Part B*, **39**, 825–853.

Kroes, E.P. and R.J. Sheldon (1988), 'Stated preference methods: an introduction', *Journal of Transport Economics and Policy*, **22**, 11–25.

Lindberg, K., B. Dellaert and C.R. Rassing (1999), 'Resident tradeoffs: a choice modelling approach', *Annals of Tourism Research*, **26**, 554–569.

Louviere, J.J. (1988), 'Conjoint analysis modelling of stated preferences', *Journal of Transport Economics and Policy*, **22**, 93–119.

Louviere, J.J. and H. Timmermans (1990), 'Stated preference and choice models applied to recreation research: a review', *Leisure Sciences*, **20**, 9–23.

Louviere, J.J. and G. Woodworth (1983), 'Design and analysis of simulated consumer choice or allocation experiments: an approach based on aggregate data', *Journal of Marketing Research*, **20**, 350–367.

Manski, C.F. and D.L. McFadden (1981), *Structural Analysis of Discrete Data with Econometric Applications*, Cambridge MA: MIT Press.

McFadden, D. and K. Train (2000), 'Mixed MNL models for discrete response', *Journal of Applied Econometrics*, **15**, 447–470.

McFadden, D.L. (1984), 'Econometric analysis of qualitative response models', in Z. Griliches and M.D. Intriligator (eds), *Handbook of Econometrics*, Volume II, Amsterdam: Elsevier Science Publishers, pp. 1395–1457.

Morley, C.L. (1992), 'A micro-economic theory of international tourism demand', *Annals of Tourism Research*, **19**, 250–267.

Morley, C.L. (1994a), 'Discrete choice analysis of the impact of tourism prices', *Journal of Travel Research*, **33** (2), 8–14.

Morley, C.L. (1994b), 'Experimental destination choice analysis', *Annals of Tourism Research*, **21** (4), 780–791.

Nevo, A. (2000), 'A practitioner's guide to estimation of random-coefficients logit models of demand', *Journal of Economics and Management Strategy*, **9**, 513–548.

Nicolau, J.L. (2010), 'Differentiated price loss aversion in destination choice: the effect of tourists' cultural interest', *Tourism Management*, doi:10.1016/j.tourman.2010.11.002.

Nicolau, J.L. and F.J. Más (2006), 'The influence of distance and prices on the choice of tourist destinations: the moderating role of motivations', *Tourism Management*, **27**, 982–996.

Sheldon, P.J. and J. Mak (1987), 'The demand for package tours: a mode choice model', *Journal of Travel Research*, **25**, 13–40.

Tapsuwan, S. (2010), 'A multivariate probit analysis of willingness to pay for cave conservation: a case study of Yanchep National Park, Western Australia', *Tourism Economics*, **16**, 1019–1035.

Verma, R. and G. Plaschka (2003), 'The art and science of customer-choice modelling: reflections, advances and managerial implications', *Cornell Hotel and Restaurant Administration Quarterly*, **44**, 156–165.

Weeks, M. (1997), 'The multinomial probit model revisited: a discussion of parameter estimability, identification and specification testing', *Journal of Economic Surveys*, **11**, 297–320.

Witt, S.F. (1980), 'An abstract mode – abstract (destination) node model of foreign holiday demand', *Applied Economics*, **12**, 163–180.

Witt, S.F. (1983), 'A binary choice model of foreign holiday demand', *Journal of Economic Studies*, **10**, 46–59.

7 Panel data analysis
Neelu Seetaram and Sylvain Petit

INTRODUCTION

Panel data sets are also known as longitudinal data or cross-sectional time series data. They have spatial (N) and temporal (T) dimensions. They constitute of a number of observations over time on a number of cross-sectional units such as individuals, firms, and countries allowing researchers to analyse the dynamics of change in short time series data. According to Baltes and Nesselroade (1979), longitudinal data and techniques involve "a variety of methods connected by the idea that the entity under investigation is observed repeatedly as it exists and evolves over time". These methods have been applied in different research disciplines. Frees (2004) posits that they have developed because important databases have become available to empirical researchers.

The term panel data was introduced by Lazarsfeld and Fiske (1938, in Frees 2004) in their study of the effect of the relationship between radio advertising and product sales, where they proposed to interview a 'panel' of consumer over time. Toon (2000 in Frees 2004), acknowledges Engel's 1857 budget surveys as the earliest application of longitudinal data. In this survey Engel collected data on the expenditure pattern from the same set of subjects over a period time. The aim was to study expenditure on food as a function of income. Panel data modelling and estimation techniques were developed in the second half of the twentieth century. Early applications of this technique are those of Kuh (1959), Johnson (1960), Mundlak (1961) and Hoch (1962) who used the fixed effect models (explained later in the text) and Balestra and Nerlove (1966) and Wallace and Hussain (1969) who used the random effect models (explained later in the text).

This chapter focuses on the application of panel data techniques in the tourism literature. The chapter is organized as follows. The next section explains panel data modelling technique emphasizing the difference between fixed and random effects. Dynamism in modelling is introduced and the implication for model estimation is discussed. The chapter then devotes a section to unit root and cointegration tests which is followed by an illustration of the application of panel data analysis in tourism research, namely, in tourism demand modelling and in explorations of the relationship between tourism and economic growth. The conclusion spells out the limitations of this technique and directions for future research.

PANEL DATA MODELLING TECHNIQUES AND BENEFITS

Panel data analysis offers several advantages. The most obvious is that inferences are performed using a larger sample and the lack of degrees of freedom is fairly unlikely to occur. According to Baltagi (2005), more complex relationships can be modelled, for example temporal changes in cross-section can be analysed. One of the most important advantages, however, is that panel data modelling allows for the control of heterogeneity in the sample.

A standard approach to model the relationship between Y (dependent variable) and X, a set of explanatory variables, is given below where ε_{it} is the stochastic error term which takes into account the variation in the expected value of Y which cannot be explained by the Xs.

$$y_{it} = x'_{it}\beta_i + \varepsilon_{it} \qquad (7.1)$$

For example in a tourism demand model, Y can stand for the number of arrivals to a particular destination while the Xs include factors affecting demand, such as income in the home country, relative prices, marketing expenditure, transportation cost and so on. The Xs or explanatory variables can be included in the model so long as they are observable and measurable. There are, however, factors such as culture and other unique characteristics of the individuals or groups under study which are not observable or measurable but which influence the outcome of expected Y. These factors are referred to as the heterogeneity and are not directly part of Equation (7.1). The effect is incorporated in the one of the βs, should they be correlated with the respective X or otherwise included in ε_{it}. As a result, in the first case, the estimated β will not reveal the true effect of the variation in X on expected Y. By modelling the relationship between X and Y, using the panel data technique, the researcher is able to separate the effect of the heterogeneity from that of β.

Suppose K number of subjects are observed over time. The response of subject Y_{1t} will tend to be similar to responses in previous years but different to the rest $Y_{2t}, Y_{3t} \ldots$ $Y_{k-1,t}$. That is, there is uniqueness in the behaviour of this subject and this is assumed to be constant over time. The uniqueness of Y_1 can be attributed to factors such as culture, and past experience (for a person) business practices, (for a firm), history, or system of government (for a country). For example, the cultural and historical links that Australia and the UK share may be expected to promote international tourism flows between the two countries. In this respect, tourism flows to Australia from the UK are expected to be influenced by factors which are unique to travellers from this source and not pertinent for travellers from other home countries. In a panel data model, the uniqueness of each market in the sample is captured by μ_i which is the unobserved heterogeneity in the sample as given in Equation (7.2) below.

$$y_{it} = \mu_i + x'_{it}\beta_i + \varepsilon_{it} \qquad (7.2)$$

The additional benefit of including μ_i in the model is that it offers a potential solution to the problem of omitted variables and measurement errors in data. Lack of data is the most common problem faced by researchers. In regression analysis, it often results in the omission of relevant variables from the model. This may give rise to potential model specification errors for example, due to difficulties in obtaining data on marketing expenditure, this variable is often omitted from tourism demand model, although a priori, it is expected to be relevant in explaining demand.

Consider Equation (7.3), where Y_{it} is determined by three variables.

$$y_{it} = \beta_1 x_{1it} + \beta_2 x_{2it} + \beta_3 x_{3it} + \varepsilon_{it} \tag{7.3}$$

omitting x_3 from the model will reduce Equation (7.3) to Equation (7.4), where the effect of X_3 is dampened by the ε_{it}. The actual model estimated is

$$y_{it} = \beta_1 x_{1it} + \beta_2 x_{2it} + \beta_3 x_{3it} + u_{it} \tag{7.4}$$

where $u_{it} = x_{3t} + \varepsilon_{it}$.

In this case the residuals include the effect of x_{3t} and will display patterns leading to the conclusion that the model may be suffering from serial correlation (Green, 1999). The implications for the $\hat{\beta}$s will depend on whether the X_{it}s are correlated with X_{3t}. If so, the estimated coefficients will be biased. If on the other hand, the covariance between X_{3t} and the X_{it}s is equal to zero, $\hat{\beta}$s will be unbiased and consistent. According to Wooldridge (2002), the panel data modelling technique offers an effective solution to this problem. The inclusion of μ_i in Equation (7.4) will solve the problem as it will absorb the effect of X_{3t}. This solution is also applicable when measurement errors are present in the data.

Taking the example of tourism model, Seetaram (2010b) explains the complexities that arise when faced with the computation of airfare elasticities. Airfare data are often plagued with measurement errors which arise mainly because of the wide array of airfares and travel class categories which are prevalent in the market. This makes the task of the researcher complex as often no choice is left but to use an average airfare to represent the transportation cost to the destination. Average airfare is not always a good representation of actual airfare. Suppose that airfare, x_{3t} is measured with errors such that the actual variable which is included in the model is $x_{3t}^* = x_{3t} + v_t$. The model estimated is given by:

$$y_t = \beta_1 x_1 + \beta_2 x_2 + \beta_3 x_{3t}^* + \eta_{it} \tag{7.5}$$

where $\eta_{it} = \varepsilon_{it} + v_t$.

In Equation (7.5), the stochastic error term is given by η_t. The cov $(\eta_i, x_{3t}^*) = -\beta\delta_v^2$ where δ_v^2 is the variance of the measurement error (Green, 1999). This violates the crucial assumption of non-correlation between any explanatory variable and the residuals of the equation (Green, 1999). As a consequence, all the Ordinary Least Squares (OLS) estimators, $\hat{\beta}$s will be biased and inconsistent and $\hat{\beta}_3$ will be attenuated. If instead the relationship between Y and the explanatory variables are modelled using the format of Equation (7.2), the measurement errors, v_t, will be absorbed by the unobserved heterogeneity μ_i leaving ε_{it} free from its effect.

Fixed Effect and Random Effects

There are two ways of modeling μ_i, namely the fixed and random effect. The choice between these two depends on whether μ_i is correlated to any of the other explanatory variables of the model (Wooldridge, 2002). Equation (7.2) is formulated using the fixed effect (FE) technique. This method assumes that the heterogeneity in the model is μ_i time invariant and specific to the individual group. In Equation (7.2), the slopes are fixed but the intercepts vary for each cross section. This is equivalent to adding a dummy specific for each cross section which is why it is also referred to as the Least Square Dummy

Variable (LSDV) method. The slopes are treated as constant across group and across time. It is however, possible to allow the slope to vary across groups, across time or both (Hsiao, 2003). The rationale behind this modelling approach is that since μ_i accounts for time invariant characteristics of the group, it removes the pernicious effect of omitted variables (Allison, 2005). Fixed effect is often chosen as a precaution against omitted variable bias. The drawback is that μ_i cannot be used to assess the effect of characteristics which change overtime.

The FE technique explores the relationship between explanatory and dependent variables within one individual group. For each group, the variations of the all variables from their mean values are considered and the estimated coefficients are also known as the within estimates. This can be a limitation of the FE method as in-between variations are ignored. Furthermore, only the effect of variables with sufficient variability can be analysed. For example, in a longitudinal study of an individual tourist's perception of the quality of destination attributes, the effect of gender and ethnicity cannot be analysed. The modeller is expected to make a trade-off between sample variability and omitted variable bias (Allison, 2005). However, as explained before the effects of these time-invariant factors are controlled in the FE model. In circumstances when the in-between variation is not relevant, the FE model makes use of maximum information, yielding error terms with smaller variations (Allison, 2005). FE models may additionally include an error component which changes over time but not for each unit, τ_t. τ_t is treated as a constant in the model.

$$y_{it} = x'_{it}\beta + \mu_i + \tau_t + \varepsilon_{it} \tag{7.6}$$

Taking the example of the tourist demand model, consider a sample which includes arrivals from ten sources over a period of 10 years. The aim is the find the income and price elasticities of demand. Each market is a group in the sample. μ_{uk} will take into account all characteristics of the UK other than price and income that will influence arrivals to Australia. The UK as a market has certain characteristics which may or may not influence income and relative prices in the country. For example, μ_i can stand for system of government, democracy, which may or may not be related to income level in the UK. However, in the instant that there exists such a relationship, then the inclusion of μ_i controls for the effect of democracy and allows the estimation of the net effect of income on number of arrivals from the UK. The FE technique also assumes that μ is unique to the UK and is not correlated to the characteristics of other countries in the sample. Any correlations between μ_{uk} and μ_{usa} are ignored.

If, however, the μ_i's are correlated to one another and to the error terms of other groups, the resulting variance will be high making statistical inference dubious. A better approach in this case will be to use the random effect (RE) technique. In the RE approach, variation across entities is assumed to be random and uncorrelated with independent variables in the model. The RE model is given as

$$y_{it} = x'_{it}\beta + \mu_{it} + \tau_t + \varepsilon_{it} \tag{7.7}$$

μ_{it} is referred to as the between-group error. The advantage of RE is that since variation across the sample are considered, it permits the study of time invariant factors such as gender, ethnicity and race in the model. The RE method uses variations both within and between individuals and typically has less sampling variability than fixed effects methods (Allison, 2005). The problem, however, is that all relevant measurable variables need to be included in the model and data on a few may not be available therefore leading to omitted variable bias in the model.

The choice between FE and RE depends on whether μ_i is correlated to any of the other explanatory variables of the model (Wooldridge, 2002). When such a correlation exists, the fixed effect technique is superior. Otherwise, the random effect is more parsimonious and gives more efficient estimates (Wooldridge, 2002). A formal test for assessing the correlation between the unobserved heterogeneity and other explanatory variable is the Hausman (1978) specification test. In the tourism literature, the FE method has been more frequently applied since the groups under observations are often markets, or destinations which have characteristics which influence the other explanatory variables of the model. The rest of the chapter will focus on the FE modelling method.

Dynamic Panel Data Models

By nature, all panel data models are dynamic since they take into account the time series dimension of the sample. However, functions which specifically model the effect of lagged dependent variables are referred to as dynamic panel data models. A general dynamic panel data model with FE effect is given as Equation (7.8) below.

$$y_{it} = \gamma_i y_{i,t-1} + \beta_0 + x'_{ikt}\beta_k + \mu_i + \varepsilon_{it} \tag{7.8}$$

It is assumed that:

1. $\mu_i \sim (N, \sigma_\mu^2)$ and $\varepsilon_{it} \sim (N, \sigma_\varepsilon^2)$ where $\sigma_\mu^2 \geq 0$ and $\sigma_\varepsilon^2 > 0$
2. The explanatory variables are strictly exogenous, that is they are not correlated with the error terms. i.e., $E(\varepsilon_{it}\,\varepsilon_{js}) = 0$ for $i \neq j$ or $t \neq s$
3. The unobserved heterogeneity, if it is present, is random. i.e., $E(\mu_i\,\mu_j) = 0$ for $i \neq j$
4. The unobserved heterogeneity is uncorrelated within the countries and with the error i.e., $E(\mu_i\,\varepsilon_{js}) = 0$ for $\forall\ i, j, t, s$
5. The explanatory variables are strictly exogenous, that is they are not correlated with the error terms. i.e., $E(x_{it}\,\varepsilon_{js}) = 0$ for $\forall\ i, j, t$
6. The unobserved heterogeneity are correlated with the predetermined variables i.e., $E(x_{it}\,\mu_j) = 0$ for $\forall\ i, j, t$
7. γ_{i0} is uncorrelated with the error term i.e., $E(\gamma_{i0}\,\varepsilon_{jt}) = 0$ for $\forall\ i, j, t$
8. γ_{i0} can be correlated with the unobserved heterogeneity. i.e., $E\,(\gamma_{i0}\,\mu_j) =$ unknown for $\forall\ i, j$

Dynamic panel data analysis is becoming increasingly popular in the tourism literature modeling. In tourism demand model, γ_i accounts for destination loyalty and repeat visitations. It takes into account the extent to which current visits are dependent on the number of past visits. It takes into account the effect of habit persistence in demand and the extent to which consumer react to *ex-post* information available. γ_i is an indication of the efficiency of information diffusion through word-of-mouth.

Generally, the functional form utilized for Equation (7.8) is that of double logarithm implying that the $\hat{\beta}$s are the short term elasticities. The long term elasticities the long term elasticities $\hat{\beta}^*$ may be obtained by

$$\hat{\beta}^* = \frac{\hat{\beta}}{1 - \gamma} \qquad (7.9)$$

The most widely used estimation technique for dynamic panel data sets in the tourism literature has been has been the Arellano Bond (1991). Examples of studies which have applied this technique are Garín-Muños (2006), Khadaroo and Seetanah (2007) and Eugenio-Martín et al. (2004).

Estimation Technique

Estimating $\hat{\beta}$ using standard LSDV method yields biased and inconsistent estimators. $\hat{\beta}_{\text{LSDV}}$ estimator, also referred to as the covariance estimator, is given by:

$$\hat{\beta}_{\text{LSDV}} = \left[\sum_{i=0}^{N} \sum_{t=1}^{T} (x_{it} - \bar{x}_{it})(x_{it} - \bar{x}_{it})' \right]^{-1} \left[\sum_{i=0}^{N} \sum_{t=1}^{T} (x_{it} - \bar{x}_{it})(y_{it} - \bar{y}_{it})' \right] \qquad (7.10)$$

where $\bar{y}_{it} = 1/T\Sigma_{t=1}^{T} y_{it}$ and $\bar{x} = 1/T\Sigma_{t=1}^{T} x_{it}$, and $\hat{\beta}_{\text{LSDV}}$ is the estimated true coefficient of the exogenous variable x_{it}, $\bar{x}_{it}$ and $\bar{y}_{it}$ are the mean of x_{it} and y_{it} respectively. $\hat{\beta}_{\text{LSDV}}$ will be biased and inconsistent unless $T \rightarrow \infty$ (Anderson and Hsiao, 1981; Arellano and Bond, 1991; Judson and Owen, 1999; Kiviet, 1995; Nickell, 1981). This occurs because in Equation (7.8), y_{it-1} will be correlated with the mean of the stochastic error term models $\bar{\varepsilon}_{it}$ by construction and will be correlated to ε_{it-1} which is contained in $\bar{\varepsilon}_{it}$ (Hsiao, 2003).

Anderson and Hsiao (AH) (1981) and Arellano and Bond (AB) (1991) show that the bias may be reduced by first differencing Equation (7.8) and using the lagged level values of the y_{it} as instruments. Consider Equation (7.11) below which is similar to Equation (7.8) but for simplicity, the vector of exogenous variables x is left out.

$$y_{it} = \gamma y_{it-1} + \mu_i + \varepsilon_{it} \qquad (7.11)$$

$$i = 1, 2 \ldots N, t = 1, 2 \ldots T$$

μ_i is the fixed effect which is the cause of the bias in the estimation by LSDV. To eliminate μ_i, Anderson and Hsiao (1981) suggest that first difference transformation be applied to Equation (7.11). First differencing Equation (7.11) gives the following:

$$(y_{it} - y_{it-1}) = \gamma(y_{it-1} - y_{it-2}) + (\varepsilon_{it} - \varepsilon_{it-1}) \qquad (7.12)$$

$$i = 1, 2 \ldots N, t = 1, 2 \ldots T$$

Equation (7.12) is a first difference autoregressive process of order one with no exogenous regressors. $\Delta y_{it-1} = (y_{it-1} - y_{it-2})$, is correlated with the error $(\varepsilon_{it} - \varepsilon_{it-1})$. The second lag y_{it-2}, and the first difference of this second lag, $\Delta y_{it-2} = (y_{it-2} - y_{it-3})$, are possible instruments, since they are both correlated with $(y_{it-1} - y_{it-2})$ but are uncorrelated with $(\varepsilon_{it} - \varepsilon_{it-1})$, as long as the ε_{it} themselves are not serially correlated (Anderson and Hsiao, 1981). Using the second lag and the first difference of this second lag as instrumental variables, two estimators $\hat{\gamma}_{IV}$ and $\hat{\gamma}^*_{IV}$ can be developed. These are given in (7.13) and (7.14).

$$\hat{\gamma}_{IV} = \frac{\displaystyle\sum_{i=1}^{N}\sum_{t=3}^{T}(y_{it} - y_{it-1})(y_{it-2} - y_{it-3})}{\displaystyle\sum_{i=1}^{N}\sum_{t=3}^{T}(y_{it-1} - y_{it-2})(y_{it-2} - y_{it-3})} \tag{7.13}$$

$$\hat{\gamma}^*_{IV} = \frac{\displaystyle\sum_{i=1}^{N}\sum_{t=2}^{T}(y_{it} - y_{it-1})y_{it-2}}{\displaystyle\sum_{i=1}^{N}\sum_{t=2}^{T}(y_{it-1} - y_{it-2})y_{it-2}} \tag{7.14}$$

These estimators are consistent when $N \to \infty$ or $T \to \infty$ or both. AB argue that more efficient estimators can be obtained by taking in additional instruments whose validity is based on orthogonality between lagged values of the dependent variable y_{it} and the errors ε_{it}. These results are confirmed by Kiviet (1995) and Judson and Owen (1999). However the bias persists in samples with small T (Kiviet, 1995; Judson and Owen, 1999). In fact it increases with the value γ and decreases with T (Kiviet, 1995). An estimator that relies on lags as instruments under the assumption of white noise errors will lose its consistency if the errors are serially correlated (Kiviet, 1995).

Using simulations to generate data, Judson and Owen (1999) performed an exercise with a panel of varying size. The number of cross sections, N, takes the value of 20 or 100 and the number of time periods, T, is given the values of 5, 10, 20 or 30. Judson and Owen (1999) show that although the value of the bias falls as T increases, it is nevertheless still considerable at $T = 30$ and can be as high as 20 per cent of the true value of the parameter. They prove that estimates resulting from the AB technique have higher variances than the LSDV estimators supporting earlier results of Kiviet (1995).

LSDV estimates are more efficient than any other class of estimates developed for autoregressive panel data models (Judson and Owen, 1999; Kiviet, 1995). The removal of the bias in LSDV estimates opens the possibility of obtaining more robust estimates (Kiviet, 1995). Kiviet (1995) evaluated the bias in the true parameters based on a Monte Carlo study and developed a method to correct for potential bias in the estimated parameters when the true parameters are known. On a practical level, however, true parameters are seldom known, in which case Kiviet (1995) suggests that estimates be obtained using the techniques proposed by AH (1981) and AB (1991). These estimates can then be corrected for the bias by applying the Kiviet (1995) corrected LSDV (CLSDV) method. This method is only applicable to balanced samples – samples which contain the same number of observations for each cross section. In the tourism literature, authors such as Cortés-Jiménez (2008) in her study of regional tourism in Spain and Italy and Soukiazis and Proença (2008) examining regional tourism in Portugal have employed this technique.

Unit Root and Cointegration Tests

Classical statistical inferences rely on data being mean reverting. However, economic variables which tend to evolve over time are not always stationary and failure to account for this will result in spurious regression results. To circumvent such problems, unit roots are carried out to ascertain that regression results are valid. However, while testing for unit root is standard in the time series literature, it is quite recent in panel data (Baltagi, 2005). In the tourism literature although not very common, the availability of samples with fairly large time dimensions has resulted in more testing for unit root in the panel data set up, for example, Lee and Chang (2008) in a study of tourism development and economic growth and Seetaram (2010a, 2012) in the context of Australian outbound tourism.

In the panel data setup, panel unit roots tests have higher power than unit root tests based on individual time series for each of the cross section, since the later performs poorly when data periods are short (Baltagi, 2005; Banerjee, 1999; Banerjee et al., 2004; Levin et al., 2002; Im et al., 2003 and Pedroni, 1999). Several tests for unit roots in panel data have been developed. A few examples are Choi (2001), Breitung (2000) and Maddala and Wu (1999). According to Baltagi (2005), however, the two most efficient tests for stationarity in a panel data setting are Levin, Lin and Chu (hereafter LLC, 2002) and Im et al. (hereafter IPS, 2003). The fundamental difference between these two tests rests on the assumption made regarding the autoregressive process (Baltagi, 2005):

1. LLC assumes that the autoregressive process is common for all cross sections, that is $\rho = \rho_i$ in Equation (7.15) give below.
2. IPS assumes that the persistence parameter, ρ_i is allowed to vary across the cross sections.

Both tests are based on estimating the following equation:

$$\Delta y_{it} = \rho_i y_{it-1} + \sum_{j=1}^{z_i} \varphi_{ij} \Delta y_{it-j} + \varepsilon_{it} \tag{7.15}$$

y_{it} is the dependent variable being tested for unit root. Δ denotes the first difference in the dependent variable y_{it}. z_i is the number of lags to be included in the testing. ε_{it} are the error terms. ρ_i and φ_{ij} are parameters.

LLC assumes that the error term ε_{it} is independent across the units of the sample and have a fixed variance. LLC tests the hypothesis that each of the series in the panel contains a unit root against the hypothesis that all individual series are stationary. This can be written as:

H_0: $\rho = \rho_i = 0$ for all $i \sim$ *All of the individuals have a unit root.*

H_1: $\rho = \rho_i < 0$ for all $i \sim$ *All the individual series are stationary.*

The IPS test assumes that the panel is balanced. It hypothesizes that each of the series contains a unit root against the alternative hypothesis, that at least one of the series is stationary. These can be represented as follows:

H_0: $\rho_i = 0$ for all i. ~ *All the series have unit roots.*

H_1: $\begin{cases} \rho_i = 0 \text{ for } i = 1, 2, \ldots, N1 \\ \rho < 0 \text{ for } i = N + 1, N + 2, \ldots, N \end{cases}$ ~ *Some of the series have unit roots.*

are the cross sections in the panel data set. This method involves regressing the individual series for each of the cross sections. The critical value for the hypotheses is obtained by taking the average of the student t-statistics for the ρ_i from the individual regressions. This is given by:

$$\bar{t}_{NT} = \frac{\left(\sum_{i=t}^{N} t_{iT}(\rho_i) \right)}{N} \tag{7.16}$$

Series containing unit roots are non-stationary processes which have time-varying mean and variance that increases as sample size grows (Baltagi, 2005).

When variables are individually integrated of the same order, such as the ones in this study, a linear combination of these variables can still be stationary (Baltagi, 2005; Banerjee, 1999; Banerjee et al., 2004; Pedroni, 2004). If the series are found to be cointegrated then there must be at least one cointegrating vector which renders the combination of variables stationary. Furthermore, it implies that there is a long-run relationship among the variables.

The conventional cointegration tests suffer from low power when applied to samples with a small time dimension, such as the one used in this chapter (Baltagi, 2005; Banerjee, 1999; Banerjee et al., 2004 Pedroni, 2004). Panel cointegrating techniques have been developed to allow researchers to pool information regarding common long-run relationships from across the panel. In addition, such techniques allow the associated short-run dynamic and fixed effects to be heterogeneous across the different members of the panel (Baltagi, 2005; Banerjee, 1999; Banerjee et al., 2004; Pedroni, 1999, 2004). This chapter focuses on the Pedroni (1999) test as it is one of the most widely used tests for cointegration in panel data. The first step in this test is to estimate a cointegrating relationship with fixed effects and heterogeneous time trends for each of cross section of the study individually. Then the cointegration tests are performed based on the residuals obtained (Banerjee, 1999; Banerjee et al., 2004; Pedroni, 1999, 2004).

Pedroni (1999) proposes seven tests for cointegration in the panel data framework. Four of these tests are referred to as the *panel cointegrating statistics* or the *within-dimension based statistics* (Pedroni, 1999, p. 658). In these tests, he assumes that there is a common cointegrating relationship among the variables. For these four tests, the residuals are pooled across the time dimension of the panel. An autoregressive function is regressed and the autoregressive coefficient is given by υ_i. This method assumes that $\upsilon_i = \upsilon$, that is, it is common for all countries. The alternate hypothesis is that there is a cointegrating relationship for all the cross sections given as (Pedroni, 1999):

H_0: : $\upsilon = \upsilon_i = 1$ ~ *All of the individuals are not cointegrated*

H_0: : $\upsilon = \upsilon_i < 1$ ~ *All of the individuals are cointegrated*

By contrast, the remaining three tests are called the *group mean cointegrating statistics* or the between-dimension. These tests statistics are based on pooling the residuals of the regression along the cross sections of the panel (Pedroni, 1999). In these tests, estimators average the individually estimated autoregressive coefficient for each cross section (Pedroni, 1999). The hypotheses here are given by:

H_0:   : $\upsilon_i = 1$ ~ *All of the individuals are not cointegrated*

H_0:   : $\upsilon_i < 1$ ~ *All of the individuals are cointegrated*

The group mean statistics can be considered as more accurate, as they allow for more heterogeneity among the countries, and produce consistent estimates (Pedroni, 2001). The higher value of the group mean statistics can be considered to be a more accurate representation of the average long-run relationship (Pedroni, 2004).

It can be noted, however, that in general the unit root cointegration tests increase the probability of determining if data are stationary or not and whether they are cointegrated (Banerjee, 1999; Banerjee et al., 2004). However, one limitation of these tests is that they assume no cross-sectional correlation in the sample (Banerjee, 1999; Banerjee et al., 2004). Banerjee et al. (2004) showed that the results of cointegration tests were susceptible to dependence among the cross sections. This means that the power of the tests is reduced in cases where the cross sections are not independent. In spite of this, in panel data sets, the problem of spurious regression results is not expected to be as serious as in pure time series. As demonstrated by Phillips and Moon (2000), noise in time series regression is lessened by pooling cross-section and time series observations, implying that the model may be estimated in level form without risking spurious results.

APPLICATIONS OF PANEL DATA TECHNIQUES IN TOURISM DATA ANALYSIS

The empirical literature based on the panel data methods and applied to the tourism sector, can be divided into two broad areas. The first concerns the determinants of tourism demand. The topic of demand modelling is not recent and goes back to Rugg (1972). The study of international tourism arrivals and receipts is a vibrant area of research and it cannot be confined to gravity models due to factors such as seasonality, cultural links or time constraints which are particular to the consumption of tourism products. The second area consists mainly of analysis of the link between tourism and economic growth. Since, several destinations, for example, Spain, Italy and Portugal, have simultaneously experienced economic development and expansion of their tourism sector, especially following the adoption of the Millennium Goals for Economic Development, many authors have attempted to estimate the real impact of international tourism on economic growth.

In tourism demand modelling, after a short period of application of standard and classic panel data models (OLS with fixed effects or random effects), the literature is characterized by a high volume of dynamic panel models. Additionally, from the second half of 2000 onwards, several of the works employ cointegration techniques. The first empirical papers, based on the classic panel data methods, were published in the beginning of the 2000s. These studies focused generally on the prices elasticities or on the impact of political risk and violence on international tourism arrivals. For example, Ledesma- Rodríguez and Navarro-Ibáñez (2001) used annual data from 1979 to 1997 to study factors affecting arrivals to Tenerife from 13 markets. They found arrivals to be elastic with respect to income and inelastic with respect to prices and transport cost in the long run. Espinet et al. (2003) used panel data with random effects for a hedonic evaluation based on 86 000 prices between 1991 and 1998. The data concerned hotels in the southern Costa Brava region. Their results indicate a real and significant effect from the quality to the price.

Eilat and Einav (2004) used multinomial logit estimations, based on bilateral data during the period 1985–98, to study the leisure tourism determinants. This was the first study based on a three-dimensional panel data (year, destination, origin). They showed that political risk is a very important determinant of the tourist arrivals. The most recent paper based on the traditional panel data method is that of Arita et al. (2011). They analysed the impact of ADS (Approved Destination Status, beginning of the 1990s) agreements on international tourism arrivals in China. They integrated, in the estimation, fixed effects, to compare results before and after ADS and also between destinations inside and outside the ADS.

As the relevant data available is often annual, there are many empirical works which use dynamic panel data methods to test long-run relationships. The most commonly used estimation technique in the literature is that of AB although authors such as Maloney and Montes Rojas (2005) made used of General Method of Moment (GMM) suggested by Blundell and Bond (1998). They measured the tourism price elasticity in Caribbean countries, with bilateral data (tourists came from the United States, Canada, United Kingdom, Germany, Netherlands, Italy and Spain) from 1990 to 2002. They estimated a large price elasticity of 4.9.

As mentioned above, the AB technique is the most widely used in the tourism literature. For example, Neumayer (2003) estimated the effect of violence, risks, freedom and human rights violations on annual international tourism arrivals during 1977–2000. This study was based on a sample which contained more than 100 countries. Neumayer employed two methods for this estimation: a traditional data panel model with fixed effects and a dynamic panel data model. He found that in most cases, these explanatory variables had a real and significant effect on tourism. Garín-Muños and Montero-Martin (2007) studied yearly data from 1991 to 2003 to assess factors affecting the number of arrivals to the Balearic Islands. They found a high level of consumer loyalty to tourism in the Balearic Islands and recommended that suppliers of tourism products should raise the quality of their products and should improve their brand image.

Khadaroo and Seetanah (2007) used data on arrivals to Mauritius during the period 1978 to 2003 to assess the relative importance of transport infrastructure as a demand determinant. Transport infrastructure was approximated by the net investment in land, air and sea infrastructure at the current market price while non-transport infrastructures were measured by net investment at current market price on communication, energy, wastewater and defence infrastructure. Transport infrastructure was found to be an important determinant of demand for travellers from Asia, Europe and the United States while the latter two groups are also influenced by the non-transport infrastructure.

However, they use a poor proxy for prices in their model. They sought to capture the price effect by using the real value of the Mauritian rupees in US dollars. The depreciation or appreciation of the Mauritian rupee against the US dollar cannot be expected to reflect changes in the cost of holidays for visitors from Africa, Asia and Europe. It is not surprising that they found prices to be insignificant in determining international arrivals to Mauritius.

Naudé and Saayman (2005) analysed annual data from 1996 to 2000 to estimate tourism arrivals for 43 African countries. Their estimation yielded a negative coefficient for the lagged dependent variable suggesting that tourism in South Africa is taking a downward trend as currently level of arrivals was negatively related to past levels. Political stability was a key determinant of arrivals. Their model included lagged values of explanatory variables. It is not unlikely that the variables are highly collinear to their lagged values and therefore the model suffers from multicollinearity. This may explain why only a few of their estimated coefficients were statistically significant.

A dynamic data panel model has the fundamental characteristics to establish the long-run relationship between two variables. As the question of difference between short- and long-run estimation is important (the results can differ as a short-run estimation can be amplified or cancelled in the long run), the dynamic model is often used along with another method of estimation which has the objective to estimate the short-run impact. For example, Kuo et al. (2008) and Kuo et al. (2009) tried to estimate impact of infectious diseases (Avian Flu) and severe acute respiratory syndrome (SARS) on international tourist arrivals in selected Asian, African and European destinations, for the sample period of 2001 to 2006 and 2004 to 2006 respectively. The long-run estimation is based on the GMM procedure and the short-run estimation is provided by ARMAX models for each country. They established different results between short and long-run estimations: SARS had a significant impact on tourist arrivals in the long- and short-run whereas infectious diseases had only an impact on the long run. Garín-Muños (2006) used annual data from 1992 to 2002 to estimate factors affecting arrivals to the Canary Islands from 15 of its markets. Demand was found to be inelastic in the short run but income and price elasticity was greater than one in the long run. Demand was elastic with respect to changes in transport cost in the short run and in the long run.

Another way of comparing short and long-run results is to employ cointegration techniques and dynamic model. Seetaram (2010a) and Seetaram (2012) analysed tourist arrivals and departures in Australia during the period 1991–2008. After testing for stationarity and cointegration (based on the suggestion of Pedroni, 1999 and 2004), she employed GMM and Corrected Least Square Dummy Variable, CLSDV (provided by Kiviet, 1995), to calculate short-run and long-run elasticities. The justification for using this estimation technique was that the temporal dimension was relatively small. For the tourist arrivals, she found that demand is inelastic in the short-run, with respect to its determinants, and elastic in the long-run. Concerning outbound tourism, the results indicated an elasticity of migration on outbound tourism of 0.2 per cent and amplified in the long run with a value of 0.6 per cent. However, contrary to the inbound model, there were no effects detected from the price index in the outbound model.

Finally, another way is to use an estimator directly for the cointegrated model: Fully Modified Ordinary Least Squares (FMOLS) or Dynamic Ordinary Least Squares (DOLS). Seetanah (2010) employed a gravity model to test price and income elasticities. However, this paper suffers from a problem of methodology as he integrates many exogenous variables into the regression. For a set of n variables, there can be up to $n-1$ independent cointegrating vectors (Harris, 1995). If explanatory variables were cointegrated among them, there would more than $n-1$ cointegrating vectors. So it is not possible to put explanatory variables that are cointegrated simultaneously into the regression (FMOLS or DOLS).

Regarding tourism and economic growth, the lack of theoretical foundation explaining the mechanism through which tourism causes economic growth has prompted several authors to apply cointegration techniques in order to explain the causality between the two variables. This has resulted in a small but growing number of empirical studies using dynamic panel data techniques. The first studies have analysed the effect of a growing tourism sector on the economic growth of the destination (tourism growth → economic growth). Eugenio-Martín et al. (2004) estimated the effect from growth of tourism per capita to income per capita with a sample including 21 Latin American countries from 1985 to 1998. They used a dynamic panel data model with AB estimator and they categorized the countries into three groups based on their respective income per capita: rich, medium and poor. The results established that tourism led to economic growth for medium and poor countries while the reverse was true for rich countries.

Cortés-Jiménez (2008) analysed the impact of international and domestic tourism arrivals on economic growth (by using the GDP per capita) for 17 regions of Spain and 20 regions of Italy during the period 1990–2000. She used two estimators for the dynamic panel model: GMM and CLSDV. She found that tourism impacted positively on economic growth in coastal and Mediterranean regions. Her results are, however, surprising for the inland regions in her sample. Here she found that while domestic tourism fostered economic growth, international tourism had the reverse effect.

Soukiazis and Proença (2008) studied the effect of tourism activity on the economic convergence of Portuguese regions between 1993 and 2001. Convergence was approximated by the difference of GDP per capita. Three estimators were applied: GMM, CLSDV and GLS (with random effects). The authors used bed capacity as a proxy for tourism activity.

According to their results, a tourism capacity expansion of 1 per cent results in a supplement of 0.01 per cent economic growth. Their results also indicated that tourism accelerates economic convergence across the regions. Without tourism, the convergence was estimated to take 11 years whereas when the effect of tourism was taken into account, this reduced to only 10 years.

Sequeira and Maçãs Nunes (2008) used a sample of 94 countries (poor countries or small countries, with a population less than 5 million) for the period 1980–2002. Three indicators of tourism activity were employed (tourism arrival in population proportion, tourism receipts as a percentage of exports and tourism receipts as a percentage of GDP). They found that tourism had a positive effect on economic growth but only for the poor countries.

In the tourism literature, the panel data cointegration technique has also been employed in order to test for the causality between tourism growth and economic development. Narayan et al. (2010) used cointegration tests to estimate long-run elasticities of tourism to Pacific Islands (Tonga, Fiji, Solomon, Papua New Guinea) for the period extending from 1988 to 2004. They then analysed the causality from tourism exports to

GDP with an ECM model (as its structure permits to check at the short-run and at the long-run). The tourism literature is not clear on the direction of the causality between economic growth and tourism. There are schools of thoughts which suggest that economic growth and development can also impact on tourism demand (economic growth → tourism).

A few studies have empirically tested this link by using cointegration methods for the data panel model. For example, Lee and Chang (2008) used panel cointegration methods to determine the relationship and the causality between economic growth and tourism development in 55 countries (developed and developing countries) covering the time span of 1990 to 2002. After performing the IPS unit root and Pedroni (1999) cointegration tests, they applied FMOLS estimator to estimate the long-run relationship between tourism and economic developments. They then performed causality tests, the results of which indicated a unidirectional causality for developed countries (tourism → economic growth), whereas in developing countries there were bidirectional causality relationships.

It is interesting to note that tourism has not only benefitted economic growth but also international trade. Santana-Gallego et al. (2011) employed FMOLS and DOLS, while Keum (2011) applied multiple dynamic causal patch analysis to investigate the causality between tourism and trade. Cassette et al. (2009) and Petit (2010) developed panel data cointegration models to analyse whether international trade of goods and services had any effect on income inequalities. Their results indicate that international trade in tourism services results in income inequalities disadvantaging low-skilled workers. Whilst tourism activities seem to benefit economic growth, the low-skilled workers seem to be losing from globalization of the tourism services.

LIMITATIONS OF PANEL DATA ANALYSIS

The first disadvantage of this technique is that it is fairly complex to estimate and data requirements are high. Observing a number of individuals over a period of time usually results in data collection that can be tedious and expensive (Baltagi, 2005). From a statistical perspective, panel survey designs have some inherent disadvantages as noted in Kitamura (2000, p. 127).

1. Respondents may find it cumbersome to participate regularly in the same survey, which results in increasing non-response.
2. Attrition or dropout rate from the sample can be high.
3. Over time, the accuracy of data collection may decline. This is known as 'panel fatigue'.
4. The response of individuals may be influence by their responses from previous participations.

These disadvantages can, however, be addressed, although solutions do come at a cost. Solution proposed, include 'refreshing' the survey design and adding fresh participants at later stages. For more in-depth analysis of attrition in panel data, see Alderman et al. (2001), Fitzgerald et al. (1998) and Uhrig (2008).

CONCLUSION AND FUTURE DIRECTIONS

The use of panel data modelling techniques is becoming more common in the analysis of tourism data. In less than a decade, the literature has progressed from the development of standard static fixed effect and random effect models in the early 2000s to the more sophisticated dynamic panel data cointegration models. So far, the application of this technique has been restricted to tourism demand studies and others which have explored the relationship between the expansion of tourism sectors and economic growth or international trade. It can be extended to other topics of research within the tourism context.

One interesting area is the investigation of the supply side of the tourism industry. For example, a scrutiny of regional differences in the productivity of this industry will benefit from panel data modelling techniques, as models developed may be used to control for the heterogeneity of each region. Other types of studies where this method can prove to be useful are examinations of labour markets and their outcomes across different districts within a destination or in international comparisons of destinations. Examples of problems that can be addressed are analysis of wage differentials and gender bias, or human capital formation and return to education within the tourism industry.

While panel data techniques are powerful, and generally yield reliable estimates, they nevertheless suffer from some weaknesses. Estimations can be complex and data requirements are fairly large especially for dynamic panel models. The main limitation, however, is that the panel data survey design is inevitably subject to problems related to attrition. This drawback, however, does not seem to have affected tourism research as the existing studies are based on secondary data or 'macro' data where this occurrence is either easier to deal with or less frequent. It is expected, however, that future research may be based on survey data when researchers seek to find answers to the behaviour of tourists using microlevel data.

Regarding unit roots and cointegration tests, it is noted that the tests applied can be restrictive in that they assume that there is no cross-sectional correlation in the sample. In the instances that this assumption is overly binding and inappropriate, researchers may circumvent it by using alternative tests such as those of Westerlund (2007) who has designed tests which perform well on smaller samples and have higher power. Additionally, Westerlund (2006) and Westerlund and Edgerton (2006) have developed cointegration tests for panel data sets with structural breaks. These tests will be useful for researchers who are attempting to examine whether the effect of shocks on the tourism data are permanent or transitory. The exploitation of these tests will be made easier when software such as STATA, which is the dominant application for estimating panel data models, catches up with theoretical development in this field and incorporates it in newer versions of the program. Finally, it is expected that in the future, the literature will see more use of panel-ECM and that application of panel data techniques for analysing tourism data will extend to non-linear models including binary models.

REFERENCES

Alderman, H., J. Behrman, H.P. Kohler, J.A. Maluccio and S. Watkins (2001), 'Attrition in longitudinal household survey data: some tests from three developing countries', *Demographic Research*, **5** (4), 79–124.

Allison, P. (2005), *Fixed Effects Regression Methods for Longitudinal Data Using SAS*, Cary, NC: SAS Press.

Anderson, T.W. and C. Hsiao (1981), 'Estimation of dynamic models with error components', *Journal of the American Statistical Association*, **76**, 589–606.

Arellano, M. and S. Bond (1991), 'Some tests of specification for panel data: Monte Carlo evidence and an application to employment equations', *Review of Economic Studies*, **58**, 277–297.

Arita, S., C. Edmonds, S. La Croix and J. Mak (2011), 'Impact of approved destination status on Chinese travel abroad: an econometric analysis', *Tourism Economics*, **17** (5), 983–996.

Balestra, P. and M. Nerlove (1966), 'Pooling cross section and time series data in the estimation of a dynamic model: the demand of natural gas', *Econometrica*, **34** (3), 585–612.

Baltagi, B. (2005), *Econometric Analysis of Panel Data*, 5th Edition, New York: Wiley and Sons.

Baltes, P.B. and J.R. Nesselroade (1979), 'History and rationale of longitudinal research', in J.R. Nesselroade and P.B. Baltes (eds), *Longitudinal Research in the Study of Behavior and Development*, New York: Academic Press, pp. 1–39.

Banerjee, A. (1999), 'Panel data unit roots and cointegration: an overview', *Oxford Bulletin of Economics and Statistics*, **61**, 607–629.

Banerjee, A., M. Marcellino and C. Osbat (2004), 'Some cautions on the use of panel methods for integrated series of macroeconomic data', *Econometrics Journal*, **7**, 322–340.

Blundell, R.W. and S.R. Bond (1998), 'Initial conditions and moment restrictions in dynamic panel data models', *Journal of Econometrics*, **87**, 115–143.

Breitung, J. (2000), 'The local power of some unit root tests for panel data', in B. Baltagi (ed.), *Advances in Econometrics, Vol. 15: Nonstationary Panels, Panel Cointegration, and Dynamic Panels*, Amsterdam: JAI Press, pp. 161–178.

Cassette A., N. Fleury and S. Petit (2009), 'Income inequality and international trade: short and long-run evidence and the specific case of tourism services', paper presented to the 2nd Conference of the International Association for Tourism Economics, Chiang Mai, Thailand, December 2009.

Choi, I. (2001), 'Unit root tests for panel data', *Journal of International Money and Finance*, **20**, 249–272.

Cortés-Jiménez, I. (2008), 'Which type of tourism matters to the regional economic growth? The cases of Spain and Italy', *International Journal of Tourism Research*, **10**, 127–139.

Eilat, Y. and L. Einav (2004), 'Determinants of international tourism: a three dimensional panel data analysis', *Applied Economics*, **36** (12), 1315–1327.

Espinet, J.M., M. Saez, C. Coenders and M. Fluvià (2003), 'Effect on prices of the attributes of holiday hotels: a hedonic prices approach', *Tourism Economics*, **9** (2), 165–177.

Eugenio-Martín, J.L., N.M. Morales and R. Scarpa (2004), 'Tourism and economic growth in Latin American countries: a panel data approach', FEEM working paper No. 2004.26.

Fitzgerald, J., P. Gottschalk and R. Moffitt (1998), 'An analysis of sample attrition in panel data: the Michigan panel study of income dynamics', *The Journal of Human Resources*, **33**, 251–299.

Frees, E.W. (2004), *Longitudinal and Panel Data: Analysis and Applications in the Social Sciences*, West Nyack, NY: Cambridge University Press.

Garín-Muños, T. (2006), 'Inbound international tourism to Canary Island: a dynamic panel data model', *Tourism Management*, **27** (1), 281–291.

Garín-Muños, T. and L.F. Montero-Martín (2007), 'Tourism in the Balearic Island: a dynamic model for international demand using panel data', *Tourism Management*, **27** (5), 1224–1235.

Green, W. (1999), *Econometric Analysis*, 4th Edition, Upper Saddle River, NJ: Prentice Hall.

Harris, R.I.D. (1995), *Using Cointegration Analysis in Econometric Modelling*, Upper Saddle River, NJ: Prentice Hall.

Hausman, J.A. (1978), 'Specification tests in econometrics', *Econometrica*, **46** (6), 1251–1271.

Hoch, I. (1962), 'Estimation of production function parameters combining time series and cross section data', *Econometrica*, **30** (1), 34–53.

Hsiao, C. (2003), *Analysis of Panel Data*, 2nd edition, New York: Cambridge University Press.

Im, K.S., M.H. Pesaran and Y. Shin (2003), 'Testing for unit roots in heterogeneous panels', *Journal of Econometrics*, **115** (1), 53–74.

Johnson, J. (1960), *Econometric Methods*, New York: McGraw-Hill.

Judson, R. and A. Owen (1999), 'Estimating dynamic panel models: a guide for macroeconomist', *Economics Letters*, **65**, 53–78.

Keum, K. (2011), 'International tourism and trade flows: a causality analysis using panel data', *Tourism Economics*, **17** (5), 949–962.

Khadaroo, J. and B. Seetanah (2007), 'Transport infrastructure and tourism development', *Annals of Tourism Research*, **34** (4), 1021–1032.

Kitamura, R. (2000), 'Longitudinal methods', in D.A. Hensher and K.J Button (eds), *Handbook of Transport Modelling*, Netherlands: Pergamon, pp.13–29.

Kiviet, J.F. (1995), 'On bias, inconsistency and efficiency of various estimators in dynamic panel data models', *Journal of Econometrics*, **68** (1), 53–78.

Kuh, E. (1959), 'The validity of cross-sectionally estimated behavior equations in time series applications', *Econometrica*, **27** (2), 197–214.

Kuo, H.-I., C.-L. Chang, B.-W. Huang, C.-C. Chen and M. MacAleer (2009), 'Estimating the impact of avian flu on international tourism demand using panel data', *Tourism Economics*, **15** (3), 501–511.

Kuo, H.-I., C.-C. Chen, W.-C. Tseng, L.-F. Ju and B.-W. Huang (2008), 'Assessing impacts of SARS and avian flu on international tourism demand to Asia', *Tourism Management*, **29**, 917–928.

Ledesma-Rodríguez, F.J. and M. Navarro- Ibáñez (2001), 'Panel data and tourism: a case Study of Tenerife', *Tourism Economics*, **7** (1), 75–88.

Lee, C.-C. and C.-P. Chang (2008), 'Tourism development and economic growth: a closer look at panels', *Tourism Management*, **29**, 180–192.

Levin, A., C.-F. Lin and C.-S.J. Chu (2002), 'Unit root tests in panel data: asymptotic and finite-sample properties', *Journal of Econometrics*, **108** (1), 120–143.

Maddala, G.S. and S. Wu (1999), 'A comparative study of unit root tests with panel data and a new simple test', *Oxford Bulletin of Economics and Statistics*, **61**, 631–652.

Maloney, W.-F. and G.-V. Montes Rojas (2005), 'How elastic are sea, sand and sun? Dynamic panel estimates of the demand for tourism', *Applied Economic Letters*, **12**, 277–280.

Mudlak, Y. (1961), 'Empirical production function free of management bias', *Journal of Farm Economics*, **43** (1), 44–56.

Narayan, P.K., S. Narayan, A. Prasad and B.C. Prasad (2010), 'Tourism and economic growth: a panel data analysis for Pacific Island countries', *Tourism Economics*, **16** (1), 169–185.

Naudé, W.A. and A. Saayman (2005), 'Determinants of tourist arrivals in Africa: a panel data regression analysis', *Tourism Economics*, **11** (3), 365–391.

Neumayer, E. (2003), 'The impact of political violence on tourism–dynamic econometric estimation in a cross-national panel', *Journal of Conflict Resolution*, **48** (2), 259–281.

Nickell, S. (1981), 'Biases in dynamic models with fixed effects', *Econometrica*, **49** (6), 1417–1426.

Pedroni, P. (1999), 'Critical values for cointegration tests in heterogeneous panels with multiple regressors', *Oxford Bulletin of Economics and Statistics*, **61** (November), 653–670.

Pedroni, P. (2004), 'Panel cointegration; asymptotic and finite sample properties of pooled time series tests with an application to the PPP hypothesis', *Econometric Theory*, **20** (3), 597–625.

Petit, S. (2010), 'An Analysis of International Tourism: Production Fragmented, Two-Way Trade, Redistributive Effects', PhD thesis, University of Lille 1, France.

Phillips, P.C.B. and H.R. Moon (2000), 'Nonstationary panel data analysis: an overview of some recent developments', *Econometric Reviews*, **19**, 263–286.

Rugg, D. (1972), 'The choice of journey destination: a theoretical and empirical analysis', *Review of Economics and Statistics*, **55** (1), 64–72.

Santana-Gallego, M., F. Ledesma-Rodríguez and J.V. Pérez-Rodríguez (2011), 'Tourism and trade in OECD countries: a dynamic heterogeneous panel data analysis', *Empirical Economics*, **41** (2), 533–554.

Seetanah, B. (2010), 'Using the panel cointegration approach to analyze the determinants of tourism demand in South Africa', *Tourism Economics*, **16** (3), 715–729.

Seetaram, N. (2010a), 'Use of dynamic panel cointegration approach to model international arrivals to Australia', *Journal of Travel Research*, **49** (4), 414–422.

Seetaram, N. (2010b), 'Computing airfare elasticities or opening Pandora's Box', *Research in Transportation Economics, Special Issue on Tourism and Transport*, **26**, 27–36.

Seetaram, N. (2012), 'Estimating demand elasticities for Australia's international outbound tourism', *Tourism Economics*, (in press).

Sequeira, T.N. and P.M. Nunes (2008), 'Does tourism influence economic growth? A dynamic panel data approach', *Applied Economics*, **40**, 2431–2441.

Soukiazis, E. and S. Proença (2008), 'Tourism as an alternative source of regional growth in Portugal: a panel data analysis at NUTS II and III levels', *Portuguese Economic Journal*, **7**, 43–61.

Uhrig, C.N. (2008), 'The nature and causes of attrition in the British Household Panel Study', ISER Working Paper 2008–05.

Wallace, T.D. and A. Hussain (1969), 'The use of error components models in combining time-series with cross-section data', *Econometrica*, **37** (1), 55–72.

Westerlund, J. (2006), 'Testing for panel cointegration with multiple structural breaks', *Oxford Bulletin of Economics & Statistics*, **68** (1), 101–132.

Westerlund, J. (2007), 'Testing for error correction in panel data', *Oxford Bulletin of Economics and Statistics*, **69** (6), 709–748.

Westerlund, J. and D. Edgerton (2006), 'A simple test for cointegration in dependent panels with structural breaks', *Oxford Bulletin of Economics and Statistics*, **70** (5), 665–704.

Wooldridge, J. (2002), *Econometric Analysis of Cross Section and Panel Data*, Cambridge, MA: MIT Press.

8 The almost ideal demand system
Sarath Divisekera

INTRODUCTION

The classic paper by Deaton and Muellbauer (1980a) – one of the top 20 papers which appeared in *American Economic Review* during the first 100 years of its existence – is an established standard for applied demand analysis (Arrow et al., 2011). The fundamental demand model established by this paper – 'Almost Ideal Demand System' or AIDS – has found widespread application in consumer demand analysis. The attraction of AIDS is that it gives an arbitrary first-order approximation to any demand system; it satisfies the axioms of choice (almost) exactly; it aggregates perfectly without invoking the assumption of parallel linear Engel curves; and it has a functional form which is consistent with known household budget data. As within the general economics literature, the AIDS model is the principal established demand system employed by researchers in the tourism field. Beginning from the work of White (1982) – the earliest attempt to model tourism demand based on a system approach to demand modelling – to the most recent study of Wu et al. (2011), the AIDS model has been the basis for modelling and estimation of tourism demands.[1] The key contributions include: Coenen and Eekeren (2003), De Mello and Fortuna (2005), De Mello et al. (2002), Divisekera (2007, 2008, 2009a, 2009b, 2010a, 2010b, 2010c), Divisekera and Deegan (2010), Fujii et al. (1985), Han et al. (2006), Li et al. (2004), Lyssiotou (2000), Mangion et al. (2005), O'Hagan and Harrison (1984), Papatheodorou (1999), Sinclair and Syriopoulos (1993), White (1982, 1985), and Wu et al. (2011).

In addition to the original non-linear AIDS model these studies employ its variants and extensions including the linear, quadratic and dynamic versions. This may reflect, among other things, complexities arising from modelling tourism demands that require extensions to the base model, issues arising from particular data available that need modifications, and adaptation of recent advances in the econometric methodology of applied researchers. An understanding of the various issues confronting an applied researcher who relies on the AIDS model to analyse tourism demand is a must, as modifications and extensions are often made to accommodate and to deal with the practical problems the researcher faces. A systematic review of these issues in the context of tourism demand modelling is the focus of this chapter. In this review, we intend to provide a broad overview of the AIDS model focussing on its specification, properties, extensions, modifications and applications to tourism.

The remainder of this chapter is organized as follows. We begin with a brief review of the neoclassical theory of consumer behaviour, which is the cornerstone of modern consumer demand analysis and the theoretical foundation of the AIDS model. Then the specification of the AIDS model is presented and its properties are discussed. In the following section, extensions and modifications to the base AIDS model are reviewed in the light of the practical issues relating to their utilization in tourism demand analysis.

These issues include incorporation of seasonality and structural change, and the short- and long-run dynamics of tourism demands. In the final section, contributions to the tourism demand literature are reviewed in the light of the application of the AIDS model and its variants. In the final section we summarize key observations, we discuss possible implications for policy formulation, and we conclude with some suggestions for future research directions.

THEORETICAL BACKGROUND AND EVOLUTION OF THE AIDS MODEL

The empirical analysis of consumer behaviour holds a central position in economic analysis, and the underlying theory of consumer behaviour provides the structure for model formulation and data analysis (Deaton, 1986). The theory of consumer behaviour postulates that consumers choose goods and services so as to maximize utility subject to their budget constraint; the utility-maximizing consumer's demand for any commodity depends on the prices of all commodities available to them and on their total expenditure on these commodities.[2] This formulation presumes the existence of a utility function that measures the level of satisfaction an individual achieves by consuming goods and services. The utility function (u), representing consumer preferences, is defined by

$$u = u(q) \tag{8.1}$$

where $q = (q_i)$ is an n-element vector of levels of commodities consumed at a given point in time.

The utility function (8.1) is assumed well behaved, strictly increasing, strictly quasi-concave and twice continuously differentiable. The rational consumer maximizes utility subject to a budget constraint:

$$pq = m \tag{8.2}$$

where $p = (p_i)$ is the *n*-element column vector of prices and m is the consumer's total expenditure (income). Prices (and incomes) are assumed to be given. Maximization of (8.1) subject to (8.2) yields n equations of $q = q(p, m)$ which express the quantity demanded of one good as a function of income and all prices,

$$q_i = q_i(p_1, \ldots p_n, m) \tag{8.3}$$

To obtain a specific functional form for a complete set of demand equations given by (8.3), it is necessary that the underlying utility function (8.1) is strictly quasi-concave (that is, consumer preferences are convex). This poses limits on the types of preferences that can be allowed in empirical demand analysis (Deaton and Muellbauer, 1980a). However, an alternative approach not requiring strict concavity properties of consumer preferences follows from *duality* theory (Diewert, 1971, 1974; Shephard, 1953). Note that the maintained hypothesis of consumer theory is that a consumer chooses a set of goods and services that maximizes utility. The solution to the maximization problem (*the primal problem*) yields a set of quantities demanded and a maximum utility level of u^*. This problem can be formulated equivalently so as to minimize the expenditure necessary to achieve a given level of utility u^*.

Minimize:

$$m = p'q \text{ subject to } u(q) = u^* \tag{8.4}$$

The solution to this problem (*the dual*) yields the same set of quantities demanded, and the minimum expenditure m^* is equal to the given m in the primal problem. In both cases – primary and dual – the optimal value of q is being sought.[3] Since the two solutions coincide, we have:

$$q_i = q_i(p, m) = h_i(p, u^*) \tag{8.5}$$

Each of these solutions can be substituted back into their respective problems to yield first, the maximum utility achievable, given prices p and expenditure m. The corresponding function $v(p, m)$ is called the *indirect utility function*.

$$u = u[q(p, m)] = v(p, m) \tag{8.6}$$

Second is the minimum cost of achieving a fixed level of utility u at prices p. This is called the *cost* (or *expenditure*) function (which is the mathematical inverse of the indirect utility function $v(p, m)$).

$$m = (u, p) = c(u, p) \tag{8.7}$$

The duality approach to the consumer choice problem makes derivation of complete demand systems straightforward. For example, the Marshallian demand functions can be derived simply by differentiating the *indirect utility function* defined in (8.9) applying Roy's identity. The Hicksian demand functions can be derived differentiating the *cost function* defined in (8.10) using Shephard's lemma. The cost function has become a major tool in recent applications of consumer demand theory due to its attractive properties. First, the cost function is homogeneous of degree unity in prices. Second, it is increasing in u, non-decreasing in p, and increasing in at least one price. Third, the cost function is continuous in p and first- and second-order derivatives exist everywhere except possibly at specific price vectors. Fourth, the cost function is concave in prices. Most importantly, the concavity of the cost function is independent of whether consumer preferences are assumed to be strictly convex or not (Deaton and Muellbauer, 1980a; Thomas, 1987). Thus, any cost function that possesses the above properties can be regarded as representative of some underlying consumer preference ordering. Consequently, unlike the traditional approach – which imposes limits on consumer preferences – the cost function approach offers a flexible alternative in deriving demand functions. This is the approach used in specifying the AIDS model.

Approaches to the Specification of Complete Demand Systems and the Specification of the AIDS Model

Since the advent of the 'Linear Expenditure System' (Stone, 1954), a number of approaches to the specification of complete demand systems consistent with the basic postulates of consumer choice theory – *homogeneity, symmetry, negativity* and *adding-up* or *aggregation* – have been advanced.[4] One approach is to derive demand functions using a utility function which satisfies the general restrictions implied by consumer theory. The well-known examples are the *Linear Expenditure System* (LES) and the *Indirect Addilog* (for details, see Berndt et al., 1977; Frisch, 1959; Houthakker, 1960; Stone, 1954). The second approach ignores the underlying utility function and starts with a set of demand functions that do not necessarily satisfy theoretical restrictions. These are then interpreted and restricted in the light of consumer demand theory. Powell's *System of Additive Preferences* and the *Rotterdam Demand System* (RTDS) belong to this class of direct demand functions (Powell, 1966; Theil, 1975). The third approach is to employ *flexible* functional forms.[5] This method may be considered as an attempt to combine the two early approaches by approximating utility functions (direct or indirect) and cost functions. Flexible functional forms belong to the Translog family. The *Translog Demand System* of Christensen et al. (1975) and the *Almost Ideal Demand System* of Deaton and Muellbauer (1980a) belong to this class.[6]

The Almost Ideal Demand System (AIDS)

Deaton and Muellbauer (1980a) start the specification of the AIDS model with a class of consumer preferences known as the *Price Independent Generalized Log-Linear* (PIGLOG) form. This class of preferences is known to represent market demands as if they are the outcome of decisions by a rational representative consumer (Deaton and Muellbauer; 1980a). The preferences are represented by a cost function, $c(u, p)$ that defines the minimum expenditure necessary to attain a specific level of utility, u, at given prices, p, and is given by:

$$\text{Log } c(u, p) = (1 - u) \log [a(P)] + u \log [b(P)] \qquad (8.8)$$

where u denotes utility and P is a vector of prices. Note that the utility index can be scaled to correspond to cases of subsistence ($U = 0$) and bliss ($U = 1$), in which case, $a(P)$ and $b(P)$ can be interpreted as representing the cost of subsistence and bliss. Deaton and Muellbauer use Translog and Cobb–Douglas functions to approximate $a(P)$ and $b(P)$ respectively. The resulting cost function takes the following form:

$$\log c(u, p) = \alpha_0 + \sum_{i=1}^{n} \alpha_i \log p_i + \frac{1}{2} \sum_{i=1}^{n} \sum_{j=1}^{n} \gamma_{ij}^* \log p_i \log p_j + u\beta_0 \prod_{i=1}^{n} p_i^{\beta_i} \qquad (8.9)$$

where p_i is the vector of prices, u is the level of utility and α_0, α_i, β_0, β_i and γ_{ij}^* are parameters ($i, j = 1, \ldots, n$). By logarithmic differentiation of (8.9), compensated (Hicksian) demand functions can be obtained and the resulting AIDS demand model – expressing expenditure shares (w_i) as a function of prices and utility (u) – takes the following form:

$$w_i = \alpha_i + \sum_j \gamma_{ij} \log p_j + \beta_i u \beta_o \prod_i p_i^{\beta_i} \tag{8.10}$$

where

$$\gamma_{ij} = \frac{1}{2}(\gamma^*_{ij} + \gamma^*_{ji}), \quad w_i = \frac{p_i q_i}{\sum p_i q_i}.$$

The behavioural demand system given in (8.10) with the unobservable u can be converted into an observable market demand system using the indirect utility function associated with (8.9):

$$u = \frac{\log X - \alpha_0 - \sum_{i=1}^{n} \alpha_i \log p_i + \frac{1}{2}\sum_{i=1}^{n}\sum_{j=1}^{n} \gamma^*_{ij} \log p_i \log p_j}{u \beta_0 \prod_{i=1}^{n} p_i^{\beta_i}} \tag{8.11}$$

where $\log X = \log c(u, p)$. By substituting (8.11) for u in (8.10), uncompensated (or Marshallian) market demand functions (in expenditure or budget share form) are obtained. The resulting AI demand functions are:

$$w_i = \alpha_i + \sum_j \gamma_{ij} \log p_j + \beta_i \log (X/P) \tag{8.12}$$

where w_i ($w_i \equiv p_i q_i / X$) is the share of expenditure of the ith commodity, p_j is the price of jth commodity, X is the total expenditure on all goods and services ($X = \Sigma p_i q_i$), and P is an aggregate price index defined as:

$$\log P = \alpha_0 + \sum_i \alpha_i \log p_i + \frac{1}{2}\sum_i \sum_j \gamma_{ij} \log p_i \log p_j \tag{8.13}$$

Linear homogeneity of the cost function, symmetry of the second-order derivatives and adding-up across the share equations implies the following set of (equality) restrictions.

$$\sum_{i=1}^{n} \alpha_i = 1, \ \sum_{i=1}^{n} \gamma_{ij} = 0, \ \sum_{i=1}^{n} \beta_i = 0; \ \sum_j \gamma_{ij} = 0, \ \gamma_{ij} = \gamma_{ij} \tag{8.14}$$

Given the parameter restrictions, Equations (8.12) and (8.13) represent a system of demand functions which add up to total expenditure ($\Sigma_i w_i = 1$), are homogeneous of degree zero in prices and total expenditure, and satisfy Slutsky symmetry.

Demand and substitution elasticities can be computed based on the estimated model parameters. The implied expenditure elasticities, η_i, reflecting the sensitivity of demands to changes in expenditure, can be calculated using the formula:

$$\eta_i = \frac{\%\Delta q_i}{\%\Delta x} = \frac{\partial q_i}{\partial x} \cdot \frac{x}{q_i} = \frac{\beta_i}{w_i} + 1 \tag{8.15}$$

where x is the total expenditure.

Price elasticities of demand are defined as:

$$\varepsilon_{ij} = \frac{\%\Delta q_i}{\%\Delta p_j} = \frac{\partial q_i}{\partial p_j} \cdot \frac{p_j}{q_i} \tag{8.16}$$

where ε_{ij} is the price elasticity of demand (cross-price elasticity for $i \neq j$ and own price elasticity (for $i = j$), p_i is the price on the ith good, and q_i is the quantity demanded for the ith good. Price elasticities can be derived from either the Marshallian demand equation or the Hicksian demand equation. Given (8.8), the Marshallian (or uncompensated) price elasticity for good i with respect to good j is:

$$\varepsilon_{ij}^M = \frac{\gamma_{ij} - \beta_i(w_j - \beta_j \ln (X/P))}{w_i} - \delta_{ij} \tag{8.16.a}$$

where δ_{ij} is the Kronecker delta; $\delta_{ij} = 1$ if $i = j$ and 0 otherwise ($\delta_{ij} \neq 1$). Marshallian elasticities can be transformed into Hicksian (compensated) elasticities through the Slutsky equation given by:

$$\varepsilon_{ij}^H = \varepsilon_{ij}^M + w_j \eta_j \tag{8.17}$$

where η_j is the expenditure elasticity. Expenditure elasticity shows how the quantity purchased changes in response to a change in the consumer's expenditure/budget. Uncompensated price elasticities indicate how a change in the price of a commodity affects its own demand (own price elasticity) and the demands for all other commodities (cross-price elasticities) included in the group. Compensated elasticities measure these effects, assuming that real expenditures are held constant. Cross-price elasticities allow the classification of commodity pairs to be substitutes or complements; negative cross-price elasticities indicate that the two commodities are complements; positive values indicate substitutes.

The AIDS model given by (8.12) and (8.13) is non-linear in parameters, thus complex non-linear estimation methods are needed to estimate model parameters. Deaton and Muellbauer (1980) proposed an alternative which allows the model to be estimated using linear regression methods. That is, the replacement of the non-linear price index (8.13) with an alternative price index that can be defined outside the AIDS system, thus leaving a linear system of share equations. The proposed alternative was that of the Stone's price index, the values of which can be calculated prior to the estimation as:

$$\log P = \sum_{i=1}^{n} w_i \log p_i \tag{8.18}$$

This version of the AIDS model is known as the *Linear Approximate* AIDS model or LA-AIDS. With the use of the Stone price index approximation, Marshallian price elasticities can be calculated using the following formula (White, 1985; Pashardes, 1993):[7]

$$\varepsilon_{ij} = (1/w_i)(\gamma_{ij} - \beta_i w_j) - \delta_{ij} \tag{8.19}$$

Model Extensions and Modifications

Over the years, several extensions and (or) modifications to the two versions of the AIDS model have been proposed. Key modifications include the inverse version (IAIDS) due to Eales and Unnevehr (1993, 1994), and the quadratic version Q-AIDS proposed by Banks et al. (1997). The refinements include dynamic versions of the base AIDS model due to Anderson and Blundell (1983), and error-correction versions of the LA-AIDS models due to Attfield (1997), Karagiannisa and Mergos (2002), Ng (1995) and others.

Inverse AIDS (IAIDS) Model

As opposed to the conventional direct demand functions, inverse demand systems explain price variations as functions of quantity variations. The particular version of the IAIDS model proposed by Eales and Unnevehr (1993, 1994) considered applications where the quantities tended to be fixed in the short run, and thus prices adjusted to clear the market. The development of the IAIDS proceeds with the dual of the cost function, the *distance function*. The distance function measures the proportion by which quantities must be scaled back to reach a particular indifference curve (Deaton 1979). It possesses the same properties as the cost function; it is linear homogeneous, concave, and non-decreasing in quantities (as opposed to prices), and it is decreasing in utility (as opposed to increasing) (Diewert, 1982). The distance function is defined as:

$$U\{q/D(u, q)\} = u \tag{8.20}$$

where u equals utility, q is quantity and D is distance. The distance function is defined in a manner analogous to the AIDS expenditure function:

$$\log D(u, q) = \alpha_0 + \sum \alpha_j \ln q_j + \frac{1}{2} \sum_i \sum_j \gamma_{ij}^* \ln q_i \ln q_j + u\beta_0 \prod_j q_j^{-\beta_i} \tag{8.21}$$

Differentiation of the distance function (8.21) with respect to a quantity of a particular good yields the compensated 'inverse' demand for that good, in the same way that differentiation of the cost function with respect to a particular price yields a compensated demand function. Substitution of the inverted distance function (which is equivalent to the direct utility function) uncompensate the functions and yields a system of inverse demand share equations of the form:

$$w_i = \alpha_i + \sum_j \gamma_{ij} \ln q_j + \beta_i \ln Q \tag{8.22}$$

where

$$\ln Q = \alpha_0 + \sum_j \ln q_j + \frac{1}{2} \sum_i \sum_j \gamma_{ij} \ln q_i \ln q_j \tag{8.23}$$

The model may be estimated by replacing the non-linear quantity index with a linear one, such as Stone's quantity index. With inverse demand models, sensitivities (elasticities) are typically measured by *flexibilities*. Eales and Unnevehr (1993) provide the relevant formulas for the flexibilities when estimating the linear version (i.e., using Stone's quantity index) of the inverse AIDS model.

$$f_{ij} = -\delta_{ij} + \{\gamma_{ij} - \beta_i w_j\}/w_i \tag{8.24}$$

$$f_i = -1 + \beta_i/w_i \tag{8.25}$$

Equation (8.24) is defined for all own and cross flexibilities, where δ_{ij} is the Kronecker delta that equals 1 if $i = j$. This is analogous to the uncompensated own and cross-price elasticities in the LA-AIDS model. Own price flexibilities describe the percentage change in the price of the ith good when the quantity demanded of that good increases by 1 per cent. The demand for the ith commodity is flexible (inflexible) if a 1 per cent increase in the consumption of that commodity leads to a greater (less) than 1 per cent decrease in the marginal consumption value (its normalized price). Similarly, cross-price flexibility is defined as the percentage change in the price of a good, where the quantity demanded of competing good increases by 1 per cent. Goods are gross quantity-substitutes (*q*-substitutes) if their cross-price flexibility is negative, and are gross quantity-complements (*q*-complements) if their cross-price flexibility is positive. Equation (8.25) is the analogue of the expenditure elasticity of the base AIDS model. It is interpreted as a scale flexibility that measures the percentage change in the price of a good brought about by a proportional change in the aggregate quantity or scale of consumption. Scale flexibilities that are greater (less) than 1 in absolute value are necessities (luxuries) (Eales and Unnevehr, 1993). The IAIDS model provides a viable alternative to the conventional direct demand functions as it can be used to model tourist numbers as a measure of tourist demand (as opposed to tourist expenditure).

Quadratic AIDS (QUAIDS)

Another extension to the AIDS model was proposed by Banks et al. (1997) who introduced a quadratic version of the standard AIDS model. This may be considered an attempt to improve the flexibility of the base AIDS model, which assumes linear Engel curves. The rationale for the proposed extension is that the relationship between budget shares and income is not always linear (however, nor is it always non-linear). Banks et al. (1997) develop their quadratic version to be flexible enough so that the non-linear Engel curve specification does not have to be applied to each good. The specification of the QAIDS model starts with adding a quadratic logarithmic income term and nests the standard AIDS model specification. The resulting QUAIDS model is given by share equations of the form:

$$w_i = \alpha_i + \beta_i \log(x/a(p)) + \frac{\lambda_i}{\prod_k p_k^{\beta_k}}(x/a(p))^2 + \sum_j \gamma_{ij} \log p_j \tag{8.26}$$

for $i = 1, \ldots, n$ and where $\log a(p)$ can be approximated by the Stone price index (8.18), the QUAIDS budget shares reduce to those of AIDS if $\lambda_i = 0$ for all i.

Coenen and Eekeren (2003) used QUAIDS to analyse the demand for tourism goods and services by Swedish households. Among other modifications, there are several attempts to redress one limitation of the AIDS model, namely its failure to satisfy the global regularity condition (that is, the AIDS cost function is not globally concave), although it can be regular over a restricted range (that is, locally flexible) (Diewert and Wales, 1987; Lau, 1986). Although this is trivial, as Deaton (1986) noted, it is possible to improve the regularity of the AIDS model by either imposing restrictions prior to estimation, or by modifying the underlying cost functions (for example, see Chalfant, 1987; Cooper and McLaren, 1988; Cooper et al., 1991).[8] Chalfant (1987) proposed a globally flexible, almost ideal demand system by using the Fourier flexible form in place of the Translog to approximate budget share equations. To improve the curvature property within AIDS, Cooper and McLaren (1992) developed a modified version of the AIDS model (MAIDS), while Moschini (1998) developed a semi-flexible AIDS specification. While these contributions are important in terms of guaranteeing global curvature conditions, as implied in the consumer theory of choice, as Lau (1986) has shown flexibility and regularity are incompatible. Thus, if regularity is to be incorporated into a flexible functional form, it is at the expense of flexibility. Further, such modifications appear to have implications for the economic plausibility of some derived elasticity parameters as well.[9] Therefore, any attempt to improve regularity is likely to impose some restrictions on the preference structure, and the resulting parameter estimates could be biased, as they are conditional upon prior restrictions.

Discussed above are key modifications to the AIDS model proposed in the literature which are aimed at improving its flexibility. In addition, there are several other proposed refinements that are necessitated by, or are consequences of, accommodating specific issues arising when implementing and (or) applying the model to study particular issues. These include the way in which applied researchers treat theoretical restrictions during the estimation, the nature and issues related to the types of data used for estimation, and the aim of the study.

An important property of the AIDS (and flexible functional forms in general) is that they afford the estimation of complete demand systems consistent with the consumer theory of choice, that is, models can be estimated while imposing theoretical restrictions a priori as maintained hypotheses. Likewise, models may be estimated unrestricted and the validity of the theoretical restrictions implied in the consumer theory of demand can be tested. The imposition of theoretical restrictions is usually made as restrictions on the AIDS model parameters (for example, Equation (8.14)).

(1) The *adding-up* (aggregation) restriction implying that all budget shares sum to unity, requires:

$$\sum_{i=1}^{n} \alpha_i = 1, \quad \sum_{i=1}^{n} \gamma_{ij} = 0, \quad \sum_{i=1}^{n} \beta_i = 0 \qquad (8.27)$$

(2) The *homogeneity* restriction implying the absence of money illusion requires:

$$\sum_{j} \gamma_{ij} = 0 \qquad (8.28)$$

(3) The *symmetry* restriction guaranteeing the consistency of consumer choice requires:

$$\gamma_{ij} = \gamma_{ij} \qquad (8.29)$$

(4) A final restriction following from the theory, *negativity*, is satisfied if the Slutsky matrix, s_{ij}, of compensated price derivatives is negative semi-definite:

$$s_{ij} = \gamma_{ij} - \beta_i\beta_j \log (X/P) - w_i\delta_{ij} + w_iw_j \qquad (8.30)$$

where δ_{ij} is the Kronecker delta ($\delta_{ij} = 1$, if $i = j$; and $\delta_{ij} = 0$, otherwise), and w_i is the predicted value of the ith budget share.

Of the four theoretical restrictions, the adding-up condition is automatically satisfied in a system of share equations by the way of construction. The negativity condition can be tested for its validity, but it cannot be directly imposed as a constraint upon econometric estimation of the AIDS model.[10] The remaining two restrictions of homogeneity and symmetry can be imposed prior to the estimation or tested for their validity. While some researchers estimate empirical models imposing theoretical restrictions – homogeneity and symmetry – as maintained hypotheses, others estimate unrestricted versions and then test for the validity of the restrictions based on estimated model parameters. Although no study has been specifically designed to test for the validity of the basic postulates of demand theory, many such tests have failed to verify the empirical validity of the two theoretical restrictions (for a detailed discussion, see Keuzenkamp and Barten, 1995). Among the two restrictions, homogeneity is the one more often rejected. Of the various explanations, errors associated with dynamic misspecification of empirical models are the ones which led researchers to incorporate dynamic consumption behaviour into the AIDS model.[11]

Anderson and Blundell (1982) introduced a dynamic version of the AIDS model by incorporating habit persistence. They showed that restrictions implied by economic theory are not rejected when tested on the long-run dynamic structure. Thus, dynamic modelling is claimed to be a better alternative in modelling demand using time series data compared to static modelling. The first attempt to model tourism demands using this dynamic version was by Lyssiotou (2000) who investigated the UK demand for tourism in the United States, Canada, and 16 European destinations. An alternative explanation advanced by Ng (1995) proposes that time-series issues – unit roots being present – are partly responsible for the rejection of homogeneity.[12] Thus she proposes the application of recently developed techniques for estimating cointegrating vectors to account for dynamic misspecification (see also Attfield, 1997; Karagiannisa and Mergos, 2002; Lewbell and Ng, 2005). This led to another empirical version of the LA-AIDS model, often coined the error-correction LAAIDS model (ECLAAIDS). This version is the most widely used in recent empirical studies of tourism demand, including the studies of Durbarry and Sinclair (2003), Li et al. (2004), Mangion et al. (2005) and Cortés-Jiménez et al. (2009).

Depending on the specific issues being investigated and the particular nature of data available, some minor modifications to the model structure are usually introduced by altering and (or) adding model parameters. For example, issues relating to seasonality and structural change may arise in applications using data collected over time. This is particularly the case with regard to tourism, given the apparent seasonality associated with tourist demand (see for example, Divisekera, 2009a, 2010b; Lyssiotou, 2000). Further, demand for tourism may be affected by random events including political disturbances, social unrest, natural disasters and health concerns. These could lead to exogenous shifts in tourism demand, and thus they need to be accounted for in the modelling (see for example, Divisekera, 2003; Han et al., 2006; Lanza et al., 2003). In addition, if data are extracted from household surveys and the focus is on household demand for tourism, data aggregated across households may raise questions regarding the aggregation properties of a particular demand model (see, for example, Coenen and Eekeren, 2003).

The standard practice is to use dummy variables in the basic share equations to capture the effects of structural change, seasonality, and (or) any other exogenous shifts (Divisekera, 2003; Han et al., 2006; Lyssiotou, 2000). In relation to linear trends, the common approach is to add a simple linear trend to the share equations, which is analogous to allowing the intercept term of each share equation to trend (see for example, Fujii et al.1985; Lyssiotou, 2000; White, 1985). The same intuition carries over to more complex factors that allow the intercept to shift according to the quarter or season of the year of the observation, or even other things such as structural breaks in the time series, and changes in tastes and preferences (Holt and Goodwin, 2009). When adding exogenous intercept shift variables, one needs be mindful that their addition does not violate the adding-up condition. Usually, time trend, seasonality, and structural shifts are incorporated by replacing the intercept term α_i (in Equation (8.12)) with α_{it} (that is, their effect is measured as a deviation from the intercept):

$$\alpha_{it} = \alpha_{0i} + \delta_{0i}t + \sum_s \delta_{is}D_s \tag{8.31}$$

where $t = 1, \ldots, T$; D_s are seasonal dummy variables, $S = 1, \ldots, 4$ and $\Sigma_s \delta_{is} = 0$. The parameters δ_{0i} are interpreted as reflecting exogenous shifts in preferences (Lyssiotou, 2000).

The use of deterministic dummy variables to capture seasonal shifts in demands, however, could lead to biased parameter estimates when turning points of the seasonal time series are changing (Fraser and Moosa, 2002; Carlos et al., 2004). The proposed alternative is to incorporate trigonometric variables to account for seasonality. This approach allows the seasonal cycle to be dictated by the data, rather than using the deterministic dummy variables that define the season. This is particularly appealing when there are clear structural shifts in seasons. The application of this method is carried out by augmenting the share equations (Equation (8.12)) with seasonal trigonometric variables and a time trend (Divisekera, 2009b; 2010a):

$$w_i = \alpha_i + \sum_j \gamma_{ij} \log p_j + \beta_i \log(X/P) + a_i^c \cos\frac{2\pi t}{4} + a_i^s \sin\frac{2\pi t}{4} + a_i^t t \tag{8.32}$$

where a_i^c and a_i^s represent parameters on the trigonometric variables, and a_i^t is the parameter on the time trend variable. To ensure that the adding-up condition is not violated these parameters should satisfy the following conditions:

$$\sum_{i=1}^n \alpha_i^c = 0, \quad \sum_{i=1}^n \alpha_i^s = 0, \quad \sum_{i=1}^n \alpha_i^t = 0 \tag{8.33}$$

Once the demand system is specified incorporating all of the relevant variables and exogenous shift variables where necessary, the next step involves estimation.

The Stochastic Specification and Estimation Methods

The model estimation is usually preceded by adding a stochastic random disturbance or error term u_{it} to the share equations. The general stochastic version of the model in vector form is:

$$w_{it} = \dot{u}_i(f_{it}, \beta) + u_{it} \tag{8.34}$$

where w_{it} is the ith budget share at time t, f_{it} is the set of explanatory variables, β is the parameters to be estimated, and u_{it} is a random disturbance term. Let $\tilde{u}_t'$ denote the n-vector of disturbances at time t and the contemporaneous covariance matrix Ω. Following convention, the covariance matrix for the share disturbance is assumed to be the same for all observations, $E(\tilde{u}_t\tilde{u}_t') = \Omega$ and the disturbances are uncorrelated across observations, $E(\tilde{u}_t\tilde{u}_s) = 0$ for $s \neq t$. Note that given the dependent variables are shares (w_i) and that they add to unity implies that $\Sigma_i u_{it} = 0$ for each t. Thus, the errors cannot be distributed independently across equations and the Ω is singular (Barten, 1969; Pollak and Wales, 1992). Due to the singularity of Ω, the density of $\tilde{u}_t$ may be expressed in terms of the density of any $(n - 1)$ equations by deleting any arbitrary element. The resulting parameter estimates are independent of the deleted equation (Barten, 1969).

The joint estimation of parameters may be carried out using a non-linear estimation method such as the Maximum Likelihood (ML) Estimator, the only known method which yields an estimator invariant with respect to the equation which is dropped during the estimation (Barten, 1969).[13] With the arbitrary deletion of the nth equation, let Ω be the corresponding covariance matrix and u_t' be the vector of disturbances. Then, under the assumption that these independent disturbances are normally distributed with zero mean and covariance matrix Ω, the log of likelihood function for t observations on the $(n - 1)$ independent equations is given by:

$$\log L = \frac{T}{2}\left(-(n - 1)\log(2\pi) - \frac{1}{2}\log|\Omega|\right) - \frac{1}{2}\sum_{t=1}^{T} u\Omega^{-1}u_t \tag{8.35}$$

where

$$u_t = (w_t - f_t); \; w_t = (w_{1t}\ldots w_{n-1t});$$

$$f_t = \begin{bmatrix} f_{1t}(p_t, x_t; \alpha, \beta, \gamma) \\ \cdot \\ \cdot \\ f_{n-1,t}(p_t, x_t; \alpha, \beta, \gamma) \end{bmatrix}$$

$p_t = (p_{1t}, \ldots p_{nt}); \; X_t = (\Sigma_i = 1, p_{it}x_{it}); \; \alpha = (\alpha_1 \ldots \alpha_n); \; \beta = (\beta_1 \ldots \beta_n); \; \gamma = (\gamma_{11} \ldots \gamma_{n1}, \ldots \gamma_{nn})$

ML estimation consists of choosing values of unknown parameters α, β, γ and Ω in order to maximize the log-likelihood function L. The ML procedure has attractive properties: estimators are consistent, asymptotically efficient, and asymptotically normally distributed (Judge et al., 1980; Malinvaud, 1980).

APPLICATIONS OF THE AIDS MODEL AND ITS VARIANTS IN TOURISM DEMAND MODELLING

As stated at the outset, the AIDS model has been the principal and most widely used established demand system employed by researchers in the tourism field.[14] The available empirical studies may be broadly classified into two categories: (1) destination choice or demand for tourist destinations, and (2) the studies that seek to analyse the demand for tourism goods and services. The former group of studies attempts to evaluate the effects of incomes and prices as determinants of tourism demand for a group of destinations. This has been the central focus of most of the early empirical studies of tourism demand. In terms of a modelling strategy, except for the inverse AIDS model, all other versions and (or) modifications of the AIDS model have been employed. The latter group of studies investigates the aspects of tourism demands that focus on the demand for destination-specific tourism goods and services. More specifically, they attempt to analyse tourists' consumption behaviour or allocations of tourists' spending among various goods and services at the destinations they visited. The economic parameters associated with *ex-post* tourist demand are important for destination management and for developing destination-specific strategies to maximize gains from tourism.

Empirical Analysis of Demand for International Tourism (Destination Choice)

The first attempt to model international demand for tourism in the system context undertaken by White (1982, 1985) was based on the LAAIDS version of the model. In this pioneering study, White analysed the demand for travel and tourism in Western Europe by US residents. This was followed by O'Hagan and Harrison (1984), White (1985), Sinclair and Syriopoulos (1993), and Papatheodorou (1999) who employed the LAIDS model to study the US, European and international demands for tourism in Mediterranean destinations. De Mello et al. (2002) concentrated on UK demand for tourism in France, Portugal and Spain. This was followed by Divisekera (2003) who developed multi-country demand systems for the demand for tourism to Australia from Japan, New Zealand, the United Kingdom and the United States. In his most recent study, Divisekera (2009c) modelled travel and tourism demands simultaneously for the same group of countries.

Of the studies based on the LAAIDS model, the pioneering study of White (1982, 1985) modelled US demand for travel to Western Europe. The model consisted of eight equations and one representing demand for travel. The study provides a comprehensive set of expenditure, own, and cross-price elasticities among the eight Western European destinations included in the model. White used consumer price indices (CPI) as a proxy for destination prices; a proxy for travel prices between the United States and Western Europe was constructed using airlines' revenue data. The results allow the classification of regions/destinations of Western Europe as substitutes or as complements according to the preferences of travellers. The price elasticities are relatively low for France, Belgium, the Netherlands and Luxembourg. France and the United Kingdom exhibited high price substitution effects as did France and Germany. Travel to most other countries might be classified as complementary with respect to travel to France, and substitutes with respect to travel to the United Kingdom. The expenditure elasticities allow the classification of goods as 'normal' or 'luxury' goods.[15] The expenditure elasticity for travel to Spain and Portugal is estimated to be 1.3 and the expenditure elasticity for Norway, Sweden and Denmark is 1.2. This indicates that among destinations, these countries could be considered 'luxury' destinations. The other countries (as well as transportation) have expenditure elasticities that are not significantly different from one. Therefore, the share of travel expenditures in these groups is not expected to increase as total expenditures increase.

All of the studies below follow a similar modelling strategy; they use CPIs as their proxy for tourism prices and they ignore travel costs. The only exception is Divisekera (2003) who estimated four demand systems focussing on Japanese, New Zealand, UK and US demand for Australian tourism. Divisekera (2003) departed from the rest of the available empirical studies in several respects. First, he specified the model in the context of a preference-consistent utility maximization framework. Second, his study uses tourism price indices along with observed average daily spending to construct tourism prices, a significant departure from the commonly used consumer price indices. Third, his study incorporates the cost of international travel, a key economic determinant of international tourism demand that was largely ignored by other researchers. Estimated models are in conformity with the basic postulates of consumer theory, homogeneity and symmetry. Derived elasticities reveal substantial cross-demand effects, reflecting the diversity of preferences of tourists from different origins.

All of the forgoing studies were based on the LAAIDS version; the first to use an alternative version was Lyssiotou (2000) who employed a dynamic version of the AIDS model of Anderson and Blundell (1983). The focus of the study was British demand for tourism to the United States, Canada and 16 European destinations. The key issue examined was the extent to which current tastes are formed through past consumption behaviour. The results show that price and expenditure elasticities of the various holiday destinations differ between the short run and the long run. For example, UK tourism demand for France is price inelastic in the short run but elastic in the long run. In the case of Greece–Italy the demand is found to be price inelastic both in the short run and the long run. Also, US–Canada appears to be a luxury holiday destination in the long run, although is not so according to the short-run expenditure elasticity. Overall, the long-run expenditure elasticities appear to be close to 1 everywhere suggesting that in the long run all the destinations included in the analysis benefit equally from an increase in British tourism expenditure. These findings are consistent with Divisekera (1995) who examined short- and long-run dynamics in tourism demand.

Durbarry and Sinclair (2003) investigated the demand for tourism by French nationals in Italy, Spain and the United Kingdom. They employ a linear version of the dynamic error-correction AIDS model of Anderson and Blundell (1983) (henceforth EC-LAAIDS). They estimate short-run and long-run demand elasticities. However, due to poor statistical fit, only the long-run elasticities are reported and evaluated. The results indicate that it is changes in relative effective own price competitiveness, rather than in the tourists' budget, that are the main drivers of changes in the destination countries' shares of the French tourism market. Li et al. (2004) used this approach to model UK demand for tourism in neighbouring Western European countries. The estimated expenditure elasticities show that travelling to most major destinations in Western Europe is a luxury for UK tourists in the long run. The demand for travel to these destinations is also found to be relatively more price elastic in the long run than it is in the short run. The calculated cross-price elasticities suggest that the substitution and (or) complementarity effects vary from destination to destination. The UK demand for tourism in the Mediterranean destinations of Malta, Cyprus and Spain was the focus of the study by Mangion et al. (2005). They applied the EC-LAAIDS model and their particular emphasis was on price competitiveness among these three destinations which are perceived as strong competitors. The results showed that – in terms of price competitiveness – Malta is the most price-sensitive destination, followed by Cyprus and Spain. The results failed to reveal any significant short-run demand effects. Han et al. (2006) model US tourism demand for four European destinations – France, Italy, the UK and Spain. The results show that price competitiveness is important for US demand for France, Italy and Spain but it is relatively unimportant in US tourism demand for the UK. France and Italy are regarded as substitutes by US tourists, as are Spain and Italy. As US expenditure rises, the market shares of Spain and the UK decline, while France and Italy benefit. Han et al. (2006) show further that that the static LAIDS model gives empirically better results than does the EC-LAIDS model. Somewhat contrary evidence is found by Cortés-Jiménez et al. (2009) who studied Italian demand for tourism in four European destinations – France, Germany, the UK and Spain. This study, based on monthly data, incorporates seasonality using dummy variables and accounts for preference changes using a linear time trend. While the study estimates both long- and short-run dynamic versions of the model, demand elasticities are reported only for the short run. This is somewhat puzzling because it is the long-run model that appears to be theoretically consistent (in terms of the acceptance of homogeneity and symmetry restrictions). The short-run elasticities revealed unusually high price-elastic demands ranging from -8.7 for France, to -8.6 for Germany and -5.8 for Spain. The empirical plausibility of these estimates needs to be questioned, as one would expect tourists to adjust to price changes slowly in the short run. Further, the statistical fit of the restricted EC model used for deriving elasticities is poor (only four of the ten own and cross-price coefficient ($c_{ij}s$) effects are statistically significant and none of the expenditure coefficients ($b_i s$) are statistically significant.

Empirical Analysis of Demand for Tourism Goods and Services (*Ex-post* Demands)

The second group of demand studies concern the demand for destination-specific tourism goods and services. More specifically, they attempt to analyse tourists' consumption behaviour or allocations of tourist spending among various goods and services at the destinations they visited. The economic parameters associated with *ex-post* tourist demands are important for destination management and for developing destination-specific strategies to maximize gains from tourism. Of the available research, one group of studies focus on demands by landed foreign tourists and the others focus on demands by domestic tourists. The studies that focus on *ex-post* demands include Divisekera (2007, 2009b, 2010a), Divisekera and Deegan (2010), Fujii et al. (1985), Sakai (1988) and

Wu et al. (2011). The studies investigating domestic demand for tourism goods and services include Coenen and Eekeren (2003), Divisekera (2007, 2009a, 2009b, 2010a, 2010b) and Pyo et al. (1991).

The first attempt to model *ex-post* tourism demand was Fujii et al. (1985). Based on the LAIDS model, they estimated demand for six categories of goods and services purchased by visitors to Hawaii. These categories were food and drink, lodging, recreation and entertainment, local transport, clothing and other. Their estimated expenditure elasticities are all positive, indicating that all goods purchased by visitors are normal goods. All the own price elasticities are negative and significantly different from 0. Based on the non-linear AIDS model, Divisekera (2009b) investigated the economic parameters underlying the *ex-post* demand for Australian tourism goods and services from ten source markets in Asia, Europe and North America.[16] These are respectively: China, Korea, Hong Kong, Malaysia, Taiwan, Indonesia, Singapore, Thailand, Germany and Canada. Five broad commodity aggregates representing a tourist's consumption bundle were used: accommodation, food, transport, shopping and entertainment. The necessary data were obtained from quarterly International Visitor Surveys conducted by *Tourism Australia* which provides itemized consumption expenditure data on a quarterly basis. Price indices were constructed for each broad commodity aggregate using detailed price data obtained from the Australian Bureau of Statistics. The study revealed substantial differences in consumption patterns by tourists from different source countries in Asia, North America and Europe. For example, expenditure elasticities of demand for the food and shopping aggregate are broadly similar across the source markets, with elasticity coefficients around unity in magnitude. However, elasticities with respect to accommodation varied across the markets. In general, demand for accommodation is the most expenditure-elastic across all of the commodity aggregates, with the exception of Chinese demand. Significant differences in the elasticities of demand for transportation are also evident, in the majority of cases demands are unitary elastic; the exceptions are Taiwanese, Thai, Korean and Chinese demands. Expenditure elasticities of demand for entertainment are around unity across the markets, with the exceptions of Singapore and China with elasticities greater than unity. In general, demands by tourists from all regions were found to be price inelastic, implying that all goods are necessities from a tourist's point of view. This result is consistent with the empirical reality that once tourists arrive at a destination, they are bound to consume the available goods and services. The cross-price elasticities reveal a gross complementarity of demands. This indicates that tourists tend to purchase a bundle of goods and services, and that all of them are necessary for the maximization of their utility from the visit. Divisekera (2010b) employed the same methodology to examine the consumption behaviour of foreign tourists from the four major source markets to Australia – New Zealand, Japan, the UK and the United States. The results from this study are consistent with the general findings of Divisekera (2009b) in that tourist demands for the bundle of goods and services are price inelastic, while expenditure elasticities varied across the commodity groups and among source markets.

Divisekera and Deegan (2010) provided further evidence on the consumption behaviour of foreign tourists in their analysis of the demand for Irish tourism goods and services. Using the non-linear AIDS model, they estimated five demand systems, with four representing the major source markets of tourists to Ireland. These were Great Britain, North America, mainland Europe and the rest of the world, and an aggregate model based on a pooled sample. Each system included six commodity aggregates including food, lodging (accommodation), transportation, shopping, sightseeing and (or) entertainment and a miscellaneous category. The data on various commodities consumed by tourists were obtained from the Irish Tourist Board (*Failte Ireland*) based on sample surveys. One finding of this study that is broadly consistent with the two previous studies is the apparent insensitivity of foreigners' demand in response to commodity prices. While there are notable variations in the consumption patterns of tourists from different source markets – reflecting differences in consumer preferences and consumption habits – in general, tourists' demand for the various Irish tourism goods and services is found to be price inelastic. Similarly, the cross-price elasticity values for all commodities across the source markets indicate gross complementarity. In relation to expenditure elasticities, substantial variations across the source markets are found. For example, the elasticity of demand for shopping is the highest among all commodities for the British tourists, whereas in the case of North American tourists, demand for accommodation is, relatively, the most expenditure elastic. In general, the North American demands for most Irish tourism goods and services are expenditure elastic, except for the demand for transportation, which is a necessity for North American tourists.

Wu et al. (2011), the most recent study on *ex-post* demands, concentrate on foreign demand for tourism goods and services in Hong Kong. Based on the EC-LAAIDS model, they estimate eight demand systems for Hong Kong's inbound tourism representing the source markets of Australia, the UK, the United States, Japan, South Korea, Singapore, Taiwan and mainland China. They classify tourist spending into four categories: shopping, hotel accommodation, meals outside hotels and other. Evaluation of demand parameters is carried out under three groups: long-haul destinations – Australia, the UK and the United States – and the short-haul markets – Japan, South Korea, Singapore, Taiwan and mainland China. The empirical results reveal different types of consumption behaviour among the eight source markets. For example, expenditure elasticities reveal an elastic demand for shopping by the tourists from the long- and short-haul haul markets implying that the tourists from these markets perceive shopping in Hong Kong as a luxury. In contrast, mainland Chinese tourists regard shopping in Hong Kong as a necessity, but view hotel accommodation as a luxury. In relation to price elasticities, the analysis is based on compensated elasticities and reveals relatively price-inelastic demand across the commodity groups. All the statistically significant cross-price elasticities are positive implying that the three commodity groups are substitutes. Overall, the empirical findings in of this study in relation to the own price and expenditure elasticities are consistent with those of Divisekera (2009b, 2010a) and Divisekera and Deegan (2010), however, the cross-price effects reveal contrary evidence.[17]

Analysis of Domestic Tourism Demands

The second group of studies addressing the consumption behaviour of tourists focus on domestic demands. The related studies based on the AIDS model include Coenen and Eekeren (2003) who studied Swedish demand and Divisekera (2008, 2009a, 2010c).[18] The first attempt to model domestic demand for tourism goods and services using the AIDS model was by Coenen and Eekeren (2003). They used a quadratic version of the AIDS model to analyse the demand for domestic tourism by Swedish households.

Using microeconomic data drawn from the Swedish tourism and travel database, they estimated ten individual demand systems, one aggregate demand and six additional systems distinguished by demographic (five income groups) and household compositional factors (four household groups). Each system included five commodity aggregates: groceries, restaurant meals, accommodation, transportation and shopping. The model for total expenditure (their aggregate model) shows that income elasticities for domestic tourism demand for the different household categories were all around 1, while the price elasticities reveal highly elastic demand. Price elasticities of demand for accommodation were the highest among the five commodity aggregates and the lowest is for restaurants.

Based on the non-linear AIDS model – using expenditure data collected from Australian National Visitor Surveys – Divisekera estimated a number of demand models focussing on different aspects of domestic demand for tourism by Australian households. These include the regional demand for domestic tourism (Divisekera, 2008, 2010c), aggregate demand for domestic tourism (Divisekera, 2009a) and leisure versus non-leisure tourism demands (Divisekera, 2010b). Each variant contained five commodity aggregates; these are food, accommodation, local transport, shopping and entertainment. In relation to regional demand overall, the estimated own price elasticities across the eight states and territories reveal relatively price inelastic demand for the five commodity aggregates, while the demands were found to be relatively expenditure elastic. The degree of sensitivity of demands to expenditure and prices, however, varied significantly across the eight states and territories. These variations may reflect the diversity of the preferences of the tourists from different origins.

In relation to leisure and non-leisure tourist demand, the demands by the leisure tourists are found to be relatively more sensitive to prices than are those of the non-leisure tourists. The cross-price elasticities derived from both models reveal gross complementarities of demands, implying that tourists' overall utility depends on their (joint) consumption of a bundle of goods and services. The observed price inelastic demands, coupled with the apparent complementarities of demands, may reflect the possibility of a latent price sensitivity associated with tourist demand.

CHALLENGES AND CONCLUSIONS

The AIDS model devised by Deaton and Muellbauer (1980) has come to be the industry standard in modern empirical demand analysis. Since its publication in 1980, several modifications and extensions have been proposed. The extensions include dynamic, inverse, quadratic and error correction versions. All of these variants of the AIDS model except the inverse AIDS have been employed by researchers of tourism demand. The AIDS model dominates as the single most widely used complete demand system by researchers in the tourism field. In addition to its attractive theoretical properties and flexibility, the popularity of this model among the applied researchers who rely on established demand systems to analyse specific issues of interest is due largely to the ease of estimation afforded by its linear version. This version, known as the LAAIDS, avoids the need for using complex non-linear estimation methods compared with a similar class of models such as the Translog demand systems of Christensen et al. (1975).[19] It is this version of the AIDS model (and its variants) that has been the principal base model used by researchers in tourism. The exceptions are Lyssiotou (2000) and studies by Divisekera (2009a, 2010a) that used the non-linear AIDS model.

The array of empirical studies using various versions of the AIDS model has explored different aspects of tourism demands, including international, domestic, and regional demands. Of the available empirical studies based on the AIDS model, the first group of studies attempt to evaluate the effects of incomes and prices as determinants of tourism demand for a group of destinations. Thus, international or destination-choice studies have been the central focus of most early empirical studies. The second group of studies focus on the demand for destination-specific tourism goods and services or *ex-post* tourism demands. They attempt to analyse tourists' consumption behaviour or allocations of tourist spending among various goods and services at the destinations they visited. The economic parameters associated with the *ex-post* tourist demands are important for destination management and for developing destination-specific strategies to maximize the gains from tourism. The second group of studies addressing the consumption behaviour of tourists focus on domestic demands.

These latter studies have generated a large number of economic parameters enriching our knowledge and understanding about the dynamics of this important activity that generates multiple socio-economic benefits. Regardless of the particular version of the model employed, the data used for estimation and their focus, all studies provide similar if not identical sets of economic parameters associated with tourism demands. They are, respectively, expenditure and (or) income elasticities and price elasticities. Expenditure elasticities highlight the effects of total tourist spending and (or) incomes on demand, and how sensitive their choices are to changes in total spending. Likewise, price elasticities indicate how the prices of tourist products affect the demand for a given product (own price elasticities) and the cross-price effects (cross-price elasticities) or interactions among and between alternative products.

The AIDS methodology allows evaluations of price effects in a consistent manner from two theoretical perspectives: Marshallian or uncompensated, and Hicksian or compensated price effects. Marshallian elasticities indicate how consumers (tourists) react to changes in the market price of a product, and the Hicksian price elasticities reveal the same effects under the proposition that consumers (tourists) have been compensated for price changes. The latter implies that a consumer's real income remains unchanged (following a price change), thus the Hicksian price elasticities reveal pure substitution effects of a price change, whereas the Marshallian elasticities reflect both income and substitution effects associated with price changes. The relevance of the two elasticity concepts as a guide to understanding market behaviour, or to develop appropriate policy measures in response to them, and (or) to exploit them for own advantage is different. For example, if the focus is to develop pricing and other strategies to exploit market conditions, the appropriate guide is provided by the Marshallian price elasticities. Alternatively, if the focus is on the welfare of consumers and the consideration is to ensure that price changes leave consumers unaffected in terms of their level of consumption (after the price change), then the concept of Hicksian price elasticities is the relevant concept that should be used as a guide to develop appropriate compensation measures.

The empirical studies of tourism demands reviewed in the preceding sections of this chapter report both types (in majority of cases), or at least one type of elasticity. Most of these studies are specific in the sense that the focus is demand from a given origin to a group of destinations or countries. Most early studies concentrated on US demand for international travel to European and Mediterranean destinations (Han et al., 2006; O'Hagan and Harrison, 1984; Papatheodorou, 1999; Sinclair and Syriopoulos, 1993; White, 1982, 1985). De Mello et al. (2002) and Li et al. (2004) concentrated on UK demand for tourism in Europe. All of these studies are based on the AIDS model and use similar types of price measures; often the real exchange rate is used as a proxy for destination prices.

Despite the fact that almost all of the studies use the same methodology and similar types of explanatory variables, there is hardly any agreement in terms of the observed price and expenditure effects. For example, in the case of UK demand, the expenditure elasticity for Portugal was estimated at 0.04 by Papatheodorou (1999) compared to 1.58 by Syriopoulos and Sinclair (1993). Li et al. (2004) report a very high elasticity for Greece (-2.75), whereas Papatheodorou (1999) found a relatively low value (-0.93) for the same country. The same applies to many other available international demand studies. The variations in elasticities between studies are so plain that no generalization can be made about the nature and magnitudes of elasticities of demands from a given origin to chosen destinations. Thus, for specific purposes such as developing policy measures to exploit or correct prevailing market conditions, demand parameters need to be estimated by taking into account both prevailing market conditions and they must use the most current data.

Most attention among researchers in recent times appears to be on keeping up with the changing econometric methodology, rather than on improving the modelling process. For example, none of the studies except for White (1985) and Divisekera (2003, 2009c) attempted to incorporate one crucial cost factor affecting international tourism demands, namely the cost of transport. Similarly, all the studies continue to use the CPI (adjusted for exchange rates) as a proxy for tourism prices. This is a major drawback, as they grossly overestimate or underestimate the real cost of tourism goods and services. Thus, there is a need to develop appropriate tourism price indices as inputs for demand model estimation. Future studies need to concentrate on improving databases and developing reasonable price measures that capture both the costs of travel and tourism goods which are the key determinants of tourism demands.

NOTES

1. Of the other existing demand systems, two of the studies (Bakkal, 1991; Bakkal and Scaperlanda, 1991) were based on the *Translog* demand system and three on the *Linear Expenditure System* (Pyo et al., 1991; Sakai, 1988; Smeral, 1988).
2. The neoclassical view of consumer demand has several important underpinnings. A central concept is the neoclassical view of the consumer as a rational choosing agent who is motivated to seek the highest level of satisfaction or utility. A consumer's wants depend on the level of utility that a particular purchase will generate. This implies that the value of a particular good is dictated not solely by its price, but by a consumer's subjective feelings toward it. The neoclassical theory of consumer behaviour is well documented in the work of Hicks (1956) and Samuelson (1947). An extensive treatment of consumer theory leading to systems of demand functions can be found in Barten (1977), Deaton (1986), Deaton and Muellbauer (1980a), Goldberger (1967), Phlips (1974), Powell (1974) and Theil (1975, 1976).
3. Note, however, that the resulting demand functions are different. In the primal case, the solution is a set of Marshallian or uncompensated demand functions, and in the dual case they are Hicksian, or compensated, demand functions.

4. The consumer's maximization problem implies four constraints on the demand equations. The first is *demand homogeneity* which states that an equiproportional change in prices has no effect on the quantities demanded when real income is held constant. The second constraint is symmetry of the substitution effects, or *Slutsky symmetry*. This states that when real income is held constant, the effect of a \$1 rise in the price of commodity *x* on the consumption of commodity *y* is exactly equal to the effect on *x* consumption of a \$1 rise in the price of *y*. The third is the negativity condition (the law of demand, namely that demand curves slope down when real income remains constant). A fourth is the aggregation or *adding up restriction*. The adding up condition implies that expenditures on individual goods must 'add up' to total expenditure ($\Sigma p_i q_i = m$).

5. A functional form for a complete system of demand functions is said to be flexible if at any given set of non-negative prices, incomes, and parameters, demand functions can be chosen so that the own, cross-price and income elasticities are capable of assuming arbitrary values, subject only to the requirement of theoretical consistency (Pollak and Wales, 1992).

6. Other available flexible functional forms include the *Generalized Leontief* (Diewert, 1971, 1974) and the *Generalized Cobb–Douglas* (Gallant, 1984; Lewbel, 1987). These are not widely used in the empirical literature. For an excellent review of alternative flexible functional forms see Thompson (1988).

7. Despite its popularity and wide applications, the relative merits of the LA-AIDS have been debated and one particular issue concerns the calculation of price elasticities (for details, see Green and Alston, 1990; 1991; Pashardes, 1993; and Buse, 1994). This linear version is the most widely used AIDS variant in the literature. Despite its popularity and wide application, the relative merits of LA-AIDS have been debated on several grounds. One issue concerns the specification and estimation of price elasticities (for details, see Buse, 1994; Pashardes, 1993; Green and Alston, 1990, 1991). Another concerns the overall properties of the LA-AIDS model (for details see Buse, 1998; Eales and Unnevehr, 1988; LaFrance, 2004; Moschini, 1995). In any event, as Holt and Goodwin (2009) pointed out, all issues pertaining to the specification, estimation, and interpretation of the LA-AIDS model are rendered moot if instead the Translog price index $a(p)$ in (8.12) is simply used in estimation.

8. According to Lau (1986), among the five criteria the only area where a compromise can be made is in the domain of applicability (regularity). This is because most practical applications can be accommodated, even if the functional form is not globally theoretically consistent, as long as it is theoretically consistent within a sufficiently large subset of the space of independent variables. For another detailed review of flexible functional forms and selection criteria see Thompson (1988).

9. A comparison of expenditure elasticities – in relation to necessities derived from a version of a regular flexible functional form (McFadden and Cobb–Douglas) with the LES and AIDS – revealed some interesting evidence. The movements in expenditure elasticities in relation to food (also clothing and tobacco) derived from the Cooper–McLaren model and the LES follow the same trends. The expenditure elasticity of food, for example, rose from 0.33 to 0.70 from 1953–54 to 1990–91 as in the case of the elasticities derived from the LES (in the LES case, the elasticities increased from 0.42 to 0.64). By contrast, the elasticities derived from the AIDS took the opposite trend, declining from 0.64 to 0.39. The movements in the expenditure elasticities derived from the AIDS are closer to the observed facts (that is, when real incomes grow all goods, and in particular necessities, become less luxurious (Flood et al., 1984). The Chalfant (1987) results, drawn from his globally regular version of the AIDS, also indicate irregularities.

10. An implication of the negativity condition is that Hicksian or compensated demand functions will be non-increasing in own price (that is, the Slutsky matrix will be negative semi-definite). Thus, a simple rule of thumb to test empirically whether the negativity condition is met is to verify that the compensated own price elasticities are negative. An alternative suggested in the literature is to re-parameterize the Slutsky matrix so that the negativity condition may be directly imposed at a point during estimation (for details, see Diewert and Wales, 1988a; 1988b; Moschini, 1998; Ryan and Wales, 1998).

11. The literature offers several explanations for the over-rejection of the homogeneity condition. These include particular parameterization of demand systems (see, for example, Byron, 1970a, b), aggregation biases in commodity groups (Parikh, 1988), misspecifications caused by omitted variables (such as changes in taste), systematic errors associated with price and quantity data, and errors associated with dynamic misspecification (Anderson and Blundell (1982).

12. Using techniques developed for estimating cointegrating vectors in the presence of deterministic trends, Ng (1995) finds that homogeneity holds in many cases.

13. Given the additivity of regression disturbances, one can use the Zellner (1962) method of Seemingly Unrelated Regressions (SUR) to obtain parameter estimates. However, under this procedure estimates depend on the equation dropped during estimation (Pollak and Wales, 1992).

14. A few authors have used two alternative models, the *Linear Expenditure System* (LES) (Pyo et al., 1991; Sakai, 1988; Smeral, 1988) and the *Translog Demand System* (Bakkal, 1991; Bakkal and Scaperlanda, 1990). All other studies are based on the *Almost Ideal Demand System* (AIDS) and its variants.

15. Expenditure elasticity shows how the quantity purchased changes (how sensitive it is) in response to a change in the consumer's expenditure/budget (a proxy for income). In the AIDS context, where demand is measured in terms of expenditure/budget shares, expenditure elasticity refers to changes in expenditure/budget share of a commodity (say share of expenditure on a particular destination) arising from a change in the travel budget of a traveller. This is represented by the ratio between percentage change in quantity demanded and percentage change in expenditure. If the percentage change in the quantity demanded is greater than the percentage change in consumer expenditure, demand is said to be expenditure elastic or responsive to changes in consumer expenditure. If the percentage change in the quantity demanded is less than the percentage change in consumer expenditure, the demand is said to be expenditure inelastic or not responsive to changes in consumer expenditure. The higher the expenditure elasticity, the more sensitive consumer demand is to expenditure changes. Although, the measure of expenditure elasticity is different from that of income elasticity (which is calculated using changes in the income of the traveller), it is customary to interpret expenditure elasticities as analogous with income elasticities. If the income (expenditure) elasticity of demand is positive, the good is considered a normal good, and if the income (expenditure) elasticity of demand is negative, the good is classified as an inferior good. Similarly, if the percentage change in the quantity demanded is greater than the percentage change in consumer income (expenditure), the demand is said to be income (expenditure) elastic, or responsive to changes in consumer income (expenditure). If the percentage change in the quantity demanded is less than the percentage change in consumer income (expenditure), the demand is said to be income (expenditure) inelastic, or not responsive to changes in consumer income (expenditure). Those commodities with income (expenditure) elasticities greater than unity are classified as 'luxuries' and the commodities with income (expenditure) elasticities less than one (positive in value) are classified as 'necessities'.

16. Chronologically, the next to follow was the study by Sakai (1988) who estimated two demand systems for business and pleasure travellers based on the *Linear Expenditure System* for Hawaii. Sakai used microexpenditure data from individual tourist parties to Hawaii drawn from the Hawaii Visitors Bureau expenditure surveys. Broad commodity groups included food, lodging, recreation, local transportation, clothing and a miscellaneous category. Sakai found that for business travellers, lodging is a luxury good. For pleasure travellers, lodging and transportation are luxury goods, while food and recreation are necessities. Further, he found that business travellers' demands are less price sensitive than pleasure travellers' demands are.

17. It should be noted that no strict comparison is warranted here, given that the present study concerns only a comparatively limited number of commodity groups. Further, the analysis is based on compensated demand elasticities (cross-price) which measure the pure substitution effect of a price change. This means either that the real expenditure is held constant, or the consumer has been compensated for the loss of income associated with the change in the price of the commodity in question.

18. Pyo et al. (1991) were the first to examine the demand for tourism goods and services by domestic tourists. Based on the *Linear Expenditure System* they estimated US domestic tourist demand for five commodity groups: transportation, lodging, food, entertainment and recreation and other goods and services. Transportation is found to be the most price sensitive of all, and they argued further that the widely held perception that tourism products are luxuries may result from the income effect on transportation.

19. Each of these demand systems has identical properties: both have budget share Engel curves that are linear in the log of total expenditures, and similar aggregation properties; and they have indirect utility functions that are built up of polynomials in log prices. Moreover, as Lewbel (1989) has shown, the AIDS and Translog demand systems are almost equal in terms of explanatory power and goodness of fit.

REFERENCES

Anderson, G. and R. Blundell (1983), 'Testing restrictions in a flexible dynamic demand system: an application to consumers' expenditure in Canada', *The Review of Economic Studies*, **50**, 397–410.
Anderson, G.J. and R.W. Blundell (1982), 'Estimation and hypothesis testing in dynamic singular equation systems', *Econometrica: Journal of the Econometric Society*, 1559–1571.
Arrow, K.J., B.D. Bernheim, M.S. Feldstein, D.L. McFadden, J.M. Poterba and R.M. Solow (2011), '100 years of the American Economic Review: the top 20 articles', *The American Economic Review*, **101** (1), 1–8.
Attfield, C.L.F. (1997), 'Estimating a cointegrating demand system', *European Economic Review*, **41** (1), 61–73.
Bakkal, I. (1991), 'Characteristics of West German demand for international tourism in the northern Mediterranean region', *Applied Economics*, **23** (2), 295–304.

Bakkal, I. and A. Scaperlanda (1991), 'Characteristics of US demand for European Tourism: a translog approach', *Weltwirtschaftliches Archiv*, **127**, 119–137.

Banks, J., R. Blundell and A. Lewbel (1997), 'Quadratic Engel curves and consumer demand', *Review of Economics and Statistics*, **79** (4), 527–539.

Barten, A.P. (1969), 'Maximum likelihood estimation of a complete system of demand equations', *European Economic Review*, **1**, 7–73.

Barten, A.P. (1977), 'The systems of consumer demand functions approach: a review', *Econometrica*, **45**, 23–51.

Berndt, E.R., M.N. Darrough and W.E. Diewert (1977), 'Flexible functional forms and expenditure distributions: an application to Canadian consumer demand functions', *International Economic Review*, **18** (3), 651–675.

Buse, A. (1994), 'Evaluating the linearized almost ideal demand system', *American Journal of Agricultural Economics*, 781–793.

Buse, A. (1998), 'Testing homogeneity in the linearized almost ideal demand system', *American Journal of Agricultural Economics*, **80**, 208–220.

Byron, R.P. (1970a), 'A simple method for estimating demand systems under seperable utility assumptions', *Review of Economic Studies*, **37**, 271–274.

Byron, R.P. (1970b), 'The restricted aitken estimation of sets of demand functions', *Econometrica*, **38**, 816–830.

Carlos, A., P. Daniel and M. Gehlhar (2004), ' Locating seasonal cycles in demand models', *Applied Economics Letters*, **11**, 533–535.

Chalfant, J.A. (1987), 'A globally flexible, almost ideal demand system', *Journal of Business & Economic Statistics*, **5** (2), 233–242.

Christensen, L.R., D.W. Jorgenson and L.J. Lau (1975), 'Transcendental logarithmic utility functions', *The American Economic Review*, **65** (3), 367–383.

Coenen, M. and L. Van Eekeren (2003), 'A study of the demand for domestic tourism by Swedish households using a two-staged budgeting model', *Scandinavian Journal of Hospitality and Tourism*, **3** (2), 114–133.

Cooper, R.J. and K.R. McLaren (1988), 'Regular alternatives to the almost ideal demand system', Department of Econometrics Working Paper No. 12/88, Monash University.

Cooper, R.J. and K.R. McLaren (1992), 'An empirically oriented demand system with improved regularity properties', *Canadian Journal of Economics*, **25** (3), 652–668.

Cooper, R.J., K.R. McLaren and P. Parameshwaran, (1991), 'A system of demand equations satisfying effectively global curvature conditions', Department of Econometrics Working Paper No. 7/91, (Revised Version 1992), Monash University.

Cortés-Jiménez, I., R. Durbarry and M. Pulina (2009), 'Estimation of out bound Italian toursim demand: a monthly dynamic EC-LAID model', *Toursim Economics*, **15** (3), 547–565.

De Mello, M.M. and N. Fortuna (2005), 'Testing alternative dynamic systems for modelling tourism demand', *Tourism Economics*, **11**, 517–537.

De Mello, M.M., A. Pack and M.T. Sinclair (2002), 'A system of equations model of UK tourism demand in neighbouring countries', *Applied Economics*, **34**, 509–521.

Deaton, A. (1979), 'The distance function in consumer behavior with applications to index numbers and optimal taxation', *Review of Economic Studies*, **46** (July 1979), 391–405.

Deaton, A. (1986), 'Demand Analysis', in Z. Griliches and M.D. Intrilligator (eds), *Handbook of Econometrics*, Vol III, Amsterdam: North-Holland, pp. 1767–1839.

Deaton, A. and J. Muellbauer (1980a), 'An almost ideal demand system', *American Economic Review*, **70** (3), 312–326.

Deaton, A. and J. Muellbauer (1980b), *Economics and Consumer Behavior*, Cambridge: Cambridge University Press.

Diewert, W.E. (1971), 'An application of the Shephard duality theorem: a generalized Leontief production function', *Journal of Political Economy*, **79**, 481–507.

Diewert, W.E. (1974), 'Applications of duality theory', in M.D. Intrilligator and D.A. Kendrick (eds), *Frontiers of Quantitative Economics*, Vol. II, Amsterdam: North-Holland, Chapter 3.

Diewert, W.E. (1982), 'Duality approaches to microeconomic theory', in K.J. Arrow and M.D. Intrilligator (eds), *Handbook of Mathematical Economics*, Vol II, Amsterdam: North Holland.

Diewert, W.E. and T.J. Wales (1987), 'Flexible functional forms and global curvature conditions', *Econometrica*, **55**, 43–68.

Diewert, W.E. and T.J. Wales (1988a), 'Normalized quadratic systems of consumer demand functions', *Journal of Business & Economic Statistics*, **6** (3), 303–312.

Diewert, W.E. and T.J. Wales (1988b), 'A normalized quadratic semi flexible functional form', *Journal of Econometrics*, **37**, 327–342.

Divisekera, S. (1995), 'An econometric model of international visitors flows to Australia', *Australian Economic Papers*, **34** (65), 291–308.

Divisekera, S. (2003), 'A model of demand for international tourism', *Annals of Tourism Research*, **30**, 31–49.
Divisekera, S. (2007), *Modelling And Estimation of Tourism Demand Elasticities: A Study of Tourist Expenditure Allocation in Australia*, Gold Coast, Australia: CRC Sustainable Tourism.
Divisekera, S. (2008), 'Modelling regional demand for tourism services: an analysis of regional demand for domestic tourism in Australia', *Global Business & Economics Anthology*, **2**, 318–326.
Divisekera, S. (2009a), 'Economics of domestic tourism: a study of Australian demand for tourism goods and services', *Tourism Analysis*, **14** (3), 279–282.
Divisekera, S. (2009b), 'Ex-post demands for Australian tourism goods and services', *Tourism Economics*, **15** (1), 153–180.
Divisekera, S. (2009c), 'An analysis of demand for international air transportation and tourism: interactions and dependencies', presented at the second conference of the International Association for Tourism Economics (IATE), Chiang Mai, Thailand.
Divisekera, S. (2010a), 'Economics of tourist's consumption behaviour: some evidence from Australia', *Tourism Management*, **31** (5), 629–636.
Divisekera, S. (2010b), 'Economics of leisure and non-leisure tourist demand: a study of domestic demand for Australian tourism', *Tourism Economics*, **16** (1), 117–136.
Divisekera, S. (2010c), 'Regional variations in tourist consumption patterns: a model of tourist expenditure allocation', *Global Business & Economics Review*, **2**, 101–111.
Divisekera, S. and J. Deegan (2010), 'An analysis of consumption behaviour of foreign tourists in Ireland', *Applied Economics*, **42**, 1681–1697.
Durbarry, R. and Sinclair, M.T. (2003), 'Market shares analysis: the case of French tourism demand', *Annals of Tourism Research*, **30** (4), 927–941.
Eales, J.S. and L.J. Unnevehr (1988), 'Demand for beef and chicken products: separability and structural change', *American Journal of Agricultural Economics*, **70** (3), 521–532.
Eales, J.S. and L.J. Unnevehr (1993), 'Structural change in U.S. meat demand', *American Journal of Agricultural Economics*, **75**, 259–268.
Eales, J.S. and L.J. Unnevehr (1994), 'The inverse almost ideal demand system', *European Economic Review*, **38** (1), 101–115.
Flood, L.R., R. Finke and M.C. Rosalsky (1984), 'How trustworthy are the standard errors of translog coefficients?', *Economics Letters*, **16**, 59–62.
Fraser, I. and I.A. Moosa (2002), 'Demand estimation in the presence of stochastic trend and seasonality: the case of meat demand in the United Kingdom', *American Journal of Agricultural Economics*, **84**, 83–89.
Frisch, R. (1959), 'A complete scheme for computing all direct and cross demand elasticities in a model with many sectors', *Econometrica*, **27**, 177–196.
Fujii, E., M. Khaled and J. Mark (1985), 'An almost ideal demand system for visitor expenditures', *Journal of Transport Economics and Policy*, **19**, 161–171.
Gallant, A.R. (1984), 'The Fourier flexible form', *American Journal of Agricultural Economics*, **66**, 204–208.
Goldberger, A.S. (1987), *Functional Form and Utility. A Review of Consumer Demand Theory*, Boulder, CO: West View Press.
Green, R. and J. Alston (1990), 'Elasticities in AIDS models', *American Journal of Agricultural Economics*, **72**, 442–445.
Green, R. and J. Alston (1991), 'Elasticities in AIDS models: a clarification and extension', *American Journal of Agricultural Economics*, **73**, 874–875.
Han, Z., R. Durbarry and M.T. Sinclair (2006), 'Modelling US tourism demand for European destinations', *Tourism Management*, **27** (1), 1–10.
Hicks, J.R. (1956), *A Revision of Demand Theory*, Oxford: Oxford University Press.
Holt, M.T. and B.K. Goodwin (2009), 'The almost ideal and translog demand systems', in D.J. Slottje (ed.), *Quantifying Consumer Preferences (Contributions to Economic Analysis, Volume 288)*, Bradford, UK: Emerald Group Publishing Limited, pp. 37–59.
Houthakker, H.S. (1960), 'Additive preferences', *Econometrica*, **28**, 244–257.
Judge, G.G., W.E. Griffiths, C.R. Hill and T.-C. Lee (1980), *The Theory and Practice of Econometrics*, New York: John Wiley.
Karagiannisa, G. and G.J. Mergos (2002), 'Estimating theoretically consistent demand systems using cointegration techniques with application to Greek food data', *Economics Letters*, **74**, 137–143.
Keuzenkamp, H.A. and A.P. Barten (1995), 'Rejection without falsification, on the history of testing the homogeneity condition in the theory of consumer demand', *Journal of Econometrics*, **67** (1), 103–127.
LaFrance, J.T. (2004), 'Integrability of the linear approximate almost ideal demand system', *Economic Letters*, **84**, 297–303.
Lanza, A., P. Temple and G. Urga (2003), 'The implications of tourism specialization in the long run: an econometric analysis for 13 OECD economies', *Tourism Management*, **24**, 315–321.

Lau, L. (1986), 'Functional forms in econometric model building', in Z. Griliches and M.D. Intriligator (eds), *Handbook of Econometrics*, Amsterdam: North-Holland, pp. 1516–1566.

Lewbel, A. (1987), 'Fractional demand systems', *Journal of Econometrics*, **36**, 331–337.

Lewbel, A. (1989), 'Nesting the AIDS and translog demand systems', *International Economic Review*, **30**, 349–356.

Lewbell, A. and S. Ng (2005), 'Demand systems with non-stationary prices', *Review of Economics and Statistics*, **87**, 479–494.

Li, G., H. Song and S.F. Witt (2004), 'Modelling tourism demand: a dynamic linear AID approach', *Journal of Travel Research*, **43** (22), 141–150.

Lyssiotou, P. (2000), 'Dynamic analysis of British demand for tourism abroad', *Empirical Economics*, **25**, 421–436.

Malinvaud, E. (1980), *Statistical Methods of Econometrics*, Amsterdam: North-Holland.

Mangion, M.L., R. Durbarry and M.T. Sinclair (2005), 'Tourism competitiveness: price and quality', *Tourism Economics*, **11** (1), 45–68.

Moschini, G. (1995), 'Units of measurement and the stone index in demand system estimation', *American Journal of Agricultural Economics*, **77**, 63–68.

Moschini, G. (1998), 'The semi flexible almost ideal demand system', *European Economic Review*, **42**, 349–364.

Ng, S. (1995), 'Testing for homogeneity in demand systems when the regressors are non-stationary', *Journal of Applied Econometrics*, **10**, 147–163.

O'Hagan, J.W. and M.J. Harrison (1984), 'Market shares of US tourist expenditure in Europe: an econometric analysis', *Applied Economics*, **16**, 919–931.

Papatheodorou, A. (1999), 'The demand for international tourism in the Mediterranean region', *Applied Economics*, **31** (5), 619–630.

Parikh, A. (1988), 'An econometric study on estimation of trade shares using the almost ideal demand system in the world link', *Applied Economics*, **20**, 1017–1039.

Pashardes, P. (1993), 'Bias in the estimating the almost ideal demand system with the Stone index approximation', *The Economic Journal*, **103**, 908–915.

Phlips, L. (1974), *Applied Consumption Analysis*, 2nd edition, Amsterdam: North-Holland.

Pollak, R.A. and T.J. Wales (1992), *Demand System Specification and Estimation*, Oxford: Oxford University Press.

Powell, A.A. (1966), 'A complete system of demand equations for the Australian economy fitted by a model of additive preferences', *Econometrica*, **34**, 661–675.

Powell, A.A. (1974), *Empirical Analytics of Demand Systems*, Lexington, Washington, DC: D.C. Heath.

Pyo, S.S., M. Uysal and R.W. McLellan (1991), 'A linear expenditure model for tourism demand', *Annals of Tourism Research*, **18**, 443–454.

Ryan, D.L. and T.J. Wales (1998), ' A simple method for imposing local curvature in some flexible consumer–demand systems', *Journal of Business and Economic Statistics*, **16**, 331–338.

Sakai, M.Y. (1988), 'A micro-analysis of business travel demand', *Applied Economics*, **20**, 1481–1495.

Samuelson, P. (1947), *Foundations of Economic Analysis*, Cambridge, MA: Harvard University Press.

Shephard, R. (1953), *Cost and Production Functions*, Princeton, NJ: Princeton University Press.

Sinclair, M.T. and T.C. Syriopoulos (1993), 'An econometric study tourism demand: the AID model of U.S. and European tourism in Mediterranean countries', *Applied Economics*, **25** (12), 1541–1552.

Smeral, E. (1988), 'Tourism demand, economic theory and econometrics: an integrated approach', *Journal of Travel Research*, **26**, 38–42.

Stone, R. (1954), 'Linear expenditure systems and demand analysis: an application to the pattern of British demand', *The Economic Journal*, **64**, 511–527.

Theil, H. (1975), *Theory and Measurement of Consumer Demand*, Vol. I, Amsterdam: North-Holland.

Theil, H. (1976), *Theory and Measurement of Consumer Demand*, Vol. II, Amsterdam: North Holland.

Thomas, R.L. (1987), *Applied Demand Analysis*, London and New York: Longman.

Thompson, G.D. (1988), 'Choice of flexible functional forms: review and appraisal', *Western Journal of Agricultural Economics*, **13** (2), 169–183.

White, K.J. (1982), 'The demand for international travel: a system-wide analysis for US travel to Western Europe', Discussion Paper No. 82/28, University of British Columbia, Department of Economics.

White, K.J. (1985), 'An international travel demand model, US Travel to Western Europe', *Annals of Tourism Research*, **12** (4), 529–545.

Wu, D.C., G. Li and H. Song (2011), 'Analyzing tourist consumption: a dynamic system-of-equations approach', *Journal of Travel Research*, **50** (1), 46–56.

Zellner, A. (1962), 'An efficient method of estimating seemingly unrelated regressions and tests for aggregation bias', *Journal of the American Statistical Association*, **57**, 348–368.

9 Hedonic price analysis
Andreas Papatheodorou, Zheng Lei and
Alexandros Apostolakis

INTRODUCTION

Pricing is a strategic choice for all firms. It not only generates revenue for a company to survive but can also be used as a communicator, as a bargaining tool and a competitive weapon. The consumer can use price as a means of comparing products, judging relative value for money or product quality (Brassington and Pettitt, 2007). In tourism, pricing decisions are often complex. For example, the price of a hotel room is normally affected by seasonality, type of the room, facilities provided, or even attributes of the external environment such as noise, pollution, distance from a specific landmark, or outside views.

From a managerial perspective, it is critically important to understand consumer perceptions of each of the attributes associated with the price: characteristics that a customer is willing to make an extra payment for and those which are irrelevant in the determination of consumer choices and preferences (Chen and Rothschild, 2010). Hedonic price analysis (HPA) makes it easier to discern which characteristics are valued by consumers and to what extent (Falk, 2008). In addition, HPA is also able to put a price estimate onto non–market product or service characteristics. For example, Mahan (1997) found that proximity to river streams had a significant influence on willingness to pay (i.e., respondents valued the proximity to river streams equal to $13.81 per foot). Hence, this technique is particularly useful for managerial decision making and evaluating individual preferences. In this chapter, we will explain the theory of HPA, followed by an illustration of its application in tourism research, and concluded by a discussion of managerial implications.

NATURE OF HEDONIC PRICE ANALYSIS AND ITS EVOLUTION

HPA is an economic valuation technique based on revealed preferences. Economic valuation has received considerable attention in the tourism literature recently as a result of various developments in the sector. On the one hand, increased levels of competition in the industry (emergence of new destinations, expansion of the boundaries of the tourism economy) imply that suppliers of tourism products and services have to improve their competitiveness in relation to close rivals and incumbents. Practically, this means that suppliers need to identify the aspect of their business that generates a competitive advantage and capitalize on it. To do so, tourism suppliers have to evaluate individual preferences for particular attributes of the product or service they bring to the market. The above rationale is equally applicable to both destinations and specific tourist attractions or resources.

On the other hand, the recent emergence of the 'evidence based' principle in tourism policy and decision making (Banks, 2009; The Countryside Agency, 2006) implies the need for further justification of public investment or private expenditure in tourism. In other words, the need for accountability regarding expenditure levels in tourism has driven stakeholders to adopt economic valuation techniques that reveal individual willingness to pay for a given level of product characteristic. A positive willingness to pay for a particular product attribute or characteristic is taken to signify a positive contribution to individual utility levels. Thus, the positive contribution of a given change in the product's or service's configuration merits or justifies the allocation of additional financial resources on the basis of improving individual welfare levels.

On these grounds, HPA is used to estimate economic values for attributes or product characteristics that directly affect prices for tourism products and services in the marketplace. Revealed preference methods use information from tourists' expressed preferences on existing markets to make statements regarding the demand for tourism goods and services. As such, revealed preference methods are quite useful in making inferences regarding the effect of a number of variables or explanatory factors on tourist expenditure patterns (Apostolakis and Jaffry 2009).

BACKGROUND AND TYPE OF PROBLEMS THAT HEDONIC PRICE ANALYSIS IS DESIGNED TO HANDLE

The HPA has its origin in Lancaster's (1971) theory of consumer demand. "The theory holds that consumer products are essentially bundles of 'separable' characteristics – such as comfort, convenience and reliability – that can be assessed accurately by value-conscious consumer" (Schwieterman, 1995, p. 292). The theory of HPA was formally formulated by Rosen (1974) in a seminal paper where he uses a conventional utility-maximizing approach to derive implicit attribute prices for multi-attribute goods under conditions of perfect competition (Andersson et al., 2010). The value that consumers attach to the characteristics is reflected in the price of the differentiated product.

HPA thus aims to disentangle the impact of the various attributes on implicit prices where positive attributes are expected to boost the overall price and have a positive effect on individual utility levels. Correspondingly, negative attributes exert downward pressure on the price and have a negative effect on utility levels (Thrane, 2005). Tourism resources are characterized as multi-attribute and multi-value resources (Oh, 2009; Riganti and Nijkamp, 2008), so the application of HPA in this setting offers considerably better and richer results as compared to other economic valuation techniques.

Another problem addressed by HPA is when researchers have to evaluate non-market elements of the tourism offering. Increasingly these days the interaction of tourism and the environment has become more complex than ever before. This is mainly due to changing consumer preferences and lifestyle and greater environmental awareness. The increasing "convergence" between tourism and the environment implies that a rising number of tourism product attributes cannot be evaluated using conventional market-based methods, simply because there is no established market for these attributes or resources. Hence, traditional market-based approaches cannot really capture the effect of an unspoilt ecosystem, or the existence of an area of natural outstanding beauty in the tourist destination. At the same time, we know that tourists derive pleasure by visiting or vacationing in or near pristine and unspoilt environments (Maddison and Bigano, 2003). HPA offers a solution to this conundrum by establishing surrogate markets to place a premium to the effect of non-market-based attributes on the tourism product or service on offer (Lise and Tol 2002, Maddison 2001). Regression techniques make it easier to estimate the implicit price for each attribute (Andersson et al., 2010) with the parameter of the hedonic price function revealing the marginal value consumers place on each of the individual attributes (Rigall-I-Torrent and Fluvia, 2011). While semi-logarithmic, log-linear, and linear Box–Cox functional forms of the regression model are all compatible with the theory of hedonic price analysis, most of the previous research seem to have followed Rosen's (1974) advice using the semi-log form (Andersson et al., 2010). The latter implies that the dependent variable (price of the evaluated product or service) is of a logarithmic form, whereas all the explanatory variables enter the equation in a linear format. The relationship between a tourist product or service attributes and its associated price may not be a linear one simply because the market may not be in long run equilibrium. In tourism, this may arise due to supply side disequilibrium conditions, or temporal variations in supply and product/ service quality.

A basic hedonic price model for the price of a tourism product may be specified as a function of a number of attributes:

$$\ln P_i = \alpha + \beta X_{ij} + \varepsilon_i \tag{9.1}$$

where $\ln P_i$ is the natural logarithm of the price of a particular tourism product i; X_{ij} is a vector of attributes j associated with the tourism product; α is the intercept; and ε_i is a random error term which is independent and identically distributed with zero expectation and constant variance. X_{ij} may be measured in logs or levels. The partial derivative of P_i with respect to each of the characteristics j, $\partial P_i/\partial X_{ij}$, refers to the marginal implicit price, which represents the consumer's valuation of (or willingness to pay for) the particular attribute of the tourism product. The predicted price can also be compared with the observed price to reveal whether the tourism product is significantly over- or underpriced (Falk, 2008).

A unique feature of hedonic price analysis is the extensive use of dummy variables to measure the qualitative attributes of a product. To provide precise explanation of each coefficient associated with the dummy variables, it is necessary to transform the estimated coefficient by $e^{\beta-1}$, where β is the coefficient and e is the base of the natural logarithm. This transformation gives the estimated effect of the dummy in percentage terms, while the monetary values can be obtained by multiplying $e^{\beta-1}$ by the average level value of the dependent variable in the sample (Monty and Skidmore, 2003). Moreover, and while the traditional HPA precludes the introduction of non-attribute variables into the econometric function, the relaxation of this constraint can offer useful insight from a competitiveness and/or marketing perspective. For example, in a HPA study of Mediterranean tourism, Papatheodorou (2002) used as explanatory variables not only characteristics of holiday packages but also dummy variables to represent specific tour operators and destinations. In this case, a negative coefficient must imply either a bargain or a poor brand image; conversely, a positive coefficient is consistent with both bad-value-for-money and a strong brand name. To resolve the conundrum further information on the prevailing demand conditions is required.

HPA requires a considerable degree of data homogeneity that would allow relevant comparisons possible. In a study to measure how the overall price of a sun-and-beach package holiday was determined by the choice of tour operator, choice of destination, and a number of different attributes associated with the package tour, Thrane (2005) adopted the following measures to homogenize the data. First, only tours to the Canary Islands from Oslo airport in Norway were considered. This is because the airfare is a major determinant of the price of a package holiday. With approximately equal travel distance from Oslo to the four Canary Islands examined, the effect of distance on the airfare has been minimized. Second, recognizing that seasonality has a significant effect on package price, Thrane selected the same week, i.e. the first week of November 2003 as a departure date to control for the effect of seasonality. Finally, as all four Canary Islands are Spanish, the tourism-production costs at the destinations are assumed at least partially constant.

APPLICATIONS OF HEDONIC PRICE ANALYSIS IN TOURISM

The hedonic price valuation approach has seen wide applications in the environmental economics literature (Boyle et al., 1999; Earnhart, 2001; Gibbons et al., 2011; McConnell and Walls, 2005). In fact, the majority of the applications of the technique are drawn from the wider environmental economics and management literature (Hunt et al. 2005). This is mainly due to the multi-attribute nature of the evaluated resources. HPA has also been extensively used for housing, computer equipment, and agricultural products (Hamilton, 2007). Recently, there has been a growing interest in applying this method in tourism research.

Espinet et al. (2003) examined how holiday hotel prices are affected by different hotel characteristics in the sun-and-beach segment. The effect on price is estimated under the hedonic function perspective by random effect models. Table 9.1 shows a comprehensive list of attributes considered by these authors.

The study reveals that compared to the reference 4-star hotels, prices were 64 percent lower for 1-star, 61 percent lower for 2-star, and 50 percent lower for 3-star hotels. Hotels located in front of the beach were more expensive, while distance to the town center had no significant effect. With regards to hotel services, availability of parking space increased prices by 8.5 percent, but recent renovation, special room equipment, availability of a garden, swimming pool, or sporting facilities had no significant effect on price.

In a study of 73 hotels in Taipei, Chen and Rothschild (2010) separated hotel rates into weekdays and weekends. The authors found that internet access and the presence of a fitness center had a significant effect on weekday rates, while room size had a significant effect on weekend rates. In contrast to the Espinet et al. (2003) study, Chen and Rothschild (2010) found that in Taipei there was a negative relationship between proximity to city center and room rates, on both weekdays and weekends: this is probably due to the fact that hotels outside the city often offer a wider range of amenities such

Table 9.1   List of attributes considered in Espinet et al. (2003)

Town in which hotel is located	Parking place
Star category	Hairdresser
Number of rooms	Outdoor swimming pool
Accepts credit cards	Indoor swimming pool
Special access for disabled	Music or radio in the room
Admits pets	Conference halls
Air-conditioning	Sauna
Satellite TV	Hairdryer in the room
Lift	24-hour service
Cafeteria	Medical care
Shops	Squash
Safe	Telephone in the room
Heating	TV set in the room
Money change	Tennis court
Close to town centre	Simultaneous translation
Discotheque	Video in the room
Located in a historical building	Games and recreational activities
Located in a picturesque building	Casino
Car repair	Recently renovated
Gymnasium	Water and wine included in full board price
Golf	Number of operators including it in their catalogue
Kindergarten	Children's swimming pool
Suites with living room	Restaurant
Garden or terrace	Close to the beach
Bicycle rental	Balcony in the room
Mini golf	View to the sea
Mini-bar in the room	Year of first opening
Park for children	

Source: Espinet et al. (2003).

as hot springs and sports facilities, hence a positive impact on the price, while the more competitive environment in the city center exerts a downward pressure on room rates.

In another study, Hamilton (2007) specifically focused on the effect of the coastal landscape on hotel prices. She found that an increase in the length of open coast in Schleswit-Holstein, Germany resulted in a rise in the average price of accommodation, while an increase in the length of dikes would lead to a reduction in the average price of accommodation. Complementing the above studies, Monty and Skidmore (2003) examined the willingness to pay for bed and breakfast amenities in southeast Wisconsin in the United States. The findings showed willingness-to-pay for specific characteristics such as a hot tub, a private bath, and a larger room. Location and spatial characteristics (such as day of the week, and period of the year) were also found to be important. However, fireplaces, architectural themes, scenic views, and room service were not statistically significant determinants of price. In another study, Garcia-Pozo et al. (2011) applied a hedonic model to the analysis of campsites in Spain. The results revealed that the variables with the greatest influence on prices were coastal location, the quality of the facilities, quality certification, and managerial compliance with ecological procedures.

As tourism products are often consumed and produced simultaneously, the physical environment may have a substantial effect on prices (Rigall-I-Torrent and Fluvia, 2011). Consider for example, two hotels of the same quality and standards, where one is located in a run-down environment, while the other is located in the same city but in a more pleasant environment with the presence of attractive cultural facilities and good provision of restaurants and pubs. The latter is more likely to command a price premium to reflect its location advantage. To measure the effects of the so-called "public" attributes on hotel prices, Rigall-I-Torrent and Fluvia (2011) used a sample of 279 coastal hotels in Catalonia, Spain. A number of "public" attributes were considered, including exclusivity (population), complementary products and services (cultural and sports facilities, restaurants, marinas), crowdedness, natural environment (caves), and public safety. They found that most of these public attributes have significant impact on hotel prices.

HPA has also been applied to study competitiveness levels among holiday resorts. Using brochure information, Papatheodorou (2002) examines destination competitiveness in the Mediterranean region. The price of holiday packages is regressed on a number of package characteristics as well as operator and location factors for core and periphery destinations, defined by their popularity as featured in the selected tour operators' brochures. Those characteristics that are statistically significant are subsequently used in a correlation analysis, providing useful insights into the observed price differentials among core and peripheral holiday destinations. The evidence from the empirical results suggests that fewer than half of core tourist destinations command a (statistically significant) price premium as compared to the benchmark tourist destination (Es Cana, Spain). In particular, the two Cypriot destinations (Paphos and Protaras) are associated with the higher willingness to pay, equal to 9.10 percent and 10.3 percent, respectively. On the other hand, Hammamet in Tunisia and Bugibba in Malta were sold at the highest discount prices (11.6 percent and 20.9 percent less, respectively). Moreover, the effect of the hotel chain affiliation is positive on peripheral but negative on core destinations (positive effect). This difference may be justified in terms of the brand name effect on less familiar and standardized destinations. An alternative but conceptually similar explanation could be attributed to the effect of information asymmetries between known and less well-known destinations.

Compared to the growing number of HPA studies in the hotel and tour operating sectors, research into other areas of tourism is somewhat limited. In a study using a sample of 10 000 published airfares, Schwieterman (1995) explored the relationship between carrier reputation for service quality and the price of air travel in the US market. The study demonstrated that airlines established prices on the basis of 23 service attributes ranging from ticketing restrictions to flight frequency and travel requirements. Based on a database of 84 ski resorts, Falk (2008) investigated the relationship between lift ticket prices and the ski resorts' characteristics. The results indicated that ski runs, transport capacity, share of modern high-speed chairlifts and gondolas, measures of snow conditions, and access to neighboring ski areas covered by the same lift pass all had a positive and significant effect on the price of a 1-day lift ticket and a 6-day ski pass. A ranking of the ski resorts according to their quality characteristics was also conducted.

ADVANTAGES AND LIMITATIONS OF HEDONIC PRICE ANALYSIS CONCEPTUALLY AND FOR POLICY FORMULATION

There are a number of factors explaining the popularity of HPA in tourism research. First, tourism competitiveness is, inter alia, a function of the various destination characteristics (Dwyer et al., 2000). In this respect, regressing tourist expenditure on a destination's characteristics could reveal useful information to policy makers on how to improve competitiveness. Taking advantage of the product characteristics background, the HPA is more capable of focusing on non-price competitive practices (Rosiers and Theriault, 1996; Vanslebrouck et al., 2005). This is because consumers (tourists) explicitly provide an account of how important a particular product characteristic is to their (positive) appreciation of a destination. The evidence generated from HPA applications can assist tourism policy makers in identifying those characteristics enhancing financial returns from tourist activity. Tourism practitioners can then use this information for destination management purposes. Hence, HPA is particularly adept in dealing with the high degree of competitiveness in the contemporary tourism sector (Andropoulos 2011).

Second, HPA is considered a better alternative for the economic evaluation of tourism resources than other techniques as tourism products and services are dependent upon natural (and thus non-market) characteristics. For example, the attractiveness of a Mediterranean destination or resort is largely dependent upon the climate and the nice weather. In addition, the probability of a tourist visiting an archaeological site (e.g., Pompeii in Italy, Knossos Palace in Greece, or Stonehenge in Britain) is also dependent upon natural and weather conditions. The fact that HPA is not solely dependent upon the price attribute means that it can offer useful insights to managers and practitioners regarding the effect of non-price attributes of a product's or a service's marketing mix on tourist choice and preference patterns. For example, Aguiló et al. (2001) have found that certain hotel attributes were significant predictors of the overall price that tourists were willing to pay.

Third, the technique is more flexible and accommodating compared to other more traditional approaches to tourism demand. This is because HPA has the ability to incorporate both demand and supply-side market characteristics (Apostolakis and Jaffry, 2009; Chen and Rothschild, 2010; Monty and Skidmore, 2003). In tourism, as in any service-related industry, demographic characteristics (e.g., size of family, existence of dependents) are as important as the quality of product characteristics. By involving and interacting demand- and supply-side influences, HPA provides more realistic estimates. Finally, the HPA tourism literature review proves that this is particularly versatile and adapted to consider several possible interactions in terms of incorporating individual characteristics and interactions between market goods and environmental quality (Champ et al., 2003; Cheshire and Sheppard, 1998; Gibbons et al., 2011).

As for the limitations of HPA one issue arises out of the *ex-post* (or retrospective) nature of the technique compared to other economic evaluation methodologies. In particular, HPA is limited to evaluating the *current* state of the world. Although useful, this information offers little opportunity to managers, practitioners, and policy makers regarding the exploitation of potential competitive advantage a destination or a resort may have. Thus, HPA offers little guidance regarding future policy initiatives and how these may affect tourist preferences and choice patterns. The ability to offer an insight on the effect of future policy and managerial decision making on prices and willingness to pay would be particularly appreciated in a highly competitive tourism industry.

Another issue is related to price changes. In practice, HPA assumes that the price dependent variable adjusts automatically to changes in the nature of the product/service attributes. In reality, a time lag may exist between price changes occurring as a result of attribute changes. This problem may also appear when dealing with new or evolving tourist destinations, as the number of visitors is still small and there is little information on product attributes and set prices. In other words, there is heavy dependence of the technique on data availability and the strong assumption of perfect information from the consumer perspective to evaluate the effect of changes in product or service attributes on price levels in an accurate way.

From an econometric perspective, multicollinearity is another problem that may arise. It may well be the case that superior quality hotels and resorts are only found in green and environmentally unspoilt locations and environments, whereas lower quality small establishments with rundown stock of facilities tend to be located in underdeveloped or poor environments. In such situations, it is difficult for the HPA researcher to disentangle environmental conditions from the nature of the hotel and its facilities in an accurate and convincing way. The dependence of the HP valuation methodology on spatial effects (Paez et al. 2001) and the existence of spatial autocorrelation and heterogeneity preclude the straightforward use of the technique (Long et al. 2007).

FURTHER DEVELOPMENTS AND APPLICATIONS OF HEDONIC PRICE ANALYSIS IN TOURISM RESEARCH

The previous discussion on the hedonic price analysis may be of particular interest to policy makers and practitioners focusing on the marketing of specific tourism products, services and destinations: knowing whether and why these are sold at a discount or a premium can provide useful insight for the strategy to be followed in terms of market positioning, pricing, and branding. Interestingly, the hedonic price framework may also be used in the context of competition analysis to examine market power abuse as a result of dominance and/or to appraise the pricing effects of potential mergers especially of horizontal nature. The critical and ultimate question to be answered by every competition inquiry is whether the business entities under investigation can (or have already) profitably abuse(d) their market power by raising their prices to the detriment of consumer welfare (Stabler et al., 2010). In the presence of horizontal (i.e., variety) and vertical (i.e., quality) disparities in the market, purged prices should be first obtained before focusing on the actual competitive conduct. On these grounds, the hedonic price framework has been used to quantitatively evaluate the fundamentals behind the observed car price differentials in the European Union (LECG, 1999). So far, however, and to the best of this authors' knowledge, the framework has not been used in the context of tourism-related industries in spite of the existence of powerful oligopolies and oligopsonies especially in the transport for tourism, hotel and tour operations sectors (Papatheodorou, 2006).

In the following, the application of the technique in the context of a potential merger appraisal between two airlines (A and B) of the same country is highlighted. For simplicity, we will assume that both airlines share airport hub C as the main base of their fleet and operations. Airport C is the most important hub in the country; moreover, the joint market share of A and B in airport C is highly dominant. A and B announce their intention to hypothetically merge on 1 June 2011 and the Competition Commission in charge decides to undertake the hedonic price analysis 6 months later, i.e., in early December 2011 (this time gap is regarded as normal in competition inquiries), to find out whether the proposed merger would result in a substantial lessening of competition and higher prices thus harming passengers and tourism in general. The sample should refer to monthly data for at least the last 36 months and the estimation method should best rely on panel data analysis comparing the results of Pooled Ordinary Least Squares (POLS) with models incorporating the existence of fixed and/or random effects (Lei and Papatheodorou, 2010).

The dependent variable can be average fare on a monthly basis per operating airline for all domestic and international city pairs using airport hub C as a point of origin or destination. From a commercial perspective, this is equivalent to the average passenger revenue per route on a monthly basis: for example, what was the average fare of airline A for the itinerary C–D in March 2011; or what was the average fare of airline B for the itinerary E–C in November 2011? The implementation of yield management techniques may render the calculation of average fares a difficult task; however, knowing the load factor and the revenue per leg can prove of great help. Ideally, the average fare should be provided on a single ticket (i.e., per leg) basis, i.e., the C–D fare should be quoted separately from the D–C. The analysis should be based on net fares but taxes and other charges should also be considered separately. Moreover, all city pairs to/from C where A and B operate should be taken into account. The focus on C stems from the concerns regarding the potential abuse of market power by the two airlines in their hub airport. The Competition Commission in charge does have the legal power to ask A and B to provide the suitable data. Alternatively, these may be purchased by Global Distribution Systems operators (such as Amadeus, Galileo, etc.) who store such data on Marketing Information Data Transfer (MIDT) tapes.

The first set of independent variables should consider cost factors. Ideally, the Competition Commission in charge should be provided with explicit cost data by the airlines under investigation; nonetheless, the reliability of such data is not always easy to validate. As an alternative, four major variables should be included: (1) average jet fuel price on a monthly basis, (2) representative type of operating aircraft per leg on a monthly basis, (3) average load factor per leg on a monthly basis, and (4) block time (i.e., flight time plus taxiing) involved in each city pair. Fuel cost is undoubtedly of major importance in the aviation industry. Moreover, airline productivity is largely affected by the type of aircraft whereas the load factor can provide an indication of the average cost. Finally, block time may provide a proxy for labor, maintenance, and other costs. These independent variables are expected to be positively associated with the dependent variable.

The second group of independent variables should consider the general macro-economic environment. Three major variables may be included, i.e., inflation (expected to have a positive association with the dependent variable); unemployment (expected to have a negative association), and GDP growth rate (expected to have a positive associa-tion) – all expressed on a monthly basis. Given the existing concerns about the level of sovereign debt in various countries, the interest rate spread between the government bond and a risk-free benchmark may also be used as a macroeconomic indicator.

The third set of independent variables should consider mode and carrier substitutability. In particular, a dummy variable can be included for mode substitutability. It can take the value of zero when the distance of a city pair is less than 500 km and surface transport is available and/or when travelling by sea is an acceptable alternative time-wise; it can take the value of one in all other cases. This dummy variable is expected to be positively related with the dependent variable, i.e., a lower degree of mode substitutability should be associated with higher prices. Regarding carrier substitutability, a variable showing the average number of airlines operating directly in each city pair on a monthly basis should be included; as a better alternative, the average monthly value of the Herfindahl–Hirschman concentration index (i.e., which is equal to the sum of the squared market shares in terms of capacity) should be used. The lower the number of operating carriers (and the higher the value of the HH index) is, the higher the average fare is expected to be. Only direct flights should be considered given the inherent inconvenience involved in indirect flights.

The fourth group of independent variables should consist of dummy variables taking the value of one when the flight is operated by a particular carrier and zero in all other cases. In line with the discussion on hedonic price analysis in previous sections of this chapter, a positive association between the dummy variables and the dependent variables is consistent with the conclusion that certain airlines can command a price premium possibly due to their strong brand name; conversely, a negative association may reveal that certain airlines sell their product at a discount possibly due to a poor brand image. It would also be advisable to add a dummy variable taking the value of zero when the flight is related to the domestic network and one when the flight is international to highlight any potential differences in the pricing policies implemented by the various airlines.

The final set of independent variables should consist of dummy variables related to time. The first dummy variable should be associated with seasonality, i.e., taking the value of one for months considered to be of peak period for the city pairs involving airport C. Understandably, this dummy variable should be positively associated with the dependent variable as a result of the use of price discrimination techniques by the airlines. Most importantly, however, another dummy variable should be included to take account of the merger announcement. This can take the value of zero for the whole sample period including 31 May 2011 and one thereafter (i.e., from 1 June 2011 when airlines A and B announced their intention to merge until the date that the hedonic price analysis is undertaken sometime in early December 2011).

In fact, the very essence of the econometric analysis lies on the coefficient of the last dummy variable. In particular:

- A statistically significant positive coefficient means that the average air fare after the merger announcement has been higher than before as a result of both unilateral (i.e., related to the fact that the merged entity can feel confident enough to plan ahead its pricing strategy without considering the interdependence with other carriers) and coordinated (i.e., related to the increased possibility of collusion among the incumbent airlines as a result of the reduction in the number of participating carriers in the market due to the merger) effects. A fortiori, if airlines A and B found it profitable to increase their average fare after the announcement but *before* the actual approval of the merger it is almost certain that they would continue doing so *after* the approval of the merger. In other words, a positive coefficient means that the competitive pressure has been reduced allowing market partici- pants to increase prices. As a result and using backward induction logic, it will be possible to consistently argue that airlines A and B are neighboring competitors. In conjunction with the coefficients of the cost variables, substitutability and vari- ables related to company brand name and nature of network, it will be possible to derive concrete conclusions on whether there are differences between domestic and international flights and whether the proposed merger will result in cost savings for the consumers or not.

- A statistically significant negative coefficient means that the average air fare after the merger announcement has been lower than before. This is consistent with a benevolent stance of the airlines under investigation as a result of increased efficiency or alternatively a manipulative behavior to secure merger approval. In this case and to avoid "witch-hunting", it would be appropriate to conduct sup- plementary qualitative analysis possibly based on the implementation of a Delphi technique with focus groups of experts expressing their opinions on the possible impacts of the merger. Supplementary analysis should also be undertaken, if the coefficient proves to be statistically insignificant.

Having the above in mind, the hedonic price analytical framework can be applied as a valid technique in competition analysis to appraise among others the effect of a poten- tial merger on prices. Given the existence of large oligopolies (and oligopsonies) in the tourism sector as well as the complementarity which characterizes the various compo- nents of the aggregate tourism product, HPA may prove useful to tourism competition economists in the future.

CONCLUSIONS

This chapter presented the basic foundations of hedonic price analysis applied in tourism research. HPA is an economic valuation approach that, conceptually speaking, belongs to the revealed preferences family. It is based on Lancaster's characteristics approach and postulates that price differences among competing tourism destinations or resources reflect differences in the benefits or value to the consumer derived from the consumption of various characteristics in each destination or resource. The methodological reliance of the technique on Lancaster's characteristics approach, make hedonic price analysis particularly adept to the study of a multi-attribute and multi-value sector such as the tourism industry (Papatheodorou, 2001). The effect of each individual attribute or char- acteristic could be measured through the use of regression analysis. In particular, coef- ficients with a positive sign are taken to imply a positive effect on prices (and consumers' valuation of the tourist resource), whereas the opposite is the case for coefficients with a negative sign.

HPA has received considerable attention in tourism recently due to two main reasons. First, increased levels of competition both within the industry and as a result of the expansion of the boundaries of the tourism economy make it imperative to estimate properly the effect of each component of the tourism product on offer. Second, the expansion of the evidence based requirement in terms of justification of tourism-related policy making makes the technique particularly appealing to managers, practitioners and policy makers (Rigall-I-Torrent and Fluvia, 2011). In addition, the recent convergence of tourism and non-market environmental resources (illustrated through the increasing popularity of the sustainability concept in tourism operations, environmentally friendly tourism practices, and ecotourism resources) necessitates the need for an evaluation approach that would allow to estimate the associated value placed by consumers/tourists on these non-market based characteristics of the tourism product or service on offer. Again, HPA is well suited to accommodate this need. The technique is based on the construction of surrogate markets to evaluate the effect of each product or service attribute on implicit prices consumers/tourists are willing to pay. In this respect, and despite a number of caveats discussed earlier, HPA offers a valid alternative method of examining demand patterns compared to other (market-based) methods.

REFERENCES

Aguiló, P., J. Alegre and A. Riera (2001), 'Determinants of the price of German tourist packages on the island of Mallorca', *Tourism Economics*, **7**, 59–74.

Andersson, D.E., O.F. Shyr and J. Fu (2010), 'Does high-speed rail accessibility influence residential property prices? Hedonic estimates from southern Taiwan', *Journal of Transport Geography*, **18**, 166–174.

Andropoulos, C. (2011), 'Latest developments at EU level concerning tourism competitiveness', The 10th European Tourism Forum, Krakow Poland, The European Commission.

Apostolakis, A. and S. Jaffry (2009), 'Examining expenditure patterns of British tourists to Greece', *International Journal of Tourism Policy*, **2** (3), 187–205.

Banks, G. (2009), 'Evidence based policy making: what is it? How do we get it?', Australian Government Productivity Commission, Canberra.

Boyle, K., J. Poor and L. Taylor (1999), 'Estimating the demand for protecting freshwater lakes from eutrophication', *American Journal of Agricultural Economics*, **81** (5), 1118–1122.

Brassington, F. and S. Pettitt (2007), *Essentials of Marketing* 2nd edition, Harlow: Pearson Education.

Champ, P.A., K.J. Boyle and T.C. Brown (2003), *A Primer on Nonmarket Valuation*, Boston: Kluwer Academic Press.

Chen, C. and R. Rothschild (2010), 'An application of hedonic pricing analysis to the case of hotel rooms in Taipei', *Tourism Economics*, **16** (3), 685–694.

Cheshire, P. and S. Sheppard (1998), 'Estimating the demand for housing, land and neighbourhood characteristics', *Oxford Bulletin of Economics and Statistics*, **60** (3), 357–382.

Dwyer, L., P. Forsyth and P. Rao (2000), 'The price competitiveness of travel and tourism: a comparison of 19 destinations', *Tourism Management*, **21**, 9–22.

Earnhart, D. (2001), 'Combining revealed and stated preference methods to value environmental amenities at residential locations', *Land Economics*, **77** (1), 12–29.

Espinet, J.M., M. Saez, G. Coenders and M. Fluvia (2003), 'Effect on prices of the attributes of holiday hotels: a hedonic prices approach', *Tourism Economics*, **9** (2), 165–177.

Falk, M. (2008), 'A hedonic price model for ski lift tickets', *Tourism Management*, **29**, 1172–1184.

Garcia-Pozo, A., J.L. Sanchez-Ollero and D.M. Marchante-Lara (2011), 'Applying a hedonic model to the analysis of campsite pricing in Spain', *International Journal of Environmental Research*, **5** (1), 11–22.

Gibbons, S., S. Mourato and R. Guilherme (2011), 'The amenity value of English Nature: a hedonic price approach', Spatial Economics Research Centre (SERC) Discussion Paper DP0074, London School of Economics and Political Science.

Hamilton, J.M. (2007), 'Coastal landscape and the hedonic price of accommodation', *Ecological Economics*, **62**, 594–602.

Hunt, L., P. Boxal, P. Englin and W. Haider (2005), 'Remote tourism and forest management: a spatial hedonic analysis', *Ecological Economics*, **53**, 101–113.

Lancaster, K.J. (1971), *Consumer Demand: A New Approach*, New York: Columbia University Press.

LECG (1999), *Quantitative Techniques in Competition Analysis*, Hayes, UK: Office of Fair Trading.

Lei, Z. and A. Papatheodorou (2010), 'Measuring the effect of low-cost carriers on regional airports' commercial revenue', *Research in Transportation Economics*, **26**, 37–43.

Lise, W. and R. Tol (2002), 'Impact of climate on tourism demand', *Climatic Change*, **55** (4), 429–449.

Long, F., A. Paez and S. Farber (2007), 'Spatial effects in hedonic price estimation: a case study in the city of Toronto', Centre for Spatial Analysis Working Paper Series N.020, McMaster University.

McConnell, V. and M. Walls (2005), *The Value of Open Space: Evidence from Studies of Nonmarket Behaviour*, Washington DC: Resources for the Future.

Maddison, B. and A. Bigano (2003), 'The amenity value of the Italian climate', *Journal of Environmental Economics and Management*, **45** (2), 319–332.

Maddison, D. (2001), 'In search of warmer climates? The impact of climate change on flows of British tourists', *Climate Change*, **49** (2), 103–208.

Mahan, B. (1997), 'Valuing wetlands: a property pricing approach', in Evaluation of Environmental Investments Research Group, US Army Corps of Engineers, Portland, USA.

Monty, B. and M. Skidmore (2003), 'Hedonic pricing and willingness to pay for bed and breakfast amenities in Southeast Wisconsin', *Journal of Travel Research*, **42**, November, 195–199.

Oh, C. (2009), 'Assessing tourists' multi-attribute preferences for public beach access', *Coastal Management*, **37** (2), 119–135.

Paez, A., T. Uchida and K. Miyamoto (2001), 'Spatial association and heterogeneity issues in land price models', *Urban Studies*, **38** (9), 1493–1508.

Papatheodorou, A. (2001), 'Why people travel to different places?', *Annals of Tourism Research*, **28** (1), 164–179.

Papatheodorou, A. (2002), 'Exploring competitiveness in Mediterranean resorts', *Tourism Economics*, **8** (2), 133–150.

Papatheodorou, A. (2006), 'Corporate rivalry, market power and competition issues in tourism: an introduction', in A. Papatheodorou (ed.) *Corporate Rivalry and Market Power: Competition Issues in the Tourism Industry*, London: IB Tauris, pp. 1–19.

Rigall-I-Torrent, R. and M. Fluvia (2011), 'Managing tourism products and destinations embedding public good components: a hedonic approach', *Tourism Management*, **32**, 244–255.

Riganti, P. and P. Nijkamp (2008), 'Congestion in popular tourist areas: a multi-attribute experimental choice analysis of willingness to wait in Amsterdam', *Tourism Economics*, **14** (1), 25–44.

Rosen, S. (1974), 'Hedonic prices and implicit markets: product differentiation in pure competition', *Journal of Political Economy*, **82** (1974), 34–55.

Rosiers, F. and M. Theriault (1996), 'Rental amenities and the stability of hedonic prices: a comparative analysis of five market segments', *The Journal of Real Estate Research*, **12** (1), 17–36.

Schwieterman, J. (1995), 'A hedonic price assessment of airline service quality in the US', *Transport Reviews*, **15** (3), 291–302.

Stabler, M., A. Papatheodorou and T. Sinclair (2010), *The Economics of Tourism*, 2nd edition, London: Routledge.

The Countryside Agency (2006), 'Planning for sustainable settlements in the High Weald AONB; evidence based policy making', High Weald Area of Outstanding Natural Beauty Authority.

Thrane, C. (2005), 'Hedonic price models and sun-and-beach package tours: the Norwegian case', *Journal of Travel Research*, **43** (2005), 302–308.

Vanslebrouck, I., G.V. Huylenbroeck and J.V. Meensel (2005), 'Impact of agriculture on rural tourism: a hedonic pricing approach', *Journal of Agricultural Economics*, **56** (1), 17–30.

10 Factor analysis
Lindsay W. Turner and Chau Vu

INTRODUCTION

Factor analysis as a generic term that is increasingly used to encompass all forms of analysis intended to uncover latent structure within a set of data. The very intent of such an analysis is fundamental to a wide variety of problems encountered in tourism because, as a social science, there is significant requirement to measure unstructured concepts, as opposed to structured items with readily measurable attributes such as height, weight, length, and width. In tourism the concepts requiring measurement relate to social systems involving values, attitudes, motivations, risks, satisfaction, and beliefs. Tourism is a combination of study fields in the social sciences where a great many problems contain such unstructured elements.

Consequently, there is a huge body of published research in tourism that uses factor analytic methods. The objective of this chapter is to discuss the background of the methods involved, explain how the methods work, highlight some examples of their applications and discuss their advantages and limitations.

EVOLUTION OF FACTOR ANALYSIS

Spearman (1904) is given the recognition for developing the factor analysis technique but like all complex methods there is a history of considerable research development reaching through to current use. Spearman's model focused upon deriving just one common function to derive intellectual activity. The work continued through to 1930 with the major contributors Cyril Burt, Karl Holzinger, Truman Kelly, Karl Pearson, and Godfrey Thomson. It was Pearson in 1901 who was arguably the first to develop a practical method for factor analysis when he proposed the method of principal axis factoring. By 1930 the idea of a single function was understood to be too limiting in describing latent structure. In 1937 Holzinger and Swineford developed bi-factoral theory whereby there remained one single overall factor for all variables, but also several other factors describing subsets of variables in the total set of variables. The most significant development of modern factor analysis was made by Thurstone (1931, 1938, 1947) when he developed the centroid calculation method (1931) commonly used before the development of computers, and the concept of simple structure (1947).

The description of simple structure is stated technically by Harman (1976, p. 87):

> The truly remarkable contribution of Thurstone was the generalization of Spearman's tetrad-difference criterion to the Rank of the correlation matrix as the basis for determining the number of common factors. He saw that a zero tetra-difference corresponded to the vanishing of a second-order determinant, and extended this notion to the vanishing of higher order determinants as the condition for more than a single factor.

It is thought likely here that this statement explains nothing to most tourism readers. Therefore the approach taken in the further discussion tends to be less technical.

Thurstone set conditions for simple structure and these conditions mean that, ideally, only one factor should contribute substantially to a given variable, and the other factors should contribute not at all. The definition of contribution set the scene for much debate. The value of contribution set as 1 is considered overly restrictive and unlikely, but the condition should still be high, and is commonly interpreted to be between 0.6 and 0.8. So a factor should load highly for one variable (0.8) and hardly at all on the other factors, preferably zero or close to zero. Hence, with several variables related to a single factor and all variables relating to a much smaller set of factors the factors have the capacity to be defined (named) as constructs and derive simple structure.

This early development occurred before computers, and so the calculations were theoretical, for example at that time a regression line of best fit would be selected *by eye from a graph*. The development of computers allowed for the application of the centroid method, and was aided by Hotelling (1933) who developed the mathematics for principal components. So from the late 1950s just about every unstructured set of data was analysed and the methods moved beyond principal components to image factor analysis (Guttman, 1953), canonical factor analysis (Harris, 1962; Rao, 1955), alpha factor analysis (Kaiser and Caffrey, 1965) and minres (Harman and Jones, 1966). The development away from principal components is possibly best defined by Jöreskog (1966, 1967, 1969, 1970) who used earlier work by Bock and Bargmann (1966) and Lawley (1940) to test hypotheses, and developed confirmatory factor analysis.

A more detailed discussion of this history is given in an excellent text by Lindeman (1980).

Hence, several different factor analytic methods developed under the general heading "factor analysis" with different intent, and these differences have caused considerable confusion ever since. Many tourism research articles do not clearly specify which technique is used, although in more modern times this is not so much the case. Moreover, the development of hypotheses is often necessarily vague in factor analysis and leads to further confusion. Finally, it is not adequate to replace the specific method title such as principal components analysis (PCA) or confirmatory factor analysis (CFA) with the generic title "factor analysis", because this leaves the reader uncertain, and it is not necessary to do so.

TYPES OF METHOD

Principal Component Analysis (PCA) is the most common use of factor analysis because it is descriptive, but provides significant insight into the latent structure of data that can often be used for further analysis, for example in structural equation modeling (SEM). The SEM software can also be used specifically to do factor analytic methods. Consequently, having described the latent structure in one set of data, hypotheses could be developed to use CFA analysis on a different set of data, or if the sample is large enough, on a subset of the original sample. In PCA, the factors are used to account for all of the variance for each variable, including variance shared with other variables (covariance). Consequently, there must be the same number of factors as variables in order to explain all the variance both unique to a variable and shared between them because, at least theoretically, each variable will have some variance unique to itself. However, the objective is to reduce the number of original variables to a smaller set of components that describes hidden structure within the data set, so that only the components with several variables with high simple structure loadings are the components that are named.

In more technical terms the analysis uses the complete correlation matrix of the original data with one on the diagonals. A covariance matrix could be used if the volume of the data has special relevance such as the volume of tourist arrivals. Principal components analysis calculates the component accounting for the most variance first and stepwise successively less variance each time, so the last components extracted can be expected to have only one variable loaded to them which must represent just the unique variance for that variable.

Mathematically, PCA is clean and avoids the question of estimating communalities that form the diagonal of the reduced correlation matrix in CFA. PCA also allows component scores to be directly calculated. The wide range of topics analysed in tourism are given by example in Table 10.6. **Confirmatory Factor Analysis (CFA)** is used to determine whether a particular set of hypotheses defining the number and type of factors applies to particular data. The hypotheses require specific theoretical definition, presumably justified by previous research, or theoretical construction such as a conceptual framework or definition from PCA. At the very least, the factors must be named in advance on the basis of theory, and possibly the variables defining these names at least suggested. As such, CFA is potentially more powerful in deriving conclusions to research problems. The method analyses only the variance in the correlation matrix that is shared (common) with other (not necessarily all) variables. Consequently, the number of factors extracted may be less than the number of variables, which in research terms is more parsimonious in defining the original data set as founded on underlying structure. The problem is determining the shared variance (covariance) in the first place.

The most common method is to calculate the squared multiple correlation coefficient of each variable against all the other variables to create the diagonal in the matrix (communality), so the sum of these diagonal elements becomes the total common variance. This is a reasonable guess of the communality but is not theoretically pure. The consequence of this process is to weight the importance of each variable by the strength of its correlation with all other variables. When the factors are extracted they are pulled closer to those variables with the higher communalities. Özgener and İraz (2006) studied customer relationship management in small and medium sized tourism enterprises using CFA and Susskind et al. (2003) examined consumer apprehensiveness toward internet use.

Image Factor Analysis (IFA) is an alternative method of calculating the common variance and as such is an alternative to CFA. It uses multiple regression to predict the values of each variable using the other variables as independent variables. The part of the variable that can be predicted becomes the image and the rest the anti-image. The R^2 values become the communalities in the diagonal of the matrix and the off diagonal elements are adjusted so no eigenvalues (see below) are negative (referred to as gramian). There are few examples of the method and it can be argued to have the same diagonals as CFA as a starting point so there is no particular advantage in using the method.

Alpha Factor Analysis assumes the variables are randomly sampled from a large set of variables to test for reliability in the factors generated. It uses Cronbach's alpha which is a measure of the intercorrelations between the variables as a measure of reliability, and only factors obtaining positive alphas are extracted in the order highest to lowest. Generally, few factors are extracted and this makes an analysis structure difficult to interpret.

Canonical Factor Analysis, termed Rao's canonical factoring, involves re-scaling the correlation matrix by the unique variance. The higher the uniqueness of a variable the less weight it has in the re-scaling. In this way the variables that have the highest common variance have more weight in extracting the factors. The factors that are derived and their scores are invariant of scale and this is the main reason for selecting this technique, because it removes the decision as to whether a correlation or covariance matrix is used. However, this aspect is also evident in both image and alpha factoring and is not unique to this method. In the methods above the fundamental differences are as follows.

PCA uses the correlation matrix with one in the diagonal; CFA uses the correlation matrix with communalities in the diagonal; IFA uses the covariance matrix with squared multiple correlations in the diagonal, and anti-image factor analysis uses the covariance matrix with one minus the squared multiple correlations in the diagonal; and canonical factor analysis uses a matrix of correlations divided by the product of the standard deviations of the uniqueness. As such there is a strong mathematical relationship between these techniques as shown by Harris (1962).

Another interesting aspect is that, in analysis conditions, the results from PCA and CFA are often similar, and indeed as the level of unique variance declines the closer the results become. This adds yet another potential confusion to factor analysis. However, this issue cannot be used to justify indiscriminant use of the methods as they are distinctly different.

Factor Regression Analysis is a combination of a factor analysis and regression. The main reason for doing this is to overcome multicollinearity between independent variables. PCA can reduce a number of correlated variables to a smaller number of uncorrelated latent variables provided the analysis remains orthogonal, refer to Massy (1965).

ANALYSIS

In order to explain clearly the analytic procedure an example using a simple random data set is used. It is more mathematically direct to use an example of PCA as a starting point because it avoids the need to calculate communalities, it allows factor scores to be directly calculated rather than estimated, there is an empirically based method for determining the number of components and most of the discussion equally relates to all forms of factor analysis.

Correlations

The discussion above has assumed the reader understands correlation, and it is necessary to take the discussion to some further detail and this is done here in graphic form, or geometrically, to avoid the more technical approach of matrix algebra.

Assuming we have two variables X_1 and X_2 and the correlation between these two variables is 0.75 then $r_{12} = r_{21} = 0.75$. Assuming the data for the two variables are normally distributed then the mean is zero and the standard deviation (S) is one.

Hence we can show the correlation between the two variables as a straight line:

Figure 10.1   Correlation between two variables

so that the correlation r = 0.75 is three quarters of the length of the standard deviation. Of course if the correlation was perfect then the value of r would be 1 and both lines would be the same length.

For the two lines to be compared on the same diagram they must have the same origin point, but this requires knowledge of the angle between the two lines. The geometric rule is that a perpendicular line from the three-quarters point (in this case) on each variable must meet the end of the line representing the standard deviation. It is common to think of this as one line casting a shadow on the other, in this case, with a length of 0.75, see Figure 10.2.

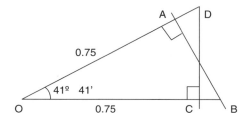

Figure 10.2   Comparison of lines

Basic trigonometry can be used to calculate the angle, where the cosine of the angle between the two lines represents the correlation between the two variables. Cosines like correlations range between −1 and +1. A cosine of zero is equal to an angle of 90° or an r = zero. A line at 90° or a right angle is termed orthogonal and represents an orthogonal relationship. So $\cos^{-1} 0.75 = 41° 41'$.

The lines representing the correlations in a correlation matrix will almost certainly create a diagram in three-dimensional space. So assuming the values given in Figure 10.3.

	Correlation Matrix				Angles		
	X_1	X_2	X_3		X_1	X_2	X_3
X_1	1.00	0.69	0.92	X_1	0	46	23
X_2	0.69	1.00	0.20	X_2	46	0	79
X_3	0.92	0.20	1.00	X_3	23	79	0

Figure 10.3   Correlation matrix and angles

It is not possible to draw three lines in two-dimensional space, whereby X_3 is both 23° from X_1 and 79° from X_2, but it is possible in three-dimensional space. The number of dimensions is equal to the number of variables.

Extracting Components

The objective in deriving the components is to derive new variables that represent groups of existing variables. Each grouping variable (component) theoretically represents whatever is described by the group of variables as loading on the component; or stated otherwise, the underlying hidden (latent) structure described by that group of variables that is not described until the group is identified to exist. This process is similar to calculating the mean of a set of data.

Each component is extracted in turn with the first component as the line that is as close as possible to all the lines representing all the variables at the same time using the centroid method. Given our correlation matrix, Figure 10.4.

	X_1	X_2	X_3	
X_1	1.00	0.69	0.92	
X_2	0.69	1.00	0.20	
X_3	0.92	0.20	1.00	
SUM	2.61	1.89	2.11	6.6 = Total Sum
	1.01	0.74	0.82	= SUM/$\sqrt{Total\ Sum}$
	0°	42°	35°	= Angles

Figure 10.4   Correlation matrix

The ratio of the sum of the correlations for each variable to $\sqrt{TS}$ is the correlation of each variable with the component or how close it is to the average. The angles and other values are rounded, and given the component is also the same as an existing variable, it has a standard deviation of one and hence the same line length.

The matrix above shows that X_1 has the highest intercorrelation at 2.61 with all the other variables including itself. The highest possible value for the total sum (TS) is the number of variables squared (n^2) assuming the highest correlation possible ($r = 1$), or $3^3 = 9$. So the maximum sum for each variable is $\sqrt{TS} = \sqrt{9} = 3$. Therefore $\sqrt{TS}$ is the new variable (principal component).

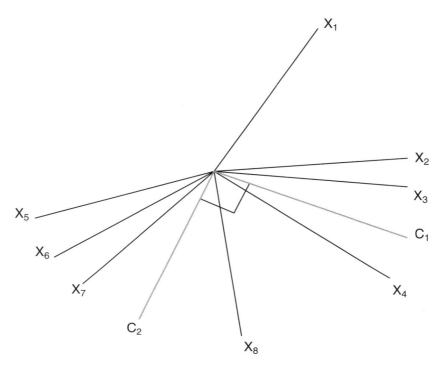

Figure 10.5   The centroid method

This centroid method is not fully accurate, so it is not used given the capacity to conduct fast matrix algebra calculations by computer. However, the result is the same in terms of locating the new variable in multi-dimensional space. In order to demonstrate the procedure of locating each component a matrix greater than order three (as used in the simple example above) is required, because we need to locate more than one principal component and to do this we need at least six variables. For each of the eight variables in the following example three separate values are calculated:

(1)   The correlation (cosine of the angle)
(2)   The angle between the first component and each variable.
(3)   The correlation squared (coefficient of determination r^2) which is the proportion of the variance associated with the component for each variable.

The correlations are termed component loadings and interpreted the same way as Pearson product moment coefficients, so that the square of the component loading (L) shows the proportion of the variance for each variable associated with the component (C_1). In the example above the highest contributor to the component one is variable X_4 with 97 percent of the variance in C_1 related to X_4. The sum of the squared component loadings is the eigenvalue, usually referred to as lambda and here lambda one (λ_1) for the first component.

Consequently the formula for an eigenvalue is:

$$\lambda_i = \sum_{j=1}^{n} L_{ij}^2 \tag{10.1}$$

Table 10.1   Correlation and angle values

Variable	Correlation (r)	Angle	r^2
X_1	0.1736	80	0.0301
X_2	0.8910	27	0.7939
X_3	0.9511	18	0.9046
X_4	0.9659	15	0.9330
X_5	−0.7986	143	0.6378
X_6	−0.6428	130	0.4132
X_7	−0.4695	118	0.2204
X_8	0.4848	61	0.2350
			$\Sigma = 4.1680 = \lambda_1$

Where: L_{ij} is the loading for variable j on the component i; and λ_i is the eigenvalue for component i.

The eigenvalue must be compared to the total variance in the correlation matrix to be interpreted. As already stated the correlation matrix is made up of a number of variables (n) each with a standardized variance of one, so the total variance is $n \times 1.0^2 = n$. Also note that the variance is the square of the standard deviation. Therefore the eigenvalue can be expressed as a percentage of n, and for the first component becomes:

$$100/(\lambda_1/n) = 100(4.1680/8) = 52.10\%$$

Therefore, component 1 accounts for 52 percent of the total unique and common variance in the analysis. Component 1 is the first average variable and the component loadings (equivalent to correlation coefficients) state how much of the variance for each variable is accounted for by component 1. In this case the variables that load highly are X_4, X_3, X_2, and X_5, but what of X_6? This question becomes an issue of debate discussed later, the question being how high does a variable need to load on a component to be a significant contributor to account for the variance of a given component? There is no test of significance for factor analysis and this is an issue of criticism. If a variable loads above 0.5 then it is not possible for any other loading on any other component to be higher, because there is only 0.49 or so residual variance. However, components can theoretically be equally explained by equal proportions of one variable.

To move on and derive the second component, which seems a likely prospect, because $100 - 52.10 = 47.90\%$ of the total variance is residual and remains unaccounted for, we assume the correlation $r_{12} = 0.6743$ and take $L_1 = 0.1736$ (the first loading for X_1 on the first component) and $L_2 = 0.8910$; with $L_1^2 = 0.0301$ as part of the correlation r_{11} associated with component one, $L_2^2 = 0.7939$ as part of r_{22} associated with component one, and $L_1 \times L_2$ as part of r_{12} associated with the component then:

$$0.1736 \times 0.8910 = 0.1547$$

Table 10.2   Possible values for the second component

Variable	Correlation (r)	Angle	r^2
X_1	−0.9848	170	0.9698
X_2	−0.6691	132	0.4477
X_3	−0.3420	110	0.1170
X_4	−0.1737	80	0.0302
X_5	0.4226	65	0.1786
X_6	0.7660	40	0.5868
X_7	0.9063	25	0.8214
X_8	0.7193	44	0.5174
			$\Sigma = 3.6689 = \lambda_2$

and

$$r_{12} - (L_1)(L_2) = 0.6743 - 0.1547 = 0.5196$$

Thus, the correlation between X_1 and X_2 with the correlation of the first component removed is 0.5196. This correlation is termed a partial correlation. The influence of the first component is removed in the above manner to produce a new correlation matrix made up of partial correlations ($r_{ij} - (L_i)(L_j)$, where i and j are variables).

In the calculation of the residual variance the partial correlations are low for variables that have already correlated highly with component 1, and potentially higher for successive new components, where the variable has not already correlated highly with component 1. Also the successive components must be orthogonal to the previous component, because the residuals are not correlated with the previous component(s) (otherwise they would not be residual). So on Figure10.5 the second component is depicted at right angles to the first component.

The second component from a correlation matrix is thus the average pattern among the residuals of the first component, and the second eigenvalue is less than the first, because the amount of variance available for the second component is less than the first, and so each successive component will have lower eigenvalues. Given the sum of the first two eigenvalues:

$$4.1680 + 3.6689 = 7.8369$$

Nearly all the total variance (n = 8) is explained by the two components.

Communality

A loadings matrix results from the analysis and is commonly presented in the form of Table 10.3.

The communality is the sum of the squared loadings for each variable (h_{18}). It is the proportion of the variance for each variable accounted for by all the components. The communalities in Table 10.3 are close to one because the two components account for 97.96 percent of the variance. This is not usual because in most studies there are a larger

Table 10.3   Loadings matrix

				Loadings			
		C_1	C_2	C_3	. . .	n	h^2
Variable	X_1	0.1736	−0.9848	−	. . .	−	1.0
	X_2	0.8910	−0.6691	−	. . .	−	
	X_3	0.9511	−0.3420	−	. . .	−	
	X_4	0.9659	−0.1737	−	. . .	−	
	X_5	−0.7986	0.4226	−	. . .	−	
	X_6	−0.6428	0.7660	−	. . .	−	
	X_7	−0.4695	0.9063	−	. . .	−	
	X_8	0.4848	0.7193	−	. . .	−	
Eigenvalue		4.1680	3.6689	−	. . .	−	
	%	52.10	45.86	−		−	
Cumulative	%	52.10	97.96	−		−	

number of variables in the study and unless the number of components extracted equals the number of variables the communality will be less than one. If a communality value is greater than one this indicates there is a technical problem with the analysis, such as a sample size that is too small.

Component and Factor Scores

Scores give the strength of the relationship between each case in the sample and each principal component. It is common practice to standardize the scores as Z scores with a mean of zero and standard deviation of one, so that they are comparable with each other.

The interpretation for isolating outlier cases is similar to analysing the residuals from regression. The larger the score the further away the case is from the "line of best fit" or the mean line which is the component. It is possible to determine if there are any patterns in the sample data (characteristics of particular cases) that cause particular components to load in a particular way. There will be as many scores as there are cases times the number of components *K*.

Since the total explained variance of a component is given as the eigenvalue the standard deviation of all the non-standardized scores on a component is equal to the eigenvalue in principal components. Therefore, the simplest way to standardize component scores is to divide the raw score by the eigenvalue. Drey and Sarma (2010) used standard scores in the information search for motivation based tourism, and Vu and Turner (2009) used component scores to list 150 countries comprising different development structures, based on different components, and to assess the economic structure of world tourism.

Factor scores cannot be directly calculated because CFA factors contain only common variance, whereas the components have all variance both common and unique. Factor scores must be derived from regressing the original data matrix onto the loadings matrix. This assumes that, on average, the proportions of common and unique variance are the same for each observation and this is likely not the case. The only way around this problem is to use image factor analysis, which uses only the common variance after

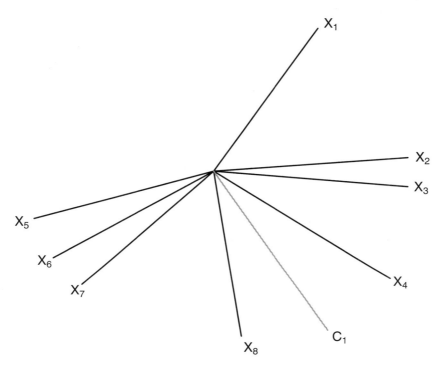

Figure 10.6   Alternative location for original specification

the unique variance has been removed, so the factor scores can be calculated directly. However, because only the unique variance is used in image factor analysis the original data has been transformed and the loadings matrix is different to CFA. Correia et al. (2008) used CFA factor scores in a second order analysis to assess satisfaction with quality and price in hospitality examining satisfaction with the gastronomic experience.

Rotation

The initial solution may not be optimal because the mean location for the first component or factor may miss obvious variable groupings. For example, what if the original specification had placed the first location as in Figure 10.6.

This is a reasonable mean location for all the variables and misses the potential for the two groups identified previously. However, the calculation of the loadings may be as given below with an eigenvalue of 2.8, which is much lower than the previous eigenvalues calculated originally for components 1 and 2.

The obvious solution to the problem is to rotate the components, probably clockwise, but at the same time maintaining their orthoganality to achieve a better solution. Originally this was done by eye but obviously this creates the problem that different analysts could determine different rotations for the same data.

The first issue to determine is the objective of the rotation. The objective is given by Thurstone (1947) is the description of simple structure, whereby variables would load

Table 10.4   Correlation and angle values

Variable	Correlation (r)	Angle	r^2
X_1	−0.0872	95	0.0052
X_2	0.5736	55	0.3290
X_3	0.6691	48	0.4477
X_4	0.9272	22	0.8597
X_5	−0.4540	117	0.2061
X_6	−0.3420	110	0.1170
X_7	−0.2588	105	0.0670
X_8	−0.8746	29	0.7649
			$\Sigma = 2.7966 = \lambda_1$

Table 10.5   Ideal simple structure

	Factor		
Variable	1	2	3
1	X	0	0
2	X	0	0
3	X	0	0
4	0	X	0
5	0	X	0
6	0	X	0
7	0	0	X
8	0	0	X

highly on only one component and close to zero on all others, so that an ideal simple structure would be as shown in Table 10.5.

Where there are three components accounting for the eight original variables in descending order of importance from 1 to 3. Alternatively, the objective could simply be to define more distinct groupings.

The rotation of principal components strictly speaking makes little sense because the centroid method should have already located optimally, and the concept of simple structure as a target for rotation is not relevant to principal components analysis, because it relates only to common variance. The issue is a difficult one, and confusing because what is rotated within a principal components analysis is the smaller set of components that have highly loaded variables on them, with the other components ignored. When this smaller set of variables is rotated this is akin to factor analysis and this is why there is often little difference between the results of either method on the same data.

Rotation of components will likely improve the fit of the components to the variables and allows principal components to be the best method for group identification. However, if the objective is to achieve simple structure (and this should already be hypothesized to exist) then CFA is the better method.

The significant issue with rotation is to find an objective procedure for the rotation, and there are several choices, but only two general groupings orthogonal and oblique rotation. Orthogonal rotation keeps the components or factors at right angles as they rotate and oblique rotation allows the angle to be other than 90°.

Orthogonal Rotation

The original orthogonal rotation (Carroll, 1953; Ferguson, 1954; Neuhaus and Wrigley, 1954; Saunders, 1953) was termed Quartimax. It works on the row loadings on the basis that the optimal result occurs when the factor (component) passes directly through the variable. So if b_1 and b_2 are the co-ordinate locations of the variable, if a factor (component) passes directly through the point its product will be minimized. The term Quartimax refers to maximizing the sum of the fourth powers of the rotated factor coefficients, and this can be shown to be equivalent to maximizing the sum of variances of the squared factor loadings in the rows of the loading matrix.

An alternative is Varimax rotation (Kaiser, 1956, 1958), which is superior in terms of achieving simple structure. Varimax works on the column loadings as opposed to the row loadings. Varimax maximizes the sum, over the m factors, of the column variances of the squared coefficients of the loading matrix. If all the coefficients in the column are either 0 or 1, then one aspect of simple structure is achieved of maximized variance. Most importantly, Kaiser showed that the solution is factorally invariant. That is if successive samples are drawn from the same population the factor loadings remain invariant using Varimax. This gives the method strength or power, because it allows for inferences about the total population to be made from a sample set of measures. Examples of tourism research using varimax rotation are widespread and include Chu and Choi's (2000) examination of factors determining perceived hotel performance and satisfaction, Lee et al.'s (2006) examination of the motivations of gamblers, and Yuan et al.'s (2004) examination of the motivations of wine festival attendees.

There are other less used orthogonal rotation methods including Transvarimax, which contains Equamax and Ratiomax (Saunders, 1962), and Parsimax (Crawford, 1967).

Oblique Rotation

Oblique rotation may result in obtaining a closer fit to simple structure and as such is more relevant to CFA. By allowing the angle between the factors to change from 90° in a general sense there is a higher likelihood of identifying groups according to simple structure, but the difference between these groups may not be high (orthogonal) and so there is a built in assumption that the resulting factor structure is yielding truly independent latent measures, which may not always be the case. Ultimately, it follows that if all the factors are rotated, that groups originally identified will be subdivided by subsequent rotations and ultimately all the variables will each have their own factor.

There are two main oblique methods, Oblimin (Carroll, 1960) and direct Oblimin (Jennrich and Sampson, 1966). Oblimin is the most commonly used method and it is a trial and error procedure to determine if there is a better fit to simple structure. The method was used by Galloway (2002) for the psychographic segmentation of park visitors, and by Lim (2010) to analyse the variables affecting e-marketing adoption by UK independent hotels. In oblique rotation two factor loadings are obtained, the structure loading and pattern loading. The structure loading is the same as the orthogonal loading matrix in regard to interpretation, where it describes the proportion of the variance associated by a given variable to a given factor. The pattern loading identifies the correlation between the variable and the factor independent of other factors, and as such is a partial correlation. As such the pattern loading explains how much of the proportion of the structure matrix is unique variance.

The communalities, eigenvalues and sums of squared loadings are not interpretable from an oblique rotation.

Other methods of oblique rotation include Little Jiffy (Kaiser, 1970), Oblimax (Saunders, 1961), Promax (Hendrikson and White, 1964), and Maxplane (Cattell and Muerle, 1960). There are few research articles in tourism using these rotations although some published studies have used Promax including Snyman and Saayman (2009) who attempt to identify the key factors influencing foreign direct investment in the South African tourism sector, and Yoo and Chon (2008) who assess the factors affecting convention participation decision making.

CONFIRMATORY FACTOR ANALYSIS USING LISREL AND AMOS

The alternative to using a standard statistical package for estimating a CFA is to use the LISREL or Amos software developed from modeling by Karl Jöreskog. Amos is the more commonly used package (although it is less sophisticated than LISREL) because it is interfaced with SPSS. The terminology used by Amos differs to the standard factor analytic terms, whereby loadings are referred to as weights and variables are sometimes referred to as common factors. The method used is not principal factoring as described above, but the Maximum Liklihood method (ML). The main drawback is that the method assumes the data is normally distributed. If the data is strongly distributed away from normal this method is questionable (Curran et al., 1996; Hu et al., 1992). These methods derive a CFA based upon oblique rotation and that assumes the resulting factors are correlated and not orthogonal. The degree of correlation can be measured, and this aspect, along with the capacity to define the specific hypothesized relationship to be tested (which variables account for which factor) and to define this relationship by a path diagram (graphically) provides added strength to undertaking factor analysis, provided that the factors do not need to be orthogonal, and provided that the theory tested is quite strongly founded. Examples of the many studies include Chu (2008) who used Lisrel 8.3 to study the work values of hospitality students, and Reisinger and Turner (1999a) who studied the cultural dimensions of Japanese tourism. The analysis result from graphics defined theory based relationships can also be displayed graphically in standardized form, and this is also a significant advantage. For a fictional analysis of motivations the outcome might be two latent dimensions (factors) of Risk and Escape defined by three explanatory variables each. This relationship is displayed graphically in Figure 10.7 where the value on the curved line gives the squared multiple correlation weight between the two factors as 0.55. The loadings (weights) are given as squared multiple correlations so that 87 percent of the variance in Freedom is accounted for by the factor Escape. The remaining 13 percent is not accounted for and comprises error.

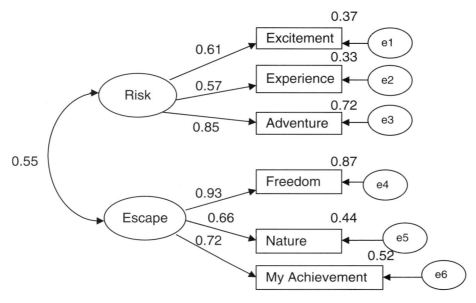

Figure 10.7   Analysis of motivations

The model allows for additional statistical measures of the reliability of the resulting model. There are several measures and the most commonly reported measures are Chi-square (CMIN) and its associated *p*-value, GFI (General Fit Index), NFI (Normed Fit Index), CFI (Comparative Fit Index), RFI (Relative Fit Index), (PNFI) (Parsimonious Normed Fit Index) and RMSEA (Root Mean Squared Error of Approximation).

Chi-square is a measure of the overall fit of the model but is very sensitive to sample size. In particular, if the sample size exceeds 300 the likelihood of a small chi-square is defined as unlikely (Hakstian et al., 1982; Harris and Harris, 1971, MacCallum, 1990). Additionally, if the data is not normally distributed then chi-square can inflate. So in most applications chi–square is not appropriate (Jöreskog and Sörbom, 1989). The GFI measures the relative amount of the variance and covariance accounted for by the model and varies between 0 and 1 where the marginal acceptance level is 0.9. It is better adjusted for degrees of freedom as the AGFI. The NFI, CFI, and RFI are all relative values comparing the model against a baseline model (independence model) which is a particularly bad model fit. The values tend to range between zero and one, or are forced to, so values close to one indicate the better fit relative to the baseline model. There are several options for the baseline model and it can be argued the independence model is not the best choice. It also needs to be understood that these measures are not absolute measures of fit. Therefore, a successful measure close to one may only indicate that the model is relatively better than a very poor option, but not that the model is intrinsically a good fit. The general argument is that the value of NFI should be 0.9 or higher, and this tends to imply the same for the other measures. The PNFI is the NFI adjusted by degrees of freedom and this is done as a parsimony adjustment of the degrees of freedom for the model, divided by the degrees of freedom for the baseline model times the NFI. The RMSEA is a useful statistic to allow for data size and a large number of variables and factors (that is a complex model) because F0 (a reliability measure which incorporates no penalty for model complexity) is adjusted as the RMSEA by degrees of freedom, and gives an approximation of the error in the path diagram. The RMSEA should be below 0.08 and certainly not above 0.1.

This model is very simple and can be made more complex with second order constructs, and the identification of correlation between the variables. As such, it is very easy to re-run the model with adjustments to derive the best fit. This issue becomes debatable and is not to be recommended, because the loss of theory that this adjustment implies creates a data-mining solution that might have little relationship to the original theory. Refer to Reisinger and Turner (1999b) for a detailed discussion on the use of the methodology in tourism.

Because SEM allows the modeling of factors as predictors there is no need to calculate factor scores, and this is another advantage of this technique, as it overcomes the problem of estimating factor scores from CFA.

APPLICATIONS IN TOURISM

There are many examples of factor analysis used in tourism research and too many to examine all publications. Taking a sample from the *Journal of Travel Research* (JTR) from 2000 (Volume 39) to July 2011 (Volume 50) there are 61 articles published using factor analysis of the 587 articles published in total, or 10 percent of all articles used factor analysis. JTR provides a good example of a cross section of tourism research, as it is a quality general tourism research journal publishing across a wide range of study fields.

Table 10.6 displays a summary of the articles published in JTR, including the area of study. These papers exclude studies that use factor analysis as a preliminary step to structural equation modeling (SEM). This is somewhat ambiguous, and it could be argued SEM is a form of regression extension to factor analysis, but since the objective is different in the conceptual frame, these studies are excluded. Studies that use regression as a further or preliminary step in the analysis either of the factor (component) scores, or the original data, are noted.

Table 10.7 provides a summary of the papers in JTR that use the Jöreskog (ML regression) approach to CFA.

Table 10.6 provides several insights into the use of factor analysis in tourism research.

(1) Although the articles tend not to discuss the issue specifically, there is a large ratio between the number of variables and cases. On average 19 cases are used for each original variable.
(2) The vast majority of papers use PCA, and the vast majority of papers are clear in stating what type of factor analysis is used.
(3) Most papers use a Varimax rotation and are intending to maximize the difference between the derived components.
(4) Most papers present the loadings, eigenvalues, and levels of explained variance and where they do not it is often possible to calculate the statistics from the information provided.
(5) Cronbach's alpha is the most common measure of reliability.

Table 10.6 Summary of factor analysis 2000–2011 in Journal of Travel Research

Authors	Vol. No. Yr	Sample (N)	Vars.	Type	Factors	Rotation	Eigen-values	% var.	Loadings	Reliability	Corr. Cut	Criteria	Regres-sion	Study Area
Jang et al.	38 (3) 2000	523	13	PCA		Oblique	Yes	Yes	Yes	Cronbach KMO Kaiser	0.298	+ One Scree	Scores	Gambling
Henthorne	38 (3) 2000	1500	19	PCA		Varimax	No	No	Yes	No	0.587	NS	No	Marketing
Phillips and Moutinho	38 (4) 2000	100	18	CFI	6	Varimax	Yes	Yes	Yes	Cronbach	0.61	+ One 60% var Scree	Scores	Planning
Heung and Cheng	38 (4) 2000	220	15	PCA	4	Varimax	Yes	Yes	Yes	Cronbach	0.4	+ One	Scores	Retail Perception
Nicholson and Pearce	39 (4) 2001	1300	20 20 20 20	PCA PCA PCA PCA	4 5 5 6	Varimax	Yes	Yes	Yes	Cronbach	0.408	+ One	No	Events Motivations
Burnett and Baker	40 (1) 2001	NS	30	PCA	4	Oblique	Yes	Yes	Yes	NS	0.59	+ One	No	Disability Attitudes Beliefs
Baloglu and Shoemaker	40 (1) 2001	234	14 13	PCA PCA	4 7	NS	Yes Yes	Yes Yes	Yes Yes	NS	0.4	+ One	Yes	Senior Travellers Motivations Preferences
Pennington-Gray and Kerstetter	40 (1) 2001	485	27	PCA	9	Varimax	Yes	Yes	Yes	Cronbach	0.465	+ One	No	Women Travellers Benefits
Wong and Lau	40 (1) 2001	200	13	PCA	4	Varimax	Yes	Yes	Yes	KMO Bartlett Cronbach	0.6	+ One	No	Culture Values
Juric et al.	40 (3) 2002	636	15	PCA	1	Varimax	No	No	No	Cronbach	0.573	NS	Scores	Ecotourism
Reisinger et al.	40 (3) 2002	618	73	PCA	5	Oblique R	No	Yes	Yes	Cronbach	0.61	+ One	No	Culture Rules Values Interaction Perceptions Satisfaction

Table 10.6 (continued)

Authors	Vol. No. Yr	Sample (N)	Vars.	Type	Factors	Rotation	Eigen-values	% var.	Loadings	Relia-bility	Corr. Cut	Criteria	Regres-sion	Study Area
Johns and Gyimóthy	40 (3) 2002	1099	12	PCA	4	Varimax	No	Yes	Yes	Cronbach	0.527	Scree	No	Marketing
			19	PCA	4	Varimax	No	Yes	Yes	Cronbach	0.543	Scree		
			30	PCA	4	Varimax	No	Yes	Yes	Cronbach	0.491	Scree		
Hsu and Lee	40 (4) 2002	817	55	PCA	6	Varimax	Yes	Yes	Yes	Cronbach	0.4	+ One	No	Senior Travellers Attributes
Perdue	41 (1) 2002	6342	3	PCA	1	Varimax	Yes	No	No	Cronbach, KMO Bartlett	0.6	+ One	No	Skiing Crowding Satisfaction
			4	PCA	1	Varimax					0.5			
Sirakaya et al.	41 (1) 2002	464	82	PCA	7	Varimax	Yes	Yes	Yes	Cronbach	0.4	+ One	Scores	Development Attitudes Perceptions
		464	24	PCA	2	Varimax	Yes	Yes						
Kim and Crompton	41 (2) 2002	2688	6	PCA	2	Varimax	Yes	Yes	Yes	Cronbach	0.5	+ One	Yes	Marketing Behaviour Loyalty
		2373	5	PCA	1	Varimax	Yes	Yes	Yes	Cronbach	0.57			
Vincent and Thompson	41 (2) 2002	969	27	PCA	5	Varimax	Yes	Yes	Yes	Bartlett Cronbach	0.3	+ One Scree	No	Ecotourism Perceptions
Sonmez and Sirakaya	41 (2) 2002	552	56	PCA	6	Varimax	Yes	Yes	Yes	Cronbach	0.45	+ One	No	Destination Image
			26	PCA	4	Varimax	Yes	Yes	Yes	Cronbach	0.51	KMO		
			17	PCA	2	Varimax	Yes	Yes	Yes	Cronbach	0.49			
Susskind et al.	41 (3) 2003	518	25	PCA	2	NS	Yes	Yes	Yes	Cronbach	0.4	Scree	Yes	Internet Apprehension
		243	21	CFA	2	NS	Yes	Yes	Yes	Cronbach	0.4	Scree		
		329	14	CFA	2	NS	Yes	Yes	Yes	Cronbach	0.4	Scree		
Morais et al.	41 (4) 2003	279	40	PCA	1	Promax	Yes	Yes	Yes	Cronbach	0.416	+ One	No	Resource Theory Perceptions
		279	29	PCA	2	Promax	Yes	Yes	Yes	Cronbach				
Benckendorff and Pearce	42 (1) 2003	407	10	PCA	3	Varimax	Yes	Yes	Yes	Cronbach	0.401	+ One	No	Attractions Perceptions
Revilla and Dodd	42 (1) 2003	139	25	PCA	5	Varimax	Yes	Yes	Yes	Cronbach	0.39	+ one Scree	No	Authenticity Perceptions

Study	Issue (Year)	N	Variance	Extraction	Factors	Rotation	(1)	(2)	(3)	Reliability	Value	Criterion	(4)	Construct
Poria et al.	43 (1) 2004	304	NS	PCA	3	Oblimin	No	Yes	Yes	Cronbach	0.4	NS	No	Heritage Motivations
Poria et al.	43 (1) 2004	136	NS	PCA	3	Oblimin	No	Yes	Yes	Cronbach	0.4	NS	No	
Reisinger and Movondo	43 (3) 2005	582	NS	PCA	3	Varimax	Yes	Yes	Yes	Cronbach	0.6	+One	Yes	Travel Risk
Pearce and Lee	43 (3) 2005	1012	74	PCA	14	Varimax	Yes	Yes	Yes	KMO / Cronbach	0.4	+One	No	Motivations to travel
Choi and Sirakaya	43 (4) 2005	308	54	PCA	7	Varimax	Yes	Yes	Yes	KMO / Bartlett / Cronbach	0.442	+One	No	Sustainable Tourism Attitudes
Choi and Sirakaya	43 (4) 2005		48	PCA	7	Varimax	Yes	Yes	Yes		0.540	+One	No	
Kwan and McCartney	44 (2) 2005	519	30	PCA	8	Varimax	Yes	Yes	Yes	Cronbach	0.43	+One / Scree	No	Gaming Perceptions
Poria et al.	44 (3) 2006	282	17	PCA	5	Oblique	Yes	Yes	Yes	Cronbach	0.505	+One	No	Heritage Motivations
Formica and Uysal	44 (4) 2006	135	20	NS	4	NS	Yes	Yes	Yes	Cronbach	0.427	+One	Yes	Destination Attractions
Hsu et al.	44 (4) 2006	464	16	NS	3	Varimax	Yes	Yes	Yes	Cronbach / KMO / Bartlett	0.429	+One	No	Marketing Benefits Sought
Hudson and Ritchie	44 (4) 2006	140	31	PCA	4	NS	No	Yes	Yes	Cronbach	0.7	+One	Yes	Film Tourism Marketing Initiatives
Ekinci and Hosany	45 (2) 2006	250	27	PCA	3	Varimax	No	Yes	Yes	KMO / Bartlett / Cronbach	0.45	+One	No	Branding Perceptions
Ollenburg and Buckley	45(4)2007	250	15	PCA	5	Varimax / Oblimin	No	Yes	Yes	Bertlett / KMO	0.5	+One	No	Farm Tourism Motivations
Murphy et al.	46 (1) 2007	124	20	NS	4	NS	Yes	Yes	Yes	NS	0.455	+One	No	Branding Personality
Murphy et al.	46 (1) 2007	126	20	NS	3	NS	Yes	Yes	Yes		0.430	+One	No	
Walters et al.	46 (1) 2007	180	NS	NS	2	NS	NS	Yes	Yes	Cronbach	0.691	NS	No	Marketing
Reichel et al.	46 (2) 2007	579	32	PCA	8	Varimax	NS	Yes	Yes	Cronbach	0.55	NS	No	Perceived Risk
Luo and Deng	46 (4) 2008	335	15	PCA	3	Varimax	Yes	Yes	Yes	Cronbach	0.54	+One	No	Environment Beliefs
Luo and Deng	46 (4) 2008		14	PCA	4	Varimax	Yes	Yes	Yes		0.48		No	Motivations

Table 10.6 (continued)

Authors	Vol. No. Yr	Sample (N)	Vars.	Type	Factors	Rotation	Eigen-values	% var.	Loadings	Relia-bility	Corr. Cut	Criteria	Regres-sion	Study Area
Rittichai-nuwat	46 (4) 2008	251	19	PCA	4	Promax	Yes	Yes	Yes	Cronbach	0.51	+ One	No	Motivations
Wang and Pfister	47 (1) 2008	130	20	PCA	2	Varimax	Yes	Yes	Yes	KMO Cronbach	0.43	+ One	No	Attitudes
Yoo and Chon	47 (1) 2008	279	42	PCA	6	Promax	Yes	Yes	Yes	Cronbach	0.47	+ One Scree	No	Conventions Decision-making
Brey et al.	47 (2) 2008	2716	18	PCA	3	Varimax	Yes	Yes	Yes	Cronbach	0.451	+ One	No	Hospitality Ratings
Vong	47 (3) 2009	495	21	PCA	5	Varimax	Yes	Yes	Yes	Cronbach	0.47	+ One	No	Gambling Attitudes
Stepchen-kova et al.	47 (4) 2009	540	100	PCA	15	Direct	No	Yes	Yes	Cronbach	0.416	NS	No	Destination Image
		540	100	PCA	15	Oblimin	No	Yes	Yes					
Gil et al.	47 (4) 2009	252	16	PCA	5	Varimax	No	Yes	Yes	Cronbach	NS	NS	Yes	Museum Image
			7	PCA	1	Varimax	No	Yes	Yes	KMO	0.524	Scree		Motivations
			13	PCA	4	Varimax	No	Yes	Yes	Bartlett	NS			Satisfaction
			3	PCA	1	Varimax	No	Yes	Yes		0.919			
Zhou and Ap	48 (1) 2009	1165	26	PCA	4	Varimax	Yes	Yes	Yes	KMO Cronbach	0.427	+ One	No	Olympics Perceptions
Poria et al.	48 (1) 2009	166	NS	PCA	2	Promax	Yes	Yes	Yes	Cronbach Bartlett	0.553	+ One Scree	No	Heritage Preferences
Woosnam et al.	49 (3) 2010	69	71	PCA	4	Varimax	Yes	Yes	Yes	KMO	0.481	+ One	No	Beliefs
		69	71	PCA	4	Varimax	Yes	Yes	Yes	Bartlett	0.439	Scree		Behavior Interaction Solidarity
		455	71	CFA	4	NS	NS	NS	Yes	Validity	0.513			
Hosany et al.	49 (4) 2010	200	44	PCA	3	Varimax	Yes	Yes	Yes	NS	0.55	+ One	No	Destination Emotions
Bronner and de Hoog	50 (1) 2011	419	20	PCA	5	Varimax	No	Yes	Yes	Cronbach	0.53	+ One	No	Internet Motivations
Wilkins	50 (3) 2011	300	7	PCA	2	Oblique	No	No	Yes	Cronbach	0.508	NS	No	Souvenirs Attitudes

Table 10.7 Summary of CFA using LISREL (Amos) 2000–2011 in Journal of Travel Research

Authors	Vol. No. Yr.	Sample (N)	No. Vars.	Type Analysis	Number of Factors	Measures of Reliability	Study Area
Petrick and Backman	41 (1) 2002	325	7	SAS	2	CMIN, CFI, GFI, NFI	Golf Tourism Perceived Value
Morais et al.	41 (4) 2003	279	14	SAS	4	CMIN, CFI, NNFI	Resource Theory Perceptions
Petrick	43 (1) 2004	792	25	EQS	5	CFI, NFI, RMSEA	Perceived Value
Al-Sabbahy et al.	42 (3) 2004	116 120	12 12	LISREL VIII LISREL VIII	2 2	GFI, AGFI, NFI, CFI, RMSEA, Cronbach	Hospitality Perceived Value
Snepenger et al.	45 (2) 2006	353	12	AMOS 5.0	1 to 2	CMIN, GFI, CFI, NFI, RFI, PNFI, RMSEA	Motivations
Nyaupane and Andereck	46 (4) 2008	332	10	LISREL 8.2	3	CMIN, GFI, CFI, RMSEA, Cronbach	Travel Constraints
Sirakaya-Turk et al.	46 (4) 2008	1817	7	LISREL 8.72	7	CMIN, GFI, AGFI, CFI, NFI, RMSEA Cronbach	Sustainable Tourism Attitudes
Yoo and Chon	47 (1) 2008	279	25	LISREL 8.3	5	CMIN, GFI, CFI, NN FI, RMSEA	Conventions Decision Making
Woosnam and Norman	49 (3) 2010	455	37	EQS 6.1	4	CFI, RMSEA, Cronbach	Beliefs, Behavior, Interaction, Solidarity
Hosany et al.	49 (4) 2010	200	23	LISREL 8	5	CMIN, GFI, AGFI, NNFI, CFI, RMSEA, SRMR	Destination Emotions
Wilkins	50 (3) 2011	300	7	NS	7	CMIN, AGFI, CFI, RMSEA, SRMR, Cronbach	Souvenirs Attitudes

(6)   The cut-off for significant components is mostly determined by an eigenvalue of one.
(7)   The level of variable allocation to a component is in most cases very low at 0.4.
(8)   There is a wide range of study areas examined using the technique.

Limitations

These points raise several questions about the use of factor analysis in tourism research.

(1)   What sample size is required?
(2)   Is the correct type of analysis applied to the problem?
(3)   Is the correct validation given for the choice of rotation?
(4)   What statistics should be reported? What reliability is required?
(5)   What cut-off determines the number of useable components?
(6)   What level of loading is required for a variable on a component?

It is not necessarily correct to say that current practice, as sampled by the articles in JTR, are the required standards.

The *sample size* required depends upon several factors including the size of the original population of data. In tourism the population sizes are usually very large because they relate to total numbers of tourists. In this case the accuracy of the sampling frame can be more important than the number of cases and a carefully selected representative sample might not be large. Consequently, the manner in which the sample is selected can be just as important as the ratio of cases to variables. If the selection of the cases is random then it is generally argued that the ratio is excellent at 20:1 or above, good at 10:1, and acceptable only at 5:1. Despite the high overall average of cases to variables in the JTR sample there are many examples where the sample size is very small relative to the number of variables analysed. However, just because a recommendation on ratios can be found in a statistics text does not make it correct; for example Gorsuch (1983) recommends a sample size of 5:1 and Nunnally (1978) and Everitt (1975) recommend 10:1. These ratios are assuming that a multivariate analysis technique is to be used. Another approach is suggested by MacCallum et al. (1996) of calculating the sample size required by determining the power level required from the analysis, given a population size estimate. Another strategy is to compare the sample characteristics to the known population equivalents, to ensure sample representation of the population which in turn may allow for a smaller sample.

In the sample of JTR papers most of the factor *analysis types* are PCA and there is a clear understanding that the analysis is exploratory or to reduce the number of variables. The PCA is sometimes followed by a CFA analysis on a second sample (if the sample size is very large the sample might be split in half to conduct the exploratory and then confirmatory analyses), and these papers are more common in Table 10.7. There appears to be no confusion as to the type of factor analysis to use. However, in presenting research this point still needs to be explained. There is confusion in the general literature arguably resulting from a conflict in opinion about which is better PCA or CFA, when really there is no better or worse option. PCA is superior for data reduction and exploratory work and CFA to test hypotheses. Both are capable of identifying latent constructs (despite arguments to the contrary in the general literature) within these contexts, and so both are a form of factor analysis.

The type of *rotation* used in the tourism sample with PCA is mostly Varimax and the intention is to describe orthogonal components. Varimax is recognized as the best form of orthogonal rotation. Where an oblique rotation is used there should be more explanation as to why it is used. Also there is nothing to stop an oblique rotation from deriving an orthogonal solution, and the ML method described above provides the advantage of measuring the correlation between the factors in a CFA. Where the ML method shows there is correlation between factors, this might suggest a higher order of constructs exists, although this point is often missed by researchers. Promax oblique is actually a little more common than Oblimin in the JTR sample, but this may not be representative of all tourism factor analysis publications. Promax derives its name from Procrustean rotation. It uses Varimax as the target rotation and uses a least square fit to obtain the oblique rotation, and as such is computationally more direct.

The question of *what statistics* should be reported is reasonably straightforward for most types of analysis and includes eigenvalues and explained variance along with factor loadings.

The question of *reliability* is less certain. Cronbach's alpha is the most common reliability measure followed by KMO and Bartlett. Alpha measures the degree to which a set of variables explain a latent construct, and a measure above 0.7 in the range 0 to 1 is considered sufficient while a measure of 0.8 is considered good, and as such it is akin to a measure of correlation. The main problem with the measure is that it is affected by the number of items in the scale, and so it does vary in accuracy becoming less accurate as the number of variables increases. The Kaiser–Meyer–Oklin (KMO) statistic measures the proportion of variance among the variables that might be common variance. The measure ranges between 0 and 1 and 0.5 and above is considered adequate to proceed with a factor analysis, although Kaiser has recommended a much higher value of 0.7 or above. KMO compares the magnitude of the correlation coefficients against the magnitude of the partial correlation coefficients.

None of the papers use the MSA which measures the common variance for each variable, and this is quite reasonable as the MSA is not easily interpreted as a measure of reliability.

Bartlett's test of sphericity tests whether the correlation matrix is an identity matrix (made up of ones in the diagonal and zeros off the diagonal). If all the correlations are one on the diagonal the variables are perfectly correlated with themselves and if zero off diagonal, they are totally uncorrelated with any other variable and there can be no common variance. It is a chi-square approximate test and the objective is to reject the null hypothesis of no correlation. This test suffers from the problem of sample size, and becomes less valid with smaller sample sizes. The Bartlett test is not highly discriminating and usually always rejects.

On balance the Cronbach's alpha value and KMO are the better reliability measures. When an ML analysis is used with CFA, the test statistics are larger in number and the suggested minimum number of statistics to report is given in the section discussing ML analysis.

The question of *what cut-off* should be used to determine the number of components to be rotated is reasonably straightforward. Components with eigenvalues greater than one should be selected. In the case of CFA the number of factors to be rotated should be selected from the correlation matrix with one on the diagonals not the reduced matrix with communalities. Obviously if an eigenvalue is very close to one, it is valid to round the eigenvalue up from 0.5 (0.95 = 1) but doing this needs to be noted and is not ideal. The logic for this stated criterion is sound because the sum of all eigenvalues is equal to the number of variables, so a value of one is average, and for another component to be selected it should exceed the average of one.

The alternative of using the scree plot by Cattell (1966) should be avoided, as it is subjective and often not conclusive. There is a suspicion that the scree plot is referenced in research to justify the use of components below an eigenvalue of one, in order to strengthen research discussion and in this context the use would be invalid. Ideally the scree plot should be presented if used, regardless of the journal editor's desire to keep an article short, so that the cutoff point is clearly obvious and justified. The main advantage of the scree method is with CFA analysis, because it applies to the reduced matrix with communalities and not the original matrix and so reflects directly on the CFA factors.

There is a third method called parallel analysis (Horn, 1965; Humphreys and Ilgen, 1969; Montanelli and Humphreys 1976) but it is not available in current programs, and is difficult to apply. The method has not been used in published tourism research, and it is recommended that further reference is made to Lidesma and Valero-Mara (2007) for a detailed discussion on how to apply the methodology.

The process of selecting the number of relevant factors in ML analysis using SEM is more subject to issues of data mining and must be done more carefully. The process is one of trial and error running the analysis several times with different numbers of factors, and attempting to maximize the fit statistics. The process is accepted generally, but raises the question of tailoring the results to the hypotheses being tested. So justification of the process needs careful explanation in theory. Quite often the adjustments yield only a small improvement and raise the question of whether they are necessary at all.

The question of the *required loading* of each variable for it to be allocated as significantly loaded on a component is the most vexing question. The original answer that is accepted in an unquestioning manner by tourism researchers was given by Stevens (1986) and is usually referenced in Hair (various editions with 1992 most commonly cited in the tourism literature, although in later editions this rises to 0.5) that a loading must at least be 0.4, because it is suggested that would indicate at least 30 percent of the variation in a variable loaded on a single factor. This was then followed by Comrey (1988) who stated that this might only apply if the loading of 0.4 was unique to only one factor. Consequently, the rule is often applied of accepting a value as low as 0.4 provided there is no other factor loading close to 0.4 for the same variable.

Given the loading in a PCA is a correlation statistic, it is difficult to see that 0.4 is an acceptable level of loading and in the literature on the evolution of factor analysis this low value was not accepted. In a regression analysis or correlation analysis a correlation of 0.4 would never be accepted, yet it is universally accepted in factor analysis. Although many tourism articles use the 0.4 criterion they usually state at least 0.4 and often have a lowest loading above 0.4 up to 0.55. There is an inconsistency in quoting one rule and then using another, simply because that was the computational result. It is also clear that a loading of 0.4 is far lower than a loading of 0.8, yet in the interpretation of the meaning of a component the variables loaded on the component receive an equal weighting for importance, carrying the same weight in the naming of the component. An equal weighting of importance might be acceptable if the cutoff value is 0.6 or higher, but not 0.4 or 0.5. A cut off of 0.4 or lower may also be acceptable if the PCA is a preliminary analysis for a CFA because the role of the PCA is simply to reduce the number of variables and give direction to the research. Results from the analysis need to be careful in defining the meaning of a component with careful interpretation of the meaning of the variables that load onto it, taking into account the relative weight of each loading variable from the strength of the loading. There is not much evidence of this happening in tourism research from the sample of articles examined.

CONCLUSION

Factor analysis is a complex methodology that provides an objective way of determining latent (hidden) concepts within social data and as such it is an important tool for analysing tourism data, and potentially solving tourism-related problems. There is a need for researchers to understand the technique, how it is calculated at least to some degree, and what the main features are of the procedure. A researcher needs to be aware of the types of applications suited to factor analytic analysis and the limitations to the methodology.

In the current published literature there are now so many factor analysed data sets that it is becoming possible to compare results on similar problems across different data surveys. More needs to be done developing hypothetical structures from previous studies and confirming constant relationships in future research. In order to aid this process there needs to be agreement and understanding of the basic elements from analysis that are to be reported, what statistics and survey elements should be clearly evident, and what standards of interpretation are required.

The major limitation in the method is interpretation of the meaning of the latent structures and more effort is needed in explaining the meaning of the survey items and the meaning and relevance of the latent constructs that are derived. Too often a meaning to a latent construct is stated with little or no justification of why the variables loading on the construct can be interpreted to have the given meaning. Alternatively, a discussion approach could be taken that gives more than one potential meaning to a latent construct, and debate follow as to the likely better interpretation.

Factor analysis will continue as a major tourism research tool but there is room for improvement in the use of the technique to raise the standard of research analysis and consequent findings.

REFERENCES

Al-Sabbahy, H.Z., Y. Ekinci and M. Riley (2004), 'An investigation of perceived value dimensions: implications for hospitality research', *Journal of Travel Research*, **42** (3), 226–234.

Baloglu, S. and S. Shoemaker (2001), 'Prediction of senior travelers' motorcoach use from demographic, psychological, and psychographic characteristics', *Journal of Travel Research*, **40** (1), 12–18.

Benckendorff, P.J. and P.L. Pearce (2003), 'Australian tourist attractions: the links between organizational characteristics and planning', *Journal of Travel Research*, **42** (1), 24–35.

Bock, R.D. and R.E. Bargmann (1966), 'Analysis of covariance structures', *Psychometrika*, **31**, 507–534.

Brey, E.T., D.B. Klenosky and A.M. Morrison (2008), 'Standard hospitality elements at resorts', *Journal of Travel Research*, **47** (2), 247–258.

Bronner, F. and R. de Hoog (2011), 'Vacationers and eWOM: who posts, and why, where, and what?', *Journal of Travel Research*, **50** (1),15–26.
Burnett, J.J. and H.B. Baker (2001), 'Assessing the travel-related behaviors of the mobility-disabled consumer', *Journal of Travel Research*, **40** (1), 4–11.
Carroll, J.B. (1953), 'An analytical solution for approximating simple structure in factor analysis', *Psychometrika*, **18**, 23–28.
Carroll, J.B. (1960), 'IBM 704 program for generalized analytic rotation solution in factor analysis', unpublished manuscript, Harvard University.
Cattell, R.B. (1966), 'The scree test for the number of factors', *Multivariate Behavioral Research*, **1**, 245–276.
Cattell, R.B. and J.L. Muerle (1960), 'The "maxplane" program for factor rotation to oblique simple structure', *Educational and Psychological Measurement*, **20**, 569–590.
Choi, H.C. and E. Sirakaya (2005), 'Measuring residents' attitude toward sustainable tourism: development of sustainable tourism attitude scale', *Journal of Travel Research*, **43** (4), 380–394.
Chu, K.H. (2008), 'A factorial evaluation of work value structure: second-order confirmatory factor analysis and its implications', *Tourism Management*, **29**, 320–330.
Chu, R.K.S. and T. Choi (2000), 'An importance-performance analysis of hotel selection factors in the Hong Kong hotel industry: a comparison of business and leisure travelers', *Tourism Management*, **21**, 363–377.
Comrey, A.L. (1988), 'Factor-analytic methods of scale development in personality and clinical psychology', *Journal of Consulting and Clinical Psychology*, **56**, 754–761.
Correia, A., M. Moital, C. Ferreira da Costa and R. Peres (2008), 'The determinants of gastronomic tourists satisfaction: a second-order factor analysis', *Journal of Foodservice*, **19**, 164–176.
Crawford, C. (1967), 'A general method of rotation for factor analysis', paper presented at the meeting of the Psychometric Society, April.
Curran, P.J., S.G. West and J.F. Finch (1966), 'The robustness of test statistics to nonnormality and specification error in confirmatory factor analysis', *Psychological Methods*, **1**, 16–29.
Drey, B. and M.K. Sarma (2010), 'Information source usage among motive-based segments of travelers to newly emerging tourist destinations', *Tourism Management*, **31**, 341–344.
Ekinci, Y. and S. Hosany (2006), 'Destination personality: an application of brand personality to tourism destinations', *Journal of Travel Research*, **45** (2), 127–139.
Everitt, B.S. (1975), 'Multivariate analysis: the need for data, and other problems', *British Journal of Psychiatry*, **126**, 237–240.
Ferguson, G. (1954), 'The concept of parsimony in factor analysis', *Psychometrika*, **19**, 281–290.
Formica, S. and M. Uysal (2006), 'Destination attractiveness based on supply and demand evaluations: an analytical framework', *Journal of Travel Research*, **44** (4), 418–430.
Galloway, G. (2002), 'Psychographic segmentation of park visitor markets: evidence for the utility of sensation seeking', *Tourism Management*, **23** (6), 581–596.
Gil, S.M. and J.R. Brent Ritchie (2009), 'Understanding the museum image formation process: a comparison of residents and tourists', *Journal of Travel Research*, **47** (4), 480–493.
Gorsuch, R.L. (1983), *Factor Analysis*, 2nd edition, Hillside, NJ: Erlbaum.
Guttman, L. (1953), 'Image theory for the structure of quantitative variates', *Psychometrika*, **18**, 277–296.
Hair, J.F. (1992), Multivariate data analysis, 3rd edition, New York: Macmillan.
Hakstian, A.R., W.T. Rogers and R.B. Cattell (1982), 'The behavior of number-of-factors rules with simulated data', *Multivariate Behavioral Research*, **17**, 193–219.
Harman, H.H. (1976), *Modern Factor Analysis*, 3rd edition, Chicago, IL: University of Chicago Press.
Harman, H.H. and W.H. Jones (1966), 'Factor analysis by minimizing residuals (minres)', *Psychometrika*, **31**, 351–368.
Harris, C.W. (1962), 'Some Rao-Guttman relationships', *Psychometrika*, **27**, 247–263.
Harris, M.L. and C.W. Harris (1971), 'A factor analytic interpretation strategy', *Educational and Psychological Measurement*, **31**, 589–606.
Hendrikson, A.E. and P.D. White (1964), 'PROMAX: a quick method of rotation to oblique simple structure', *British Journal of Mathematical and Statistical Psychology*, **17**, 65–70.
Henthorne, T.L. (2000), 'An analysis of expenditures by cruise ship passengers in Jamaica', *Journal of Travel Research*, **38** (3), 246–250.
Heung, V.C.S. and E. Cheng (2000), 'Assessing tourists' satisfaction with shopping in the Hong Kong Special Administrative Region of China', *Journal of Travel Research*, **38** (4), 396–404.
Holzinger, K. and F. Swineford (1937), 'The bi-factor method', *Psychometrika*, **2**, 41–54.
Horn, J.L. (1965), 'A rationale and technique for estimating the number of factors in factor analysis', *Psychometrika*, **30**, 179–185.
Hosany, S. and D. Gilbert (2010), 'Measuring tourists' emotional experiences toward hedonic holiday destinations', *Journal of Travel Research*, **49** (4), 513–526.

Hotelling, H. (1933), 'Analysis of complex statistical variables into principal components', *Journal of Educational Psychology*, **24**, 417–441; 498–520.

Hsu, C.H.C. and E. Lee (2002), 'Segmentation of senior motorcoach travelers', *Journal of Travel Research*, **40** (4), 364–373.

Hsu, C.H.C., S.K. Kang and T. Lam (2006), 'Reference group influences among Chinese travelers', *Journal of Travel Research*, **44** (4), 474–484.

Hu, L., P.M. Bentler and Y. Kano (1992), 'Can test statistics in covariance structure analysis be trusted?', *Psychological Bulletin*, **112**, 351–362.

Hudson, S. and J.R.B. Ritchie (2006), 'Promoting destinations via film tourism: an empirical identification of supporting marketing initiatives', *Journal of Travel Research*, **44** (4), 387–396.

Humphreys, L.G. and D.R. Ilgen (1969), 'Note on a criterion for the number of common factors', *Educational and Psychological Measurements*, **29**, 571–578.

Jang, H., B. Lee, M. Park and P.A. Stokowski (2000), 'Measuring underlying meanings of gambling from the perspective of enduring involvement', *Journal of Travel Research*, **38** (3), 230–238.

Jennrich, R.I. and P.F. Sampson (1966), 'Rotation for simple loadings', *Psychometrika*, **31**, 313–323.

Johns, N. and S. Gyimóthy (2002), 'Market segmentation and the prediction of tourist behavior: the case of Bornholm, Denmark', *Journal of Travel Research*, **40** (3), 316–327.

Jöreskog, K.G. (1966), 'Testing a simple structure hypothesis in factor analysis', *Psychometrika*, **31**, 165–178.

Jöreskog, K.G. (1967), 'Some contributions to maximum likelihood factor analysis,' *Psychometrika*, **32**, 443–482.

Jöreskog, K.G. (1969), 'A general approach to confirmatory maximum likelihood factor analysis', *Psychometrika*, **34**, 183–202.

Jöreskog, K.G. (1970), 'A general method for analysis of covariance structures', *Biometrika*, **57**, 239–251.

Jöreskog, K.G. and D. Sörbom (1989), *LISREL-7 User's Guide*, Mooresville, IN: Scientific Software.

Juric, B., T.B. Cornwell and D. Mather (2002), 'Exploring the usefulness of an ecotourism interest scale', *Journal of Travel Research*, **40** (3), 259–269.

Kaiser, H. (1956), 'The Varimax method of factor analysis', unpublished PhD dissertation, University of California, Berkley.

Kaiser, H. (1958), 'The Varimax criterion for analytic rotation in factor analysis', *Psychometrika*, **23**, 187–200.

Kaiser, H. (1970), 'A second generation little-jiffy', *Psychometrika*, **35**, 401–415.

Kaiser, H. and J. Caffrey (1965), 'Alpha factor analysis', *Psychometrika*, **30**, 1–14.

Kim, S. and J.L. Crompton (2002), 'The influence of selected behavioral and economic variables on perceptions of admission price levels', *Journal of Travel Research*, **41** (2), 144–152.

Kozak, M. and M. Rimmington (2000), 'Tourist satisfaction with Mallorca, Spain, as an off-season holiday destination', *Journal of Travel Research*, **38** (3), 260–269.

Kwan, F.V.C. and G. McCartney (2005), 'Mapping resident perceptions of gaming impact', *Journal of Travel Research*, **44** (2), 177–187.

Lawley, D.N. (1940), 'The estimation of factor loadings by the method of maximum likelihood', *Proceedings of the Royal Statistical Society of Edinburgh*, **60**, 64–82.

Lee, C., Y. Lee, B.J. Bernhard and Y. Yoon (2006), 'Segmenting casino gamblers by motivation: a cluster analysis of Korean gamblers', *Tourism Management*, **27**, 856–866.

Lidesma, R.D. and P. Valero-Mara (2007), 'Determining the number of factors to retain in an EFA: an easy to use computer program for carrying out parallel analysis', *Practical Assessment, Research and Evaluation*, **12** (2), 1–11.

Lim, W.M. (2010), 'Factor analysis of variables affecting e-marketing adoption by UK independent hotels', in U. Gretzel, R. Law and M. Fuchs (eds), *Information and Communication Technologies in Tourism 2010*, New York, Springer, pp. 39–50.

Lindeman, R.H. (1980), *Introduction to Bivariate and Multivariate Analysis*, London: Scott, Foresman and Company.

Luo, Y. and J. Deng (2008), 'The new environmental paradigm and nature-based tourism motivation', *Journal of Travel Research*, **46** (4), 392–402.

MacCallum, R.C. (1990), 'The need for alternative measures of fit in covariance structure modeling', *Multivariate Behavioral Research*, **24**, 59–69.

MacCullum, R.C., M.W. Browne and H.M. Sugawara (1996), 'Power analysis and determination of sample size for covariance structure modelling', *Psychological Methods*, **1**, 130–149.

Massy, W.F. (1965), 'Principal components regression in exploratory statistical research', *Journal of the American Statistical Society*, **60**, 234–256.

Montanelli, R.G. Jnr. and L.G. Humphreys (1976), 'Latent roots of random data correlation matrices with squared multiple correlations on the diagonal: a monte carlo study', *Psychometrika*, **41**, 341–348.

Morais, D.B., S.J. Backman and M.J. Dorch (2003), 'Toward the operationalization of resource investments made between customers and providers of a tourism service', *Journal of Travel Research*, **41** (4), 362–374.

Murphy, L., G. Moscardo and P. Bekerndorff (2007), 'Using brand personality to differentiate regional tourism destinations', *Journal of Travel Research*, **46** (1), 5–14.

Neuhaus, J.O. and C. Wrigley (1954), 'The Quartimax method: an analytical approach to orthogonal simple structure', *British Journal of Mathematical and Statistical Psychology*, **7**, 81–91.

Nicholson, R.E. and D.G. Pearce (2001), 'Why do people attend events: a comparative analysis of visitor motivations at four South Island events', *Journal of Travel Research*, **39** (4), 449–460.

Nunnally, J.C. (1978), *Psychometric Theory*, 2nd edition, New York: Mc Graw-Hill.

Nyaupane, G.P. and K.L. Andereck (2008), 'Understanding travel constraints: application and extension of a leisure constraints model', *Journal of Travel Research*, **46** (4), 433–439.

Ollenburg, C. and R. Buckley (2007), 'Stated economic and social motivations of farm tourism operators', *Journal of Travel Research*, **45** (4), 444–452.

Özgener, Ş. and R. İraz (2006), 'Customer relationship management in small-medium enterprises: the case of Turkish tourism industry', *Tourism Management*, **27**, 1356–1363.

Pearce, P.L. and U. Lee (2005), 'Developing the travel carer approach to tourist motivation', *Journal of Travel Research*, **43** (3), 226–237.

Pearson, K. (1901), 'On the lines and planes of closest fit to systems of points in space', *Philosophical Magazine*, **6**, 559–572.

Pennington-Gray, L.A. and D.L. Kerstetter (2001), 'What do university-educated women want from their pleasure travel experiences?', *Journal of Travel Research*, **40** (1), 49–56.

Perdue, R.R. (2002), 'Perishability, yield management, and cross-product elasticity: a case study of deep discount season passes in the Colorado ski industry', *Journal of Travel Research*, **41** (1), 15–22.

Petrick, J.F. (2004), 'First timers' and repeaters' perceived value', *Journal of Travel Research*, **43** (1), 29–38.

Petrick J.F. and S.J. Backman (2002), 'An examination of the construct of perceived value for the prediction of golf travelers' intentions to revisit', *Journal of Travel Research*, **41** (1), 38–45.

Phillips, P.A. and L. Moutinho (2000), 'The strategic planning index: a tool for measuring strategic planning effectiveness', *Journal of Travel Research*, **38** (4), 369–379.

Poria, Y., A. Biran and A. Reichel (2009), 'Visitors' preferences for interpretation at heritage sites', *Journal of Travel Research*, **48** (1), 92–105.

Poria, Y., R. Butler and D. Airey (2004), 'Links between tourists, heritage, and reasons for visiting heritage sites', *Journal of Travel Research*, **43** (1), 19–28.

Poria, Y., A. Reichel and A. Biran (2006), 'Heritage site perceptions and motivations to visit', *Journal of Travel Research*, **44** (3), 318–326.

Rao, C.R. (1955), 'Estimation and tests of significance in factor analysis', *Psychometrika*, **20**, 93–111.

Reichel, A., G. Fuchs and N. Uriely (2007), 'Perceived risk and the non-institutionalized tourist role: the case of Israel student backpackers', *Journal of Travel Research*, **46** (2), 217–226.

Reisinger, Y. and F. Movondo (2005), 'Travel anxiety and intentions to travel internationally: implications of travel risk perception', *Journal of Travel Research*, **43** (3), 212–225.

Reisinger, Y. and L.W. Turner (1999a), 'A cultural analysis of Japanese tourists: challenges for tourism marketers', *European Journal of Marketing*, **33** (12), 1203–1227.

Reisinger, Y. and L.W. Turner (1999b), 'Structural equation modeling with LISREL: application in tourism', *Tourism Management*, **20** (1), 71–88.

Reisinger, Y. and L.W. Turner (2002), 'Cultural differences between Asian tourist markets and Australian hosts, Part 1', *Journal of Travel Research*, **40** (3), 295–315.

Reisinger, Y. and L.W. Turner (2003), *Cross-Cultural Behaviour in Tourism, Concepts and Analysis*, Oxford: Butterworth Heineman.

Revilla, G. and T.H. Dodd (2003), 'Authenticity perceptions of Talavera pottery', *Journal of Travel Research*, **42** (1), 94–99.

Rittichainuwat, B.N. (2008), 'Responding to disaster: Thai and Scandinavian tourists' motivation to visit Phuket, Thailand', *Journal of Travel Research*, **46** (4), 422–432.

Saunders, D.R. (1953), 'An analytical method for rotation to orthogonal simple structure', *Educational Testing Service Research Bulletin* RB-53-10.

Saunders, D.R. (1961), 'The rationale for an "Oblimax" method of transformation in factor analysis', *Psychometrika*, **26**, 317–324.

Saunders, D.R. (1962), 'Trans-varimax', *American Psychologist*, **17**, 395.

Sirakaya, E., V. Teye and S. Sonmez (2002), 'Understanding residents' support for tourism development in the Central Region of Ghana', *Journal of Travel Research*, **41** (1), 57–67.

Sirakaya, E., M. Uysal and C.F. Yoshioka (2003), 'Segmenting the Japanese tour market to Turkey', *Journal of Travel Research*, **41** (3), 292–304.

Sirakaya-Turk, E., Y. Ekinci and A.G. Kaya (2008), 'An examination of the validity of SUS-TAS in cross cultures', *Journal of Travel Research*, **46** (4), 414–421.

Snepenger, D., J. King, E. Marshall and M. Uysal (2006), 'Modeling Iso-Ahola's motivation theory in the tourism context', *Journal of Travel Research*, **45** (2), 140–149.

Sonmez, S. and E. Sirakaya (2002), 'A distorted destination image? The case of Turkey', *Journal of Travel Research*, **41** (2), 185–196.

Spearman, C. (1904), 'General intelligence, objectively determined and measured', *American Journal of Psychology*, **15**, 201–293.

Stepchenkova, S., A.P. Kirilenko and A. Morrison (2009), 'Facilitating content analysis in tourism research', *Journal of Travel Research*, **47** (4), 454–469.

Stevens, J. (1986), *Applied Multivariate Statistics for the Social Sciences*, Hillsdale, NJ: Erlbaum.

Snyman, J.A. and M. Saayman (2009), 'Key factors influencing foreign direct investment in the tourism industry in South Africa', *Tourism Review*, **64** (3), 49–58.

Susskind, A.M., M.A. Bonn and C.S. Dev (2003), 'To look or book: an examination of consumers' apprehensiveness toward internet use', *Journal of Travel Research*, **41** (3), 256–264.

Thurstone, L.L. (1931), 'Multiple factor analysis', *Psychological Review*, **38**, 406–427.

Thurstone, L.L. (1938), 'Primary mental abilities', *Psychometric Monographs*, **1**, Chicago, IL: University of Chicago Press.

Thurstone, L.L. (1947), *Multiple Factor Analysis*, Chicago, IL: University of Chicago Press.

Vincent, V.C. and W. Thompson (2002), 'Assessing community support and sustainability for ecotourism development', *Journal of Travel Research*, 153–160.

Vong, F. (2009), 'Changes in residents' gambling attitudes and perceived impacts at the fifth anniversary of Macao's gaming deregulation', *Journal of Travel Research*, **47** (3), 388–397.

Vu, C.J. and L.W. Turner (2009), 'The economic structure of world tourism', *Tourism Economics*, **15** (1), 5–21.

Walters, G., B. Sparks and C. Herington (2007), 'The effectiveness of print advertising stimuli in evoking elaborate consumption visions for potential travelers', *Journal of Travel Research*, **46** (1), 24–34.

Wang, Y. and R.E. Pfister (2008), 'Residents' attitudes toward tourism and perceived personal benefits in a rural community', *Journal of Travel Research*, **47** (1), 84–93.

Wilkins, H. (2011), 'Souvenirs: what and why we buy', *Journal of Travel Research*, **50** (3),239–247.

Woosnam, K.M. and W.C. Norman (2010), 'Measuring residents' emotional solidarity with tourists: scale development of Durkheim's theoretical constructs', *Journal of Travel Research*, **49** (3), 365–380.

Wong, S. and E. Lau (2001), 'Understanding the behavior of Hong Kong Chinese tourists on group tour packages', *Journal of Travel Research*, **40** (1), 57–67.

Yoo, J.J. and K. Chon (2008), 'Factors affecting convention participation decision-making: developing a measurement scale', *Journal of Travel Research*, **47** (1), 113–122.

Yuan, J., L.A. Cai, A.M. Morrison and S. Linton (2004), 'An analysis of wine festival attendees' motivations: a synergy of wine, travel and special events?', *Journal of Vacation Marketing*, **11** (1), 41–58.

Zhou, Y. and J. Ap (2009), 'Residents' perceptions towards the impacts of the Beijing 2008 Olympic Games', *Journal of Travel Research*, **48** (1), 78–91.

11 Cluster analysis
Liz Fredline

INTRODUCTION

The purpose of this chapter is to describe and illustrate the analytical technique known as cluster analysis and to outline its application in tourism research. This technique can be extremely useful for certain research questions, but a review of literature shows that its application has been quite infrequent. The chapter begins with a brief summary of the nature of the technique followed by a summary of some of the tourism literature which has employed cluster analysis. Following on from this is a summary of a worked example (using IBM SPSS 19.0) of a two-stage cluster analysis procedure. Finally, the chapter concludes with a discussion of the advantages and limitations of the technique as well as the possible future advances in tourism research which may be possible with the application of cluster analysis.

Cluster analysis is a family of multivariate techniques useful for analysing cases based on their scores on a range of measured variables. Essentially the technique identifies cases with a comparable pattern of responses that can be regarded, for the purposes of the analysis, as similar. In so doing a large number of individual cases are summarized into a smaller, more manageable number of clusters. The outcome of a successful cluster analysis would be a small number of highly homogeneous clusters that are substantially different to each other (Hair et al., 1998). Cluster membership can then be used as a variable for further analysis aimed at understanding the clusters and the bases on which they were formed.

In the tourism context there are many possible applications for cluster analysis. It is useful in any situation where the researcher wants to identify groups of cases that are similar to each other but different from other groups, that is, segmentation of the population. This segmentation can be based on any variables that are regarded as important for discriminating between groups and could include simple demographic characteristics or psychographic characteristics such as attitudes, perceptions, and motivations. The populations being studied may be tourism or hospitality customers (see for example, Arimond and Elfessi, 2001; Jurowski and Reich, 2000; Ryan and Huyton, 2000) or residents of a region that is visited by tourists (Davis et al., 1988; Fredline and Faulkner, 2000, 2002; Madrigal, 1995; Perez and Nadal, 2005). This latter application is quite common in the tourism literature aimed at assessing residents' perceptions of the impact of tourism.

NATURE OF CLUSTER ANALYSIS AND ITS EVOLUTION

Cluster analysis has its origins in the biological sciences where it was first used in taxonomical studies to classify flora and fauna into phyla, classes and orders. Gilmour (1951) describes its development from the mid-1800s. However, it was not until the second half of the twentieth century that advances in the use of computers for statistical analysis allowed the technique to be updated for modern application. Authors such as Sneath and Sokal (1973) and Anderberg (1973) were instrumental in this process (cited in Jurowski and Reich, 2000).

Cluster analysis is an 'interdependence' rather than a 'dependence' technique. This means that it does not aim to assess the relationship between independent and dependant variables; rather it is focused on the underlying structure of variables and the usefulness of this structure in categorizing cases (Hair et al., 1998). Thus, it does not have a specific test of significance indicating the outcome of the analysis. For this reason many researchers inexperienced in its use are sometimes uncomfortable with it as they are used to having a definitive indication of the solution. Instead interpretation of the results of cluster analysis must be based on researcher knowledge and experience, as well as the logic of the solution and the extent to which clusters demonstrate high internal homogeneity and high external heterogeneity. As Jurowski and Reich (2000, p. 69) suggest the technique can be 'considered an art as well as a science'.

Like any analysis there are a number of options and therefore several decisions the researcher must make. First, the data must be assessed for their suitability for analysis. Cluster analysis does not hinge on assumptions about the distribution of the data so normal considerations about the normality, linearity and homoscedasticity of the data are not relevant (Hair et al., 1998). However, there are three issues which do require some consideration; outliers, multi-collinearity and the extent to which the data are representative of the population being studied.

Outliers can substantially affect the results so it is important to try to identify multivariate outliers (those which represent an unusual combination of scores on the linear combination of variables) and remove these. Mahalanobis distance can be used for this purpose and can be accessed through the regression procedure in SPSS. Multicollinearity is a problem to the extent that if two or more variables included in the analysis are highly correlated, while other variables are not, then those variables have more weight in determining the outcome. Any high correlations need to be examined and if two variables are determined to be effectively the same, then one should be removed or the two variables could be collapsed together into a composite. Like any other analytical technique, the results will only be generalizable beyond the specific cases included in the analysis if the sample was representative of the population of interest (Aldenderfer and Blashfield, 1984). Consideration of representativeness should reflect on the sampling procedures used as well as the response rate. If response rates were low, then some check should be made of non-response bias.

If the variables to be analysed are not measured on the same scale then consideration should be given to standardizing them prior to analysis. This is because variables with a much larger range will have a greater influence on the solution than those with a smaller range. For example, if one variable is measured on a scale ranging from 1–100 while another ranges from 1–10, then the former could potentially carry far more weight in determining the similarity or differences between cases. Standardization will ensure that all variables are having a similar impact on the outcome (Hair et al., 1998).

The next decision that researchers need to consider is how the variables which are to form the basis of segmentation should be combined into a composite score known as a cluster variate. There are three main choices here: correlational measures, distance measures, and association measures. The choice depends on the form of the variables and the purpose of the research. If the data are non-metric, then association measures are most appropriate. Metric data can be combined using either correlation measures, if the aim is to identify patterns in the data set, or distance measures, if the aim is to identify cases which are closest together (Hair et al., 1998).

The next decision, and possibly the most fundamental one, is between hierarchical and non-hierarchical clustering, as these represent quite different approaches to segmentation. The former begins with each case in its own cluster and in the first step it joins together the two closest cases based on their scores on the cluster variate. In each step there is one less cluster and the process continues until all cases are joined together in a single cluster. It is quite a computationally intensive technique, as the centroids (the multivariate means of the scores on the variate) must be recalculated as each new cluster is formed. Thus a large number of cases and/or variables will require substantial computational power.

Once the analysis is complete it is then necessary to select which solution, that is, which number of clusters, is the best. SPSS produces two outputs that can help in this regard: the agglomeration schedule and the dendrogram. The agglomeration schedule shows the clustering coefficient at each step. A small increase in the coefficient indicates that the clusters being combined are relatively homogeneous, while a large increase indicates that they were fairly heterogeneous, so the basic principle involves stopping the analysis just before a large increase. However, Hair et al. (1998) suggest that this may tend to indicate too few clusters. The dendrogram shows the distances between clusters being combined at each stage. Similarly, the idea would be to select a solution just before a large distance is observed.

The researcher can then examine the solution at each point to determine where the explanation is most appropriate. It is typical to start by examining the two-cluster solution and work backwards. The researcher should look at the means of the two clusters on the original variables to see how these differ. Then the three cluster solution should be examined. This solution will contain one cluster that was present in the two cluster solution, while to other two will have resulted from the splitting of another so it is useful to try and understand the basis for this split. The researcher must then ask themselves whether this split results in a more interpretable and useful segmentation than the two cluster solution. If they feel this to be the case then they should proceed to the four cluster solution and so on until it is felt that the outcome provides good discrimination into manageable and meaningful groups. This process, in combination with the interpretation of the agglomeration schedule and/or dendrogram, should help researchers to decide on the most appropriate solution.

One weakness associated with the method is that cases can become 'trapped' in a cluster. Once a case is allocated to a cluster it must stay there even if, by the process of recalculating centroids at each step, a new cluster later emerges that it would be closer to. As Arimond and Elfessi (2001, p. 391) suggest, 'hierarchical methods only provide a starting point and do not consistently produce clusters that are clearly homogeneous and well balanced'.

The alternative method, non-hierarchical clustering (also known as quick cluster or K-means clustering), takes a quite different approach. In this case, the researcher must pre-specify the number of clusters to be derived and a starting variate score (or seed) for

Table 11.1   Advantages and disadvantages of hierarchical and non-hierarchical techniques

	Hierarchical	Non-hierarchical
Advantages	Can be used to determine the best number of clusters	Allows cases to be reassigned Provides additional diagnostic tables
Disadvantages	Computationally intensive Cases can become trapped	Most suitable when the researcher has some knowledge about the number of clusters and their starting points

Table 11.2   Clustering algorithms

Hierarchical	Non-hierarchical
Single Linkage – joins clusters based on shortest distance to any case within the cluster. Also known as nearest neighbour. **Complete Linkage** – joins clusters based on longest distance between any two cases. **Average Linkage** – joins clusters based on the average distance between all cases. Less affected by outliers. **Centroid Method** – joins clusters based on the distance between centroids. **Ward's Method** – joins clusters based on the sums of squares within the clusters. Tends to produce clusters of a similar size.	**Sequential Threshold Method** – selects seeds one at a time and includes all cases within a specified distance. Then moves onto the next seed. **Parallel Threshold Method** – processes all cluster seeds simultaneously and assigns cases to the closest seed. **Optimizing Procedure** – similar to the parallel method but allows reassignment of cases.

each cluster. For this reason non-hierarchical clustering is far more successful if there is a substantial body of previous literature to inform these decisions. It is possible to randomly select seeds but these will substantially affect the outcome. It is likely that different randomly selected seeds will produce somewhat different results.

A key benefit of non-hierarchical clustering is that it allows cases to be reassigned if they become closer to a different cluster centroid. Also the non-hierarchical clustering method in IBM SPSS 19.0 provides some diagnostic tables which facilitate better understanding of the adequacy of the solution.

Thus, each method has its advantages and disadvantages as summarized in Table 11.1. For this reason, a common approach is to use a combination of the two; hierarchical clustering followed by non-hierarchical. This allows the researcher to select the most appropriate solution in terms of number of clusters, and then ensure the best possible allocation of cases to clusters.

The next decision for the researcher is which clustering algorithm to use. There are many choices here. In hierarchical clustering the options include single linkage, complete linkage, average linkage, Ward's method and the centroid method. The methods differ in how they decide which clusters should be joined together at each iteration of the analysis. In non-heirarchical clustering the options include sequential threshold, parallel threshold and optimization. Table 11.2 provides a brief explanation of these but a fuller description can be found in many multivariate statistics textbooks such as Hair et al. (1998) and Jobson (1991).

APPLICATIONS OF CLUSTER ANALYSIS IN TOURISM

As mentioned previously, the two most common applications of cluster analysis in tourism research are market segmentation and segmentation of host community attitudes or perceptions toward tourism. Below is a brief summary of some of the work in these two fields.

Market Segmentation

A common application of cluster analysis in tourism is market segmentation as the technique has been adopted from more mainstream marketing research where it has been widely used. In this form, the analysis allows tourism researchers and operators to better understand the various groups that exist within their market and therefore to modify their product to specifically target selected markets or alternatively to attempt to meet the differing needs of all segments. It allows more efficient allocation of resources which should then lead to the generation of additional income.

An excellent example of this type of study is Jurowski and Reich (2000) who classified potential hotel customers based on 24 items relating to their interest in entertainment options which might be offered in the future by a casino in Arizona. They used hierarchical clustering (with between groups linkage as the method and squared Euclidean distances as the measure) to identify three clusters which they described as 'diners', 'dancers' and 'drinkers'. The results of the study provided valuable information to the property developers on the interests of different market segments and how these segments could be best targeted. The authors identified that the cluster most likely to increase patronage in response to the development of new facilities was the 'dancers' and therefore, if this market segment were targeted then the potential for additional revenue could be maximized.

Jurowski and Reich (2000) also provide a very good discussion of the application of cluster analysis with detailed discussion on the selection of methods and interpretation of output from SPSS.

Cha et al. (1995) used cluster analysis to examine the travel motivations of Japanese outbound tourists. They initially used factor analysis to reduce 30 motivational items to 6 motivational factors, and then used the factor scores in an hierarchical analysis of 5 per cent of the cases. The means observed were then used in a non-hierarchical analysis of all 1199 cases. Although the authors do not explicitly mention a reason for this approach, it is likely that the large number of cases and items was beyond the computational power of their desktop computers as this research was conducted more than 20 years ago. The use of factor analysis prior to clustering was very common in early research most likely for this reason. However, Rolph (1970, cited in Hair et al., 1998) says there is evidence to suggest the variables which truly discriminate between underlying groups are not well represented in many factor solutions. In recent years most clustering has been conducted on original variables. Following on from the cluster analysis, Cha et al. (1995) used multiple discriminate analysis to explain the differences between the three cluster they identified; 'sport seekers', 'novelty seekers' and 'family/ relaxation seekers'.

Another application of cluster analysis to market segmentation is found in Ryan and Huyton (2000). These researchers used 28 items relating to desired tourism experiences in the Northern Territory, Australia, to identify seven market segments and their differing levels of interest in aboriginal tourism products.

Mueller and Lanz Kaufmann (2000) conducted an interesting study on the health tourism market. They used a two-stage process (hierarchical followed by non-hierarchical) to identify four clusters based on the importance ratings of various wellness components offered by hotels in Switzerland. These included tangible components such as swimming pools, saunas and medical centres, as well as intangibles such as information, courses and medical advice. The identified clusters included 'demanding health guests', 'independent infrastructure users', 'care intensive cure guests' and 'undemanding recreation guests'.

Arimond and Elfessi (2001) used an interesting combination of multiple correspondence analysis followed by a non-heirarchical clustering procedure. This was because of the format of their data, which was non-metric categorical data. The seven variables all related to desired services and benefits that customers seek when staying at a bed and breakfast accommodation property, and for each variable respondents were asked to select only the most desirable option, rather than rate each option on a Likert type scale. The results from the multiple correspondence analysis were then input into the non-hierarchical clustering procedure. Because the researchers were unsure about the appropriate number of clusters they undertook a number of analyses and the solutions were compared. The researchers settled on a four cluster solution which produced the clearest distinguishable segments.

Najimi et al. (2010) used cluster analysis to segment the market of tourists to Iran based on two variables: profitability and cultural compatibility. Using the average linkage method and Euclidean distances as the measure, they identified three clusters: semi-compatibles, compatibles and dissatisfied. They then undertook a further segmentation of the compatibles cluster into Iranian-compatibles and Arab-compatibles based on a common sense approach, and the fact that this delineation would be more useful in targeting appropriate tourists. This demonstrates the application of 'art' in cluster analysis rather than just 'science' as described by Jurowski and Reich (2000).

The above studies demonstrate the usefulness of cluster analysis in market segmentation as it helps to identify important sub-groups of the total market which have different needs and wants. However, as each application is in a very different tourism market, the literature does not really form a body of knowledge beyond development of the methods used. The next example application, however, resident perceptions of tourism, does form a body of knowledge, because although the case studies are in different locations, people are similar all over the world and there are commonalities in their reactions to tourism.

Cluster Analysis in Host Community Attitude/Perception Research

The assessment of how residents of a host community feel about tourism has seen numerous applications of cluster analysis with the aim of understanding the impacts of tourism on host communities.

An early example of this application was Davis et al. (1988) who used cluster analysis to segment Florida residents in terms of their attitudes toward tourism development. Using a hierarchical procedure they identified five clusters labelled as 'haters', 'lovers', 'cautious romantics', 'in betweeners' and 'love 'em for a reason'. The first two groups obviously represented extreme opposite opinions, while 'cautious romantics' appeared to be in favour of tourism but not pro-growth. The 'in betweeners' had middle of the road opinions, while members of 'love 'em for a reason' had similar responses to lovers but not as strong.

Similarly, Madrigal (1995) examined community reactions to tourism in two different types of cities in the United States and United Kingdom, finding three clusters, 'haters', 'lovers' and 'realists'. 'Haters' agreed primarily with the negative impacts of tourism, 'lovers' primarily with the positive impacts, whereas 'realists' agreed with both positive and negative impacts.

Fredline and Faulkner (2000) used a similar approach to segment the host community in terms of their perceptions of the impact of a motorsport event. They employed a two-stage cluster analysis (hierarchical followed by non-hierarchical) and, using 36 event impact statements measured on a Likert-type scale, identified five clusters labelled as 'ambivalent supporters', 'haters', 'realists', 'lovers' and 'concerned for a reason'.

In a follow up study, Fredline and Faulkner (2002) conducted a similar analysis, this time comparing the host community's reactions to different motorsport events in different cities. Like Madrigal's (1995) comparison they found that similar clusters can be observed in different locations indicating that perceptions of the impacts of tourism (and events) have some common elements regardless of the context. Fredline and Faulkner (2002) then used logistic regression to explain cluster membership.

Other studies which have used cluster analysis in a similar way include Andriotis and Vaughan (2003), Perez and Nadal (2005), Ryan and Montgomery (1994) and Williams and Lawson (2001). In all these cases between three and five clusters were identified representing different perceptions held by various segments of the community.

AN EXAMPLE OF CLUSTER ANALYSIS IN TOURISM RESEARCH

The following is a worked example of an application of cluster analysis in tourism market segmentation. The data were collected from competitors in a sport tourism event, the Asia Pacific Masters Games. This is a multi-sport event held biennially on the Gold Coast, Australia. The surveys were included in the participants' registration packages along with a reply paid envelope. There was a total of 1936 responses and 1905 of these contained all data necessary for inclusion in the analysis.

The variables used to segment the market were the responses to nine statements enquiring about competitors' motivations for attending the event. The list of motivations

Table 11.3 Motivation items used in cluster analysis with means and standard deviations

		Mean	Std. Deviation
A	I wanted to participate in my sport	5.45	1.797
B	I wanted to participate in the social activities of the event	2.63	2.691
C	I wanted to see the Gold Coast	0.96	1.883
D	I wanted to spend time with my family or friends	2.48	2.852
E	I wanted to meet new friends	2.88	2.673
F	I wanted to relax and escape from everyday life	2.93	2.918
G	I wanted to do something different	2.27	2.713
H	I wanted to have fun	4.97	2.460
I	I wanted to learn new things	1.83	2.584

is presented in Table 11.3. Each item was measured on a seven point Likert-type scale ranging from 'not very important' to 'extremely important'.

The raw responses to the motivation items exhibited low variance as shown in Table 11.3, so the scores were standardized in order to magnify the differences. Thus the scores represent deviations from the mean rather than a specific point on the scale.

A two-stage cluster procedure was used utilizing a hierarchical procedure followed by non-hierarchical. The hierarchical procedure used Ward's method and squared Euclidean distances as the measure. A distance measure was selected because the aim was to identify cases closest together in terms of their motivations. Ward's method was selected because of its tendency to produce more evenly sized clusters. Most other measures have a tendency to produce one large and numerous much smaller clusters which is less useful for market segmentation (Hair et al., 1998).

As mentioned previously the hierarchical process produces $n - 1$ solutions but for the sake of parsimony it makes sense for the researcher to begin with the two cluster solution and work backwards to select the smallest possible solution that appears to adequately explain differences between the groups based on the means for each group on the original variables. The agglomeration schedule suggested a three cluster solution as the percentage change in coefficient at this step was 2.5 per cent compared with 0.7 per cent at the previous stage. However, interpretation of the means showed a meaningful split into four clusters, and given Hair et al.'s (1998) suggestion that agglomeration coefficients can underestimate the number of clusters, a decision was made to proceed with the four cluster solution.

In the second stage, the means of each of the four clusters identified in the first stage were used as starting points or seeds for a non-hierarchical (quick cluster) procedure. This allowed for the reclassification of cases so that they could move to the closest cluster which is not possible in the hierarchical procedure. In this analysis, just over 16 per cent of cases were reassigned, most of these moving from cluster one to the other three groups.

In SPSS the quick cluster procedure produces a number of output tables which can provide other useful information. One of these is a table showing one-way ANOVA tests of difference between the clusters on the original variables as shown in Table 11.4. While it is inappropriate to use these to confirm the adequacy of the solution (it is a tautological argument given that the clusters were derived by trying to maximize the differences on

Table 11.4   Mean scores for each cluster and ANOVA results

I wanted to . . .	Cluster One – Fun and Novelty Seekers	Cluster Two – Fun and Friend Seekers	Cluster Three – Relaxation Seekers	Cluster Four – Sport Focused	ANOVA results
A. Participate in my sport	0.61	1.10	0.68	2.29	$F_{(3, 1905)} = 530.58, p<0.001$
B. Participate in the social activities of the event	−0.51	0.14	0.01	−0.24	$F_{(3, 1905)} = 77.365, p<0.001$
C. See the Gold Coast	−1.21	−0.68	−0.84	−0.32	$F_{(3, 1905)} = 134.032, p<0.001$
D. Spend time with my family or friends	−0.54	−0.15	0.20	−0.23	$F_{(3, 1905)} = 80.604, p<0.001$
E. Meet new friends	−0.16	0.18	−0.06	−0.25	$F_{(3, 1905)} = 32.046, p<0.001$
F. Relax and escape from everyday life	0.23	−0.77	0.80	−0.32	$F_{(3, 1905)} = 934.003, p<0.001$
G. Do something different	0.63	−0.60	−0.64	−0.31	$F_{(3, 1905)} = 487.809, p<0.001$
H. Have fun	0.80	1.26	0.87	−0.35	$F_{(3, 1905)} = 744.516, p<0.001$
I. Learn new things	0.15	−0.47	−1.02	−0.27	$F_{(3, 1905)} = 314.130, p<0.001$

these variables), it does provide some insight into which of the variables best explain the differences between the groups.

In this study the greatest differences were observed with regard to items F (Escape), H (Have Fun) and A (Participate in Sport). This can also be observed in a line chart of the means for each cluster as presented in Figure 11.1.

Another interesting output table produced in SPSS is the distance between final cluster centres. Theses distances have been reproduced in Table 11.5 along with the mean distances of each case from its cluster centroid on the diagonal. This facilitates comparison of the 'within' and 'between' group variability of the solution. As can be seen, Cluster Four is the most homogeneous as its members have a mean distance from their cluster centroid of 1.14. Conversely, the least homogeneous is Cluster One. A clear discrimination between the groups cannot be claimed as the average distance of cluster one members from the centroid is the same as the distance between centroids one and three. However, this is to be expected given the highly specific nature of the event and the low variance observed in the original variables. It does not create a problem for interpretation given that the purpose of the study is to better understand market segments rather than to definitively classify specific cases into groups for some further action.

The next step in interpretation of the analysis is to consider what is now known about the clusters identified. In this case the mean scores on the original variables is the logical starting point as these describe the motivations of the different segments. Figure 11.1 displays these means, making it clear what the main motivating factors for each group were. Following on from this a more useful interpretation of the clusters can be explored if additional data exist for the cases. In this study, a number of demographic and sport-related variables were collected and these can be examined for differences between and relationships with cluster membership to facilitate a fuller understanding of the clusters. A brief discussion of these results is shown below as an example.

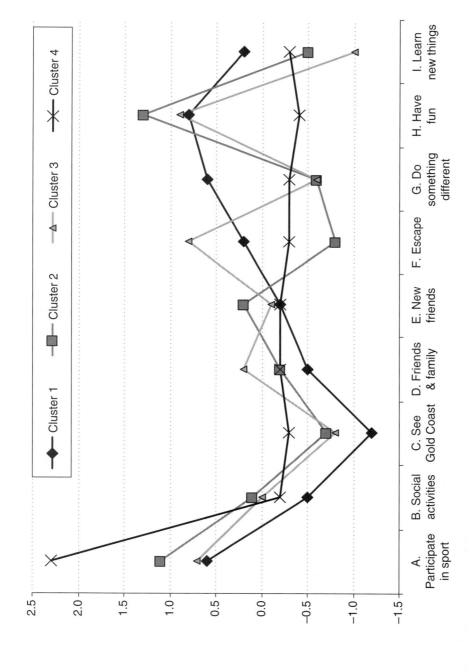

Figure 11.1 Means of clusters

Table 11.5   Comparison of the within and between group variability

Cluster	1	2	3	4
1	*2.07*			
2	2.08	*1.81*		
3	2.07	1.82	*1.93*	
4	2.54	2.19	2.561	*1.14*

Cluster One: Fun and Novelty Seekers

The first group has been labelled as 'Fun and Novelty Seekers', as these are the motivations they rated as being relatively more important (not including sport participation which was rated highly by all groups). They rated social activities, spending time with family and friends and seeing the Gold Coast as unimportant factors. Relationships between cluster membership and other variables were examined in contingency tables evaluated using the chi-square statistic. These results are shown in Table 11.6.

Table 11.6 indicates that people in the fun and novelty group were more likely to be younger and female, with dependent children at home. A larger than expected proportion had part time jobs (based on the standardized residuals in the chi-square contingency table analysis). They were most likely to be attending their first Masters Games event, and a large proportion had been participating in their sport for less than 5 years. They were more likely than other groups to rate their abilities as below average, and less likely to be aiming to win their events.

Cluster Two: Fun and Friend Seekers

The next group rated fun and sport participation as the most important motivators for attending the event, but the scores that differentiate them from other groups are for social activities and meeting new friends. While most groups rated these as unimportant factors, cluster two (on average) saw them as moderately important factors. Table 11.6 shows that they are somewhat more likely to be locals (Gold Coast residents) who are older and retired.

Cluster Three: Relaxation Seekers

Like the other groups, the third cluster was highly motivated by sport and fun, but they were also highly motivated by a desire for relaxation and escape from everyday life. This group was the most likely to be working full time, and to have dependent children, so perhaps they see the event as an opportunity to get away from life's pressures. This group was more likely to include repeat attendees at this type of event, with nearly half having attended two or more Masters Games in the past. They were more likely to have commenced played sport at a young age (childhood or 20s) and therefore more likely to have been playing for many years.

Table 11.6 *Cross tabulations of cluster membership with demographic and event related variables*

		Cluster One – Fun and Novelty Seekers n = 515	Cluster Two – Fun and Friend Seekers n = 573	Cluster Three – Relax- ation Seekers n = 532	Cluster Four – Sport Focused n = 285	Total N = 1905
Gender	Male	45.5↓	57.9	53.8	68.8↑	1048
$\chi^2(3)$ = 42.8, p<0.05	Female	54.5↑	42.1	46.2	31.2↓	856
Age	Up to 40 years	28.9↑	20.9	23.9	15.2↓	435
$\chi^2(6)$ = 91.2, p<0.05	40–60 years	62.7	61.6	67.4	55.8	1182
	Over 60 years	8.4↓	17.5↑	8.7↓	29.0↑	270
Dependant children?	Yes	59.2↑	47.1	60.5↑	37.6↓	996
$\chi^2(3)$ = 54.6, p<0.05	No	40.8↓	52.9	39.5↓	62.4↑	894
Employment status	Full time employed	57.8	55.9	63.7	50.9	1090
$\chi^2(21)$ = 104.0, p<0.05	Part time employed	23.0↑	15.2	18.4	13.8	339
	Unemployed seeking work	1.0	0.9	0.6	2.1	19
	Retired	6.3↓	15.3↑	6.7↓	24.4↑	223
	Home duties	6.1	6.3	6.1	3.5	109
	Student	1.4	0.7	0.2	0.4	13
	Volunteer worker	0.8	1.4	1.5	0.7	22
	Other	3.7	4.2	2.9	4.2	70
Place of origin	Local	19.6	32.6↑	12.6↓	26.0	429
$\chi^2(3)$ = 68.1, p<0.05	Non-local	80.4	67.4↓	87.4↑	74.0	1476
Previous event	First event	54.6↑	41.4	29.7↓	35.1	776
attendance	Second event	22.1	24.8	21.8	22.8	435
$\chi^2(12)$ = 96.8, p<0.05	2–5 previous events	15.7	22.7	30.5↑	26.7	449
	6–10 previous events	6.6↓	8.7	15.0↑	12.6	200
	More than 10 previous events	1.0↓	2.4	3.0	3.5	45
Type of event	Team events	57.3	58.4	70.3↑	45.8↓	1129
$\chi^2(6)$ = 60.6, p<0.05	Individual events	28.7	26.3	21.6↓	41.9↑	530
	Both	14.0	15.3	8.1↓	12.3	237
Age commenced in sport	Childhood/20s	39.3	41.7	48.8↑	37.5	784
$\chi^2(6)$ = 33.0, p<0.05	30s/40s	50.8	44.2	43.2	43.7	843
	Over 40	9.9	14.1	8.1↓	18.8↑	221
Years of participation	Less than 5 years	34.8↑	30.6	24.0↓	22.8	529
in sport	5–10 years	15.6	10.5	13.7	12.7	241
$\chi^2(9)$ = 30.8, p<0.05	10–20 years	19.4	21.6	21.9	25.4	399
	More than 20 years	30.2↓	37.3	40.4	39.1	673
Perception of ability	1 – Very Low	1.6	1.6	1.7	0.7	28
$\chi^2(18)$ = 42.2, p<0.05	2	3.4	2.1	2.3	2.5	48
	3	8.1↑	6.6	3.4↓	4.3	108
	4 – Average	28.8	24.7	25.0	19.4	470
	5	30.8	27.0	31.3	29.5	554

Table 11.6   (continued)

		Cluster One – Fun and Novelty Seekers n = 515	Cluster Two – Fun and Friend Seekers n = 573	Cluster Three – Relax- ation Seekers n = 532	Cluster Four – Sport Focused n = 285	Total N = 1905
	6	19.6↓	26.0	25.4	27.0	454
	7 – Very High	7.7↓	11.9	10.8	16.5↑	209
Achievement aspirations	I wanted. . . to win	17.3↓	24.3	18.5	32.3↑	417
$\chi^2(15) = 57.4$, p<0.05	. . .to get a place in my (our) event	26.5	20.5	23.3	24.5	445
	. . . to perform better than ever before	26.8	22.2	20.3	23.4	439
	. . . to perform as well as usual	16.9	19.6	22.2	14.2	357
	I didn't care for myself but did not want to let the team down	7.2	7.0	9.8↑	3.5↓	139
	Not at all concerned	5.3	6.5	6.0	2.1↓	102

Notes: ↑ and ↓ denote standardized residuals greater than or less than expected

Cluster Four: Sport Focused

The final group is clearly the most focused on sport and has rated all other motives as relatively unimportant. As shown in Table 11.4, they rate fun as being much less impor-tant than any of the other groups, and rate participating in sport as being much more important. This group is predominantly male, and more likely to be older with 29 per cent over 60 years of age. They are therefore more likely to be retired and less likely to have dependent children. This group are more often involved in individual sports rather than team sports and a relatively large proportion of them commenced in their sport at over 40 years of age. Over half the group aspired to winning or placing in their event, and they tended to rate their ability highly with a significantly higher proportion rating their ability as very high.

Implications

As the above results show, this kind of analysis would be very valuable to the organizers of this event in determine the future direction. They could elect to concentrate on one or two of these clusters or alternatively to attempt to cater to the needs and wants of all these groups. For example, they may wish to offer more associated social functions to facilitate meeting new friends for the 'fun and friend seekers'. Alternatively they could offer more 'sport focused' activities such as training and nutrition seminars if they feel this is the target market they would prefer to pursue.

ADVANTAGES AND LIMITATIONS OF CLUSTER ANALYSIS

The main advantage of cluster analysis is that it provides an effective and meaningful reduction of data. All tourism customers have slightly different needs and wants but it is impossible to treat them all as individuals. For this reason it has been common practice to either assume they all have the same needs or to segment them based on geographic or demographic variables. Cluster analysis provides a better segmentation approach that allows groups to be defined by their needs and therefore identifies groups who can be targeted in a similar way because they are genuinely similar.

Similarly, in resident perception research, the tendency has been to consider the majority opinion so that if more than 50 per cent of the population appear to support a tourism issue then no problem is perceived. However, the cluster analysis approach provides a much deeper understanding of gradations in perceptions of tourism and the specific issues that appear to be of concern. This may encourage policy makers to consider attempting to better cater to all segments of the community rather than just the majority.

One of the major disadvantages of the technique in terms of its application is that the solution is not definitive. That is, there is no single correct solution, all possible cluster solutions are correct, it is just that some do not explain the data in a manner that is as easy to interpret and use. Researchers who are looking for a 'black and white' solution can become frustrated with this lack of certainty.

Therefore it can be quite a labour-intensive process for the researcher to identify the 'best' solution, that is, the one that summarizes and simplifies the data set in a way that makes it most manageable and provides insights that are useful.

FURTHER DEVELOPMENTS AND APPLICATIONS OF CLUSTER ANALYSIS

In earlier days, the computational requirements of hierarchical analysis often meant that researchers with data sets comprising many variables and cases would have to compromise by analysing only a subset of these. Obviously as desktop computers continue to advance in terms of their capacity to process information such compromises will be reduced.

Given the rapid pace of development of online surveys and handheld mobile devices which can be used for field surveys there is potential for researchers to embed cluster analysis into their data collection phase. Respondents could answer a range of questions and it may be possible for the data to be processed during the survey so that respondents could be assigned to a cluster immediately (using a variation of a non-hierarchical approach). They could then be funnelled to a specific bank of questions applicable to their cluster. This could either reduce the length of the questionnaire because the questions are only asked of those they are applicable to, or alternatively could lead to much richer data being collected.

CONCLUSION

This chapter has attempted to provide an overview of the usefulness of cluster analysis in tourism research. A full discussion of the technicalities of the technique is beyond the scope of this chapter but researchers who are interested in learning more are directed to the many good texts on multivariate statistical techniques. Hair et al. (1998) is a particularly good example for non-mathematicians as its explanations of various issues are simple and clear.

The chapter has also summarized some of the work in two areas which represent the most common applications of cluster analysis in tourism research: market segmentation and resident perceptions of tourism. It is hoped that researchers in these fields will continue to advance knowledge through the application and further development of cluster analysis.

REFERENCES

Aldenderfer, M. and R. Blashfield (1984), *Cluster Analysis*, Newbury Park, CA: Sage Publications.
Andriotis, K. and R. Vaughan (2003), 'Urban residents' attitudes toward tourism development: the case of Crete', *Journal of Travel Research*, **42**, 172–185.
Arimond, G. and A. Elfessi (2001), 'A clustering method for categorical data in tourism market segmentation research', *Journal of Travel Research*, **39**, 391–397.
Cha, S., K. McCleary and M. Uysal (1995), 'Travel motivations of Japanese overseas travellers: a factor–cluster segmentation approach', *Journal of Travel Research*, **34**, 33–39.
Davis, D., J. Allen and R. Cosenza (1988), 'Segmenting local residents by their attitudes, interest and opinions toward tourism', *Journal of Travel Research*, **27** (2), 2–8.
Fredline, E. and B. Faulkner (2000), 'Host community perceptions: a cluster analysis', *Annals of Tourism Research*, **27** (4), 763–784.
Fredline, E. and B. Faulkner (2002), 'Resident's reactions to the staging of major motorsport events within their communities: a cluster analysis', *Event Management*, **7**, 103–114.
Gilmour, G. (1951), 'The development of taxonomic theory since 1851', *Nature*, **168**, 400–402.
Hair, J., W. Black, B. Babin, R. Anderson and R. Tatham (1998), *Multivariate Data Analysis*, Upper Saddle River, NJ: Prentice-Hall.
Jobson, J. (1991), *Applied Multivariate Data Analysis, Volume II: Categorical and Multivariate Methods*, New York: Springer-Verlag.
Jurowski, C. and A. Reich (2000), 'An explanation and illustration of cluster analysis for identifying hospitality market segments', *Journal of Hospitality and Tourism Research*, **24**, 67–91.
Madrigal, R. (1995), 'Residents' perceptions and the role of government', *Annals of Tourism Research*, **22**, 86–102.
Mueller, H. and E. Lanz Kaufmann (2001), 'Wellness tourism: market analysis of a special health tourism segment and implications for the hotel industry', *Journal of Vacation Marketing*, **7** (1), 5–17.
Najimi, M., A. Sharbatoghlie and A. Jafarieh (2010), 'Tourism market segmentation in Iran', *International Journal of Tourism Research*, **12**, 497–509.
Perez, E.A. and J.R. Nadal (2005), 'Host community perceptions: a cluster analysis', *Annals of Tourism Research*, **32** (4), 925–941.
Ryan, C. and J. Huyton (2000), 'Who is interested in Aboriginal tourism in the Northern Territory? A cluster analysis', *Journal of Sustainable Tourism*, **8** (1), 53–88.
Ryan, C. and D. Montgomery (1994), 'The attitudes of Bakewell residents to tourism and numbers in community responsive tourism', *Tourism Management*, **15**, 358–369.
Williams, J. and R. Lawson (2001), 'Community issues and resident opinions of tourism', *Annals of Tourism Research*, **28**, 269–290.

12 Input–output and SAM models
Clemente Polo and Elisabeth Valle

NATURE OF THE TECHNIQUE AND ITS EVOLUTION

Input–output (IO) and social accounting matrix (SAM) models are tools that economists have used for many decades to measure sectoral interdependencies, compare the economic structure of economies, quantify production impacts, measure structural and productivity changes, study the effects of redistribution policies, calculate the energy content of commodities, estimate CO_2 emissions, etc. The IO model is a simple linear model first proposed by Leontief (1937) to determine production quantities and prices in a set up where commodities are produced with commodities. It was as Leontief himself put it 'an attempt to apply the economic theory of general equilibrium – or rather, general interdependence – in an empirical study of the interrelationships between different parts of the economy . . .'. In Leontief's model quantities of different commodities and prices were treated as variables and 'the technical and natural conditions of production and the tastes of consumers' as data.

The applied nature of his endeavour and the lack of detailed technological investigations to cover 'the entire field of agricultural, mineral and industrial production' led Leontief to specify 'the technical set up of each industry by as many homogeneous linear equations as there are separate cost factors involved'.[1] Following Walras, Leontief termed 'coefficients of production' the parameters included in those linear equations and assigned them numerical values employing a statistical table constructed for the United States that included detailed information on 'quantitative input and output relations' for 44 industries in 1919 (Leontief, 1936). The first 'tableau economique' based on observed data, or an IO table, of a national economy and the first numerical general equilibrium model based on observed data had been born.

The first contributions of Leontief spurred the construction of IO tables to analyse a wide range of issues with IO models.[2] Stone (1961) pioneered the integration of IO tables in the National Accounts framework taking the disaggregation of the production account as a starting point. Stone's report also included a self-contained account of the algebra of the so-called Leontief's open and closed quantity and price models, extensions of the basic model in various directions (restricted, dynamic and interregional models) and a review of some applications to real economies. Other statements of IO analysis can be found in Bulmer-Thomas (1982), Leontief (1966), Miernyk (1965) and Miller and Blair (1985, 2009).

The extension of the IO table and Leontief's open model into a SAM and SAM model, respectively, was a quite natural development. In 1969, the new system of national accounts elaborated by the Statistical Office of the United Nations (SNA, 1969) first included a square matrix representation of national accounts. Each account is fully described by a row where revenues from all accounts are recorded and a corresponding column where expenditures to all accounts are recorded. The matrix representation is not only a more transparent and efficient way to present national accounts but also a very flexible tool since accounts can be easily subdivided.

It was only a matter of time until disaggregated national accounts were presented in a matrix form to integrate the institutional accounts with the IO table and that they were employed to specify numerically economic models. Pyatt et al. (1972) and Thorbecke and Sengupta (1972) were the first to use it to analyse redistribution policies and growth. Keuning and Ruijter (1988) signal Pyatt and Thorebecke's (1976) study of Bangladesh as the first comprehensive presentation of a SAM and its uses. Other classical references are Cohen (1989), Pyatt (1988), Pyatt and Round (1977, 1979), Pyatt et al. (1977) and Thorbecke (2000).[3]

SAM models have two main advantages over IO models. First, the household(s) and capital (savings–investment) accounts are balanced and the 'induced' effects caused by income generation (consumption and savings–investment) can be analysed in a more consistent way than in extended IO models. Second, SAM models can analyse the distributive consequences of injections, a subject that has no room in the IO models. There are disadvantages too. On the one hand, SAM models require a SAM and only a few Statistical Offices that routinely elaborate IO tables for national or regional economies also compile SAMs. On the other hand, the extension of fixed coefficients beyond the production sphere is even more questionable than in the IO model.

The chapter is divided in four sections. The next section presents the basic algebra employed in IO and SAM applications. Then how the models can be applied to tourism and numerous IO and SAM applications to tourism since the 1970s are discussed. The strengths and weaknesses of the models are then considered. The final section includes a quest for improving the data sets and the way research results are presented. It also discusses how tourism satellite accounts and some environmental approaches can be combined with IO models, two topics that have received considerable attention in the last decade.

BACKGROUND AND TYPES OF PROBLEMS THAT THE TECHNIQUE IS DESIGNED TO HANDLE

Since the 1970s, IO models have been employed to asses tourism impacts. More recently SAM models have also been used. In this section, we briefly present the algebra of IO and SAM models and discuss their numerical specification.

A Basic IO Model

There are 1, 2, . . ., M sectors in the economy. Sector i produces product i employing intermediate products $(X_{ji})_{j=1,2,...,M}$ and labour L_i and capital services K_i. The ith sector's output is determined by a Leontief linear homogeneous production function

$$Y_i = \min\left(\frac{X_{1i}}{a_{1i}}, \frac{X_{2i}}{a_{2i}}, \ldots, \frac{X_{Mi}}{a_{M1}}, \frac{L_i}{l_i}, \frac{K_i}{k_i}\right) \qquad (12.1)$$

where $(a_{ji})_{j=1, 2,..., M}$, l_i and k_i are sector's i technical coefficients (Leontief's 'production coefficients') or unitary requirements of all products, labour and capital, respectively. It follows that the amount of inputs that minimize the cost of production

$$X_{ji} = a_{ji}Y_i, \quad L_i = l_iY_i, \quad K_i = k_iY_i, j, i = 1, 2, ..., M \tag{12.2}$$

are independent of production and factor prices.

The production level Y_i that satisfy a given set of net (final) demands $D_i \geq 0$, $i = 1, 2, ..., M$ is therefore

$$Y_i = \sum_j^N a_{ij}Y_j + D_i, i, j = 1, 2, ..., M. \tag{12.3}$$

The equilibrium conditions (12.3) can be expressed in matrix notation

$$y = Ay + d \tag{12.4}$$

where A is the $M \times M$ matrix of technical or unit requirement coefficients and y and d the column vectors of production and exogenous final demand, respectively. The elements in the ith column of matrix A are the unit requirements of sector i. The solution (provided A is invertible) of the system of Equation (12.4)

$$y = (I - A)^{-1}d = Md \tag{12.5}$$

is a linear transformation of the vector of final demands. M is known as Leontief's multiplier matrix and it can be easily checked that

$$M = I + A + A^2 + \ldots = \sum_{i=0}^{\infty} A^i = I + \sum_{i=1}^{\infty} A^i \tag{12.6}$$

Substituting (12.6) in (12.5)

$$y = d + Ad + A^2d + \ldots = d + \sum_{i=1}^{\infty} A^id$$

total output is broken down into two terms: output required to satisfy final demand and output used by other sectors (indirect or intermediate demand). Since Equation (12.5) is valid for any nonnegative d, the elements of the ith column of M, $m \cdot i = (m_{ji})_{j=1, 2, ..., M}$, can be interpreted as sector j production needed to produce one net unit of i. This property of matrix M led to define interdependency indexes (Beynon et al., 2009; Chenery and Watanabe, 1958; Rasmussen, 1956) known as backward and forward linkages employing the column and row totals of M, respectively.

Labour and capital inputs required to produce d are also linear transformations of output and therefore of final demand

$$L = \sum_{i=1}^{M} l_i Y_i = l^T y = l^T M d = l^T d + \sum_{i=1}^{\infty} l^T A^i d$$

$$K = \sum_{i=1}^{M} k_i Y_i = k^T y = k^T M d = k^T d + \sum_{i=1}^{\infty} k^T A^i d \qquad (12.7)$$

As in the case of output, labour and capital requirements to produce d can be split into direct and indirect labour and capital requirements.

A more detailed account of output, labour and capital requirements can be obtained substituting vector d by a diagonal matrix $\hat{D}$ where the ith diagonal element $\hat{a}_{ii} = d_i$

$$\hat{Y} = M\hat{D}, \hat{l} = l^T M\hat{D}, \hat{k} = k^T M\hat{D} \qquad (12.8)$$

where $\hat{Y}_{ji}$ indicates the amount of product j required to produce d_i units of i, and $\hat{l}_i$ and $\hat{k}_i$ the total amount of labour and capital, respectively, required by all sectors to produce d_i units of i.[4] Since (12.5), (12.7) and (12.8) are linear transformations, the impact of discrete changes in d are

$$\Delta y = M\Delta d, \Delta L = l^T M\Delta d, \Delta K = k^T M\Delta d \qquad (12.9)$$

(12.3), (12.7) and (12.9) can be used to calculate the amounts of output, labour and capital required to produce d or Δd, provided A, l and k remain unchanged.[5]

The basic open model just presented can be partially closed. Leontief (1937) already treated 'households as any other "industry"'. The household 'industry' can be endogenized assuming it produces a composite consumption good that is required by all other industries. Thus, Equation (12.4) becomes

$$y = A^* y + \underline{d} \qquad (12.10)$$

where A^* is a $(M + 1) \times (M + 1)$ coefficients' matrix and $\underline{d}$ is the final demand vector net of households' consumption. The $M + 1$ column of A^* includes the technical coefficients of the household industry employed to produce the composite consumption commodity and the $M + 1$ row the composite consumption requirements by all industries.[6] As households are included as an industry the new $(M + 1) \times (M + 1)$ multiplier matrix

$$M^* = (I - A^*)^{-1}$$

captures not only the direct and indirect effects but also those induced by the new 'industry'.

The basic model presented has intentionally ignored that products can be distinguished by origin. Following the national accounts identity, exports of different products are included in d while product imports are added to domestic production to insure equality of supply and demand

$$y = Ay + d - m \qquad (12.11)$$

where m is the vector of equivalent imports. We shall come back to this point later.

Numerical Specification of the IO Table

IO tables present the identity of the production account for each sector: the value of domestic production plus imports equals the value of intermediate consumption plus final demand. Leontief (1936) presented the first IO table for the US economy in 1919 and his work spurred the construction of similar tables for other countries, states and regions. A standard IO table includes an intermediate transactions matrix $(\widetilde{X}_{ji})$, a factor matrix F that shows sectoral payments to labour, capital, government and foreign sectors and a final demand matrix D that provides the breakdown of private and public consumption, investment and exports (excluding tourism exports). From the information in the IO table, expenditure coefficients can be obtained for each sector

$$\widetilde{a}_{ji} = \frac{\widetilde{X}_{ji}}{\widetilde{Y}_i} = \frac{p_j X_{ji}}{p_i Y_i}, \quad \widetilde{l}_i = \frac{\widetilde{L}_i}{\widetilde{Y}_i} = \frac{w L_i}{p_i Y_i}, \quad \widetilde{k}_i = \frac{\widetilde{K}_i}{\widetilde{Y}_i} = \frac{r K_i}{p_i Y_i} \tag{12.12}$$

If units for products, labour and capital are chosen in such a way that their prices are equal to 1 $(p_i = w = r = 1)$, then the technical coefficients are equal to the expenditure coefficients. Therefore, if Δd is measured in the same units, (12.9) can be interpreted as changes in output, labour and capital quantities. Notice that column totals of M add up quantities of different products; however, since prices are equal to 1 they can be interpreted as the total value of output. For the same reason,

$$m_{ji} = \frac{\Delta Y_j}{\Delta d_i} = \frac{p_i \Delta Y_j}{p_j \Delta d_i}$$

can be interpreted as the increase in the value of production of sector j brought about by one additional unit spent in product i.

SAM and SAM Models

Let X be a SAM, i.e., a square $N \times N$ matrix that records transactions arising in the circular flow of income (production, income generation, income distribution and income expenditure) of an economy. The elements in the ith row indicate the sources of income accruing to the ith account, and those in the ith column its expenditures. Thus, row (column) sums indicate the total income accruing (spent or saved) by accounts. In a SAM, row totals (revenues) equal column totals (outlays):

$$\sum_{j=1}^{N} \widetilde{X}_{ij} \equiv \widetilde{Y}_i \equiv \sum_{j=1}^{N} \widetilde{X}_{ji} \tag{12.13}$$

A SAM may include accounts for industries, commodities, institutional sectors (households, non-profit institutions, corporate sector, public administrations and foreign sectors), capital (savings–investment), and as many auxiliary accounts as needed. Equation (12.13) implies that the value of sales equals total costs in any industry; the value of demands equals the value of supply for commodities; and total revenues equal total expenditures and savings for institutions.

Expenditure coefficients can be defined as

$$\tilde{a}_{ij} \equiv \frac{\tilde{X}_{ij}}{\tilde{Y}_j} \tag{12.14}$$

and (12.13) can be expressed in terms of them

$$\tilde{Y}_i \equiv \sum_{j=1}^{N} \tilde{a}_{ij} \tilde{Y}_j \tag{12.15}$$

The right hand term in Equation (12.15) can be split in two terms: one for the income accruing from the accounts the first M accounts, considered endogenous, and the other for remaining accounts taken as exogenous:

$$Y_i \equiv \sum_{j=1}^{M} \tilde{a}_{ij} Y_j + \sum_{j=M+1}^{N} \tilde{a}_{ij} Y_j \ i = 1, 2, \ldots, M \tag{12.16}$$

Identities (12.16) become a system of equations when the exogenous incomes and the expenditures coefficients are assumed to be fixed. Assuming that units of products, commodities and factors are chosen so that their prices are equal to 1, some fixed expenditure coefficients (interindustry, industry–commodity, primary factors) can be interpreted as technical coefficients and the results obtained with SAM models compared with those of IO models.[7] For unitary prices, balance conditions (12.16) can be interpreted as zero profit conditions for industries, demand and supply equilibrium conditions for commodities and budget constraints for institutions. Having made these assumptions we drop the tilde from the coefficient expenditures.

Once the partition of accounts is done, matrix A can be partitioned accordingly

$$A = \begin{pmatrix} A_{mm} & A_{mn} \\ A_{nm} & A_{nn} \end{pmatrix}$$

and (12.16) be written as

$$y^m = A_{mm} y^m + A_{mn} \bar{y}^n \tag{12.17}$$

where y^m and $\bar{y}^n$ are the vectors of endogenous and exogenous income, respectively. From Equation (12.17) one can derive the vector of endogenous income

$$y^m = (I - A_{mm})^{-1} A_{mn} \bar{y}^n = M_m A_{mn} \bar{y}_n = M_m d_m \tag{12.18}$$

being d_m the vector of exogenous income $A_{mn} y^n$. As in the IO model, M_m is the multiplier matrix and m_{ji} can be interpreted as the increase in income of account j brought about by a unit injection into account i.

Income Redistribution

The effects of exogenous injections on relative incomes can be easily calculated. First, the vector of relative incomes is written in matrix form

$$y = \frac{y^m}{\sum\limits_{j=1}^{M} Y_j} = \frac{M_m d}{e^T y^m} \tag{12.19}$$

being e^T a row vector of ones. Then variation of the vector of relative incomes resulting from exogenous injections is given by the redistribution matrix

$$R = \frac{\partial y}{\partial d} = \begin{pmatrix} \dfrac{\partial y_1}{\partial d_1} & \dfrac{\partial y_1}{\partial d_2} & \cdots & \dfrac{\partial y_1}{\partial d_m} \\[2mm] \dfrac{\partial y_2}{\partial d_1} & \dfrac{\partial y_2}{\partial d_2} & \cdots & \dfrac{\partial y_2}{\partial d_m} \\[2mm] \cdots & & & \\[2mm] \dfrac{\partial y_m}{\partial d_1} & \dfrac{\partial y_m}{\partial d_2} & \cdots & \dfrac{\partial y_m}{\partial d_{2m}} \end{pmatrix} = \frac{M_m e^T y^m - y^m e^T M_m}{(e^T y^m)^2} = \frac{1}{e^T y^m}\left(M_m - \frac{y^m e^T M_m}{e^T y^m}\right) \tag{12.20}$$

whose r_{ji} is

$$\frac{\partial y_j}{\partial d_i} = \frac{1}{e^T y^m}\left(m_{ji} - \frac{Y_j \sum\limits_{k=1}^{M} m_{ki}}{\sum\limits_{k=1}^{M} Y_k}\right) \tag{12.21}$$

The sign is determined by the parentheses and is positive if and only if

$$\frac{m_{ji}}{\sum\limits_{k=1}^{M} m_{ki}} \geq \frac{Y_j}{\sum\limits_{k=1}^{M} Y_k}$$

i.e., if the marginal relative effect on j (the term on the left-hand side of the equality) is greater than the relative income of j (the right-hand term of the inequality). It can easily be checked that the sum of the elements of each column of the redistribution matrix is zero

$$e^T \frac{\partial y}{\partial d} = \frac{1}{e^T y^m}\left(e^T M_m - \frac{e^T y^m e^T M_m}{e^T y^m}\right) = 0$$

APPLICATIONS OF THE TECHNIQUE TO TOURISM

Economists' interest in tourism came to age when the rapid increase in per capita income in the western economies and the reduction of transportation costs after World War II gave rise to mass international and domestic tourism. By the 1970s, servicing international tourism had become a key export 'industry' that accounted for large shares of output, income, labour and tax revenues in the recipient countries (Archer, 1982). At the same time, domestic tourism had also become an important source of revenues for regions, counties, cities and recreational areas (Archer, 1978). Not surprisingly, IO models (or approaches inspired by it) were used since the 1960s to quantify the impact of international tourism in large, medium and small national economies as well as in regions, counties, cities and recreational areas all over the world. In the last two decades, SAM and CGE models have also been applied to that end.

How to Apply the Models

Leaving aside for the moment concerns about the underlying assumptions made in IO and SAM models, the fact is that they have been routinely employed to measure the weight of tourism in the economy and quantify tourism impacts on output, income and employment. These models can be applied if the appropriate information is available: an IO table (or a SAM) for the economy at hand and a vector of tourists' expenditures by sector d valued at the base year prices. Of course, one may subdivide the tourists' vector into as many vectors ($d = d_1 + d_2 + \ldots + d_K$) as types of tourists data allows to differentiate and calculate their individual contributions and impacts using Equations (12.5), (12.7), (12.9), (12.19) and (12.21).[8]

If an IO table is available, the only difficulty to apply the model is to cast tourists' expenditures into a vector d congruent with the classification employed and the way transactions are valued in the IO table. To begin with, when the IO table is dated at year t and the impact occurs at $t + s$, vector e_{t+s} has to be valued at time t prices.[9] Moreover, tourists' expenditures include distribution and transportation margins and product taxes that need to be eliminated to make them congruent with IO tables. Reported expenditures categories are often too broad to be assigned to specific IO sectors (Khan et al., 1990). Moreover, as Cooper and Pigram (1984) point out, they have be valued as transactions are in the table, i.e., excluding margins and taxes. In the case of domestic tourism, adjustments have also to be made to deduct expenditures that would have been made anyway and add pre-trip expenditures not included in reported tourists' expenditures. The development of Tourism Satellite Accounts (TSA) can provide adequate estimates of tourists' demand to be used jointly with IO tables to analyse its impact on the economy. We shall return to this point.

A final point refers to the treatment of import leakages since not all tourists' expenditures are demand for local products and not all inputs employed by industries are of domestic origin. As indicated earlier, an accepted solution to that problem (Lee and Taylor, 2005) is to deduct imports from final demand as in (12.11). However, a more accurate way to deal with imports is replace Equation (12.5) and (12.7) by their domestic counterparts

$$y_I = (I - A_I)^{-1}d_I = M_I d_I \tag{12.5'}$$

$$L = \sum_{i=1}^{M} l_{I\cdot i} Y_{I\cdot i} = l_I^T y_I = l_I^T M_I d_I = l_I^T d_I + \sum_{i=1}^{\infty} l^T A_I^i d_I$$
$$K = \sum_{i=1}^{M} k_{I\cdot i} Y_{I\cdot i} = k_I^T y_I = k^T M_I d_I = k^T d_I + \sum_{i=1}^{\infty} k^T A_I^i d_I \tag{12.7'}$$

$$y_M = A_M y_I + d_M = A_M M_I d_I + d_M$$

where the subscript I (M) denotes the matrix of technical coefficients and the net demand vector of domestic (imported) origin. Unfortunately, even recent IO studies (Kweka et al., 2001; Mazumder et al., 2011; Steenge and Van de Steeg, 2010; and Oosterhaven and Fan, 2006) overlook import specification or apply a domestic vector d_I to the total coefficient matrix A. It should be emphasized that the distinction of products by origin can also be incorporated into a SAM model, although the distinction has been generally ignored in tourism studies.[10]

The Multipliers' Fever

IO tables are often unavailable for small national, regional and local economies. The rapid growth of tourism in the 1970s and early 1980s gave rise to a multipliers' fever and many studies were completed to calculate (personal) income and employment 'tourism multipliers' and provide 'marketing' clues to policy makers. Archer and Owen (1971) proposed a method that Henderson and Cousins (1975) perfected to calculate income and employment multipliers. Following Archer (1976) and Vanhove (1981), total income (employment) generated was the sum of direct, indirect and induced income (employment). Direct and indirect household income were approximated by

$$\sum_{k=1}^{K} \sum_{i=1}^{M} \theta_{ki} I_i \qquad (12.22)$$

where θ_{ki} is the proportion of the expenditure by tourist k directed to business i over total tourists' expenditures and I_i the direct and indirect income generated by 1 unit spent in business i. Total income was obtained multiplying (12.22) by a Keynesian multiplier defined by

$$\frac{1}{1 - c \sum_{i=1}^{M} \theta_i^r I_i}$$

where c is the average propensity to consume over disposable income and θ_i^r the ratio of residents' consumption of locally produced commodity i over total consumption.[11] I_i was in turn estimated from net of tax factor receipts and purchases to other businesses. Liu and Var (1982) for Victoria BC and Liu et al. (1984) for Turkey employed the multiplier matrix M to estimate I_i.

The typical study included the completion of two surveys: one directed to local businesses to determine their cost structure and the other to incoming tourists to estimate their expenditures. The results obtained (Archer, 1976, 1982; 1984; Milne, 1987; Vanhove, 1981; Var and Quayson, 1985) indicate that the size of multipliers depends (as expected) on three factors: the importance of import leakages, the value added coefficients of tourists' oriented sectors and the strength of linkages between tourist-oriented sectors and other sectors. Thus, income multipliers for states (Hawaii and Missouri) and small islands with a developed economic base (Dominican Republic and Hong Kong) or high value added coefficients in tourists' sectors (Bermuda and Indian Ocean) are large (0.9–1.30) while for small islands with a poor economic base (Cayman and British Virgin) and most counties in the United States and UK are small (0.3–0.6). Liu and Var's results for Turkey give a direct and indirect income multiplier of 0.79 and a total multiplier (household endogenous) of 1.87 for all visitors. Differences among various types of visitors were negligible but Turkish tourists from abroad had the largest impact.

National and Regional IO Impact Studies

The ad hoc tourism multipliers approach (Fletcher, 1989) was gradually abandoned in favour of standard IO modeling.[12] IO tables (and to a less extent SAMs) are elaborated regularly along with national accounts in many developed countries since the 1980s and IO tables have also been compiled occasionally for some African and Asian countries, regions and small islands. However, many of these databases have been constructed for other purposes and do not provide a vector of tourists' expenditures to be fed into IO and SAM models. This is so even in countries where international tourism is a major export 'industry' and domestic tourism accounts for a sizable share of total residents' expenditures.[13]

The following indicative list includes some IO studies that have analysed the structure of tourism or estimated its impact on the reference economy. At a national level, one can mention the studies of Cooper and Pigram (1984) for Australia; Henry and Deane (1997) for Ireland; IET (1997) for Spain;[14] Kweka et al. (2001) for Tanzania; Liu et al. (1984) for Turkey; Mazumder et al. (2011) for Tanzania; and Oosterhaven and Fan (2006) for China. Also from a national perspective, there are studies that focus on specific tourist activities such as those of Felsenstein and Freeman (1998) of gambling in Israel; Kim et al. (2003) of conventions in South Korea; and Lee and Taylor (2005) of a mega sport event (FIFA World Cup).[15] The IO model has also been applied to analyse tourism in regions and islands: Archer (1995) in the Bermudas; Archer and Fletcher (1996) in Seychelles; Archer and Wanhill (1980) and Archer (1985) in Mauritius; Baster (1980) in Scotland; Heng and Low (1990) and Khan et al. (1990) in Singapore; Jones and Munday (2010) in Wales; Lin and Sung (1984) in Hong Kong; Polo and Valle (2008a and 2011) in the Balearic Islands; Pratt (2011) in Hawaii; Ruíz (1985) in Puerto Rico; Steenge and Van de Steeg (2010) in Aruba; and West and Gamage (2001) in Victoria.

The studies for Australia, Turkey, Spain and Ireland differentiate international and domestic tourism. Baster (1980) for Scotland and Polo and Valle (2008a) for the Balearic Islands employ just one vector for non-residents demand, while West and Gamage (2001) distinguish four tourists' types: international, interstate, intrastate and day-trippers. In contrast, the China study and most studies of small islands and developing countries only deal with international tourism, although Archer (1995), Archer and Fletcher (1996), Heng and Low (1990) and Mazumder et al. (2011) differentiate them by nationality.

As to the integration of tourists' expenditures into the IO framework, generally national and regional IO tables present a fine sectoral breakdown that facilitates tourism impact studies. An exception is Oosterhaven and Fan that use a Chinese table with only 17 sectors. In those cases where IO tables were specifically compiled to carry out tourism' studies (Archer, 1985, 1995; Archer and Fletcher, 1996) all important tourism-oriented sectors (hotels, other tourist accommodation, restaurants, travel agencies, car renting, etc.) are included in the tables and the impact of tourists' expenditures directed to those sectors is calculated. As to the estimation of the tourists' vector, sometimes it is described in great detail (Cooper and Pigram, 1984) or dispatched in a cursory way (Oosterhaven and Fan, 2006).

It seems fair to say that less attention than desirable has been paid to model import leakages. For instance, Oosterhaven and Fan (2006) adjust consumption coefficients but say nothing on the tourists' demand vector and the coefficients matrix. What for a large developing country such as China might be understood, it can greatly distort the results obtained for regions and small islands. Archer and Fletcher (1996) indicate that 'a large quantity of additional data relating to imports by establishment had to be obtained in order to obtain a detailed breakdown of intermediate consumption into its local and imported components'. Polo and Valle (2002, 2008a) employed only domestic technical coefficients and domestic non-residents demand. Steenge and Van de Steeg (2010) also indicate that 'imports and the "taxes less subsidies on products" were removed from intermediate consumption, final consumption expenditure, gross capital formation and exports'. But in other studies, it is hard to guess what the authors actually did and how they did it.

The most complete reports provide output multipliers for the basic and extended IO models, backward and forward linkages, multipliers for value added, income and employment economy, tax revenues and imports. However, some studies include only weighted multipliers; others only output multipliers for the basic or the extended model; in one case (Henry and Deane, 1997) the Government is also endogenous; and others report only absolute impact figures. It is hard to compare results coming from such heterogeneous studies.[16] Table 12.1 presents some (average) output, income/value added and employment multipliers for the basic model (unless otherwise indicated). They are either reported in the studies or calculated by us.

As indicated, many of these studies provide other useful pieces of information on the economies studied of great interest for policy makers: backward linkages of tourism sectors; the relative importance of tourism respect to other exports; government revenues derived from tourism; imports required to satisfy tourists' demands and multipliers for different tourist services (accommodation types, non-real estate renting, food, entertainment, car renting, etc.) and different tourists' types (residents and non-residents classified by origin or trip motivation).

Some of them also calculate the production, value added and employment shares accounted for tourists' demand and measure the weight of tourism under alternative assumptions on final demand. Tourists' contributions to total income and employment (measured by GVA, GDP or GNP) go from very low levels in China (1.64 and 1.01 per cent in 1997) and Australia (2.9–2.8 and 3.3–2.6 per cent in 1974–75 and 1980–81), to medium range values for Ireland (4.5–4.9 and 5.6–6.8 per cent in 1990–95) and high values for Spain (9.33 per cent of total value added in 1992). Archer (1995) and Archer and Fletcher (1996) reported even larger values for Bermuda (45 per cent of income) and the Seychelles (23.5 per cent of GDP) with residents' consumption endogenous.

Polo and Valle (2007, 2008a) estimated with the IO model that non-residents demand accounts for 36.2 per cent of value added and 30.12 per cent of employment in the Balearic Islands in 1997, figures that increase up to 72.7 and 65.11 per cent, respec-

Table 12.1   Output, income and employment multipliers: direct + indirect

Authors, country/ island or region and base year	Output	Income/ VA[b]	Employment[c]
Liu, Var and Timur (1984): Turkey,1973[a]	–	0.79	–
Cooper and Pigram (1984): Australia (1974–75 and 1980–81)	–	–	–
IET (1997): Spain, 1992[a]	1.62	0.96	–
Henry and Deane (1997): Ireland 1990 and 1995	–	0.73–0.74	45.35–39.69
Felsenstein and Freeman (1998): Israel, 1982[a, d, f]	3.59	2.87	25.12
Tohamy and Swinscoe (2000): Egypt, 1991/92[d]	2.64	–/–	755.18
Kim, Chon and Chung (2003): South Korea, 1998[e]	1.67	0.36/0.88	105.9
Kweka, Morrisey and Blake (2001): Tanzania, 1992[e]	3.37	–/–	7.78
Lee and Taylor (2005): South Korea, 1998[d]	1.92	0.59/1.37	60.07
Oosterhaven and Fan (2006): China, 1997[d]	2.80	1.80	74.57
Baster (1980): Scotland, 1973[a]	–	0.32	24.18
Lin and Sung (1984): Hong Kong, 1973	0.98	0.59	26.7
Ruíz (1985): Puerto Rico, 1972[d]	2.08	1.24	142.10
Archer (1985): Mauritius, 1982[d]	–	1.03	5.32
Heng and Low (1990): Singapore, 1983	1.46	0.75	26.66
Khan, Seng and Cheong (1990): Singapore, 1983	1.48	0.69	24.84
Archer (1995): Bermuda, 1985[c]	n.a.	0.91	29.39
Archer and Fletcher (1996): Seychelles, 1991[d]	n.a.	0.88	17.09
West and Gamage (2001): Victoria, 1993–94[a]	1.47	1.11/1.31	8.62
Polo and Valle (2008a): Balearic Islands, 1997[a]	1.28	–/0.78	19.06
Steenge and Van de Steeg (2010): Aruba, 1999	–	0.68	n.a.
Mazumder et al. (2011): Malaysia, 2000	1.42	0.34–054	17.36
Polo and Valle (2011): Balearic Islands, 2004[a]	1.73	–/0.71	15.31
Pratt (2011): Hawaii, 2005	–	–/0.70	–

Notes:
Reported values and own calculations for foreign tourists unless otherwise indicated.
[a]   Domestic and international tourists distinguished.
[b]   Income when just one figure is reported.
[c]   Employment multipliers indicate the number of jobs created by unit of tourists' expenditures. Ireland: per million IR pound; Israel: per million $; Egypt: per million $; South Korea: per million $; Tanzania: per million TShs; China: per million Yuan; Scotland: per 1000 pound; Hong Kong: per million HK$; Puerto Rico: per million $; Mauritius: per 100000 Rs; Singapore: per million $; Bermuda: per million $; Seychelles: per 100000 SEYRs; Balearic Islands: per million €; and Malaysia per 100 million Ringitt.
[d]   Includes induced effects.
[e]   For the hotels and restaurants sector ('tourism') output and employment multipliers are 1.84 and 4.85.
[f]   International convention industry.
[g]   Casino gambling.
[h]   2002 FIFA World Cup.

tively, when consumption and depreciation investment are endogenous. Polo and Valle (2011) calculated that value added and employment shares accounted for non-residents demand were 36.59 and 32.65 per cent, respectively, in the Balearic Islands in 2004.[17] They also obtained that the value added and employment shares accounted for non-residents demand exceeds 70 per cent of value added in renting (non-real estate) and holiday home lodging and 90 per cent in lodging services and passenger supporting services. Pratt (2011) shows how value added multipliers have evolved in Hawaii since 1967 until 2005.

Small Areas, Single Resource and Event Tourism Impact IO Studies

Hundreds of studies have been done to quantify the impact of tourism in small areas and some of them have relied on the IO model (or models close to it). No matter the visitors' purpose (relax, enjoy nature, practice sports, visit cities' historical landmarks and museums, gamble in casinos, assist in events, etc.), their expenditures have economic effects on the communities where the attraction is located or the event takes place, as well as in the surrounding areas. Archer (1976) already reported all purpose 'tourism income multipliers' for a considerable number of counties in the UK and United States. Since then, the emphasis has shifted towards the assessment of a 'single tourist resource or tourist activity' (Johnson and Moore, 1993; Mescon and Vozikis, 1985).[18] Consequently, the number of studies has grown exponentially[19] and several authors have presented 'guides' to avoid methodological pitfalls (Burgan and Mules, 1992; Crompton et al., 2001; Gelan, 2003; Getz, 1989; Matheson, 2002; Mules and Faulkner, 1996; Stynes, 1999; Tyrrell and Johnston, 2001).

Indeed, the assessment of tourism impacts – whether 'all purpose', 'single resource' or 'event related' – in small economies present some peculiarities regarding both the estimation of the injection and the model employed to simulate the effect. First, recorded tourists' expenditures may not reflect the amounts really spent in the area, or those spent solely due to the resource (Johnson and Moore, 1993) or the event object of study (Burgan and Mules, 1992; Lee and Taylor, 2005; Tyrrell and Johnston, 2001).[20] Second, since small areas are generally very open economies and leakages (product imports and factor payments to nonresidents) and feedbacks (product exports and factor payments to residents) may be quite substantial, considerable attention must be paid to the delineation of the impact region (Stevens and Rose, 1985). Third, only local expenditures that would have been spent out of the area in the absence of the resource or the event should be added to visitors' expenditures (Johnson and Moore, 1993; Mules, 1999). Therefore, surveys conducted to estimate the expenditures in the destination area or due to the resource or event should take into account all these specificities.

A final problem is that IO tables are not usually available for small areas. In some cases, the estimated tourists' injection is simulated either with a regional IO model (Leistritz, et al., 1982; Mescon and Vozikis, 1985) or with a local 'input–output technical coefficient matrix' (Var and Quayson, 1985).[21] But most applications rely on ready-made models. IMPLAN, funded by the USDA Forest Services (Alward and Palmer, 1983) provides in its last version a complete set of 2008 county level SAMs with 440 sectors and 9 households, output income and employment effects, and simple and total (households endogenous) multipliers. BEA-RIMS II is a model constructed and supported by the

Bureau of Economic Analysis that calculates county level simple and total multipliers as well as output, income and employment effects. Both models regionalize the national IO model employing regional location earning quotients (BEA-RIMS II) or regional purchase coefficients and value added-output ratios (IMPLAN). The REMI model, first implemented by Treyz et al. (1980) and Treyz (1981), includes also an IO block that 'forms the core of the model' (Treyz et al., 1991), but differs from REMI and RIMS II in an important respect: prices are included in the model and interact with quantities. Bushnell and Hyle (1985) compared earlier versions of the three models and Rickman and Schwer (1995) compared their relative performance.

These models have been applied to estimate all sorts of tourist effects in regional and local economies. Here is an illustrative sample: state parks on state economies (Bergstrom et al. 1990), a single resource in a local economy (Johnson and Moore, 1993), tourism spending in Washington DC (Frechtling and Horvath, 1999) or Michigan state (Stynes, 2000), the Atlanta Olympic Games in Georgia (Humphreys and Plummer, 1995), a festival in Ocean City (Crompton et al. (2001), a youth softball tournament in (Daniels, 2004) in fairs on Washington state (WSDA 2007), etc. Daniels (2004) proposes an interesting extension of IO, occupation-based modelling, a method to assign sector labour incomes across different occupations employing the Bureau of Labor Statistics wage-occupational data bank. In the absence of an IO table, the use of ready-made models may be the only cheap alternative to evaluate minor tourism events. However, the output that comes out of these models generates probably more value added in the consultancy business than in 'the search of economic truth'.

SAM Models

SAM models have also been employed to study tourism impacts in national, regional and small economies during the last two decades. Since expenditure coefficients are ratios of SAM flows to column totals, the only requirements to estimate tourism impacts with a SAM model are a SAM of the economy studied and a vector of tourists' impacts. The fact that many national statistical offices in developed economies publish IO tables along with national accounts but only a few of them elaborate SAMs has hampered its use in tourism studies. For many developing countries, SAMs have been assembled to explore 'the links between growth, inequality and employment, and . . . how the extent of poverty and changes in it are related to familiar issues of savings and investment, balance of payments, production and distribution' (Pyatt and Thorbecke, 1976). SAMs constructed for those purposes can nevertheless be employed to quantify the role tourism in the economy and its impact on all endogenous accounts including households.

National, Regional or Local SAM-based Studies

An early application is West's (1993) analysis of tourism in Queensland (Australia) which combines a regional SAM with econometric time series analysis. The Queensland integrated model includes, along with the SAM, other blocks where labour equations, income relationships and household expenditure by commodity and sector are calculated to 'reduce the static limitations of the model and, to some extent, the linearity relations'. The SAM included the following accounts: ten sectors, two factors (labour and capital), three institutions (households, enterprises and Government), savings–investment and the foreign sector. The basic information for activities was drawn from the 1985–86 Queensland IO table while visitors expenditure, subdivided in intrastate, interstate (the largest) and overseas, was estimated with the information provided by the Queensland Tourist and Travel Corporation. Tourism impacts for the three tourists' types were calculated by comparing the values of 'various economic indicators derived by the model' with and without tourism expenditure, assuming that activities, factors and institutions are all endogenous. The following average multipliers: 0.70 for GDP; 0.53 for household income and 26.48 jobs per million AU$.

Wagner (1997) developed a SAM for Guaraqueçaba to study the impact of tourism and its effects on households. The SAM comprises four types of accounts: eight activities (rudimentary rural farms, rural entrepreneurs, construction, manufacturing, commerce, service, transportation and government); three factors (labour:households, labour:salaried, and capital rent) and indirect taxes; nine institutions (subsistence, low income, medium income and high income households; enterprises, the capital account and three accounts for local, state and federal governments); and the import–export account. A peculiarity of the Guaraqueçaba SAM is that the base year is 1989–94 instead of a single year, a decision Wagner justified by the singularity of the economy and data availability.

The basic source for activities' transactions patterns were the 1980 IO table and the 1975 SAM for Brazil. Sector totals were calculated from a 1989 Government report on value added by sector for municipalities. The distribution of capital rents and consumption expenditures relied on the 1992 budget research study conducted by the Brazilian Government. Consumption expenditures were then valued at production prices employing distribution and transportation margins from the 1980 IO table. As for labour, official statistics only provided information on workers holding formal contracts but no information was available for labourers in the informal economy that hold two or three different jobs in a year. Number of labourers with and without formal contracts and their annual salaries were obtained from structured interviews. Population data were obtained from official sources and it was estimated that 95 per cent of the working-age population worked without a formal contract. Data on the local Government receipts and expenditures came from municipal sources. Notice that although national sources were employed in many instances to obtain patterns, an effort was made to include in the SAM the local information drawn from structured interviews with experts. The SAM was balanced by adjusting the import–export entries, but taking into account that activities and final demand are mainly supplied with imports, and exports come exclusively from the rural entrepreneurs and manufacturing sectors.

Multipliers for the endogenous accounts were obtained in three scenarios: first, only productive accounts are endogenous; second, productive, labour accounts and households are endogenous; and finally, productive accounts, labour, capital payments, households and enterprises are endogenous. In the first case only intergroup effects are captured while in the other cases all intragroup (own), intergroup (closed loop) and extragroup (open loop) effects are captured. As expected, activity multipliers increase as more accounts are endogenous. The largest multiplier of private activities is that of rudimentary rural farms in all scenarios; rural: entrepreneurs and commerce and manufacturing are also large when factors' income, households and the enterprise are endogenous. Labour:households and household:subsistence multipliers are the largest in the factor income and institutions blocks, respectively.

Employing survey data on the number of visitors and average expenditure, Wagner performed the following experiment: what will be the effect of the arrival of 100 tourists who spent on average $15.15 per day? Output impacts are 1563, 2097 and 3261 dollars and employment impacts are 0.28, 0.31 and 0.43 (full time equivalent) jobs in the three scenarios. Assuming 7.500 tourist average arrivals every day to Guaraqueçaba, the total impact on output and jobs is obtained multiplying the previous figures by 75 is $244.575 worth of goods and services, $19 425 salaries and 32 full time equivalent jobs. Sensitivity analysis indicated that the results were reasonably robust to measuring errors. Wagner concluded that although tourism impact was non-negligible, it 'will do nothing to break the cycle of deficit spending by local households' and advised 'strengthen the linkages between rudimentary rural farmers and subsystem households and the rest of the economy'.

Polo and Valle (2007 and 2008a) constructed a 72 × 72 square SAM for the Balearic Islands. It included 54 sectors in the IO table, two factors of production, several auxiliary accounts for taxes, subsidies and transfers, a resident household and a non-resident household, a corporation sector, the local and general governments, the savings–investment account and one foreign sector that includes the rest of Spain and the rest of the world. Fourteen sectors that produce tourist services are included in the SAM. Unfortunately, the SAM only includes one resident and one non-resident household and does not distinguish commodities by origin.

Polo and Valle (2007) compared the effects of exogenous injections in three scenarios: one, only the 54 production accounts are endogenous (SAM: 54); two, factors accounts and the resident household account are also endogenous (SAM: 54 + F + H); and finally, the savings–investment account is also endogenous (SAM: 54 + F + H + I). They also compared the effects of a 10 per cent fall in non-residents consumption in the three models. In the first case, weighted average production falls 3.21 per cent, value added 3.61 per cent and employment 3.02 per cent. The falls when the factors, resident household and savings–investment accounts are also endogenous are much larger: 5.52, 6.0 and 5.5 per cent, respectively. Polo and Valle (2008a and 2009) compared these results with those obtained with IO models specified with domestic coefficients.

Polo et al. (2006 and 2008) also analysed the impact on employment and added value of a hypothetical change in the expenditure distribution of the non-resident consumer using both the IO and SAM models. In particular, they calculate the increase in the demand of 4–5 star hotels services needed to offset a decline in the demand in the 1–2–3 star hotels category so that neither employment nor the added value would be affected. Their results indicate that in order to keep value added constant a reduction of 1000 beds in 1–2–3 stars hotel segment requires 505 (499) extra beds in the 4–5 stars category using the IO (SAM) model, and including the complementary offer, these figures increase to 568 (562) extra beds in the 4–5 stars category. This information may be of interest for those who view in a replacement policy a way to alleviate congestion and environment degradation in a mass tourism destination.

Jones (2010) estimates the impact of tourism in Mozambique using a 'tourism-focussed' SAM. The paper only includes a highly aggregated 'standard' and 'tourism-focussed' SAMs but more details can be found in Jones (2007). The standard SAM includes 17 production activities, 20 commodities including five characteristic products (hotels, restaurants, land and air transport and travel agencies), four factors (no list provided) and 15 institutions including five taxes (although only four appear in the aggregated sum). The institutions apparently include: firms, 5 households classified by income quintiles, the government, investment and the rest of world.[22] The 'tourism-focused' SAM includes some auxiliary accounts for domestic tourists (household, firms and government, and investment) and foreign tourists (business, self-drive and other leisure type) that appear twice in the activities and the commodity blocks. Foreign tourists in the commodity block receive income from the rest of the world and give it to foreign tourists in the activity block that use it to finance the purchase of commodities. In turn, domestic tourists in the commodity block receive income from activities, the household and the investment accounts and pass it to domestic tourists in the commodity block that use it to buy commodities. Notice that the extraction of intermediate tourism from intermediate consumption distorts the production coefficients.

In the reported results, all accounts except investment and the rest of the world are considered endogenous. As indicated earlier, the element m_{ji} in the multiplier indicates the income accruing to the jth account after a unitary exogenous injection directed to the ith account and the column sum the aggregate income caused by the injection. The normalized column sums (column sums divided by the average value of all column sums) shows that the injections directed to all types of foreign visitors have above average impact whether one looks to all accounts, production accounts, household income or value added. Domestic tourism impacts are slightly over the average but for two accounts, firms and government and investment tourism, are below the average. Only government revenue multipliers are larger than average and larger than foreign tourists' multipliers. Although these results indicate that 'tourism is a sector with comparatively strong backward linkages across production, household income and value added', Jones calls the attention to two weak points: the fragility of backward linkages of domestic tourism and the shortage of scarce production factors.[23]

Small Areas Ready-made SAM-based Studies

Ready-made IMPLAN-based SAMs have also been applied to estimate tourism impacts in small areas of the United States. Croes and Severt (2007) evaluate the effects of tourism in Osceola County (Florida) and find the following average multipliers with endogenous households: 1.21 for output, 0.66 for income, 0.38 for labour income, and 17.58 jobs per million dollars spent. Mansury and Hara (2007) propose the introduction of 'organic food agritourism' at Liberty in Sullivan County (New York) and propose the convenience of implementing 'a successful campaign to promote organic agriculture' that has stronger linkages with the local economy. To simulate its effects, they increase (reduce) the local (imported) coefficients of tourists sectors and conclude that the change 'not only is expected to deliver higher production output, but also generates a more egalitarian distribution of income'. Hara and Naipaul (2008) analyse the effects of a 50 million dollar injection in tourism expenditure in four counties in the vicinity of Orlando (Florida). The estimated injection assumes that 1 per cent of all visitors to central Florida would spend two days in the area enjoying 'agritourism' activities and spent two-thirds of their average expenditure. They calculate an output multiplier with endogenous households of 1.68 and 25.76 jobs created per million dollars; nothing is said, however, on the investment required to develop agritourism activities. Daniels et al. (2004) studied the Cooper River Bridge Run a sport event (a single day annual road race) in Charleston. They compared SAM results with those obtained when labour income is distributed employing the BLS occupation-based model for three levels of disaggregation. Their results indicate that the effects on households are sensitive to the specification of the model and that 'using SAMs to estimate personal income effects across different households may be inappropriate'.

ADVANTAGES AND LIMITATIONS OF THE IO AND SAM TECHNIQUES CONCEPTUALLY AND FOR POLICY FORMULATION

It seems fair to say that the advantages and limitations of IO and SAM models are well known by now. In this section, we first examine the relative merits and shortcomings of IO models versus SAM models. Then, we address an issue that has attracted considerable attention in the last 15 years: the criticism of IO and SAM models spurred by advocates of computable general equilibrium (CGE) models. They are in part responsible for having given way to more sophisticated nonlinear models known as CGE or AGE models. First, we compare the relative merits of IO and SAM models. Then, we address an issue that has received considerable attention since IO models were applied to assess economic impacts. This section ends with some general considerations on the interest of this type of analysis.

IO Versus SAM Models

The main advantage of IO models is that all parameters involved (A, l, k) can be specified numerically with the sole aid of an IO table, and IO tables are often provided by many national (or even regional) statistical offices along with national (regional) accounts. The expenditure coefficients $(A_{mm}$ and $A_{mn})$ in a SAM model can also be specified having a SAM, but SAMs require additional information to distribute sectors' gross value added among institutions (households, corporations, government and foreign sectors) and determine their outlays (consumption and savings decisions). Unfortunately, only a few national statistical offices that compile IO tables also assemble SAMs.

On the other hand, SAM models are conceptually more satisfactory than IO models since the households and capital accounts are balanced. Although IO models can be expanded to include consumption and investment 'industries' in the model, the 'production coefficients' required by the other sectors of the added industries are rather arbitrary. It is rather more natural to make endogenous those activities when their accounts are balanced. Therefore, one may say that 'all things equal' SAM models are preferable to IO models.

The 'all things equal' condition is not satisfied when important details are lost in the process of obtaining a SAM. The IO framework usually distinguishes commodities by origin in both supply and use tables, a distinction crucial to assess economic impacts, but few SAMs incorporate this feature. In that case, the results of both models are not comparable (even when the endogenous accounts in the SAM models are just the traditional IO sectors) and IO simulations done with domestic coefficients may give more accurate results than SAM simulations performed with total expenditure coefficients. The comparison in this respect is not always favourable to IO models, however. In particular, value-added estimates obtained with sectoral value added coefficients calculated from an IO table may be too optimistic since wages and especially capital rents may go to foreigners, leakages that are taken into account in the SAM framework.

LIMITATIONS OF IO AND SAM MODELS

Since Leontief proposed his system of linear demand equations to analyse the interdependencies in production, the fixed coefficients' assumption has been considered one of the greatest limitations of IO modelling. The proportionality between inputs and outputs is a very stringent assumption in the short-run and even more so in the long-run. Production coefficients do vary as new production processes brought about by changes in relative prices and the introduction of technological innovations. It is unlikely that 'production coefficients' of industries will remain constant as energy prices soar, real wages increase and new vintages of capital goods are installed. The proportionality assumption is even less tenable when applied to factors, households, savings–investment and government 'industries' in extended IO and SAM models. Moreover, it is also questionable the use of 'tax coefficients', defined as ratios of tax revenues over total production or outlays, to calculate tax revenues in these models.

Little can be said in favour of an assumption that is obviously restrictive beyond pointing out that changes in the production coefficients of an entire industry are probably piecemeal. Thus, one can take the 'observed' technical coefficients $A(p_t, t)$, $l(w_t, r_t, t)$ and $k(w_t, r_t, t)$ derived from an IO table at the base year t, as proxies of the true technical coefficients $A(p_{t+s}, t + s)$, $l(w_{t+s}, r_{t+s}, t + s)$ and $k(w_{t+s}, r_{t+s}, t + s)$ s years later. Thus, the results of a simulation done with the 'observed' coefficients to evaluate the effects of a change in exogenous income, Δd, should be read as the impact that would have occurred at time t had the prices remained unchanged after the impact. In other words, the relevance of the simulation results increases the closer the present time is to the base year and the smaller are the price changes caused by the impact itself. From this perspective, the results of IO and SAM models can be viewed as a particular case of more general models and it is not a coincidence that the SAM framework is also known as fix-price multiplier analysis.[24] At any rate, simulation results from IO and SAM models should always be interpreted with caution.

Disregard for capacity restrictions and resource limitations have also been considered a serious limitation of IO and SAM models.[25] In response to positive exogenous shocks, IO and SAM models assume that supplies of labour and capital can be increased at will to satisfy their requirements as industries expand their outputs to clear product markets.[26] Where do they come from the extra supplies needed? People already employed may work more hours and unemployed, inactive persons and immigrants may join the labour force. Additional capital services can be obtained by increasing utilization rates or installing new capital. Probably both things take time and the results obtained with IO and SAM models probably overstate the effects of positive injections in the short-run. But as more workers and capital are added to the initial endowments, IO and SAM results may not be so far off the target. Indeed, tourism has become a key 'industry' in many regions and nations since 1960 and factor restrictions have not deterred its growth. [27]

What about the effects of negative exogenous shocks? In this case, the multiplier works in the opposite direction: labour and capital demands fall with output, unemployment rises and capacity utilization falls. It is true that in more general models, market clearing conditions for labour and capital services ensure labour and capital endowments are reallocated among sectors at the new equilibrium prices. But how long does it take to reach the new equilibrium? We guess, a great deal. A fall in tourist demand will probably result in unemployment and capacity underutilization for quite a while, as IO and SAM models suggest, and it is not obvious how capital embodied in hotels and apartments to service tourists might be cast into others types of capital useful in other industries. Polo and Valle (2008b) show that IO and SAM models' results are close to those obtained with a general equilibrium model with a Keynesian closure. In our opinion, they do a better job than standard neoclassical models in predicting short-run outcomes after a negative demand shock.[28]

Going beyond impact analysis, Burgan and Mules (1992) pointed out that IO and SAM models are not 'evaluative tools'. A tourism impact simulation only quantifies the effects on value added or employment of the injection, not the costs caused by it, and a balanced approach to tourism requires weighting benefits and costs (Burgan and Mules, 2001; Dwyer and Forsyth, 1993; and Dwyer et al., 2011). Tourism may increase congestion, raise land and real estate prices, damage the environment in different ways, increase the (cost) of providing government services, alter the income distribution, etc., that have been ignored in most studies. In our opinion, there is no objection to do so as long as the results obtained with the models are interpreted as what they are: gross estimates of the effects of tourism.

FURTHER DEVELOPMENTS AND APPLICATIONS OF THE TECHNIQUE IN TOURISM RESEARCH

As indicated in the previous section, IO and SAM modelling is a mature applied field and most users are well aware of the limitations of linear models. Some of those are intrinsic to them and little can be done about it. But yet a great deal can be gained if only an effort is made to improve the quality and timing of the databases employed in these studies and the way the results are presented in academic journals.

Quest for Better Databases and Reporting of Results

The implementation of IO and SAM models require the existence of IO tables and SAMs and national statistical offices that elaborate IO tables should take into consideration analytical needs and shorten compilation periods. On this respect, what Stone wrote in the 1961 report that played a crucial role in the gestation of the 1968 SNA has not lost its relevance:

These reports are intended to provide guidance on various conceptual issues and also to set a system of definitions and classifications of general applicability, to *indicate detail that is generally desirable for analytical purposes* and to provide a framework for assembling the data of various countries on a comparable basis. (Our emphasis.)

In our opinion, the link between the design of social accounting systems and its potential applications has become more tenuous with the passage of time. Offices in charge of national accounts seem to be more concerned in developing IO tables and SAMs to present the definitive National Accounts' estimates than in providing the *detail generally desirable for analytical purposes*. To put it shortly: IO tables and SAMs are not ends in themselves but instruments to model the economy.

The numerical specification of a model is a crucial stage and should be done with the best possible database. Archer (1978) recalled many years ago that the 'old adage of "rubbish in, rubbish out" applies to multiplier work as much as other forms of analysis'. IO and SAM modelling require counting with good IO tables and SAMs. Although great progress has been made in the last 50 years and statistical offices are aware that it is 'a suitable instrument to . . . guide the use of information in economic analysis', they seem to value more its role 'as a framework to improve the basic statistics' and 'evaluate the validity of the first estimates of the production account' (INE, 1985, pp. 97–98). Perhaps, for this reason, the information published quite often does not fit modellers' needs. In particular, those countries and regions where tourism is an important 'industry' should include all characteristic sectors and products in their IO framework.

Since IO tables have considerable delay, IO models (and all models based on IO tables like SAM and CGE models) are condemned to be specified with 'outdated' data, as critics often point out.[29] An 8 or 10 years lag is not infrequent as inspection of Table 12.1 confirms. Production coefficients do change and it is crucial to count with reliable and updated databases to increase the confidence in the simulation results. Publication lags should and can be shortened if technology and human resources are set at the task. It may be a bit expensive but it is probably more costly to keep dozens and dozens of economists working with outdated and non-reliable databases. Better data will not solve all problems, but it will eliminate one source of uncertainty.[30]

In developed countries, statistical offices responsible for the elaboration of National Accounts should also engage in the elaboration of SAMs. Individual scholars often have to build SAMs making heroic assumptions to distribute factors income among different agents. Statistical offices count with a great deal information (often undisclosed) and could do a much better job.[31] The European initiative to develop a SAM handbook (Eurostat, 2003) deserves applause and those countries that decided not to participate in the endeavour should reconsider their position. It would be naïve to think that an official SAM developed within the national accounting system will satisfy the needs of all potential users, but it would be a much better starting point, especially if modellers' needs are taken into account.

The IO model is well known but in applied work details matter and should be made explicit by the authors. The main characteristics of the IO table or SAM, the data on tourism expenditures and the adjustments made to obtain the vectors of tourists' expenditures should be clearly indicated. Academic articles should also include a precise specification of the model to avoid unnecessary confusion and facilitate results' comparisons.[32] The implementation of the model deserves much more than a few cursory remarks and the equations employed in the simulations should be presented. In this review of the literature, we have found too many papers that are equation free (or almost free) that included lots of irrelevant statistics and details about the country and tourism trends. It is a bad practice that should be abandoned. Lack of space or the need to reach a larger audience should no longer be an excuse in academic journals.

TSAs: The Promised Land?

The development of a tourism satellite account (TSA) has received a great deal of attention in the last decade (Libreros, et al., 2006). The publication of the United Nations (2008) monograph *Tourism Satellite Account: Recommended Methodological Framework* is the latest attempt to set up homogenous criteria to measure the contribution of tourism activities.[33] In essence, the TSA aims at providing a comprehensive and coherent account of tourism from the demand side (visitors' expenditure and consumption) and the supply side (production of tourists' services and employment). It also includes other accounts to measure the contribution of tourism to capital formation, collective consumption and nonmonetary indicators. Although the construction of the ten interrelated tables that comprise the TSA has an interest of its own as an extension of the SNA framework (Frechtling, 2010), the relevant issue from the viewpoint of IO, SAM and even CGE modeling is whether or not the information actually provided facilitates the inclusion of tourists' households in the models.[34]

For Van de Steeg and Steenge (2008), 'tourism is implicitly already included in the supply and use tables and . . . the TSA is developed to make tourism explicit'. For them, 'a most important contribution of the TSA framework is the construction of a final expenditure vector specific of tourism'. Blake et al. (2001) recognize that 'TSAs represent a major step forward in the measurement of the economic size of tourism' and 'provide detailed data on tourism activities that are not otherwise available in national accounts', but also point out that TSA 'do not assess the total impact of tourism'. Smeral (2006) insists that 'it is necessary to adjust the TSA results for indirect effects and intermediate consumption'. Jones and Munday (2008) also recognize that the TSA framework 'offers complementary opportunities to improve the modeling of tourism activity and policy', but they argue that 'it requires restructuring to become more useful for modeling purposes'. In other words, modelling remains essential to assess the importance of tourism and TSAs may not provide the most suitable information to analyse tourism with models.

Let us take the case of Spain – a major international tourist destination – to illustrate some of the difficulties we encounter to combine the TSA and the IO frameworks. The symmetric table provides a consumption vector by product in the territory and the use table an estimate of total non-residents consumption in the territory (NRCT). To simulate the impact of NRTC all is needed is to allocate that total among the different products. Does the Spanish TSA do the job? The answer is . . . definitely not. Although TSAs are supposed to be a satellite of the SNA and the IO framework there are substantial differences between the numbers reported by both.[35] Thus, the availability of a TSA does not solve the allocation problem of NRCT.[36] Would it not be less costly and more interesting to focus the attention in improving the measurement of NRCT (distinguishing commodities by origin) and disaggregating it into several vectors (corresponding to distinct tourists' types) that would be displayed in the final demand matrix of the IO framework? It seems that the elaboration of the TSA has become (at least in some countries) an end in itself and overlooks the 'detail that is generally desirable for analytical purpose'.[37]

Energy and Environmental Impacts of Tourism

The notion that services energy direct requirements are generally smaller than in other sectors (agriculture, manufacturing and construction) is probably behind the lack of interest in estimating energy intensity and consumption and CO_2 emissions associated with tourism. However, the picture changes considerably when indirect energy requirements are taken into account (see Alcántara and Padilla, 2007; Cardenete et al., 2011). In the case of tourism, the very concept of visitors involves the use energy-consuming services such as transportation and accommodation.

Tabatchnaia-Tamirisa et al.'s (1997) study of Hawaii used and IO model to estimate direct and indirect energy use by domestic and foreign tourists in Hawaii. Energy intensities of any tourism activity are given by the rows of the matrix $M'_{(T \times E)}$, defined as the transposed of the submatrix of M obtained by the intersection of the E energy rows and the T tourism columns of the multiplier matrix M. The intermediate energy demand vector associated with the production of the final tourist demand vector d^T is given by

$$A_E M d^T$$

where A_E is the $E \times M$ submatrix of direct energy coefficients. Finally, the total vector of energy demand y_E^T is obtained by adding to the intermediate the final energy demand vector d_E^T

$$y_E^T = A_E M d^T + d_E^T.$$

Tabatchnaia-Tamirisa et al. reported estimates of direct and indirect energy use by domestic and foreign tourists. Their calculations indicate that indirect energy use is very important both in absolute terms and as a ratio of visitors' expenditure, especially for foreign tourists.[38]

Briassoulis (1991) already signalled the 'assessment of the intangible social and environmental impacts of tourism and linking them with the input–output model' as an important research topic. Among those 'intangible' impacts, CO_2 and more generally greenhouse emissions have attracted much attention in the last decade. Having estimated the energy consumption associated with tourism, the IO and SAM models can provide estimates of, let us say, CO_2 emissions by multiplying the energy vector y_E^T by a suitable c' emissions' vector.[39] Lenzen (1998) applied the IO model to estimate energy intensities and emissions of greenhouse gases (GHG) caused by final demand in Australia. Lenzen et al. (2003) showed how the approach can also be used to assess other environmental impacts ('land disturbance', 'water use' or emission of NO_x and SO_2) involved in the construction of a second Sydney airport and their results indicate that 'total impacts are considerably higher than the on-site impacts'. For this reason, they suggest that 'input–output techniques could be incorporated as mandatory in environmental impact assessment standards'.[40]

Dwyer et al. (2007) and Lundie et al. (2009) have also employed IO analysis to provide measures of environmental indicators for different tourist market segments of inbound tourism in Australia. The direct onsite effects are estimated by the audit approach while indirect effects are estimated with an IO model of Australia specified with a 1994–95 IO table. The study distinguishes 29 fuels, 12 types of tourists, four environmental aspects (primary energy consumption, water use, GHG emissions and land disturbance) and calculates various measures of environmental yield (per visit, per visitor night and per dollar spent). Their results indicate that 'markets associated with high daily expenditure in Australia generate higher impacts to the environment compared with tourists who spend less'. UK repeaters and backpackers obtained the best scores in all environmental accounts using per visitor night indicators.

Konan and Chan (2010) applied the IO model to estimate the petroleum use and GHG emissions of tourism, Hawaii's key export industry. The model was specified with a 1997 IO table that included 131 sectors and seven fossil fuels.[41] Out of 323 trillion BTU total of primary energy consumption, direct requirements are very high in air transport (102.51), electricity generation (99.89) and residents' consumption (41.07). Visitors' direct gasoline purchases are comparatively small (2.74) that apparently avails the view that visitors GHG emissions are insignificant. However, visitors' demand of transportation, accommodation services, restaurants, etc., imply a much larger indirect demand of fuels and a greater responsibility for GHG emissions. Indeed, the IO analysis unveils that visitors are responsible for 22 per cent of total emissions and emission rates per visitor are between three and five times larger than those of residents depending on the type of fuel.

Collins et al. (2009) examined the relative merits of two approaches, environmental IO modelling (EIO) and ecological footprint (EFP) analysis,[42] to assess the environmental impacts of major sport events and presented the results obtained for the 2004 Wales Rally of Great Britain. Among the advantages of the EIO approach the authors mentioned the following: transparency and low cost, availability of IO tables and detailed environmental satellite accounts, and the possibility of comparing economic benefits and environmental costs resulting from the event. Despite the well-known limitations of IO models and the ambiguity that surrounds EFP calculations, the two methods provide two quantitative estimates that may help to compare event impacts across space and time.[43]

Kytzia et al. (2011) employed an augmented IO model to simulate the effects of changes in tourism patterns on land use efficiency indicators and employment at Davos (Switzerland). The IO table was assembled combining the information drawn from surveys that cover most sectors with an existing the IO table for an Austrian region. The situation at the status quo (2002) was that accommodation in high and medium class hotels and group accommodation are more 'efficient' (in the sense they require less *ground* floor area per overnight) than low class hotels, vacation rentals and second homes. Then, they looked at the income generated by the different types and concluded that tourists lodged in high class hotels and group accommodation establishments generate the largest income per unit of ground floor used per night. Finally, the authors simulated three scenarios: reducing seasonality;[44] increasing the number of high class tourists and occupancy rates in high class hotels; and expanding accommodation capacity. The conclusions are not too surprising when they claim that an increase in the number of tourists staying in high class hotels would 'increase land use efficiency'. A serious drawback of this approach is that the 'efficiency' indicator chosen (value added over ground floor area per overnight) does not take into account land values. It is unclear to us why value added per unit of ground floor should be preferred to the rate of return earned by different types of accommodation services as an efficiency measure.

Berners-Lee et al. (2011) used the environmental IO model supplemented with direct emissions estimates to estimate total emissions caused by small and medium size businesses in the tourism sector and evaluate the 'potential costs or savings from switching activities'. Their model that combines the 'top-down' approach characteristic of IO analysis with the process specific 'bottom-up' Life-Cycle Analysis (LCA) is applied to the characteristic tourism sectors: hotels and travel agencies. As the authors point out, LCA suffers from subjectivity in the definition of the boundaries of supply chains that may result in severe truncation errors (Lenzen, 2001).[45] In turn, IO analysis lacks specificity since industry's production coefficients are averages of different production processes. Although the authors call it a hybrid model, 'the first 10 steps relate to the IO model' and provide a total emission matrix where each column indicates the emissions resulting from producing one net unit of each product.[46] 'Steps 11 and 12 are concerned with improving the accuracy by incorporating elements of LCA'. Since the nature of those adjustments is not precisely stated, it is hard to evaluate the final result.[47]

All energy and environmental studies of tourism impact just reviewed employ the basic IO model. An obvious extension would be to estimate those effects employing extended IO and SAM models to capture induced effects. Moreover, more comprehensive approaches like EFP and LCA suggest that the concept of intermediate consumptions should be expanded to include somehow the services of produced capital goods and 'natural' resource capital required to produce tourism services.[48] Including investment coefficients along with intermediate coefficients may not be a satisfactory solution but there is a need for a better integration of fixed capital (land, construction, natural resources, etc.) in the model. Sustainability of tourism (especially in mature destinations) will continue to be an important issue in the following decades and we expect IO and SAM analysis will continue playing an important role side by side with more general models and other complementary tools.

GENERAL APPRAISAL

Is it worthwhile to continue using IO and SAM models in tourism research? Notwithstanding the limitations discussed, our answer is definitely yes. The models are easy to specify numerically and provide quantitative estimates of the weight of tourism in the economy, useful information on the interrelations between tourism characteristic products and sectors with the rest of the economy, informed predictions of the magnitude of economic permanent impacts and an assessment of some environmental consequences of tourism activities. What really matters is to count with a data basis (IO tables and SAMs) assembled from basic statistical information on production, distribution and expenditure activities. Ideally, it should be designed to be the basis of a wide range of applications displaying a fine sectoral and commodity disaggregation. At least in those countries where tourism plays an important role, the final demand should include vectors for representative domestic and foreign tourists. Moreover, tourism related investment should also be singled out (Holtz-Eakin, 2001). A lot can be done in all those areas to improve our models and their numerical specification.

It is true that linear models rule out substitution but the solution is by no means to assume (as it often happens in nonlinear models) elasticity figures whose empirical relevance for the economy studied has never been tested.[49] It is probably true that IO and SAM models overestimate the effects of positive impacts in the short run, but they give good clues of what may happen in the medium run even for large economies after labour and capacity constraints are adjusted; and their estimates in the short run can be even more accurate than those obtained with more general nonlinear models when the economy faces negative shocks and factor prices adjust slowly. It goes without saying that their results should be taken as informed estimates and compared with those provided by more general models.[50] Indeed, comparing the simulation results of IO-SAM and more general models for different types of shocks and closure rules are issues that deserve more attention in the future. What it seems undeniable is that IO and SAM models have made a great contribution to understand the multiple ways tourism impacts the economy and that they will probably continue playing an important role in the future.

ACKNOWLEDGEMENTS

The authors gratefully acknowledged financial support from the Ministry of Education of Spain, SEJ2007-61046/ECON. All errors are the responsibility of the authors.

NOTES

1. It should be noted that the 'industry' covered not only agricultural, mineral and industrial sectors but also services, household and the foreign sector.
2. Chenery and Watanabe (1958) indicated that 'at least 15 countries have now done serious input–output work although not all of the results have been published'.
3. The textbook by Hara (2008) covers the IO and SAM models.
4. Oosterhaven and Fan (2006) obtain $\hat{I}(\hat{k})$ multiplying the diagonal matrices $\hat{L}$ and $\hat{K}$ of factors' coefficients, by the vector Md.
5. Observe that labour impacts are measured in the labour units chosen. To translate those effects into number of jobs those figures need to be multiplied by the ratio of employees to labour units in the base year.
6. Although is not as common, the investment 'industry' can also be endogenized (Wolff, 1985). Henry and Deane (1997) considered endogenous household consumption and the government. For an alternative interpretation of $M + 1$th row and column see Miller and Blair (2009).
7. There are expenditure coefficients that cannot be interpreted as technical coefficients at all. A conspicuous case is the expenditure coefficient obtained when tax revenues are divided by total income.
8. They can be classified by origin (nonresidents and resident), nature of the trip (vacation, business, assistance to a singular event, etc.), lodging characteristics (hotels, furnished houses, caravans, day-trippers, etc.) and other socioeconomic considerations.
9. $\Delta d = d_{t+s}\hat{P}_{t+s}^t - d_t$ where $\hat{P}_{t+s}^t$ is a diagonal matrix whose ith element is p_{it}/p_{t+si}. An alternative is to 'inflate' the A matrix (Henry and Deane, 1997; Var and Quayson, 1985).
10. Pérez-Viéitez and Polo (2007) analysis of energy intensities in Catalonia is one of the few studies where

an IO and SAM analysis is done with domestic and total coefficients and the conclusion reached is that it matters.

11. Slightly different formulas were used to calculate the employment multiplier (Archer, 1976).

12. Vaughan has kept faithful to this approach (see Vaughan et al., 2000).

13. In Spain, for instance, the IO framework only provides the total consumption expenditures of non-residents (residents) in (out of) the territory. The situation has improved since the National Statistical Institute started publishing the Tourist Satellite Account in 2002 (INE, 2002).

14. The Institute of Tourist Studies (IET) is an organism dependent of the Ministry of Commerce and Tourism.

15. There are many more articles that the interested reader can find in the references of those included here that provide a fair representation of IO studies at different levels (nation, regions and small islands), geographical areas (Australia, Europe, Asia and Africa) and topics (general tourism and tourism events).

16. They differ in the aggregation of the IO table and the base year; the way the tourists' vector was estimated and the parameters specified; the income concept employed; (non-government income, value added, GDP, GNP, etc.) and the characteristics of the tourism 'industry' in each area.

17. Further results can be found in Polo and Valle (2007, 2008a, 2009) for 1997 and Polo and Valle (2011) for 1983, 1997 and 2004.

18. Since 'tourist resources' and 'tourists activities' attract visitors who may otherwise have gone elsewhere, city officials strive to develop such resources to reinforce the economic base of their communities. In the case of singular mega-events such as the Olympic Games, FIFA World Cup, World Exhibitions, etc., they engage in long and costly contests to host them, although the benefits of mega-events exceeds tourists' expenditures due to the event and may have significant effects on the entire state where they are held.

19. It is hard to find a festival, fair, race, game, mega-event, etc. whose impact has not been evaluated. Crompton (2006) claims that 'most economic impact studies are commissioned to legitimize a political position rather than to search for economic truth'.

20. Guidelines have helped to clarify what should be included in the expenditure vector. However, not all is clear cut. Tyrrell and Johnston (2001) indicate that if a visitor spends $15 on a meal and the reason to be there is 97 per cent due to the activity only $14.75 should be included in meal's entrance of the expenditure vector. It is doubtful that those percentages can be taken seriously.

21. Saayman and Saayman (2006) estimate the impact of the Krueger National Park in Mpumalanga province of South Africa with a national 1996 IO table and assume that provincial indirect effects are a proportion sector dependent on the national indirect effects.

22. It is not totally clear how the SAM was assembled. Apparently, it is an update to 2003 of the SAM elaborated by McCool et al. (2009) for 2001.

23. Jones (2010) defines in Appendix B (p. 696) two normalized adjusted value added multipliers defined as the ratio of the average multipliers in a column by the scarce factor multiplier. Capital and skilled labour are the two scarce factors considered. The normalized capital adjusted value added multipliers are slightly over the average for foreign visitors but the normalized skilled labour adjusted multipliers well below the average.

24. Notice, however, that this criticism also applies to CGE models that often assume Leontief production functions for intermediate inputs.

25. For a recent statement of this view, see Dwyer et al. (2004). Dwyer et al. (2005) recognize, however, that 'the input–output assumption of freely available resources is closer to the truth in the local case, because labour and capital can flow to the area from other areas'. Today, labour and capital mobility is high not only in small areas.

26. In the tourism impact literature, impact restrictions were first introduced by Wanhill (1988).

27. This is by no means a novel view. McGregor et al. (1996) claimed that the 'IO system replicates the long-run equilibria of a wide range of regional models, many of which do not operate as IO systems in the short-run'.

28. Álvarez and Polo (2011) arrive at similar conclusions with a general equilibrium model of Spain.

29. Of course, IO tables and SAMs can be updated. But this poses another question: what confidence can we have in updated tables if key sectoral information is not available when they are updated?

30. Another indication of the lack of attention to analytical needs of some national statistical offices is that published IO tables do not include auxiliary price and tax tables required to analyse productivity changes and evaluate the effects of fiscal policies.

31. It is unfortunate that some national statistical offices behave as if the statistical information collected with citizens' taxes was a private good.

32. One or two equations are sometimes included in appendixes but they are too general and therefore provide no useful information. In other cases, they are simply not correct.

33.   A detailed account of TSAs inception can be found in Frechtling (1999, 2010) and Jones and Munday (2008).
34.   TSAs have also been constructed for regions (see Jones and Munday, 2008, 2010; Jones et al., 2003; Pham et al., 2009). Canada and Australia have pioneered these undertakings.
35.   Of course, there may be important differences across countries. The following comments apply only to Spain and all figures are in million EUR and refer to 2005. First, the value of NRCT in the IO framework (38.681) differs from the inbound tourism consumption figure in the TSA (42217), a difference that may be due to the inclusion of service exports (mainly transport fares) in the TSA (INE, 2002, p. 27). Second, since total tourism demand (98389.1) in the TSA is disaggregated into 13 characteristic products (totaling 80609.9) and a single figure (17779.2) for the *rest* of the economy, we cannot calculate individual product shares. Third, for each of the characteristic products, let us say, lodging, total demand (27554.2) includes inbound (10487.5), domestic (13965.0), intermediate (3039.5) and government (62.2) demand. Thus, product shares for characteristic products are contaminated by the inclusion of intermediate and government demand. Fourth, for some commodities (i.e., lodging) the sum of inbound (10487.5) and domestic (13965) tourism consumption in the TSA is much greater than household lodging consumption expenditure (11829.9) in the symmetric table and even larger than production of the lodging branch (17110.8). The main explanation for this apparent inconsistency is that lodging household demand is masked as final demand of other products (travel agencies) in the IO framework. For all these reasons, we can conclude that the present format of the Spanish TSA does not provide the appropriate information to extract domestic and inbound tourism from the households' consumption expenditure vector in the IO framework.
36.   Neither does it solve the problem of extracting domestic tourism expenditures from the household consumption in the IO framework. Moreover, the lodging or even hotels characteristic product in the TSA and IO tables is too heterogeneous (from 5-star hotels to bed and breakfast) to analyse tourism impacts, a shortcoming that also affects other countries (Jones et al., 2003, pp. 2783–2785).
37.   Another important shortcoming of the Spanish IO framework is the lack of information on the distribution of taxes (subsidies) on products across products both in the use and the symmetric tables. This deficiency becomes especially relevant when the IO framework is embedded in a general equilibrium model to analyse tax policies. The complementary tax tables have never been published and the symmetric table is only available at basic prices.
38.   Becken et al. (2001) estimated the direct energy consumption in the accommodation sector in New Zealand but no indirect effects were calculated. They find that consumption patterns vary greatly among different accommodation types and suggest disaggregating the accommodation sector and visitors by types of accommodation.
39.   These applications have been facilitated by the availability of environmental satellite accounts. Perch-Nielsen et al. (2010) show using a NAMEA that emissions by the Swiss tourism characteristic sectors are four times greater than average.
40.   Lenzen (2003) also used the Leontief and Gosh models and Defourny and Thorbecke (1984) structural path analysis to determine key sectors and important influence paths from an environmental perspective.
41.   A more recent 2002 IO table was available but the authors could not use it because it did not include key energy sectors such as petroleum refining and electricity generation.
42.   The EFP provides an aggregate measure of resource consumption of a given population expressed in units equivalent to an hectare with average productivity known as global hectare (gha). Gösling et al. (2002) explain at length (pp. 201–205) how they applied the EFP methodology to measure the environmental impact of inbound tourism to the Seychelles. An obvious advantage of the EFP is that it tries to take into account the footprint of built-up land in transportation, accommodation, etc.
43.   Collins et al. (2009) discarded other alternatives such as environmental impact assessment, life-cycle analysis, cost–benefit analysis, etc., on the basis that 'the selected techniques are able to deal in various degrees with the environmental consequences of travel outside the event areas', provide quantitative estimates and are to some extent complementary.
44.   There are discrepancies between the figures in Table 3 and the 'status quo' column in Table 4 that are hard to interpret. Moreover, curbing seasonality means equalizing summer and winter overnight stays to the largest winter figure in the status quo column. This amounts to an increase in the summer season rather than a reduction in seasonality.
45.   In a recent paper, Filimonau et al. (2011) criticize both the EFP and EIO approaches and defend LCA as a superior alternative. Their discussion of the literature indicates that out of the six papers that have used the 'original' LCA analysis, four combine it with the EIO model. They illustrate the approach estimating CO_2 emissions of a hypothetical weekend holiday trip from London to Poole, in our view a rather anecdotal contribution.
46.   Many of those steps could have been avoided had the authors counted with a more recent and congruent IO environmental data. In some cases, the adjustments made (adjusting emissions coefficients by the CPI (step 10) the adjustments are very crude.

47. It seems that the emissions caused by organization expenditures, intermediate consumption, are evaluated using the multipliers derived from final demand.
48. León et al. (2007) for instance claim 'that the optimal trajectory of tourist consumption increases when the stock of natural resources is high and environmental attributes are preserved'.
49. CGE models present a more complex structure that includes nested production and utility functions, optimization behaviour and market-clearing conditions for all products and generally factors. In most models, the nesting and production functions chosen at each level of the nest are to a large extent arbitrary, i.e., lack any empirical backing.
50. Fixed-price models are obviously inadequate to estimate the effects of fiscal policies that affect prices and quantities. To analyse the impact of a change in VAT rates is preferable to employ a general equilibrium model (Kehoe et al., 1988) than to feed in an IO model the quantity changes estimated with ad-hoc equations (Manente and Zanette, 2010).

REFERENCES

Alcántara, V. and E. Padilla (2007), 'Subsistemas Input-Output y contaminación: Una aplicación al Sector Servicios y las Emisiones de CO_2 en España'. *II Jornadas Españolas de Análisis Input-Output Zaragoza: Crecimiento, Demanda y Recursos naturales*, Zaragoza: Libro de Comunicaciones.
Álvarez, M.T. and C. Polo (2011), 'A general equilibrium assessment of external and domestic shocks in Spain', in press.
Alward, G.S. and C.J. Palmer (1983), 'IMPLAN: an input-output analysis system for Forest Service planning', in R. Seppala, C. Row and A. Morgan (eds), *Forest Sector Models: Proceedings of the First North American Conference on Forest Sector Modeling*, pp. 131–140. Williamsburg VA: USDA Forest Service.
Archer, B.H. (1976), 'The anatomy of a multiplier', *Regional Studies*, **10**, 71–77.
Archer, B.H. (1978), 'Domestic tourism as a development factor', *Annals of Tourism Research*, **5** (1), 126–141.
Archer, B.H. (1982), 'The value of multiplier and their policy implications', *Tourism Management*, **3** (4), 236–241.
Archer, B.H. (1984), 'Economic impact: misleading multiplier', *Annals of Tourism Research*, **12**, 517–518.
Archer, B.H. (1985), 'Tourism in Mauritius: an economic impact study with marketing implications', *Tourism Management*, **6** (1), 50–54.
Archer, B.H. (1995), 'Importance of tourism for the economy of Bermuda', *Annals of Tourism Research*, **22** (4), 918–930.
Archer, B.H. and J. Fletcher (1996), 'The economic impact of tourism in the Seychelles', *Annals of Tourism Research*, **23** (1), 32–47.
Archer, B.H. and C.B. Owen (1971), 'Towards a tourist regional multiplier', *Regional Studies*, **5** (4), 289–294.
Archer, B.H. and S. Wanhill (1980), *Tourism in Bermuda: An Economic Evaluation*, Hamilton, Bermuda: Bermuda Department of Tourism.
Baster, J. (1980), 'Input–output analysis of tourism benefits. Lessons from Scotland', *International Journal of Tourism Management*, **1** (2), 99–108.
Becken, S., C. Frampton and D. Simmons (2001), 'Energy consumption patterns in the accommodation sector: the New Zeland case', *Ecological Economics*, **39**, 371–386.
Bergstrom, J.C., H.K. Cordell, A.E. Watson and G.A. Ashley (1990), 'Economic impacts of state parks on state economies in the South', *Southern Journal of Agricultural Economics*, **22** (2), 69–77.
Berners-Lee, M., D.C. Howard, J. Moss, K. Kaivanto and W.A. Scott (2011), 'Greenhouse gas footprinting for small businesses: the use of input-output data', *Science of the Total Environment*, **409**, 883–891.
Beynon, M., C. Jones and M. Munday (2009), 'The embeddedness of tourism-related activity: a regional analysis of sectoral linkages', *Urban Studies*, **46**, 2123–2141.
Blake, A., R. Durbarry, M.T. Sinclair and G. Sugiyarto (2001), 'Modelling tourism and travel using tourism satellite accounts and tourism policy and forecasting models', unpublished manuscript, Nottingham.
Briassoulis, H. (1991), 'Methodological issues. tourism input-output analysis', *Annals of Tourism Research*, **19** (4), 700–710.
Bulmer-Thomas, V. (1982), *Input-output Analysis in Developing Countries: Sources, Methods, and Applications*, Chichester, NY: John Wiley.
Burgan, B. and T. Mules (1992), 'Economic impact of sporting events', *Annals of Tourism Research*, **19**, 700–10.
Burgan, B. and T. Mules (2001), 'Reconciling cost-benefit and economic impact assessment for event tourism', *Tourism Economics*, **7** (4), 321–330.

Bushnell, R.C. and M. Hyle (1985), 'Computerized models for assessing the economic impact of recreation and tourism', in D.B. Propst (compiler), *Assessing the Economic Impact of Recreation and Tourism: Conference and Workshop*. Asheville, NC: Southeastern Forest Experiment Station.

Cardenete, A., P. Fuentes-Saguar and C. Polo (2011), 'CO_2 decomposition in the Andalusian economy', *Journal of Industrial Ecology*, in press.

Chenery, H.B. and T. Watanabe (1958), 'International comparisons of the structure of production', *Econometrica*, **26** (4), 487–521.

Cohen, S.I. (1989), 'Multiplier analysis in social accounting and input-output frameworks: evidence for several countries', in R.E Miller, K.R. Polenske and A.Z. Rose (eds), *Frontiers in Input–Output Analysis*, Oxford: Oxford University Press.

Collins, A., C. Jones and M. Munday (2009), 'Assessing the environmental impacts of mega sporting events: two options?', *Tourism Management*, **30**, 828–837.

Cooper, M.J. and J.J. Pigram (1984), 'Tourism and the Australian economy', *Tourism Management*, **5** (1), 2–12.

Croes, R.R. and D.E. Severt (2007), 'Evaluating short-term tourism economic effects in confined economies: conceptual and empirical considerations', *Tourism Economics* **13** (2), 289–307.

Crompton, J.L. (2006), 'Economic impact studies: instruments for political shenanigans?', *Journal of Travel Research*, **45** (1), 67–82.

Crompton, J.L., S. Lee and T.J. Shuster (2001), 'A guide for undertaking economic impact studies: the Springfest example', *Journal of Travel Research*, **40**, 79–87.

Daniels, M.J. (2004), 'Beyond input-output analysis: using occupation-based modelling to estimate wages generated by a sport tourism event', *Journal of Travel Research*, **43** (1), 75–82.

Daniels, M., W. Norman and M. Henry (2004), 'Estimating income effects of a sport tourism event', *Annals of Tourism Research*, **31** (1), 180–199.

Defourny, J. and E. Thorbecke (1984), 'Structural path analysis and multiplier decomposition within a social accounting matrix framework', *The Economic Journal*, **94**, 111–136.

Dwyer, L. and P. Forsyth (1993), 'Assessing the benefits and costs of inbound tourism', *Annals of Tourism Research*, **20**, 751–768.

Dwyer, L., P. Forsyth, L. Fredline, M. Deery, L. Jago and S. Lundie (2007), 'Yield measures for special-interest Australian inbound tourism markets', *Tourism Economics*, **13** (3), 421–440.

Dwyer, L., P. Forsyth and A. Papatheodorou (2011), 'Economics of tourism', *Contemporary Tourism Reviews*, 1–29.

Dwyer, L., P. Forsyth and R. Spurr (2004), 'Evaluating tourism's economic effects: new and old approaches', *Tourism Management*, **25**, 307–317.

Dwyer, L., P. Forsyth and R. Spurr (2005), 'Estimating the impacts of special events on an economy', *Journal of Travel Research*, **43**, 351–359.

Eurostat (2003), *Handbook on Social Accounting Matrices and Labour Accounts*, Leadership group SAM. Luxembourg: Eurostat Secretariat Unit E3, European Commission.

Felsenstein, D. and D. Freeman (1998), 'Simulating the impacts of gambling in a tourist location: some evidence from Israel', *Journal of Travel Research*, **37**, 145–155.

Filimonau, V., J.E. Dickinson, D. Robbins and M.V. Reddy (2011), 'A critical review of methods for tourism climate change appraisal: life cycle assessment as a new approach', *Journal of Sustainable Tourism*, **19** (3), 301–324.

Fletcher, J. (1989), 'Input–output analysis and tourism impact studies', *Annals of Tourism Research*, **16** (4), 514–529.

Frechtling, D.C. (1999), 'The tourism satellite account: foundations, progress and issues', *Tourism Management*, **20**, 163–170.

Frechtling, D.C. (2010), 'The tourism satellite account. A primer', *Annals of Tourism Research*, **37** (1), 136–153.

Frechtling, D.C. and E. Horvath (1999), 'Estimating the multiplier effects of tourism expenditures on a local economy through a regional input–output model', *Journal of Travel Research*, **37**, 324–332.

Gelan, A. (2003), 'Local economic impacts. The British Open', *Annals of Tourism Research*, **30** (2), 406–425.

Getz, D. (1989), 'Special events: defining the product', *Tourism Management*, **10** (2), 135–137.

Gösling, S., C. Borgström Hansson, O. Hörstmeier and S. Saggel (2002), 'Ecological footprint analysis as a tool to assess tourism sustainability', *Ecological Economics*, **43**, 199–211.

Hara, T. (2008), *Quantitative Tourism Industry Analysis. Introduction to Input–Output, Social Accounting Matrix Modelling and Tourism Satellite Accounts*, Amsterdam: Elsevier.

Hara, T. and S. Naipaul (2008), 'Agritourism as a catalyst for improving the quality of the life in rural regions: a study from a developed country', *Journal of Quality Assurance in Hospitality and Tourism*, **9** (1), 1–33.

Henderson, D.M. and R.L. Cousins (1975), *The Economic Impact of Tourism: A Case Study in Greater Tayside*. Edinburgh: Scottish Tourist Board.

Heng, T.M. and L. Low (1990), 'Economic impact of tourism in Singapore', *Annals of Tourism Research*, **17** (2), 246–269.

Henry, E.W. and B. Deane (1997), 'The contribution of tourism to the economy of Ireland in 1990 and 1995', *Tourism Management*, **18** (8), 535–553.

Holtz-Eakin, D. (2001), 'Capital in a tourism satellite account', *Tourism Economics*, **7** (3), 215–232.

Humphreys, J.M. and M.K. Plummer (1995), *The Economic Impact on the State of Georgia of Hosting the 1996 Olympic Games*, Georgia: Selig Center for Economic Growth.

IET (1997), *Tabla intersectorial de la economía española 1992*, Madrid: Instituto de Estudios Turísticos del Ministerio de Comercio y Turismo.

INE (1985) *'Contabilidad Nacional de España*, Madrid: Instituto Nacional de Estadística.

INE (2002), *La cuenta satélite del turismo de España. Metodología y primeras estimaciones 1996–1999*, Madrid: Instituto Nacional de Estadística.

Johnson, R.L. and E. Moore (1993), 'Tourism impact estimation', *Annals of Tourism Research*, **20**, 279–288.

Jones, C. and M. Munday (2008), 'Tourism satellite accounts and impact assessments: some considerations', *Tourism Analysis*, **13**, 53–69.

Jones, C. and M. Munday (2010), 'Tourism satellite accounts for regions? A review of development issues and an alternative', *Economic Systems Research*, **22** (4), 341–358.

Jones, C., M. Munday and A. Roberts (2003), 'Regional tourism satellite accounts: a useful policy tool?', *Urban Studies*, **40** (13), 2777–2794.

Jones, S. (2007), 'A economia de turismo em Moçambique: tamanho, impacto, e implicaçoes', DNEAP Discussion Paper 55P, Direcçao Nacional de Estudos e Análise de Políticas, Ministério de Planificaçao e Desenvolvimento, República de Moçambique.

Jones, S. (2010), 'The economic contribution of tourism in Mozambique: insights from a social accounting matrix', *Development Southern Africa*, **27** (5), 679–696.

Kehoe, T.J, A. Manresa, P. Noyola, C. Polo and F. Sancho (1988), 'A general equilibrium analysis of the 1986 tax reform in Spain', *European Economic Review*, **32** (2–3), 334–342.

Keuning S.J. and W.A. de Ruijter (1988), 'Guidelines to the construction of a social accounting matrix', *Review of Income and Wealth*, **34** (1), 71–101.

Khan, H., C.F. Seng and W.K. Cheong (1990), 'Tourism multiplier effects on Singapore', *Annals of Tourism Research*, **17**, 408–418.

Kim, S.S., K. Chon and K.Y Chung (2003), 'Convention industry in South Korea: an economic impact analysis', *Tourism Management*, **24**, 533–541.

Konan, D. and H.L. Chan (2010), 'Greenhouse gas emisisions in Hawaii: household and visitor expenditure analysis', *Energy Economics*, **32**, 210–219.

Kweka, J., O. Morrisey and A. Blake (2001), 'Is tourism a key sector in Tanzania? Input-output analysis of income, output, employment and tax revenue', TTRI discussion paper 1001/1. Tourism and Travel Research Institute, University of Nottingham, Nottingham, UK.

Kytzia, S., A. Walz and M. Wegmann (2011), 'How can tourism use land more efficiently? A model based approach to land-use efficiency for tourist destinations', *Tourism Management*, **32**, 629–640.

Lee, C. and T. Taylor (2005), 'Critical reflections on the economic impact assessment of a mega-event: the case of 2002 FIFA Worl Cup', *Tourism Management*, **26**, 595–603.

Leistritz, F.L., W. Ransom-Nelson, R.W. Rathge, R.C. Coon, R.A. Chase, T.A. Hertsgaard, S.H. Murdock, N.E. Toman, R. Sharma and P.S. Yang. (1982), 'North Dakota Economic-Demographic Assessment Model (NEDAM): Technical Description', Ag. Econ. Rpt. No. 158. Fargo: North Dakota State University.

Lenzen, M. (1998), 'Primary gases and greenhouse gases embodied in Australian final demand consumption: an input-output analysis', *Energy Policy*, **26** (6), 265–290.

Lenzen, M. (2001), 'A generalized input-output multiplier calculus for Australia', *Economic System Research*, **13** (1), 66–92.

Lenzen, M. (2003), 'Environmentally important paths, linkages and key sectors in the Australian economy', *Structural Change and Economic Dynamics*, **14**, 1–34.

Lenzen, M., S.A. Murray, B. Corteand and C.J. Dey (2003), 'Environmental assessment including indirect effects: a case study using input–output analysis', *Environmental Assessment Review*, **23**, 263–282.

León, C.J., J.M. Hernández and M. González (2007), 'Economic welfare, the environment and the tourist product lifecycle', *Tourism Economics*, **13** (4), 583–602.

Leontief, W. (1936), 'Quantitative input–output relations in the economic system of the United States', *Review of Economics and Statistics*, **18** (3), 105–125.

Leontief, W. (1937), 'Interrelation of prices, output, savings and investment', *Review of Economics and Statistics*, **19** (3), 109–132.

Leontief, W. (1966), *Input–Output Economics*, New York: Oxford University Press.

Libreros, M., A. Massieu and S. Meis (2006), 'Progress in tourism satellite account implementation and development', *Journal of Travel Research*, **45**, 83–91.

Lin, T. and Y. Sung (1984), 'Tourism and economic diversification in Hong Kong', *Annals of Tourism Research*, **11**, 231–247.
Liu, J. and T. Var (1982), 'Differential multipliers for the accommodation sector', *Tourism Management*, **3** (3), 177–187.
Liu, J., T. Var and A. Timur (1984), 'Tourist–income multipliers for Turkey', *Tourism Management*, **5** (4), 280–287.
Lundie, S., L. Dwyer and P. Forsyth (2009), 'Environmental–economic measures of tourism yield', *Journal of Sustainable Tourism*, **15** (5), 503–519.
Manente, M. and M. Zanette (2010), 'Macroeconomic effects of a VAT reduction in the Italian hotels and restaurants industry', *Economic Systems Research*, **22** (4), 407–425.
Mansury, Y. and T. Hara (2007), 'Impacts of organic food agritourism on a small rural economy: a social accounting matrix approach', *The Journal of Regional and Policy Analysis*, **37** (3), 213–222.
Matheson, V.A. (2002), 'Upon further review: an examination of sporting event economic impact studies', *The Sport Journal*, **5** (1).
Mazumder, M.NH., E. Musa Ahmed, Md. Wahid Murad and A. Quaem Al-Amin (2011), 'Identifying economically inbound markets for Malaysian tourism', *Journal of Vacation Marketing*, **17** (1), 17–31.
McCool, C., J. Thurlow and C. Arndt (2009), 'Documentation of social accounting matrix (SAM) development' in C. Arndt and F. Tarp (eds), *Taxation in a Low Income Economy: The Case of Mozambique*, London: Routledge.
McGregor, P.G., J.K. Swales and Y.P. Yin (1996), 'A long-run interpretation of regional input–output analysis', *Journal of Regional Science* **36** (3), 479–501.
Mescon, T.S. and G.S. Vozikis (1985), 'The economic impact of tourism at the port of Miami', *Annals of Tourism Research*, **12** (4), 515–528.
Miernyk W.H. (1965), *The Elements of Input–Output Analysis*, New York: Random House.
Miller, R.E. and P.D. Blair (1985), *Input–Output Analysis: Foundations and Extensions*, Englewood Cliffs, NJ: Prentice-Hall.
Miller, R.E. and P.D. Blair (2009), *Input–Output Analysis: Foundations and Extensions*, 2nd edition, Cambridge New York: University Press.
Milne, S. (1987), 'Differentiation multipliers', *Annals of Tourism Research*, **14** (3), 498–515.
Mules, T. (1999), 'Estimating the economic impact of an event on a local government area, region, state or territory', in *Valuing Tourism: Methods and Techniques*. Occasional Paper, No. 28. Canberra: Bureau of Tourism Research.
Mules, T. and Faulkner, B. (1996), 'An economic perspective on major events', *Tourism Economics*, **12** (2), 107–117.
Oosterhaven, J. and T. Fan (2006), 'Impact of international tourism on the Chinese economy', *International Journal of Tourism Research*, **8**, 347–354.
Perch-Nielsen, S., A. Sesartic and M. Stucki (2010), 'The greenhouse gas intensity of the tourism sector: the case of Switzerland', *Environmental Science and Policy*, **13**, 131–140.
Pérez-Viéitez, H. and C. Polo (2007), 'Intensidades energéticas en la economía de Cataluña: un análisis IO and SAM', unpublished manuscript, Universidad Autónoma de Barcelona.
Pham, T.D., L. Dwyer and R. Spurr (2009), 'Constructing a regional tourism satellite account: the case of Queensland', *Tourism Analysis*, **13**, 445–460.
Polo, C. and E. Valle (2002), 'Un análisis input–output de la economía balear', *Estadística Española*, **44** (151), 393–444.
Polo, C. and E. Valle (2007), 'Un análisis estructural de la economía balear', *Estadística Española*, **49** (165), 227–257.
Polo, C. and E. Valle (2008a), 'An assessment of the impact of tourism in the Balearic Islands', *Tourism Economics*, **14** (3), 615–630.
Polo, C. and E. Valle (2008b), 'A general equilibrium assessment of impact of a fall in tourism under alternative closure rules: the case of the Balearic Islands', *International Regional Science Review*, **31** (1), 3–34.
Polo, C. and E. Valle (2009), 'Estimating tourism impacts using input–output and SAM model in the Balearic Islands', in A. Matias, P. Nijkamp and M. Sarmiento (eds), *Advances in Tourism Economics. New developments*, Heildelberg: Pysica-Verlag, pp. 121–143.
Polo, C. and E. Valle (2011), 'The weight of tourism in the Balearic Islands: 1983, 1987 and 2004', *Estudios de Economía Aplicada*, **29** (3), 737–754.
Polo, C., V. Ramos, J. Rey-Maqueira, M. Tugores and E. Valle (2006), 'Employment and added value effects of upgrading hotels quality', *Annals of Tourism Research*, **33** (3), 574–577.
Polo, C., V. Ramos, J. Rey-Maqueira, M. Tugores and E. Valle (2008), 'The potential effects of a change in the distribution of tourism expenditure on employment', *Tourism Economics*, **14** (1), 709–725.
Pratt, S. (2011), 'Economic linkages and impacts across the TALC', *Annals of Tourism Research*, in press.
Pyatt, G. (1988), 'A SAM approach to modeling', *Journal of Policy Modeling*, **10** (3), 327–351.

Pyatt, G. and J.I. Round (1977), 'Social accounting matrices for development planning', *Review of Income and Wealth*, **23** (4), 239–264.
Pyatt, G. and J.I. Round (1979), 'Accounting and fixed price multipliers in as social accounting matrix framework', *The Economic Journal*, **89**, 850–873.
Pyatt, G. and E. Thorbecke (1976), *Planning Techniques for a Better Future*, Lausanne, Switzerland: International Labour Office.
Pyatt, G., J. Bharier, R. Lindley, R. Mobro and Y. Sabolo (1972), 'A methodology for development planning applied to Iran', mimeo, Warwick, England.
Pyatt, G., A.R. Roe, J.I. Round, R.M. Lindley and others (1977), *Social Accounting for Development Planning*, Cambridge: Cambridge University Press.
Rasmussen, P.N. (1956), *Studies in Intersectoral Relations*, Amsterdam: North Holland.
Rickman D.S. and R.K. Schwer (1995), 'A comparison of the multipliers of IMPLAN, REMI, and RIMS II: Benchmarking ready-made models for comparison', *The Annals of Regional Science*, **29** (4), 363–374.
Ruíz, A.L. (1985), 'Tourism and the economy of Puerto Rico: an input–output approach', *Tourism Management*, **6** (1), 61–65.
Saayman, M. and A. Saayman (2006), 'Estimating the economic contribution of visitor spending in the Kruger National Park to the regional economy', *Journal of Sustainable Tourism*, **14** (1), 67–81.
Smeral, E. (2006), 'Tourism satellite accounts: a critical assessment', *Journal of Travel Research*, **45**, 92–98.
SNA (1969), *A System of National Accounts*, Studies in Methods, Series F, No. 2 Rev. 3. New York: Statistical Office of the United Nations.
Steenge, A. and A. Van de Steeg (2010), 'Tourism multipliers for a small Caribbean island state; the case of Aruba', *Economic Systems Research*, **22** (4), 359–384.
Stevens, B. and A. Rose (1985), 'Regional input–output methods for tourism impact analysis', in D.B. Propst (ed.), *Assessing the Economic Impacts of Recreation and Tourism*, Asheville, NC: USDA Forest Service, pp. 16–21.
Stone, R. (1961), *Input–Output and National Accounts*, Paris: Organisation for Economic Cooperation and Development.
Stynes, D.J. (1999), 'Guidelines for measuring visitor spending', working paper, Michigan State University, Department of Park, Recreation and Tourism Resources.
Stynes, D.J. (2000), *Michigan Tourism Spending and Economic Impact Model (MITEIM)*, East Lansing, MI: Department of Park, Recreation and Tourism Resources, Michigan State University.
Tabatchnaia-Tamirisa, N., M. Loke, P. Leung and K. Tucker (1997), 'Energy and tourism in Hawaii', *Annals of Tourism Research*, **24** (2), 390–401.
Thorbecke, E. (2000), 'The use of social accounting matrices in modelling, (revised version)', Paper prepared for the 26th General Conference of the International Association for Research in Income and Wealth. Krakow, Poland.
Thorbecke, E. and J. Sengupta (1972), 'A consistency framework for employment output and income distribution projections applied to Colombia', World Bank, Washington.
Tohamy, S. and A. Swinscoe (2000), 'The economic impact of tourism in Egypt', working paper No. 40, The Egyptian Centre for Economic Studies.
Treyz, G.I. (1981), 'Predicting the economic effects of state policy initiatives', *Growth and Change*, **12**, 2–9.
Treyz, G.I., A.F. Friedlaender and B.H. Stevens (1980), 'The employment sector of a regional economic policy simulation model', *Review of Economics and Statistics*, **62**, 63–73.
Treyz, G.I., D.S. Rickman and G. Shao (1991), 'The REMI economic–demographic forecasting and simulation model', *International Regional Science Review*, **14** (3), 221–253.
Tyrrell, T.J. and R.J. Johnston (2001), 'A framework for assessing direct economic impacts of tourist events: distinguishing origins, destinations and causes of expenditures', *Journal of Travel Research*, **40**, 94–100.
United Nations Statistics Division, Statistical Office of the European Communities, Organisation for Economic Co-operation and Development and World Tourism Organization (2008). *2008 Tourism Satellite Account: Recommended Methodological Framework*. Madrid: World Tourism Organization.
Van de Steeg, A.M. and A.E. Steenge (2008), 'Integrating the TSA and input–output methodology in tourism impact studies', paper presented at the Intermediate Input–Output Meeting 2008, Sevilla, Spain, 8–10 July, 2008.
Vanhove, N. (1981), 'Tourism and employment', *International Journal of Tourism Management*, **2** (3), 162–175.
Var, T. and J. Quayson (1985), 'The multiplier impact of tourism in the Okanagan', *Annals of Tourism Research*, **12** (4), 497–514.
Vaughan, D.R., H. Farr and R.W. Slee (2000), 'Estimating and interpreting the local economic benefits of visitor spending: an explanation', *Leisure Studies*, **19** (2), 95–118.
Wagner, J.E. (1997), 'Estimating the economic impacts of tourism', *Annals of Tourism Research*, **24** (3), 592–608.

Wanhill, R.C. (1988), 'Tourism multipliers under capacity constraint', *The Service Industries Journal*, **8** (2), 136–142.

West, G.R. (1993), 'Economic significance of tourism in Queensland', *Annals of Tourism Research*, **20** (3), 490–504.

West, G. and A. Gamage (2001), 'Macro-effects of tourism in Victoria, Australia: a nonlinear input–output approach', *Journal of Travel Research*, **40** (1), 101–109.

Wolff, E.N. (1985), 'Industrial composition, interindustry effect and the U.S. productivity slowdown', *Review of Economics and Statistics*, **LXVII** (2), 268–277.

WSDA (2007), *Washington State Fairs and Other Fairground Activities Economic Impact Analysis*, Washington State: Northern Economics.

13 CGE modeling
Larry Dwyer and Tien Duc Pham

INTRODUCTION

There is now an extensive literature on evaluating the economic impacts of tourism. This literature seeks to show how the impacts of changes in tourism expenditure, due perhaps to improved destination marketing and promotion, development of special events or external shocks such as terrorist attacks, can be evaluated in economic terms. An economic impact analysis estimates the changes that take place in an economy due to some existing or proposed project, action, event, or policy resulting in increased income and expenditure for a range of different stakeholders, many of whom are not directly connected with the tourism industry.

As typically employed in tourism research and policy analysis, economic impact analyses trace the flows of spending associated with tourism activity in an economy through business, households and government to identify the resulting changes in economic variables such as sales, output, government tax revenues, household income, value added, and employment. A major objective of such estimates has been to inform policy makers as to the appropriate allocation of resources both within the tourism sector itself and between tourism and other industry sectors.

The effects of tourist expenditure on a tourism destination/region can be estimated using economic models that identify and quantify the linkages between the different sectors of the local economy and the linkages with other regions in the economy. Almost every industry in the economy is affected to some extent by the indirect and induced effects of the initial tourist expenditure. In CGE models, these flow-on effects determine the impact of a shock on all industries including the tourism sector in the economy. Important variables that represent the net impacts of shocks include Gross Domestic Product (GDP) (or Gross Regional Product (GRP)), value added, factor incomes, and employment. For any given injection of tourism expenditure, the increment to value-added and employment in the region will vary according to several features of the economy (Dwyer et al., 2010). These include:

- the particular industries that are the recipients of the direct expenditure
- strengths of the business linkages between tourism and other industry sectors
- the structure of the model employed
- the assumed factor constraints
- the import content of consumer goods and inputs to production
- the production and consumption relationships assumed
- changes in the prices of inputs and outputs
- changes in the exchange rate
- the workings of the labor market, and
- the government fiscal policy stance.

CGE models represent world best practice in assessing economy-wide economic impacts of changes in tourism expenditure. Proponents of CGE modeling for tourism impact analysis point out that the economy-wide, interactive effects must be taken into account in determining the impacts of increased tourism expenditure on a destination.

NATURE OF THE TECHNIQUE AND ITS EVOLUTION

The Structure of a CGE model

Computable general equilibrium (CGE) models combine the abstract Walrasian general equilibrium structure, formalized by Arrow and Debreu (1954), Debreu (1959), and Arrow and Hahn (1971), with realistic economic data to solve numerically for the levels of supply, demand and price that support equilibrium across a specified set of markets. CGE modeling involves a mathematical specification of simultaneous relationships within the economy. Many features can be built into this framework, to tailor it to the different conditions that characterize alternative real world circumstances. In this way, the framework provides a widely encompassing means of evaluating the effects of policy changes and exogenous shocks on resource allocation and can also permit assessment of the distributional effects of such changes. CGE models treat an economy as a whole, allowing for feedback effects of one sector on another. They represent the economy as a system of flows of goods and services between sectors (Bandara, 1991; Costa, 1998; Shoven and Whalley, 1992).

CGE models consist of a set of equations characterizing the production, consumption, trade, and government activities of the economy. There are four types of equations in a typical CGE model that are solved simultaneously. These are (McDougall 1995):

> *Equilibrium conditions* for each market ensure that supply is equal to demand for each good, service, factor of production, and for foreign exchange. Assuming flexible prices and wages, this enables factors of production, such as labor and capital, imports, and exports to be modeled (although some sticky prices can be assumed such as might occur in the labor market).
>
> *Income–expenditure identities* ensure that the economic model is a closed system. All earnings must be accounted for through expenditure or savings. These conditions apply to all private households, the government, firms, and any other economic agents that are modeled. These define various macroeconomic identities such as aggregate employment and the components of gross domestic product.
>
> *Behavioral relationships* state how economic agents (consumers, suppliers, investors, and so on) acting in their own best interests can lead to changes in price and income levels. For example, businesses will seek to maximize profits. Firms can retain a share of their profits. Their financing can proceed through financial markets or banks. Consumers will look for lowest prices for equivalent products. Households can deduce their supply of labor from the maximization of their utility function. The zero-pure-profits condition for production is assumed. Resource allocation is via market forces – where markets behave imperfectly unemployment may increase.

The labor market can be segmented between industries, urban and rural areas, or regions. Then, migration costs prevent perfect and instantaneous arbitrage between the wages of workers with the same skill but working in different industries. Wages can be bounded from under by a legal minimum wage. If it is above the equilibrium wages for some skills, the workers with these skills will partly be unemployed. Increasing government expenditures are met either by raising taxes or borrowing, with implications for the expenditure of other economic agents.

Production functions determine how much output is produced for any given level of factor employment. With assumptions regarding market structure, these determine what levels of labor employment, capital usage, and intermediate input usage are required to satisfy a given level of output for a given set of prices. The production assumptions allow substitution between intermediate inputs and factors of production as prices and wages change. The production functions can include firm-specific resources, which allows for decreasing returns to scale. Or they can include fixed costs, which allows for increasing returns to scale.

A CGE model is a very versatile structure, which can easily be adapted to the special features of any economy, to the questions that are asked, and to the data, which are available. Its assumptions can easily be changed so that the results of a simulation can be interpreted, for instance, as describing a short-term or long-run equilibrium.

Model Database

Figure 13.1 is a schematic representation of the CGE core's input–output database, revealing the basic structure of the CGE core. The exegesis herein is based on the study by Peter et al. (1996). The model, known as 'MMRF' divides the Australian economy into eight regional economies representing the six States and two Territories. This model has been used in various studies of the economic impact of tourism in Australia (Adams and Parmenter, 1999; Dwyer et al., 2000, 2003).

The columns in Figure 13.1 identify the following agents:

- domestic producers divided into J industries in Q regions;
- investors divided into J industries in Q regions;
- a single representative household for each of the Q regions;
- an aggregate foreign purchaser of exports;
- another demand category corresponding to Q regional governments; and
- another demand category corresponding to Federal government demands in the Q regions.

The rows show the structure of the purchases made by each of the agents identified in the columns. Each of the I commodity types identified in the model can be obtained within the region, from other regions, or imported from overseas. The source-specific commodities are used by industries as inputs to current production and capital formation, are consumed by households and governments, and are exported. Only domestically

		ABSORPTION MATRIX					
		1	2	3	4	5	6
		Producers	Investors	Household	Export	Regional Govt.	Federal Govt.
	Size	← $J \times Q$ →	← $J \times Q$ →	← Q →	← 1 →	← Q →	← Q →
Basic flows	↑ $I \times S$ ↓	BAS1	BAS2	BAS3	BAS4	BAS5	BAS6
Margins	↑ $I \times S \times R$ ↓	MAR1	MAR2	MAR3	MAR4	MAR5	MAR6
Taxes	↑ $I \times S$ ↓	TAX1	TAX2	TAX3	TAX4	TAX5	TAX6
Labour	↑ M ↓	LABR					
Capital	↑ 1 ↓	CPTL					
Land	↑ 1 ↓	LAND					
Other Costs	↑ 1 ↓	OCTS					

I = number of commodities

J = number of industries

M = number of occupation types

Q = number of domestic regions

R = number of commodities used as margins

S = 9:8 × domestic regions plus 1 × foreign import

Source: Peter et al. (1996).

Figure 13.1   The CGE core input–output database

produced goods appear in the export column. *R* of the domestically produced goods are used as margin services (domestic trade and transport and communication) which are required to transfer commodities from their sources to their users. Commodity taxes are payable on the purchases. As well as intermediate inputs, current production requires inputs of three categories of primary factors: labor (divided into *M* occupations), fixed capital, and agricultural land. The other costs category covers various miscellaneous industry expenses. Each cell in the input–output table contains the name of the corresponding matrix of the values (in some base year) of flows of commodities, indirect taxes or primary factors to a group of users. For example, MAR2 is a five-dimensional array showing the cost of the *R* margins services on the flows of *I* goods, both domestically and imported (*S*), to *I* investors in *Q* regions.

The theoretical structure of MMRF includes: demand equations are required for type of user; equations determining commodity and factor prices; market clearing equations; definitions of commodity tax rates. The CGE core equations can be grouped according to the following classification:

- producer's demands for produced inputs and primary factors;
- demands for inputs to capital creation;
- household demands;
- export demands;
- government demands;
- demands for margins;
- zero pure profits in production and distribution;
- market-clearing conditions for commodities and primary factors;
- indirect taxes;
- regional and national macroeconomic variables and price indices.

Input Demands: Current Production

Figure 13.2 illustrates the structure of a production nest for an industry in a regional economy. At the top level, the producer combines intermediate inputs, primary inputs, and all other costs in the constant shares relationship, which is often referred to as the Leontief technique in CGE modeling. For each intermediate input, the input can be sourced from the domestic economy, or from overseas countries depending on which source is *relatively* cheaper. This is governed by the constant elasticity of substitution in the production nest between *imports* and *domestic* in Figure 13.2. In a similar approach, the producer then chooses the cheapest region among all regions in the domestic economy. This is represented at the bottom of the substitution level among *region 1* to *region 8* in Figure 13.2.

The primary input bundle is also a combination of labor, capital, and land using the CES functional form in order to minimize the cost of this bundle.

Investment Demands

Capital creators for each regional sector combine inputs to form units of capital. In choosing these inputs they minimize costs subject to technologies similar to that in Figure 13.2. Figure 13.3 shows the nesting structure for the production of new units of fixed capital. Capital is assumed to be produced with inputs of domestically produced and imported commodities. No primary factors are used directly as inputs to capital formation. The use of primary factors in capital creation is recognized through inputs of the construction commodity (service) (Peter et al., 1996, p. 13).

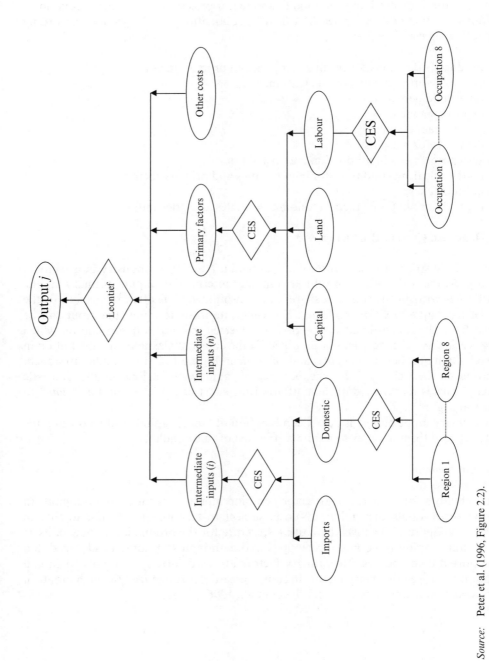

Source: Peter et al. (1996, Figure 2.2).

Figure 13.2   Production nest

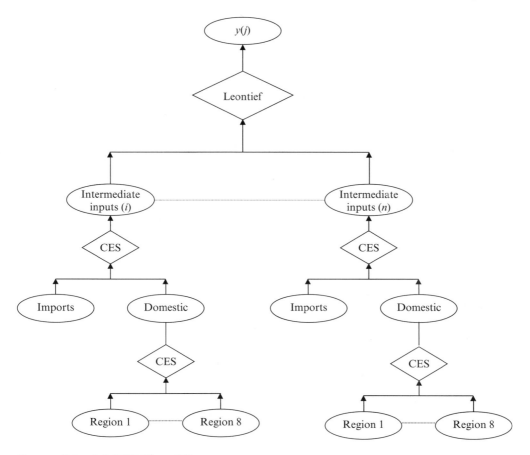

Source: Peter et al. (1996, Figure 2.3).

Figure 13.3 Structure of investment demand

Household Demands

MMRF has eight representative household sectors, one for each state. Total household expenditure in a region is driven by the regional household disposable income (a Keynesian approach) and the changes of the number of household in the region. Figure 13.4, household sector, indicates that the nesting in the household demands is nearly the same as the nesting in the investment structure, except that MMRF adopts the Stone–Geary utility function at the top level instead of a Leontief function for investment and current production (Adams, 2008; Peter et al., 1996).

Foreign Export Demands

Export demands are divided into two groups: traditional export and non-traditional export. The traditional exports include industries such as agriculture and mining that

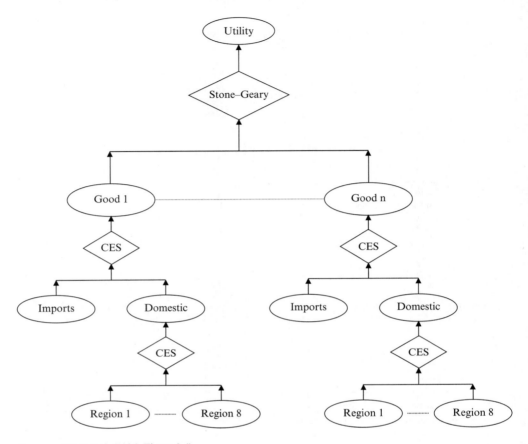

Source: Peter et al. (1996, Figure 2.4).

Figure 13.4   Household consumption nest

have large export shares in the total exports. Each traditional export commodity is modeled to have a downward sloping demand curve, driven by individual constant price elasticity for each commodity. Thus, each traditional export commodity is free to respond to price signal independently. In contrast, all non-traditional export commodities are assumed to move together as a group to maintain fixed shares in the total (aggregate) non-traditional export. The aggregate non-traditional export is modeled to have a downward sloping demand curve with a constant price elasticity. Thus, each non-traditional export commodity cannot respond freely to price signals as in the case of traditional export commodities. However, the model does have a mechanism to allow for changes to the composition of the non-traditional export commodities when needed.

Government Demands

There are two government demand groups in MMRF: one by the Federal Government and one by the State Government. The modeling of government demands is straight forward. The Federal Government demands are driven by aggregate national household consumption, while the regional government demands are driven by the regional aggregate household consumption.

Demands for Margins

Two margin commodities are recognized in MMRF: transport and communication and finance. These commodities, in addition to being consumed directly by the users (e.g., consumption of transport when taking holidays or commuting to work), are also consumed to facilitate trade (e.g., the use of transport to ship commodities from point of production to point of consumption). The latter type of demand for transport and communication and finance are the so-called demands for margins. The margin demand equations in MMRF indicate that the demands for margins are proportional to the commodity flows with which the margins are associated (Peter et al., 1996, p. 18).

Prices

The price system underlying MMRF is based on two assumptions: (1) that there are no pure profits in the production or distribution of commodities, and (2) that the price received by the producer is uniform across all customers.

The MMRF has two types of price equations: (1) zero pure profits in current production, capital creation and importing and (2) zero pure profits in the distribution of commodities to users. Zero pure profits in current production, capital creation, and importing is imposed by setting unit prices received by producers of commodities (i.e., the commodities' basic values) equal to unit costs. Zero pure profits in the distribution of commodities is imposed by setting the prices paid by users equal to the commodities' basic value plus commodity taxes and the cost of margins (Peter et al., 1996, p. 18).

Market-clearing Equations for Commodities

These impose the condition that demand equals supply for domestically produced margin and nonmargin commodities and imported commodities respectively. The output of regional industries producing margin commodities must equal the direct demands by the model's six users and their demands for the commodity as a margin. The outputs of the nonmargin regional industries are equal to the direct demands of the model's six users. Import supplies are equal to the demands of the users excluding foreigners, i.e., all exports involve some domestic value added (Peter et al., p. 20).

Indirect Taxes

For each user, the sales-tax equations in MMRF allow for variations in tax rates across commodities, their sources and their destinations.

Regional Incomes and Expenditures

At the aggregate level, Gross Regional Product from the expenditure and income sides is calculated as follows.

Gross Regional Product (expenditure side) =

+	Total household consumption	(C)
+	Total investment	(I)
+	Total government consumption	(G)
+	Total overseas export	(E)
+	Total inter-state export	(E_IS)
−	Total overseas imports	(M)
−	Total inter-state imports	(M_IS)

Gross Regional Product (income side) =

+	Total wages
+	Total gross operating surplus
+	Total net commodity taxes
+	Total net production taxes

Model Closures

Simulation results from CGE models depend largely on the adopted assumptions that are often referred to as a *closure*. For a comparative static CGE model, the solution path over time is not known. Rather, it is assumed that the economy operates within a certain timeframe either a long run or a short run, depending on the purpose of a simulation.

The two main assumptions that characterize a *short-run* closure are: (1) the economy operates in a timeframe that wage rates are rigid, changes to labor demand will be reflected by changes in employment, as often this is not long enough for sale contracts to be renegotiated for higher commodity prices in order to take into account any necessary changes to wage rates that producers have to pay to their employees; (2) there is not enough time for capital stock to be adjusted; return to capital (or the rate of return) will adjust to reflect changes in demand for capital. As investment is tied to capital stock, in this short-run closure investment is mainly fixed. In addition, the short-run closure also assumes that regional migration does not occur, therefore regional population remained unchanged. Any changes to the demand for labor will be satisfied by changes in the regional unemployment rates while labor participation rates are kept constant. In order to isolate the impact of an increase in tourism demand, all unnecessary stimuli to the regional economies are minimized thus regional government consumptions, technological changes and inventory (stocks) are fixed. A positive shock is imposed to increase tourism demand for individual selected specific tourist. Total import is determined by the domestic income level as well as how expensive domestic goods are, in relative to import prices. These movements of export and import determine the net balance of trade. Figure 13.5 presents the macro assumptions of the short-run closure. Elements in the rectangles are those which are fixed (i.e., exogenously set at zero) while the ovals are determined during simulation.

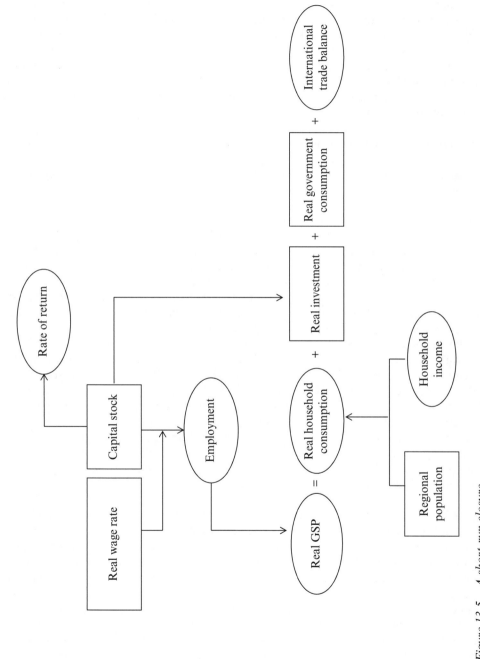

Figure 13.5   A short-run closure

The *long-run* closure adopts the opposite assumptions. For the labor market, real wage rates are now fully flexible while employment is fixed. The whole economy cannot have more than the total aggregate employment level that the labor market can offer. Any demand higher than this will be reflected by a rise in the real wage. In an adverse situation, the fixed employment implies that whoever wants a job will get employment as long as they are prepared to take whatever wage rate that is affordable by the producers. Implicitly, this assumes full employment in the economy. Thus, in a long-run closure, the total employment at the national will not change under the impact of any shocks introduced to the model. For the capital market, the economy-wide capital stock is now allowed to change in response to the demand of capital in the economy, while the national rate of return is fixed.

Static Versus Dynamic CGE Models

The majority of CGE models can be separated into two broad categories, *comparative static* and *dynamic*.

Comparative static models focus on the reactions of the economy at only one point in time. For policy analysis, results from such a model are often interpreted as showing the reaction of the economy in some future period to some external shock or policy change that the adjustment path is not known. Often the adjustment path is assumed to be in either a short-run or a long-run scenario. In the short run, it is assumed that capital stocks are fixed and the real wages are not flexible enough to settle the labor market. In contrast, the long-run scenario allows enough time for capital to build up such that economy-wide rate of return is restored; and that, real wages can adjust so that anyone who would like to work will find a job. In a favorable condition, real wages will increase to reflect a higher demand for labor; and, in an adverse condition, real wages will decrease to restore the "full employment" level in the economy. Using the ORANI-F mode (Horridge et al., 1993), Adams and Parmenter (1995) showed the effects on the Australian economy of additional (ten percent) expansion of inbound tourism in a long-run scenario. In contrast, Blake (2003b) used the Nottingham model in the short-run assumptions to measure the impacts of foot and mouth disease on the UK economy. Short-run scenarios are assumed to take place over 1–2 years. The long-run assumptions are applicable to adjustment over 3–5 years or longer. This is the approximate time scale under which all economic adjustments will have been made following an exogenous change.

Dynamic CGE models explicitly trace each variable through time, often at annual intervals so that the adjustment path of the economy can be examined. The path comprises a series of simulations, throughout a sequence of years (often referred to as recursive dynamic), linked by intertemporal equations describing investment decisions and capital accumulation. The model explicitly generates a time path of the economy following the change in the policy or introduction of a supply side or demand side shock. In a recursive dynamic scenario, it requires two series of simulations to measure the impacts. The first series portrays a business as usual case (baseline) and the second series incorporates the policy shocks that take the economy away from the baseline scenario. The deviation of the policy scenario from the baseline reflects the impacts of the policy on the economy.

Dynamic models can be used to forecast the structure of the economy as well as to assess the effects of policy and other shocks over a period of time. Blake (2005) uses a forward looking dynamic model to project the economic impacts of the London Olympics 2012, under different dynamic conditions. In particular, an unanticipated shock differs significantly to an anticipated shock. He demonstrates that the benefits of tourism are lower when a tourism boom is anticipated and this is of particular concern when considering the economic benefits of future events that can be anticipated, such as major sporting and other special events. One area where a dynamic approach is particularly useful is in modeling the effects of climate change mitigation policies (Hoque et al., 2009). Dynamic CGE models can provide a richer set of information than that available from static models, depending on the assumptions that are made about the changes that are occurring in the economy. However, they are more challenging to construct and solve since they require for instance that future changes be predicted for all exogenous variables, not just those directly targeted by a possible policy change.

The majority of case studies of CGE applications employed in a tourism context to date are static. While dynamic models can certainly offer the time path of adjustment over time, static models are essentially revealing the direction of impacts at the industry and tourism destination level that are the major concerns of policy makers with less complexity of requirement than a dynamic application. Thus, comparative static simulations are often used in practice.

CGE models can be formulated at a number of spatial levels:

- Single-country models such as ORANI (Dixon et al., 1982) or MONASH (Dixon and Rimmer, 2002) with extensions for regional disaggregation using a top-down approach.
- Stand-alone models of regional economies (Meagher and Parmenter, 1990).
- Multi-regional models such as MONASH-MRF (Adams, 2008).
- Multi-country models (Hertel, 1997).

Models of one or more of these types would be suitable for assessing most tourism impact issues.

BACKGROUND AND TYPES OF PROBLEMS THAT CGE MODELING IS DESIGNED TO HANDLE

CGE models are a standard tool of empirical analysis. They are widely used to analyse the aggregate welfare and distributional impacts of policies whose effects may be transmitted through multiple markets, or contain mixtures of different tax, subsidy, quota, or transfer instruments. CGE analysis is being employed to explore the economic impacts of policy initiatives and frameworks, and broader changes as diverse as hazardous waste management, trade liberalization, tariff protection, environment–economy interactions, structural adjustment, agricultural stabilization programs, technological change, labor market deregulation, financial market deregulation, fiscal reform, development planning, macroeconomic reform, economic transition, international capital linkages, environmental regulation, public infrastructure, and industry sector studies (Dixon and Parmenter, 1996; Gunning and Keyzer, 1995; Harrison et al., 2000).

CGE models are now increasingly used in tourism economics analysis and policy formulation (Dwyer et al., 2004). Some advantages are:

- Computable general equilibrium (CGE) models are well suited to tourism analysis and policy, given their multi-sectoral basis. In contrast to partial equilibrium approaches, CGE models can take account of the interrelationships between tourism, other sectors in the domestic economy and foreign producers and consumers.
- CGE modeling can be tailored to alternative conditions, such as flexible or fixed prices, alternative exchange rate regimes, differences in the degree of mobility of factors of production and different types of competition.
- CGE models can be used to quantify the effects of actual policies, such as changes in taxation, subsidies or government borrowing, as well as predicting the effects of a range of alternative policies or exogenous expenditure shocks. They can be used to estimate the impacts of changes in tourism expenditure under a range of alternative macroeconomic scenarios; tailoring them to alternative conditions such as flexible or fixed prices, various exchange rate regimes, differences in the degree of mobility of factors of production, different government fiscal policy stances, and different types of competition.
- CGE models are helpful to tourism policy makers who seek to use them to provide guidance about a wide variety of 'What if?' questions, arising from a wide range of domestic or international expenditure shocks or alternative policy scenarios.

APPLICATIONS OF CGE MODELING TO TOURISM

A good summary of the usefulness of CGE modeling in tourism analysis and policy development is provided by Blake et al. (2006). To highlight some of the uses of CGE modeling in tourism contexts, we classify them herein under the following headings:

- Economic impacts of changes in inbound tourism
- Economic impacts of tourism crises
- Economic impacts of special events
- Evaluation of economic policy

While the articles highlighted below comprise only some of the research by tourism economists using CGE models, they indicate the types of issues that are being addressed in the literature.

Economic Impacts of Changes in Inbound Tourism

CGE models provide information on the structural effects of tourism expansion. Adams and Parmenter (1995, 1999) were among the first researchers to provide empirical evidence to support Copeland's (1991) theoretical argument that some sectors benefit and some lose as the result of tourism expansion. They used the ORANI-F, a 117-sector general equilibrium model for Australia, to assess the effects on the Australian economy of additional expansion of inbound tourism. To highlight the effects on the economy of the increased international tourism, Adams and Parmenter compared the Australian economy in a scenario with ten percentage point increase in inbound tourism higher than the tourism growth in the base case projection of the Australian economy. The effects of the additional tourism growth rate were reported as the differences between the amended and bases case simulations.

The tourism expansion stimulates capital formation and generates an increase in the rate of growth of investment. Holding both employment growth and technical change at their base-case rates, there is a small increase in real GDP. Growth in private consumption is reduced slightly due to an increase in income tax rates. To maintain a fixed Public Sector Borrowing Requirement (PSBR), income tax rates must rise to offset rapid growth in government investment expenditure. With additional growth in aggregate real domestic absorption (consumption plus investment) exceeding additional growth in real GDP, there is an increase in the balance of trade deficit. The import content of the induced investment contributes directly to the deterioration in the trade balance. In addition, an appreciation of the real exchange rate is required to make room for the increased level of domestic demand. This generates substitution towards imports and reduces the traditional exports of mining and agricultural commodities. This reduced export growth improves the terms of trade and explains why growth in the aggregate volume of exports increases by only a very small percentage. The improvement in the terms of trade and the reduction in the activity levels of land intensive export industries allow an increase in the real wage rate.

At the sectoral level, there will be losers as well as gainers from the expansion in inbound tourism. Four groups of industries are distinguished.

Service industries catering directly to international tourists (e.g., air transport, restaurants, and hotels). These are strongly stimulated by the additional expansion in tourism. This strengthens further the industries' base-case growth implied by the strong growth assumed for tourism in the base forecasts.

Industries indirectly supplying tourism-related activities (e.g., aircraft maintenance and construction). These are also stimulated by the additional expansion of tourism. Except for construction, most of them also enjoy strong prospects in the base forecasts because of base-case growth of tourism. In the base forecasts, since investment growth is weak, especially residential investment, the additional expansion of tourism eases the adjustment problems that the construction sector would otherwise have experienced.

Non-tourism exporters (e.g., agriculture, mining, food and metals processing). Growth prospects in these industries are reduced by the appreciation of the real exchange rate produced by additional tourism expansion. However, the base forecasts are characterized by exchange rate depreciation, giving the export industries good prospects. The adverse effects of the additional tourism expansion should thus be easily accommodated.

Import-competing industries (e.g., transport equipment, chemicals, textiles, clothing and footwear). Prospects in these industries are reduced by the tourism induced appreciation of the exchange rate.

The authors also explored the consequences for the different states within Australia. The appreciation of the exchange rate adversely impacts on export-oriented activities including mining and agriculture. Three heavily export-oriented states – Queensland, Western Australia and Tasmania – are net losers from general tourism stimulation nationally.

Using a CGE model based on the ORANI model, Narayan (2003, 2004) simulated the long-run impact of a 10 percent increase in visitor expenditures on Fiji's economy. The study indicates that, for an island developing country such as Fiji, an expansion in inbound tourism can generate overall growth in real GDP but effects on the real exchange rate, real wages, and the CPI imply that the gains to tourism-related sectors are offset to some extent by losses in traditional export and import competing industries.

Zhou et al. (1997) analysed the impacts on the Hawaii state economy of a 10 percent projected *decrease* in visitor expenditure. This is projected to result in: a reduction in GSP; a small reduction in the general level of prices; output reductions in the industries servicing tourist needs, and in traditional exports, manufacturing, construction and services; a reduction in imports, particularly those associated with tourist related industries; a fall in the balance of trade; and reduced employment in the hotel industry, restaurants and bars, and transportation.

CGE modeling can be used to develop "economy-wide" yield measures of tourist "worth". Economy-wide yield measures indicate the bottom line for the economy from tourist spending when all inter-industry effects have taken place (Dwyer et al., 2007). Dwyer and Forsyth (2008) estimated three economy-wide yield measures associated with 14 of Australia's major tourism origin countries and for three regions. The yield measures were Gross Value Added (GVA), Gross Operating Surplus (GOS), and Employment. The economic impacts were then converted to yield measures by determining the economy wide effects of an additional tourist from each market. Yield measures based on CGE modeling can inform organizations in both the private and public sector about effective allocation of marketing resources and types of tourism development that meet operator and destination manager objectives (Dwyer and Forsyth, 2008).

Economic Impacts of Tourism Crises

Blake et al. (2003b) investigated the economy-wide effects of foot and mouth disease (FMD) in the UK using their 'Nottingham' CGE model. The simulations showed that FMD had considerable impacts not only on sectors directly related to tourism, but also on other industries. The policy of maintaining FMD-free status supported meat exports, but it cost the UK tourism industry substantially. The CGE tourism model of the UK economy showed that the effects of the tourism decreases were to reduce GDP in the UK by more than the loss of agricultural production. The authors concluded that a policy geared towards supporting tourism would have been far less costly than the government's policy of supporting agricultural exports by means of slaughtering animals and prohibiting access to many rural areas. The implication is that policy makers need to adopt a whole of industry approach to policy making relating to FMD and in formulating agricultural policies.

Blake and Sinclair (2003) modeled the impacts on tourism in the USA of actual and proposed policy responses of the US Government following the terrorist attacks of September 11, 2001. A major finding was that an airline production subsidy outperforms all other types in each of the criteria with the exception of the number of accommodation jobs lost. However, an airline subsidy fails to take account of job losses outside the sector that are caused by the fall in demand from tourists who would have traveled by air. The researchers also found that subsidies to accommodation establishments were reasonably effective at boosting GDP and saving jobs in this sector. These subsidies are significantly more effective than those allocated to catering and entertainment. In fact, subsidies to the latter can have the effect of worsening GDP and labor and capital adjustment, as they encourage workers to move out of the airline and accommodation sectors, thereby increasing the job losses in these sectors.

In a context of uncertainty over traveler security, tourism experienced two major crises in 2003 – the Iraq War and SARS. Acknowledging that the relative impacts of a complex array of impacts on travel decision making are almost impossible to dissect. Dwyer et al. (2006c) explored the economic effects of the SARS crisis on tourism to Australia. Although the crisis resulted in less inbound tourism, it also led to reduced outbound tourism. The net economic impacts on the nation depend upon the extent to which canceled or postponed outbound travel are allocated to savings, to domestic tourism, or to the purchases of other goods and services. Using a computable general equilibrium model of the Australian economy, simulations of the impacts of the events suggest that the net effects were not as severe as were perceived by tourism stakeholders.

Pambudi et al. (2009) employed a multi-regional CGE model for Indonesia to estimate the short-run effect of a decline in tourism following the 2002 Bali bombings on the Indonesian economy. The results suggest that of Indonesia's 26 provinces, GRP of Bali is worst affected by a negative shock to tourism exports followed by other popular tourist destinations, such as Jakarta and Yogyakarta. In Bali employment fell by 4.93 percent, household consumption by 4.68 percent, investment by 6.79 percent, exports by 16.34 percent, and imports by 8.95 percent. Within Bali the tourism-related and non-tradable sectors contain the worst affected industries while export-oriented industries, such as textiles, clothing, and footwear, and import-competing industries, such as machinery and electronics expand. The researchers concluded that policy makers and lending agencies should take into account not only the regional macroeconomic implications of the bombing, but also the sectoral results in allocating compensation packages. The results indicate that while the sectors that are most closely tied to tourism are the worst affected by the bombings, some sectors may grow even though they are in regions that lose overall. For example, while the Balinese hotel and restaurant sector shrinks by 7.7 percent, machinery and electronics grow by 2.13 percent. Thus, to have most effect, assistance should not just be allocated on a regional basis, but be sector specific.

Meng et al. (2010) studied the effects of the Global Financial Crisis (GFC) on Singapore. The CGE simulation results demonstrate that at the macro level, the CFC tends to have large negative effects on Singapore's tourism and on the Singapore economy. Although almost all economic variables are negatively affected, total exports benefit greatly. At the industry level, a negative tourism shock impacts severely on the tourism-related sectors, impacts only slightly on sectors weakly linked to tourism, but tourism-competing sectors expand. In commodity market, prices and outputs decrease for most products but real household consumption and exports increase. In the labor market, low-skilled workers are adversely affected, but some occupational groups benefit at the expense of others.

Li et al. (2010) studied the effects of the GFC on China. They note that while headline figures show that international tourism is suffering as a consequence of this economic crisis, domestic tourism is larger than in many countries and impacts through this market could be larger than through international tourism. In the context of China's tourism, the authors test the common viewpoint that an increase in domestic tourism could compensate a decline in inbound tourism, which supports the policy of focusing on the development of domestic tourism. They evaluate the magnitude of economic impact of the economic slowdown on China's tourism using computable general equilibrium modeling and then bring forward some policy suggestions on the development of China's tourism.

Pham et al. (2010) used a sub-state CGE model of the Australian economy, known as TERM (Horridge et al., 2003), and elaborated the model to incorporate the inbound and domestic tourism sectors explicitly for five tourism destinations in Australia. The model was then used to analyse the impacts of induced impacts of climate change via tourism on the destination economies. The study emphasizes that while direct climate change will have adverse impacts on the tourism destinations, the further induced impacts of climate change on tourism will exacerbate the total impacts on the tourism destinations. If the induced impacts are not taken into account, it most likely that the climate change impacts on tourism destinations are underestimated.

The findings from the above studies suggest that government subsidies can be effective in limiting the adverse effects of a major tourism crisis. However, the relative effectiveness of the different policy responses varies considerably. The overall conclusion is that directing subsidies to the sector that is most severely affected by the crisis is the most efficient policy response in terms of both GDP and the total number of jobs saved. Policy makers should be very careful in their decisions as to which sectors to assist, as the provision of subsidies for those relatively unaffected can even be counterproductive.

Economic Impacts of Special Events

Adam Blake has used a dynamic CGE model of the UK and London economies to forecast the economic impacts of the London 2012 Olympics (Blake, 2005). While the overall impacts on GDP and employment in the UK are positive, the simulations reveal that there is a loss of GDP and employment in the areas outside London. Reasons for this include: spending in London by UK residents from outside London visiting the games; movement of workers, whether migrants, commuter, or temporary migrants, into London because of higher wages in the capital; and the provision of Lottery funding, which in effect transfers money to London. The study also shows that the impact of the games will vary significantly across different sectors of the UK economy. Sectors that expand include construction, passenger land transport, business services, hotels, and restaurants. Sectors that are not directly related to the games may contract in size indirectly as a result of hosting the games. These include manufacturing, agriculture, fishing, and other services. However, these results are relative to the "No Games" scenario in which a substantial amount of growth takes place in all sectors of the economy. Thus, while no sector is predicted to contract in the time span modeled, some will grow less because of the impact of hosting the Olympics.

The simulations indicate that any changes to the UK economy associated with the Olympics 2012 will be comparatively small. Even in the Olympic year, the total economy wide effect for the UK is only 0.066 percent of total UK GDP at 2004 prices. The results of Blake's study indicate that a mega event, even of the size of the summer Olympics, is unlikely to provide any substantial boost to either the national or host-region economy.

That the type of model used to estimate the economic impacts of special events has a substantial effect on the assessment results became evident in a study by Dwyer et al. (2005, 2006a, 2006b) which compared the results of using CGE and input–output modeling to estimate the economic impacts of a special event held in Australia, namely, the Qantas Formula One Grand Prix. The simulations reveal that input–output modeling projects a much greater impact on real output for both New South Wales and Australia (A\$112.0 million and A\$120.1 million), as compared to CGE modeling (A\$56.70 million and A\$24.46 million). The output multiplier for New South Wales is 2.185 using the input–output model but only 1.106 using the CGE model. For Australia as a whole, the input–output model yields an output multiplier of 2.343 whereas the CGE model yields a substantially smaller output multiplier of 0.477. The two models give different employment projections also. The projected increase in employment using an input–output model is 521 (full-time equivalent) jobs in NSW and 592 jobs throughout Australia. Using a CGE model the projected employment effects are 318 jobs and 129 jobs, respectively.

Madden (2006) employed a multiregional CGE model to examine the effects of a mega sporting event, the Sydney 2000 summer Olympics. Simulations were conducted for three phases over a 12-year period. Careful attention was paid to the presence of constraints on labor supply and capital and on the sources of savings funding Olympic investments. Simulations were conducted under the assumption that no effects from the games remain on the debt position of Australian governments or the nation's external debt 5 years after the Sydney Games. The results indicate that provided there is not too large a financial loss on the games, inclusive of construction costs, a modest positive impact on the state hosting the games can occur. The degree to which this positive impact comes at the expense of other states depends crucially on assumed labor-market conditions.

A study by Li et al. (2011) takes the first step in applying CGE modeling to forecasting the economic contribution of tourism generated by the Beijing Olympics. The paper includes two types of estimations: *ex ante* and *ex post*. The *ex-ante* estimation was conducted before the Beijing Olympics and thus predicted the impact of international tourism based on historical data, such as previous literature and historical statistics. The *ex-post* estimation was conducted several months after the Beijing Olympics and the estimation was based on up-to-date statistics published by the China National Tourism Administration. The economic impact generated from the two types of estimations is compared. It was found that, while the economic impact of international tourism was predicted to be positive in the *ex-ante* estimation, this impact was found to be negative in the *ex-post* estimation.

Giesecke and Madden (2011) explored the issue of whether the large economic benefits predicted for Olympics host countries actually materialize. They re-examined the Sydney 2000 Olympics via historical modeling with a multiregional dynamic CGE model. Their modeling encompasses the four key economic dimensions of the games: (1) games operations; (2) construction of games facilities and associated financing; (3) spending by interstate visitors in the games year; and (4) spending by foreign visitors in the games year. It was found that the Sydney Olympics generated a loss in Australian real private and public consumption in present value terms of $2.1 billion. This does not necessarily mean that Australia should not have hosted the games. An Olympic Games is a great international sporting event that brings much enjoyment to a large number of people around the globe. There is evidence (Atkinson et al., 2008) pointing to significant positive effects on welfare from an Olympic Games such as national pride, consumer surplus on local ticket sales, and perceived improvements in various socially desirable goals (e.g. greater cultural understanding, inspiration of children, and the promotion of healthy living). Thus, although the Australian economy experienced a loss, whether Australians gained or not in welfare terms from hosting the 2000 Olympics remains an open question.

Contrary to what might be implied in much of the economic impacts literature, estimates of the economic impacts of events provide, in themselves, an imperfect basis for decisions about resource allocation (Abelson, 2011). The problem arises from a failure to distinguish clearly between the *impacts* and the (net) *benefits* of the event. A Cost-Benefit Analysis (CBA) picks up a whole range of benefits and costs which would not be picked up in a CGE model. This includes non priced effects which do not get included in the markets which are modeled-noise from an event, the consumers surplus of home patrons, loss of park amenity and traffic congestion associated with the event. The CGE modeling technique, in contrast, picks up general equilibrium effects which the partial CBA is not capable of detecting, including the increased income to households resulting from the event. Studies commissioned by the Victorian Auditor-General (2007) found that, while the Melbourne Formula One Grand Prix in 2005 increased Victorian State Product by $62.4 million (CGE result), it generated a negative net social benefit (cost) to the State of $6.7 million (CBA result). Since neither technique is completely comprehensive, both have a role in a detailed evaluation of a project or event. Dwyer and Forsyth (2009) outline a method for partially integrating the two techniques.

Evaluation of Economic Policy

CGE-related research has also considered the impact of tourism in developing countries.

CGE modeling can also provide important insights into policies relating to different types and levels of taxation. Alavalapati and Adamowicz (2000) examined the interactions between tourism, natural resources, and the environment in British Columbia, paying specific attention to the effects of an environmental tax on each sector of the economy. They considered two scenarios: one in which environmental damage occurs because of natural resource extraction activities, notably the pulp industry, and the other in which the environment deteriorates because of both natural resource extraction and tourism. The simulated results indicated that the imposition of an environmental tax on the resource sector is beneficial if the environmental damage results only from the extraction activities but that it has adverse effects if the damage results from both resource extraction and tourism. The study indicates that the policy measure should be targeted directly on the sector that is most directly affected.

Blake (2000) studied the impact of different types of taxation using a CGE model that he developed for the Spanish economy. He showed that foreign tourism activities in Spain are highly taxed relative to other sectors. In the case of domestic tourism, the tax system levies lower rates of taxation on tourism and subsidizes domestic transport. Blake examined the issue of near-marginal tax incidence in the Spanish case and found that marginal increases in taxes on foreign tourism are likely to result in higher domestic welfare, since the effect of the increases is to reduce the pre-existing distortions in the domestic economy that result from low levels of domestic taxation. The elimination of indirect taxation would benefit foreign tourists but would decrease the quantity of domestic tourism, indicating that the existing tax structure, in its entirety, has the net effect of taxing foreign tourists but subsidizing domestic tourists. The removal of value added tax from accommodation would have adverse effects on the economy. However, an increase in the tax on accommodation would be beneficial over the long run, partly because it would counteract the effects of the subsidies on domestic transport. Blake also pointed out that both the short run transition costs and any externalities associated with tax changes should also be taken into account in the process of policy formulation.

Mabugu (2002) applied a short-term computable general equilibrium model for Zimbabwe to trace the direct and indirect effects of policy on the macroeconomy and tourism. The results show that the main reason why benefits from tourism are bypassing the country is because of poorly sequenced macroeconomic policies and a negative political climate. Mabugu argues that as and when the national political situation stabilizes and the economy begins to grow again, a credible macroeconomic stabilization programme should be implemented, targeted to reduce fiscal deficits, and using flexible foreign exchange markets and tight monetary policies to address inflation. However, because Zimbabwe is in arrears, there can be no programmes or lending with the International Monetary Fund and World Bank. Getting the budget in order without aid money will be very difficult indeed, and the alternative (debt deflation by means of hyperinflation) is worse.

Sugiyarto et al. (2003) used a CGE model of the Indonesian economy to examine the effects of globalization via tariff reductions, as a stand-alone policy and in conjunction with tourism growth. Indonesia is an interesting case study as it has experienced both trade liberalization and tourism growth during the past decades The results show that tourism growth amplifies the positive effects of globalization and lessens its adverse effects. Production increases and welfare improves, while adverse effects on government deficits and the trade balance are reduced. Globalization combined with tourism does not necessarily have adverse effects on the domestic economy, in contrast to the past portrayal of the combination as "a deadly mix". Globalization and foreign tourism growth can, in fact, reduce the domestic price level and increase the amount of foreign trade and availability of products in the domestic economy, thereby stimulating further production. The end result in the Indonesian case is improved macroeconomic performance and welfare, as domestic absorption, and household consumption increase. Foreign tourists are also better off for they can consume more, given their spending level, and also benefit from the greater availability of products. The ongoing growth of foreign tourism also reduces the government's burdens as a result of embarking on globalization, by enabling it to reduce its reliance on import tariffs and indirect taxation while, at the same time, maintaining the level of income necessary to finance its expenditure. Tourism growth would, therefore, enable the government to follow a fiscal policy of revenue neutral globalization, allowing it to finance its expenditure without imposing higher taxes on the Indonesian population.

Gómez Gómez et al. (2003) formulated a dynamic GE model that examines the conditions that are required for a tourism tax to contribute a double dividend of environmental improvement and an increase in consumption. They highlight the role of the terms of trade in giving rise to a double dividend in an economy specializing in tourism. Gillham (2004) developed a dynamic model with imperfect competition that can take account of increasing returns to scale in different sectors of the Spanish economy. He used the model to evaluate the impact of foreign direct investment on tourism and other economic sectors in Spain. He also used a CGE model developed specifically for the Canary Islands to examine the interrelationships between tourism and trade and taxation policies in the islands.

Blake et al. (2003a) developed CGE models of the Maltese and Cypriot economies to quantify and compare the impact of EU accession and changes in tourism on each of the Mediterranean islands. Tourism is particularly important relative to other economic activities in these island nations, so that changes in tourism demand are likely to have considerable effects at both the macroeconomic and intersectoral levels. Results show that EU accession is beneficial to both countries, although as a percentage of GDP Malta benefits considerably more than Cyprus – in part because EU funding is more substantial in Malta when compared with GDP, but also because Malta trades a larger share of its GDP with the EU than Cyprus does. The effects of accession on tourism are negative in Malta and positive in Cyprus, because the greater effects from trade and funding allocations lead to a greater demand for factors of production in Malta that increase wage rates and take factors of production away from tourism. In Cyprus, effects that benefit tourism outweigh such general equilibrium trade-off effects.

Gooroochurn and Sinclair (2005) employed a CGE model for Mauritius to explore the effects of changes in production taxes and of sales taxes on different sectors of the economy, in alternative contexts of exogenous and endogenous tourist arrivals. The marginal economic benefit (MEB), a measure of the incremental welfare cost of raising additional revenue from a tax that is already distortionary, was found to be higher for almost all economic sectors in the case when tourist arrivals are exogenous. However, the MEB was higher for restaurants and hotels when tourist arrivals are endogenous, as the increase in welfare associated with a rise in domestic consumption outweighed the fall in welfare associated with a smaller increase in government revenue. Consideration of the distributional effects of an increase in sales tax on the tourism sector indicated that an increase in the tax rate has smaller adverse effects on poorer than on richer households. The overall results indicate that the structure of indirect taxation in Mauritius is not optimal and that tourism-related sectors appear to be under-taxed, although any tax increases should be considered in conjunction with estimates of the incidence of the tax on tourists and their price elasticity of demand.

Gooroochurn and Sinclair (2005) found that directly taxing foreign tourists to Mauritius increases domestic welfare. The authors also examined production and sales tax reforms and compare the welfare cost of raising additional revenue from a tax on a specific commodity while other taxes remain constant. They found that tourism-related sectors (restaurants/hotels and transport/communication) were undertaxed, that the cost of increasing the taxation of these sectors would be mainly born by foreign tourists, and that increasing taxes in these sectors has smaller effects on poorer than on richer households and reduces income inequality. The main driver of the last result is the higher proportion of domestic consumption from the richer household groups for tourism-related sectors. A narrow policy, taxing the highly tourism-intensive sectors extracts significantly more revenues from tourists than a broader policy where all tourism-related sectors are taxed. The narrow policy has a higher beneficial term of trade effect than the broader policy. Higher term of trade implies that the local economy can obtain more imports (hence consumption) for a given amount of exports.

Blake et al. (2008) examined the issue of how tourism affects poverty. They used a CGE model for Brazil to quantify the effects of increased inbound tourism on income distribution and poverty relief that occur via changes in prices, earnings, and government revenues. The CGE model is calibrated using a Social Accounting Matrix (SAM) that shows the payments that take place among the different industries, products, factors, households, firms, the government, and the rest of the world. The model incorporates the earnings of different groups of workers within tourism, along with the channels by which changes in earnings, prices, and the government affect the distribution of income among rich and poor households. A 10 percent increase in demand by foreign tourists in Brazil was assumed in order to investigate the effects on income distribution in the economy. The results suggest caution when generalizing the effects of tourism growth on poverty within a country. In the case of Brazil, there was a strong reinforcement effect whereby the industries that reduced their output following an increase in tourism demand were export industries that employ factors of production from the richer households. This implies that the structure of earnings in non-tourism export sectors plays a significant role in determining the net poverty effects of tourism. The authors emphasized that this type of earnings structure may not apply in other countries. Hence, it would be important to apply the model to tourism expansion in other countries, in order to investigate the effects that would occur under different types of earnings structures.

To answer the question: is tourism growth pro-poor?, Wattanakuljarus and Coxhead (2008) used a CGE model for Thailand to simulate the effects of tourism growth. The simulations indicated that capital and labor in non-agriculture are the factors that gain the most. In Thailand, corporations are the major owners of capital in non-agriculture, and corporate income accrues mainly to wealthy non-agricultural households. Similarly, since high-income non-agricultural households are the major owners of labor in non-agriculture, they are the next biggest beneficiaries. As a result, given the distribution of factor ownership across household groups, inbound tourism expansion raises incomes across the board, but the main share of the gains accrues to the non-poor. The authors conducted sensitivity analysis with different assumptions regarding factor constraints. In every scenario, however, although tourism growth benefits all household classes, the biggest gains accrue to high-income and non-agricultural households. It is concluded that tourism growth in Thailand is not pro-poor or pro-agriculture. To address this increased inequality, additional policy instruments are required to correct for the inequalities occasioning tourism growth.

Macao has been witnessing robust economic growth in recent years. According to Sheng and Tsui (2009) the ongoing boom is mainly driven by rapid tourism growth reflected in massive tourist arrivals and foreign capital inflow. Although Macao is praised as an "economic wonder", serious externalities have emerged, raising concerns about the sustainability of the city's long-term development. Using a modified simple general equilibrium model, the authors show how economic, social, environmental, and political externalities accompanying rapid tourism growth may possibly reduce the net welfare of host communities. The paper concludes that the government should keep sustainability in mind when making tourism policies, carefully taking all related social, environmental and political factors into consideration.

MMRF-GREEN (Adams et al., 2003) has been developed to estimate the greenhouse gas emissions associated with economic activity. The development of "green" CGE models is an important step towards identifying the extent of externalities associated with tourism and other industries. Based on the MMRF-GREEN model, Hoque et al. (2009) investigated the potential economic impacts of introduction by the Australian government of its proposed Carbon Pollution Reduction Scheme (CPRS). The CPRS is intended to introduce a cap and trade mechanism for reducing greenhouse gas emissions in Australia. It was intended to commence in 2011 but passage of the legislation has been delayed in Parliament. The modeling focused on a scenario called the CPRS–5 with targets aimed to achieve greenhouse gas emissions reduction by 2020 of 5 percent below 2000 level. Effects on the Australian economy and in particular the tourism sector in Australia were examined. The authors concluded that under the proposed scheme, the tourism sector will contract. Falls will occur in real tourism gross value added and tourism employment. The largest falls are projected to be in accommodation, air and water industries, and in cafes, restaurants, and food outlets. While most tourism industries experience contraction in their real value added relative to baseline values, the rail transport industry experiences an expansion because the emissions price causes substitution toward this industry against the high-emissions transport industries such as air, water, and other road transport industries. Overall, the gains experienced by some tourism industries will be heavily outweighed by contractions in some of the tourism characteristic industries.

Forsyth et al. (2011) used a CGE model to assess the impacts of Australia's Passenger Movement Charge on key economic variables, such as GDP, GNI, and economic welfare, and on tourism industry output and employment. The PMC is a tax on all persons departing Australia by air. For Australia as a whole, a rise in the PMC is positive, though it is negative for the tourism industry (which forms part of the Australia-wide effect). This effect on the tourism industry will be more negative if the reduction in outbound tourism does not help stimulate domestic tourism. The net impact on the tourism industry is small (if domestic tourism substitutes for outbound tourism) but this can go either way. However there will be a net positive impact on the economy as a whole in most cases. This comes about because of the tax effect Australia gains from foreign tourists paying Australian taxes rather than Australian residents. This effect is sufficient to outweigh other impacts. This suggests that if funds become available, reducing the PMC would not be a cost-effective way of helping the tourism industry, and that other ways, such as increasing promotion or measures directed to improving tourism industry productivity, may prove to be more cost effective for the economy as a whole.

ADVANTAGES AND LIMITATIONS OF CGE MODELING CONCEPTUALLY AND FOR POLICY FORMULATION

CGE models are sometimes said to be too difficult to use and too data demanding. While it has been the case that the application of CGE models to tourism economics has been much restrained until recently by the lack of data, the development of Tourism

Satellite Accounts (TSA) has progressively reduced this difficulty, and we have seen more and more of these applications in the recent years. This trend will certainly continue. Moreover, CGE modeling techniques and software systems are now routinely available globally. An increasing number of dynamic CGE models are now being developed, in line with improvements in software and increasing computational power. In any case, the data should be assessed in terms of its importance for the question to be investigated, other than just in terms of the ease of data mobilization.

Some critics regard the assumption of market clearing in CGE modeling as unwarranted, arguing that although there are forces pushing economies towards equilibrium, there are also forces that prevent such equilibrium outcomes from being achieved. Croes and Severt (2007) argue that the tourism product presents features difficult to align with perfect equilibrium. Market distortions reduce the role of price signals and hence affect the efficient allocation of resources. Furthermore, the presence of public goods impacts the optimizing behaviour of economic agents. Finally, extreme cases of natural hazards, such as in the case of hurricanes in Florida, can propel great external shocks to the markets to the extent that the applicability of the CGE model is rendered deficient. In response, as Blake et al. (2006) point out, this type of criticism can be leveled against the great majority of economic models. All models provide a simplified representation of reality but nevertheless provide an effective means of understanding and/or predicting economic interrelationships and outcomes. CGE analysis allows the models to be tailored to fit different real world circumstances. Thus, for example, constraints can be imposed on the model to allow for rigidities in factor prices or mobility, exchange rates or government borrowing. Similarly, alternative functional forms can be used to take account of different types of market structure and competition.

CGE models can determine an industry-level impact and show the interactions *between* industries (or sectors). However, like other models, CGE models usually do not show what happens *within* an industry or market. In such circumstances, a market-specific model is required.

CGE models provide useful guidance for policy formulation, as the above examples of research indicate. Of course, the results obtained are particularly sensitive to some of the parameter values (and assumptions) that are included in them. If such parameter values are inaccurate, the results obtained from the models are also likely to be inaccurate, as well as misleading for policy purposes. To overcome this problem, sensitivity analysis can be conducted by including alternative parameter values in the model, to determine the bounds within which the model results lie, for changes in the parameter values that are deemed to be realistic. Results from CGE models can be explained clearly in terms of straightforward economic mechanisms and properties of the data incorporated in the model. It is the responsibility of the modeler to produce such explanations for the users of the results.

FURTHER DEVELOPMENTS AND APPLICATIONS OF CGE MODELING IN TOURISM RESEARCH

Future research on CGE tourism analysis is likely to focus on four main areas (Blake et al., 2006). The first involves further research on dynamic CGE analysis. When there is an interest in the adjustment process, for example, how long it takes for a shift in tourism flows to influence other variables in the economy, then a dynamic framework is required As discussed above, dynamic models can be used to project the structure of the economy as well as to assess the effects of policy and other shocks. This is currently at the frontier of developments in tourism modeling, in terms of both theoretical and empirical contributions.

The second area concerns the incorporation of more microeconomic information into CGE models of tourism. This is an area that is in the forefront of research on CGE modeling (Bourguignon et al., 2002; Hertel et al., 2001). The incorporation of detailed information at the level of individual households' consumption and firms' production behavior and their interactions with the macroeconomic representations of economic behavior characterized by CGE models would improve the quantity and quality of data as well as the accuracy and insights available from the analysis.

Econometric models can provide more accurate estimates of the parameter values that are included in CGE models, relating to more disaggregated levels of analysis, providing improved means of policy formulation. Improved data at the regional and local levels would also assist more effective policy formulation, along with better coordination between policy making at the local, regional, national, and international levels. The building of SAM matrices including tourism activities and the application of CGE models to tourism economics, have recently become easier with the ongoing development of Tourism Satellite Accounts (TSAs) internationally. These have provided substantial increases in the quantity and quality of the data that can be used in CGE modeling. However, this information needs to be complemented by tourism modeling if they are to provide industry and governments with effective guidance for dealing with the range of events and policy decisions that have to be made on an ongoing basis.

A third area concerns the use of CGE models to estimate the "welfare effects" or "net benefits" of some demand shock. Typically, CGE models focus on measures of economic activity such as changes in GDP rather than on explicit measures of economic welfare. However, if the economy wide effects of a positive demand shock are so large that there is no change in national output then the net gains will be small. This is recognized by Dixon and Rimmer (2002) and Blake et al. (2006, 2008a) who introduce welfare measures into their economic modeling of demand shocks. The measure favored by Blake is the equivalent variation – the amount of money that leaves a person as well off as they would be after a change in economic activity. That is, it measures the amount of money required to maintain a person's satisfaction, or economic welfare, at the level it would be at after the change in economic activity. To overcome the limitations of relying solely on GDP as a measure of the benefits accruing to Australians from policy changes, Australia's Productivity Commission uses "adjusted Gross National Expenditure" as a welfare indicator. Adjusted GNE is an indicator of the real national income accruing to the residents from the current value of production (GDP). It is the income accruing to the residents from their labor and their savings invested at home and abroad. It is defined as GDP less the net income paid to foreign investors. On this measure, changes in welfare resulting from tourism demand shocks relate to changes in adjusted GNE. In contrast, Dixon (2009) estimates welfare effects with reference to taxation revenues accruing from foreign-financed capital expansion, efficiency effects, and effects of changes in the terms of trade on net exports. Recently, Coleman (2008) has discussed the superiority of real gross domestic income over GDP as an indicator of welfare in the presence of changes to the terms of trade. Analysis of the advantages and limitations of the different welfare measures may be expected to increasingly occupy the attention of CGE modelers.

A fourth area concerns policy analysis. CGE modeling can be applied to a much broader set of policy issues than at present. The agenda for future research in this area should be to extend the analysis to different tourism destinations, and to include detailed analyses of the appropriate behavioral characteristics of the economic agents that are included in model specification and of the government policy settings that determine the context for their behaviour. This could include the effects of foreign direct investment in tourism, tourism productivity, and competitiveness, fiscal policies for tourism, policies within wider international groupings such as the European Union, policies for transportation, the environment and related externalities, including the impacts of climate change on tourism. CGE tourism modeling provides a versatile and effective means of examining the wide range of scenarios that can occur.

As a result of the development of more sophisticated modeling techniques in recent years, the study of the economic impacts of tourism has become a more fertile ground for research and policy evaluation.

REFERENCES

Abelson, P. (2011), 'Evaluating major events and avoiding the mercantilist fallacy', *Economic Papers*, **30** (1), March, 48–59.

Adams, P. (2008), *MMRF: Monash Multi-Regional Forecasting Model: A Dynamic Multi-Regional Applied General Equilibrium Model of the Australian Economy*, Monash University: Centre of Policy Studies.

Adams, P.D. and B.R. Parmenter (1995), 'An applied general equilibrium analysis of the economic effects of tourism in a quite small, quite open economy', *Applied Economics*, **27** (10), 985–994.

Adams, P.D. and B.R. Parmenter (1999), '*General Equilibrium Models*', *Valuing Tourism. Methods and Techniques*, Canberra, Australia: Bureau of Tourism Research.

Adams, P., M. Horridge and G. Wittwer (2003), 'MMRF GREEN: a dynamic multi-regional applied computable general equilibrium model of the Australian economy, based on the MMR and Monash model', General Working Paper No. G-140, October, Centre of Policy Studies, Monash University, Australia.

Alavalapati, J.R.R. and W.L. Adamowicz (2000), 'Tourism impact modeling for resource extraction regions', *Annals of Tourism Research*, **27** (1), 188–202.

Arrow, K.J. and G. Debreu (1954), 'The existence of an equilibrium for a competitive economy', *Econometrica*, XXII, 265–290.

Arrow, K.J. and F.H. Hahn (1971), *General Competitive Analysis*, San Francisco: Holden-Day.

Atkinson, G., S. Mourato, S. Szymanski and E. Ozdemiroglu (2008), 'Are we willing to pay enough to "back the bid"? Valuing the intangible impacts of London's bid to host the 2012 Summer Olympic Games', *Urban Studies*, **45**, 419–444.

Bandara, J.S. (1991), 'Computable general equilibrium models for development policy analysis in LDCs', *Journal of Economic Surveys*, **5** (1), March, 3–69.

Blake, A. (2005), 'The economic impact of the London 2012 Olympics', Research Report 2005/5, Christel DeHaan Tourism and Travel Research Institute, Nottingham University Business School.

Blake, A., T. Sinclair and J. Gillham (2006), 'CGE tourism analysis and policy modeling', in L. Dwyer and P. Forsyth (eds), *International Handbook of Tourism Economics*, Cheltenham, UK and Northampton, MA, USA: Edward Elgar.

Blake, A., J.S. Arbache, M.T. Sinclair and V. Teles (2008), 'Tourism and poverty relief', *Annals of Tourism Research*, **35** (1), 107–126.

Blake, A.T. (2000), 'The economic effects of tourism in Spain', Christel DeHaan Tourism and Travel Research Institute Discussion Paper, available at http://www.nottingham.ac.uk/ttri/series.html, 2000/2.

Blake, A.T. and M.T. Sinclair (2003), 'Tourism crisis management: US response to September 11', *Annals of Tourism Research*, **30** (4), 813–832.

Blake, A., M.T. Sinclair and G. Sugiyarto (2003a), 'Tourism and EU accession in Malta, Cyprus', TTRI Discussion Paper 2003/7, University of Nottingham, Nottingham.

Blake A., M. Sinclair and G. Sugiyarto (2003b), 'Quantifying the impact of foot and mouth disease on tourism and the UK economy', *Tourism Economics*, **9** (4), 449–465.

Bourguignon, F., A. Robilliard and S. Robinson (2002), 'Representative versus real households in the macroeconomic modelling of inequality', paper presented at the Development Economics Study Group Annual Conference, University of Nottingham, available at http://www.shef.ac.uk/uni/projects/desg/cinfo/cpapers/robinson.pdf.

Coleman, W. (2008), 'Gauging economic performance under changing terms of trade: Real Gross Domestic Income or Real Gross Domestic Product?', *Economic Papers*, **27** (4), 329–342.

Copeland, B.R. (1991), 'Tourism, welfare and de-industrialization in a small open economy', *Economica*, **58**, 515–529.

Costa, M.L. (1998), *General Equilibrium Analysis and the Theory of Markets*, Cheltenham, UK, and Lyme, NH, USA: Edward Elgar.

Croes, R. and D. Severt (2007), 'Evaluating short-term tourism economic effects in confined economies: conceptual and empirical considerations', *Tourism Economics*, **13** (2), 289–307.

Debreu, G. (1959), *Theory of Value*, New York: Wiley.

Dixon, P. and B. Parmenter (1996), 'Computable general equilibrium modelling for policy analysis and forecasting', in H. Aman, D. Kendrick and J. Rust (eds), *Handbook of Computational Economics*, Vol. 1, Melbourne: Elsevier Science B.V, pp. 4–85.

Dixon, P. and M. Rimmer (2002), *Dynamic, General Equilibrium Modelling for Forecasting and Policy: a Practical Guide and Documentation of MONASH*, Amsterdam: North-Holland.

Dixon, P.B. (2009), 'Comments on the productivity commission's modelling of the economy-wide effects of future automotive assistance', *Economic Papers*, **28** (1), March, 11–18.

Dixon, P.B., B.R. Parmenter, J. Sutton and D.P. Vincent (1982), ORANI: A multisectoral model of the Australian Economy, North-Holland, Amsterdam.

Dwyer, L. and P. Forsyth (2008), 'Economic measures of tourism yield: what markets to target?', *International Journal of Tourism Research*, **10**, 155–168.

Dwyer, L. and P. Forsyth (2009), 'Public sector support for special events', *Eastern Economic Journal*, **35** (4), 481–499.

Dwyer, L., P. Forsyth and W. Dwyer (2010), *Tourism Economics and Policy*, Cheltenham, UK: Channel View Publications.

Dwyer, L., P. Forsyth, L. Fredline, L. Jago, M. Deery and S. Lundie (2007), 'Yield measures for Australia's special interest inbound tourism markets', *Tourism Economics*, **13** (3), 421–440.

Dwyer, L., P. Forsyth, J. Madden and R. Spurr (2000), 'Economic impacts of inbound tourism under different assumptions regarding the macroeconomy', *Current Issues in Tourism*, **3** (4), 325–363.

Dwyer, L., P. Forsyth, R. Spurr and T. Van Ho (2003), 'The contribution of tourism to a state and national economy: a multi-regional general equilibrium analysis', *Tourism Economics*, **9** (4), 431–448.

Dwyer, L., P. Forsyth and R. Spurr (2004), 'Evaluating tourism's economic effects: new and old approaches', *Tourism Management*, **25**, 307–317.

Dwyer, L., P. Forsyth and R. Spurr (2005), 'Estimating the impacts of special events on the economy', *Journal of Travel Research*, 43 (May), 351–359.

Dwyer, L., P. Forsyth and R. Spurr (2006a), 'Assessing the economic impacts of events: a computable general equilibrium approach', *Journal of Travel Research*, **45**, 59–66.

Dwyer, L., P. Forsyth and R. Spurr (2006b), 'Assessing the economic impacts of special events', in L. Dwyer and P. Forsyth (eds), *International Handbook of Tourism Economics*, Cheltenham, UK and Northampton, MA, USA: Edward Elgar.

Dwyer, L., P. Forsyth and R. Spurr (2006c), 'Effects of SARS crisis on the economic contribution of tourism to Australia', *Tourism Review International*, **10**, 47–55.

Forsyth, P., S. Hoque, L. Dwyer, Tien Duc Pham and R. Spurr (2011), 'The Impacts of the Passenger Movement Charge on Tourism Output and the Economy', report commissioned by Tourism Research Australia, The Centre for Economics and Policy, Sydney, Australia.

Giesecke, J.A and J.R. Madden (2011), 'Modelling the economic impacts of the Sydney Olympics in retrospect: game over for the bonanza story?', *Economic Papers*, **30** (2), June, 218–232.

Gillham, J. (2004), 'Economic interrelationships of tourism: a computable general equilibrium analysis', PhD thesis, University of Nottingham.

Gómez Gómez, C.M., J. Lozano Ibáñez and J. Rey-Maquieira Palmer (2003), 'Tourism taxation in a dynamic model of an economy specialised in tourism', Conference on Tourism Modelling and Competitiveness, Paphos, Cyprus, October.

Gooroochurn, N. and C. Milner (2003), 'Assessing indirect tax reform in a tourism-dependent developing country', Conference on Tourism Modelling and Competitiveness, Paphos, Cyprus, October.

Gooroochurn, N. and T. Sinclair (2005), 'The economics of tourism taxation: evidence from Mauritius', *Annals of Tourism Research*, **32** (2), 478–498.

Gunning, J.W. and M. Keyzer (1995), 'Applied general equilibrium models for policy analysis', in J. Behrman and T.N. Srinivasan (eds), *Handbook of Development Economics* Vol. III-A, Amsterdam: Elsevier, pp. 2025–2107.

Harrison, G., S. Jensen, L. Pedersen and T. Rutherford (2000), 'Using dynamic general equilibrium models for policy analysis', in G. Harrison, S. Jensen, L. Pedersen and T. Rutherford (eds), *Contributions to Economic Analysis* Vol. 248, Oxford and New York: Elsevier, North Holland.

Hertel, T.W. (1997), *Global Trade Analysis: Modelling and Applications*, Cambridge: Cambridge University Press.

Hertel, T.W., P.V. Preckel, J.A.L. Cranfield and M. Ivanic (2001), 'Poverty impacts of multilateral trade liberalization', unpublished research paper available from the Center for Global Trade Analysis, Purdue University, USA.

Horridge, J.M., J. Madden and G. Wittwer (2003), 'Using a highly disaggregagted multi-regional single-country model to analyse the impacts of the 2002–03 drought on Australia', Centre of Policy Studies, General Working Paper No. G-141 Oct 2003, Monash University, Australia.

Horridge, J.M., B.R. Parmenter and K.R. Pearson (1993), 'ORANI-F: a general equilibrium model of the Australian economy', *Economic and Financial Computing*, **3**, 71–140.

Hoque, S., P. Forsyth, L. Dwyer, R. Spurr and D. Pambudi (2009), 'Economic effects of an emissions trading scheme on the Australian tourism industry: a dynamic CGE analysis', paper presented at conference of International Association for Tourism Economics (IATE), Chiang Mai, Thailand, December 2009.

Li, S., A. Blake and C. Cooper (2010), 'China's tourism in a global financial crisis: a computable general equilibrium approach', *Current Issues in Tourism*, **13** (5), 435–453.

Li, S., A. Blake and C. Cooper (2011), 'Modelling the economic impact of international tourism on the Chinese economy: a CGE analysis of the Beijing 2008 Olympics', *Tourism Economics*, **17** (2), 279–303.

McDougall, R. (1995), 'Computable general equilibrium modelling: introduction and overview', *Asia-Pacific Economic Review*, **1** (1), April, 88–91.

Mabugu, R. (2002), Short-term effects of policy reform on tourism and the macroeconomy in Zimbabwe: applied CGE analysis, *Development Southern Africa*, **19**, 419–430.

Madden, J. (2006), 'Economic and fiscal impacts of mega sporting events: a general equilibrium assessment', *Public Finance and Management*, **6** (3), 346–394.

Meagher, G. and B. Parmenter (1990), 'ORANI-NT: a multisectoral model of the Northern Territory economy, The Australian National University, North Australia Research Unit, Darwin.

Meng, X., M. Siriwardana, B. Dollery and S. Mounter (2010), 'The impact of the 2008 world financial crisis on tourism and the Singapore economy and policy responses: a CGE analysis', *International Journal of Trade, Economics and Finance*, **1** (1), June.

Narayan, P.K. (2003), 'The long-run impact of coups on Fiji's economy: evidence from a computable general equilibrium model', *Journal of International Development*, **19**, 149–160.

Narayan, P.K. (2004), 'Economic impact of tourism on Fiji's economy: empirical evidence from the computable general equilibrium model', *Tourism Economics*, **10** (4), 419–433.

Pambudi, D., N. McCaughey and R. Smyth (2009), 'Computable general equilibrium estimates of the impact of the Bali bombing on the Indonesian economy', *Tourism Management*, **30**.

Peter, M., M. Horridge, G.A. Meagher, Z. Naqvi and B.R. Parmenter (1996), 'The theoretical structure of Monash-MRF', Preliminary Working Paper No. OP-85 April 1996, Centre of Policy Studies, Monash University.

Pham Tien Duc, D.G. Simmons and R. Spurr (2010), 'Tourism: adapting to climate change and climate policy', *Journal of Sustainable Tourism* Special Issue: **18** (3), 449–473.

Sheng, L. and Y. Tsui (2009), 'A general equilibrium approach to tourism and welfare: the case of Macao', *Habitat International*, **33**, 419–424.

Shoven, J.B. and J.L. Whalley (1992), *Applying General Equilibrium*, Cambridge: Cambridge University Press.

Sugiyarto, G., A. Blake and M.T. Sinclair (2003), 'Tourism and globalization: economic impact in Indonesia', *Annals of Tourism Research*, **30** (3), 683–701.

Victorian Auditor-General (2007), *State Investment in Major Events*. Melbourne: Victorian Printer.

Wattanakuljarus, A. and I. Coxhead (2008), 'Is tourism-based development good for the poor? A general equilibrium analysis for Thailand', *Journal of Policy Modeling*, **30** (6), 929–955.

Zhou, D., J.F. Yanagida, U. Chakravorty and P. Leung (1997), 'Estimating economic impacts of tourism', *Annals of Tourism Research*, **24** (1), 76–89.

14 Cost–benefit analysis
Larry Dwyer

INTRODUCTION

Decision makers need a consistent basis for assessing competing proposals and to be fully informed about the implications of using economic resources. The public sector is a major user of a destination's available resources and, as such, should ensure that it makes a significant positive contribution to the economy and society. More particularly, no new proposal, programme, project or policy should be adopted without first answering questions such as:

- What are the specific outcomes sought?
- Do the gains to people exceed the costs the sacrifices required?
- Are there better ways to achieve these outcomes?
- Are there better uses for these resources?
- Is this an appropriate area of responsibility for government?

The primary technique that should be used for the economic appraisal of actions or proposals in terms of economic efficiency is Cost–Benefit Analysis (CBA). CBA is a systematic process for identifying and assessing all costs and benefits of a policy, project or programme in monetary terms, including those costs and benefits not usually represented by dollar values, and then subtracting the costs from the benefits to show the estimated net effect of that activity. Future costs and benefits are discounted relative to present costs and benefits in a net present value sum. The policy or project is deemed to be socially acceptable if the sum of the benefits to society (including private and social benefits) exceeds the sum of the costs to society (including private and social costs).

CBA is the most comprehensive of the economic appraisal techniques. CBA is particularly important in the context of evaluating tourism policy, programmes, regulations, projects and developments. Specific examples might include regional or local tourism plans; rezoning of land for tourism purposes; and major tourism developments such as the creation of tourism shopping precincts, airport development, resorts and hotels, nature reserves and sporting facilities. As such projects generally have relatively wide economic, environmental and social implications for a community that are not captured in the basic financial analysis undertaken by project proponents.

CBA is especially appropriate to tourism because there is often a clear trade-off between economic benefits and social costs of some programme, policy, project, investment or proposal (henceforth referred to as 'proposal'). Tourism proposals that might be economically beneficial may be rejected because of their adverse environmental and/ or social impacts.

NATURE OF CBA AND ITS EVOLUTION

CBA is a commonly applicable technique in public investment assessment developed by Dupuit (1844). Throughout the last three decades, the focus on CBA as a vehicle for economic efficiency appraisal of public projects has increased. Several studies (Boardman et al., 2001; Jenkins and Harberger, 1995; Mishan, 2002) have shown the crucial role of accurate valuation of benefits and costs in public projects evaluation. CBA is a systematic process for identifying and assessing all costs and benefits of a proposal in monetary terms, as they are expected to occur through the life of a project. CBA is concerned with measuring, the change in all sources of economic welfare, whether occurring in markets or as implicit values.

Benefits and Costs

A CBA aims to estimate all the costs and benefits of an activity to a specified community. It is an evaluation method that has been designed specifically to answer welfare or public policy questions. Benefits are defined as increases in social welfare while costs are defined as reductions in social welfare. A CBA provides an estimate of the worth of a proposal relative to an accompanying estimate of what would happen in the absence of the proposal (Dwyer et al., 2010, chapter 10).

In CBA, 'value' or 'benefit' is measured by willingness to pay (WTP) or willingness to accept (WTA). Formally using the compensating variations principle, the net social benefit is the maximum net amount that residents would be willing to pay for the proposal and be just as well off with the proposal as without it. Using the equivalent variations principle, the net social benefit is the minimum amount that the community would be willing to accept as compensation for not having the proposal. The social costs of a project are measured in terms of opportunity costs – that is, the value of the marginal benefits foregone from the same resources in alternative uses. Using these two valuation principles (for benefits and costs) the analyst can determine whether the value of consumption gained is greater than the value of consumption that it has given up. The net benefit is the sum of all welfare benefits less costs. Maximizing net welfare is the standard policy objective implicit or explicit in cost–benefit studies.

All costs and benefits, including social and environmental aspects, are assigned a money value, allowing the calculation of the net benefits of different proposals as a basis for evaluating alternatives. CBA are used to include, measure, weight and compare all expected present and future benefits of a policy with all its expected present and future costs. Future costs and benefits are discounted relative to present costs and benefits in the net present value (NPV) sum. For a capital investment development, programme or policy to be socially acceptable, the sum of the benefits to society (including private and social benefits) must exceed the sum of the costs to society (including private and social costs). These net benefits/costs can then be used to rank alternative proposals quantitatively. In principle, a CBA enables agencies to compare the relative merit of alternative programs or projects in terms of their returns on the use of resources, public and private. CBA is primarily designed to answer the question 'does the expenditure of money on this particular project or programme provide a net benefit to the economy and the public, given that these resources could be applied in an alternative use?'

By quantifying the net benefits of projects, programmes and policies in a standard manner, CBA improves the information base for public sector decision making, thereby assisting in the assessment of relative priorities.

We can highlight several issues involved in CBA.

Scope and Objectives of the Analysis

The initial step in a CBA is to outline the nature of the problem to be addressed: its background, context and rationale. Every proposal to spend money must have an underlying objective. What is the programme, project or activity trying to achieve? Thus a destination manager may enquire as to the net benefits expected from an international tourism promotion campaign or the construction of additional airport capacity. These objectives should be defined, initially, in terms of the possible market failure or market imperfections that could warrant government intervention. A clear statement of objectives will provide information on whose costs and benefits are being assessed.

CBA must also identify and specify a set of alternatives. A basic principle of any type of project or proposal evaluation is the 'with–without' principle. In practice, this means that the forecast 'state of the world' with the proposal to be undertaken, is compared with the 'state of the world' that would have existed in the absence of the project (the 'do nothing' or 'status quo' option). For example, government decision makers may assess the benefits of a tourism training programme, or bilateral air services regulations by comparing scenarios with and without such schemes. A 'do nothing' option is generally required as a base because costs and benefits are always measured as incremental to what would have happened had the project or policy not been undertaken.

To ensure that all alternatives for meeting the identified objectives are feasible, various constraints that may apply need to be considered, including financial, distributional, managerial, environmental or other constraints.

Discounting

The costs and benefits flowing from a project will be spread over time. For purposes of CBA, the selection of a discount rate introduces some complexities not relevant to financial appraisal (Burgess and Zerbe, 2011). While debate continues at the theoretical level, in reality analysts use the market interest rate to discount the costs and benefits associated with different projects. The essential argument is that the government must achieve a return on investment at least equivalent to what the money would earn if left in the private sector to justify taxing the private economy to undertake public-sector investments. If the government cannot achieve this by investing in some project it would be better for the destination if the money is left untaxed in the private sector (Treasury Board of Canada, 1998). A real discount rate should be used to discount constant dollar or real benefits and costs. A real discount rate, eliminating the effects of expected inflation, can be approximated by subtracting expected inflation from a nominal interest rate. Benefits and costs should be expressed in real terms and adjusted for differential price effects where a specific resource price is expected to move at a rate different from the general inflation rate.

Decision Criteria

Various investment criteria are available to assist in reaching decisions on different proposals. In CBA, the net social benefit (NSB), or the excess of total benefit over total cost, is represented by the net present value (NPV) of the proposal. Under this decision rule, a project is potentially worthwhile (or viable) if the NPV is greater than zero, that is, the total discounted value of benefits is greater than the total discounted costs. If projects are mutually exclusive, the project which yields the highest NPV would be chosen.

Net Present Value is the sum of the discounted project benefits minus the discounted project costs. Formally, it can be expressed as follows:

$$NPV = \sum_{t=1}^{T} \frac{B_t}{(1 + r)^t} - \left(K + \sum_{t=1}^{T} \frac{C_t}{(1 + r)^t} \right) \qquad (14.1)$$

where:

Σ means summation over all the years of the project life (T years),
B_t stands for the benefits expected in the tth year,
$(1 + r)^t$ represents the discounting factor by which values expected in the future are turned into today's values.
K is the capital or construction costs (assumed to occur in the current year) and
C_t is the operation, maintenance, and repair costs expected in the tth year.
T is number of years that the benefits or costs are produced.

Under this decision rule, a project is potentially worthwhile (or viable) if the NPV is greater than zero, that is, the total discounted value of benefits is greater than the total discounted costs. If projects are mutually exclusive, the project which yields the highest NPV would be chosen.

Sometimes the decision rule takes the form of a Benefit-Cost Ratio (BCR). This is the ratio of the present value of benefits to the present value of costs. In algebraic terms, the BCR can be expressed as follows:

$$BCR = \frac{\sum_{t=1}^{T} \dfrac{B_t - C_t}{(1 + r)^t}}{K} \qquad (14.2)$$

It is conventional to split costs into two types when calculating BCRs: initial capital costs and ongoing costs. Ongoing costs in each year are subtracted from benefits in that year to identify a net benefit stream, while initial capital costs are used as the denominator.

A project is potentially worthwhile if the BCR is greater than 1, that is, the present value of benefits exceeds the present value of costs. Thus:

If BCR > 1 implementation of the project is judged to be economically worthwhile.
If BCR = 1 the project adds nothing to economic welfare.
If BCR < 1 the project reduces economic well being.

If projects are mutually exclusive, this rule would indicate that the project with the highest BCR should be chosen.

The BCR is a useful measure because, when there are a large number of proposals, there may not be enough resources available to undertake them all, even if they all have high net present values. As a rule of thumb, picking the projects with the highest BCR can ensure maximum value for money in terms of contributing to outcomes, though only if all the projects have similar time patterns of benefits and costs.

The choice of the discount rate can have a significant impact on the ranking of options/ projects and hence their choice. In general, short lived options are favoured by higher discount rates relative to long-lived options.

As the discount rate rises:

● The more are net benefits further into the future downgraded in present value terms relative to net benefits closer to hand.
● Projects with larger initial outlays become relatively less attractive compared with projects with lower initial outlays.
● Projects with lower ongoing outlays become relatively more attractive compared to projects with higher ongoing outlays.

Distributional Impacts

In reality, it is highly likely that a change in resource allocation, such as the introduction of a new tourism resort or new tourism policy or programme, will increase the welfare or well being of some people but reduce the welfare of others. One approach to recognizing this in a CBA is to identify the gainers and losers, and measure the extent of their gains and losses in monetary terms. This information is then provided to the decision maker, who then must make the distributional value judgments. Alternatively, others (Ray, 1984) have suggested that distributional weights be assigned to the benefits and costs experienced by different groups in society (for example, with higher weights being given to benefits and costs to poorer groups than benefits and costs to richer groups). These weights would be provided by the government. The criterion for proceeding with the project then depends on whether weighted benefits exceed weighted costs. While analytically this approach has its attractions, the problem of finding the appropriate weights makes it difficult to implement in practice.

Investment Horizon

The investment horizon is the end of the period over which costs and benefits are compared to ascertain whether an investment is acceptable. If costs and benefits can be identified over the useful life of the project and uncertainties are low, then this provides the best investment horizon. This will be a long time for some tourism infrastructure projects such as airports, highway systems and cruise shipping terminals. As a general rule, the period of analysis should extend over the useful life of the project.

Residual values are also an important component of the total value of a proposal and should be included in the assessment. The residual or terminal value of a project is its estimated value at the end of the analysis period. While, in theory, an asset's residual value at the end of its economic life should be zero, in practice it may not be so.

Sensitivity Analysis

The values of future costs and benefits on which the NPV is based cannot be known with certainty. While they should be forecast on expected values, it is important to test the NPV for 'optimistic' and 'pessimistic' scenarios. This is known as sensitivity analysis and is a critical component of any CBA. Sensitivity analysis can help to highlight those factors (e.g., exchange rates, salary costs, demand drivers, project timings) that require especially careful assessment or management. Sensitivity analysis is particularly useful in assessing the effects of different discount rates on NPV calculations. Thus the net benefits of developing a special event can be estimated for distinct cost scenarios based on different allocation of stadium infrastructure costs (Access Economics, 2010).

Ex-post Evaluation

Ex-post evaluations involve:

- Re-evaluation of the benefits and costs of the selected option to assess whether the anticipated benefits were realized and the forecast costs were accurate;
- Reconsideration of alternative options;
- Examination of the project design and implementation to assess the scope for improvement to the option adopted.

By re-examining these issues, *ex-post* evaluations will assist in the development and evaluation of future projects. Flyvbjerg et al. (2003) demonstrate the value of the post implementation review given the failures of megaprojects to perform according to expectations.

VALUING COSTS AND BENEFITS

All economic evaluations in CBA are based on the *incremental* costs and benefits associated with a particular proposal. These can be classified usefully into three categories:

(1) Effects which can be Readily Identified and Valued in Money Terms

These could include ticket sales to residents for a special event, revenues generated from restaurant meals, costs of waste disposal and so on. The relevant costs and benefits are typically based upon market prices as they are the easiest to identify and usually reflect implicit opportunity costs. Where competitive markets exist, prices reflect WTP at the margin for goods and the opportunity costs of resources.

While market prices provide the starting point for measuring WTP, they sometimes do not adequately reflect the true value of a good to society. Consumers are often willing to pay more than the market price rather than go without a good they consume – for example, a person might be willing to pay much more to attend a festival event than the ticket price.

When market prices exist but are distorted for some reason, we need to estimate what the prices would be in the absence of the distortions and then use these adjusted market prices. These adjusted prices are called *shadow prices* (sometimes called social prices or true prices). The use of shadow prices rather than market prices is most commonly advocated for the following market distorting situations: labour markets (when unemployment and/or underemployment exists or wages are artificially high); foreign exchange market (where the value of foreign exchange is different from the market rate); market power (distortion of market prices by monopoly seller or monopsony buyer); government regulations, taxes and subsidies. While theoretically interesting, the above types of distortions may not have much effect on the CBA estimates. In many cases given the potentially small changes that result to the net benefit calculation it may not be worthwhile for the analyst to confront the difficult measurement problems associated with shadow pricing.

(2) Effects which can be Identified and Measured in Physical Terms but which Cannot be Easily Valued in Money Terms Because of the Absence of Market

These could include the value of preserving a wilderness area, the cost of noise from airport or hotel construction, time savings to travellers from a new transport link or greenhouse gas emissions from motor coaches and so. There are often cases where a market does not exist for the goods and services flowing from a project, or market prices are not directly observable or easy to estimate. This makes it difficult to estimate costs and benefits (or even to determine to whom the costs and benefits accrue). For example, undertaking a project may result in benefits received or costs incurred by others not associated with the activity and for which payment is neither given nor received. Such spillovers are termed 'externalities' (also referred to as social effects or third party effects). Externalities are impacts on third parties that are not the primary parties (producers or consumers) in an economic exchange and hence are not required to pay for a cost imposed or benefit received. This is particularly the case for policies and programmes that generate social and/or environmental impacts. Examples of negative spillovers abound in tourism. The construction of a golf course resort hotel that discharges residues into a nearby river will have a negative impact on people who use the river downstream of the resort. Similarly, the greenhouse gas emissions from aircraft affect the environment of people on the ground.

The two main general approaches to valuing externalities are the 'revealed preference' and 'stated preference' methods.

Revealed preference
Revealed preference is based on consumer behaviour in related markets, and compares situations where people have made trade-offs between a cost and some form of benefit. This information indicates the extent to which people are prepared to pay for a given benefit. Revealed preference techniques are based on preferences from actual, observed, market-based information. These preferences for environmental goods and services are revealed indirectly when individuals purchase marketed goods which are related to the

environmental good in some way. For example, there are markets for certain goods to which environmental commodities are related, as either substitutes or complements to the goods in question. In this way people's purchasing behaviour in actual markets reflect, to a certain extent, their preferences for environmental assets. Thus, people often pay a higher price for a hotel room with a view of the ocean, or will take the time to travel to a special spot for swimming or bird watching. These kinds of expenditures can be used to place a lower bound on the value of the view or the recreational experience. Two approaches often used in valuing tourism related benefits and costs are the Travel Cost Method and Hedonic Pricing.

Travel cost method   The travel cost method (TCM) estimates the economic values associated with environmental attributes or sites that are used for recreation. Thus, peoples' WTP to visit the site can be estimated based on the number of trips that they make given different travel costs. This is analogous to estimating peoples' WTP for a marketed good based on the quantity demanded at different prices. A basic assumption is that the time and travel cost expenses that people incur to visit a site represent the 'price' of access to the site. The cost of travel is considered to be a proxy for WTP (Bedate et al., 2004; Rosato, 2008; Ward and Beal, 2000). The TCM has been applied to demand estimation in various tourism contexts including: hiking and biking (Hesseln et al., 2003); fishing (Morey and Breffle, 2006); snorkeling (Park et al., 2002), visits to islands (Chen et al., 2004), national parks (Liston-Heyes and Heyes, 1999), beach resorts (Bell and Leeworthy, 1990), coral reefs (Carr and Mendelsohn, 2003); and the demand for rock climbing (Shaw and Jakus, 1996).

Hedonic pricing   The hedonic pricing method (HPM) assumes that people value the attributes of a good, or the services it provides, rather than the good itself. The price that a person pays will reflect the value of the set of attributes that he/she considers important when purchasing the good. On this assumption, we can value any individual attribute of any good by looking at how the price people are willing to pay for it changes when that attribute changes. In valuing environmental attributes tourism researchers have used HPM to estimate the value of aircraft noise (Espey and Lopez, 2000; Rahmatian and Cockerill, 2004), scenic views (Baddeley, 2004; Monty and Skidmore, 2003), urban wetlands (Mahan et al., 2000), recreational and aesthetic value of water (Lansford and Jones, 1995), beach pricing (Wilman, 1981); and clean air (Harrison and Rubinfeld, 1978).

Stated preference
Stated preference techniques involve asking people about their preferences to identify the trade-offs they are prepared to make as regards costs and benefits under certain hypothetical scenarios. The approach simulates a market by estimating a consumer's WTP for the good or service, or WTA compensation to tolerate a negative or adverse economic outcome. The two basic stated preference approaches that use surveys to elicit value through peoples' responses to given hypothetical situations are *contingent valuation* and *contingent choice*.

Contingent valuation   The contingent valuation method (CVM) is the most widely used method for estimating non-use value. The basic principle of CVM is that people have preferences in relation to all goods including goods that are not available in any existing market. CVM attempts to reveal these hidden preferences by means of questionnaires. People are asked the maximum amount of money they are willing to pay (or willing to accept as compensation) for a hypothetical change in the quantity or quality of a good. It is assumed that this professed willingness to pay would equate to actual willingness if a real market for the good did exist. The method is called 'contingent' valuation because people are asked to state their willingness to pay (accept), contingent on a specific hypothetical scenario and description of the environmental amenity. CVM can be used to put dollar values on non-market values of the environment, including everything from the basic life support functions associated with ecosystem health or biodiversity, to the enjoyment of a scenic vista or a wilderness experience, to appreciating the option to go hiking, fishing or rafting in the future or the right to bequest those options to one's grandchildren. It also includes the value people place on simply knowing that elephants, whales and rainforests exist. CVM studies have been published on wildlife and the environment (Chase et al., 1998; Giraud et al., 2002; Nunes and Nijkamp, 2009), the value of coral reefs (Brander et al. (2006) and various outdoor recreation and ecotourism settings :value of forests (Bostedt and Mattsson (1995); marine reserve management (Bhat, 2003); nature-based tourism resources (Lee, 1997); landcape (Willis and Garrod, 1993); national parks (Bateman and Langford, 1997); protected areas (Dharmaratne et al., 2000); ecotourism resources (Lee et al., 1998); wildlife (Solomon et al., 2004), and the economic benefits of rare and endangered species (Loomis and White, 1996). CVM has also been applied to valuing cultural heritage (Beltran and Rojas, 1996; Bille Hansen, 1997; Chambers et al., 1998; Lockwood et al., 1996; Pollicino and Maddison, 2001; Noonan, 2003; Salazar and Marques, 2005).

Contingent choice   The Contingent Choice Method (CCM) asks respondents to state a preference between one group of environmental attributes, at a given price or cost to the individual, and another group of environmental attributes at a different price or cost. WTP (accept) can then be inferred from the hypothetical choices that include cost as an attribute (Hanley et al., 2001; Louvier et al., 2000). CCM, also referred to as *conjoint analysis*, measures preferences for different attributes of a multi-attribute choice. CCM is similar to CVM, in that it can be used to estimate economic values for many environmental services, but differs in that it does not directly ask individuals to state their values. Instead, values are inferred from the hypothetical choices or trade-offs that people make between sets of attributes. Because it focuses on trade-offs among scenarios with different characteristics, CCM is especially suited to policy decisions where a set of possible actions might result in different impacts on natural resources or environmental services (Rahim, 2008).

(3) Effects that are Known to Exist but Cannot be Precisely Identified and Accurately Quantified, Let Alone Valued

These could include crime prevention effects of tourist police programmes, outcomes of a publically funded tourism and hospitality training programme, aesthetic effects of streetscape beautification programmes, loss to humans from species extinction and so on. Costs and benefits that cannot be valued in money terms are often described as 'intangibles'. Examples of 'intangibles' in tourism projects include the development of special 'themed' events to improve 'destination image', 'branding' or 'community pride'. Similarly the construction of a large-scale hotel adjacent to an attractive beach might be 'aesthetically displeasing' or 'socially alienating' to local residents. Lost assets as a result of tourism development may be considered to have 'heritage value'. Effects that cannot reasonably be quantified in monetary terms should not be ignored in the CBA. If the externalities are unable to be quantified, they should at least be identified and explained to decision makers. Intangible benefits and costs can sometimes be significant in relation to the quantitative impacts, and heavily influence the final accept–reject decision. If they appear to be significant, they should be explicitly highlighted and explained in the analysis so that decision makers are aware of the values underpinning a particular option. This explanation can be quantitative, qualitative, descriptive, or some combination.

While it is desirable to give a monetary value to as many benefits and costs as possible within the resource and time constraints, often not all benefits and costs require valuation in order to obtain relevant information from benefit cost analysis. For instance, in some situations the valuation of only some benefits may be sufficient to indicate that benefits exceed costs.

APPLICATIONS OF CBA TO TOURISM

CBA can be used to guide a wide range of decisions on types of tourism development, especially within the following four broad contexts:

Analysing Capital Expenditure

Many projects involve capital expenditure for new or replacement facilities. Such projects might include airport construction or expansion, the development of cruise shipping terminals, a resort development or highway construction. Larger capital projects, including buildings, equipment and other forms of infrastructure and productive investment, should be subjected to an analysis of their costs and benefits over their lifetime. Key questions are whether or not to undertake the investment, whether to undertake it now or later, and which option to choose. It is in the transportation area that most CBA appear to have been conducted (Litman, 2010). Examples of tourism related CBA studies include assessment of options for expanding capacity (runways and terminal facilities) at Heathrow airport (Department of Transport, 2009); investment in high speed rail infrastructure (De Rus, 2011); estimating the benefits of tourism development in a National Park in Madagascar (Mercer et al., 1995); tourism development in South Carolina (Hefner et al., 2001); economic evaluation of the Channel Tunnel (Anguera, 2006).

Analysing a Policy Option

In principle, any proposal or policy option can be subjected to CBA. A basic principle of any type of project evaluation is the 'with–without' principle. In practice, this means that the forecast 'state of the world' with the proposal to be undertaken, is compared with the 'state of the world' that would have existed in the absence of the project (the 'do nothing' or 'status quo' option). Thus, a government may wish to estimate the costs and benefits of some policy regarding requirements for tourist visas, bilateral aviation agreements, tourism and hospitality training programmes or restrictions on the use of migrant labour. Policies almost always confer benefits on some parties and impose costs on others. CBA helps to uncover unanticipated costs and benefits of projects. It explicitly estimates the size of gains and losses for affected individuals and groups. This information is important in public sector decision making and should be made explicit because it is important to identify those who stand to gain and lose from a programme or project. These costs and benefits can be valued in the same way as costs and benefits arising from capital expenditures. Recent tourism examples are CBA of protection of the northern beaches of Australia's Gold Coast (Raybould and Mules, 1999); road safety measures (Elvik, 2001); and a smoking ban in the Dutch hotel and catering sector (Spreen and Mot, 2008).

Retaining or Disposing of an Existing Asset

CBA can be undertaken where an agency is considering the retention or disposal of an existing asset. A government agency may be considering closing a rail link to a tourist region or closing a museum, cruise terminal facilities or zoo. CBA can address issues such as whether or not to sell land, whether to relocate facilities, and whether to repair an asset or to replace it. The potential benefit of an economic appraisal of assets is to improve the allocation of public sector resources to ensure the government's objectives are met to the maximum extent as are community benefits. Tourism-related examples include assessing the economic benefits of removing dams and restoring rivers (Loomis, 1996) and the benefits to inter-urban rail passenger services of retaining a railroad (Joray and Kochanowski, 1978).

Post-evaluation of a Project or Program

CBA provides a means of determining whether or not a particular programme or project has generated a net benefit for the community. Thus, tax concessions offered to hotel developers or tourism and hospitality training programmes may be reviewed to assess the net benefits, and a government agency may investigate whether its decision to provide financial support for a special event such as a Formula One Grand Prix event or an Olympic Games generates an appropriate return on public funds. CBA is particularly well suited to evaluating special events. Examples include CBAs of the Eurovision Song Contest in Israel (Fleischer and Felsenstein, 2002), V8 Car Races in the Australian Capital Territory (ACT Auditor General, 2002), the Vancouver Winter Olympics 2010 (Shaffer et al., 2003); a Formula One Grand Prix event in Melbourne (Victorian Auditor General, 2007). On the basis of a CBA, it is possible for the decision maker to make a judgment of whether the economic benefits of the event are greater than the costs, and to also judge whether the event would represent the best use of the funds, when funds are limited and alternative calls on funds exist. In the case of the Vancouver Winter Olympics and both car races, the CBA revealed that net losses to society would occur even though economic impact analyses projected positive effects on GDP and employment. Clearly, there are many potential effects of events that are often not accounted for in a standard economic impact analysis. In order for the government to be more comprehensively apprised event assessments need to be broadened to take, where practicable, a more comprehensive approach embracing not only economic but social and environmental factors. Once these wider effects of events are acknowledged we can appreciate why estimation of the economic impacts of events is only part of the evaluation story. To determine the extent (if any) of government assistance to be provided, it is necessary that the cost of these funds be compared to the wider costs and benefits from the event (Abelson, 2011).

ADVANTAGES AND LIMITATIONS OF CBA

CBA has a number of strengths but also limitations.

Strengths

A systematic method
CBA is a systematic and consistent evaluation method that facilitates comparisons between different options. It has a well-developed theoretical foundation – neoclassical welfare economics – which is based on the individual being the best judge of their own welfare and the welfare of society being the sum of the welfare of individuals. Its use promotes the efficient use of resources. The template character of CBA permits the decision maker to determine the adequacy of the information collected and see important information is missing. This knowledge provides the decision maker with valuable insight into the level of ignorance regarding important attributes of the policy. CBA makes proponents consider costs and benefits that are external to the proponent. It forces the decision maker to think in a rational way about the costs and benefits of alternative actions. It can provide a clear focus on net benefits of a proposal without regard to who wins and who loses from projects and programmes. CBA encourages clear consideration of the true *value added* from a proposal by focusing on incremental net benefits. Its emphasis on the quantification of costs and benefits on a comparable basis can provide a useful 'hard edge' to an evaluation strategy.

Transparent
The results of a well-executed CBA can be clearly linked to the assumptions, theory, methods and procedures used in it. This transparency can add to the accountability of public decisions by indicating where the decisions are at variance with the analysis. It can also improve the political process by uncovering gains and losses which might otherwise be neglected in the bargaining process between different stakeholders of some project, programme or policy.

Comparability
CBA attempts to capture in a single index all the features of a policy decision that affects the well being of society. The single-metric approach permits the comparison of policies

that affect different attributes of well being differently, that is, it permits the decision maker to compare 'apples' and 'oranges' on the basis of a single attribute (the index of social welfare) common to both.

Limitations

Some values can't be monetized
CBA often includes subjective assumptions regarding non-economic values. While the analysis usually highlights the various qualitative costs and benefits, assessing the actual quantitative values can be quite contentious. Where the use of value judgments and assumptions becomes unavoidable, the quantification of intangibles is particularly susceptible to manipulation. Environmental protection is often desirable for reasons that cannot be quantified – social, spiritual, and psychological values that defy monetization. And what is the economic value of a country's enhanced international reputation and standing following the hosting of a mega event, or the destruction of aspects of cultural heritage through tourism development, or of increases in customer and employee satisfaction? In sum, there are things that humans cannot put a price tag on. The upshot is that CBA can yield dramatically different numbers, especially as different methodologies for assigning economic values to non-economic benefits can vary significantly.

By way of response, exponents of CBA should of course endeavour to value whatever can be quantified and valued reliably within the resource constraints of the situation. The remaining intangible effects should be listed and described as fully as possible, and some consideration given to the impact of the intangible component of the CBA on the results. Economic values are inferred from the choices made by individuals. The worth of a rainforest might be inferred from the things that one gives up to see the rainforest (e.g., the cost of travel to the location). To economists, the importance of things (tangible or intangible) is revealed by what a person will give up to obtain them. The lower bound on the value of the item obtained is equated to what is given up. It is sometimes suggested that some non-market effects cannot be valued or have infinite values. However, finite values for non-market effects are routinely explicit in government decisions and the behaviour of consumers. For difficult to quantify values, it is therefore important that analysts make their assumptions clear and that margins for error be identified or sensitivity testing be undertaken.

Individual versus social welfare
Critics highlight the presumption of CBA that the well being of society can be defined as some aggregation of the well being of individual members of that society, and the methods by which the aggregation is performed. As Sagoff (1998) argues, economists use the term 'social welfare' as a proxy for the 'satisfaction of preferences' and then trivially and speciously argue that the 'satisfaction of preferences' produces social welfare. On the contrary, common wisdom suggests that it is not the satisfaction but the content and quality of desires that correlate with what people mean by welfare or well being. The criticism here is relatively straightforward – that the economic value of something is not related to the well being that a person enjoys

as a result of that thing. Researchers do not seem to have adequately addressed this type of criticism of CBA.

Future generations

It is sometimes argued that the activity of discounting implies that the needs of future generations are given less weight than those of the current generation. Traditional CBA tends to give little weight to costs that occur far in the future and overly emphasizes short-term gain. Critics have argued that intergenerational equity is fostered if the discount rate is low and some claim that this is appropriate when environmental sustainability is an issue. In response, it should be noted that a low discount rate can make projects seem profitable and can encourage their implementation even if they are at odds with sustainability. Assuming no irreversible environmental effects are involved, a project with a high rate of return when all of its costs and benefits are counted is better for the present generation and, through reinvestment, better for future generations as well. Only when benefits are non-renewable and consumed rather than reinvested is there conflict across generations, with one generation paying and another benefitting (Treasury Board of Canada, 1998).

It is important that intertemporal equity issues form an integral part of each decision-making process in CBA and research is progressing in respect of this issue. Approaches to selecting real discount rates fall into two broad groups, both of which have given rise to a wide range of recommended rates – a 'descriptive' approach based on the opportunity cost of drawing funds from the private sector; and – a 'prescriptive' approach that derives from ethical views about intergenerational equity. Debate on this issue continues (Harrison, 2010).

Equity considerations

It is often argued that CBA takes the existing distribution of income as given and does not consider the equity implications of the policies that it seeks to evaluate. This criticism emphasizes the anonymous manner in which the welfare changes of individuals are aggregated to obtain estimates of the change in social welfare. Efficiency is measured without regard to who would get the benefits and who would incur the costs. Questions related to distribution of income are not taken up for consideration. The criticism is valid as far as it goes. Anonymous weighting of individual welfare does not take equity into account. However, distributional information can be supplied as an adjunct to CBA. One way in which distributional aspects can be integrated into CBA is by assigning weights to benefits received and costs borne by different socio-economic groups, e.g., giving higher weight to the poorer categories. Another way of handling the distributional aspect is to establish distributional constraint as an additional criterion. It is then up to decision makers and the political process to identify the appropriate trade-off between equity and efficiency.

Complexity

CBA has been criticized for being complex and too onerous in its information requirements. Not surprisingly, there are many gaps in the scientific knowledge and many deficiencies in the analytic techniques necessary to complete these analyses. However, in some situations this may simply reflect the complexity of public decisions and, in most cases, unnecessary complexity should and can be avoided. Use of CBA in tourism contexts may generally be less onerous on data collection and analysis than for environmental decision making. Even simple applications of the technique can yield valuable information for proponents and decision makers.

FURTHER DEVELOPMENTS AND APPLICATIONS OF CBA IN TOURISM RESEARCH

The discussion indicates that there is substantial scope for greater use of CBA in tourism contexts. To date, there has been relatively little attempt to undertake detailed CBA studies of plans, policies or regulations that either directly or indirectly affect tourism stakeholders. The preferred technique among tourism economists appears to be economic impact analysis. However, estimates of the economic impacts of tourism plans, policies, developments or programmes provide, in themselves, an imperfect basis for decisions about resource allocation. While economic impact analysis (CGE modelling) picks up general equilibrium effects which the partial CBA is not capable of detecting, including changes in income to households, CBA picks up a whole range of benefits and costs due to non priced effects arising from the absence of markets for some goods and services affected which would not be included in economic impact analysis.

CBA is not without its challenges as the discussion of limitations highlights. Each type of limitation is being addressed in the research literature and CBA remains the primary technique for informing policy makers of the net benefits of different strategies to achieve objectives associated with 'the public good'.

One area of tourism in which CBA is expected to play an increasingly important role is in the assessment of special events. The success or contribution of a particular event should not be measured only by its direct financial contribution but needs to consider the wider economic, social and environmental impacts that are invariably associated with it. There is a growing awareness among researchers that event assessment which focuses only on economic impacts is too narrow in scope to provide sufficient information to policy makers and government funding agencies and that, where practical, a more comprehensive approach should be employed to embrace the importance of social and environmental impacts in addition to economic impacts. Similar reasoning supports greater use of CBA generally in tourism research.

REFERENCES

Abelson, P. (2011), 'Evaluating major events and avoiding the mercantilist fallacy', *Economic Papers*, **30** (1), 48–59.
Access Economics (2010), 'Cost benefit analysis of the FIFA 2022 World Cup', report by Access Economics Pty. Ltd for Department of Resources, Energy and Tourism, Canberra, Australia.
ACT Auditor General (2002), 'ACT Auditor General's Office Performance Audit Report V8 Car Races in Canberra: Costs and Benefits', Canberra, ACT.
Anguera, R. (2006), 'The Channel Tunnel: an ex post economic evaluation', *Transportation Research Part A: Policy and Practice*, **40** (4), 291–315.
Baddeley, M.C. (2004), 'Are tourists willing to pay for aesthetic quality? An empirical assessment from Krabi Province, Thailand', *Tourism Economics*, **10** (1), 45–61.

Bateman, I. and I. Langford (1997), 'Non-users willingness to pay for a national park: an application and critique of the contingent valuation method', *Regional Studies*, **31** (6), 571–578.
Bedate, A., L.C. Herrero and J.Á. Sanz (2004), 'Economic valuation of the cultural heritage: application to four case studies in Spain', *Journal of Cultural Heritage*, **5** (1), 101–111.
Bell, F. and V. Leeworthy (1990), 'Recreational demand by tourists for Saltwater Beach days', *Journal of Environmental Economics and Management*, **18**, 189–205.
Beltran, E. and M. Rojas (1996), 'Diversified funding methods in Mexican archeology', *Annals of Tourism Research*, **23** (2), 463–478.
Bhat, M. (2003), 'Application of nonmarket valuation to the Florida Keys Marine Reserve management', *Journal of Environmental Management*, **67**, 315–325.
Bille Hansen, T. (1997), 'The willingness-to-pay for the Royal Theatre in Copenhagen as a public good', *Journal of Cultural Economics*, **21**, 1–28.
Boardman, A.E., D.H. Greenberg, A.R. Vining and D.L. Weimer (2001), *Cost–Benefit Analysis. Concepts and Practice*, 2nd edition, Upper Saddle River, NJ: Prentice Hall.
Bostedt, G. and L. Mattsson (1995), 'The value of forests for tourism in Sweden', *Annals of Tourism Research*, **22** (3), 671–680.
Brander, L.M., P van Beukering and S.J. Cesar (2006), 'The recreational value of coral reefs: a meta-analysis', IVM Working Paper: IVM 06/07, Institute for Environmental Studies, Amsterdam.
Burgess, D.F. and R.O. Zerbe (2011), 'Appropriate discounting for benefit-cost analysis', *Journal of Benefit-Cost Analysis*, **2** (2), 1–18.
Carr, L. and R. Mendelsohn (2003), 'Valuing coral reefs: a travel cost analysis of the Great Barrier Reef', *Ambio*, **32** (2), 353–357.
Chambers, C., P. Chambers and J. Whitehead (1998), 'Contingent valuation of quasipublic good: validity, reliability, and application to valuing a historic site', *Public Finance Review*, **26** (2), 137–154.
Chase, L., D. Lee, W. Schulze and D. Anderson (1998), 'Ecotourism demand and differential pricing of national park access in Costa Rica', *Land Economics*, **74** (4), 466–482.
Chen, W., H. Hong, Y. Liu, L. Zhang, X. Hou and M. Raymond (2004), 'Recreation demand and economic value: an application of travel cost method for Xiamen Island', *China Economic Review*, **15**, 398–406.
Department for Transport (2009), 'Adding capacity at Heathrow Airport: impact assessment', DfT Publications, London, January.
De Rus, G. (2011), 'The BCA of HSR: should the government invest in high speed rail infrastructure?', *Journal of Benefit-Cost Analysis*, **2** (2), 1–26.
Dharmaratne, G.S., F. Yee Sang and L.J. Walling (2000), 'Tourism potentials for financing protected areas', *Annals of Tourism Research*, **27** (3), 590–610.
Dupuit, A.J.É.J. (1844), *De la mesure de l'utilité des travaux publics*, Annales des ponts et chaussées, Second series, 8. Translated by R.H. Barback as 'On the measurement of the utility of public works', International Economic Papers, 1952, **2**, 83–110.
Dwyer, L., P. Forsyth and W. Dwyer (2010), *Tourism Economics and Policy*, Cheltenham, UK: Channel View Publications.
Elvik, R. (2001), 'Cost-benefit analysis of road safety measures: applicability and controversies', *Accident Analysis and Prevention*, **33**, 9–17.
Espey, M. and H. Lopez (2000), 'The impact of airport noise and proximity on residential property values', *Growth and Change*, **31**, 408–419.
Fleischer, A. and D. Felsenstein (2002), 'Cost-benefit analysis using economic surpluses: a case study of a televised event', *Journal of Cultural Economics*, **26** (2), 139–156.
Flyvbjerg, B., N. Bruzelius and W. Rothengatter (2003), *Megaprojects and Risk: An Anatomy of Ambition*, Cambridge: Cambridge University Press.
Giraud, K., B. Turcin, J. Loomis and J. Cooper (2002), 'Economic benefit of the protection program for the Steller sea lion', *Marine Policy*, **26**, 451–458.
Hanley, N., S. Maurato and R. Wright (2001), 'Choice modelling approaches: a superior alternative for environmental valuation?', *Journal of Economic Surveys*, **15** (3), 435–462.
Harrison, D., Jr., and D.L. Rubinfeld (1978), 'Hedonic housing prices and the demand for clean air', *Journal Environmental Economics and Management*, **5**, 81–102.
Harrison, M. (2010), 'Valuing the future: the social discount rate in cost-benefit analysis', Visiting Researcher Paper, Productivity Commission, Canberra.
Hefner, F., J. Crotts and J. Flowers (2001), 'The cost–benefit model as applied to tourism development in the state of South Carolina', *Tourism Economics*, **7** (4), 163–175.
Hesseln, H., J.B. Loomis, A. Gonzalez-Caban and S. Alexander (2003), 'Wildfire effects on hiking and biking demand in New Mexico: a travel cost study', *Journal of Environmental Management*, **69**, 359–368.
Jenkins, G. and A.C. Harberger (1995), *Cost-Benefit Analysis of Investment Decisions*, Cambridge, MA: Harvard Institute for International Development.

Joray, P. and P. Kochanowski (1978), 'Inter-urban rail passenger service: social benefits of retaining the South Shore Railroad (Chicago)', *Logistics and Transportation Review*, **14** (1), 81–89.

Lansford, N.H. Jr. and L.L. Jones (1995), 'Recreational and aesthetic value of water using hedonic price analysis', *Journal of Agricultural and Resource Economics*, **20** (2), 341–355.

Lee, C. (1997), 'Valuation of nature-based tourism resources using dichotomous choice contingent valuation method', *Tourism Management*, **18**, 587–591.

Lee, C., J. Lee and S. Han (1998), 'Measuring the economic value of ecotourism resources: the case of South Korea', *Journal of Travel Research*, **36** (Spring), 40–47.

Liston-Heyes, C. and A. Heyes (1999), 'Recreational benefits from the Dartmoor National Park', *Journal of Environmental Management*, **55**, 69–80.

Litman, T. (2010), 'Transportation cost and benefit analysis', Victoria Transport Policy Institute (www.vtpi.org).

Lockwood, M., K. Tracey and N. Klomp (1996), 'Analyzing conflict between cultural heritage and nature conservation in the Australian Alps: a CVM approach', *Journal of Environmental Planning and Management*, **39** (3), 357–370.

Loomis, J. (1996), 'Measuring the economic benefits of removing dams and restoring the Elwha River: results of a contingent value survey', *Water Resources Research*, **32**, 441–447.

Loomis, J. and D. White (1996), 'Economic benefits of rare and endangered species: summary and meta-analysis', *Ecological Economics*, **18** (3), 197–206.

Louvier, J., D. Henscher and J. Swait (2000), *Stated Choice Methods: Analysis and Applications*, Cambridge: Cambridge University Press.

Mahan, B.L., S. Polasky and R.M. Adams (2000), 'Valuing urban wetlands: a property price approach', *Land Economics*, **76** (1), 100–113.

Mercer, E., R. Kramer and N. Sharma (1995), 'Rainforest tourism: estimating the benefits of tourism development in a new national park in Madagascar', *Journal of Forest Economics*, **1** (12), 239–269.

Mishan, E.J. (2002), 'On the conceptual underpinning of a cost-benefit analysis', *The Singaporean Economic Review*, **47** (1), 1–16.

Monty, B. and M. Skidmore (2003), 'Hedonic pricing and willingness to pay for bed and breakfast amenities in Southeast Wisconsin', *Journal of Travel Research*, **42**, 195–199.

Morey, E.R. and W.S. Breffle (2006), 'Valuing a change in a fishing site without collecting characteristics data on all fishing sites: a complete but minimal model', *American Journal of Agricultural Economics*, **88** (1), 150–161.

Noonan, D. (2003), 'Contingent valuation and cultural resources: a meta-analytic review of the literature', *Journal of Cultural Economics*, **27** (3–4), 159–176.

Nunes, P. and P. Nijkamp (2009), 'Contingent valuation method', Encora Coastal Portal, available at http://www.coastalwiki.org.

Park, T., J.M. Bowker and V.R. Leeworthy (2002), 'Valuing snorkeling visits to the Florida Keys with stated revealed preference models', *Journal of Environmental Management*, **65**, 301–312.

Pollicino, M. and D. Maddison (2001), 'Valuing the benefits of cleaning Lincoln Cathedral', *Journal of Cultural Economics*, **25**, 131–148.

Rahim, K.A. (2008), 'Non-market valuation techniques', Economic Valuation of the Goods and Services of Coastal Habitats The Regional Training Workshop, March 24–28, 2008, Samut Songkram Province, Thailand.

Rahmatian, M. and L. Cockerill (2004), 'Airport noise and residential housing valuation in Southern California: a hedonic pricing approach', *International Journal of Environmental Science & Technology*, **1** (1), 17–25.

Ray, A. (1984), *Cost Benefit Analysis*, Washington DC: The World Bank.

Raybould, M. and T. Mules (1999), 'A cost-benefit study of protection of the northern beaches of Australia's Gold Coast', *Tourism Economics*, **5** (2), 121–139.

Rosato, P. (2008), 'Travel cost method', Encora Coastal Portal, http://www.coastalwiki.org.

Sagoff, M. (1998), 'Aggregation and deliberation in valuing environmental public goods: a look beyond contingent pricing', *Ecological Economics*, **24**, 213–230.

Salazar, S. and J. Marques (2005), 'Valuing cultural heritage: the social benefits of restoring an old Arab tower', *Journal of Cultural Heritage*, **6**, 69–77.

Shaffer, M., A. Greer and C. Mauboules (2003), 'Olympic costs and benefits', Canadian Centre for Policy Alternatives Publication, February.

Shaw, W. and P. Jakus (1996), 'Travel cost models of the demand for rock climbing', *Agricultural and Resource Economics Review*, **25**, 133–142.

Solomon, B., C. Corey-Luse and K. Halvorsen (2004), 'The Florida Manatee and ecotourism: toward a safe minimum standard', *Ecological Economics*, **50**, 101–115.

Spreen, M. and E. Mot (2008), '*Een rookverbod in deNederlandse horeca, Een kosten-batenanalyse* [A smoking

ban in the Dutch hotel and catering sector, a cost-benefit analysis]', Netherlands Bureau for Economic Analysis, Document 159, February (English summary, main report only in Dutch).
Treasury Board of Canada (1998), 'Benefit-cost analysis guide', Treasury Board of Canada Secretariat Ottawa.
Victorian Auditor General (2007), 'State investment in major events', Victorian Government Printer, Victoria.
Ward, F.A. and D. Beal (2000), *Valuing Nature with Travel Cost Method: A Manual*, Cheltenham, UK and Northampton, MA USA: Edward Elgar.
Willis, K. and G. Garrod (1993), 'Valuing landscape: a contingent valuation approach', *Journal of Environmental Management*, **37** (1), 1–22.
Wilman, E. (1981), 'Hedonic prices and beach recreation values', in V. Smith (ed.), *Advances in Applied Microeconomics*, Volume 1, Greenwich, CT: JAI Press.

PART II

QUALITATIVE RESEARCH METHODS

Gayle R. Jennings

QUALITATIVE RESEARCH: ITS NATURE AND EVOLUTION

Qualitative research is a well-established approach to researching phenomena in the social sciences. Comparatively, its application in the fields of tourism studies and management is a more recent occurrence dating from the late 1970s and 1980s. Increasingly, however, in the early decades of the twenty-first century, qualitative research is gaining broader acceptance within those fields. This acceptance is due to the ability of qualitative research to provide rich, in-depth knowledge from multiple viewpoints along with its emphasis on *verstenhen*, 'empathetic understanding', especially, with regard to the 'how' and 'why' of tourism related phenomena and experiences.

In the past, the fields of tourism studies and management have tended to emphasize quantitative research. That emphasis still continues in the early 2010s. Quantitative research places an emphasis on *erklären*, 'causal or nomethetic (rule or law related) explanation', particularly, 'who, when, what, where', along with 'how' and 'why'. Qualitative research distinguishes itself from quantitative research by nature of the former's emic approach to research. Emic approaches acknowledge the subjectivity of the researcher within research processes as well as shape research to include the researcher as a subjectively embedded being in the research process. Emic research has also been described as insider research since the researcher usually brings background experiences that have complementarity and/or empathy with the focus of the study. Rather than distort the research, such background commonality facilitates the interpretive processes of the research act and adds to the depth and diversity of interpretations.

On the other hand, quantitative research is associated with etic approaches to research. Specifically, etic approaches are objectively situated and may best be framed as research conducted from a neutral stance, that is, an outsider perspective. Such a stance is assumed to remove or reduce bias from and distortions to analyses and findings. In discussing emic and etic approaches, we are starting to consider aspects associated with axiological positions upon which research may be situated.

Axiology is the study of values and ethics (Jennings, 2009), in this case, with respect to research processes. Axiology is one of four frames that guide research processes (Guba 1990; Jennings, 2009). The other frames are ontology (world view), epistemology (science of knowledge generation as well as the nature of the 'relationship between the researcher and that which is to be known' (Jennings, 2009, p. 674; see also Guba, 1990) and methodology (principles for guiding the conduct of research). Each of these four frames enables us to understand the differing suites of paradigms used in tourism studies and management research.

PARADIGMS INFORMING TOURISM STUDIES RESEARCH

Broadly speaking, there are two clusters of paradigms. Those associated with qualitative research that use qualitative methodologies and those linked to quantitative research, that predominantly use quantitative methodologies. Within the latter set, there are approaches that use mixed methods by drawing on both quantitative and qualitative methods of research. Quantitative research is associated with the paradigms of positivism and post-positivism.

Qualitative research is generally associated with (social) constructivism, interpretivism critical theory orientation and participatory paradigms (Jennings 2009, 2010; Lincoln et al. 2011; Schwandt, 2000). Examples of use of social constructivism in tourism studies are found in the works of Gurney and Humphreys (2006) and Jennings (1999). Discussion of social constructivism also occurs in O'Gorman's (2005) work. An interpretive approach is demonstrated in the work of Gurung (2008) and Jennings and Stehlik (2009). Critical theory orientation as a research tool is used by Fox (2007) and Kensbock (2012/13) as well as considered in the writings of Chambers (2007). An example of a participatory approach is provided in the research of Bennett (2004) and Jennings et al. (2010). The approach is also discussed in the writings of Darcy (2006) and Westwood (2007).

Amongst social science and tourism scholars, debates remain as to what should or should not be included within the cluster of paradigms associated with qualitative research. For example, feminist perspectives, cultural studies, queer theory, critical race theory and postmodern paradigms are variously considered as part of the cluster of qualitatively associated paradigms. Others argue regarding the inclusion of mixed methods approaches. Refer to Denzin and Lincoln (2011), Jennings (2009), Lincoln et al. (2011) for further consideration of this debate.

Despite the preceding debates, within the fields of tourism studies and management, the dominant, hegemonic research paradigms are positivism and post-positivism. The cluster of paradigms bearing complementarity with qualitative research continues in the meantime to grow in application within tourism studies and management research. The difference between post/positivistic paradigms and paradigms that associate around social constructivism are now considered further.

What distinguishes post/positivistic paradigms from social constructivism? The preceding discourse has hinted at some differences – etic versus emic approaches; and quantitative versus qualitative methodological approaches. There are other differences arising from the respective paradigms' attitudes to ontology, epistemology, methodology and axiology. Generally, post/positivistic paradigms adopt:

- an ontology that views truth and laws as universal (positivism) or immutable and shaped by historical and social circumstances (post-positivism);

- an epistemology that is objective (positivism) or objective but recognizes the potential for researcher bias (post-positivism);
- primarily a quantitative methodology. Some post-positivistic research may use mixed methods; and
- an axiology predicated on value-free attitudes and a focus on the extrinsic value of research processes and outcomes. Some post-positivistic research may embrace an emancipatory role for research.

As already noted, there is a suite of paradigms that constitute those associated with a qualitative methodological research approach. For comparative purposes with post/ positivism, social constructivism has been selected from that suite. Social constructivism adopts:

- an ontology that embraces multiple realities;
- an inter-subjective epistemology;
- a focus on qualitative methodologies; and
- a value-laden axiology, which emphasizes the intrinsic value of research processes and research outcomes.

Table II.1 provides an overview of positivism and post-positivism, the hegemonic paradigms, along with critical theory orientation, social constructivism and participatory paradigms, the burgeoning paradigms. The table does not present all paradigms in use. For fuller discussion, readers are referred to Denzin and Lincoln, 2011, Jennings (2009, 2010) and Lincoln et al. (2011).

Which paradigm should a researcher use? The answer should be determined by the nature of the research questions, issues and tourism/leisure phenomena of interest. It should not be determined based only on hegemonic research practice with regard to paradigm selection. Cohen (1988), Goodson and Phillimore (2004), Hollinshead (1996), and Jennings (2010), Riley and Love (2000), Walle (1997) advocate that qualitative methodologically informed research can contribute to understanding tourism phenomena and should be used. Qualitative research serves to complement quantitative research's focus on explanation by emphasizing understanding. Both types of research have and do make significant contributions to our development of knowledge in the fields of tourism studies and management. The first section of this book has provided readers with insights into the various research approaches and methods associated with positivism and post-positivism. This, the second section of the book, considers a range of qualitative research methods and approaches connected with social constructivism and related paradigms.

A COMMENTARY ON TOURISM STUDIES AND MANAGEMENT RESEARCH

Before moving on to the background and research foci of qualitative research, as tourism researchers, we need to take stock of significant criticism that has been directed at global research efforts. Tourism studies and management research, like other disciplinary and fields of studies research, is predicated on western-centric research processes. This

Table II.1 Comparison of major paradigms used in tourism studies and management research

Examples of paradigms	Positivism	Post-Positivism	Critical Theory	Constructivism/ Interpretivism	Participatory
Ontology (world view, perspective on the nature of reality)	Universal truths and laws.	Fallible truths that are influenced by social and historical circumstances.	Realities are socially and historically framed and reflect power relations.	Realities and perspectives are multiple in nature.	Realities are constructed collectively via engagements between individuals and others.
Epistemology (science of knowledge construction; relationship between 'researcher' and 'researched' or 'participants')	Objective, etic	Objective, etic whilst recognizing potential biases inherent in researcher decision-making processes.	Subjective–objective (emic–etic) unless post-positivist critical theory (objective).	Intersubjective (emic)	Reflexive, situated and embodied. Critical subjectivity. Emic and etic. Hermeneutic.
Methodology (research guidelines)	Quantitative	Quantitative (Use of mixed methods)	Qualitative Some quantitative	Qualitative	Qualitative. Quantitative. Mixed method.
Axiology (study of values and ethics)	Value free. Research projects' purposes are extrinsic in nature.	Value free emphasizes albeit fallibility of researcher recognized. Extrinsic nature of research purposes albeit some approaches lean toward emancipatory roles of research.	Value laden research agendas. Intrinsic research foci, political agendas, emancipatory and transformative in nature.	Value laden. Research projects associated with intrinsic foci.	Value laden. Transformation.

Source: Derived from Denzin and Lincoln (2011), Guba (1990), Jennings (2009, 2010), Lincoln and Guba (2000), Lincoln et al. (2011), and Schwandt (2000).

predication has been critiqued in various disciplinary and fields of studies extant literature, see, for example, Bourdieu (1990), Bourke (1995), Foley (2003), Ivanitz (1999), Laclau (1990), Scheurich (1997), Smith (1999, 2005), Stanfield II (1994) and Urry (1990, 1996, 2002). Within tourism literature, the key critiques are associated with:

- ignoring tourism phenomena external to western cultural and social knowledge constructions (Berno, 1996; Hollinshead, 1992);
- limited use of a variety of culturally bounded sign systems and their meanings to collect, interpret and/or analyse empirical materials and/or data beyond western-centric systems and meanings (Echtner, 1999);
- paucity of integrated multicultural studies (Echtner, 1999);
- need for 'emic', context-based and temporally situated research designs when comparing tourist settings and tourism cultural differences (Cohen, 1979; Dann et al., 1988; Jennings 2007a; Sofield, 2000; Tribe, 2006);
- need to acknowledge indigenous epistemologies and use indigenous methodologies (Denzin et al., 2008; Kuokkanen, 2003; Schaper et al., 2007);
- need for inclusion of differing ontologies, epistemologies, methodologies and axiologies in tourism research beyond western-centric ones (Jennings, 2003, 2009).

As researchers we need to be cognizant of these critiques as well as address them in our research enterprises. This is especially important when considering that qualitative research seeks to achieve in-depth, empathetic understandings. In this book, Carla Santos provides readers with her thoughts on cross-cultural research.

QUALITATIVE RESEARCH: BACKGROUND AND RESEARCH FOCI

As already noted, qualitative research is predicated on *verstenhen*, empathetic understanding. It aims to gain detailed insights into phenomena by adopting worldviews (ontologies) that recognize the multiplicity of 'realities' and the manner in which these realities are constructed. Knowledge (epistemology) is generated variously through subjective–objective orientations in the case of critical theory orientation, intersubjectivity in social constructivism, and reflexive and hermeneutic processes in participatory research. In each case, the embodied and situated nature of participants and researchers contribute to the co-construction of knowledge in interactions that are founded on tenets of reciprocity (mutual exchange). Methodologically, as would be expected, the paradigms that associate under the umbrella of qualitative research predominantly utilize qualitative methodologies. Qualitative methodologies are focused on amassing empirical materials (data) drawn from the empirical world.

A methodology is a set of guidelines for conducting research, in this case qualitative research. The guidelines for qualitative methodologies are (Jennings, 2010):

- use of an inductive approach to explore the nature of reality in real world contexts;
- assumption of an ontological perspective that advocates multiple world views and realities;

- emphasis on intersubjective relationships between research participants and researcher(s);
- embracing an axiology, which values propositional, transactional, experiential knowledge that will facilitate social change and/or emancipation;
- adoption of an intersubjective epistemology, which results in value laden ethics;
- perception of researchers as insiders by study participants;
- flexible, emergent research designs to enable researcher responsiveness to field settings;
- study-specific research designs grounded in the setting being studied;
- researcher(s) focus/foci on emblematic themes arising during study processes and stages;
- non-probability sampling methods, where every person in the study population does not have an equal chance of participation unless complete participation is the focus;
- collection of written, oral and visual empirical materials that are amassed as textual units, instead of numeric representations;
- interpretation/(re)construction of empirical materials to elicit key themes and motifs synergistic with study participants' world experiences;
- representation of the findings using 'narrative'-based written text forms, use of first person active voice by the researcher(s); along with visual and performative texts, as well as practices and praxes for participatory paradigms;
- acknowledgment that the capture and representation of a 'slice of life' from the study setting is specific to only that study setting.

These guidelines in turn inform the methods of empirical material collection used. For the purpose of this chapter, a method is deemed to be the tools for empirical material collection and interpretation/(re)construction (Jennings, 2010).

METHODS OF EMPIRICAL MATERIAL COLLECTION

Qualitative research has a wide range of methods that may be used for empirical material generation. These include fieldwork, diaries, journals, memo-ing and note-making, participant observation, interviewing, visual methods, focus groups, documentary and archival analysis and computer-mediated methods of empirical material collection (Jennings, 2010).

METHODS OF EMPIRICAL MATERIAL INTERPRETATION

Qualitative research draws on a suite of methods for empirical material interpretation. The most used forms tend to be successive approximation, constant comparison, grounded theory interpretations, content analysis and deconstruction (Jennings, 2010).

QUALITATIVE EMPIRICAL MATERIAL COLLECTION AND INTERPRETATION

While the ensuing chapters address a variety of methods for empirical material collection and interpretation, in this chapter, I want to highlight five aspects of which qualitative researchers must be cognizant during qualitative research processes. The particular aspects to which I refer are qualitative vocabulary, qualitative sampling, reciprocity, triangulation/crystallization and reflexivity.

I emphasize here that these are my perspectives informed by the perspectives and discourses of others drawn from the broader area of social sciences research. Readers should note that these five aspects may not be considered or addressed by the authors of the following chapters. In fact, the authors may write using a vocabulary which is contrary to the one I articulate below. It is for them to justify the use of their chosen vocabulary and/or terminology just as I intend to do.

Qualitative Vocabulary

Qualitative research tends to use a different vocabulary than quantitative research to describe elements and aspects of the research processes. Rather than use the term data, often you will see the term empirical materials used. The terms interpretation and (re)construction may be applied instead of analysis. Participants, co-researchers rather than subjects, respondees or interviewees will be applied. Why this different usage. Essentially, the terms data, analysis and subjects imply a passive role within research processes. They resonate with actions occurring over which 'that which is to be researched' has no power. The research act is heavily imbued with power. Without our participants or access to empirical materials we have no basis for research. Power is vested in our participants or gatekeepers who hold access keys to other empirical materials, such as, documents and records. The research process is far from being a passive, objective process.

Moreover, the qualitative research act is a social process of meaning making where 'that which is to be researched' actively engages with the researcher(s). Specifically, the act is a co-construction of knowledge arising from intersubjective relationships between participants and researcher(s). What is being created as knowledge in the qualitative research act is not data but empirical world knowledge and realities originating in and arising from empirical world materials. Such knowledge and realities are subjectively and actively co-constructed.

You also will find that terms such as trustworthiness, authenticity, groundedness, participant checks, resonance, originality, credibility, dependability, usefulness, transferability, confirmability, goodness of fit and boundedness are used to discuss the outcomes of qualitative research processes. Terms used in quantitative research, such as, reliability, validity and levels of confidence, and limitations, for example, are not used as qualitative research adopts differing ontological, epistemological, methodological and axiological principles. Being different does not mean of lesser value or less rigorous in research processes. It just means using different principles and attendant vocabulary to match those principles.

Qualitative 'Sampling'

Qualitative research uses the principles of 'non-probability sampling'. Qualitative research is not about a specific set of numbers, cases or participants. It is about targeted research, which includes participants and other empirical materials, which have relevance to the research focus or foci. Such sampling is referred to as purposive sampling. Selection of participants occurs bearing several points in mind: size, nature and accessibility of the population of interest (Jennings, 2010). While various authors advocate a specific number of participants for qualitative research, in reality, there is no standard. Qualitative researchers continue to amass empirical material while simultaneously interpreting/(re)constructing the empirical materials until they reach a 'qualitative informational isomorph' (Lincoln and Guba, 1985, pp. 233–4). This is also referred to as 'theoretical saturation'. At this stage, further amassment of empirical materials will yield no further insights into the study phenomena. The interpretations are then participant checked for authenticity with participant lived experiences of the research phenomena.

Reciprocity

Qualitative research is an intersubjective experience. Reciprocity is giving something back in the research exchange. This means that during empirical material collection and interpretation/(re)construction researchers actively engage in the research process. For instance, interviews and focus groups are exchanges and rightfully, participants can ask researchers about their opinions. Principles of reciprocity require researchers to share their thoughts and insights with the participants.

Other forms of reciprocity may include gift giving as a thank you for the participant's time. Such gift giving could include chocolates, cakes, food items, books, gift vouchers and a chance to win cash prizes. Careful consideration of gift giving needs to be undertaken, the researcher wants participants to participate because they are interested in sharing their insights with the researcher rather than as a means to receive a gift.

Triangulation/Crystallization

Previously, with regard to qualitative research, the term 'triangulation' was used. In fact, it is still a term used today. Triangulation is associated with establishing a fixed point as an established reality. From a qualitative research perspective, such a reality is questionable given an ontological worldview of multiple realities. Consequently, a contrary term has gained more currency. That term is crystallization. The term emanates from the work of Richardson (1994). Crystallization refers to the practice of using various methods to illuminate as much of study phenomena as possible. Richardson (1994) tells us that when viewing any phenomena we will only achieve partial views of it, somewhat like trying to view the many facets of a crystal at the one time in a snapshot.

Relatedly, there cannot be a singular fixed reality within qualitative research. Knowledge and reality are constantly being constructed and reconstructed and interpreted and reinterpreted. Realities and knowledges are always in flux and are part of social processes, which are heavily value-laden because of the subjective and embodied beings, who participate in knowledge construction. Subsequently, due to multiple realities and perspectives, a better term for use is crystallization rather than triangulation (see Jennings, 2010).

Reflexivity

Reflexivity refers to constantly looking back on the researcher's roles and presence in the field and the research process. Qualitative researchers are constantly questioning themselves about the course of their research and the empirical materials that they gather and the interpretations that unfold. When writing qualitative research texts, researchers should incorporate reflections of reflexivity in their work. They should also address aspects of their researcher 'social situatedness' with regard to the research phenomena and/or participants. Readers need to be informed of the background, knowledge and experiences that the researcher(s) bring(s) to the research setting. This enables readers to become co-interpreters of the research during the course of reading research texts, whether the text is an article, conference paper, thesis or technical report. It also enables readers to be informed upon what bases the researcher's proximity to the research focus has informed interpretations, which as mentioned before should always be reflexively articulated in qualitative texts.

In considering these five aspects of qualitative research, I have set the stage for consideration of what elements or criteria should be used to judge the quality of qualitative research.

CRITERIA FOR JUDGING QUALITATIVE RESEARCH

The following list provides a series of points, which can be used to determine the overall quality of qualitative research. The list is intended primarily for evaluations of written works. The list also may have applicability to oral and performative texts. The degree to which each of these criteria is addressed will be influenced by:

(1) Audience, for example, academic, practitioner, general public, stakeholder group, community, examiners, reviewers;
(2) Language, specifically, level of language, style of language, cross-cultural considerations;
(3) Genre of the text, report, article, conference paper, poster, thesis, news-media report/article, play, film, multimedia presentation;
(4) Context of the presentation, such as, conference, congress, workshop, performance, gallery, stage, multimedia settings;
(5) Time limits in the case of oral presentations and performance;
(6) Word limits in the case of written texts.

Needless to say, in academic written contexts, the majority of the following criteria should be addressed.

- Research aim is clearly articulated;
- Research design complements research aim;

- Researcher appears informed concerning area being researched (background literature, theoretical constructs, methodology and methods of empirical material collection and interpretation);
- Theoretical paradigm has been articulated and supported with lucid arguments regarding relationship with research aim/focus;
- Unpacking of ontology, epistemology, methodology and axiology has occurred;
- Approach to ethics has been articulated;
- Methods of empirical material collection clearly described, justified, supported with examples of field notes, memos and text units (visual, aural, oral and print based);
- Methods of empirical material interpretation clearly described, justified and exemplified;
- Theoretical sampling explained;
- Theorizing clearly outlined and supported beyond initial first level of codings;
- Evidence that the theory has been grounded with participants or has 'goodness of fit', authenticity and trustworthiness;
- Theory considered in regard to related extant literature, especially literature beyond tourism and hospitality studies;
- Researcher social situatedness explicitly stated so readers can follow interpretations made;
- Reflexive processes identified and discussed;
- Research setting and context clearly described and considered;
- Recruitment of participants explained, access, ethics;
- Numbers of participants explained and justified;
- Reciprocity explained;
- Writing follows a narrative style befitting qualitative research;
- Writing adopts a first person active voice stance;
- Reader hears the voices of participants or feels close to the phenomena being shared.

In addressing the above points, researchers should provide readers with more than just a checklist style of writing. They should incorporate a narrative style, which simultaneously fully integrates these elements and informs the reader.

Limitations

The discussion of limitations is a 'hangover' from post/positivistic research. In choosing qualitative research, the researcher has determined that it is the best approach for illuminating the research focus or achieving insights into a research study's aim(s). Consequently, there are no limitations to the research. There are, however, boundaries. Each qualitative researcher explains to readers and stakeholders the bounded nature of their study. The study is what the study is – qualitative research does not masquerade as being more than it is. Qualitative research focuses on providing a slice of life and offers multiple perspectives and does not profess to identify a truth for all.

The bounded nature of qualitative research is influenced by research topic, researcher insider-ness and social situatedness with regard to the research topic, connectedness of researcher(s) to participants and empirical materials, access to research participants and materials, research scope and resources such as time, human, financial and material resources. Obviously with regard to resources, qualitative research experiences similar exposure to elements that bound research when using quantitative and mixed methods research: time, human financial and material resources. When using the term, material resources, I refer to technological equipment, audio, video recorders, cameras, computer-related programs, applications and diverse databases.

QUALITATIVE RESEARCH: APPLICATIONS IN TOURISM STUDIES

At the beginning of this chapter, I presented examples of applications of qualitative research used in tourism studies based on paradigms. The studies that I selected were chosen because of their demonstration of commensurability with qualitative research. Readers are directed to each of the references associated with those examples for further information. In the course of writing this chapter, I have also referred to seminal works beyond the field of tourism studies as evidenced in the reference list. As researchers, we are all required to familiarize ourselves with seminal and past works within and beyond our field of study. There are no short cuts. To convince readers that you are an informed qualitative researcher, you need to think, write, talk and act like one. So ensure that you familiarize yourself and understand the related methodological literature as well as the works that use qualitative research in tourism studies.

Following this chapter, a range of studies that have used qualitative research in tourism studies are presented. In this section of the book, the authors of chapters highlight their perspectives on a number of qualitative methods that may be utilized in the course of qualitative research. A number of these authors focus on qualitative research approaches, notably: archival research, Dallen Timothy; community case studies, Dianne Dredge and Rob Hales; and cross cultural approaches, Carla Santos and Changsup Shim. Others provide insights into the use of a range of qualitative methods of empirical material collection: ethnographic approach, Kathleen Adams; participant observation, Nuno Ribeiro and Eric Foemmel; interview techniques, Nancy McGehee; and focus groups, Carl Cater and Tiffany Low. Olga Junek and Les Killion, focus on qualitative research empirical material collection and interpretation in their chapter on grounded theory.

Beyond these chapters, tourism and hospitality journals provide additional models, demonstrations and applications of qualitative research. As you read such works, be critical and do not take all articles at face value. There are articles that have been published that profess to be qualitative research which are not. Use the information contained in this chapter and the following chapters to critically read and evaluate such works.

Additionally, critiques of published qualitative and quantitative research are useful to iterate here. Bear these critiques in mind when you are preparing to share your research with others. As you draft your writing, use these critiques as well as the previous criteria for judging the quality of qualitative research as useful checks of your own writing. The critiques note that authors of articles do not provide insights into their epistemological stance or methodological processes (Weed, 2005), or paradigmatic positioning (Botterill,

2001). Others do not familiarize readers with the theoretical relevance of their analyses and interpretations (Dann et al., 1988). Still other research has been critiqued for 'conceptual weakness and fuzziness' (Cooper, 2003, p.1). Ensure that you address these critiques and when conducting your methodological literature review, remember, not all work published is quality work. Endeavour to make sure your work is quality work.

QUALITATIVE RESEARCH AND POLICY FORMULATION

The first decades of the twenty-first century have continuously highlighted the complexities of a globalized connected world, in which unexpected and unprecedented events are becoming the norm and are constant challenges for governments, communities, environments, tourism experience consumers and providers.

Unpacking the 'how' and 'why' of tourism and hospitality phenomena and experiences with in-depth insights grounded in the multiple realities of the participants and the complexity of the worlds in which they live are critical for policy formulation and maintenance of quality of life of stakeholders now and for the future. Qualitative research provides a slice of life, which enables policy makers to clearly understand the lived experiences, expectations, needs and wants of their constituents. Qualitative research enables creative developments of empirical material collection and interpretation. Creativity and innovation is part and parcel of the qualitative research process because of the emergent design embedded in qualitative research processes. Creativity and innovation is an area that has been underdeveloped in educational systems and so qualitative research enables researchers to develop these skill sets and capacities, which in turn enable creative and innovative responses and strategies to be developed for planning and policy purposes.

QUALITATIVE RESEARCH: FURTHER DEVELOPMENTS AND APPLICATIONS FOR TOURISM RESEARCH

Essentially, here I wish to emphasize the need for two particular developments with regard to tourism research. First, the development and use of emic, holistic approaches to research and, second, the facilitation of wider worldviews in tourism research enterprises.

Emic and Holistic Approaches

Given the complexity of the opening decades of the twenty-first century, questions have to be raised regarding the use of etic (outsider/objective) models that are based on dimensional delimitation. Such delimitation tends to focus on uni- (Pearce, 1993), two-dimensional, or selected-dimensional perspectives and/or unicausal analysis (Ryan, 1991). This results in fragmented understandings of tourism phenomena – a holistic perspective is and will not be achieved. To achieve holistic perspectives, an emic (insider/subjective) approach is required. Holistic-oriented approaches are able to deconstruct the 'complexity' (Lee et al., 1994) inherent in tourism phenomena. Qualitative research assists with achieving holistic views.

Over time, tourism research has variously supported an emic approach (see for example Banner and Himmelfarb, 1985; Graburn, 1983, p. 28; Jennings, 1999, 2009; Ryan and Kinder in Ryan, 1997). Yet wide-scale adoption of emic approaches lags behind the unquestioning adherence to hegemonic tourism research practices premised on etic practices. Research in tourism studies needs to adopt holistic and emic based research in order to move beyond limited dimensional studies. The chapters in this section of this book provide a number of examples to inform readers regarding how to advance this agenda. Research courses and programmes need to be reviewed and revised to equally privilege qualitative and quantitative research processes and to ensure emergent researchers are versed in both approaches to research.

Wider World Views

As already noted, our reflexive lenses on tourism phenomena have been heavily founded in western developed world contexts. The application of western-centric concepts and dimensions assumes that these are universal and that different cultures and peoples of the world use the same lenses to understand and interpret the world. Such universalizing is akin to imperialism and colonialism (Bourdieu, 1990; Laclau, 1990; Smith, 2005). Western epistemologies are insufficient to support alternate knowledge bases with regard to tourism phenomena. Tourism research needs to incorporate and promote ways of knowing and researching that are not just predicated on western worldviews (Jennings, 2007b). Finally, tourism research needs to embrace multicultural research teams and multicultural studies, which are emically focused and are contextually and temporally situated.

REFERENCES

Banner, D.K. and A. Himmelfarb (1985), 'The work/leisure relationship toward a useful typology', *Leadership and Organization Development Journal*, **6** (4), 22–55.

Bennett, J. (2004), 'Indigenous entrepreneurship, social capital and tourism enterprise development: lessons from Cape York', unpublished PhD thesis, La Trobe University, Australia.

Berno, T. (1996), 'Cross-cultural research methods: content or context? A Cook Island example', in R. Butler and T. Hinch (eds), *Tourism and Indigenous Peoples: Issues and Implications*, London: International Thomson Business Press, pp. 376–395.

Botterill, D. (2001), 'The epistemology of a set of tourism studies', *Leisure Studies*, **20**, 199–214.

Bourdieu, P. (1990), *The Logic of Practice*, R. Nice (trans.), Cambridge: Polity Press.

Bourke, E. (1995), 'Dilemmas of integrity and knowledge: protocol in Aboriginal research', Paper presented at the Indigenous Research ethics, Townsville. September.

Chambers, D. (2007), 'Interrogating the "Critical" in critical approaches to tourism research', in I. Ateljevic, N. Morgan and A. Pritchard (eds), *The Critical Turn in Tourism Studies: Innovative Research Methodologies*, Amsterdam: Elsevier.

Cohen, E. (1979), 'Rethinking the sociology of tourism', *Annals of Tourism Research*, **6**, 18–35.

Cohen, E. (1988), 'Traditions in the qualitative sociology of tourism', *Annals of Tourism Research*, **15**, 29–46.

Cooper, C. (2003), 'Progress in tourism research', in C. Cooper (ed.), *Classic Reviews in Tourism*, Aspects of Tourism Series, Number 3, Bristol, UK: Channel View Press.

Dann, G., D. Nash and P. Pearce (1988), 'Methodology in tourism research', *Annals of Tourism Research*, **15**, 1–28.

Darcy, S. (2006), 'Setting a research agenda for accessible tourism', Technical Report, Australia: CRC for Sustainable Tourism.

Denzin, N.K. and Y.S. Lincoln (2011), 'Introduction: the discipline and practice of qualitative research', in N.K. Denzin and Y.S. Lincoln (eds), *The Sage Handbook of Qualitative Research*, 4th edition, Thousand Oaks, CA: Sage Publications, pp. 1–20.

Denzin, N.K., S. Lincoln and L.T. Smith (eds) (2008), *Handbook of Critical and Indigenous Methodologies*, Thousand Oaks, CA: Sage.

Echtner, C.M. (1999), 'The semiotic paradigm: implications for tourism research', *Tourism Management*, **20**, 47–57.

Foley, D. (2003), 'Indigenous epistemology and Indigenous standpoint theory', *Social Alternatives*, **22** (1), 44–52.

Fox, K. (2007), 'Critical theory and Katrina', *City*, **11** (1), 81–99.

Goodson, L. and J. Phillimore (2004), 'The inquiry paradigm in qualitative tourism research', in L. Goodson and J. Phillimore (eds), *Qualitative Research in Tourism: Ontologies, Epistemologies and Methodologies*, London: Routledge, pp. 30–45.

Graburn, N.H.H. (1983), 'The anthropology of tourism', *Annals of Tourism Research*, **10**, pp. 9–33.

Guba, E. (1990), 'The alternative paradigm dialog', in E. Guba (ed.), *The Paradigm Dialog*, Newbury Park, CA: Sage.

Gurney, P.M. and M. Humphreys (2006), 'Consuming responsibility: the search for value at Laskarina holidays', *Journal of Business Ethics*, **64**, 83–100.

Gurung, H.B. (2008), 'Fusioning', PhD thesis, Griffith University, Gold Coast Australia.

Hollinshead, K. (1992), '"White" gaze, "red" people-shadow visions: the disidentification of "Indians" in cultural tourism', *Leisure Studies*, **11** (1), 43–64.

Hollinshead, K. (1996), 'The tourism researcher as bricoleur: the new wealth and diversity in qualitative inquiry', *Tourism Analysis*, **1**, 67–74.

Ivanitz, M. (1999), 'Culture, ethics, and participatory methodology in cross-cultural research', *Australian Aboriginal Studies*, **2**, 46–58.

Jennings, G.R. (1999), 'Voyages from the centre to the margins: an ethnography of long term ocean cruisers', PhD thesis, Murdoch University, Murdoch, Australia.

Jennings, G.R. (2003), 'Tourism research: theoretical paradigms and accountability', Targeted Research: The Gateway to Accountability: TTRA 34th Annual Conference Proceedings [CD Rom], 15–18 June, St Louis, Missouri.

Jennings, G.R. (2007a), 'Tourism perspectives towards regional development and Asia's Values', paper presented at Dong-Eui University, 22–23 October, Busan, South Korea.

Jennings, G.R. (2007b), 'Advances in tourism research: theoretical paradigms and accountability', in A. Matias, P.A. Neto and P. Nijkamp (eds), *Advances in Modern Tourism Research*, Economic Perspectives, Heidelberg: Springer, Physica-Verlag, pp. 9–35.

Jennings, G.R. (2009), 'Methodologies and methods' in T. Jamal and M. Robinson (eds), *Handbook of Tourism Studies*, Thousands Oaks, CA: Sage Publications, pp. 672–692.

Jennings, G.R. (2010), *Tourism Research*, 2nd edition, Brisbane: John Wiley.

Jennings, G.R. and D. Stehlik (2009), 'Farm stay enterprises: (re)interpreting public/private domains and "home" sites and sights', in P. Lynch, A. McIntosh and H. Tucker (eds), *The Commercial Home: International Multidisciplinary Perspectives*, London: Routledge, pp. 50–59.

Jennings, G.R., S. Kensbock and U. Kachel (2010), 'Enhancing "education about and for sustainability" in a tourism studies enterprise management course: an action research approach', *Journal of Teaching in Travel & Tourism*, **10** (2), 163–191.

Kensbock, S. (2012/13), 'The employment experiences of hotel room attendants at five star hotels on the Gold Coast of Queensland, Australia', PhD thesis, Griffith University, Gold Coast Australia.

Kuokkanen, R. (2003), 'Toward a new relation of hospitality in the academy', *American Indian Quarterly*, **27** (1&2), 267–295.

Laclau, E. (1990), *New Reflections on the Revolution of our Time*, London: Verso.

Lee, Y., J. Datillo and D. Howard (1994), 'The complex and dynamic nature of leisure experience', *Journal of Leisure Research*, **26**, 195–211.

Lincoln, Y.S. and E.G. Guba (1985), *Naturalistic Inquiry*, Newbury Park, CA: Sage.

Lincoln, Y.S. and E.G. Guba (2000), 'Paradigmatic controversies, contradictions, and emerging confluences', in N.K. Denzin and Y.S. Lincoln (eds), *Handbook of Qualitative Research*, 2nd edition, Thousand Oaks, CA: Sage, pp. 163–188.

Lincoln, Y.S., S.A. Lynham and E.G. Guba (2011), 'Paradigmatic controversies, contradictions, and emerging confluences, revisited', in N.K. Denzin and Y.S. Lincoln (eds), *Handbook of Qualitative Research*, 4th edition, Thousand Oaks, CA: Sage, pp. 97–128.

O'Gorman, K.D. (2005), 'Modern hospitality: lessons from the past', *Journal of Hospitality and Tourism Management*, **12** (2), 141–151.

Pearce, P.L. (1993), 'Fundamentals of tourist motivation', in D.G. Pearce and R.W. Butler, *Tourism Research*, London: Routledge.

Richardson, L. (1994), 'Writing: a method of inquiry', in N. Denzin and Y.S. Lincoln (eds), *Handbook of Qualitative Research*, 2nd edition, Thousand Oaks, CA: Sage, pp. 516–529.

Riley, R.W. and L.L. Love (2000), 'The state of qualitative tourism research', *Annals of Tourism Research*, **27** (1), 164–187.

Ryan, C. (1991), *Recreational Tourism, a Social Sciences Perspective*, London: Routledge.

Ryan, C. (ed.) (1997), *The Tourist Experience, a New Introduction*, Studies in Tourism Series, London: Cassell.

Schaper, M., J. Carlsen and G. Jennings (2007), 'Reflections on researching Indigenous enterprises', in J. Buultjens and D. Fuller (eds), *Striving for Sustainability: Case Studies in Indigenous Tourism*, Lismore, Australia: Southern Cross University Press, Chapter 2, pp. 37–66.

Scheurich, J.J. (1997), *Research Methods in the Postmodern*, London: The Falmer Press.

Schwandt, T.A. (2000), 'Three epistemological stances for qualitative inquiry: interpretivism, hermeneutics, and social constructionism' in N.K. Denzin and Y.S. Lincoln (eds), *Handbook of Qualitative Research*, 2nd edition, Thousand Oaks, CA: Sage, pp.189–213.

Smith, L.T. (1999), *Decolonizing methodologies: Research and Indigenous Peoples*, London: Zed Books.

Smith, L.T. (2005), 'On tricky ground: researching the native in the age of uncertainty', in N.K. Denzin and Y.S. Lincoln (eds) *Handbook of Qualitative Research*, 2nd edition, Thousand Oaks, CA: Sage, pp. 85–107.

Sofield, T.H.B. (2000), 'Re-thinking and re-conceptualising social and cultural issues of tourism development in South and East Asia', Institute for Sustainability and Technology Policy, Case Study. Murdoch University, Australia, available at http://sustainability.murdoch.edu.au/casestudies/Case_Studies_Asia/toursea/toursea.htm.

Stanfield II, J.H. (1994), 'Ethnic modelling in qualitative research', in N.K. Denzin and Y.S. Lincoln (eds), *Handbook of Qualitative Research*, 1st edition, Newbury Park, CA: Sage, pp. 175–188.

Tribe, J. (2006), 'The truth about tourism', *Annals of Tourism Research*, **33** (2), 360–381.

Urry, J. (1990), *The Tourist Gaze, Leisure and Travel in Contemporary Societies*, London: Sage.

Urry, J. (1996), 'Sociology of time and space', in B.S. Turner (ed.), *The Blackwell Companion to Social Theory*, Oxford: Blackwell, pp. 369–395.

Urry, J. (2002), *The Tourist Gaze*, 2nd edition, London: Sage.

Walle, A.H. (1997), 'Quantitative versus qualitative tourism research', *Annals of Tourism*, **24** (3), 524–536.

Weed, M. (2005), 'Sports tourism, theory and method: concepts, issues and epistemologies', *European Sport Management Quarterly*, **5** (3), 229–242.

Westwood, S. (2007), 'What lies beneath? Using creative, projective and participatory techniques in qualitative tourism inquiry', in I. Ateljevic, N. Morgan and A. Pritchard (eds), *The Critical Turn in Tourism Studies: Innovative Research Methodologies*, Advances in Tourism Research, Amsterdam: Elsevier, pp. 293–316.

15 Grounded theory
Olga Junek and Les Killion

INTRODUCTION

Grounded theory (GT) as a research approach seeks to *induce* theory from empirical material through the ongoing interpretation of that material. In the development of a theory or theoretical framework, continual integration between the participants, the empirical materials, the researcher and the interpretation takes place (Strauss and Corbin, 1994). Since its origin in 1965 (Glaser and Strauss, 1965, 1967), and following a number of methodological and philosophical arguments and contested meanings, grounded theory has undergone a number of substantive changes.

In the last decade, grounded theory has become a popular and increasingly important research methodology in tourism studies, thus acknowledging the multi-disciplinary nature of tourism and the moving away from a previously dominant business and quantitative focus. Using grounded theory in tourism studies provides researchers with a lens into tourist behaviour at a specific time, and, in particular, behaviour that may not have been studied before from a qualitative perspective (Birks and Mills, 2011). Grounded theory is also used when there is no a priori theory to explain an area or phenomenon of interest, or when the existing theory does not adequately take account of the social or temporal contexts of tourist behaviour (Hobson, 2003; Junek, 2004; Mehmetoglu and Olsen, 2003).

In briefly noting some of the debates surrounding its development, this chapter draws the distinction between grounded theory as an alternative qualitative paradigm, and grounded theory methods which now form the basis of methodologies in a broad range of approaches to social enquiry. The chapter sees grounded theory as being founded upon the premise that emergent explanatory theories can be formulated during the ongoing interplay between gathering and analysing empirical materials. Tourism research, once founded firmly upon positivist perspectives and paradigms and the testing of a priori theory, has, in contrast to other disciplines, only recently embraced the principles and precepts of grounded theory. The chapter examines some of the more recent tourism-related investigations in which grounded theory approaches have been implemented. One such area is that of tourism policy formulation and implementation and the chapter argues that grounded theory approaches offer the potential to achieve collaborative research outcomes reflecting the inputs of the wide spectrum of industry stakeholders whose performance within the industry are influenced both directly and indirectly by tourism policies and the wider ambit of public policy decisions. Such collaborative research efforts have the potential to generate Mode 2 Knowledge 'characterised by the constant flow back and forth between the fundamental and the applied, between the theoretical and the practical' (Gibbons et al., 1994, p. 19). Through the adoption of grounded theory methods and approaches it is considered that trans-disciplinary research and the generation of Mode 2 Knowledge provides a way forward in seeking insights into the issues that challenge tourism in the twenty-first century.

NATURE OF GROUNDED THEORY

While adopted by a diverse range of disciplines, grounded theory approaches (and qualitative research more generally) remain somewhat undervalued in certain areas of enquiry. Within interpretivist social sciences paradigms, grounded theory approaches focus on the realities of peoples' social experiences (Bryant and Charmaz, 2007; Charmaz, 2006). Grounded theory approaches aim to develop a situation specific emergent theory founded upon the construction and interpretation of the experiential stories of informants who are at the centre of the investigation. Formulating theory through inductive reasoning was a response to the critique that quantitative positivist paradigms did not provide in-depth understanding of social phenomena.

While accepted as a popular and robust methodology amongst social science researchers, many researchers in other fields of study such as in business, especially novice researchers and those doing their doctoral dissertations, are still often confronted with scepticism when using grounded theory methodologies. Trepidation, fear, misunderstanding and misgivings about using grounded theory are common issues confronting researchers using this methodology.

As is the case with any methodology, grounded theory has inherent strengths and weaknesses. Its use depends on both the paradigmatic considerations of the researcher and objectives of the research. The strengths of grounded theory lie in the closeness of the researcher to the empirical materials throughout the information collection and analysis stages of research. In grounded theory approaches, the two stages of collection and analysis are inseparable and often referred to as the process of data generation. They occur concurrently allowing for an openness and creativity for the researcher in foregrounding the emergent theory. This is not to say that the analysis is not systematic. On the contrary, to be able to validate and support the emerging theory, grounded theory researchers need to convince themselves and others that the emergent theory is founded upon the classification, categorization and conceptualization of the empirical materials.

A major difference between grounded theory and other methodologies, and often the cause of much confusion and consternation amongst novice researchers is the role of the literature review. Since Glaser and Strauss (1967) postulated that the grounded theory researcher should not review the literature relevant to the field of study before collecting and analysing empirical materials, many grounded theory researchers have argued the place of the literature review and preconceived theories emanating from the literature. The notion that a researcher enters the field with as little knowledge as possible had been initially strongly defended by Strauss and Corbin (1990). Their stand changed as grounded theory evolved, with their subsequent advocacy of some literature being reviewed in the early stages of research (Dunne, 2011; Wiener, 2007).

Contrariwise, Glaser (1998) and many of his followers still argue that no extensive literature review should be undertaken (Nathaniel, 2006). Faced with this rather prescriptive requisite of purist grounded theory methodology, doctoral students often faced the prospect of not fulfilling candidature requirements if a substantial literature review was not submitted when seeking confirmation of candidature. To some degree this has now changed. Through discussion, and informed justification, several prominent grounded theory advocates have turned away from the prescriptive Glaserian guidelines and have arrived at a 'middle ground' regarding literature review (Dunne, 2011, p. 117). Grounded theory researchers have found their own ways of using the literature review while still ensuring they enter the research field with openness without prejudging their research results. In relation to the place of literature Dunne (2011), for instance, discusses several important positions, aspects and ideas as how best to make 'proper use of previous knowledge' (Struebing, 2007, p. 587).

It is important at this point to draw attention to the terminology used to distinguish between grounded theory, that is, the theory that emerges from the empirical materials, and grounded theory method (GTM), the methods and processes employed to gather, analyse and interpret empirical materials that can lead to the development or emergence of a grounded theory. GTM today exists in many different versions, based on a number of similarities but just as many differences among researchers, the disciplines in which they are working, and their research objectives (Hood, 2007; Locke, 2001; Stern, 2007; Wiener, 2007). Bryant and Charmaz (2007) see these similarities and differences as 'a family of methods' (p. 11) based on Wittgenstein's (1953) ideas about family resemblances.

As a first step, investigators who base their research on a grounded theory method generally gather the necessary information in naturalistic settings through collaboration with those participating in the study using informal, conversational interviews based upon open-ended, minimally structured questions to focus the discussion. The information thus gained is often referred to as 'empirical materials' as distinct from 'data', a term that is seen to have positivistic, quantitative overtones. In general, empirical materials gathered through a grounded theory method take the form of transcribed records of such interviews and conversations. Theorizing and finding meaning within the empirical materials then adopts an inductive (as opposed to deductive) approach in order to generate a theory grounded in those materials. In order to establish 'distinct units of meaning' (Goulding, 2002, p. 74), and subsequently to generate theory in this way, the empirical materials must be broken down through a system of codification. Based upon her insights into the seminal works of Glaser and Strauss (1967) and Glaser (1992), Goulding (2002) provides a useful summary of the codings achieved through constant comparison. That is, by sampling (theoretical sampling) from within the empirical materials that research participants have provided, comparing 'incident with incident, and incident with concept, to emerge more categories and their properties' (Glaser, 1992, p. 38). Through such theoretical sampling, similarities and differences across incidents found within the empirical materials can be identified. Initially, open coding is employed to 'open up the interview data by fragmenting it, identifying concepts and [using] constant comparison to scrutinize the data for every meaning' (Stevenson et al., 2008, p. 9). The initial codes are labelled with descriptive labels to generate concepts that, as Goulding (2002) explains, can then be aggregated into descriptive categories which, in turn, can be further grouped into higher order concepts (Strauss and Corbin, 1998). Importantly, throughout the coding processes, memos ('memo-ing') are written as a basis for highlighting comparisons between incidents contained in the empirical materials with those recalled from experience and from the literature. In depicting the further steps of a grounded theory method, Goulding (2002, p. 169) then notes that axial coding is required 'which seeks to identify incidents which have a relationship to each other'. Through axial coding a higher order of abstraction is sought as the basis for understanding the relationships between identified concepts. In that sense, axial coding can be seen as 'reassembling' the empirical materials that were initially broken down in the process of open coding. As Goulding (2002, p. 169) has explained, the descriptive codes are subsumed into a higher order category that 'unites the theoretical concepts to offer an explanation or theory of the phenomenon' under investigation.

It is important to acknowledge that the procedures of constant comparison, theoretical sampling, coding, categorizing and memo-ing form the basis of GTM. However, while based on the use of these fundamental approaches, not all research using GTM results in a *grounded theory*. GTM may just as readily lead to the formulation of hypotheses, propositions, theoretical frameworks or conceptual themes for subsequent investigation. In contrast, only when a theory that is grounded in the empirical materials of the research emerges can it be claimed that *grounded theory* (as opposed to grounded theory approaches) as a methodology has been used.

BACKGROUND AND EVOLUTION OF GROUNDED THEORY

Grounded theory is now considered to be one of the most used methodologies within qualitative research (Morse et al., 2009). Since its origins in 1967 as a response to the hegemony of quantitative research and the positivist paradigm, grounded theory and GTM have evolved from the original foci on illness and its effects on caregivers (Charmaz, 2007) to encompass a wide number of other social science areas. The original writings of Glaser and Strauss (1965) focussed heavily on the GTM – that is how to conduct research using these methods – and as such provided a rather dogmatic approach to conducting research. However, the foundations of grounded theory were laid and many of the original characteristics still remain despite the well-documented arguments between the two authors. There now exist 'multiple interpretations of the tradition' (Jennings and Junek, 2009, p. 199) led by the new, second-generation of authors who have adapted grounded theory according to their own research paradigms and their particular research aims.

Amongst the second generation of authors who have progressed the use of grounded theory and have used this methodology 'as a launching pad for their own iterations' (Birks and Mills, 2011, p. 3) while also providing seminal writings, and pragmatic guidance, Charmaz (1997, 2000, 2003, 2006), Corbin (2008, 2009) and Clarke (2009) are prominent. Corbin (2008, 2009) sees methodology as a 'dynamic, living thing' (2008, p. 37) and in light of that dynamic process her research reflects changes in her approaches to grounded theory whilst staying rooted in the original ideas and processes of Glaser and Strauss's (1967) grounded theory. Charmaz's (2006, 2007, 2009) constructivist grounded theory 'assumes a relativist epistemology, sees knowledge as socially produced, acknowledges multiple standpoints . . . and takes a reflexive stance toward our actions, situations and participants in the field setting – and our analytic constructions of them' (2009, p. 129). Epistemologically, in the constructivist grounded theory approach theorists and informants are co-creators of knowledge. It is the *emergent, constructivist* characteristics of GTM stressed by Charmaz (2003) that are central to the constructivist grounded theory.

Clarke (2005, 2009), the third of the three major influential members of the second generation of authors on grounded theory, took yet another direction with situational analysis, grounded in 'symbolic interactionist sociology . . . to be understood as a 'theory/methods package' (Clarke, 2009, p. 197). In situational analysis using grounded theory, so Clarke argues (2009), human element is not enough and attention needs to be paid to non-human objects to fully research the situation or problem.

It was this second generation of writers who approached grounded theory with distinct philosophical frameworks of epistemological, ontological, axiological and methodological paradigms (Birks and Mills, 2011) in their quest to use grounded theory as a methodology as well as a set of interrelated methods and approaches.

The further development of grounded theory has not only been about the evolution of methodology and methods. It has also been about an expanding range of areas of research inquiry that have embraced grounded theory. Originally used in the areas of health care, particularly palliative care and nursing, grounded theory has moved into other areas of social research including human development, education, social justice, indigenous studies and to a lesser, although steadily growing extent, business studies, in particular organizations, tourism and marketing.

APPLICATION TO TOURISM AND TOURISM RELATED STUDIES

Several reasons exist to explain the relatively recent adoption of grounded theory in tourism studies. Tourism as a field of study has traditionally been placed within the business schools of universities where quantitative and positivistic paradigms tend to predominate as the guiding methodologies (Cohen, 1988; Jennings, 2001; Jennings and Junek 2009; Riley and Love, 2000; Walle, 1997). Furthermore, even within qualitative research there has been a noticeable lack of researchers using grounded theory to progress the field of tourism studies from a social studies interpretivist paradigm. However, since the 1990s more and more research has been undertaken using grounded theory and grounded theory methods.

Some of the early grounded theory researchers in the area of tourism explored travel prestige (Riley, 1995); travel experiences of cruisers (Jennings, 1997, 1999, 2005); heritage site visitors (Daengbuppha, et al., 2004; Goulding, 1999); backpacker travellers in Australia (Hillman, 2001); visitor perceptions of theme parks (Johns and Gyimothy, 2002); commodification (Goulding, 2000) and authenticity in the tourist experience (Mehmetoglu and Olsen, 2003). The common research characteristics of these studies were the in-depth explanations and understandings of the phenomena and experiences being studied. As well as an increase in the use of grounded theory research in tourism studies, there has also been a recognition of the need for more qualitative research methodologies in tourism studies (including grounded theory) as discussed by Connell and Lowe (1997); Hobson (2003) and Junek (2004); Riley (1995).

In the last decade grounded theory and GTM have continued to play an important part in tourism studies research and have become even more important, as tourism studies and tourism researchers embrace a more interdisciplinary approach. Some of these studies include Belhassen et al.'s (2007) research on the use of cannabis amongst vacationers; village residents' attitude towards tourism (Lepp, 2007); tourist behaviour (Drew and Woodside, 2008); volunteer tourism (Alexander, 2009); tourism jobs (Jiang and Tribe, 2009); slow travel (Lumsdon and McGrath, 2011) and online holiday reviews (Papathanassis and Knolle, 2011). As tourism as a field of studies has increasingly incorporated a number of different perspectives beyond the commercial and business perspective, the listed studies contribute to the widening areas of the social, the personal and the psychological perspectives. In terms of the personal and the psychological perspectives in particular, grounded theory offers an in-depth exploration of the lived experiences of tourists and tourism, an exploration that has broadened our understanding of the complexities and inter relationships amongst tourism stakeholders.

It has thus become evident that research using grounded theory makes important contributions to the field of tourism studies. In summary these include:

- Theory building as opposed to theory testing (Alexander, 2009; Drew and Woodside, 2008)
- Greater insight and in-depth understanding of many different types of tourists and tourism, whether this be backpackers, cruising, slowtravellers, volunteer tourists (Alexander, 2009; Lumsdon and McGrath, 2011) or memorable tourism experiences (Tung and Ritchie, 2011)
- Understanding behaviour and social processes within a particular context (Belhassen et al., 2007; Jiang and Tribe, 2009).

The legitimacy of grounded theory as a robust and widely accepted research methodology is reflected in the number of research articles founded on such approaches that have been published in prestigious, peer-reviewed tourism journals such as *Annals of Tourism Research*, *Tourism Management* and *Journal of Sustainable Tourism*. This has been a significant change from the 1990s and early 2000s when researchers often had to resort to conference publications and lower-ranked journals to have their grounded theory studies published.

Tourism, tourists and tourist behaviour exist within many social contexts and embrace a number of different stakeholders. It is therefore important to understand the multi-faceted nature of tourism as a business but also as a sociological phenomenon. Grounded theory, through its methods and as an approach resulting in an emergent theory can provide a holistic picture of tourist behaviour and tourism but it can also be used to add deeper insight to studies using quantitative methodology, whether this be in the form of mixed methods or using existing studies as a basis for a more qualitative understanding of the research topic or area. The areas of policy formulation, implementation and evaluation, for instance, offer an emergent field of enquiry in which grounded theory approaches offer potential contributions.

ADVANTAGES AND LIMITATIONS OF GROUNDED THEORY APPROACHES: CONCEPTUALLY AND FOR POLICY FORMULATION

Founded upon the central precepts and paradigms of qualitative research, grounded theory approaches offer a number of advantages in tourism research projects aimed at achieving insights into unexplored questions, or complementing quantitative data with the richness that a qualitative approach can contribute to further explanation and/or confirmation of previously investigated social phenomena. Despite these acknowledged advantages, like many qualitative research approaches, grounded theory research can sometimes be seen as limited through its focus on situation-specific phenomena.

The Advantages and Contributions of Grounded Theory Approaches to Tourism Research

Congruent with the purpose and aims of an investigation, grounded theory approaches may contribute to tourism research in several ways:

1. Exploratory: where no a priori theories exist, grounded theory approaches may be employed to explore the situation from the perspectives of those involved and generate emergent theory by constructing and interpreting of empirical materials obtained through informal interviews and observations. For example, in a host community such as the Sisters of St Joseph residing in Mount Street, North Sydney, Australia, who were engaging with mass tourism for the first time following the Beatification of Saint Mary MacKillop, the community's responses to visitor impacts were explored through grounded theory approaches (Killion, 2003). Earlier, Jennings (1999) employed an ethnographic methodology to theorize about the social realities and lived experiences of long-term ocean cruisers.
2. Explanatory: where phenomena are already known, grounded theory approaches may facilitate new explanations, for example, of the responses made by tourism operators seeking to recover from the impacts of the 2011 floods in Queensland, Australia. Radel (2010) employed a grounded theory approach in order to account for factors which have contributed to the successful operation of the Dreamtime Cultural Centre, an Indigenous tourism enterprise located in Rockhampton, Australia.
3. Confirmatory: finally, grounded theory approaches, through their application to specific research contexts, may confirm (or refute) established knowledge as found in the literature, mindful that in grounded theory methodologies engagement with pertinent literature occurs after the initial formulation of emergent explanatory theory.

The Limitations of Grounded Theory Approaches

Grounded theory approaches have been seen as freeing researchers 'from the tyranny of verifying theory and instead instruct[ing] them to focus on generating theory' (Wagenaar, 2003) founded upon the construction of empirical materials and reflexivity to produce '*thick description*' of social reality. Such a postpositivist paradigm provided 'systematic inductive guidelines for collecting and analyzing data to build middle-ground theoretical frameworks that explain the collected data' (Charmaz, 2000, p. 509). The view of Glaser and Strauss (1967) from the genesis of grounded theory approaches was, and is, that theory is not a final statement about some social phenomenon or activity, but a strategy for handling data informed by real-world social realities.

The limitations of grounded theory approaches reflect the critiques of much postpositivist, qualitative research that the emergent theory, supported and justified by the generated empirical materials, is project-specific and is inherent to these approaches. Critics then question the extent to which such emergent theory can be generalized to other contexts. Eichelberger (1989), however, argues that through subsequent engagement with relevant literature, the findings derived from one investigation can be integrated and compared with others who have studied the same, or similar experiences and phenomena as the basis for substantive theory. That is, as described by Flick (2002), a preliminary and relative version of the world. In a similar vein, Jafari (1987) and Kerr et al. (2001) recommend case specific studies to develop thick description and improve understanding in a specific context rather than attempting to develop universal models.

Project and temporal specificity make replication of findings in the positivist tradition difficult for grounded theorists. This has also engendered criticism of such approaches. Such criticism fails to appreciate the nature of interpretivist qualitative paradigms. Stevenson et al. (2008) explain that grounded theory approaches provide systematic procedures and rigorous methodologies akin to those of positivist persuasion for collecting and analysing qualitative data, and enable investigators to build theory 'from the bottom up' from the actions, words and behaviour of the research informants. Grounded theory approaches emphasize the need 'to get out in the field' (Glaser, 1998) to study phenomena using the perspectives or voice of those studied, collect and analyse data simultaneously and refine theory using a wider range of data (Goulding, 2002). The systematic and constant comparison of data through open and then axial coding allows grounded theorists to identify incidents that have a relationship to each other, and to achieve a level of abstraction that leads to appreciation of dynamic relationships between concepts (Goulding, 2002). Subsequent engagement with the wider literature then aims for further substantiation or refutation of the emergent theory.

Grounded Theory Approaches and Policy Making

Policy makers and those tasked with evaluating the impacts and consequences of policy decisions, favoured process models of policy making and were more inclined to follow positivist paradigms and quantitative data to measure their efforts. In investigating policy formulation and implementation, grounded theory approaches have made only relatively recent contributions. The reasons for this exist at two interrelated levels, underscoring the need for greater knowledge of policy dynamics at all stages. First, less than perfect understanding of policy-making processes driven by diverse stakeholder groups within and beyond government; and second, the apparent lack of success of policy decisions in achieving desired policy outcomes. In both instances, grounded theory approaches offer levels of understanding extending beyond those gleaned only from quantitative approaches.

In considering the applications of grounded theory approaches to policy formulation in their study of Leeds city, Stevenson et al. (2008) emphasize that 'policy making is essentially a social process, involving communication and negotiation between people in the context of wider change' and 'between many people in a variety of different organisations'. Policy making can be considered a social conceptualization or social construct and 'further research should investigate the communications involved in producing policy' (Stevenson et al., 2008). Noting that 'policy means different things to different people', Dredge and Jenkins (2007, p. 14) also describe policy making and planning as:

> dynamic, socially constructed activities that involve a wide range of agents and organisations characterised by varying degrees of interest and commitment to tourism. Tourism planning and policy development takes place in multi-actor settings, and it is important to understand how different conceptions of tourism and different values and ideas are mediated in planning and policy processes.

Policy is formulated in a dynamic environment. The consequences of change may provide the rationale for the formulation of policy positions in the first place. Whether in public or private sectors, in formulating policy, policy makers respond to 'the facts' of a given situation. Whatever these may be, facts reflect the social realities of those engaged in policy making, and the intended recipients of policy provisions. 'Facts' are social constructs formed on the basis of interactions between policy observers, policy advocates, the communities of which they are also members, and the wider world. The ways in which 'facts' are configured and perceived reflect the social realities and experiences of all parties. Likewise, and as Stevenson et al. (2008) observe, the making of policy is a complex social process that involves interaction and communication between a large number of people from different backgrounds and organizations – political parties, lobby groups, industry stakeholders, consumers, community members – any or all of whom may facilitate or constrain the formulation and implementation of policy. Unsurprisingly, multiple perspectives and multiple social realities find their way into the policy processes as policy is developed, enacted, implemented and evaluated. Understanding how these 'policy actors' (Dredge and Jenkins, 2007; Hall, 2010) relate, interact and communicate makes a fertile field for the development of emergent theories founded upon grounded theory approaches.

Weed's (2005) study of sport and tourism policy responses further exemplifies the application of grounded theory approaches in a longitudinal investigation of tensions in the policy process at three levels: the macro- (or context level); the meso- (or setting and situated activity level); and, the micro- (or 'self' level). The grounded theory model based upon empirical materials collected through the discussion of policy issues among key stakeholders, points to the value of supplementing quantitative data with the depth and richness of understanding that grounded theory approaches can contribute.

While critical of the 'questionable quality of much qualitative work in European policy research', Wagenaar (2003, pp. 1–2) considers much policy research 'abounds in grandiose, abstract, a priori theoretical statements (often with a strong normative ring to it) and small, badly executed empirical studies that have the tacked-on quality that Glaser and Strauss warn us for'. In these terms, Wagenaar is critical of iterative models of the 'policy process' such as that offered by Althaus et al. (2007), for example. He criticizes such process models and frameworks because they largely neglect the wider range of actors who directly and indirectly influence the development and implementation of policy, but whose interpretations and social realities are often not considered (Nagel, 1999).

Wagenaar (2003) presents three reasons for applying grounded theory approaches in such investigations. His reasons reflect some of the advantages which such methodologies offer policy researchers. First, policy, claims Wagenaar, is a good subject for grounded theory, especially in studies aiming to show how policies work and/or what the social impacts of a policy might be. In this Wagenaar agrees with Goulding (2002) in outlining the advantages of grounded theory approaches in business, management and marketing research. Second, Wagenaar notes the return of policy studies to the contextual analysis advocated by Lasswell and Lerner (1951) in encouraging a holistic understanding of policy processes, consequences and impacts. Third, and importantly, Wagenaar argues grounded theory approaches force the development of an intimate and detailed familiarity with 'the world that is the object of particular policy' (p. 4). He argues that while those directly engaged in political action may not require such intimate familiarity with social realities, it enables advisors to policy decision makers and those evaluating policy outcomes:

> to grasp the meaning that policy measures have for those affected by them, and thereby to better understand how they will adapt to them in their everyday practices. In the final analysis, it allows him [sic] to grasp the value of lay, experiential knowledge as it intersects with the more abstract knowledge that informs policy programs, and to involve this in the understanding of complex, evolving policy situation. (Wagenaar, 2003, p. 4.)

FURTHER DEVELOPMENTS AND APPLICATIONS OF GROUNDED THEORY APPROACHES IN TOURISM RESEARCH

The tourism industry comprises complex networks of key stakeholders including public and private sector and not-for-profit owners and operators of all elements of the destination mix; tourists; and, the host community. Each of these functions and interacts within an industry well known for its competitiveness and the dynamics and turbulence of change processes. Some of these can be reasonably anticipated while others, such as the hurricanes and floods of Australia's summer of 2011, less so. Knowledge of how stakeholders function, interact and behave is less than complete. Abstract extant theories seemingly provide only limited explanations.

Adopting the central precepts of a grounded theory approach, in his study of tourism development in Malta, Bramwell (2006) advocated the 'actor perspective' to investigate interactions between different stakeholder groups. The future applications of grounded theory approaches will continue to focus on the interpretation of lived social realities as the basis for inductive theorizing. Moreover, as Bramwell and Meyer (2007) suggest with reference to policy making and policy research, grounded theory forms the basis of a 'relational approach' that is holistic in its intentions to understand the contexts and realities of informants and participants. By placing people at the centre of the investigation, grounded theory approaches emphasize the social realities and social interactions that are fundamental to the process. Referring to the tourism policy of the city of Leeds (UK), Stevenson et al. (2008, p. 748) note that 'policy making is a soft intuitive human process rather than a rational scientific process'. Grounded theory approaches provide a direct focus on the vagaries of human intuition.

Grounded Theory Approaches, Transdisciplinary Research and Mode 2 Knowledge

Grounded theory approaches to tourism research carry the possibility of generating Mode 2 Knowledge through the integrated transdisciplinary collaborative efforts of academics and industry stakeholders. Transdisciplinary research embraces approaches such as grounded theory to integrate the knowledge, epistemologies and methods of established academic disciplines with real world experiences and situations to generate Mode 2 Knowledge that combines scientific knowledge derived from established disciplines with extra-scientific real world (or 'life-world') experiences and practices in problem-solving (Mittelstrass, 2001). Knowledge production is not confined to academic disciplines but also emanates from various organizations, communities, groups and individuals outside of academia as people undertake their day-to-day functions and interactions. Mode 2 Knowledge is generated at the intersections between academic disciplines (the 'horizontal plane') and the life-world experiences of people and groups outside academia (the 'vertical plane') (Mittelstrass, 2001).

CONCLUSION

While direct findings in the form of emergent theory are context specific, grounded theory approaches provide further insights and understandings of the complex social phenomena associated with tourism. The lived social experiences of tourists themselves, tourism operators and other stakeholders within the industry, and members of host communities, provide extended insights into and understandings of an industry that is highly competitive, dynamic and subject to the influences of wider social change processes. Quantitative approaches founded upon the traditions of positivist paradigms have provided important baseline data. The insights gained through the applications of GT and GTM provide fresh information and the prospects of transdisciplinarity capable of generating Mode 2 Knowledge. This is of significance to those who formulate, implement and evaluate tourism policy to resolve contemporary issues and prepare for the future.

REFERENCES

Alexander, Z. (2009), 'Understanding voluntourism: a Glaserian grounded theory', *The voluntourism effect: case studies and investigations*, 18–20 March, 2009, San Diego, CA.

Althaus, C., P. Bridgeman and G. Davis (2007), *The Australian Policy Handbook*, 4th edition, Sydney, Australia: Allen & Unwin.

Belhassen, Y.S., A.S. Santos and N. Uriely (2007), 'Cannabis usage in tourism:a sociological perspective', *Leisure Studies*, **23** (3), 303–319.

Birks, M. and J. Mills (2011), *Grounded Theory: A Practical Guide*, London: Sage.

Bramwell, B. and D. Meyer (2007), 'Power and tourism policy relations in transition', *Annals of Tourism Research*, **34** (3), 766–788.

Bramwell, W. (2006), 'Actors, power and discourses of growth limits', *Annals of Tourism Research*, **26** (2), 392–415.

Bryant, A. and K. Charmaz (2007),'Introduction grounded theory research: methods and practices', in A. Bryant and K. Charmaz (eds), *The SAGE Handbook of Grounded Theory*, Thousand Oaks, CA: Sage, pp. 1–28.

Charmaz, K. (1997), 'Identity dilemmas of chronically ill men', in A. Strauss and J. Corbin (eds), *Grounded Theory in Practice*, Thousand Oaks, CA: Sage, pp. 35–63.

Charmaz, K. (2000), 'Grounded theory: objectivist and constructivist methods', in N.K. Denzin and Y.S. Lincoln (eds), *Handbook of Qualitative Research*, Thousand Oaks, CA: Sage, pp. 509–535.

Charmaz, K. (2003), 'Grounded theory: objectivist and constructivist methods', in N.K. Denzin and Y.S. Lincoln (eds), *Strategies of Qualitative Inquiry*, Thousand Oaks, CA: Sage, pp. 249–291.

Charmaz, K. (2006), *Constructing Grounded Theory: A Practical Guide through Qualitative Analysis*, Thousand Oaks CA: Sage.

Charmaz, K. (2007), 'Constructionism and grounded theory', in A.J. Holstein and J.F.Gubrium (eds), *Handbook of Constructionist Research*, New York: Guilford Publishers, pp. 397–412.

Charmaz, K. (2009), 'Shifting the grounds: constructivist grounded theory methods', in J.M. Morse, P.N. Stern, J. Corbin, B. Bowers, K. Charmaz and A.E. Clarke, *Developing Grounded Theory: The Second Generation*, Walnut Creek, CA: Left Coast Press, pp. 127–192.

Clarke, A. (2005), *Situational Analysis: Grounded Theory after the Postmodern Turn*, Thousand Oaks, CA: Sage.

Clarke, A. (2009), 'From grounded theory to situational analysis: what's new? Why? How?', in J.M. Morse, P.N. Stern, J. Corbin, B. Bowers, K. Charmaz and A.E. Clarke, *Developing Grounded Theory: The Second Generation*, Walnut Creek, CA: Left Coast Press, pp. 194–234.

Cohen, E. (1988), 'Traditions in the qualitative sociology of tourism', *Annals of Tourism Research*, **15**, 29–46.

Connell, J. and A. Lowe (1997), 'Generating grounded theory from qualitative data: the application of inductive methods in tourism and hospitality management research', *Progress in Tourism and Hospitality Research*, **3** (2), 165–173.

Corbin, J. (2008), *Basics of Qualitative Research: Techniques and Procedures for Developing Grounded Theory*, 3rd edition, Thousand Oaks, CA: Sage.

Corbin, J. (2009), 'Taking an analytic journey', in J.M. Morse, P.N. Stern, J. Corbin, B. Bowers, K. Charmaz and A.E. Clarke, *Developing Grounded Theory: The Second Generation*, Walnut Creek, CA: Left Coast Press, pp. 35–54.

Daengbuppha, J., N. Hemmington and K. Wilkes (2004), 'Using grounded theory approach: theoretical and practical issues in modelling heritage visitor experience', in K.A. Smith and C. Schott (eds), *Proceedings of the New Zealand Tourism and Hospitality Research Conference 2004*, 8–10 December, Wellington, New Zealand, pp. 64–78.

Dredge, D. and J. Jenkins (2007), *Tourism Planning and Policy*, Milton, Queensland: John Wiley and Sons Australia Ltd.

Drew, M. and A. Woodside (2008), 'Grounded theory of international tourism behaviour', *Journal of Travel and Tourism Marketing*, **24** (4), 245–258.

Dunne, C. (2011), 'The place of the literature review in grounded theory research', *International Journal of Social Research Methodology*, **14** (2), 111–124.

Eichelberger, R.T. (1989), *Discipline Inquiry: Understanding and Doing*, Educational Research, New York: Longmans.

Flick, U. (2002), *An Introduction to Qualitative Research*, 2nd edition, London: Sage Publications.

Gibbons, M., C. Limoge, H. Nowotny, S. Schwartzman, P. Scott and M. Trow (1994), *The New Production of Knowledge: The Dynamics of Science and Research in Contemporary Societies*, London: Sage Publications.

Glaser, B. (1992), *Basics of Grounded Theory Analysis: Emergence vs Forcing*, Mill Valley, CA: Sociology Press.

Glaser, B. (1998), *Doing Grounded Theory: Issues and Discussions*, Mill Valley, CA: Sociology Press.

Glaser, B.G. and A.L. Strauss (1965), *Awareness of Dying*, Chicago, IL: Aldine.

Glaser, B.G. and A.L. Strauss (1967), *The Discovery of Grounded Theory Strategies for Qualitative Research*, New York: Aldine Publishing Company.

Goulding, C. (1999), 'Heritage, nostalgia and the "grey" consumer', *Journal of Marketing Practice: Applied Marketing Science*, **5** (6/7/8), 177–199.

Goulding, C. (2000), 'The commodification of the past, postmodern pastiche, and the search for authentic experiences at contemporary heritage attraction', *European Journal of Marketing*, **34** (7), 835–853.

Goulding, C. (2002), *Grounded Theory: A Practical Guide for Management, Business and Market Researchers*, Thousand Oaks CA: Sage.

Hall, C.M. (2010), 'Politics and tourism: interdependency and implications in understanding change', in R. Butler and W. Suntikul (eds), *Tourism and Political Change*, Oxford: Goodfellow Publishers, pp. 7–12.

Hillman, W. (2001), 'Searching for authenticity and experience: backpackers travelling in Australia', *TASA Conference*, University of Sydney.

Hobson, J.S.P. (2003), 'The case for more exploratory and grounded tourism research', Martin Oppermann Memorial Lecture 2001, *Pacific Tourism Review*, **6** (2), 73–81.

Hood, J. (2007), 'Orthodoxy vs. power: the defining traits of grounded theory', in A. Bryant and K. Charmaz (eds), *The SAGE Handbook of Grounded Theory*, London: Sage, pp. 151–164.

Jafari, J. (1987), 'Tourism models: the socio-cultural aspects', *Tourism Management*, **9** (1), 82–84.
Jennings, G.R. (1997), 'The travel experience of cruisers', in M. Oppermann (ed.), *Pacific Rim 2000: Issues, Interrelations, Inhibitors*, London: CABI International, pp. 94–105.
Jennings, G.R. (1999), 'Voyages from the centre to the margins: ethnography of long term ocean cruisers', PhD thesis, Murdoch University, Murdoch, Australia.
Jennings, G.R. (2001), *Tourism Research*, Brisbane, Australia: John Wiley.
Jennings, G.R. (2005), 'Caught in the irons: one of the lived experiences of cruising women', *Tourism Research International*, **9** (2), 177–193.
Jennings, G.R. and O. Junek (2009), 'Grounded theory: innovative methodology or a critical turning from hegemonic methodological praxis in tourism studies?', in I. Ateljevic, A. Pritchard and N. Morgan (eds), *The Critical Turn in Tourism Studies: Innovative Research Methodologies*, Oxford: Elsevier, pp. 197–210.
Jiang, B. and J. Tribe (2009), 'Tourism jobs – short lived professions: student attitudes towards tourism careers in China', *Journal of Hospitality, Leisure, Sport and Tourism Education*, **8** (1), 4–19.
Johns, N. and S. Gyimothy (2002), 'Mythologies of a theme park: an icon of family life', *Journal of Vacation Marketing*, **8** (4), 320–331.
Junek, O. (2004), 'A qualitative inquiry into leisure and travel patterns of international students. Part 1: background and methodology', The 2nd Asia-Pacific CHRIE (APacCHRIE) Conference & the 6th Biennial Conference on Tourism in Asia, 2004, Conference Proceedings. 27–29 May, Phuket, Thailand, 2004.
Kerr, B., G. Barron and R. Wood (2001), 'Politics, policy and regional tourism administration: a case examination of Scottish Area Tourist Board Funding', *Tourism Management*, **22** (6), 649–657.
Killion, E.L. (2003), 'More than a miraculous journey – an interpretivist study of the Sisters of the Congregation of St. Joseph and their experiences of visitor impacts following the beatification of Blessed Mary MacKillop', PhD thesis, Rockhampton CQUniversity Australia.
Lasswell, H.D. and D. Lerner (eds) (1951), *The Policy Sciences*, Palo Alto, CA: Stanford University Press.
Lepp, A. (2007), 'Residents' attitude towards tourism in Bigodi village, Uganda', *Tourism Management*, **28**, 876–885.
Locke, K. (2001), *Grounded Theory in Management Research*, London, Sage.
Lumsdon, L. and P. McGrath (2011), 'Developing a conceptual framework for slow travel: a grounded theory approach', *Journal of Sustainable Tourism*, **19** (3), 265–279.
Mehmetoglu, M. and K. Olsen (2003), 'Talking authenticity: what kind of experiences do solitary travelers in the Norwegian Lofoten Islands regard as authenticity?', *Tourism, Culture and Communication*, **4** (3), 137–152.
Mittelstrass, J. (2001), 'On trans-disciplinarity', in *Science and the Future of Mankind*, Vatican City: Pontifical Academy of Sciences, 495–500, available at http://www.vatican.va/roman_curia/pontifical_academies/acd-scien/documents/sv%2099(5of5).pdf.
Morse, J.M., P.N. Stern, J. Corbin, B. Bowers, K. Charmaz and A.E. Clarke (2009), *Developing Grounded Theory: The Second Generation*, Walnut Creek, CA: Left Coast Press.
Nagel, S. (ed.) (1999), *Policy Analysis Methods*, New York: New Science Publishers.
Nathaniel, A. (2006), 'Thoughts on the literature review and GT', *Grounded Theory Review*, **5** (2/3), 35–41.
Papathanassis, A. and F. Knolle (2011), 'Exploring the adoption and processing of online holiday reviews: a grounded theory approach', *Tourism Management*, **32**, 215–224.
Radel, K. (2010), 'The Dreamtime Cultural Centre: A Grounded Theory of Doing Business in an Indigenous Tourism Enterprise', PhD thesis, Rockhampton CQUniversity Australia.
Riley, R.W. (1995), 'Prestige-worthy behaviour', *Annals of Tourism Research*, **22** (3), 630–649.
Riley, R.W. and L.L. Love (2000), 'The state of qualitative tourism research', *Annals of Tourism Research*, **27** (1), 164–187.
Stern, P. (2007), 'On solid ground: essential properties of growing grounded theory' in A. Bryant and K. Charmaz (eds), *The SAGE Handbook of Grounded Theory*, London: Sage, pp. 114–126.
Stevenson, N., D. Airey and G. Miller (2008), 'Tourism policy making: the policy-makers' perspective', *Annals of Tourism Research*, **35** (3), 732–750.
Strauss, A.L. and J. Corbin (1990), *Basics of Qualitative Research Grounded Theory Procedures and Techniques*, Newbury Park, CA: Sage.
Strauss, A.L. and J. Corbin (1994), 'Grounded theory methodology: an overview', in N.K. Denzin and Y.S. Lincoln, *Handbook of Qualitative Research*. Thousand Oaks, CA: Sage, pp. 273–285.
Strauss, A.L. and J. Corbin (1998), *Basics of Qualitative Research Techniques and Procedures for Developing Grounded Theory*. Thousand Oaks, CA: Sage.
Struebing, J. (2007), 'Research as pragmatic problem-solving: the pragmatist roots of empirically-grounded theorising', in A. Bryant. and C. Charmaz (eds), *The SAGE Handbook of Grounded Theory*, London: Sage, pp. 580–601.
Tung, V. and J. Ritchie (2011), 'Exploring the essence of memorable tourism experiences', *Annals of Tourism Research*, **38** (4), 1367–1386.

Wagenaar, H. (2003), 'The (re-)discovery of grounded theory in postpositivist policy research', paper presented for the ESF Workshop Qualitative Method for the Social Sciences, Vienna.

Walle, A.H. (1997), 'Quantitative versus qualitative tourism research', *Annals of Tourism Research*, **24** (3), 524–536.

Weed, M. (2005), 'A grounded theory of the policy process for sport and tourism', *Sport in Society: Cultures, Commerce, Media, Politics*, **8** (2), 356–377.

Wiener, C. (2007), 'Making teams work in conducting grounded theory', in A. Bryant (ed.), *The SAGE Handbook of Grounded Theory*, London: Sage, pp. 293–310.

Wittgenstein, L. (1953), *Philosophical Investigations*, Oxford: Blackwell.

16 Ethnographic methods
Kathleen M. Adams

INTRODUCTION

Although ethnographic methods derive from the discipline of sociocultural anthropology, because of their potential for producing insights into human actions and behaviors they have come to be embraced by sociologists, psychologists, and other social scientists interested in gaining insights into human behavior. Ethnographic methods fall into the broader category of qualitative methodologies and are aimed at understanding cultural practices, human beliefs and behaviors, and sociocultural changes over time. As such, ethnographic methods are particularly apt for tourism-related research and for tourism policy planning, as noted by a number of recent tourism scholars (Cole, 2005; Graburn, 2002; Nash, 2000; Palmer, 2001, 2009; Salazar, 2011; Sandiford and Ap, 1998). This chapter (1) introduces the key elements of ethnographic methodologies, (2) examines the types of tourism research problems for which this research strategy is suited, (3) reviews challenges entailed in using ethnographic methods in tourism settings, (4) surveys key tourism studies grounded in ethnographic research, and (5) closes with a discussion of new visions for this technique in tourism research.

NATURE AND EVOLUTION OF ETHNOGRAPHIC METHODS

Anthropologists use the term ethnography in two senses. In the first sense, an ethnography is a written account of the socio-cultural dynamics animating a particular human population. In the second sense, doing ethnography (or ethnographic research) entails long-term fieldwork and draws on a mixture of qualitative research techniques all aimed at generating insights into sociocultural relationships and the "native[s]'s point[s] of view" (Geertz, 1976; Malinowski, 1922). As Fife notes, in this context "native" refers not to a concept of aboriginality but rather to "anyone who has grown up within a specific cultural milieu" (Fife, 2005, p. 71). In broad terms, ethnographic research methods are ideally suited for describing or analysing cultural practices, beliefs and behaviors, including encounters between different groups. Most ethnographic research does not entail theory-testing per se. Instead, it draws on "grounded theory", which entails conducting field research on broad themes and drawing on the data collected to develop compelling theories.

Foremost among the techniques that comprise the ethnographic approach is that of participant observation (to be explained below). But ethnographic research draws upon a variety of other research techniques, including in-depth unstructured interviews, structured interviews, questionnaires, focus groups, mapping, photography, and video-documentation. Ethnographic researchers also collect and analyse various materials produced by, for, and about the group being studied, including brochures, newsletters, visitor and locally produced blogs, web pages, historical archival material, handicrafts, museum exhibits, and so forth.

Perhaps more than any other research strategy, the roots of ethnographic methods lie in travel and displacement. The earliest ethnographic researchers all lived amongst the people under study and participated to varying degrees in their daily activities. Franz Boas (1858–1942), a German-born scholar considered one of the "fathers" of American anthropology, spent a year in the mid-1880s living on Baffin Island where he researched the Inuits' adaptation to their physical environment (Boas, 1888). In keeping with the German tradition, Boas' data-collection strategy stressed the importance of direct observation (Ellen, 1984, p. 42). His subsequent fieldwork trips were generally shorter and often team projects wherein assistants adept in the local languages gathered, transcribed, and interpreted local community members' explanations of their cultural practices. Although Boas tended to make repeat research trips to the same areas, long-term immersion in the field and participation in local activities were not yet essential components of ethnographic methods (Eriksen and Nielsen, 2001, pp. 39–40).

Participant observation, the cornerstone of ethnographic methods, was not developed until anthropologist Bronislaw Malinowski's (1888–1942) landmark research amongst the Trobriand Islanders in the South Pacific. Although Malinowski had not initially envisioned a 2-year immersion in his research setting, as a Pole from Austria-Hungary visiting British-controlled Melanesia when World War I erupted, Malinowski opted for exile in the Trobriand Islands over internment for the duration of the war. Partially as a result of this inadvertent long-term fieldwork, Malinowski came to believe that the most effective approach to researching cultures was that of participant observation. He laid out the principles underlying this methodology in his classic ethnography of the Trobriand Islanders (Malinowski, 1922).

Revolutionary in its day, one of the key ideas underlying Malinowski's vision of participant observation was that researchers armed with "real scientific aims" reside with the people being studied for an extended period of time (usually at least a year to enable observation of the annual cycle of events). As Malinowski wrote, "Living in the village with no other business but to follow native life, one sees the customs, ceremonies and transactions over and over again, one has examples of their beliefs as they are actually lived through, and the full body and blood of actual native life fills out soon the skeleton of abstract constructions" (Malinowski, 1922, p. 18). Malinowski believed that it was only through participating in and observing everyday life over a long period of time that anthropologists could hope to begin to see and experience the world through the eyes of those whose lives one seeks to understand. Likewise, he reasoned that as the community under study becomes more accustomed to the anthropologist's presence, the less likely the anthropologist is to inadvertently alter community members' normal activities. Malinowski also emphasized that long-term participant observation enabled anthropologists to come to recognize the differences between societal rules for behavior and actual behavior (what has been dubbed the difference between ideal culture and real culture).

Also, in a departure from the then-standard anthropological practice of relying heavily on interpreters, Malinowski stressed the need for researchers to become proficient in the local language. In his view, one could not possibly achieve ethnography's aim – "to grasp the native's point of view, his relations to life, to realize his vision of his world" (Malinowski, 1922, p. 25) – without mastery of the local lingua franca. Today, particularly for those who study global processes such as tourism, this means that ethnographic researchers (ethnographers) must often be multi-lingual, with proficiency in a local language, national language, and some of the languages of international visitors. As Malinowski and others have stressed, ethnographers' culturally contextualized translations of quotations drawn from informal and formal conversations are a key form of ethnographic data, and are heavily used in ethnographies.

For Malinowski, one of the main points of the ethnographic methods was to collect "concrete data over a wide range of facts", recording it meticulously in a fieldwork log. As he emphasized, "the obligation is not to enumerate a few examples only, but to exhaust as far as possible all the cases within reach" (Malinowski, 1922, pp. 13–14). He directed anthropologists to gather data on local activity patterns, institutions, folklore, and even what he termed the "inponderabilia" of everyday life which included "things such as the routine of a man's working day, the details of the care of his body, the manner of taking food and preparing it; the tone of conversation and social life . . ., the existence of strong friendships or hostilities, and of passing sympathies or dislikes between people; the subtle yet unmistakable manner in which personal vanities and ambition are reflected in the behaviour of the individual and in the emotional reactions of those who surround him" (Malinowski, 1922, pp. 18–19). All of these, he stressed, were things which could not possibly be recorded via interviews or via documents, but only through participant observation (Malinowski, 1922, p. 18). These "facts", Malinowski emphasized, should not be simply recorded as detailed listings, but "with an effort at penetrating the mental attitude expressed in them" (Malinowski, 1922, p. 19). That is, ethnographic methods should entail a rich and diverse array of data and cases that, taken together, reveal the "emic" or cultural insider's perspective (Pike, 1967). Thus, with Malinowski's invention of participant observation, it was no longer acceptable for anthropologists to conduct their research as distant observers working with translators and relying solely on interviews (Eriksen and Nielsen, 2001, p. 42). Rather, ethnographic methods became an enterprise that centered on immersion, language mastery, participation, and cultural interpretation.

By the early 1970s ethnographic research began to be envisioned as entailing "thick description", a concept that was popularized by anthropologist Clifford Geertz (1973).[1] For Geertz, "thick description" involves unearthing and explicating the multiple, nuanced, and layered webs of meaning of cultural behaviors, relationships, activities, rituals, and productions. This contrasts with "thin description" which tends to be "favoured by low-in-context conventional linear styles of research, and which are prone to focusing exclusively upon the cause-and-effect power of single variables" (Hollinshead, 2004, p. 92). As Geertz tells us, "From the point of view . . . of the textbook, doing ethnography is establishing rapport, selecting informants, transcribing texts, taking genealogies, mapping fields, keeping a diary, and so on. But it is not these things, techniques and received procedures that define the enterprise. What defines it is the kind of intellectual effort it is: an elaborate venture in . . . 'thick description'" (Geertz, 1973, p. 6).[2]

Dating back to the days of Malinowski, a major concern in ethnographic research methods has been with finding ways to ensure the reliability of data collected via ethnographic research methods. Malinowski's early directive for field researchers to constantly check one's data with multiple sources, rather than rely on a single "informant" (the term used in Malinowski's day: today anthropologists prefer the terms "mentor", "collaborator", or "consultant") was echoed and elaborated upon by Raymond Firth, who cautioned that individuals' assertions should not simply be accepted as truths, but instead should be approached as "reflections of the position and interests of the people who give them" (Firth, 1965, p. 3, cited in Duranti, 1997, p. 91). Many researchers draw on the strategy of respondent validation, a process of presenting one's interpretations and write-ups of findings to various participants for checking (for a tourism study that draws on and discusses this strategy, see Cole, 2005, p. 64).

The mid-1980s blossoming of the post-modernist movement brought new attention to the ways in which the researcher's racial, class, national and gender identity, and personality shape the data-collection and interpretation processes, producing not objective scientific reports but what some termed "partial truths", a mixture of objective and subjective observations (see Clifford and Marcus, 1986). Since this crisis moment in the evolution of ethnographic methods, most who embrace ethnographic methods have sought to compensate for these biases in various ways. Many ethnographers adopt a self-reflexive stance, revealing the particulars of their identity and the circumstances of their field research and embracing the first person singular in their writings to signal their positionality. For an example of effective use of this strategy in tourism research, see Causey's (2003) penetrating study of Toba Batak carvers and tourist interactions in the handicraft market. In this study, Causey shares his experiences of his informal apprenticeship with a Toba Batak carver and in so doing readers come to better understand the challenges local artisans face and the ways in which ways in which they adjust their stories and products to the tourist market. As Simonds et al. (2012) summarize, "in the end, ethnographers are content to recognize that their observations are at once subjective interpretations of a mere fragment of their own constrained perceptions of social experiences and at the same time sensitive and intensely engaging but fleeting glimpses of life as it is lived by others."

A discussion of ethnographic research methods would not be complete without addressing ethics. It is essential to ensure that those we are studying are not compromised by our research, or made unwitting participants. Researchers are ethically required to secure permission for their research from the relevant gate-keepers (human subjects boards, national and local governments, etc.), and to reveal their research aims to those whose communities they are studying. Additionally, informed consent forms are the norm (Spradley, 1980, pp. 20–25). Generally, ethnographers are also careful to ensure the anonymity of community members, and use coded names in field notes and other writings, unless they determine that participants prefer to be named in their research publications.

BACKGROUND AND TYPES OF PROBLEMS THAT ETHNOGRAPHY IS DESIGNED TO HANDLE

As many have noted, the clearest value of ethnography is in terms of its relationship to developing theories pertaining to social life (see Hammersley and Atkinson, 1991, p. 23). Engaging in ethnographic methods enables researchers to recognize their own misleading preconceptions concerning the motives underlying human behavior. Long-term immersion in the research setting inevitably forces the researcher to reassess his or her prior understandings of the dynamics at play in the cultural setting under study. As the researcher's understanding shifts over time, he or she "can begin to develop theory in a way that provides much more evidence of the plausibility of different lines of analysis than is available to the 'armchair theorist', or even the survey researcher or experimentalist" (Hammersley and Atkinson, p. 24).

Ethnographic research methods are also ideally suited for tapping into local points of view. Ethnography can effectively unearth local peoples' perceptions regarding changes, challenges and triumphs in their worlds. Local voices – particularly those of minority groups who may speak different languages, be illiterate, impoverished and relatively disenfranchised from their nations – are notoriously difficult to access via classic survey methods and questionnaire-based interviews. Fear of giving the "wrong" answer, mistrust of outsiders, reluctance to speak honestly (and critically) to unknown temporarily visiting researchers, and power imbalances can compromise the validity of other research methodologies. As Berno observed in her discussion of her research on tourism in the Cook Islands, due to "a lack of familiarity with structured questionnaires and social science research in general, subjects tended to acquiesce, and a positive response bias was evident on questions that dealt with satisfaction with tourism and tourists" (Berno, 1996, p. 384, cited in Cole, 2004, p. 295). Long-term participant observation, however, enables researchers to gain the trust of the community members whose lives, perceptions, and attitudes they aspire to understand. Describing her ethnographic research in Eastern Indonesia, Cole underscores that "spontaneous, indoor fireside chats were a more successful technique than attempting to carry out questionnaire-based interviews . . . [and] disclosed information on topics that were not openly discussed at other times" (Cole, 2004, pp. 295–6).

This methodology is especially valuable for offering insights into how people conceptualize themselves vis-á-vis others, as well as into how groups are organized and how they perceive newcomers, be they migrants, tourists, new businesses, or new development projects. These attributes make ethnographic research particularly useful for gaining understandings of the dynamics underlying conflict situations. Ethnographic research can offer fuller data on the issues lurking behind the scenes of questionnaires and quantified surveys (Simonds et al., 2012). Members of disgruntled groups may be unwilling to fully air their critiques in surveys or formal interviews (particularly when they are unsure about the extent to which confidentiality will be maintained), but more likely to convey their frustrations to a long-term field researcher who has gained the trust of the community. The experience of participant observation enables the ethnographer to gain a first-hand appreciation of the basis of the conflict. As both insider and outsider, the ethnographer is well situated to identify possible avenues for conflict resolution between local groups and external agencies, be they private or governmental (see Adams, 2011).

APPLICATIONS OF ETHNOGRAPHIC METHODS TO TOURISM STUDIES

As noted above, ethnographic research strategies yield rich and nuanced understandings of how people make sense of and engage with the world. In this regard, they are valuable for understanding tourists' perspectives on their travel experiences, as well as on the broader ritualized meanings of their voyages vis-à-vis the rest of their lives. Nelson Graburn observes that this methodological emphasis on meaning "might not reveal much about . . . [tourists'] spending, demonstration effects or other measures of impact; nor does it necessarily relate to their satisfaction or the likelihood of their return, though it might. More importantly, meaning has to do with the feelings experienced and the values expressed by temporary travelers, almost always in relation to their whole . . . lives" (Graburn, 2002, p. 30). In this regard, ethnographic methods have been used by tourism scholars to illuminate how travel experiences can impact tourists' perceptions of other nations as well as prompt reassessments, reaffirmations or transformations of their own personal, religious, or national identities. For example, Shaul Kelner's (2010) study of Israeli birthright tourism draws on his participant observation on homeland tours for Jewish young adults that are sponsored by North American Jewish organizations and the State of Israel. These free tours are designed to foster diaspora Jewish engagement with Israel. In addition to participating in these tours, Kelner also spent time with guides and observed guiding program activities. As Kelner concludes, although these diaspora tours may not necessarily change young travelers' identities, they can foster emotionally compelling, embodied experiences that "re-ground" these young visitors' process of self-creation. The on-tour activities "encourage non-Israeli Jews to strike symbolic roots in a place where they do not live . . . through their actions they inscribe place onto self and self onto place, recreating their understandings of themselves and of Israel in the meeting of the two" (Kelner, 2010, p. 198).

Tourism scholars have also drawn on ethnographic methods to examine on-the-ground dimensions of tourism's relationship to nation-building and nationalism (see Adams, 1998; Babb, 2011; Bruner, 2001; Cohen, 2010; Edensor, 1998; Sanchez and Adams, 2008). For example, the differences between the practices and orientations of domestic and international tourists in Asia were seldom addressed by scholars and planners until several researchers engaged in participant observation and chronicled their varying interpretations of what they were seeing. Nelson Graburn's field research in Japan (1983) prompted the realization that the language and framing of domestic tourism in Japan was quite different from that of international tourism. Likewise, my participant observation in Indonesia's ethnic tourism destination of Tana Toraja identified and examined the different framings and meanings underlying domestic and international tourists' visits to this Indonesian hinterland region. Whereas the Indonesian government frames domestic tourism in terms of reaffirming regional and national inter-ethnic ties (contrasting with the ways in which international travelers' visits are framed), my participant observation revealed that government visions of building cross-cutting ties via domestic tourism were often complicated and confounded by prior inter-ethnic or religious tensions. In short, despite governmental framing of tourism as an avenue for strengthening the ties between the diverse groups within the nation, domestic tourism does not automatically build inter-ethnic bridges: sometimes it reignites long-simmering tensions (Adams, 1998).

In a similar vein, several tourism scholars have engaged in participant observation at Indonesia's Taman Mini ethnic theme park and elaborated on the complex ways in which this park, designed to foster nation-building and nationalism, challenges some of our key tourism theories (Bruner, 2005; Hitchcock, 1998). For instance, Bruner notes that when Toba Batak tourists visit the Batak section of this ethnic theme park in their nation's capital, they do not go with Urry's "tourist gaze" seeking experiences different from those of their everyday life, but rather they go to see "what they know they are. They do not discover the other but rather witness a performance of themselves in a different context" (Bruner, 2005, p. 227). In this sense, then, ethnographic methods have effectively enabled us to better understand how tourism can foster "self-construction".

More broadly, ethnographic field methods are well suited for shedding light on tourism's role in shaping particular communities and cultures, insights that are less likely to be culled from questionnaires and surveys. For instance, Hazel Tucker's (2003) long ethnographic research in Goreme, Turkey revealed some of the new cultural forms arising out of encounters between tourists and locals: her findings challenge the dominant stereotype of tourism as a force that uniformly disempowers locals: rather, relationships between insiders and outsiders are constantly negotiated. With regards to tourism and gender relations, Tucker notes that romantic relationships between tourist women and local men are creating new expanded ideas about gender relations in the village (Tucker, 2003). Likewise, Maribeth Erb's long-term participant observation on the Eastern Indonesian island of Flores enabled her to observe, document, and interpret local debates surrounding the rebuilding of traditional houses with an eye to the potential to attract tourists. This methodological approach led Erb to understand that these processes were not instances in which the tourism was "destroying" traditional culture, but rather instances in which interactions with foreign tourists (as well as foreign priests and the state) were introducing new yardsticks for authenticity and enabling local people to make claims for different kinds of authenticity in different contexts (Erb, 1998, 2009). Still other scholars have used ethnographic methods to document the reorganization of local labor, artistic meanings, and conceptions of traditions when ethnic crafts and music are marketed to tourists (see Causey, 2003; Cohen, 2000; Forshee, 2001).

Ethnographic data gathering methods have also offered rich illustrations of how tourism transforms or reaffirms ethnic and racial hierarchies (see Adams, 2006; Guerrón-Montero, 2006; Stronza, 2008; van den Berghe, 1994). For example, Pierre van den Berghe's pioneering ethnographic research in Peru enabled us to recognize that tourism is always superimposed on pre-existing structures of ethnic hierarchies (van den Berghe, 1980). Van den Berghe's more recent fieldwork on ethnic tourism in San Cristobal, Mexico, revealed a tri-partite tourism arena comprised of wealthier foreign and urban Mexican tourists, predominantly *ladino* middlemen who tend to reap the greatest financial gains from tourism and indigenous Maya "tourees" who are the objects of tourists' attention (van den Berghe, 1994). Ultimately, his fieldwork underscores the ways in which ethnic divisions of labor can underlie and sustain tourism in various destinations.

Finally, ethnographic methods are also particularly well suited for gathering data on delicate subjects such as money. For instance, in her study of how tourism employment has transformed Bulgarian women's lives, Kristen Ghodsee recounts how her attempts to gather income information via surveys yielded worthless data. It was only via participant observation and informal interviews that she came to fully appreciate the inappropriateness of the questions that framed her earlier survey (Ghodsee, 2005, pp. 66–7). Likewise, while Ghodsee did not feel comfortable asking direct questions about illicit sources of tourism-related income, participant observation and informal conversations enabled her to learn about income-supplementing strategies of over-charging and short-changing foreign tourists (Ghodsee, pp. 72–3).

One last advantage of ethnographic research methods is worth underscoring before turning to review the limitations of this methodology. As some scholars have noted, the "multi-stranded" nature of ethnographic research (which combines long-term participant observation with interview, archival and other data) forms a solid basis for triangulation and enables researchers to systematically compare data culled from various sources (Hammersley and Atkinson, 1991, p. 24). Hammersley and Atkinson underscore that "this avoids the risks that stem from reliance on a single kind of data: the possibility that one's findings are method-dependent" (Hammersley and Atkinson, 1991, p. 24).

ADVANTAGES AND LIMITATIONS OF ETHNOGRAPHIC RESEARCH METHODS

Ethnographic research methods have potential value for policy formulation and planning that has yet to be fully tapped. First, ethnographic work is particularly adept at giving voice to minorities and at mapping out competing regimes of power at tourism sites. Tapping into this sort of data early can result in the formulation of policies that are more likely to circumvent inequities and conflict at tourism sites slated for development. More generally, ethnography produces a more textured appreciation of the varied responses to prospective tourism development projects in any given community.

Second, ethnographic research methods can also yield insights into the underlying dynamics of on-going clashes at established tourism destinations and this information is valuable for wise policy formulation. Ethnographic research demands that one be attentive to the diverse groups interacting in and beyond the tourist sites, be they domestic tourists, foreign tourists, guides, hoteliers, crafts-makers, souvenir sellers, restaurant and bar employees, local residents, planners, tour organizers, transport workers, or travel writers. Ethnography can shed light on the different visions each of these groups has of a tourist site, and how these visions may clash (see Bruner, 1993, 1996; Notar, 2006). For instance, Bruner's study of tourism at Ghana's slave castles revealed dramatic contrasts between Ghanaian visions of the slave castles as a route to development, African-American tourists' conception of the slave castles as sacred pilgrimage space that should not be commercialized, and other foreign or domestic tourists interest in the slave castles due to their historic roles as other things (past Dutch and British colonial headquarters, site where an important Asante king was imprisoned in 1896, etc). As Bruner (1993) observed, conflicts and frustrations are aroused when different claims about the significance of the space were made simultaneously. His study points towards the challenge faced by planners: how to represent dynamic spaces with long histories to vastly different audiences in such a way that all (or at least many) are satisfied? Via the ethnographic data, however, planners can gain clues as to how to avoid some of the pitfalls inherent in this challenge.

Third, ethnographic research can potentially point towards avenues for bridge-building between diverse stake-holders in touristic settings. Ethnography's orientations towards the broader cultural and political contexts in which tourism unfolds means we engage in participant observation not only *in* the arenas of tourism enterprise, but well *outside* the areas directly tied to the tourism industry. And, sometimes, we find that avenues for tourism conflict resolution lie in spaces and institutions that, on the surface, have little connection to tourism, per se. For example, as part of my field research in the California mission tourism town of San Juan Capistrano (Adams, 2011) I began attending a weekly "coffee chat" that had begun as a journalist's short-cut for gathering local news stories. These open café gatherings soon blossomed into an arena that drew into dialogue both powerful and minority community members and called to mind Habermas's observations on the historic role of British coffee houses in fostering democratic civic engagement. On several occasions, the coffee chat became a forum for constructive tourism problem resolution. It is worth underscoring that the pivotal role of the coffee chat as an arena for bringing together diverse stakeholders in dialogue and ultimately resolving potentially explosive tourism-related conflicts could not have been uncovered easily without ethnographic fieldwork, since the coffee chat forum did not have any obvious relation to tourism. It is in these sorts of ways that the broader "community and beyond" scope of ethnographic research can help steer policy makers and planners towards unexpected new avenues for fostering constructive dialogue between diverse stakeholders in tourism sites.

There are, however, some limitations of this technique that are worth noting. First, ethnographic research is tremendously time-consuming. Policy makers cannot always wait a year for ethnographic data to be gathered and still more months for the researcher to analyse the massive amount of data produced by ethnographic research (for a fuller discussion of this critique, see Yin, 1989, pp. 21–2). Second, as with other qualitative methods, some feel that the "danger of researcher bias" inherent in ethnographic methods render them less appealing than statistical material or survey responses (Sandiford and Ap, 1998, p. 11). In short, some have critiqued ethnographic methods as a "soft" methodology (Phillimore and Goodson, 2004, pp. 3–4).[3] Third, perhaps ironically, ethnographic research's ability to produce rich, nuanced accounts of people's understandings of tourist sites has also been envisioned by some as one reason for its limitations for policy formulation (Filippucci, 2009, p. 321). As Paola Filippucci notes, the diverse narratives we collect in tourist settings can often reveal contradictory perspectives that are "impossible to translate into recommendations to public policy agencies charged with developing 'local' heritage" (Filippucci, 2009, p. 319). Finally, still others have critiqued ethnographic research methods as "too specific to be replicated or applied generally" (Alder and Alder, 1994, cited in Hollinshead, 2004).

FUTURE DEVELOPMENTS

While efforts to accurately predict the future are notoriously difficult due to the many variables on which such predictions are based (Prideaux, 2002, p. 221), some recent developments have indicated new directions in the evolution of ethnographic methods that are pertinent to tourism studies. These include social scientists' growing recognition of the ways in which local sites are tethered to distant regions of the globe, new computer technology, new tweakings of ethnographic methods themselves, and increasing expectations on the part of local stakeholders to have a say in tourism development policies.

This section briefly addresses the potential ramifications of these developments for ethnographic field research methods in tourism studies.

In recent years, scholars have become increasingly cognizant of the ramifications of accelerated globalization for tourism studies: the communities tourism ethnographers study are tethered to global flows, and that tourists are not the only ones to be moving in and out of these destinations: local guides go for training sessions outside the region (see Salazar, 2010), romances with foreign tourists may result in tourates relocating to distant nations (Brennan, 2004), traders move ethnic art wares and tourist souvenirs across great distances (see Forshee, 2001), and even tourism campaigns and slogans travel the globe. In tandem with these developments, tourism ethnographers have grappled with new methodological challenges and have begun what some have dubbed a "post-local" era, casting their ethnographic lens to multiple locales to foster richer, more complex understandings of the workings of tourism in our hyper-global era. One pioneering example of this new development in qualitative research methods is Noel Salazar's multi-sited ethnography, which draws on two years of what he terms "glocal ethnography" (Salazar, 2011) to examine tour guide training and performance in Yogyakarta, Indonesia, and Arusha, Tanzania. Salazar's ethnography is deeply rooted in the destinations he considers and offers rich documentation of how tour guides' practices, narratives, and aspirations are informed by globally circulating "imaginaries" of the past and the future (Salazar, 2010). Drawing on multi-sited ethnographic research techniques to study the local-to-global dynamics of tourism processes, as well as the power trail of touristic systems is clearly a productive avenue for future research.

New technological developments, in tandem with a global economic and ecological crisis, also have implications for the evolution of ethnographic research methods suitable for studying new tourism trends. As Prideaux (2002) has noted, future tourists may be alternating between real and cyber experiences. In his words, "harsh political and/or economic realities may force a retreat of the tourist to more confined areas, and the taste for real-time travel may be restricted or substituted by cybertourism experiences" (p. 324). Such a scenario poses new challenges for adapting ethnographic research techniques to the highly individualized and personalized experiences of this new genre of tourism. Some scholars have begun exploring the methodological terrain of virtual ethnography, or netography (see Hall, 2011; Kozinets, 2010). In addition, one possible avenue for adapting ethnographic methods to fit these new forms of tourism is that of auto-ethnography. Auto-ethnography is a newer form of ethnographic research that draws on the researcher's own experience as a source of data. This approach has already been productively applied to tourism topics by various scholars (see Morgan and Pritchard, 2005; Walsh and Tucker, 2009). For instance, Morgan and Pritchard (2005) have examined their uses and narratives of their own collections of tourist arts amassed over lifetimes of travel, ultimately shedding light on the relations between material things, tourism, and constructions of self-identity. It is likely that future tourism researchers will be increasingly adding auto-ethnography to their methodological toolkit.

Finally, in an era where local communities are increasingly expecting to have a say in tourism planning decisions that will impact their lives, a growing number of tourism researchers are drawing on ethnographic research methods to facilitate this process (see Cohen, 2010; Jamal and Stronza, 2009; Stronza, 2005, 2010). For instance, Amanda Stronza (2005) has engaged in participatory ethnographic research (what some term collaborative ethnographic methods) in a Peruvian Amazon ecotourism destination to shed light on and help steer planning in the direction that local stakeholders envision for ecotourism development. This is a promising path for future tourism scholars, as insights culled from collaborative ethnographic research methods can lead us to find ways to skirt the classic problems by tourism development, yielding more contented stakeholders and tourists.

NOTES

1. This expression derives from the British philosopher Gilbert Ryle's lectures (1971). Norman Denzin (1989) further explicated the scope of thick description in qualitative ethnographic research, delineating and offering examples of 11 genres of thick description. For a full exploration of the origins and evolution of this concept in qualitative research, see Ponterotto (2006).
2. Hollinshead (1991) offers a discussion and adjustment of Geertz's vision of ethnography for tourism scholars.
3. However, qualitative researchers would rebut that surveys are also susceptible to researcher bias and that fully objective research is a cultural myth, not a reality.

REFERENCES

Adams, K.M. (1998), 'Domestic tourism and nation-building in South Sulawesi, Indonesia', *Indonesia and the Malay World*, **26** (75), 77–97.
Adams, K.M. (2006), *Art as Politics: Re-crafting Identities, Tourism and Power in Tana Toraja, Indonesia*, Honolulu: University of Hawaii Press.
Adams, K.M. (2011), 'Public interest anthropology, political market squares, and re-scripting dominance: from swallows to "race" in San Juan Capistrano, CA', *Journal of Policy Research in Tourism, Leisure and Events*, **3** (2), 147–169.
Alder, P.A. and P. Alder (1994), 'Observation technique', in N.K. Denzin and Y.S. Lincoln (eds), *Handbook of Qualitative Research*, Thousand Oaks, CA: Sage.
Babb, F. (2011), *The Tourism Encounter: Fashioning Latin American Nations and Histories*, Stanford, CA: Stanford University Press.
Berno, T. (1996), 'Cross-cultural research methods: content or context? A Cook Island example', in R. Butler and T. Hinch (eds), *Tourism and Indigenous Peoples*, London: International Thompson Business Press
Boas, F. (1888), 'The Central Eskimo', Sixth Annual report of the Bureau of American Ethnology, Smithsonian Institution, Washington DC.
Brennan, D. (2004), *What's Love Got to do with It? Transnational Desire and Sex Tourism in the Dominican Republic*, Durham, NC, and London: Duke University Press.
Bruner, E. (1993), 'Tourism in Ghana: the representation of slavery and the return of the black diaspora', *American Anthropologist*, **98** (2), 290–304.
Bruner, E. (1996), 'Lincoln's New Salem as a contested site', *Museum Anthropology*, **17** (3), 14–25.
Bruner, E. (2001), 'The Maasai and the Lion King: authenticity, nationalism and globalization in African tourism', *American Ethnologist*, **28** (4), 881–908.
Bruner, E. (2005), 'Taman Mini: self constructions in an ethnic theme park in Indonesia', in E. Bruner, *Culture on Tour*, Chicago, IL: University of Chicago Press, pp. 211–230.
Causey, A. (2003), *Hard Bargaining in Sumatra: Western Travelers and Toba Bataks in the Marketplace of Souvenirs*, Honolulu: University of Hawaii Press.
Clifford, J. and G.E. Marcus (1986), *Writing Culture: The Poetics and Politics of Ethnography*, Berkeley, CA: University of California Press.
Cohen, B.C. (2010), *Take Me to My Paradise: Tourism and Nationalism in the British Virgin Islands*, Piscathaway, NJ: Rutgers University Press.
Cohen, E. (2000), *The Commercialized Crafts of Thailand: Hill Tribes and Lowland Villages*, London: Curzon Press and Honolulu: University of Hawaii Press.
Cole, S. (2004), 'Shared benefits: longitudinal research in Eastern Indonesia', in J. Phillimore and L. Goodson

(eds), *Qualitative Research in Tourism: Ontologies, Epistemologies and Methodologies*, Abingdon, UK: Routledge, pp. 292–310.

Cole, S. (2005), 'Action ethnography: using participant observation', in B.W. Ritchie, P. Burns and C. Palmer (eds), *Tourism Research Methods: Integrating Theory With Practice*, Wallingford, UK, and Cambridge, MA: CABI Publishing, pp. 63–72.

Denzin, N.K. (1989), *Interpretive Interactionism*, Newbury Park, CA: Sage.

Duranti, A. (1997), *Linguistic Anthropology*, Cambridge and New York: Cambridge University Press.

Edensor, T. (1998), *Tourists at the Taj: Performance and Meaning at a Symbolic Site*, London: Routledge.

Ellen, R.F. (1984), *Ethnographic Research*, London: Academic Press Inc.

Erb, M. (1998), 'Tourism space in Manggarai, Western Flores, Indonesia: The house as a contested place', *Singapore Journal of Tropical Geography*, **19** (2), 177–198.

Erb, M. (2009), 'Tourism as glitter', in P. Toe, T.C. Chang and T. Winter (eds), *Asia on Tour: Exploring the Rise of Asian Tourism*, London: Routledge, pp. 170–182.

Eriksen, T.H. and F.S. Nielsen (2001), *A History of Anthropology*, London and Sterling, VA: Pluto Press.

Fife, W. (2005), *Doing Fieldwork: Ethnographic Methods for Research in Developing Countries and Beyond*, New York and Hampshire, UK: Palgrave Macmillan.

Filippucci, P. (2009), 'Heritage and methodology: a view from social anthropology', in M.L.S. Sørensen and J. Carman (eds), *Heritage Studies: Methods and Approaches*, Hoboken, NJ: Routledge, pp. 319–325.

Firth, R. (1965), *Primitive Polynesian Economy*, New York: Norton.

Forshee, J. (2001), *Between the Folds: Stories of Cloth, Lives and Travels from Sumba*, Honolulu: University of Hawaii Press.

Geertz, C. (1973), *The Interpretation of Cultures: Selected Essays*, New York: Basic Books.

Geertz, C. (1976), 'From the natives' point of view: on the nature of anthropological understanding', in K. Basso and H. Selby (eds), *Meaning in Anthropology*, Albuquerque, NM: University of New Mexico Press, pp. 221–238.

Ghodsee, K. (2005), *The Red Riviera: Gender, Tourism and Postsocialism on the Black Sea*, Durham, NC: Duke University Press.

Graburn, N. (1983), *To Pray, Pay, and Play: The Cultural Structure of Japanese Domestic Tourism*, Aix-en-Provence, France: Centre des Hautes Etudes Touristiques.

Graburn, N.H.H. (2002), 'The ethnographic tourist', in G. Dann (ed.), *The Tourist As Metaphor of the Social World*, Wallingford, UK and Cambridge, MA: CABI Publishing, pp. 19–38.

Guerrón-Montero, C. (2006), 'Can't beat me own drum in me own native land: Calypso music and tourism in the Panamanian Atlantic coast', *Anthropological Quarterly*, **79** (4), 633–663.

Hall, C.M. (2011), 'In cyberspace can anybody hear you scream? Issues in the conduct of online fieldwork', in C.M. Hall (ed.), *Fieldwork in Tourism: Methods, Issues and Reflections*, Abingdon, UK, and New York: Routledge, 267–288.

Hammersley, M. and P. Atkinson (1991), *Ethnography: Principles in Practice*, London and New York: Routledge.

Hitchcock, M. (1998), 'Tourism, Taman Mini, and national identity', *Indonesia and the Malay World*, **26** (75), 124–35.

Hollinshead, K. (1991), 'The scientific nature of anthropology', *Annals of Tourism Research*, **18**, 653–660.

Hollinshead, K. (2004), 'Ontological craft in tourism studies: the productive mapping of identity and image in tourism settings', in J. Phillimore and L. Goodson (eds), *Qualitative Research in Tourism: Ontologies, Epistemologies and Methodologies*, Abingdon, UK: Routledge, pp. 83–101.

Jamal, T. and A. Stronza (2009), 'Collaboration theory and ecotourism practice in protected areas', *Journal of Sustainable Tourism*, **17** (2):169–189.

Kelner, S. (2010), *Tours That Bind: Diaspora, Pilgrimage and Israeli Birthright Tourism*, New York and London: New York University Press.

Kozinets, R. (2010), *Netography: Doing Ethnographic Research Online*, London: Sage.

Malinowski, B. (1922), *Argonauts of the Western Pacific: An Account of Native Enterprise and Adventure in the Archipelagoes of Melanesian New Guinea*, London: Routledge and Kegan Paul.

Morgan, N. and A. Pritchard (2005), 'On souvenirs and metonymy: narratives of memory, metaphor and materiality', *Tourist Studies*, **5** (1), 29–53.

Nash, D. (2000), 'Ethnographic windows on tourism', *Tourism Recreation Research*, **25** (3), 29–35.

Notar, B. (2006), *Displacing Desire: Travel and Popular Culture in China*, Honolulu: University of Hawaii Press.

Palmer, C. (2001), 'Ethnography: a research method in practice', *International Journal of Tourism Research*, **3** (4), 301–312.

Palmer, C. (2009), 'Reflections on the practice of ethnography within heritage tourism', in M.L.S. Sørensen and J. Carman (eds), *Heritage Studies: Methods and Approaches*, Hoboken, NJ: Routledge, pp. 123–139.

Phillimore, J. and L. Goodson (2004), 'Progress in qualitative research in tourism: epistemology, ontology, and methodology', in J. Phillimore and L. Goodson (eds), *Qualitative Research in Tourism: Ontologies, Epistemologies and Methodologies*, Abingdon, UK: Routledge, pp. 3–29.

Pike, K.L. (1967), 'Etic and emic standpoints for the description of behavior', in D.C. Hildum (ed.), *Language and Thought: An Enduring Problem in Psychology*, Princeton, NJ: D. Van Norstrand Company, pp. 32–39.

Ponterotto, J. (2006), 'Brief note on the origins, evolution, and meaning of the qualitative research concept "thick description"', *Qualitative Research*, **11** (3), 538–549.

Prideaux, B. (2002), 'The cybertourist', in G. Dann (ed.), *The Tourist As Metaphor of the Social World*, Wallingford, UK, and Cambridge, MA: CABI Publishing, pp. 317–339.

Ryle, G. (1971), *Collected Papers, Volume II, Collected Essays 1929–1968*, London: Hutchingson.

Salazar, N. (2010), *Envisioning Eden: Mobilizing Imaginaries in Tourism and Beyond*, New York and Oxford: Berghahn Books.

Salazar, N. (2011), 'Studying local-to-glocal tourism dynamics through glocal ethnography', in C.M. Hall (ed.), *Fieldwork in Tourism: Methods, Issues and Reflections*, Abingdon, UK and New York: Routledge, pp. 177–187.

Sanchez, P. and K. Adams (2008), 'The Janus-faced character of tourism in Cuba: ideological continuity and change', *Annals of Tourism Research*, **35** (1), 27–46.

Sandiford, P.J. and J. Ap (1998), 'The role of ethnographic techniques in tourism planning', *Journal of Travel Research*, **37** (1), 3–11.

Simonds, L.M., P.M. Camic and A. Causey (2012), 'Using focused ethnography in psychological research', in H. Cooper, P.M. Camic, D.L. Long, A.T. Panter, D. Rindskopf and K. Sher (eds), *American Psychological Association Handbook of Research Methods in Psychology: Vol. 2: Research designs: Quantitative, Qualitative, Neuropsychological, and Biological*, Washington DC: American Psychological Association.

Spradley, J.P. (1980), *Participant Observation*, New York: Holt, Rinehart, and Winston.

Stronza, A. (2005), *Trueque Amazónico: Lessons in Community-based Ecotourism*, Washington DC: Critical Ecosystem Partnership Fund.

Stronza, A. (2008), 'Through a new mirror: reflections on tourism and identity in the Amazon', *Human Organization*, **67** (3), 244–257.

Stronza, A. (2010), 'Commons management and ecotourism: ethnographic evidence from the Amazon', *International Journal of the Commons*, **4** (1), 56–77.

Tucker, H. (2003), *Living With Tourism: Negotiating Identities in a Turkish Village*, London: Routledge.

van den Berghe, P. (1980), 'Tourism as ethnic relations: a case study of Cuzco, Peru', *Ethnic and Racial Studies*, **3** (4), 375–392.

van den Berghe, P. (1994), *The Quest for the Other: Ethnic Tourism in San Cristobal, Mexico*, Seattle, WA: University of Washington Press.

Walsh, N. and H. Tucker (2009), 'Tourism "things": the travelling performance of the backpack', *Tourist Studies*, **9** (3), 223–239.

Yin, R.K. (1989), *Case Study Research: Design and Methods* (revised edition), London: Sage.

17 Focus groups
Carl Cater and Tiffany Low

NATURE OF THE TECHNIQUE AND ITS EVOLUTION

Focus groups are one of the core methods in the qualitative researcher's toolkit, for their ability to canvass opinions of a range of stakeholders in a relatively efficient format. In their simplest form they take the format of a group of people discussing a particular issue, with the researcher acting as facilitator. Although there is an issue or topic under debate, the method is relatively unstructured, relying on the interaction of participants to keep the discussion moving. Despite the fact that they are quick to complete, Bosco and Herman (2010) argue that focus groups are one of the most engaging research methods available. In this chapter we explore the development of focus groups, and their potential for collaborative research. Applications of the technique within tourism research are discussed, alongside some of the advantages and disadvantages of the technique. It seems apparent, however, that focus groups have been underutilized in tourism research, particularly in their critical form, and yet they have much to offer.

Focus groups are particularly useful when used in combination with other methods. They may be useful in the early stages of research for providing a broad overview of a topic and generating questions that can be tested by other methods. Alternatively they may be used to test generalizations and theories that are generated by other methods. As Goss (1996, p. 113) demonstrates, they are of use throughout the research process, from orienting the researcher to a new field; generating hypotheses that can be tested by quantitative research; identifying appropriate concepts for the development of questionnaires; following up surveys and helping in the interpretation of quantitative data; and presenting results to the community for validation.

Focus groups have their modern origin as an evaluative method developed to assess audience reactions to radio programs, although they may have existed informally much earlier. The structuring of the method developed to assess US Army training and propaganda films during World War II (Goss, 1996). The focus here was a specific piece of media which the researcher had already analysed, and discussion was moderated by a trained facilitator working from a guide. Continuing from its inception, focus group research is extensively used in marketing and media studies, although this format tends to be of a more structured style. In consumer research storyboards or other scenarios are used to evaluate the effectiveness of media messages. In the movie industry focus groups are often used with test screenings of films to assess audience reaction, and feedback may often result in significant changes to film storylines prior to general release. However, these marketing-oriented focus groups have come under some critique for their Fordist approach to data collection, particularly where they are used in support of business and commercial pursuits (Bosco and Herman, 2010;).

In critical academic work, focus groups have been most developed within sociology, with the pioneer of the technique being recognized as Robert K. Merton (Bosco and

Herman; 2010 Goss, 1996). Building on work conducted with the homeless during the Great Depression, Merton refined his technique as the focussed interview, developed with the backdrop of an interest in the sociology of knowledge, and a growing interest in phenomenological approaches. In later years Merton had concerns about the application of his technique without such a theoretical background, lacking the ability to extend prediction of audience response to examination of human behaviour (Bosco and Herman, 2010). Nevertheless, Merton was keen to stress the wide application of focus groups, emphasizing that the 'focussed interview is a generic technique, that could and would be applied in every sphere of human behavior and experience, rather than largely confined to matters of interest in marketing research' (Merton, 1987, p. 551).

BACKGROUND AND TYPES OF PROBLEMS THAT FOCUS GROUPS ARE DESIGNED TO HANDLE

It is clear that there is a division between 'traditional' focus groups commonly used in marketing studies, and in-depth groups more useful for critical research (Bosco and Herman, 2010). The ability for the latter to present a more grounded form of research is highly important. As Weber (2001) suggests, many previous approaches to the study of tourism have been dominated by etic research, imposing theoretical conceptualizations of the experience upon the study community. Historically there have been fewer attempts at more emic research, which would seek to uncover tourism from the view of the subject, and in particular recognize the variety in individuals' experiences. Similar to interviews, focus groups are qualitative in nature, and provide rich material for analysis. However, their more unstructured nature does 'allow the respondents to impart their own reality . . . cataloguing the socially constructed knowledge of informants rather than the hypothesising of the investigator' (Riley, 1995, p. 636). In this sense, the voices of respondents in focus groups are representative of the emic approach that Weber (2001) supports. By combining the academic's 'perception with an insider's view of the way of life under consideration, the researcher can thus get behind the statistical shapes and patterns . . . studying them from the value terms of the people themselves, in their own terms and on their own ground' (Pryce, 1979, p. 279). This fits with the theory of symbolic interaction which treats theory as something that should be brought into line with the empirical world of lived experience, rather than the other way round (McCall and Becker, 1990).

The dynamic nature of focus groups is grounded in an interactionist tradition which pays attention to the intersubjective ways in which people understand their lived experience (Cloke et al., 1991). The goal of focus groups is not to create one single meaning, but to develop multiple meanings from shared discussion (Finn et al., 2000). In a focus group there is the opportunity for the researcher to interact directly with respondents and each other in a social setting. This further justifies an interactionist approach, where 'any human event can be understood as the result of the people involved continually adjusting what they do in the light of what others do, so that each individual's line of action "fits" into what the others do' (McCall and Becker, 1990, p. 3). Indeed, the *conversations* among participants are the distinguishing elements of focus groups (Bosco and Herman, 2010). This acknowledgement of change attempts to 'connect mobile, moving, shifting minds (and their representations) to a shifting, external world' (Denzin, 1997, p. 32). Following Bodens' observations on conversational analysis, focus groups must therefore be 'centrally concerned with temporality, with duration, with action, and with, as it were, the pulse' (1990, p. 265) of the conversation.

Focus groups therefore are a collaborative research method, as the outcome is dependent on the interactions of group members as well as interactions with the facilitator. However, this should be seen as a strength, not a weakness, as interviewers are themselves implicated in the construction of meanings with their interviewees. Such intertextuality is crucial and unavoidable, and the data which results is essentially collaborative (Cloke, 2002). Indeed, experience suggests that respondents tend to enjoy focus groups as they feel that they are part of the project, assisting in collaborative and generative enquiry. There are also opportunities for all stakeholders to engage in learning through focus group participation.

In line with their collaborative nature, focus groups tend to be useful for engaging with a defined community of interest. For example, focus groups are useful when the study group of interest is small and would not be represented fairly in a larger survey (Veal, 2006). In addition, they are also important for their ability to engage with minority groups, and indeed can form part of a broader process of empowering marginalized communities. Onyx and Benton (1995, p. 50) define empowerment as essential in community development and connected to 'concepts of self-help, participation, networking and equity'. These principles are embedded within critical focus group approaches. As focus groups involve the sharing of knowledge, education is a critical consideration in research design, as 'education theory argues that knowledge is power, and advocates of community empowerment contend that increased levels of community and individual awareness about tourism lead to levels of all types of empowerment' (Friedmann, 1996, cited in Timothy, 2007, p. 209). Therefore there should be consideration of reciprocity in focus groups, following the work of Cole (2006), who advocates a research approach that ensures adequate contribution to the capacity of the researched. Focus groups can form part of such a strategy, although they cannot be relied upon as a sole empowerment method.

A number of researchers in the critical social sciences have called for greater flexibility in the focus group method, and are wary of the rules that specify the ideal form of the focus group discussion, including: group composition, that is the number, gender, age, social status and life experience of participants; the communication skills and personality of the moderator; the nature of topic and questions under discussion; and the timing, setting, seating arrangements and provision of refreshments (Goss, 1996). Therefore, any guidelines should be treated only as such, and any researcher using the focus group method should employ their own reflexivity in their design.

One of the main barriers to effective focus groups can be arranging them in the first instance. Whilst the discussion itself and data generation are relatively swift, their organization may take many months. Finn et al. (2000, p. 79) suggest that this is behind a greater use of focus groups in academic research, but less in undergraduate study, due to the requirements for cooperation, organization, time and resources that few students have access to. A major part of this is having access to communities of interest, through 'gatekeepers', who control avenues of opportunity (Hammersley and Atkinson, 1995).

Following access issues there are concerns with sampling and recruitment, which are often overlooked in qualitative research. Sampling here is just as important as in other methods, even if the community of interest is very specific. There has been debate within the literature with regard to the homogeneity of focus group members. Conradson (2005) explains that a general design principle in setting up focus groups is one of intra-group homogeneity (in terms of gender, race, age, class or occupational sector). This is echoed in much of the literature, with experienced users of the technique such as Burgess (1996) recommending this strategy, with the reasoning behind this being so that respondents feel relaxed in an atmosphere of similar views. In some cases it may be appropriate to have members from specific marginalized groups together so that their voices can be heard. However, there has been some recent critique of this strategy, for it assumes a shared identity, a view which contrasts with the focus group approach where it is surmized that identities are relational (Bosco and Herman, 2010). Furthermore, although Finn et al. (2000) suggest that the atmosphere needs to be relaxed, in some cases a more charged atmosphere may generate fruitful discussion, although one would wish to avoid outright conflict, and this should be considered in risk assessments.

There is no fixed number for a focus group, although one needs to be cognizant of the need to have enough people to generate discussion, without so many that it becomes difficult for the facilitator to involve all participants. Experience suggests that between five and ten participants is a workable number. Consideration also needs to be given to the location, and discursive locales in which focus groups take place (Pryce, 1979). As focus groups are attempting to create as open and comfortable an environment as possible, this should be considered in the design of the interview space. Again there are parallels with community planning strategies, for example those used by Gill and Williams (1994) in their 'living room' approach to assessing community concerns. In this study 18 focus groups or 'living-room meetings' were held with 187 Whistler residents who met in small groups ranging from 6 to 15 individuals in the informal settings of private homes to discuss community growth issues. Such informal settings have also been used in the digital villages project described below. Similarly there also needs to be consideration of timing of focus groups, and how this may influence recruitment and participation. Time of day, other commitments, or timing in relation to an event or issue under consideration are all elements worthy of acknowledgement, not just for logistical reasons, but perhaps more importantly for the influence these factors may have on data generated.

The format of the focus group itself is largely up to the individual, and the priorities of the research project, although it is hoped that the examples provided below will provide some food for thought. Some form of structure is normal, with an introduction to the research, as well as ensuring that all participants are adequately informed as to the purpose of the study. Discussion may then be framed around specific subtopics, and the researcher may wish to impose a rough time limit on these if it is necessary that all areas are to be covered. One of the major roles of the facilitator is to ensure that everyone in the focus group has adequate opportunity to participate. It is important to note that it is not necessarily equal time on the floor that all participants should share, rather that there is equal opportunity to share ideas and opinions. Individuals differ greatly in their ability and desire to articulate, and the facilitator needs to be mindful of this in steering conversations. As Timothy (2007) points out, it is rare all stakeholders in a community will have homogenous views about tourism, the important thing is that everyone enjoys an equal opportunity to participate. This may also involve politely steering the conversation away from topics of limited interest when required. Of course, deciding what is of interest, and what is of relevance is an important but difficult determination to make, and one which can undoubtedly change the outcome of the focus group.

It may not be solely conversations with purpose (Bosco and Herman, 2010) that are generated from the focus group process. There has been a growing interest in using visual techniques in tourism (Garrod, 2008) which can be used in combination with the focus group method. Photographs, either researcher or respondent generated, can be used as an additional prompt for discussion. In community tourism planning in the Rinjani National Park on Lombok, Indonesia, focus groups generated a range of stakeholder maps which were combined to form a planning and tourism information resource (Cater 2012). These maps reflected the beliefs, interests and issues of most concern to these different sectors, for example, indigenous female residents were most interested in where their crops and water sources were located, whereas parks authority representatives took a much more scientific approach to the landscape.

It is normal for focus groups to be recorded, either with tapes or more usually with digital media. The researcher should ensure that the microphones are appropriately located and all participants are recorded clearly. Given the other demands made on the facilitator, it would be problematic for them to attempt to record the discussion on paper at the time. Nevertheless, the facilitator may wish to keep a paper record of the focus group to note any other observations from the discussion. These may be body language, assessments of emotions or relationships or any ancillary points to follow up outside of the discussion. As Denzin (1997, p. 38) suggests, it is often 'the unsaid, the assumed, and the silences in any discourse (which) provide the flesh and bone – the backdrop against which meaning is established'. Indeed, it may be helpful to have a second researcher involved assisting in the administration of the group, acting as observers and to note material which is supplementary to the text. This would be particularly appropriate if for some reason recording was not possible. Burgess (1996, p. 133) emphasizes the importance of a 'debrief' session with facilitators and observers following the focus group to discuss and record 'what was going on, how individuals responded, the themes and topics that came up (or did not come up), our initial ideas about the significance of particular issues'.

There are some concerns that in the transcribed focus groups the physical body of respondents is absent, along with their self image and speaking repertoire (Denzin, 1997). Hammersley and Atkinson (1995) suggest that recordings may present a distorted sense of 'the field', by focussing data collection on what can be recorded, and concentrating attention on the analysis of spoken action. Therefore consideration may be given to the use of video cameras, whilst recognizing the no less representational shortcomings of this technique. There should also be adequate consideration of the ethical aspects of this technology, as well as inhibitions that this may or may not place on participants.

APPLICATIONS OF THE TECHNIQUE TO TOURISM

Focus groups came relatively late to tourism research, even in their less critical marketing form. Indeed, for Peterson (1994) general marketing methods were underutilized in travel and tourism marketing research until the 1990s. Research that presented focus groups as a conversation were also lacking, as tourism scholarship has historically neglected the personal voice of either the subject or the analyst in the analysis (Swain, 1995). One of the earliest applications of the focus group method was by Simmons (1994) who incorporated it in a participatory approach to understanding the role of community participation in tourism planning. In this instance, the focus groups were preceded first by a series of informal interviews and subsequently by a postal survey. It was seen that the adoption of these three complementary methods allowed the researcher to continually refine the research focus as the project developed. Specifically, the researcher's focus groups consisted of small groups of people ($n = 8$–12) who met the prerequisite of having completed the second-stage postal survey. Focus groups were held at three locations within the defined geographical area of interest of the project in order to represent a spectrum of tourism and opportunity (Simmons, 1994). The focus groups themselves took on a three-phase structure, where participants were first given the opportunity to review and interpret the results from the aforementioned postal survey. It was felt this provision of information provided a quantitative framework from which participants could generate specific tourism development proposals. Following this, more definitive tourism development options were developed by focus group participants and subsequently ranked using the 'nominal group technique' (NGT). This technique involves every member of the group giving their view of the solution, in this case to tourism development, and then any duplicate solutions are eliminated from the list of all solutions. Group members then proceed to rank these solutions, first, second, third, fourth, and so on. The third and final phase of the focus groups involves a discussion around key planning constraints which might shape future tourism developments in the area. As the focus of this study was primarily concerned with community participation in the formation of tourism planning decisions, the outcomes of the study noted that of all three stages of investigation, focus groups were seen as the most satisfactory mechanism to encourage participation amongst the community. Importantly, the results of this study demonstrated that through the provision of information (survey results) to focus group participants, the group came to resemble that of an advisory group which was found to be one of the preferred mechanisms for participation identified in the survey.

Despite a few examples, the utilization of focus groups as a research tool from the mid-1990s in tourism was scarce. Not until recently and particularly from the second half of the 2000s has the adoption of focus groups become more widespread. Examples of recent research topics using focus groups in tourism include destination marketing in the context of major UK cities, namely London and Edinburgh (Fyall and Leask, 2006), resident attitudes towards tourism in Lao People's Democratic Republic (Suntikul et al., 2010), evaluation of the development and management of rural tourism projects in Great Britain and South Africa (Briedenhann, 2009), experiences of eating-out for Norwegian solo female travellers (Heimtun, 2010) and cross-cultural analysis of sport tourism between Chinese-Canadians and Anglo-Canadians (Hudson et al., 2010). In her study examining perceptions of international air travel's impact on global climate change, Becken (2007) used focus groups as a means of exploring a consensus on this topic. In this instance, five focus groups were held ($n = 4$–8) lasting on average for two hours. Her focus groups were facilitated by one researcher, and observed by another, and in addition were audio and video taped for later analysis. Focus group participants were also provided with snacks and refreshments as an incentive to participate. As in the earlier example, a structured approach for convening the focus groups was adopted with the use of a quiz, role-play and a general discussion. At the outset, participants were briefed with an introduction to climate change and how tourism relates to it, with consideration given to choice of language and content so as not to influence or prime participants. The purpose of a climate and travel quiz was to introduce facts on climate change and tourism at the start of the discussion and to stimulate debate about the issues (Becken, 2007). The quiz was seen as a way of testing participant knowledge on the subject area in a relaxed environment, as well as providing an opportunity for discussion through the provision of multiple choice answers. The second phase of the session involved the use of role-play. Scenarios which formed the basis for the role-plays were based on contemporary policy discussions, recent studies on emissions trading, emission charges and energy or carbon budgets. Participants were asked to choose pre-defined roles, defined through a few key points. The role-play was seen as a means of reducing the impact of response desirability where participants were seen to be more comfortable presenting answers/arguments as their hypothetical alias than they might otherwise be. The final phase of these focus groups involved a general discussion element. Becken (2007) notes that at the conclusion of the role play activity participants were comfortable giving their *own* opinions on the topic, and as such only loose facilitation and guidance was needed. In conclusion, the researcher noted that because of the specific nature of participants and the structured format of the focus groups that the findings do not allow for wider conclusions about tourists in general to be made. Findings from this research generally pointed towards a desire for more information on the environmental impacts of international air travel by tourists.

A further recent study concerning customer-derived value in the timeshare industry in Australia (Sparks et al., 2007) also used focus groups as one of its core methods of data collection. Sparks and her colleagues employed the use of focus groups because of their ability to canvass a range of opinions at one time, as well as allowing for the collection of a broad range of information from two major sub-groups simultaneously. They note that this qualitative group interviewing process enabled the collection of rich data about the derived customer value of timeshare ownership, whilst also allowing other participants to add cumulatively to the data. As such, this cumulative approach also had the effect of permitting group members to challenge and verify what other participants were saying, "thus providing an iterative yet interactive dialogue" (Sparks et al., 2007, p. 31). In their study, Sparks et al. (2007) recruited three focus groups (*n* = 16, consisting of eight couples) with the help of an industry body, as well as three major timeshare firms. For each focus group, a pre-prepared interview schedule was used, which had been devised in consultation with the aforementioned industry panel members. They noted that this structure consisted of both structured and unstructured interviewing approaches, and in doing so, attempts were made to maintain equal contributions from all participants. Each focus group lasted for between 60 and 75 minutes, and, as in the previous example, was also audio-taped and later transcribed. The analysis of results for this study was undertaken with the use of a software program (NVivo2.0, QSR International, 2002), where the first stage involved two researchers assessing the transcribed audio for comments related to customer-derived value and used an iterative process to differentiate group explanations of consumer value. From this, a codebook was developed and another researcher then recoded text based on final classifications, with an inter-rater reliability of 90 per cent realized. The results from this analysis were then presented to the expert industry panel. In the main, consumers' opinions were found to be in line with Holbrook's (1999) relativistic-preferential definition of consumer value, where participants often compared the value of timeshare against other products they could have purchased, or another leisure experience they had undertaken.

Jennings et al. (2009) carried out focus groups in their study of quality in adventure tourism experiences from the perspectives of adventure travellers and providers on Australia's Gold Coast. The specific aims of this study were to determine the nature of 'quality adventure tourism experiences' for adventure travellers; to determine the nature of 'quality tourism experiences' for adventure travel providers and to develop a quality adventure tourism experience evaluation tool. The research was conducted in partnership with a group of hostels and activity providers serving this sector. Focus groups were identified as being a suitable method for investigation as it would allow rich discussion on issues of quality contrasting with existing quantitative methods such as SERVQUAL (Parasuraman, 1991). The research took place within two specific time periods, a peak summer season, and a quieter off peak period, to assess the relationship between capacity and quality. Given that the adventure youth travel market was defined as people aged between 18–29 years, who were travelling in Australia outside of family units, not for business, and not primarily to visit friends or relatives, whose travel included at least one overnight stay and purchase of adventure travel products, services or experiences, this formed the sampling frame for the focus groups. As many of the industry partners were hostels, they agreed access to their guests and provided facilities in which to hold discussions. The focus groups for the adventure travel providers were held at a central location which was neutral in regards to offering adventure travel experiences. Breakfast and afternoon tea were supplied depending on the time of day that the focus group was being held. The timing of the focus group was based on industry preferences and convenience – either early morning or late afternoon.

As there was a team of researchers involved in this project, it was important to create guidelines for the administration of the focus groups. This included the introduction given to focus group participants, so that all of the participants had the same prior knowledge about the project. Incentives were used to increase traveller participation. The focus groups included the provision of food and beverages, and tourism souvenirs (for example, t-shirts and caps). The focus groups were held around the late afternoon at the accommodation venues when the travellers were between the end of day activities and start of evening activities. As such these focus groups could be loosely described as a 'conversation-based working evening-meal' (Jennings, 2009). The focus groups used in this project were augmented with the use of individual interviews and travel diaries. From interpreting (analysing) the information derived from the focus groups, interviews and traveller diaries, the research team identified five higher order concepts, which highlighted and determined the nature of a quality adventure tourism experience. Those concepts are (1) personal connectivity; (2) social connectivity; (3) experience delivery; (4) combining experiences; and (5) inter-connectivity of the entire adventure travel experience (Jennings, 2009). These concepts were derived by constant comparison of themes generated from the initial and successive analysis of dominant themes.

Focus groups can also be useful in teaching feedback and development, as in a project carried out at Griffith University, Australia, on the teaching of ethics and responsible practice to tourism students (Hornby et al., 2007). The purpose of this project was to develop a resource to assist and facilitate teaching staff to train and educate students in fieldwork courses in ethics and responsible practice. A driver for this project was anticipation that the release of the 2007 National Statement on Ethical Conduct in Human Research would designate an institutional responsibility for the training and educating of students carrying out research. Thus this project aimed to develop good practice in delivery of training and education for students doing fieldwork courses, by developing a resource to assist and facilitate that delivery. To achieve best practice, a team was formed that included members experienced in running fieldwork courses, and members experienced in training, advising and administering research ethics and responsible practice in the university.

After the 2006 delivery of the resources in the undergraduate and postgraduate courses, students were given the opportunity to anonymously participate in focus groups and/or surveys regarding the resource and delivery of materials from the resource. A total of 34 students participated in the survey, while three focus groups were held. These focus groups found that delivery of the materials was successful in increasing awareness and understanding of ethics and responsible practice issues, and this assisted students in complying. However, they also identified that there was a need to demonstrate more application to the students' projects; a need for more class time and depth on the topic; and a need to include issues of subjectivity and cultural influences. Thus a second round of focus groups was conducted following a second implementation of the resource. Such a longitudinal application of the focus group method is particularly useful when examining change.

ADVANTAGES AND LIMITATIONS OF FOCUS GROUPS

Given the usual low overall numbers of participants in focus groups and the 'rich' transcripts that result, it would normally be inappropriate for there to be any quantitative analysis of focus group material. Indeed, one possible challenge of focus groups is the potentially large amounts of material that are generated and seeking meaning within this. This emphasizes the importance of keeping some degree of 'focus' during the discussion phase! The initial approach to analysis is to produce a transcript of the focus group discussion, although as Veal (2006) suggests there is a requirement not just to identify interviewer and interviewee, but also different members of the focus group, which may be difficult from the recording alone. Some researchers advocate producing a summary of the focus group identifying salient themes directly from the recording. If this is done as the notes are being taken then 'the analysis is effectively proceeding at the same time . . . since the note-taker must be drawing out key elements of the discussion in light of the objective of the study' (Veal, 1997, p. 139). Care should therefore be taken as to the accurate representation of themes, and it is recommended that there are multiple listenings to the recording or another person should be used to validate the analysis. Technological developments including software developments in programs such as ATLAS Ti (Scientific Software Development, 1993) and Nvivo (QSR International, 1999) have also enabled researchers to code directly from audio, still images and even video. However, developments such as these have applied quantitative techniques to the evaluation of data, a path which some researchers have criticized.

One of the main concerns regarding focus groups, and indeed one of the main reasons for their use is their ability to uncover power relations. However, in its application one must ensure that there is not simply a replication of existing power structures, or assumptions about where they might exist. Geographical examinations of the scalar nature of power by, for example, Allen (2003) and Herod and Wright (2002) stress that there is no certainty to power or the scales at which it manifests itself. Thus there needs to be consideration both within focus groups and outside as to the application of the process. The former is relatively easier by ensuring that discussion is not dominated by one or two vociferous members of the group (Veal, 2006). However, the balanced external application of focus groups in a policy context is an altogether trickier proposition. For example in the case of the community mapping exercise discussed earlier (Cater, 2012), there has been concern by observers that despite a notionally inclusive process, participation in the benefits of tourism is still limited. As Schellhorn (2010) shows, indigenous residents have limited position of power in the tourism industry, with outsiders and migrants controlling the business of tourism. Nevertheless, focus groups do provide the opportunity to to revise and re-work theories and concepts from the ground up, together with participants, providing a more transparent lens to knowledge construction. In this 'focus groups provide an opportunity to challenge traditional divisions between theory and methodology and between data and interpretation' (Bosco and Herman, 2010, p. 195).

FURTHER DEVELOPMENTS AND APPLICATIONS OF FOCUS GROUPS IN TOURISM RESEARCH

There is certainly opportunity for more use of focus groups within critical tourism studies, particularly in longitudinal research applications. Here there may be parallels with the Delphi method which uses expert opinion in order to answer specific research questions. The Delphi method relies on an expert panel being questioned over a number of rounds, with each member being given feedback on the answers provided by the other panellists between each round. In that sense the Delphi method is also a collaborative research strategy. However, Garrod (2012) highlights a lack of rigour often applied by those using Delphi, which could be shared by focus group applications. Indeed, 'studies using the Delphi method can be very sensitive to the manner in which the experts are recruited, the expertise that is then represented on the panel and how this expertise is exploited' (Garrod, 2012). In particular Garrod points to the problem of panel attrition in Delphic methods, and questions the validity of studies where attrition is too high. Validity in focus group research comes through rigour in design and analysis. Thus the call for flexibility in focus group design described in this chapter should not be mistaken for a lack of process.

Technology also offers significant opportunity for development of the focus group method. Software such as Skype offers the ability to have group conversations remotely with up to ten participants (Skype, 2011). The company suggests that 'video makes communications richer helping you to develop more collaborative relationships' (Skype, 2011, p. 2), and there are clear opportunities for focus groups here. Recruitment and participation may be increased as there is no need for all participants to be physically located in the same space. Digital video recording of the focus group may also be easier. However, there are some issues of concern, for example, how the facilitator maintains control over the discussion, as the group dynamics may be less clear. A lack of 'presence' may mean that there is less 'potential to shift the balance of power away from the researcher towards the participants and allow for supportive and reflexive encounters' (Bosco and Herman, 2010, p. 194). Although video is a step up from just speech as discussed above, such technology may miss much of the non-verbal expressions such as silences, attitudes and emotions (Bosco and Herman, 2010), central to the qualitative method. One also should be wary of possible exclusion of respondents who are not able, for whatever reason, to engage with this technology. Some of the issues in using Skype for focus groups were encountered by the digital villages project which targeted Information and Communication Technology (ICT) use in the home and community in villages in Cleveland, northern England (Digital Villages Research Network, 2011). Issues encountered were space requirements, sound and picture quality and broadband speeds. Nevertheless there were felt to be significant advantages in providing a relaxed 'home' environment as well as flexible catering opportunities (Digital Villages Research Network, 2011).

It would appear that the use of focus groups in tourism research is now accepted, although there is much potential for their future refinement. A review of the use of focus groups in the tourism literature indicates greatest satisfaction when used with other complementary methods and we would stress that methodological triangulation is important for any research project. However, focus groups are certainly unusual in their ability to generate a great deal of information relatively quickly, and one of their greatest strengths is in the collaborative nature of the outputs. Whilst this chapter has presented a number of cases where focus groups have been employed, we have shied away from a list of focus groups 'dos and don'ts'. In line with concerns in the social sciences, we feel that it is more important to employ a degree of reflexivity and rigour in methodological design appropriate to the project in question. Nevertheless, we do also contend that it is perhaps time for tourism researchers to do less borrowing from other areas of study, and create their own innovations in focus group methodology. Many of the cases in this chapter exemplify this innovation. Lastly, it is worth remembering that the skills gained from employing focus groups are useful in many other areas of inquiry. Indeed, as academics we may often find ourselves in informal focus groups with tourism professionals at industry or networking functions. The insights from these interactions contribute to shaping our understanding of the tourism phenomenon, and are part of the collaborative knowledge generation that is the pillar of focus group research.

REFERENCES

Allen, J. (2003), *Lost Geographies of Power*, Oxford: Blackwell.
Becken, S. (2007), 'Tourists' perceptions of international air travel's impact on the global climate and potential climate change policies', *Journal of Sustainable Tourism*, **15** (4), 351–368.
Boden, D. (1990), 'People are talking: conversation analysis and symbolic interaction', in M. McCall and H. Becker (eds) *Symbolic Interaction and Cultural Studies*, Chicago, IL: University of Chicago Press, pp. 244–273.

Bosco, F.J. and T. Herman (2010), 'Focus groups as collaborative research performances', in D. DeLyser, S. Herbert, S. Aitken, M. Crang and L. McDowell (eds) *The SAGE Handbook of Qualitative Geography*, New York: Sage, pp. 220–236.

Briedenhann, J. (2009), 'Socio-cultural criteria for the evaluation of rural tourism projects: a Delphi consultation', *Current Issues in Tourism*, **12**, (4), 379–396.

Burgess, J. (1996), 'Focusing on fear', *Area*, **28** (2), 130–136.

Cater, C. (2012), 'Community involvement in trekking tourism: the Rinjani Trek Ecotourism Programme, Lombok, Indonesia', in B. Garrod and A. Fyall. (eds) *Contemporary Cases in Tourism Volume 1*, Oxford: Goodfellow, pp. 191–212.

Cole, S. (2006), 'Information and empowerment: the keys to achieving sustainable tourism', *Journal of Sustainable Tourism*, **14** (6), 629–644.

Conradson, D. (2005), 'Focus groups', in R. Flowerdew and D. Martin (eds), *Methods in Human Geography: A Guide for Students Doing a Research Project*, Harlow, UK: Pearson pp. 111–126.

Cloke, P., C. Philo and D. Sadler (1991), *Approaching Human Geography*, London: Paul Chapman.

Cloke, P.J. (2002), 'Deliver us from evil? Prospects for living ethically and acting politically in human geography', *Progress in Human Geography*, **26** (5), 587–604.

Cloke, P.J., I. Cook, P. Crang, M. Goodwin, J. Painter and C. Philo (2004), *Practising Human Geography*, London: Sage.

Denzin, N.K. (1997), *Interpretative Ethnography: Ethnographic Practices for the 21st Century*, London: Sage.

Digital Villages Research Network (2011), http://digitalvillage.org.uk/using-a-skype-link-for-a-small-focus-group/.

Finn, M., M. Elliott-White and M. Walton (2000), *Tourism and Leisure Research Methods: Data Collection, Analysis, and Interpretation*, Harlow, UK: Pearson.

Fyall, A. and A. Leask (2006), 'Destination marketing: future issues – strategic challenges', *Tourism and Hospitality Research*, **7** (1), 50–63.

Garrod, B. (2008), 'Exploring place perception a photo-based analysis', *Annals of Tourism Research*, **35** (2), 381–401.

Garrod, B. (2012), 'Applying the Delphi method in an ecotourism context: a response to Deng et al.'s "Development of a point evaluation system for ecotourism destinations: a Delphi method"', *Journal of Ecotourism*, forthcoming.

Gill, A. and P. Williams (1994), 'Managing growth in mountain tourism communities', *Tourism Management*, **15** (3), 212–220.

Goss, J.D. (1996), 'Introduction to focus groups', *Area*, **28** (2), 113–114.

Hammersley, M. and P. Atkinson (1995), *Ethnography: Principles in Practice*, 2nd edition, London: Routledge.

Heimtun, B. (2010), 'The holiday meal: eating out alone and mobile emotional geographies', *Leisure Studies*, **29** (2), 175–192.

Herod, A. and M.W. Wright (eds) (2002), *Geographies of Power: Placing Scale*, Oxford: Blackwell.

Holbrook, M. (1999), 'Introduction to consumer value' in M. Holbrook (ed.), *Consumer Value: A Framework for Analysis and Research*, London: Routledge, p. 5.

Hornby, G., G. Jennings, G. Allen, C. Cater and K. Toohey (2007), 'Educational resource to assist with delivery of training in ethical principles and responsible practise', Unpublished Report, Circulation, Griffith University.

Hudson, S., T. Hinch, G. Walker and B. Simpson (2010), 'Constraints to sport tourism: a cross-cultural analysis', *Journal of Sport & Tourism*, **15** (1), 71–88.

Jennings, G.R., Y.-S. Lee, C. Cater, A. Ayling, C. Ollenburg and B. Lunny (2009), 'Quality tourism experiences: reviews, reflections, research agendas', *Journal of Hospitality and Leisure Marketing*, Special Issue: Experience Marketing, **18** (2–3), 294–310.

McCall, M.M. and H.S. Becker (eds) (1990), *Symbolic Interaction and Cultural Studies*, Chicago, IL: University of Chicago Press.

Merton, R.K. (1987), 'The focussed interview and focus groups: continuities and discontinuities', *Public Opinion Quarterly*, **51**, 550–665.

Merton, R.K., M. Fiske and P.L. Kendall (1956), *The Focussed Interview*, Glencoe, IL: Free Press.

Onyx, J. and P. Benton (1995), 'Empowerment and ageing: toward honoured places for crones and sages', in G. Craig and M. Mayo (eds), *Community Empowerment: A Reader in Participation and Development*, London: Zed Books.

Parasuraman, A.A., L.L. Berry and V.A. Zeithaml (1991), 'Refinement and reassessment of the SERVQUAL scale', *Journal of Retailing*, **67** (4), 420–450.

Peterson, K.I. (1994), 'Qualitative research methods for the travel and tourism industry', in J.R. Ritchie and C.R. Goeldner (eds), *Travel, Tourism and Hospitality Research*, New York: John Wiley, 75–92.

Pryce, K. (1979) *Endless Pressure: A Study of West Indian Lifestyles in Bristol*, London: Penguin.

Riley, R. (1995), 'Prestige-worthy tourism behaviour', *Annals of Tourism Research*, **22**, 630–649.

Schellhorn, M. (2010), 'Development for whom? Social justice and the business of ecotourism', *Journal of Sustainable Tourism*, **18** (1), 115–135.

Simmons, D. (1994), 'Community participation in tourism planning', *Tourism Management*, **15** (2), 98–108.

Skype (2011), 'Group video calling product datasheet', available at http://download.skype.com/share/business/guides/gvc-product-datasheet.pdf.

Sparks, B., K. Butcher and G. Pan (2007), 'Understanding customer-derived value in the timeshare industry', *Cornell Hotel and Administration Quarterly*, February 2007, 28–45.

Suntikul, W., T. Bauer and Song, H. (2010), 'Towards tourism: a Laotian perspective', *International Journal of Tourism Research*, **12**, 449–461.

Swain, M.B. (1995), 'Gender in tourism', *Annals of Tourism Research*, **22** (2), 247–266.

Timothy, D.J. (2007), 'Empowerment and stakeholder participation in tourism destination communities', in A. Church and T. Coles (eds), *Tourism, Power and Space*, London: Routledge, pp. 199–216.

Veal, A.J. (1997), *Research Methods for Leisure and Tourism: A Practical Guide*, 2nd edition, Harlow, UK: Prentice Hall.

Veal, A.J. (2006), *Research Methods for Leisure and Tourism: A Practical Guide*, 3rd edition, Harlow, UK: Pearson.

Weber, K. (2001), 'Outdoor adventure recreation. A review of research approaches', *Annals of Tourism Research*, **28** (2), 360–377.

18 Interview techniques
Nancy Gard McGehee

NATURE OF THE TECHNIQUE AND ITS EVOLUTION

Throughout history, people have attempted to make sense of the human condition through narratives, putting words to their experiences. Some argue that the original paradigm of human inquiry and the archetypical research method is, in fact, the act of conversation between two people (Heron, 1981). Interviewing as a research technique has roots in anthropology and sociology (Seidman 2006) and has been well-regarded in those disciplines for decades.

The term "interviewing" includes a broad range of techniques, spanning from highly structured, standardized, closed questions, to unstructured, open-ended conversations. The focus for this chapter will be upon the latter, most often referred to as in-depth interviewing. In-depth interviewing "uses individuals as the point of departure for the research process, assumes that individuals have unique and important knowledge about the social world that is ascertainable, which can be shared through verbal communication" (Hesse-Biber and Leavy, 2011, p. 94). With this approach, the researcher typically loosely follows an interview schedule of open-ended, broad questions, with the goal of guiding the informant toward her/his reconstruction and interpretation of the topic of study.

Interviewing is primarily located within the qualitative epistemology of research methods, particularly the critical and interpretive paradigms (Goodson and Phillimore, 2004). Those who identify with these paradigms and engage in the interview technique believe that "all research is influenced by the philosophical position of the researcher, the nature of the project, and its intended audience" (Jordan and Gibson, 2004), and view research as a unique, context-specific product, co-created between the researcher and the informant. It is important to note, however, that more positivist, quantitative researchers sometimes utilize the interview technique as well.

BACKGROUND AND TYPES OF PROBLEMS THAT THE INTERVIEW TECHNIQUE IS DESIGNED TO HANDLE

The effectiveness of any research technique is dependent on its fit with the research question. The interview technique is useful for a variety of research scenarios. As with most qualitative techniques, interviewing is especially effective when the research question at hand requires depth and specificity. This method is well-suited for issue-oriented research questions or problems, or when the researcher wants to learn about the experience and perceptions of the informant. Interviewing is valuable when the researcher wants to capture an informant's ideas, thoughts, and experiences in their own words. Perhaps the most important role of interviewing is its ability to give voice to the experiences of persons who are often marginalized in traditional, survey-based quantitative studies. The interview method is also flexible in that it can yield descriptive, explanatory, and/or exploratory data.

APPLICATIONS OF THE INTERVIEW TECHNIQUE TO TOURISM

In many ways, the tourism experience facilitates opportunities for interviews, particularly with the tourists themselves. Persons actively engaged in the act of tourism are often in a position to share their discretionary time with researchers while on vacation. In other words, informants can afford the time to talk. Additionally, the subject matter of tourism is one that many tourists are eager to discuss; they enjoy analysing or recounting their travel experiences.

On the supply-side, tourism industry stakeholders are often very busy people, but they also tend to be immersed and involved in their work, and as such are eager to share their thoughts. From a practical perspective, the relative youth of the industry, along with a lack of clean, systematic, quantitative data measuring the tourism industry also contributes to the usefulness of the interview technique in tourism. As researchers begin to gain an appreciation of the complexity surrounding the relationship between the tourism industry and the rest of the community, the interview technique offers a way to capture residents' varied experiences and perceptions of tourism. Finally, this is an era where researchers are finding average survey response rates to be plunging (Sheehan, 2001), often due to survey fatigue. The interview technique may incite a more welcome response from potential tourism study subjects of all types.

The in-depth interview technique has been applied in a number of ways to research in tourism. Some utilize it as a sole method of study, while others triangulate it with a variety of qualitative techniques, either sequentially or simultaneously (multi-method). Still others utilize it as a precursor to quantitative research methods (mixed methods). Buzinde et al. (2010) provide an excellent example of the application of interviews as the sole data collection method. They utilize the technique known as funneling (Patton, 1990) as part of the interview process surrounding their work that targets visitor's perceptions of beach reclamation efforts at a coastal resort in Mexico. Buzinde et al.'s use of the funneling process begins with broad questions about the landscape and then follows up with more specific queries about particular circumstances or situations as a means to explore the contested meanings that emerge from the human–environment relationship. White and White (2007) also utilize interviews solely in their study of the changing notions of "home" and "away" amongst tourists in the context of today's internet connected world. They find that tourists who stay in contact with family and friends at home through inexpensive fixed telephone services and/or internet cafés experienced a blurring of lines between their everyday environment of home and life on the road. Informants reported both positive and negative elements of connectivity: positive in that they could maintain established relationships, but negative in that communication in this context could be upsetting and lead to re-assessment of contentious relationships.

While these are excellent examples of the use of the interview technique as a stand-alone method for a study, tourism researchers also utilize interviews as one component of a multi-method study, triangulating the interview findings with other qualitative data collection techniques (Aas et al., 2005; Brown, 2009; Muzaini, 2006; Palmer, 2005). This is commonly utilized in the ethnographic approach, whereby researchers combine participant observation, field diaries, conversations, systematic lurking, and/or other qualitative methods with in-depth interviews (Fetterman, 1998). For example, Muzaini (2006) utilizes interviews in concert with field diaries in a fascinating study of backpackers in Southeast Asia and their strategies for achieving a high level of cultural immersion in order to have what they perceive as an authentic experience. This study provides an especially good example of how to classically merge interview results with other techniques.

The mixed method approach is similar to the multi-method approach, but utilizes a mix of both qualitative and quantitative methods. One very innovative use of the interview method as part of a mixed-method study may be found with Pan and Fesenmaier's (2006) exploration of the online information search as part of the vacation planning process. Interviews were used as a way to follow-up on a vacation planning exercise conducted with a group of 15 individuals that included the audio and video recording of the online planning process as well as computer and internet activity monitoring using specialized quantitative software. The interviews were extremely valuable as they provided insight and clarity into the perspectives of the research subjects.

There is certainly a more traditional positivistic area of the literature where in-depth interviewing is utilized as a way to develop quantitative variables, scales and survey items (Hung and Petrick, 2010; Rittichainuwat, 2011; Yang, 2011) or as a form of reconnaissance to determine if a tourist site is appropriate for the research problem (Williams and Soutar, 2009). In other words, the interview is used to lay the groundwork or act as a precursor to the primary quantitative study. Hung and Petrick (2010) provide a classic example of this in their development of a measurement scale for constraints to cruising, as does Rittichainuwat (2011) in an interesting study that uses interviews of a travel writer, journalist, tour operator, and tsunami survivors to develop a scale to measure possible deterrents from visiting tsunami-hit destinations.

These aforementioned studies provide rigorous examples of the various uses of the interview technique in the area of tourism. But what do we know about overall trends in the use of the interview technique in tourism research? As with qualitative research overall, the interview method has gained considerable ground in the study of tourism over the past 20 years (Goodson and Phillimore, 2004). At the time this chapter was written, over 130 peer-reviewed articles from the top three tourism journals (*Journal of Travel Research*, *Annals of Tourism Research*, and *Tourism Management*) were found to have utilized the interview method within the last decade (2000–2010). In the decade previous to that, less than half that number were found. The majority of recent interview-focused research seems to be located within the visitor behavior/consumer psychology and heritage/culture areas of study, but the method has also been utilized in the areas of destination development, policy and planning, tourism industry management, resident attitudes, and host–guest relations.

Much work that utilizes the interview technique is being conducted in the broad area of visitor behavior/consumer psychology, including park usage (Cochrane, 2006), risk (Elsrud, 2001; Uriely and Belhassen, 2006), tourist satisfaction (Moyle and Croy, 2007; Rodriguez Del Bosque and San Martin, 2008), constraints to travel (Hung and Petrick, 2010; Rittichainuwat, 2011), study abroad (Brown, 2009), niche and/or marginalized groups (Andriotis, 2009; Gibson, 2002; Hecht and Martin, 2006; Heuman, 2005; Lane and Waitt, 2007; Sin, 2009; White and White, 2007), motivation (Maoz, 2007), and the postmodern tourist (Maoz and Bekerman, 2010). One of the most interesting studies from this area of tourism research is Uriely and Belhassen's (2006) work in the area of drugs and risk-taking in tourism. By utilizing in-depth interviews, the researchers are able to delve deeply into the rationale used by tourists who commonly seek out destinations based on the availability of drugs. Findings reveal that the informants are very aware of the risks associated with drug use when they are far from home, but informants also have a sense that in some ways being a tourist provides greater protection from those risks. Given the sensitivity of this subject matter, and the difficulty of finding a large sample of informants, the interview technique is a very appropriate method.

A variety of issues surrounding the interface of heritage and culture with tourism have been analysed using the interview method within the past decade: the social and political construction of heritage (Chronis, 2005; Park, 2010; Santos and Yan, 2008), authenticity (Kim and Jamal, 2007; Martin, 2010), commodification (Cole, 2007), identity (Goulding and Domic, 2009; Light, 2007; Palmer, 2005), tourism and performance (Mordue, 2005), and cross-cultural relations (Raymond and Hall, 2008), to name a few. Light's (2007) use of the interview technique in his work focusing on the social construction of a Dracula-centered cultural identity in Romania is an excellent example of the value of the interview method in this area of tourism research. Light is interested in how tourism planning and policy making was conducted during the socialist era, and how it in turn constructed and supported the myth of Transylvania. As very little documentation is accessible to him from that secretive time in Romanian history, he utilizes the interview method as a way to gain knowledge from former policy makers during that era. Thus he is able to access information and explore the contradictions between the myth of Dracula and the image that Romania was attempting to portray to the world during that time that otherwise would not have been accessible.

In the area of destination development, interview based research is being conducted in the topics of eco-tourism (Cruz et al., 2005; Jones, 2005), rural tourism (Cawley and Gillmore, 2008; Nepal, 2007; Saxena and Ilbery, 2009), race/ethnicity/gender and tourism development (Buzinde and Santos, 2009; Carr, 2007; Gentry, 2007), dependency (Lacher and Nepal, 2010), conflict (Lee et al., 2010), and community participation (Li, 2006; Matarrita-Cascante, 2010; Sebele, 2010). As mentioned previously, the interview technique is especially useful for capturing the perspectives and complexities of marginalized groups normally excluded from the conversation. Gentry (2007) utilizes the method to explore Belizean women's experiences in a wide range of employment (both tourism and non-tourism), and by doing so is able to tease out the complex interactions between development and culture in the context of gender. For example, while the Belizean cultural cornerstones of gender segregation and housewifization of labor are often reinforced and magnified in the workplace, employment opportunities in tourism do, in some cases, reduce the reliance of women on the male heads of households as the sole financial decision maker and give them greater economic independence. Gentry is able to focus on women (in this case a marginalized group) through the interview technique and capture these differences and contradictions that might otherwise be missed in a male-dominated culture.

Some work utilizing the interview technique is found in the area of policy, although not as prominent as in the three previous topics. Categories include stakeholders (Aas et al., 2005), politics (Airey and Chong, 2010; Altinay and Bowen, 2006) power (Bramwell and Meyer, 2007), social policy (Stevenson et al., 2008) and governance (Yuksel et al., 2005). Bramwell and Meyer (2007) interview key decision makers and utilize discourse analysis to explore the networks, strategies, and power relations involved in the tourism development of an island in the former East Germany. The interview process allows the researchers to conduct multiple interviews of a purposive sample of 21 key informants, and triangulate that data with informal conversations with 53 local residents, published and unpublished reports, internal documents, and newspaper articles. From the data, Bramwell and Meyer discovered unique tensions and difficult transitions, most of which are a result of the political changes brought about by a formerly socialist region being absorbed into a capitalist democratic state. Bramwell and Meyer also exposed the dialectics of power relations that existed during the process of tourism development on the island.

Interview-based research targeting the area of tourism industry management is difficult to categorize. Ethics (Lahdesmaki, 2005; Lovelock, 2008), sustainability (Vernon, 2000; Vernon et al., 2005), product development (Lumsdon, 2006), performance measurement (Phillips and Louvieris, 2005), risk (Wang et al., 2010), knowledge transfer (Weidenfeld et al., 2010; Wong and McKercher, 2011), and business networks (O'Brien, 2006; Paget et al., 2010; Tinsley and Lynch, 2001) are only a few of the categories discovered while conducting a literature review in this area. While all of these areas are important, one of the most important (yet difficult to study) is knowledge transfer. Weidenfeld et al. (2010) use the interview technique to examine innovation and knowledge transfer within the under-studied attractions segment of the tourism industry in the region of Cornwall, England. Perhaps the most interesting element of this study is the way in which framework analysis is used to analyse 32 interviews of a variety of stakeholders, which involved the

> familiarization, classification, and indexation that allowed the identification of different themes and their coding, using Non-numerical Unstructured Data Indexing Searching and Theory-building. . . . Each knowledge transfer or innovation process identified was named, classified as product innovation, process innovation or other form of knowledge transfer. Each pair (knowledge provider and receiver) was classified as "neighbours" when both enterprises were located in the same cluster, and "distant" when not. Attractions were classified thematically as product-similar or product-different in terms of the attractions that they received or supplied knowledge to. (Weidenfeld, Williams & Butler, 2010, p. 613.)

Findings from the study indicate that at the local and regional level, spatial proximity, product similarity, and market similarity generally facilitate knowledge transfers and innovation spillovers.

While some quantitative studies of resident attitudes toward tourism (McGehee and Andereck, 2004; Vargas-Sánchez et al., 2011) conclude with a call for more qualitative work in the area, very little has been published in the top-tier journals within the last decade. In fact, only one resident attitude article is found: a study of residents' attitudes toward tourism in a small village in Uganda by Lepp (2008), which provides an excellent example of the usefulness of the interview technique in locales where literacy rates may be low, survey research may be unfamiliar to the targeted research population, and/or resources needed for survey research are scarce or unavailable. Lepp utilizes the method of constant comparison to analyse the interview data, which is the process origi- nally developed by Glaser and Strauss (1967) as the methodology for grounded theory. Constant comparison consists of (1) collecting and analysing data, (2) developing tentative conclusions, hypotheses, and themes, (3) collecting and analysing additional data, (4) testing against the initial hypotheses and themes, (5) purposefully seeking out additional new perspectives and data sources, and (6) continuing the process until you reach data saturation (you are not learning anything new from your data collection). As a result of his use of constant comparison, Lepp is able to capture the complexity of some seemingly simple responses regarding tourism. For example, while many farmers interviewed express frustration with the issue of crop raiding by protected wildlife from a nearby preserve, they view that as a by-product of conservation rather than tourism, and that the revenue from tourism is actually a positive compensation for the inevitable crop raiding. This perspective has not been captured in previous research in this area of study.

In the area of host–guest relations publications in top-tier journals are limited (de Albuquerque, 2001; Maoz, 2007; Salazar, 2005). Given the legacy of Smith (1989), this is quite surprising. Maoz (2007) conducted a long-term study of Israeli backpackers in India that included in-depth interviews and participant observation to present the notion of the "mutual gaze" (Maoz, 2007, p. 221). She posits that not only is there a tourist gaze whereby tourists objectify local residents, the opposite occurs among the Indian hosts of the large numbers of Israeli backpackers.

As conclusion to this section, it is important to note that while the focus was on citing works from top-tier journals, a great deal of valuable work utilizing the interview technique is situated in more topic-specific journals, book chapters, and monographs. Focusing on the top-tier journals is simply utilized as a way to manage the large quantity of work that exists in this area.

ADVANTAGES AND LIMITATIONS OF INTERVIEW TECHNIQUE CONCEPTUALLY AND FOR POLICY FORMULATION

As with any research method, there are advantages and limitations to the use of in-depth interviews. Jordan and Gibson (2004, pp. 222–3) provide a thorough overview of these in their study of solo women travel experiences, as does Seidman (2006) in his guide of interviewing techniques targeting researchers in education. To summarize its advan- tages, interviewing:

- is adaptable to a wide range of themes and topics
- enables researchers to account for body language and non-verbal forms of com- munication often missed in other forms of data collection
- can provide background for studies using multiple methods
- can create rich, descriptive data and illustrative examples of the human experience
- the iterative nature of interviewing can ensure its validity and accuracy.

Limitations to the interviewing technique include:

- poor data quality if the possible power differentials and status differences (including class, gender, race and ethnicity) between the researcher and the informant are not taken into consideration
- the potential for failure and misunderstandings if a partnership is not established early on between the researcher and informant
- the time-consuming nature of the method, both the interviewing process itself as well as the pre-interview process, which includes conceptualizing the research problem, gaining entre' with informants, scheduling (and often re-scheduling) interviews, and the post-interview transcription and analysis
- the investment of training, experience, and confidence to implement
- the monetary expense, including researcher travel and compensation of informants for their time
- political pitfalls for the researcher in choosing the "paradigmatic road less traveled", and for the informant if the subject is sensitive to family, friends, co-workers, and her/his community
- the dependency on the honesty of the informant to the success of the interview and the research project overall.

There are a number of strategies that can be employed to maximize the advantages and minimize the disadvantages of the interview technique. They include:

- appropriate selection of the sample or panel
- the role of triangulation and other methods of trustworthiness
- finding the appropriate length and structure for the interview
- conducting an ethical study that accounts for the respect of and confidentiality for the informants
- applying active listening techniques and taking advantage of the iterative nature of interviewing.

First, selection of informants is extremely important. Who you choose to interview will have a very powerful impact on your research. It is vital that the researcher recognize and appreciate why she/he wants to study the selected sample. Researchers should be cognizant of a number of possible issues, including bias (both positive and negative), prejudice, familiars versus strangers as informants, and snowball versus purposive sampling. One example of how these issues may be addressed is found in Zahra and McGehee's (in press) study of volunteer tourism in the Philippines and its impact on community capital. Zahra has over 20 years experience working with the communities and organizations purposefully selected for the study, which provided a very strong level of access and trust, but while the primary researcher was aware that her familiarity and 'entre' into the community was vital to the success of the study, she also was aware of any potential bias that she might introduce given her strong ties with the organizations and the community. To combat this, she immersed herself in the volunteer tourism literature (particularly the area of critical theory), worked hard to allow for a wide spectrum of voices in the interviews, and intentionally sought out a co-researcher whom she felt would be as unbiased as possible.

Second, the inclusion of criteria for trustworthiness is vital to all forms of qualitative research, including interviews (Lincoln and Guba, 1985). Special care should be taken in the development of the research design to assure Maxwell's (2005) parameters for validity in qualitative research, which is also in alignment with Lincoln and Guba's (1985) typology. This includes four criteria for qualitative inquiry: credibility, transferability, dependability, and confirmability (DeCrop, 2004, p. 159). Credibility, which "relates to the quantitative criterion of internal validity" (DeCrop, 2004, p. 159), may be enhanced using techniques of prolonged engagement, persistent observation, and member checks. Transferability (much like external validity) may be accounted for through purposive sampling. Dependability mirrors quantitative reliability. Dependability may be increased through the development of a detailed research plan which can include an audit trail of the transcripts, a personal journal of the research process kept by the researcher, prolonged engagement, and/or the inclusion of a research auditor. The research audit process is also useful to assess confirmability, e.g., assurances that a variety of explanations about the phenomenon are being studied. Additionally, the role of triangulation is important to any type of qualitative research; the interviewing technique is no exception. This may include data, method, investigator, and/or theoretical triangulation (DeCrop, 2004). Triangulation simply means the use of more than two data sources (data triangulation), methodological approaches (method), researchers (investigator), or theoretical perspectives (theoretical) to approach a problem as a way to increase confidence in the results.

Third, determining the appropriate length and structure of the interview format is also an important means of maximizing the advantages while minimizing the limitations of the method. In general, 90 minutes is seen as a typical length for interviews, but as with much of qualitative research there are no "cookbook" rules. Informants notice, appreciate, and respond to researchers who respect their time and resources by keeping the interview on task but not regimental, structured but not rigid, and appropriate but not constrained. Similarly, the fourth element of conducting an ethical research program and assuring the respect toward and confidentiality of informants is tantamount to the success of the interview techniques. Hesse-Biber and Leavy (2011, p. 83) provide a practical and insightful "Checklist of Questions for Conducting an Ethical Research Project" that includes such important elements as the importance of explaining the purpose of your study to your informants, any risks that the informants may incur by participating in the project, exactly the parameters and expectations of confidentiality, who will have access to the data, and what ethical framework informs the research project.

Fifth, the role of the researcher as active listener is crucial to gaining the trust of the informant and obtaining honest answers, but must be carefully approached (Hesse-Biber and Leavy, 2011). Active listeners are interviewee focused, supportive but non-interruptive, non-judgmental, accepting of difference, allowing for and listening to the importance of silences, and resisting the need to "fill in the blanks" by putting words into the informant's mouth. Active listeners keep asking questions until they fully understand the informant, probing and exploring, taking advantage of the iterative nature of the interview format. For fledgling researchers, this can be difficult. A few "starter questions" are always valuable to keep nearby as a guide, should the interview begin to lose momentum. These include: tell me a story about _____; tell me more about _____; draw a picture that reflects _____; can you explain that a bit more for me?; and is there an example you can think of?

FURTHER DEVELOPMENTS AND APPLICATIONS OF THE INTERVIEW TECHNIQUE IN TOURISM RESEARCH

It is hoped that tourism research as a whole will continue to become more sophisticated and multi-faceted, reaching beyond the sometimes overused survey method to include a wider variety of techniques. In this manner tourism researchers can work toward richer, more robust solutions to the myriad problems of tourism development, to better understand the behavior of the tourist, and to give voice to the under-served and marginalized groups on both sides of the host–guest dichotomy.

In the specific area of in-depth interviews, while some have utilized a pre- and post-event interview technique (Maoz, 2007), there is very little research in tourism that utilizes the classic three interview structure (Schuman, 1982; Seidman, 2006) quite often used in interpretivist phenomenological research (Schutz, 1967). Phenomenology is the study of structures of experience or consciousness. Phenomenologically based interviewing combines life history interviewing with in-depth interviewing. While a number of studies in tourism have utilized the phenomenological perspective (Andriotis, 2009; Pernecky and Jamal, 2010; Wang, 1999), the author could find no tourism studies where the three interview structure was employed. Designed by Schuman (1982), this technique includes a first interview, whereby the participant's life history is placed in the context of the research topic; a second interview, whose purpose is to focus on the concrete details of the informants present, lived experience; and a third interview, which focuses on meaning-making, or the intellectual and emotional connections between the topic at hand and the person's life. Each interview is important, in that it facilitates putting the informant's life experience into language (Seidman, 2006) as well as creating a rapport between the researcher and the informant.

In addition to the need for interview-based tourism research that includes multiple interviews with each informant, there also seems to be a paucity of practice and pilot interviews utilized as a way to refine and improve the interview quality. Just as researchers conduct pilot surveys, pilot interviews are also valuable.

The interview technique allows tourism researchers to approach issues in the field in a deep, rich way not possible within many quantitative methods. As noted earlier, the interview method may act as a stand-alone technique, or it can work in concert with other methods, both qualitative and quantitative. As with any method, paying careful attention to the appropriate ways to utilize the technique will minimize its limitations and maximize its strengths.

REFERENCES

Aas, C., A. Ladkin and J. Fletcher (2005), 'Stakeholder collaboration and heritage management', *Annals of Tourism Research*, **32** (1), 28–48.

Airey, D. and K. Chong (2010), 'National policy-makers for tourism in China', *Annals of Tourism Research*, **37** (2), 295–314.

Altinay, L. and D. Bowen (2006), 'Politics and tourism interface: the case of Cyprus', *Annals of Tourism Research*, **33** (4), 939–956.

Andriotis, K. (2009), 'Sacred site experience: a phenomenological study', *Annals of Tourism Research*, **36** (1), 64–84.

Bramwell, B. and D. Meyer (2007), 'Power and tourism policy relations in transition', *Annals of Tourism Research*, **34** (3), 766–788.

Brown, L. (2009), 'The transformative power of the international sojourn: an ethnographic study of the international student experience', *Annals of Tourism Research*, **36** (3), 502–521.

Buzinde, C. and C. Santos (2009), 'Interpreting slavery tourism', *Annals of Tourism Research*, **36** (3), 439–458.

Buzinde, C., D. Manuel-Navarrete, E. Yoo and D. Morais (2010), 'Tourists' perceptions in a climate of change: eroding destinations', *Annals of Tourism Research*, **37** (2), 333–354.

Carr, A. (2007), 'Māori nature tourism businesses: connecting with the land', in R. Butler and T. Hinch (eds), *Tourism and Indigenous Peoples: Issues and Implications*, Oxford: Elsevier, pp. 113–127.

Cawley, M. and D. Gillmore (2008), 'Integrated rural tourism: concepts and practice', *Annals of Tourism Research*, **35** (2), 316–337.

Chronis, A. (2005), 'Coconstructing heritage at the Gettysburg storyscape', *Annals of Tourism Research*, **32** (2), 386–406.

Cochrane, J. (2006), 'Indonesian national parks: understanding leisure users', *Annals of Tourism Research*, **33** (4), 979–997.

Cole, S. (2007), 'Beyond authenticity and commodification', *Annals of Tourism Research*, **34** (4), 943–960.

Cruz, R., E. Baltazar, G. Gomez and E. Lugo (2005), 'Social adaptation: ecotourism in the Lacandon Forest', *Annals of Tourism Research*, **32** (3), 610–627.

de Albuquerque, K. (2001), 'Tourist harassment: Barbados survey results', *Annals of Tourism Research*, **28** (2), 477–492.

DeCrop, A. (2004), 'Trustworthiness in qualitative tourism research', in J. Phillimore and L. Goodson (eds), *Qualitative Research in Tourism: Ontologies, Epistemologies, and Methodologies*, London: Routledge, pp. 156–169.

Elsrud, T. (2001), 'Risk creation in traveling: backpacker adventure narration', *Annals of Tourism Research*, **28** (3), 597–617.

Fetterman, D. (1998), *Ethnography*, London: Sage.

Gentry, K. (2007), 'Belizean women and tourism work: opportunity or impediment?', *Annals of Tourism Research*, **34** (2), 477–496.

Gibson, H. (2002), 'Busy travelers: leisure-travel patterns and meanings in later life', *World Leisure*, **44** (2), 11–20.

Glaser, B.G. and A. Strauss (1967), *The Discovery of Grounded Theory: Strategies for Qualitative Research*, 3rd edition, Madison, WI: Sociology Press.

Goodson, L. and J. Phillimore (2004), 'The inquiry paradigm in qualitative tourism research', in J. Phillimore and L. Goodson (eds), *Qualitative Research in Tourism: Ontologies, Epistemologies, and Methodologies*, London: Routledge, pp. 30–46.

Goulding, C. and D. Domic (2009), 'Heritage, identity and ideological manipulation: the case of Croatia', *Annals of Tourism Research*, **36** (1), 85–102.

Hecht, J.A. and D. Martin (2006), 'Backpacking and hostel-picking: an analysis from Canada', *International Journal of Contemporary Hospitality Management*, **18** (1), 66–77.

Heron, J. (1981), 'The philosophical basis for a new paradigm', in P. Reason and J. Rowan (eds), *Human Inquiry*, New York: Wiley, pp. 19–35.

Hesse-Biber, S.N. and P. Leavy (2011), *The Practice of Qualitative Research*, 2nd edition, Thousand Oaks, CA: Sage.

Heuman, D. (2005), 'Hospitality and reciprocity: working tourists in Dominica', *Annals of Tourism Research*, **32** (2), 407–418.

Hung, K. and J. Petrick (2010), 'Developing a measurement scale for constraints to cruising', *Annals of Tourism Research*, **37** (1), 206–228.

Jones, S. (2005), 'Community-based ecotourism: the significance of social capital', *Annals of Tourism Research*, **32** (2), 303–324.

Jordan, F. and H. Gibson (2004), 'Let your data do the talking: researching the solo travel experiences of British and American women', in J. Phillimore and L. Goodson (eds), *Qualitative Research in Tourism: Ontologies, Epistemologies, and Methodologies*, London: Routledge, pp. 215–235.

Kim, H. and T. Jamal (2007), 'Touristic quest for existential authenticity', *Annals of Tourism Research*, **34** (1), 181–201.

Lacher, R.G. and S. Nepal (2010), 'Dependency and development in Northern Thailand', *Annals of Tourism Research*, **37** (4), 947–968.

Lahdesmaki, M. (2005), 'When ethics matters: interpreting the ethical discourse of small nature-based entrepreneurs', *Journal of Business Ethics*, **61** (1), 55–68.

Lane, R. and G. Waitt (2007), 'Inalienable places: self-drive tourists in Northwest Australia', *Annals of Tourism Research*, **34** (1), 105–121.

Lee, T., M. Riley and M. Hampton (2010), 'Conflict and progress: tourism development in Korea', *Annals of Tourism Research*, **37** (2), 355–356.

Lepp, A. (2008), 'Tourism and dependency: an analysis of Bigodi village, Uganda', *Tourism Management*, **29** (6), 1206–1214.

Li, W. (2006), 'Community decision-making: participation in development', *Annals of Tourism Research*, **33** (1), 132–143.

Light, D. (2007), 'Dracula tourism in Romania: cultural identity and the State', *Annals of Tourism Research*, **34** (3), 746–765.

Lincoln, Y.S. and E. Guba (1985), *Naturalistic Inquiry*, Beverly Hills, CA: Sage.

Lovelock, B. (2008), 'Ethical travel decisions: travel agents and human rights', *Annals of Tourism Research*, **35** (2), 338–358.

Lumsdon, L. (2006), 'Factors affecting the design of tourism bus services', *Annals of Tourism Research*, **33** (3), 748–766.

McGehee, N.G. and K. Andereck (2004), 'Factors influencing rural resident's support of tourism', *Journal of Travel Research*, **43** (2), 131–140.

Maoz, D. (2007), 'Backpackers' motivations: the role of culture and nationality', *Annals of Tourism Research*, **34** (1), 122–140.

Maoz, D. and Z. Bekerman (2010), 'Searching for Jewish answers in Indian resorts: the postmodern traveler', *Annals of Tourism Research*, **37** (2), 423–439.

Martin, K. (2010), 'Living pasts: contested tourism authenticities', *Annals of Tourism Research*, **37** (2), 537–554.

Matarrita-Cascante, D. (2010), 'Beyond growth: researching tourism-led development', *Annals of Tourism Research*, **37** (4), 1141–1163.

Maxwell, J.A. (2005), *Qualitative Research Design: An Interactive Approach*, 2nd edition, Thousand Oaks, CA: Sage.

Mordue, T. (2005), 'Tourism, performance and social exclusion in "Olde York"', *Annals of Tourism Research*, **32** (1), 179–198.

Moyle, B. and G. Croy (2007), 'Crowding and visitor satisfaction during the off-season: Port Campbell National Park', *Annals of Leisure Research*, **10** (3/4), 518–531.

Muzaini, H. (2006), 'Backpacking Southeast Asia: strategies of "looking local"', *Annals of Tourism Research*, **33** (1), 144–161.

Nepal, S. (2007), 'Tourism and rural settlements: Nepal's Annapurna region', *Annals of Tourism Research*, **34** (4), 855–875.

O'Brien, D. (2006), 'Event business leveraging: the Sydney 2000 Olympic Games', *Annals of Tourism Research*, **33** (1), 240–261.

Paget, E., F. Dimanche and J. Mounet (2010), 'A tourism innovation case: an actor-network approach', *Annals of Tourism Research*, **37** (3), 828–847.

Palmer, C. (2005), 'An ethnography of Englishness: experiencing identity through tourism', *Annals of Tourism Research*, **32** (1), 7–27.

Pan, B. and D. Fesenmaier (2006), 'Online information search: vacation planning process', *Annals of Tourism Research*, **33** (3), 809–832.

Park, H. (2010), 'Heritage tourism: emotional journeys into nationhood', *Annals of Tourism Research*, **37** (1), 116–135.

Patton, M. (1990), *Qualitative Evaluation and Research Methods*, 2nd edition, Newsbury Park, CA: Sage.

Pernecky, T and T. Jamal (2010), 'Phenomenology in tourism studies', *Annals of Tourism Research*, **37** (4), 1055–1075.

Phillips, P. and P. Louvieris (2005), 'Performance measurement systems in tourism, hospitality, and leisure small medium-sized enterprises: a balanced scorecard perspective', *Journal of Travel Research*, **44** (2), 201.

Raymond, E. and C. Hall (2008), 'The development of cross-cultural (mis)understanding through volunteer tourism', *Journal of Sustainable Tourism*, **16** (5), 530–543.

Rittichainuwat, B. (2011), 'Ghosts: a travel barrier to tourism recovery', *Annals of Tourism Research*, **38** (2), 437–459.

Rodriguez Del Bosque, I. and H. San Martin (2008), 'Tourist satisfaction a cognitive-affective model', *Annals of Tourism Research*, **35** (2), 551–573.

Salazar, N. (2005), 'Tourism and glocalization: local tour guiding', *Annals of Tourism Research*, **32** (3), 628–646.

Santos, C. and G. Yan (2008), 'Representational politics in Chinatown: the ethnic other', *Annals of Tourism Research*, **35** (4), 879–899.

Saxena, G. and B. Ilbery (2009), 'Integrated rural tourism: a border case study', *Annals of Tourism Research*, **35** (1), 233–254.

Schuman, D. (1982), *Policy Analysis, Education, and Everyday Life*, Lexington, MA: Health.

Schutz, A. (1967), *The Phenomenology of the Social World*, G. Walsh and F. Lenhert (trans.), Chicago, IL: Northwestern University Press.
Sebele, L.S. (2010), 'Community-based tourism ventures, benefits and challenges: Kham Rhino Sanctuary Trust, Central District, Botswana', *Tourism Management*, **31** (1), 136–146.
Seidman, I. (2006), *Interviewing as Qualitative Research: A Guide for Researchers in Education and the Social Sciences*, New York: Teachers College Press.
Sheehan, K. (2001), 'E-mail survey response rates: a review', *Journal of Computer-Mediated Communication*, **6** (2).
Sin, H.L. (2009), 'Volunteer tourism: "Involve me and I will learn"?', *Annals of Tourism Research*, **36** (3), 480–501.
Smith, V. (1989), *Hosts and Guests Revisited: The Anthropology of Tourism*, Philadelphia, PA: University of Pennsylvania Press.
Stevenson, N., D. Airey and G. Miller (2008), 'Tourism policy making: the policymakers' perspectives', *Annals of Tourism Research*, **35** (3), 732–750.
Tinsley, R. and P. Lynch (2001), 'Small tourism business networks and destination development', *International Journal of Hospitality Management*, **20** (4), 367–378.
Uriely, N. and Y. Belhassen (2006), 'Drugs and risk-taking in tourism', *Annals of Tourism Research*, **33** (2), 339–359.
Vargas-Sánchez, A., N. Porras-Bueno and M.A. Plaza-Mejia (2011), 'Explaining residents' attitudes toward tourism: is a universal model possible?', *Annals of Tourism Research*, **38** (2), 460–480.
Vernon, J. (2000), 'Barriers to sustainability in tourism-related businesses in South-East Cornwall: results of discussion groups with tourism business owners', Working Paper No.1. University of Plymouth: Department of Geographical Sciences.
Vernon, J., S. Essex, D. Pinder and K. Curry (2005), 'Collaborative policymaking: local sustainable projects', *Annals of Tourism Research*, **32** (2), 325–345.
Wang, K., P. Jao, H. Chan and C. Chung (2010), 'Group package tour leader's intrinsic risks', *Annals of Tourism Research*, **37** (1), 154–179.
Wang, N. (1999), 'Rethinking authenticity in tourism experience', *Annals of Tourism Research*, **26** (2), 349–370.
Weidenfeld, A., A. Williams and R. Butler (2010), 'Knowledge transfer and innovation among attractions', *Annals of Tourism Research*, **37** (3), 604–626.
White, N. and P. White (2007), 'Home and away: tourists in a connected world', *Annals of Tourism Research*, **34** (1), 88–104.
Williams, P. and G.N. Soutar (2009), 'Value satisfaction and behavioral intentions in an adventure tourism context', *Annals of Tourism Research*, **36** (3), 413–438.
Wong, C. and B. McKercher (2011), 'Tourist information center staff as knowledge brokers: the case of Macau', *Annals of Tourism Research*, **38** (2), 481–498.
Yang, L. (2011), 'Ethnic tourism and cultural representation', *Annals of Tourism Research*, **38** (2), 561–585.
Yuksel, F., B. Bramwell and A. Yuksel (2005), 'Centralized and decentralized tourism governance in Turkey', *Annals of Tourism Research*, **32** (4), 859–886.
Zahra, A. and N. McGehee (2012), 'Host perceptions of volunteer tourism: a community capital perspective', *Annals of Tourism Research*.

19 Participant observation
Nuno F. Ribeiro and Eric W. Foemmel

NATURE OF PARTICIPANT OBSERVATION AND ITS EVOLUTION

A cornerstone research method of cultural anthropology and sociology, and widely used in a number of other social sciences, participant observation falls under the broad umbrella of ethnographic fieldwork (Bernard, 2006). Participant observation consists of engaging in regular and prolonged interaction with the people the researcher seeks to study – immersing oneself in the participants' local environment – in order to learn more about obvious and not-so-obvious aspects of their lives and culture. DeWalt and DeWalt (2011, p. 1) define it as "a method in which an observer takes part in the daily activities, rituals, interactions, and events of the people being studied as one of the means of learning the explicit and tacit aspects of their culture." Moreover, by observing and participating in daily life as much as possible, the researcher is able to overcome participants' natural distrust towards outsiders, becomes part of the living landscape and as a result is able to collect a myriad of data that would be impossible to obtain otherwise. Thus the researcher is saddled with a dual task: she is at the same time the investigator and the data collection instrument.

Both distinct from and complementary to other means of data collection such as semistructured and structured interviewing, questionnaire research, focus groups, and so forth, the nature of participant observation is primarily qualitative (Jennings, 2001; but see Schensul et al., 1999), although the data produced through participant observation can be analysed by both qualitative and quantitative means (Bernard, 2006; LeCompte and Schensul, 1999; see also Oakes, 1998). Participant observation data arises primarily from field notes of what the researcher observes and participates in, as well as his interpretation of the events that occurred (Emerson et al., 1995). The field notes are then compiled, analysed, and contrasted with data acquired through other means (e.g., photographs, interview transcripts, survey data), with the end result being an ethnography, or written account of a given culture or people (LeCompte and Schensul, 1999).

While the origins of participant observation can be traced back to the work of early sociologists such as Beatrice Webb (1926), William Foote Whyte (1943), and others at the then emerging Chicago School in the 1920s (e.g., Park et al., 1925; for an historical overview of the Chicago School, see Bulmer, 1986), Bronislaw Malinowski is generally credited with encoding the principles and merits of participant observation (Bernard, 2006). In his seminal *Argonauts of the Western Pacific* (1922[1984]), Malinowski described "the proper conditions for ethnographic work" thus:

> cutting oneself off from the company of other white men, and remaining in as close contact with the natives as possible, which can only be achieved by camping right in their villages . . . by means of this natural intercourse, you learn to know him, and you become familiar with

his customs and beliefs far better than when he is a paid, often bored, informant (. . .) There is all the difference between a sporadic plunging into the company of natives, and being really in contact with them. What does the latter mean? On the Ethnographer's side, it means that his life in the village, which at first is a strange, sometimes unpleasant, sometimes intensely interesting adventure, soon adopts a natural course very much in harmony with his surroundings. (pp. 6–7)

In spite of its colonialist and racist overtones, Malinowski's description of fieldwork in the Trobriands contains several of the characteristics of modern participant observation: (1) prolonged immersion in the field; (2) gradual acquaintance and building of trust between researcher and informant; (3) familiarization with the local language and/ or dialect(s); and (4) the acquisition of data in as much detail as possible. Such characteristics have not changed in almost a century, and they remain hallmarks of sound participant observation.

If the core of the method itself has known little change from the days of Malinowski (Bernard, 2006), participant observation has nonetheless evolved, with a growing number of fields of research – such as tourism – adopting it as a valid research methodology. While space limitations preclude us from delving into the evolution and growing popularity of participant observation in detail (a propos, see Agar, 1996; Atkinson and Hammersley, 1994; Becker, 1958; Delamont, 2004; DeWalt and DeWalt, 2011; Jorgensen, 1989; Platt, 1983), it is nonetheless necessary to identify four moments in the history of the use of this research method.

The first period, comprising the early attempts of ethnographers to participate in local communities' daily life in order to better understand them and record their characteristics before they disappear (i.e., "salvage ethnography" – see Barnard, 2000), lasted almost a century from the late 1800s until the early 1980s. In fact, the term "participant observation" did not appear until the 1920s (DeWalt and DeWalt, 2011). With a few notable exceptions (e.g., Cushing and Green, 1981 [1879]; Mead, 1928 [1961]; Lindeman, 1924; McCall and Simmons, 1969), during this period little effort was devoted by researchers towards systematizing the methodological knowledge necessary in order to conduct participant observation. During this period, the researcher was supposed to go out into the field and simply "do it". The apocryphal and outdated tales of dissertation advisors counseling the young researcher about to go into the field to "take plenty of quinine and stay away from village women" – in lieu of rigorous training in participant observation methods – find a parallel in today's lack of formal coursework in ethnographic field methods in a number of graduate programs in the social sciences.

The second period spanned roughly a decade (the 1980s) and saw the emergence of a number of important treatises on the topic of participant observation, such as Spradley's (1980) and Jorgensen's (1989) volumes both entitled *Participant Observation*, Polkinghorne's *Methodology for the Human Sciences* (1983), and Van Maanen's edited volume on *Qualitative Methodology* (1983). The contribution of these works towards the legitimization of participant observation as a reputed method of data collection in the social sciences was considerable. Issues such as gaining entry to the field, the researcher's positioning along a continuum ranging from complete outsider to complete insider, covert and overt observation, the importance of key informants and gate keepers, participant observation ethics, and many other topics which until then were privy to a handful of veteran researchers and accordingly passed from one generation of field workers to

Complete Observer ⟶ Observer as Participant ⟶ Participant as Observer ⟶ Complete Participant

Source: Gold (1969), Jorgensen (1989).

Figure 19.1   The participant observation continuum

the next were finally discussed, systematized, and brought to the attention of a wider audience of scholars.

Among these topics, the participant observation continuum (Jorgensen, 1989) is particularly worthy of discussion (Figure 19.1). Depending on the goals of the research and the researcher's intentions/skills, the researcher will adopt one of four postures in the field that correspond to different levels of involvement between the researcher and the research participants. Thus, the researcher may choose to exclusively observe, taking no part in what is going on; or he may participate to a small extent; he may also choose to participate to a greater degree; or lastly, the researcher may become a complete participant and thus virtually indistinguishable from those he seeks to study, as Sally Cole (1991) did when she worked alongside fishermen's wives in a Portuguese coastal community dealing with the early impacts of tourism development in the Mediterranean basin.

In regard to tourism research, the 1980s also marked the beginning of the legitimization of tourism as a reputable field of inquiry in the social sciences, and coincidentally or not, many of tourism's most prominent advocates came from backgrounds where participant observation was an important, if not crucial, method of data collection, such as sociology, anthropology, and human geography (e.g., Cohen, 1984; Crick, 1989; Dann et al., 1988; Dumont, 1984; Graburn, 1983; Hartmann, 1988). Moreover, a number of seminal tourism studies using participant observation were published in this period, such as Boynton's (1986) study of tourism impacts on Amish communities, Esman's (1984) analysis of tourism as an ethnic preservation tool, Foster's (1986) study on short-lived societies, and Kemper et al.'s (1983) analysis of tourism as a cultural domain.

The third period (1990s–2000s) was marked by the interpretivist/postmodern challenge (for an overview, see Barnard, 2000), which forced researchers in the social sciences and elsewhere to adopt a more reflexive stance regarding the communities they were studying on the one hand, and on themselves and the product of their research, on the other. With respect to participant observation, there was an explosion of scholarly literature on the topic, with an increasing number of researchers publishing the insights garnered from the encounter between the researcher and the "other" (i.e., the researched). Earlier works such as Paul Rabinow's *Reflections on Fieldwork in Morocco* (1977) had set the tone for a host of studies on post-modernity, colonialism, semiotics, representation, and power with participant observation as the preferred method of research, and with an increasing emphasis on self-reflection by the researcher, in what Tedlock (1991) dubbed the "observation of participation".

This vigorous publication period had obvious effects on the use of participant observation in tourism research, which in turn reflected the then dominant self-reflexive stance of ethnographic fieldwork. First, participant observation was used to dissect the encounter between the tourist and "the other" (the host) in all its nuances, with particular emphasis being put in the dénouement of power dynamics between the (often wealthy) tourists and the (often impoverished) hosts, and paying also close attention to the symbolic nature of the tourism activity (e.g., Abram et al. 1997; Bruner, 1996; Chambers, 1997; Hoskins, 2002; Smith and Brent, 2001). Second, there was a surge in the interest in research methods by tourism researchers, resulting in the publication of several "how-to" research manuals, which included participant observation as an important method of data collection (e.g., Jennings, 2001; Veal, 1992). And third, it forced the question of whether the researchers were all that different from the tourists they were studying (Errington and Gewertz, 1989).

The last period, ranging from the early 2000s to the present, saw the coming of age of multi-sited ethnographic fieldwork, which had emerged in the mid-1990s (Marcus, 1995). With the accelerated impacts of globalization and the increased connectivity of local events and global processes, fieldworkers no longer could work within the narrow confines of "secluded villages", and were forced to place their findings within broader economic, political, and social contexts (Durrenberger, 2003; Vandegriff, 2008). Nelson Graburn's (2002) notion of the "ethnographic tourist" stands out as a perfect example of the effects of multi-sited ethnography on tourism research, as does Noel Salazar's (2010) "glocal" ethnographic study of tourism in Indonesia and Tanzania.

BACKGROUND AND TYPES OF ISSUES PARTICIPANT OBSERVATION IS DESIGNED TO HANDLE

Observing and participating in a group's activities (e.g., a group tour's behavior while on vacation), a researcher gains intimate knowledge of the group as the researcher goes "from being a complete outsider to a complete insider" (Creswell, 1997, p. 123; see also Figure 19.1). This intimate knowledge provides the researcher with the context needed to explain differences in behavior that may be influenced by the group's assembly.

When tourism researchers immerse themselves in the field to conduct participant observation, they begin to understand "the context and the associated interactions of natural surroundings" (Riley and Love, 2000, p. 5). This understanding gives the researcher the information needed to posit theories and also suggest ways to mitigate conflicts in communities that may be experiencing negative impacts caused by tourism. Wallace and Diamente (2005) argue that the dialectic dynamics between economics, ecotourism, and conservation efforts may have detrimental effects on local communities, and that anthropology may be the voice of reason in addressing the conflicting agendas of tour operators, conservationists and local residents. As stated earlier, participant observation is a useful method in conducting research that may offer reasonable solutions to issues in tourism management when in-depth, detailed knowledge of local conditions is of consequence.

Participant observation requires that the researcher do more than simply hang out and observe the group she is studying. Gaining access to the population under study is critical. The researcher is a virtual outsider when entering the field for the first time, and will definitely be noticed by the individuals of a group as he takes notes and asks questions. It is useful to identify and befriend a gatekeeper who will assist the researchers' entry into the field or introduce them to people who will be essential for successful data collection. Depending on the group and the situation, the researchers may want to formally introduce themselves to the gatekeepers and follow up the meeting with a detailed, professional letter of introduction explaining their research goals and methods. Connecting a face with a letter explaining the research and asking the informants' consent to participate in the research may help instill a familiarity between the researcher and the key informants. In other cases, such formalities are not necessary and may even be detrimental to the research project, such as when the researcher is interested in marginal/illegal tourism activities, such as sex tourism (e.g., Brennan, 2004).

During her time in the field, the researcher takes notes on the surroundings, interactions, conversations, habits, customs, and daily routines of the group she is studying. These notes are the raw data the researcher uses to write a detailed and thick description of the group. The researcher should write a faithful description of the surroundings, events, people and interactions that will give the reader a vivid understanding of this social group within the context of their environment.

Direct observation will also give the researcher valuable data needed to confirm or disprove hypotheses. After an extensive literature review, the researcher should have relevant research questions and an excellent understanding of theories that pertain to his study. Prolonged participant observation gives the researcher the opportunity to watch a group and determine the veracity of current literature or theories. As Sandiford and Ap (1998) remark, "although ethnography is often considered most appropriate in the early stages of theory development, hypothesis testing can also be carried out by field-workers at a later stage using focused observations" (p. 8).

It is not unforeseeable that two researchers will have different accounts after conducting participant observations at the same field site. Although both accounts may be valid, participant observation is not a method that can be easily replicated by numerous researchers and yield the exact same results. The most famous example is Derek Freeman's (1999) refutation of Margaret Mead's descriptions of Samoa in her seminal work *Coming of Age in Samoa* (1928 [1961]) as a stress free utopia complete with free love and little conflict. Margaret Mead concluded that adolescent Samoan woman raised in this environment do not have the tumultuous teenage experiences of American adolescents. After extensive participant observation in Mead's same research setting, Freeman interviewed Mead's informants, who confessed they had lied to her. Freeman also pointed out that there were cultural and social norms that place limitations on the sexual relationships of adolescent Samoan women (Freeman, 1999). The difference in their accounts has led to heated debates (e.g., Tcherkézoff, 2001).

In tourism research, we are unaware of controversies equivalent to the Mead–Freeman debate, but nonetheless there are points of discord which participant observation has helped resolve (or in some cases exacerbated). For instance, the panacea-for-all-evils approach to tourism as an engine of economic prosperity common in post-World War II Europe was challenged by ethnographical accounts of the impacts of unbridled tourism development in communities on the receiving end of mass tourism in Crete (Andriotis, 2001), Goa (Wilson, 1997), Portugal (Cole, 1991), and Spain (Rozenberg, 1990), thus shedding light on a much more nuanced tourism reality.

Participant observation is a craft in the sense that the researcher must develop excellent note-taking skills, record events in a field journal, and diligently write about her observations and experiences each time she exits the field. It is best to write one's notes right after leaving the field as details will be easier to recall (Bernard, 2002). Moreover, taking field notes (or using more intrusive methods such as audio and visual recordings) may predispose those the researcher is attempting to study against him. Nonetheless, with time these constraints will fade as the researcher gains the trust of the group under study. In addition to the tenacity and skill needed to conduct participant observation, the researcher must develop the social skills needed to establish rapport with the group she is studying. These skills, combined with rigorous methods of analysis of ethnographic data (LeCompte and Schensul, 1999), can make a profound contribution to the study of the topic at hand. Although as an outsider it may be possible to observe a group of individuals, the researcher will only be able to collect superficial data. Participant observation allows the researcher to become immersed in the group and collect data that are not apparent to the casual observer. This gives the researcher the background she needs to explain the structure, culture, and behavior of a group. The researcher conducting participant observation has a more in-depth understanding of a phenomenon with his analysis than findings from a standard questionnaire or survey, which may have problems with accuracy and internal validity (Bernard, 2002).

APPLICATIONS OF PARTICIPANT OBSERVATION IN TOURISM RESEARCH

From Dennis O'Rourke's *Cannibal Tours* (1988) to the successive editions of *Hosts and Guests* (Smith, 1977[1989]; Smith and Brent, 2001), and to the more recent surge in ethnographic accounts of postmodern encounters between the tourist and the host (e.g., Bruner, 2005; Edensor, 1998; Ness, 2003; Salazar, 2010; Urry, 1990; Yamashita, 2003), uses of participant observation in tourism research have been plentiful. Participant observation has been used to study topics as diverse as the impacts of tourism on an Australian indigenous community (Dyer et al., 2003), vacation cruising (Foster, 1986; Yarnal and Kerstetter, 2005), trader tourism in Eastern Europe (Konstantinov et al., 1998), community involvement in tourism development in Nepal and China (Nyaupane et al., 2006; see also Stonich, 2005), music tourism in Goa (Saldanha, 2002), effects of tourism development in post-revolutionary Nicaragua (Babb, 2004), tourist consumer satisfaction (Bowen, 2002), dark tourism in Alcatraz and Robben Island (Strange and Kempa, 2003), ecotourism (Wallace and Diamente, 2005; see also Weil, 1997), and sport tourism (Costa and Chalip, 2005).

The vast majority of tourism studies that have used participant observation, however, have used this technique to look into the impact of tourism development in host communities, on the one hand; and investigate the complexities of the host–guest relationship, on the other. In the case of the former, there is a substantial body of research on the impact of tourism development on traditional economic activities, such as fishing (Cole, 1991; Kottak, 1983 [2005]; Johnson and Orbach, 1990), weaving (Boynton, 1986), and agriculture (Davis and Morais, 2004). In regard to the dynamics between hosts and tourists, a number of recent studies have brought to light the increasing complexities of the encounter between local communities and the tourists (e.g., Gmelch, 2004[2009]).

For instance, Kottak (2005) conducted ethnographic fieldwork in Arembepe (northeastern Brazil) over the course of more than 30 years (1962–2004). Making extensive use of participant observation, Kottak and his research assistants (2005) were able to chronicle the changes that occurred in Arembepe from a subsistence economy in the 1970s to an international tourism destination with a "sustainable diversified economy" in the early 2000s (Kottak, 2004, p. 501). Kottak's successive revisits to the research site allowed an almost-unparalleled longitudinal and detailed study of the conditions under which international tourism impacts local communities and, moreover, how these communities are able to minimize its potential harmful aspects (e.g., commodification of culture, excessive urban development, mono-employment) and maximize its advantages (e.g., attraction of foreign currency, decreased unemployment rates, economic diversification). Moreover, the extended permanence in the field over the course of almost four decades forced the author to reflect on tourism as both an agent and a product of change; if the first edition of Kottak's study (1983) decried the commodifying and de-characterizing effects of tourism as an agent of social change, its later editions (1999, 2005), place tourism within the nexus of global economic forces, and acknowledge the multiple advantages that tourism brought to the people of Arembepe.

Other studies that used participant observation have been more critical of tourism's overall impacts in local communities and economies (e.g., Chambers, 2000; Crick, 1989; Smith 1977[1989]; Stocker, 2007). In an oft-quoted article, Greenwood (1977[1989]) decried the selling of "culture by the pound" that tourism activities had brought to Hondarribia, Spain. Set out to study the Alarde ritual, Greenwood was able to describe in minute detail how the sudden interest by outsiders (tourists) had commercialized and, in his opinion, devalued what was an emblematic part of Hondarribian character and culture. Yet the same author, a few decades later, revised his earlier findings and debated whether or not his desire to protect a culture he admired from the effects of tourism had not played a part in his discussion of the phenomenon (Greenwood, 2004).

Participant observation has also been useful in deconstructing travel imagery, from glossy magazine adverts of tourism resorts to discount group travel brochures that portray tourism destinations as idyllic and unidimensional landscapes where the local community is all but willing to satisfy the tourist's every whim, and contrasting it with factual and participatory accounts of host–guest interactions in tourism destinations (e.g., Bruner, 2005; Peaslee, 2010; Roland, 2010). Perhaps the most famous of these studies is Edward Bruner's (1996) account of the postmodern encounter between US and European tourists with a Ghanaian tourism attraction (Elmina Castle) that emphasized the brutal conditions under which African slaves were kept before being sent to the colonies of the New World. Through participant observation (as a tourist, ethnographer, and consultant for one of the agencies in charge of preserving and managing the attraction), in-depth interviews with key informants, and focus groups, Bruner shed light on the many layers of meaning that the castle and its past held for the Ghanaian population and the tourists that originated from several countries, all of which with a colonial past (United States, United Kingdom, the Netherlands). Their often conflicting views and actions were made visible by the use of participant observation, and the use of this research method also provided a rich context imbedded in meaning that would have been difficult to obtain otherwise.

Overall, tourism studies that have used participant observation as a research method were helpful in revealing the multifaceted and ambiguous nature of tourism as a human activity. As Wallace (2005) rightly points out, whereas the early ethnographic tourism studies of the 1970s and 1980s concentrated on the negative impacts of tourism on host communities and cultures (e.g., Smith, 1977 [1989]), the last 20 years gave way to a host of research highlighting the positive aspects of tourism development (e.g., Lanfant et al., 1995; Smith and Brent, 2001). This ambiguous character of tourism activity was evidenced thanks in no small part to the use of participant observation as a research methodology. In turn, the use of ethnographic research methods has contributed not only to move the field forward theoretically (Jafari, 2001), but has also been extremely useful in the elaboration and implementation of tourism policies.

ADVANTAGES AND LIMITATIONS OF PARTICIPANT OBSERVATION CONCEPTUALLY AND FOR POLICY FORMULATION

Witnessing the impacts of tourism, researchers can voice concerns and steer policies to address issues seen in the field. Participant observation offers tourism researchers the experience and insight needed to make valid statements based on locally produced (i.e., emic) knowledge. Moreover, participation observation gives the researcher the opportunity to obtain "a general understanding of how any social institution of organization works" (Bernard, 2002, p. 355). Participating and writing field notes on the interactions and behaviors of a group and their culture, the researcher collects valuable data from within the field. The researcher uses this data to provide a "thick description" of the group and their social norms (Geertz, 1973), and also to communicate to the reader how a culture operates. This first-hand experience, knowledge and understanding of the group's culture, coupled with an intimate knowledge of the research site, are critical components of the foundation needed to obtain an expert knowledge of the field. Within the context of tourism, valid statements and findings about successful tourism operations, a group's attitudes about tourism, and positive policy developments in tourism stem from this expert knowledge.

Researching an innovative tourism operator, Paget et al. (2010) used participant observation methods to study tourists' consumer behavior and the operations of Delta, a tourism operator providing alternative winter activities in France – such as dinners in tepees in remote areas. The success of Delta's programs depended on using existing resources in unconventional ways. To understand the complexity of this research site and Delta's operations, these researchers observed the entire "tourismscape". Not only did the researchers observe the interactions between the tourists and tour operators, they collected data on the natural resources or quality of the ski slopes, the infrastructure of the town and its ability to host tourists, the amenities of ski resorts and their lifts, and the promotion and advertizing of the area as a winter destination (Paget et al., 2010). They reported that the constant presence of the researchers in the field made it possible for them to establish a rapport with the participants and gain access to previously inaccessible data and "participate in several strategic company meetings" (Paget et al., 2010, p. 835). This level of interaction using participant observation as a method "provided opportunities to better explain complex processes" and allowed the team of researchers to understand how Delta was able to offer and successfully provide tourists with winter activities other than skiing.

In another study, Mason (2005) commented on the benefits of using participant observation when assessing tourist destinations. In the development of the Erie Canal National Heritage Corridor in the United States, participant observation gave the planners the information they needed to reallocate resources to improve facility use. Mason (2005) reports the canal was primarily used for industrial shipping in the nineteenth century, but was revitalized as a heritage park offering recreational activities in the twenty-first century. By observing and interviewing the visitors, the researchers discovered that inadequate information about waterway facilities was proving frustrating to visitors. With this data, a tourism developer at the Erie Canal Heritage Corridor would have the information needed to allocate resources to meet the actual needs of the land-use visitors, and to effectively inform visitors about existing water-based recreational resources that were not being used to their fullest potential.

Participant observation as a research method offers the researcher an opportunity to spend a prolonged amount of time in the field, become accepted as a participant, become acquainted with the host community's perspective, and understand their beliefs and attitudes. All of these factors have a positive influence on data collection and analysis as the researcher will gain an insight into the group's behavior and understand subtleties in the development of attitudes that may challenge existing theories. Understanding (and ultimately predicting) human behavior is a critical goal of tourism research. It is imperative to understand the behavior of tourists, and the behavior of the host community. Interactions between the tourists and hosts, whether harmonious or volatile, are better understood when researchers identify the attitudes and intent of both parties. Lepp (2007) studied the residents' attitudes about tourism in a Bigodi village in Uganda, and he felt the use of participant observations and other qualitative methods gave him the data that improved his understanding of their attitudes and the prediction of their behavior. After observing participants in the field, Lepp identified the economic benefits tourism brought to this rural Ugandan community, and he observed that everyone in the community seemed to benefit from tourism. The tourists brought an outside source of income when they paid for food. They paid for lodging and other services from farmers and merchants, who then spent their earnings in the community. What is more, Lepp (2007, p. 883) suggested that "positive attitudes toward tourism would increase intentions to behave in a manner conducive to tourism and this would lead to an increase in protourism." Lepp's findings demonstrate how participant observation can be used to provide an insightful explanation of human behavior in tourism settings.

The usefulness of participant observation in collecting pertinent data does not end with making valid statements about the success of tourism programs or the ability to effectively predict and explain human behavior. Data collected by an objective researcher using participant observation gives planners the information needed to formulate and implement policies that consider the values and concerns of the community hosting tourists, and the needs and expectations of tourists visiting a destination. Considering both parties, ethnocentric biases of the host community and the tourists are mitigated. The cultural values or social norms of all parties are considered and none are privileged at the expense of others.

Using participant observation and other qualitative research methods typically associated with anthropology to tourism development, Lalone (2005) has coined the term "anthro-planning", which has benefited communities developing heritage parks and tourism sites. Anthro-planning facilitates "design projects that plan 'with' and 'for' people, groups, and communities" (Lalone, 2005, p. 136). In contrast, developers may forgo this type of research and formulate policies and ignore the need to consult with anyone in the community. In a sense, developing policy in this manner is primarily "developercentric". According to Lalone (2005) "a successful research design will use anthropological techniques to study the social, economic, and political patterns and groupings within the target community and will apply that knowledge in ways that seek representative, participatory involvement from the public" (p. 137). Objective observations require the researcher to suspend personal values and judgments based on cultural norms that may not apply to the community being observed. Planners developing tourism policies with data collected from participant observation can create seamless connections between relevant research and the formulation of policy.

On the other hand, exclusive reliance on participant observation methods instead of more holistic/mixed methods approaches may hinder the success of tourism planning and development initiatives. Because participant observation data is seldom generalizable beyond the sample of individuals/groups studied (but see Bernard, 2006), it would be a crucial error to suggest and/or enforce tourism policies based solely on data obtained via the researcher's observations and actions in the field. Moreover, excessive permanence in the field may result in significant emotional and institutional ties, which may compromise the objectivity of tourism policies based on participant observation. Consciously or inadvertently, the researcher may be more prone to suggest policies that benefit "his" people, as opposed to more equitable tourism development guidelines (on the ethical quagmires of conducting participant observation in tourism studies, see Adams, 2005). DeWalt et al. (1998) recommend that self-reflection and use of additional research methods should be employed to reduce potential researcher bias.

Nonetheless, participant observation is an effective method that puts the tourism researcher in the field. This offers the researcher a vantage point to collect data from key informants, observe subtle nuances in behavior, test theories, and gain insight needed to develop inclusive policies that acknowledge both the host community and the tourists (Nyaupane et al., 2006). Participant observation is an exciting and effective way to collect detailed emic data, with the added benefit of necessitating the active involvement of the researcher with the object of study. In turn, such involvement often generates additional insights which are helpful in the formulation of tourism policy and tourism product development and appraisal (Bowen, 2002; Bowie and Chang, 2003).

FURTHER DEVELOPMENTS AND APPLICATIONS OF PARTICIPANT OBSERVATION IN TOURISM RESEARCH

It seems unlikely that participant observation will experience any dramatic developments in the near future. Its main precepts (prolonged immersion in the field, direct contact with the participants, emphasis on emic models of knowledge, focus on meaning and interpretation) are unlikely to change or be replaced by others. The deceptive simplicity of this research technique is one of its greatest strengths, and one that makes it particularly suitable for tourism research.

Conversely, recent developments in the application of participant observation are noteworthy. First, in recent years there has been a push towards rapid assessment (RAP) research (i.e., "quick ethnography" – Handwerker, 2002; see also Beebe, 2001), whereby ethnographic methods such as participant observation are still desirable, but time and budget constraints limit their application over the course of typical time frameworks (i.e., a year or more). Thus researchers have developed variations of a wide range of qualitative methods – such as participant observation – which can be used in a shorter time span while still retaining many of its strengths (Handwerker, 2002). Thus far, RAP uses in tourism research have been limited to environmental impact assessment of tourism activities (e.g., Ervin, 2003; Kikuchi et al., 2003), but it is likely that, particularly in times of budget constraints and fiscal austerity, RAP will see an increase in its popularity in tourism research.

Second, there has long been an interest in increasing the external validity (i.e., the possibility of generalization of results) of ethnographic methods such as structured observation, which involves collecting participant observation data at pre-defined, regular intervals (DeWalt and DeWalt, 2011; Kawulich, 2005). Techniques such as instantaneous spot sampling and random spot checks (Bernard, 2006) have also been used to bolster the possibility of inference from small, non-randomly sampled data. To our knowledge, only our most recent work (Ribeiro and Foemmel, 2012; Ribeiro et al., 2011) has made use of these techniques within a tourism setting, but hopefully more tourism studies will employ them. The use of recent technological advances, such as hand-held computers, is also likely to play a role in future uses of participant observation when external validity is a concern (Ice, 2004).

Lastly, mirroring a growing trend in the social sciences towards the blurring of the divide between quantitative and qualitative research (Creswell and Clark, 2007; Johnson and Onwuegbuzie, 2004; Tashakkori and Teddlie, 1998), there has been an increase in the adoption by tourism scholars of mixed methodologies of research (MacKay and Campbell, 2004; Lemelin, 2006; Pansiri, 2005; Riley and Love, 2000). Taking into account the multi and inter-disciplinary nature of tourism research, one expects the use of mixed-methods research methods to increase among tourism scholars in years to come, with participant observation playing a crucial role in the process.

REFERENCES

Abram, S., J., Waldren and D.V. Mcleod (eds) (1997), *Tourists and Tourism: Identifying with People and Places*, Oxford: Berg.
Adams, K.M. (2005), 'Generating theory, tourism, and "world heritage" in Indonesia: ethical quandaries for anthropologists in an era of tourist mania', *NAPA Bulletin*, **23**, 45–59.
Agar, M. (1996), *The Professional Stranger: An Informal Introduction to Ethnography*, 2nd edition, Beverly Hills, CA: Sage Publications.
Andriotis, K. (2001), 'Tourism planning and development in Crete: recent tourism policies and their efficacy', *Journal of Sustainable Tourism*, **9** (4), 298–316.
Atkinson, P. and M. Hammersley (1994), 'Ethnography and participant observation', in N.K. Denzin and Y.S. Lincoln (eds), *Handbook of Qualitative Research*, Los Angeles, CA: Sage, pp. 248–261.
Babb, F.E. (2004), 'Recycled *Sandanistas*: from revolution to resorts in the new Nicaragua', *American Anthropologist*, **106** (3), 541–555.
Barnard, A. (2000), *History and Theory in Anthropology*, New York: Cambridge University Press.

Becker, H.S. (1958), 'Problems of inference and proof in participant observation', *American Sociological Review*, **23** (6), 652–660.

Beebe, J. (2001), *Rapid Assessment Process: An Introduction*, Thousand Oaks, CA: AltaMira Press.

Bernard, H.R. (2002), *Research Methods in Anthropology: Qualitative and Quantitative Approaches*, 3rd edition, Lanham, MD: AltaMira Press.

Bernard, H.R. (2006), *Research Methods in Anthropology: Qualitative and Quantitative Approaches*, 4th edition, Lanham, MD: AltaMira Press.

Bowen, D. (2002), 'Research through participant observation in tourism: a creative solution to the measurement of consumer satisfaction/dissatisfaction (CS/D) among tourists', *Journal of Travel Research*, **41** (1), 4–14.

Bowie, D. and J.C. Chang (2003), 'Tourist satisfaction: a view from a mixed international guided package tour', *Journal of Vacation Marketing*, **11** (4), 303–322.

Boynton, L.L. (1986), 'The effect of tourism on Amish quilting design', *Annals of Tourism Research*, **13**, 451–564.

Brennan, D. (2004), *What's Love Got to do With it? Transnational Desires and Sex Tourism in the Dominican Republic*, Durham, NC: Duke University Press.

Bruner, E.M. (1996), 'Tourism in Ghana: the representation of slavery and the return of the Black diaspora', *American Anthropologist*, **98** (2), 290–304.

Bruner, E.M. (2005), *Culture on Tour: Ethnographies of Travel*, Chicago, IL: The University of Chicago Press.

Bulmer, M. (1986), *The Chicago School of Sociology*. Chicago, IL: University of Chicago Press.

Chambers, E. (1997), *Tourism and Culture: An Applied Perspective*, Albany, NY: SUNY Press.

Chambers, E. (2000), '*Native Tours: An Applied Perspective*, Albany, NY: SUNY Press.

Cohen, E. (1984), 'The sociology of tourism: approaches, issues, and findings', *Annual Review of Sociology*, **10**, 373–392.

Cole, S.C. (1991), *Women of the Praia: Work and Lives in a Portuguese Community*, Princeton, NJ: Princeton University Press.

Costa, C.A. and L. Chalip (2005), 'Adventure sport tourism in rural revitalization: an ethnographic evaluation', *European Sport Management Quarterly*, **5** (3), 257–279.

Creswell, J.W. (1997), *Qualitative Inquiry and Research Design: Choosing Among Five Traditions*, Thousand Oaks, CA: Sage.

Creswell, J.W. and V.L. Clark (2007), *Designing and Conducting Mixed Methods Research*, Thousand Oaks, CA: Sage.

Crick, M. (1989), 'Representations of international tourism in the social sciences: sun, sex, sights, savings, and servility', *Annual Review of Anthropology*, **18**, 307–344.

Cushing, F.H. and J. Green (eds) (1981) [1879], *Zuni: Selected writings of Frank Hamilton Cushing*, Winnipeg, Manitoba: Bison Books.

Dann, G., D. Nash and P. Pearce (1988), 'Methodology in tourism research', *Annals of Tourism Research*, **15**, 1–28.

Davis, J.S. and D.B. Morais (2004), 'Factions and enclaves: small towns and socially unsustainable tourism development', *Journal of Travel Research*, **43** (1), 3–10.

Delamont, S. (2004), 'Ethnography and participant observation', in G. Gobo, J.F. Gubrium and D. Silverman (eds), *Qualitative Research Practice*, London: Sage, pp. 205–217.

DeWalt, K.M. and B.R. DeWalt (2011), *Participant Observation: A Guide for Fieldworkers*, 2nd edition, Lanham, MD: AltaMira Press.

DeWalt, K.M., B.R. DeWalt and C.B. Weyland (1998), 'Participant observation', in H.R. Bernard (ed.), *Handbook of Methods in Cultural Anthropology*, Walnut Creek, CA: AltaMira Press, pp. 259–300.

Dumont, J. (1984), 'A matter of touristic "indifférance"', *American Ethnologist*, **11** (1), 139–151.

Durrenberger, E.P. (2003), 'Global processes, local systems', *Urban Anthropology*, **32** (3–4), 253–279.

Dyer, P., L. Aberdeen and S. Schuler (2003), 'Tourism impacts on an Australian indigenous community: a Djabugay case study', *Tourism Management*, **24**, 83–95.

Edensor, T. (1998), *Tourists at the Taj: Performance and Meaning at a Symbolic Site*, New York: Routledge.

Emerson, R.M., R.I. Fretz and L.L. Shaw (1995), *Writing Ethnographic Fieldnotes*, Chicago, IL: University of Chicago Press.

Errington, F. and D. Gewertz (1989), 'Tourism and anthropology in a post-modern world', *Oceania*, **60** (1), 37–54.

Ervin, J. (2003), 'Rapid assessment of protected area management effectiveness in four countries', *BioScience*, **53** (9), 833–841.

Esman, M.R. (1984), 'Tourism as ethnic preservation: the Cajuns of Louisiana', *Annals of Tourism Research*, **11**, 451–467.

Foster, G.M. (1986), 'South Seas cruise: a case study of a short-lived society', *Annals of Tourism Research*, **13**, 215–238.

Freeman, D. (1999), *The Fateful Hoaxing of Margaret Mead: A Historical Analysis of her Samoan Research*, Boulder, CO: Westview.

Geertz, C. (1973), *The Interpretation of Cultures*, New York: Basic Books.

Gmelch, S.B. (ed.) (2004 [2009]), *Tourists and Tourism: A Reader*, 2nd edition, Prospect Heights, IL: Waveland Press.

Gold, R.L. (1969), 'Roles in sociological field observations', in G.J. McCall and J.L. Simmons (eds), *Issues in Participant Observation*, Reading, MA: Addison-Wesley, pp. 30–39.

Graburn, N.H. (1983), 'The anthropology of tourism', *Annals of Tourism Research*, **10**, 9–33.

Graburn, N.H. (2002), 'The ethnographic tourist', in G.M. Dann (ed.), *The Tourist as a Metaphor of the Social World*, Wallingford, UK: CABI Publishing, pp. 19–40.

Greenwood, D.J. (1977 [1989]), Culture by the pound: an anthropological perspective on tourism as cultural commoditization', in V.L. Smith (ed.), *Hosts and Guests: The Anthropology of Tourism*, 2nd edition, Philadelphia: University of Pennsylvania Press, pp. 171–185.

Greenwood, D.J. (2004), 'Culture by the pound: an anthropological perspective on tourism as cultural commoditization', in S. Gmelch (ed.), *Tourists and Tourism: A Reader*, Prospect Heights, IL: Waveland Press, pp. 157–169.

Handwerker, W.P. (2002), *Quick Ethnography: A Guide to Rapid Multi-Method Research*, Walnut Creek, CA: AltaMira Press.

Hartmann, R. (1988), 'Combining field methods in tourism research', *Annals of Tourism Research*, **15**, 88–105.

Hoskins, J. (2002), 'Predatory voyeurs: tourists and "tribal violence" in remote Indonesia', *American Ethnologist*, **29**, 797–808.

Ice, G.H. (2004), 'Technological advances in observational data collection: the advantages and limitations of computer-assisted data collection', *Field Methods*, **16** (3), 352–375.

Jafari, J. (2001), 'The scientification of tourism', in V.L. Smith and M. Brent (eds), *Hosts and Guests Revisited: Tourism Issues of the 21st Century*, New York: Cognizant Communication Corporation, pp. 28–41.

Jennings, G. (2001), *Tourism Research*. Milton, Australia: Wiley.

Johnson, J.C. and M.K. Orbach (1990), 'A fishery in transition: the impact of urbanization on Florida's spiny lobster fishery', *City & Society*, **4** (1), 88–104.

Johnson, R.B. and A.J. Onwuegbuzie (2004), 'Mixed methods research: a research paradigm whose time has come', *Educational Researcher*, **33** (7), 14–26.

Jorgensen, D.L. (1989), *Participant Observation: A Methodology for Human Studies*, Thousand Oaks, CA: Sage Publications.

Kawulich, B.B. (2005), 'Participant observation as a data collection method', *Forum: Qualitative Social Research*, **6** (2), art. 43.

Kemper, R.V., J.M. Roberts and R.D. Goodwin (1983), 'Tourism as a cultural domain: the case of Taos, New Mexico', *Annals of Tourism Research*, **10**, 149–171.

Kikuchi, R.K., Z.A. Leão, V. Testa, L.X. Dutra and S. Spano (2003), 'Rapid assessment of the Abrolhos Reefs, Eastern Brazil', *Atoll Research Bulletin*, **496**, 172–187.

Konstantinov, Y., G.M. Kressel and T. Thuen (1998), 'Outclassed by former outcasts: petty trading in Varna', *American Ethnologist*, **25** (4), 729–745.

Kottak, C.P. (2004), 'An anthropological take on sustainable development: a comparative study of change', *Human Organization*, **63** (4), 501–510.

Kottak, C.P. (2005), *Assault on Paradise: The Globalization of a Little Community in Brazil*, 4th edition, New York: McGraw-Hill.

Lalone, M. (2005), 'An anthro-planning approach to local heritage tourism: case studies from Appalachia', *NAPA Bulletin*, **23**, 135–150.

Lanfant, M.-F., J.B. Allcock and E.M. Bruner (eds) (1995), *International Tourism: Identity and Change*, London: Sage.

LeCompte, M.D. and J.J. Schensul (1999), *Analyzing and Interpreting Ethnographic Data*, Walnut Creek, CA: AltaMira Press.

Lemelin, R.H. (2006), 'The gawk, the glance, and the gaze: ocular consumption and polar bear tourism in Churchill, Manitoba, Canada', *Current Issues in Tourism*, **9** (6), 516–534.

Lepp, A. (2007), 'Residents' attitudes towards tourism in Bigodi village, Uganda', *Tourism Management*, **28**, 876–885.

Lindeman, E.C. (1924), *Social Discovery: An Introduction to the Study of Functional Groups*, New York: Republic Publishing Group.

McCall, G.J. and J.L. Simmons (eds) (1969), *Issues in Participant Observation*, Reading, MA: Addison-Wesley.

MacKay, K.J. and J.M. Campbell (2004), 'A mixed-methods approach for measuring environmental impacts in nature-based tourism and outdoor recreation settings', *Tourism Analysis*, **9** (3), 141–152.

Malinowski, B. (1922 [1984]), *Argonauts of the Western Pacific: An Account of Native Enterprise and Adventure in the Archipelagoes of Melanesian New Guinea*, Prospect Heights, IL: Waveland Press.

Marcus, G. (1995), 'Ethnography in/of the world system: the emergence of multi-sited ethnography', *Annual Review of Anthropology*, **24**, 95–117.

Mason, A. (2005), 'Applied anthropology and heritage tourism: working for the Western Erie Canal Heritage Corridor planning committee', *NAPA Bulletin*, **23**, 159–169.

Mead, M. (1928 [1961]), *Coming of Age in Samoa*, New York: Morrow Quill.

Ness, S.A. (2003), *Where Asia Smiles: An Ethnography of Philippine Tourism*. Philadelphia, PA: University of Pennsylvania Press.

Nyaupane, G.P., D.B. Morais and L. Dowler (2006), 'The role of community involvement and number/type of visitors on tourism impacts: a controlled comparison of Annapurna, Nepal and Northwest Yunnan, China', *Tourism Management*, **27**, 1373–1385.

O'Rourke, D. (director) (1988), *Cannibal Tours* [motion picture]. Australia: Institute of Papua New Guinea Studios.

Oakes, M.P. (1998), *Statistics for Corpus Linguistics*, Edinburgh, UK: Edinburgh University Press.

Paget, E., F. Dimanche and J. Mounet (2010), 'A tourism innovation case: an actor-network approach', *Annals of Tourism Research*, **37** (3), 828–847.

Pansiri, J. (2005), 'Pragmatism: a methodological approach to researching strategic alliances in tourism', *Tourism Planning and Development*, **2** (3), 191–206.

Park, R.E., E.W. Burgess and R.D. McKenzie (1925), *The City*, Chicago, IL: The University of Chicago Press.

Peaslee, R.M. (2010), '"The man from New Line knocked on the door:" tourism, media power, and Hobbiton/Matamata as boundaried space', *Tourist Studies*, **10** (1), 57–73.

Platt, J. (1983), 'The development of the "participant observation" method in sociology: origin, myth and history', *Journal of the History of the Behavioral Sciences*, **19** (4), 379–393.

Polkinghorne, D. (1983), *Methodology for the Human Sciences*, Albany, NY: State University of New York Press.

Rabinow, P. (1977), *Reflections on Fieldwork in Morocco*, Berkeley, CA: University of California Press.

Ribeiro, N.F., E.W. Foemmel (2012, June), 'A map of the tourists' mind? Using Graphic Layout Algorithm (GLA) to visualize on-site destination image perception', Proceedings of the 43rd Travel and Tourism Research Association (TTRA) Annual Conference, Virginia Beach, VA.

Ribeiro, N.F., E.W. Foemmel and T. Liechty (2011), 'Using a variety of methods to compare related free lists and investigate the relationship between perceptions of meaning and behavior of a leisure experience', Proceedings of the 13th Canadian Congress of Leisure Research (CCLR) Annual Conference, St. Catharines, ON.

Riley, R.W. and L.L. Love (2000), 'The state of qualitative tourism research', *Annals of Tourism Research*, **27** (1), 164–187.

Roland, L.K. (2010), 'Tourism and the commodification of Cubanidad', *Tourist Studies*, **10** (1), 3–18.

Rozenberg, D. (1990), *Tourism et utopie aux Baléares*, Paris: L'Harmattan.

Salazar, N.B. (2010), *Envisioning Eden: Mobilizing Imaginaries in Tourism and Beyond*, New York: Berghahn Books.

Saldanha, A. (2002), 'Music tourism and factions of bodies in Goa', *Tourist Studies*, **2** (1), 43–62.

Sandiford, P.J. and J. Ap (1998), 'The role of ethnographic techniques in tourism planning', *Journal of Travel Research*, **37**, 3–11.

Schensul, S.L., J.J. Schensul and M.D. LeCompte (1999), *Essential ethnographic methods: Observations, interviews, and questionnaires*, Walnut Creek, CA: AltaMira Press.

Smith, V.L. (ed.) (1989), *Hosts and Guests: The Anthropology of Tourism* 2nd edition, Philadelphia, PA: University of Pennsylvania Press.

Smith, V.L. and M. Brent (eds) (2001), *Hosts and Guests Revisited: Tourism Issues of the 21st Century*, New York: Cognizant Communication.

Spradley, J. (1980), *Participant Observation*, New York: Holt, Rinehart, & Winston.

Stocker, K. (2007), 'Identity as work: changing job opportunities and indigenous identity in the transition to a tourist economy', *Anthropology of Work Review*, **28** (2), 18–22.

Stonich, S.C. (2005), 'Enhancing community-based tourism development and conservation in the Western Caribbean', *NAPA Bulletin*, **23**, 77–86.

Strange, C. and M. Kempa (2003), 'Shades of dark tourism: Alcatraz and Robben Island', *Annals of Tourism Research*, **30** (2), 386–405.

Tashakkori, A. and C. Teddlie (1998), *Mixed Methodology: Combining Qualitative and Quantitative Approaches*, Thousand Oaks, CA: Sage.

Tcherkézoff, S. (2001), *Le mythe occidental de la sexualité polynésienne: 1928–1999 Margaret Mead, Derek Freeman et Samoa*, Paris: PUF.

Tedlock, B. (1991), 'From participant observation to the observation of participation: the emergence of narrative ethnography', *Journal of Anthropological Research*, **47** (1), 69–94.

Urry, J. (1990), *The Tourist Gaze*, London: Sage.

Vandegriff, D. (2008), '"This isn't paradise – I work here:" Global restructuring, the tourism industry, and women workers in Caribbean Costa Rica', *Gender & Society*, **22** (6), 778–798.

Van Maanen, J. (ed.) (1983), *Qualitative Methodology*, Beverly Hills, CA: Sage.

Veal, A.J. (1992), *Research Methods for Leisure and Tourism: A Practical Guide*, London: Longman.

Wallace, T. (2005), 'Tourism, tourists, and anthropologists at work', *NAPA Bulletin*, **23**, 1–26.

Wallace, T. and D.N. Diamente (2005), 'Keeping the people in the parks: a case study from Guatemala', *NAPA Bulletin*, **23**, 191–218.

Webb, B. (1926), *My Apprenticeship*, London: Longmans.

Weil, J. (1997), 'An *Ecomuseo* for San Vicente: ceramic artisans and cultural tourism in Costa Rica', *Museum Anthropology*, **21** (2), 23–38.

Whyte, W.F. (1943), *Street Corner Society*, Chicago, IL: University of Chicago Press.

Wilson, D. (1997), 'Paradoxes of tourism in Goa', *Annals of Tourism Research*, **24** (1), 52–75.

Yamashita, S. (1999 [2003]), *Bali and Beyond: Explorations in the Anthropology of Tourism*, J.S. Eades (transl.), New York: Berghahn Books.

Yarnal, C.M. and D.K. Kerstetter (2005), 'Casting off: an exploration of cruise ship space, group tour behavior, and social interaction', *Journal of Travel Research*, **43**, 368–379.

20 Cross-cultural approaches
Carla Almeida Santos and Changsup Shim

NATURE OF THE CROSS-CULTURAL APPROACH AND ITS EVOLUTION

Traditionally utilized in psychology, the emphasis of cross-cultural research is on the comparative examination of individuals from different countries or ethnic groups. Largely, such research approaches culture as an underlying influence that collectively directs individuals' beliefs, norms, values, customs, and ideological perspectives; all of which serve to govern individuals' behavior. Accordingly, such a view of culture assumes a collective framework of experiences and beliefs that serve to construct a common consensus of not only what to expect, but also how to behave in any given setting (Hofstede, 2001; Kim et al., 2002). Culture, therefore, has largely been thought of as a standardized, causal, and constant system of meanings shared by and amongst its group members. The result has been a considerable body of cross-cultural research that serves to categorize national cultures along a set of standard cultural dimensions (Hofstede, 2001). Such work has significantly contributed and furthered our knowledge and understanding of consumer behavior and marketing. Indeed, the study of cross-cultural difference reveals its importance and centrality largely for its ability to account for consumer behavior, as well as suggest effective and efficient marketing strategies and tools aimed at a variety of targeted markets (Hsieh and Tsai, 2009). In particular, and as it relates to the focus of this book, such understanding has proven central in travel and tourism research given the proposed role of cultural and national uniqueness in shaping tourist demand and behavior (Crotts and Erdmann, 2000; Graburn, 1995; Pizam and Sussman, 1995; Reisinger and Turner, 2003).

From this perspective, it naturally follows that the vast majority of published cross-cultural research conceptualizes culture as a variable, with statistical comparisons that allow for description of the range and distribution of cross-cultural variation, as well as the testing of hypotheses proposed to explain the variation recorded (Jackson and Niblo, 2003; van de Vijver and Leung, 1997). Consequently, extant cross-cultural research has largely been premised on the assumption of universal principals governing the relationship between culture and behavior. In other words, a defining assumption of traditional cross-cultural research designs is that members of a given cultural group share specific characteristic behaviors and patterns of traits. In so doing, the perspective inherent in such research designs is that individuals who share the same culture always and necessarily share an automatic tendency toward one or another form of behavior and patterns of traits. Such an approach naturally favors universal laws and assumes culturally comparable constructs. However, criticism has increasingly mounted for this approach to culture and its lack of sensitivity toward understanding behavior as universal versus cultural specific. In particular, there is increasing recognition that scientific knowledge does not necessarily reflect and describe cultural reality, nor that culture can be studied, recognized and understood as existing in a vacuum.

Consequently, guided by a distrust of shared, cohesive cultural systems, social science and humanities scholars began problematizing dominant cross-cultural research approaches. They proposed that the assumption of universal principles governing the relationship between culture and behavior failed to recognize cultural intricacies, complexities and paradoxes, as well as differential identities and dynamics among members of a given cultural group (Stanfield, 1993). To address such limitations, they proposed that cross-cultural research embrace a variety of epistemological and methodological approaches that consider how cultural perspectives and social situations are continuously produced, negotiated and modified (Gupta and Ferguson, 1997; Jackson and Niblo, 2003). Qualitative research approaches were deemed particularly appropriate in answering this call given that their methods often generate descriptive data that can assist in investigating and identifying local, social, cultural and political processes as they unfold and shift (Denzin and Lincoln, 2008; Hall and Kulig, 2004; Liamputtong, 2008, 2009; Papadopoulos and Lees, 2002; Smith, 2008; Tillman, 2006). As Morris suggests, qualitative research is at "the sociological vanguard" for investigating cross-cultural issues (2007, p. 410).

Seeking to answer the abovementioned call, cross-cultural qualitative research approaches have developed around specific theory and application (e.g., ethnography, grounded theory). Central to these approaches is the notion that culture is not something that individuals "possess"; instead, a variety of cultures serve to form an inherent part of each individual and are articulated in a variety of ways across multiple social settings. Largely, these approaches, when put into practice, do share a significant overlap in data collection methods. Cross-cultural qualitative research approaches are, therefore, less reflective of a particular technique and instead more reflective of a particular epistemology that serves to guide data collection and analysis. With this in mind, this chapter discusses a particular technique used extensively in cross-cultural qualitative research data collection: cross-cultural interviewing. The decision to focus on cross-cultural interviewing is attributable to the fact that interviewing is one of the most fundamental techniques used in qualitative research; and as a result, the large majority of qualitative research makes use of individual or group interviews as one of its principal data collection methods. However, at the onset it should also be noted that it is not the intent of this chapter to offer a prescriptive orthodoxy with regard to cross-cultural interviewing. To be sure, the specifics of interviewing in cross-cultural research are identical to other kinds of interviews (specifics such as building strong rapport with research participants, thoughtful probing of research participants, maintaining visibility in the studied community, and so on). Instead, this chapter introduces a practical discussion regarding cross-cultural qualitative research, as well as some of the distinctive issues and practices associated with cross-cultural interviewing that are often missing from published research.

BACKGROUND AND TYPES OF PROBLEMS THAT A CROSS-CULTURAL APPROACH IS DESIGNED TO HANDLE

In any given investigation methodological appropriateness is largely contingent upon a variety of factors such as the issue being investigated, the knowledge available to the researchers, and the participants' degree of recognition and acceptance of the techniques used in the study. In general, when the objective is to generalize results or facilitate comparisons mixed or exclusively quantitative approaches in cross-cultural research are best suited (Bhawuk and Triandis, 1996). However, when the objective is to investigate and understand culturally unknown scenarios either from an in-depth or unique perspective, qualitative approaches in cross-cultural research are best suited (Bhawuk and Triandis, 1996). Qualitative research is, therefore, traditionally proposed as essential when investigating "questions of subjective experience and situational meaning" because it provides "a better opportunity for conveying sensitivity" (Davies et al., 2009, p. 6).

Seeking to investigate and convey cultural sensitivities, a variety of principles serve to guide cross-cultural qualitative research. Some of those principles are: (1) that research participants generally know more about the topic, its complexities and paradoxes than the researcher; (2) that those doing the interpreting – be they the researcher or participant – ultimately affect the interpretation; and (3) that problematizing and understanding more significantly contributes to advancing knowledge than does prediction and control. In particular, cross-cultural qualitative research investigates subjective human experiences from the perspective that "understanding of reality can change over time and in different social contexts" (Dew, 2007, p. 434). Seeking to problematize and understand meanings and interpretations, as well as the resulting experiences, qualitative research emphasizes flexibility, fluidity, and interpretation in its approaches (Denzin and Lincoln, 2008; Liamputtong, 2009).

A particular data collection technique frequently employed in cross-cultural qualitative research is cross-cultural interviewing. This technique has proven particularly helpful and central for investigating cross-cultural values, as well as perceptions and interactions between individuals from different cultural backgrounds, information gathering processes, and processes of meaning making amongst others. One research area in which cross-cultural interviewing is particularly useful is the study of cross-cultural values (e.g., the basis for why individuals hold certain values). As Chan proposes, "whereas theory posits that values influence consumer behavior, empirical research fails to establish a strong link between values and consumer behavior, particularly in cross-cultural contexts" (2009, p. 322); to address this issue, he advocates for a qualitative approach to the measurement of cross-cultural values. Specifically, Chan (2009) proposes that the investigation of cross-cultural values is best addressed by cross-cultural interviewing. Moreover, he proposes that cross-cultural interviews are better positioned to avoid the problems of conceptual, functional, and translation equivalence that permeate much of the existing cross-cultural research. Indeed, interviews play a vital role in the investigation of cross-cultural values because amongst others, they permit further elaboration and probing on both the interviewer's questions and the participant's answers; in turn allowing the researcher to capture and grasp the manifold aspects of the complex construct of cross-cultural values.

Another focus area in cross-cultural qualitative research where interviews are particularly useful is the study of perception and interaction between individuals from different cultural backgrounds. Looking to engage with recent criticisms of the dominant approach to the study of cross-cultural perception, Heijes (2011) investigates the role of power dynamics on cross-cultural perception. Specifically, he examines the role of power and power differences between European Dutch and African Curaçaoans. He proposes that changes in cross-cultural perception between the two groups is largely based on the amount of power imbalance. In particular, he explains that perceptions between European Dutch and African Curaçaoans change "depending on the amount of power asymmetry between the groups, whereas the diminution of power asymmetry led to the possibility of effectively bridging the cultural differences by Curaçaoans" (Heijes, 2011, p. 670). As the study sought to describe perception and interaction between respondents, Heijes (2011) employed cross-cultural interviews which started with open-ended questions and gradually moved toward semi-structured interviews so as to provide continuous structure and focus to data collection and interpretation. The findings further promote the notion that research on cross-cultural perception must take into account power dynamics between relevant groups; and that such dynamics are best studied, recognized and understood when examined via the use of interviews.

APPLICATIONS OF THE CROSS-CULTURAL APPROACH TO TOURISM

Culture is often proposed as playing a significant role in tourism-related decisions, including where to travel and how to behave, as well as perceptions regarding quality of tourism services and experiences (Crotts and Erdmann, 2000; Crotts and Litvin, 2003; Pizam and Sussman, 1995; Reisinger and Turner, 2003). To be sure, extant studies affirm that tourist decision making, behavior, and expectations are affected by cultural factors (Chen, 2000; Gursoy and Chen, 2000; Hsieh and Tsai, 2009; Kim and Prideaux, 2005; Lee and Lee, 2009; Lee and Sparks, 2007; MacKay and Fesenmaier, 2000; Richardson and Crompton, 1988). For example, Graburn (1995) suggests that the Japanese are more likely to travel in groups due to their low sense of cultural confidence, while Europeans and North Americans are more likely to travel on their own due to their high sense of cultural confidence. Pizam and Sussman (1995) also propose that the Japanese, French and Italians, unlike North Americans, are less tolerant of uncertainty. While Tsang and Ap (2007) argue that, whereas Asian tourists place more emphasis on the quality of service encounters as a key factor in their travel experience, Western tourists place more emphasis on goal completion, efficiency, and time saving as key factors in their travel experience. Therefore, given the proposed role of cultural and national uniqueness in shaping tourist decision making, behavior, and expectations, cross-cultural research has proven central in travel and tourism literature. Such research, however, is not without its criticism both in terms of its adoption of universal and deterministic values, as well as methodological approaches (Dimanche, 1994; Peabody, 1985). Indeed, while cross-cultural tourism research continues to support the investigation of the role of culture on tourist decision making, behavior, and expectations, it increasingly recognizes that culture is a fluid construct "with a limited lifespan for marketing purposes" (Laing and Crouch, 2005, p. 211).

Although extant cross-cultural tourism research continues to adopt universal and deterministic values in regard to culture as its starting point, an increasing number of scholars are calling for tourism studies to go beyond these dimensions (Chang et al., 2010; Laing and Crouch, 2005; Maoz, 2007; Santos and Buzinde, 2007; Uriely et al., 2009). Such research calls for an understanding of the social and cultural contexts and lived experiences of both the tourists and the toured, and largely falls into one of three approaches. The first, and most traditional approach to cross-cultural qualitative tourism research, is comparative studies that investigate cultural differences between different groups of individuals. Such studies focus mostly on issues that are strongly influenced by a tourist's particular ethnicity or nationality. For example, from a grounded theory approach, Laing and Crouch (2005) conducted a cross-cultural qualitative analysis of frontier travel experiences (i.e., travel to the most remote and amazing places on earth, such as the poles, the harshest deserts, or the peaks of the highest mountains). In order to compare the cultural differences in these travelers' motivations as well as understand the role of cultural background, in-depth interviews were conducted with frontier travelers from Great Britain, America, and Australia. The analysis identified several major themes: challenge/goal setting, self-actualization, novelty, and childhood influences. Although they mainly sought to identify cross-cultural differences between the three nationalities, they also found that, across all themes, participants from all three countries shared similar motivations largely based on a common tradition of exploration in British and Australian history, as well as the frontier myth in North American history.

Some comparative cross-cultural tourism studies do not seek to identify differences between groups of tourists. They instead focus on the relationship between international tourists and host community members. For example, Uriely et al. (2009) explored the northern region of Sinai, which is largely frequented by Jewish-Israeli tourists. They focused on what they called "the bubble of serenity" which resulted from the encounter between Israeli tourists and their Egyptian hosts. The authors used a variety of qualitative data collection methods including participant observation, semi structured in-depth interviews, and informal conversations with Israeli tourists and their Egyptian hosts. The questions addressing Israeli tourists included their motivation to travel to Sinai, their feelings during the stay, and their interactions with the local hosts. At the same time, Egyptian hosts were asked about the nature of their work, their feelings as service providers, and their interaction with Israeli tourists. The results propose that Israeli tourists desire an inexpensive and calm vacation, while Egyptians are willing to supply it in exchange for economic benefits. Moreover, both parties were aware of their mutual interests and readily served in line with them. The authors identify five main practices for avoiding possible impediments to peaceful encounters: perceiving Sinai as an ex-territory; avoiding politics; making friends; stressing similarities; and, finally, distinguishing between "Good Guys" and "Bad Guys".

The second approach to cross-cultural qualitative tourism research investigates groups of tourists from a particular national or ethnic background. The focus of such studies is largely on how cultural background influences tourist motivation, behavior, and satisfaction. The main purpose of these studies is to gain a deeper understanding of a given group of individuals, as well as that group's differences from others. For example, Chang et al. (2010) examined Chinese tourists' food preferences by employing focus-group interviews and on-site observations. The study focused on international tourists from Mainland China, Hong Kong, and Taiwan; all of whom are thought to share a similar food culture. Rather than large group discussions, small group interviews with three to five tourists were decided upon to prevent the discussion from getting too broad. Based on the interpretive analysis of the interviews, the authors presented their four main findings: food preferences and underlying motivation; a typology of the Chinese tourists' tourism dining behavior; the influence of Chinese food culture; and, finally, intergroup disparities. The authors proposed that Chinese food culture strongly influences tourism dining behavior; while at the same time there are some disparities in terms of patterns between the participants from Mainland China, Hong Kong, and Taiwan. Another example is Maoz's (2007) study, in which she examined Israeli backpackers' motivations and travel patterns, and compared them to backpackers from several other countries. As a participant observer, the author, an avid backpacker, conducted interviews as well as stayed in guesthouses, spent time with backpackers in their favorite restaurants, tea houses, and gathering places. After collecting data on Israeli backpackers, and then comparing them to other backpackers, the results indicated that Israeli backpackers have a highly collective orientation, tend to be patriotic, and are inclined to disregard local norms.

The third approach to cross-cultural qualitative tourism research investigates the cultural characteristics and dynamics of a particular tourist destination and its community. Hence, most of these studies focus on the host community rather than on the tourists who visit the community. More specifically, these studies examine the interrelationship between tourism phenomena and the community influenced by the phenomena. For example, from the perspective of colonialism, Lujan (1993) explored Taos Pueblo, one of the most traditional Indian Pueblos in New Mexico, to understand the impact of the increasing number of tourists on the ethnic community where 2000 tribal members reside. The sample consisted of lifetime residents of the pueblo who were enrolled as members in the pueblo. Several questions were asked during interviews, including questions about the tribal members' general feelings about tourists, their experiences with tourists, social changes in the pueblo due to tourism, and personal changes due to tourism. In addition, informal interactions and observations were included in the analysis. The results showed that although there were some differences between age groups, tourism largely led the Native Indians to become more aware of their own culture and to maintain their traditional lifestyle due to economic benefits, their strong cultural and religious foundation, and a strong sense of community and responsibility. Similarly, from a symbolic interactionist perspective, Santos and Buzinde (2007) examined the Puerto Rican neighborhood of Humboldt Park, Chicago. Their study investigated how tourism influenced Humboldt Park's representation of its Puerto Rican cultural identity. Interviews were conducted with individuals residing in the ethnic neighborhood. Their approach focused on how participants defined their own situation to create the reality they perceived and from which they acted. The authors found that there were three main ways in which Puerto Rican residents represented their cultural identity for tourism purposes: invoking historical details; calling on elaborate architectural features; and focusing on the neighborhood's rich legacy, presence, and persistence in Humboldt Park.

ADVANTAGES AND LIMITATIONS OF THE CROSS-CULTURAL APPROACH

The growing influence of globalizing tendencies and competing research cultures call for the development of culturally sensitive research methodologies. And while, to date, the large majority of cross-cultural studies employ quantitative research methodologies, increasingly cross-cultural qualitative studies can be found in tourism (e.g., Laing and Crouch, 2005; Lujan, 1993; Uriely et al., 2009). Accompanying this growth in cross-cultural qualitative research, there are some distinctive issues and practices associated with cross-cultural interviewing that must be considered. To begin, there is the issue of understanding that culture serves to influence interviewing techniques, strategies, and question interpretation; and, therefore, must be taken into account in research design. Indeed, to increase their value, interviewing practices such as providing participants the opportunity to choose their preferred languages for the interviews are often implemented. Also, seeking to avoid interviewer bias and recognizing that the ethnic background of the interviewer can at times affect the respondents' answers – particularly when the topic and focus of the questions is culture (Weeks and Moore, 1981) – cross-cultural qualitative research often employs interviewers who vary in gender and ethnic background. In addition, another common practice is the use of local interpreters. However, while such practices are of great benefit to advancing cross-cultural tourism research, there are certainly issues that arise; one them being the concern that interviewers, research participants, and interpreters often interpret questions and answers in very different ways.

We should also note that while cross-cultural interviewing is often thought of as interviewing that is conducted by a national or cultural outsider with a national or cultural insider, such a narrow approach is proving increasingly problematic. Indeed, there are countless fieldwork accounts that illustrate the insider–outsider challenges faced by researchers conducting interviews within their own societies (Bhopal, 2000; Phellas, 2000; Warren, 1977). To be sure, the insider–outsider challenge "is generic to all forms of interviewing conducted under the auspices of cultural difference, whether ethnicity or culture writ large mediates the relationship between interviewer and interviewee" (Ryen, 2003, p. 430). Nonetheless, there are those who propose that within the context of cross-cultural differences, the insider–outsider challenge is likely to grow uneven given the homogenizing influence of globalization forces. We must, however, consider the possibility that "increasing transnational flows of culture seem to be producing, not global homogenization, but the growing assertion of heterogeneity and local distinctiveness" (Sibley, 1995, pp. 183–4).

Another distinctive issue associated with cross-cultural interviewing is the necessity of establishing good field relationships. As Kvale suggests, for valid interview data collection, "it is up to the interviewer to create in a short period of time a contact that allows the interaction to get beyond merely a polite conversation or exchange of ideas" (1996, p. 125). And while establishing good field relationships is central in any study, the issue is greatly exacerbated in cross-cultural interviewing given that rapport is necessary for "valid cultural understanding. Rapport, however, is the outcome of communication and is not established once and forever. Rather, and especially in cross-cultural contexts, it is mediated by the complex external and internal ingredients of day-to-day involvement" (Ryen, 2003, p. 431). Therefore, cross-cultural interviewers must continuously work out their roles and relationships with the community they are studying. Moreover, this process is further complicated by the researcher's own search for insider status (Rutten, 1995; Tadria, 1991). However, as Panini notes, the search for insider status "is like chasing a mirage" (1991, p. 8). As such, in cross-cultural interviewing, the interviewer must come to terms with the fact that "their place in society . . . is negotiated from the existing cultural shock of knowledge and action available to define and cope with stran-gers" (Warren, 1988, p. 189).

Other distinctive issues associated with cross-cultural interviewing are the potential problems caused by the assumption that in sharing a common language one also shares an agreement and understanding of the nonverbal elements of communication. As von Raffler-Engel (1988) suggests, one of the most significant challenges in cross-cultural research is understanding that there are a number of communicative practices that lie below consciousness and as such cannot easily be understood by simply sharing a common language. Such sensitivity toward, and understanding of the dynamics and complexities of cross-cultural communicative practices can significantly diminish the usual tendency by cross-cultural researchers to focus on verbal communication while disregarding the central role of nonverbal elements of communication (Kvale, 1996). Moreover, those conducting cross-cultural interviews are best served by remembering that even within cultures who share the same language there are still vast differences in linguistic, interpretive and signalling behavior. Indeed, as Gumperz suggests, "Only by looking at the whole range of linguistic phenomena that enter into conversational man-agement can we understand what goes on in an interaction" (1982, p. 186).

Finally, it is imperative that cross-cultural qualitative researchers take into account that life narratives themselves are rarely straightforward. Cross-cultural interviews can certainly generate a significant amount of data. Such interview data is often in the form of a gamut of life narratives with their very own beginning and ending points, and rarely do fit together into a harmonious whole. One approach to unpacking such complex narratives is to allow interviews in their earlier stages to be as unstructured as possible, while progressively moving toward more structured lines of questioning that allow the researcher to more purposely explore themes of interest. In addition, it is essential that in the process of gathering qualitative data, cross-cultural researchers extend beyond the very limitations of cross-cultural interviewing by incorporating into their research design both oral and written materials, as different genres of communication allow for different interpretive advantages.

FURTHER DEVELOPMENTS AND APPLICATIONS OF THE CROSS-CULTURAL APPROACH IN TOURISM RESEARCH

A major challenge for contemporary cross-cultural tourism research will continue to be the fact that the world is becoming more and more interconnected; at times blurring cul-tural differences and threatening the existence of a distinctive national culture. As Kasfir and Yai (2004) suggest, global diasporas have transformed contemporary society into a global community where distinct national cultures continue to diminish while global governance continues to increase. To address such shifts and challenge traditional, universal, and deterministic approaches to culture, cross-cultural tourism researchers have begun to engage with a variety of qualitative methodological approaches that allow for the study of culture without disconnecting it from its context. One particular approach we believe holds promise for tourism research is the multiple case-study project approach with its respective joint analysis strategies, originally developed by Miles and Huberman (1994). This detailed and systematic approach calls for a team of researchers, each one working in a different site. Projects begin with a set of shared research questions and data-coding schemes. What follows are frequent case analysis meetings where the researchers come together to jointly share and discuss their ongoing experiences and emerging themes. During these meetings possible interpretations, explanations and hypotheses are recorded and debated by the team. Based on the discussion, the team then decides on the next steps regarding data collection, follow-up questions, coding schemes, and any other required actions. This process continues until the project is completed. "Thus, analysis feeds into further data collection, leading to further analysis" (Troman and Jeffrey, 2007, p. 513). However, we should note that given the considerable amount of time required to have the type of debates and discussions essential for sorting out conflicting interpretations across different languages, the Miles and Huberman model can also prove difficult to implement in cross-cultural projects (Somekh and Pearson, 2002).

Finally, contemporary cross-cultural tourism research must continue to advance notions of culture as a dynamic, open, and shifting system. Indeed, given the increasing recognition that "the diversity of human experience in social groups and communities, with languages and epistemologies, is undergoing profound cultural and political shifts" (Smith, 2008, p. 137), cross-cultural tourism research can no longer simply rely on universal value-based approaches to culture. Instead, cross-cultural tourism research has to take into account the power dynamics between tourists and the toured, both within contemporary society as a whole, as well as within the specific communities where tourists and the toured engage as a result of the tourism phenomena. Although the focus of cross-cultural qualitative tourism studies varies significantly, the majority employ individual or group interviews as the primary data collection method so as to clarify differential identities and dynamics between cultural groups. Indeed, data generated from interviews has the ability to interrupt past assumptions regarding tourism phenomena, as well as contribute to the development of culturally relevant theories of tourism phenomena. Specifically, to date, the use of interviews in cross-cultural tourism research has furthered our ability to investigate and convey cultural sensitivities as it relates to the social and cultural contexts, as well as lived experiences, of both tourists and the toured.

REFERENCES

Bhawuk, D. and H. Triandis (1996), 'The role of culture theory in the study of culture and intercultural training', in D. Landis and R.W. Brislin (eds), *Handbook of Intercultural Training*, Thousand Oaks, CA: Sage, pp. 17–34.
Bhopal, K. (2000), 'Gender, "race" and power in the research process: South Asian women in East London', in C. Truman, D.M. Mertens and B. Humphries (eds), *Research and Inequality*, London: UCL, pp. 67–79.
Chan, A. (2009), 'Measuring cross-cultural values: a qualitative approach', *International Review of Business Research Papers*, **5** (6), 322–337.
Chang, R.C.Y., J. Kivela and A.H.N. Mak (2010), 'Food preferences of Chinese tourists', *Annals of Tourism Research*, **37** (4), 989–1011.
Chen, J.S. (2000), 'Cross-cultural differences in travel information acquisition among tourists from three Pacific-rim countries', *Journal of Hospitality Tourism Research*, **24**, 239–251.
Crotts, J.C. and R. Erdmann (2000), 'Does national culture influence consumers' evaluation of travel services? A test of Hofstede's Model of cross-cultural differences', *Managing Service Quality*, **10** (6), 410–419.
Crotts, J.C. and S.W. Litvin (2003), 'Cross-cultural research: are researchers better served by knowing respondents' country of birth, residence or citizenship?', *Journal of Travel Research*, **42** (2), 186–190.
Davies, B., J. Larson, N. Contro, C. Reyes-Hailey, A.R. Ablin, C.A. Chesla, B. Sourkes and H. Cohen (2009), 'Conducting a qualitative culture study of pediatric palliative care', *Qualitative Health Research*, **19** (1), 5–16.

Denzin, N.K. and Y.S. Lincoln (2008), 'Introduction: the discipline and practice of qualitative research', in N.K. Denzin and Y.S. Lincoln (eds), *Strategies of Qualitative Inquiry*, 3rd edition, Thousand Oaks, CA: Sage Publications, pp. 1–44.

Dew, K. (2007), 'A health researcher's guide to qualitative methodologies', *Australian and New Zealand Journal of Public Health*, **31** (5), 433–437.

Dimanche, F. (1994), 'Cross-cultural tourism marketing research: an assessment and recommendations for future studies', in M. Uysal (ed.), *Global Tourist Behavior*, Binghamton, NY: Haworth Press.

Graburn, N. (1995), 'Tourism, modernity and nostalgia', in A.S. Ahmed and C. Shore (eds), *The Future of Anthropology: Its Relevance to the Contemporary World*, London: Athlone.

Gumperz, J.J. (1982), *Discourse Strategies*, Cambridge: Cambridge University Press.

Gupta, A. and J. Ferguson (1997), 'Beyond "culture": space, identity, and the politics of difference', in A. Gupta and J. Ferguson (eds), *Culture, Power, Place*, Durham, NC: Duke University Press, pp. 33–51.

Gursoy, D. and J.S. Chen (2000), 'Competitive analysis of cross-cultural information search behavior', *Tourism Management*, **21** (6), 583–590.

Hall, B.L. and J.C. Kulig (2004), 'Kanadier Mennonites: a case study examining research challenges among religious groups', *Qualitative Health Research*, **14** (3), 359–368.

Heijes, C. (2011), 'Cross-cultural perception and power dynamics across changing organizational and national contexts: Curaçao and the Netherlands', *Human Relations*, **64** (5), 653–674.

Hofstede, G. (2001), *Cultural Consequences*, 2nd edition, Thousand Oaks, CA: Sage.

Hsieh, A. and C. Tsai (2009), 'Does national culture really matter? Hotel service perceptions by Taiwan and American tourists', *International Journal of Culture, Tourism and Hospitality Research*, **3** (1), 54.

Jackson, M.S. and D.M. Niblo (2003), 'The role of qualitative methodology in cross-cultural research', *Qualitative Research Journal*, **3** (1), 18–27.

Kasfir, S.L. and O.B.J. Yai (2004), 'Authenticity and diaspora', *Museum International*, **56** (1–2), 190–197.

Kim, S.S. and B. Prideaux (2005), 'Marketing implications arising from a comparative study of international pleasure tourist motivations and other travel-related characteristics of visitors to Korea', *Tourism Management*, **26** (3), 347–357.

Kim, S.S., B. Prideaux and S.H. Kim (2002), 'A cross-cultural study on casino guests as perceived by casino employees', *Tourism Management*, **23** (5), 511–520.

Kvale, S. (1996), *Interviews: An Introduction to Qualitative Research Interviewing*, Thousand Oaks, CA: Sage.

Laing, J.H. and G.I. Crouch (2005), 'Extraordinary journeys: an exploratory cross-cultural study of tourists on the frontier', *Journal of Vacation Marketing*, **11** (3), 209–223.

Lee, G. and C. Lee (2009), 'Cross-cultural comparison of the image of Guam perceived by Korean and Japanese leisure travelers: importance–performance analysis', *Tourism Management*, **30**(6), 922–931.

Lee, S. and B. Sparks (2007), 'Cultural influences on travel lifestyle: a comparison of Korean Australians and Koreans in Korea', *Tourism Management*, **28** (2), 505–518.

Liamputtong, P. (2008), 'Doing research in a cross-cultural context: methodological and ethical challenges', in P. Liamputtong (ed.), *Doing Cross-Cultural Research: Ethical and Methodological Perspectives*, Dordrecht, the Netherlands: Springer, pp. 3–20.

Liamputtong, P. (2009), *Qualitative Research Methods*, 3rd edition, Melbourne, Australia: Oxford University Press.

Lujan, C.C. (1993), 'A sociological view of tourism in an American Indian community: maintaining cultural integrity at Taos Pueblo', *American Indian Culture and Research Journal*, **17**(3), 101–120.

MacKay, K.J. and D.R. Fesenmaier (2000), 'An exploration of cross-cultural destination image assessment', *Journal of Travel Research*, **38** (4), 417–423.

Maoz, D. (2007), 'Backpackers' motivations: roles of culture and nationality', *Annals of Tourism Research*, **34** (1), 122–140.

Miles, M.B. and A.M. Huberman (1994), *Qualitative Data Analysis*, 2nd edition, Thousand Oaks, CA: Sage.

Morris, E.W. (2007), 'Researching race: identifying a social construction through qualitative methods and an interactionist perspective', *Symbolic Interaction*, **30** (3), 409–425.

Panini, M.N. (1991), 'Introduction: reflections in feminism and fieldwork', in M.N. Panini (ed.), *From the Female Eye: Accounts of Women Fieldworkers Studying Their Own Communities*, Delhi: Hindustan Publishing, pp. 1–10.

Papadopoulos, I. and S. Lees (2002), 'Developing culturally competent researchers', *Journal of Advanced Nursing*, **37** (3), 258–264.

Peabody, D. (1985), *National Characteristics*, Cambridge: Cambridge University Press.

Phellas, C.N. (2000), 'Cultural and sexual identities in in-depth interviewing', in C. Truman and E.M. Bruner (eds), *Research and Inequality*, Urbana, IL: University of Illinois Press, pp. 52–64.

Pizam, A. and S. Sussman (1995), 'Does nationality affect tourist behaviour?', *Annals of Tourism Research*, **22** (2), 901–917.

Rabinow, P. (1977), *Reflections on Fieldwork in Morocco*, Berkeley, CA: University of California Press.

Reisinger, Y. and L. Turner (2003), *Cross-Cultural Behaviour in Tourism: Concepts and Analysis*, Oxford: Butterworth Heinemann.

Richardson, S.L. and J. Crompton (1988), 'Vacation patterns of French and English Canadians', *Annals of Tourism Research*, **15** (3), 430–450.

Rutten, M. (1995), *Farms and Factories: Social Profile of Large Farmers and Rural Industrialists in West India*, Delhi: Oxford University Press.

Ryen, A. (2003), 'Cross-cultural interviewing', in J.A. Holstein and J.F. Gubrium (eds), *Inside Interviewing: New Lenses, New Concerns*, Thousand Oaks, CA: Sage Publications, pp. 429–448.

Santos, C.A. and C. Buzinde (2007), 'Politics of identity and space: representational dynamics', *Journal of Travel Research*, **45**, 322–332.

Sibley, D. (1995), *Geographies of Exclusion: Society and Difference in the West*, London: Routledge.

Smith, L.T. (2008), On tricky ground: researching the native in the age of uncertainty', in N.K. Denzin and Y.S. Lincoln (eds), *The Landscape Of Qualitative Research*, 3rd edition, Thousand Oaks, CA: Sage Publications, pp. 113–143.

Somekh, B. and M. Pearson (2002), 'Intercultural learning arising from Pan-European collaboration: a community practice with a "hole in the middle"', *British Educational Research Journal*, **28** (4), 483–484.

Stanfield, J. (1993), 'Epistemological considerations', in J. Stanfield (ed.), *Race and Ethnicity in Research Methods*, London: Sage, pp. 16–36.

Tadria, H.M. (1991), 'Challenges of participation and observation: fieldwork experience among some peasants in Uganda', in M.N. Panini (ed.), *From the Female Eye: Accounts of Women Fieldworkers Studying Their Own Communities*, Delhi: Hindustan Publishing, pp. 88–98.

Tillman, L.C. (2006), 'Researching and writing from an African-American perspective: reflective notes on three research studies', *International Journal of Qualitative Studies in Education*, **19**(3), 265–287.

Troman, G. and B. Jeffrey (2007), 'Qualitative data analysis in cross-cultural projects', *Comparative Education*, **43** (4), 511–525.

Tsang, N.K. and J. Ap (2007), 'Tourists' perceptions of relational quality service attributes: a cross-cultural study', *Journal of Travel Research*, **45** (3), 355–363.

Uriely, N., D. Maoz and A. Reichel (2009), 'Israeli guests and Egyptian hosts in Sinai: a bubble of serenity', *Journal of Travel Research*, **47** (4), 508–522.

van de Vijver, F.J.R. and K. Leung (1997), *Methods and Data Analysis for Cross-Cultural Research*, Newbury Park, CA: Sage.

von Raffler-Engel, W. (1988), 'The impact of covert factors in cross-cultural communication', in F. Poyatos (ed.), *Cross-cultural Perspectives in Nonverbal Communication*, Toronto: C.J. Hogrefe, pp. 71–104.

Warren, C.A. (1977), 'Fieldwork in the gay world: issues and phenomenological research', *Journal of Social Issues*, **33** (4), 93–107.

Warren, C.A. (1988), *Gender Issues in Field Research*, Newbury Park, CA: Sage.

Weeks, M.F. and R.P. Moore (1981), 'Ethnicity-of-interviewer effects on ethnic respondents', *The Public Opinion Quarterly*, **45** (2), 245–249.

21 Archival research
Dallen J. Timothy

INTRODUCTION

Archives are one of the oldest and most utilized sources of data known to researchers. For centuries scholars have used written texts and visual images to piece together histories of salient events in a nation's development, lives of prominent citizens, or occurrences of interest to the general population. Today, archived data are best known for their value in historical research, but archives-based studies are becoming more mainstream in many academic fields, including tourism, as postpositivist methods have gained more traction in the realm of empirical research. In particular, archival data help develop understandings of how tourist destinations grow and decline, the long-term impacts of tourism in destinations, how certain populations have dealt with travel in the distant and recent past, and how policies and legislative actions affect the industry's growth throughout the world.

Archival research itself is not an analytical method but rather a set of approaches to understanding physical data and their meanings. Archives are data sources, and the methods that can be used to interpret archival data are manifold. Content analysis, regression analysis, factor analysis, semiotics, and historical documentation are a few of the most prevalent analytical methods for studying archived information. Since several of these are discussed elsewhere in the book, this chapter does not delve too deeply into any one analytical or interpretive method. It does, however, describe the nature of archival research and its various forms, and it provides a background for the technique and its application in tourism. It highlights several studies that have utilized archival sources and outlines the main advantages and limitations associated with undertaking archives-based scholarship.

USE OF ARCHIVAL DATA AND RESEARCH

In very general terms, archival research entails the use of data which the investigators did not collect themselves; the data already existed when the study was started (Jackson, 2009). The researcher's role is to select which information to use and how to analyse it (McBurney and White, 2010). In the words of Dane (2011, p. 274), "archival researchers deal with people's products rather than with the people themselves." It is an unobtrusive research endeavor and involves the use of "physical evidence" (Babbie, 2010) wherein the unit of analysis is any public record or artifact.

There are two general types of archive data sources. The first is numerical data sets that were collected by someone else. These are usually created to fulfill the needs of a public or private agency, such as the Census Bureau or the Ministry of Tourism. For the agency that collected it, the primary purpose of this information is to gauge trends and patterns in certain populations. In the tourism context these data sets are compiled to help understand global or regional travel trends, or demand for destinations or a particular tourism product.

The second type of archival data derives from a variety of records, images, and artifacts that have remained in collections from bygone eras or from more recent times. These are records of the activities of individuals, organizations, or groups, which can be used to study people and events by examining their recorded history (Hill, 1993). Unlike the numerical data sets mentioned earlier, this second type of archived data is less interested in causal relationships and more interested in exploration, description, and explanation. Like numerical data sets, these artifacts are also produced and held in reserve by someone other than the researcher. A few key examples of these sources include newspapers, websites, historic and contemporary maps, cultural artifacts and souvenirs, photographs and postcards, gravestones, brochures and books, posters, personal journals, ship manifests, oral histories, transcripts, planning documents, recorded music and speeches, tax and land records, letters, guest registries, poetry, birth certificates, marriage licenses, legal documents, and death records (Danto, 2008; Galgano et al., 2008; Williams, 2007). Of all research approaches utilized by tourism scholars, this is one of the most creative and flexible, as almost anything remaining from the past can be mined as a data source, depending upon the research questions being investigated and the availability of the source.

Archival sources can be direct or indirect (Howell and Prevenier, 2001). Direct sources are usable in their original form or derived directly from their creators. Letters written by an immigrant, poems penned by an aspiring poet, or photographs taken during a late nineteenth-century vacation are examples of direct sources. Indirect sources include things such as inventories of someone's collection, which then can help identify the person's interests and help understand his or her history.

Archival data have been used for centuries. Within the first three centuries of the Christian era, ecclesiastical leaders and historians compiled the New Testament from various gospel sources and letters from the apostles (Riches, 2000). This is probably one of the more famous uses of archived data. As well, there are many accounts of parliaments and congresses around the world basing laws and constitutions on historical records. The United States, the United Kingdom, Canada, Australia, and New Zealand have based many elements of their respective constitutions and laws on one of the most famous historic documents in the world: the Magna Carta, which limited royal powers and promoted human rights. Even during the medieval period, scholars were already using books, letters, and other records to compile histories and document colonial successes (de Hamel, 1986).

Historians and geographers were heavily engaged in archival research in the nineteenth century as they compiled histories and historical geographies of places that were still under colonial rule and in their initial stages of industrialization (Milne, 1898; Ratzel, 1896). Today, nearly all historians and many social scientists from a wide range of disciplines engage in archival research, including that associated with tourism. It is seen as a valuable approach to understanding historical problems, telling stories, unfolding important events, understanding people's lives and travel experiences, explaining tourism's impacts, and identifying past and present patterns of supply and demand.

Although archives are essentially collections of documents held by a person or organization, the term also refers to the place where they are kept. There are thousands of archives throughout the world under the ownership or stewardship of public agencies, private companies and organizations, churches and other religious societies, cultural clubs, libraries, non-profit organizations, and universities.

Until quite recently, archival work was done by hand, searching through card catalogs, folders, and boxes of stored items to find facts that helped tell stories or to identify key words and symbols. Later, however, a significant breakthrough occurred as many organizations began photographing and recording their collections on microfilm or microfiche, which people could access by visiting the archives and utilizing microform readers. The research process evolved even further when many organizations began lending, or selling copies of, their microforms to other institutions and even to private individuals. The use of microforms to store visual and textual data was an important breakthrough, and in many cases researchers no longer had to travel away from their home base to glean data from historical documents and artifacts.

The process has been improved even more in recent years with the digitization of archival records and data sets that can be accessed from anywhere in the world through the internet. Organizations have scanned millions of old birth certificates, census records, newspapers, and the like to be digitized for mass consumption. Today, direct and indirect secondary sources no longer have to be old and dusty but can be utilized by a wider range of users. This digital revolution has brought about new ways for people to relate to history and place (Meethan, 2008, p. 101), thus affecting both academic researchers and the general public. This democratization of public and private records and the concomitant increase in information accessibility has spread the use of archival research beyond the domain of historians and historical geographers to include many other disciplines, such as mainstream tourism studies.

ARCHIVAL METHODS

As noted already, archival research is not a method. Archives are sources of data that can be assessed using a variety of analytical and interpretive methods, which can be classified into several broad types. Quantitative analysis of existing data, content analysis, semiotic analysis, and historical fact finding are a few examples.

Existing Data Sets

Existing information, such as border-crossing data provided by a government agency, can be analysed in many ways. Descriptive statistics, such as measures of central tendency or frequencies, are often used to understand basic distribution patterns. Different variables within existing data sets can also be analysed with bivariate or multivariate tests to understand causal relationships between selected variables, as long as adequate information was collected to represent the desired variables.

Content Analysis

Content analysis is a well-established research method that helps make inferences about theoretically pertinent problems (Dane, 2011; Neuendorf, 2002). It is used in studying archived materials to record the occurrence and frequency of certain words, images, names, events, or ideas. Broadly speaking, all forms of archival research involve content analysis, because signs, symbols, patterns, and meanings are sought from archived materials regardless of the methodological approach utilized. Content analysis is an observational technique used to analyse symbolic or actual content of all forms of recorded material (Hall and Valentin, 2005). This method in tourism studies has tended to concentrate on visual images and advertising, such as brochures and websites, although more scholars today are beginning to examine recurring concepts in novels, guidebooks, movies, and other textual sources.

Content analysis can be done quantitatively or qualitatively. From a quantitative perspective, frequency counts can provide simple descriptive statistics, which help researchers understand the occurrences and distributions of key words and concepts. Bivariate and multivariate tests may also be used in analysing the frequency of variables in texts, documents, and visual images, and checking their relationships with other variables.

There are several qualitative methods used to interpret content data. Template analysis is often used to interpret archived data. This technique requires the researcher to develop a coding template, which encapsulates various themes identified by the researcher as important for the research questions, and allows these themes to be organized in a meaningful way (King, 1998). Broad themes envelop narrower and more specific themes, which are often identified (e.g., based upon a literature review) ahead of time as being relevant to the study. When data bits appear in the archived texts or images, they are coded according to the most relevant a priori theme. To check for reliability, this process is typically undertaken by at least two independent assessors to assure consistency in the coding and theming. Once all transcripts have been coded the template of themes becomes the foundation for interpreting the data and summarizing the findings (King, 1998).

Semiotic Analysis

Qualitative content analysis may also include semiotics, discourse analysis, or textual analysis. Semiotic analysis refers to the study of signs, and in the context of tourism it has focused overwhelmingly on understanding the symbolisms and communicative elements of visual images. Semiotics researchers are particularly interested in the meanings of signs and symbols, their real and symbolic social contexts and their effects on the people who produce and/or consume them. The meanings of signs and how these meanings are transmitted are key in understanding archived objects such as photographs or souvenirs. Researchers must decode the messages of signs found in physical objects and texts to identify meanings that will help make sense of a medium and reveal the significance of its production and social relations (Chandler, 2007; Danesi, 2007; Metro-Roland, 2009). Physical objects may be read as 'texts' just as written documents are considered texts (Geertz, 1973).

Overlapping concepts include discourse and textual analysis, which focus on understanding written or spoken language and have been useful in understanding archived written texts, such as speeches, planning documents, books, diaries, and newspapers. Like other forms of semiotic analysis, discourse analysis is interested in the underlying meanings of texts and their contexts. This approach views language and text as very important and emphasizes the social frameworks within which various discourses are embedded (Gee, 2005). Textual analysis describes how the existence or absence of information creates meaning (Buzinde, 2010).

Fact Finding/Historical Approach

Historical fact finding is another approach to archives-based research. For centuries historians have documented the lives of individuals, important events, and the spatial and temporal development of places via historical documentation. Historians construct meanings and contextualize information from archival sources. They uncover facts to help tell a story or reveal the bigger picture of an event or place. This kind of work can be highly subjective, as each historian creates his or her own depiction of the past based upon the bits and pieces of history they are able to verify (Howell and Prevenier, 2001). History researchers identify a historical problem or need. They then gather as much pertinent information as possible about the issue, organize the evidence and verify its authenticity inasmuch as possible. Once the information is organized, conclusions are drawn and written into an expressive narrative (Busha and Harter, 1980).

THE MESSAGE IN THE MEDIUM

As already noted, there are multiple data sources and units of analysis involved in archival research. According to Dane (2011, p. 274), "any record of information is fair game for archival research." This section examines several of these resources and provides examples of their use in the context of tourism.

Secondary Data Sets

Analysis of existing data sets usually means using the data for a different purpose than that for which they were collected (Dane, 2011). Among the most commonly used secondary data sets in tourism research are visitor satisfaction and perception data, arrival numbers, tourist demographics, transport-related data, and other such information that is deemed important and useful by various public and private agencies. As already noted, any number of analytical approaches can be used on secondary data to test hypotheses or reveal descriptive and causal relationships between variables.

Based on a secondary data set from Canada, Murphy et al. (2000) assessed the effects of visitors' experiences and trip quality on trip value and intension to return. The data were collected by Tourism Victoria, the destination tourism agency of Victoria, British Columbia, based on a convenience sample of 3088 tourists as they were leaving the city. For Tourism Victoria, these data were collected to provide an understanding of tourists' perceptions of the city's environment, service quality, and value. Just over 600 of these surveys were used by Murphy and his colleagues in the study. They employed a Partial Least Squares regression analysis and found that destination quality and infrastructure were important factors in determining trip value. They also found that destination quality and experience quality were important predictors of one's intention to revisit Victoria, although trip value was not.

Newspapers

Newspapers and other popular print material (e.g., magazines) are rich sources of data. They reveal much about public thinking, or at least the media's views of public thinking, regarding a variety of topics. There has been a long and rich history of scholars analysing newspaper content to understand the public's view of tourism-related issues (Frew, 2009; West, 2007; Wise, 2011).

Morgan et al. (2011) analysed the effects of newspaper coverage of "red tide" (algae bloom) at a beach and park on Florida's coast. They searched for the key words 'red tide' in the daily newspapers (online versions) of Fort Myers and Naples, Florida, between the years 2002 and 2004, and compared these findings to secondary data related to visitor use of Lovers Key State Park. Because of its usefulness in interpreting time series data, a multiple regression analysis was employed by Morgan and her colleagues. They concluded that there was a significant negative impact on park attendance when red tide was mentioned in the local newspapers in the range of between 398 and 416 visitors, and financial losses for the county of some 4.5 million dollars.

From a qualitative perspective, Andriotis (2010) used a template analysis to appraise public debates about the behavior of British travelers in the Greek Islands. His use of a template resulted in four categories of bad behavior and community perceptions of it as noted in newspapers. The categories included binge drinking, sexual behavior, risk taking, and destination community reactions. After identifying these types of behaviors and reactions, he highlighted examples and manifestations of each type based on quotes and descriptions from the newspapers.

Journals, Letters and Other Written Sources

Old, hand-written letters, journals, and other primary sources have long been a favored information well for historians, genealogists, and social scientists. These documents provide a glimpse of what life was like in the past and how people experienced life events and the world around them (Richards, 2008). Life histories and event histories have long relied on these important resources.

One study in Ghana revealed some very interesting patterns associated with the experiences of African-Americans at a slave heritage site (Timothy and Teye, 2004). The data source for the study was the guest registry at Elmina Castle, one of the most notorious slave trading forts in West Africa built in the fifteenth century by the Portuguese. At the conclusion of their visits, tourists are invited to record their thoughts and feelings in a guest book. The books' contents were provided to the study's authors for the decade of the 1990s and included some 14 120 entries, which were sorted and analysed qualitatively into nationalities. American visitors were further divided into whites and African-Americans, and a textual analysis was undertaken to assess the slave site experience of each group of US tourists. Textual and template analysis resulted in seven themes, which epitomized the experiences of African-Americans: grief and pain, good versus evil (black versus white), revenge, forgiveness and healing, coming home, in memory of our ancestors, and God and holy places.

Historical analysis of travelers during various periods of history is also popular in tourism studies. In particular, with the rapid growth in feminist scholarship since the

1980s, more attention has been paid to women travelers and their struggles to go beyond socially dictated gender roles, to be taken seriously as recognized explorers and adventurers. Feminist histories of travel are prominent illustrations of how historical researchers have utilized the travel journals and diaries of allocentric women exploring parts of the world that had historically been the domain of men (Kolocotroni and Mitsi, 2008; Nittel, 2001; Squire, 1995; Towner, 1988, 1995).

Information in travel diaries and letters has also been widely used to illustrate the history of the Grand Tour, one of the most salient eras in tourism history – one that has received a great deal of academic attention (Black, 1992; Brodsky-Porges, 1981; Towner, 1984, 1985, 1988, 1996) and is often highlighted as a precursor of today's phenomena of cultural tourism, educational travel, independent travel, and backpacker tourism.

Books and Guidebooks

There has been growing interest in recent years about how places and travel are depicted in various types of best-selling novels. Through content and semiotic analyses, researchers have attempted to understand how tourist destinations are portrayed in popular books (Beaulieu and Lévy, 2003; Cate-Arries, 2000). Likewise, we have seen a growth in the number of studies that provide discourse and other semiotic analyses of the content of specialized tourist guide books (Laderman, 2002; Lew, 1992).

Using a semiotic textual analysis, Buzinde (2010, p. 224) analysed the discursive construction of slavery at historic plantations in the American south as depicted in a Lonely Planet guide book. She first prepared the raw data in a way that would more easily accommodate cross comparisons. Second, she conducted an in-depth review of the text to understand the narrative for the period in question. The third step entailed a closer reading of the text and extrapolation of recurring themes and language that spoke about plantation life. Finally, Buzinde interpreted the emergent themes within the larger context of the study. The process resulted in the author identifying and supporting with quotes and examples three main themes: deflection from slavery, presencing slavery, and critical reflections on slavery. The findings suggest that the United States still bears the burden of racial inequalities in its tourism narratives and that more dialogue is needed to reach more balanced race relations in a country that prides itself on being a post-racial society.

Photographic Images

Tourism and photographs go hand-in-hand. Tourists take photographs, and photos have long been used by governments and the private sector to promote places and businesses (Garrod, 2009). Postcards, brochures, and websites are all popular users of place-based pictures that promote destinations and create images abroad. Photographs, postcards, and tourist brochures stimulate strong interest among tourism scholars, primarily because of the messages and image representations they portray (Burns and Lester, 2005; Cohen, 2001; Echtner, 2002; Jokela and Raento, 2011). Semiotic analyses and other forms of content analysis have been key in past research that has analysed tourism visual images. Feighery (2009) argues that tourism organization stock photos, which are utilized in promotional materials, can be helpful in understanding how places, bodies, and spaces are scripted through tourism. In this regard there are clear political implications in terms of image creation and power relations between a place's heritage identity and what tourism and public officials want to portray to visitors. Similarly, semiotic analyses often highlight political undertones as readings of postcards and other photographic images help create "imaginative geographies" and contrived, idealized tourist spaces (Larsen, 2006; Timothy, 2011).

Vespestad's (2010) content analysis of brochures used to market Norway abroad, found that tangible assets and snapshots of nature tend to dominate most of the advertizing media Norway produces. Despite a rich built and living cultural heritage, this illustrates how the country sells itself to British and Russian tourists as a primarily nature-based destination. Istanbul, Turkey, highlights cultural heritage in its brochures. One study of Istanbul brochures found that local tourism officials and the Turkish Ministry of Tourism prefer to depict the city as a 'historically dynamic' place where visitors can 'travel through time' via depictions of many of the civilizations that have flourished there through the centuries (Özdemir, 2010).

Since the 1800s, postcards have been an important part of the tourist experience. Postcard images traditionally have represented what destinations and postcard producers have wanted the outside world to accept as being part of the destination (Arreola, 2001). In an interesting study of Christmas postcards, Cohen (2007) argued that they have the potential to influence travelers' decision making. He found that Thai Christmas postcards depict Santa Claus enjoying the tropics and concluded that they contribute to tourism promotion by encouraging northerners to get out of the cold and spend their winter holidays in balmy Thailand.

Stokowski (2011) used both semiotic analysis and quantitative content analysis to assess photographs published in local newspapers in two small Colorado communities over a 22-year period while gambling tourism was the towns' development focus. Her aim was to understand the number of photos published on the front page of the newspaper, the number of pictures that included scenes with people, and the number of pictures that depicted people smiling in relation to "key moments" in gaming development. Her content analysis entailed tabulating raw numbers and percentages of each type of picture, compared across years. She found that the number of photos published on the papers' front pages declined over the years and that the proportion of photographs with people in them went up and down in relation to the establishment and growth of gambling tourism. Similarly, the depiction of people smiling in the photos declined during the 22-year period. Stokowski's semiotic analysis suggests that as gaming tourism grew, the communities became more serious as discontent and antagonism set in. In the initial stages of tourism development, smiles were more prominent on the faces of community members and decreased as gaming tourism matured.

Souvenirs

Like the photographs noted above, souvenirs are an important part of material culture that reveal considerable meaning about places and can influence visitors' experiences (Collins-Kreiner and Zins, 2011; Timothy, 2005). In this sense, souvenirs and handicrafts can also be viewed as an archival medium. Souvenirs research has typically involved tabulating the range of gift items for sale in a given destination, shop, or museum. Much of the research associated with souvenirs and handicrafts has centered on the materials, styles, designs, places, and crafters and how these reinforce or undermine the authenticity of cultural artifacts for sale to tourists (Asplet and Cooper, 2000; Littrell et al., 1993). Most of this line of inquiry, however, derives from tourists' perceptions of authenticity rather than the researchers' own content analysis of the objects.

In terms of the cultural artifacts themselves, content analyses can be done to examine the frequency of certain characteristics of a single type of souvenir or across a range of souvenirs available in a destination. Semiotic approaches have been utilized in the past, although not enough, in souvenir studies. Gordon's (1986) analysis resulted in a typology of souvenirs based on their forms, functions, and meanings for tourists: pictorial images, piece-of-the-rock items, symbolic shorthand, markers, and local products. Shenhav-Keller (1993) undertook a semiotic textual analysis of archived Israeli souvenirs at a craft and souvenir market and concluded that the country's attitude toward its recent and ancient heritage, views of religion and culture, and relations with the Palestinians were all expressed in the souvenirs on display. The analysis suggests that souvenirs in Israel emphasize the boundary between Jews and non-Jews. They also contribute to the anonymity of Palestinian crafters by utilizing Arab-made souvenirs as representative of the state of Israel and in so doing ignore the cultural identity of the original Palestinian crafters.

Electronic Archives and Modern Technology

Since the 1990s there has been growing interest in the use of web-based media for archival research. The internet itself is likely the world's largest archive, as so much textual and visual data is stored within it. Online archives nowadays allow for easier content analysis because they enable scholars to search for key words in titles or textual bodies, as well as sources and date ranges (Hall and Valentin, 2005). Many traditional archives have been scanned and logged into digital formats that can be accessed via the internet. Likewise, new web-based media themselves may also be seen as archives that provide abundant data for qualitative or quantitative inquiry. Website images, tourism marketing web pages, social media, online photo banks, and webcams are all examples of internet archives that are now receiving widespread research coverage (Alderman and Modlin, 2008; Choi et al., 2007; Tang et al., 2011; Timothy and Groves, 2001).

Social media, such as Facebook, Twitter, and blogs have become a significant outlet for people logging their travel behaviors and experiences. Some tourism service providers have also jumped on the bandwagon and are using these as inexpensive marketing tools. These social media, together with web-based services such as Google Earth, Flickr, WikiMapia, OpenStreetMap, and Mapapedia have created a new type of electronic archive that allows members of the general public to create and share their own maps, photographs, stories, and daily travel experiences. These new abilities and archival spaces have been dubbed variously neogeography (Turner, 2006) or VGI (volunteered geographic information) (Goodchild, 2007). These virtual venues now allow tourists to make available an astonishing amount of geographic and destination attribute data to other potential tourists (Sui, 2008).

There is an emerging literature that uses various textual analyses, content analysis, and semiotic assessments to understand aspects of travel blogs and other social media networks (Enoch and Grossman, 2010; Leung et al., 2011; Pudliner, 2007). Paris (2011) followed eight backpacker tourist bloggers and used a content analysis to examine their online behavior. His aim was to understand the role of social media in the travel experience; the content analysis enabled him to formulate social media maps that defined travel bloggers' virtual spaces and meanings. Using a template approach, Timothy and Groves (2001) analysed the image content of 300 webcams and illustrated the value of webcam pictures for tourism research from the perspective of context/setting (site-specific attractions, natural scenery, resorts, cruise ships and ports, shopping centers, infrastructure, border crossings, tourist services, and special events), data types (weather, crowd density, changes in facilities, changes in infrastructure, and car number plates) and influential factors that affect the researcher's ability to glean reliable visual data (update frequency, image resolution, range/distance of coverage, and quality of coverage/obscured images).

ADVANTAGES AND DISADVANTAGES OF ARCHIVAL RESEARCH

As with any research approach or data-collection method, the use of archives has both benefits and drawbacks. One of the most commonly cited advantages is that researchers do not have to interact with study participants (Jackson, 2009). This, in effect, diminishes the reactivity between the researcher and the researched. Thus it is unobtrusive and non-reactive (Keppel et al., 1992), so that answers are recorded and not influenced by what the subject feels the researcher might want to hear.

A second advantage is that archives-based investigations are less time consuming and usually less expensive. When considering secondary data sets, the data are already collected, saving time, effort, and cost (Jackson, 2009; Keppel et al., 1992). In most cases, to address research questions archived documents can be used without large budgets, thus allowing researchers to identify trends and patterns that exist in physical evidence or historical documents without having to collect primary data.

Another benefit is that secondary data sets are sometimes based on entire populations rather than just samples at a single point in time (Keppel et al., 1992). Many researchers see this as being more reliable, or at least more desirable in undertaking empirical research. Total visitor arrivals at a museum or across an international border are good tourism examples that allow researchers to work with aggregate data that reflect a fairly accurate total accounting of the test population.

Despite the multitude of advantages of archival research there are also some notable drawbacks. One of the most glaring limitations of archival data is the source, and in the case of data sets, the methods with which the data were collected. Most archived data sets were collected for the use of whatever agency commissioned their collection. Thus, the data were typically acquired for non-scientific purposes and might not have been done as randomly or systematically as a researcher would normally desire (McBurney and White, 2010). Secondary data sets are also less flexible. The variety of questions a researcher wants to ask might not have been included. Studies are therefore constrained by the questions that were asked in the original data collection exercise. It is sometimes difficult to derive conceptually rich information from data that are only produced for marketing or general informational purposes. Data in a study commissioned by the US

National Park Service, for instance, which aims to gauge visitors' use of a heritage trail would be difficult to use for understanding attachment to place concepts if related questions were not included on the original questionnaire. Because all archive-based research derives conclusions based upon information collected by another person or agency, there is "no control in terms of who is studied or how they were studied" (Jackson, 2009, p. 86).

Another problem is that many private archives are closed to scholars and can only be accessed by permission from the owners, some of whom are unwilling to provide entry except in exceptional circumstances. The vast archives in the Vatican City are home to large collections of pilgrimage-related accounts, travel diaries, and ancient books that would be of interest to many tourism historians, but the microstate is reticent to allow researchers into its documents rooms. Although the vaults are opening up to more researchers with special permission, access to the Vatican archives is still heavily restricted (Boyle, 2001; Coombs, 1989).

Another glaring drawback is subjectivity. Information published in some newspapers and on the internet is filtered and biased by reporters, editors, and web designers, who do not always write occurrences verbatim or in their precise chronological order (Keppel et al., 1992). Thus, depictions of past events, places, and people are often filtered through selective memory mechanisms in favor of more positive twists or in ways that make the event or person more heroic than they really were (Timothy, 2011). In archive-speak this is known as "selective deposit". Likewise, "selective survival" refers to the limited number of archived items available for analysis (Keppel et al., 1992), which can result in incomplete pictures of the past being revealed in historical narrative and other analyses.

CONCLUSION

Archives have been used as sources of data for centuries and will likely continue to be an important element of social science and historical research for centuries to come. Their primary value is the provision of information that does not have to be collected first-hand by the researcher; the information already exists in numerical, textual, visual, or physical form. In them are volumes of data about people's lived experiences and travel accounts, the successes and failures of service providers, images of place, and destinations' touristification processes, to name but a few.

These extant data can be analysed quantitatively via statistical tests and content analysis, or qualitatively through various semiotic interpretations and deconstructionist frameworks or historical storytelling. There is a growing literature elucidating the meanings and contexts of many archived documents and images using many different types of analysis. Some of those described here have focused on brochures, travel diaries, newspapers, photographs, online blogs, guide books, websites, souvenirs, and secondary numerical data sets.

Despite this emerging interest in archival research among tourism scholars, there is a need to delve more deeply into the meanings of physically archived objects, texts and images. How are destinations trying to depict themselves to the world by way of their website images, postcards, and brochures? What underlying power relations exist between key players, souvenir producers, and marketers? How can archived sources provide better understandings of tourism development in different parts of the world? These are only a few of the multitudinous examples of questions that need to be addressed with more analyses of archival data. There is an urgent need in academic research to understand place identity and sense of place in tourism settings, power, and politics, transformational tourism, and many other pressing issues of today. Archival research can help address these and many more important scholarly debates. As long as humans inhabit the earth and tourism continues to grow and develop, there will be texts, pictures, or objects to archive. As the world continues to transform through technological changes and globalization, adaptations will need to be made to traditional archival approaches, but archives will undoubtedly continue to be important sources of data to understand the tourism phenomenon.

REFERENCES

Alderman, D.H. and E.A. Modlin (2008), '(In)visibility of the enslaved within online plantation tourism marketing: a textual analysis of North Carolina websites', *Journal of Travel and Tourism Marketing*, **25** (3), 265–281.
Andriotis, K. (2010), 'Brits behaving badly: template analysis of newspaper content', *International Journal of Tourism Anthropology*, **1** (1), 15–34.
Arreola, D.D. (2001), '*La Cerca y las Garitas de Ambos Nogales*: a postcard landscape exploration', *Journal of the Southwest*, **43**, 505–541.
Asplet, M. and M. Cooper (2000), 'Cultural designs on New Zealand souvenir clothing: the question of authenticity', *Tourism Management*, **21**, 307–312.
Babbie, E. (2010), *The Practice of Social Research*, 12th edition, Belmont, CA: Cengage.
Beaulieu, I. and J.J. Lévy (2003), 'Tourism, sexuality and eroticism in a few contemporary novels', *Téoros, Revue de Recherche en Tourisme*, **22** (1), 44–50.
Black, J. (1992), *The British Abroad: The Grand Tour in the Eighteenth Century*, New York: St Martin's Press.
Boyle, L.E. (2001), *A Survey of the Vatican Archives and of its Medieval Holdings*, Toronto: Pontifical Institute of Mediaeval Studies.
Brodsky-Porges, E. (1981), 'The grand tour travel as an educational device 1600–1800', *Annals of Tourism Research*, **8** (2), 171–186.
Burns, P. and J. Lester (2005), 'Using visual evidence: the case of *Cannibal Tours*', in B.W. Ritchie, P. Burns and C. Palmer (eds), *Tourism Research Methods: Integrating Theory with Practice*, Wallingford, UK: CABI, pp. 49–61.
Busha, C. and S.P. Harter (1980), *Research Methods in Librarianship: Techniques and Interpretations*, New York: Academic Press.
Buzinde, C.N. (2010), 'Discursive constructions of the plantation past within a travel guidebook', *Journal of Heritage Tourism*, **5** (3), 219–235.
Cate-Arries, F. (2000), 'Changing places: travel and tourism in Manuel Vázquez Montalbán's detective novels', in H.M. Fraser and B.D. Willis (eds), *Essays on Hispanic and Luso-Brazilian Literature and Film in memory of Dr. Howard M. Fraser*, pp. 83–90. Mobile, AL: University of South Alabama Publications.
Chandler, D. (2007), *Semiotics: The Basics*, London: Routledge.
Choi, S.J., X.Y. Lehto and A.M. Morrison (2007), 'Destination image representation on the web: content analysis of Macau travel related websites', *Tourism Management*, **28** (1), 118–129.
Cohen, C.B. (2001), 'Island is a woman: women as producers and products in British Virgin Islands Tourism', in Y. Apostolopoulos, S. Sonmez and D.J. Timothy (eds), *Women as Producers and Consumers of Tourism in Developing Regions*, Westport, CT: Praeger, pp. 47–72.
Cohen, E. (2007), 'From benefactor to tourist: Santa on cards from Thailand', *Annals of Tourism Research*, **34** (3), 690–708.
Collins-Kreiner, N. and Y. Zins (2011), 'Tourists and souvenirs: changes through time, space and meaning', *Journal of Heritage Tourism*, **6** (1), 17–27.
Coombs, L.A. (1989), 'A new access system for the Vatican Archives', *American Archivist*, **52** (4), 538–546.
Dane, F.C. (2011), *Evaluating Research: Methodology for People Who Need to Read Research*, Thousand Oaks, CA: Sage.

Danesi, M. (2007), *The Quest for Meaning: A Guide to Semiotic Theory and Practice*, Toronto: University of Toronto Press.

Danto, E.A. (2008), *Historical Research*, New York: Oxford University Press.

de Hamel, C. (1986), *A History of Illuminated Manuscripts*, Oxford: Phaidon Press.

Echtner, C. (2002), 'The content of third world tourism marketing: a 4A approach', *International Journal of Tourism Research*, **4** (6), 413–434.

Enoch, Y. and R. Grossman (2010), 'Blogs if Israeli and Danish backpackers to India', *Annals of Tourism Research*, **37** (2), 520–536.

Feighery, W. (2009), 'Tourism, stock photography and surveillance: a Foucauldian interpretation', *Journal of Tourism and Cultural Change*, **7** (3), 161–178.

Frew, E. (2009), 'Festival image creation: the role of local and interstate newspapers', *Tourism Analysis*, **14** (2), 221–230.

Galgano, M.J., J.C. Arndt and R.M. Hyser (2008), *Doing History: Research and Writing in the Digital Age*, Boston, MA: Thomson.

Garrod, B. (2009), 'Understanding the relationship between tourism destination imagery and tourist photography', *Journal of Travel Research*, **47** (3), 346–358.

Gee, J.P. (2005), *An Introduction to Discourse Analysis: Theory and Method*, London: Routledge.

Geertz, C. (1973), *The Interpretation of Cultures*, New York: Basic Books.

Goodchild, M. (2007), 'Citizens as sensors: the world of volunteered geography', *GeoJournal*, **69**, 211–221.

Gordon, B. (1986), 'The souvenir: messenger of the extraordinary', *Journal of Popular Culture*, **20** (3), 135–146.

Hall, C.M. and A. Valentin (2005), 'Content analysis', in B.W. Ritchie, P. Burns and C. Palmer (eds), *Tourism Research Methods: Integrating Theory with Practice*, Wallingford, UK: CABI, pp. 191–209.

Hill, M.R. (1993), *Archival Strategies and Techniques*, Newbury Park, CA: Sage.

Howell, M.C. and W. Prevenier (2001), *From Reliable Sources: An Introduction to Historical Methods*, Ithaca, NY: Cornell University Press.

Jackson, S.L. (2009), *Research Methods and Statistics: A Critical Thinking Approach*, 3rd edition, Belmont, CA: Cengage.

Jokela, S. and P. Raento (2011), 'Collecting visual materials from secondary sources', in T. Rakić and D. Chambers (eds), *An Introduction to Visual Research Methods in Tourism*, London: Routledge, pp. 53–69.

Keppel, G., W.H. Saufley and H. Tokunaga (1992), *Introduction to Design and Analysis: A Student's Handbook*, New York: W.H. Freeman and Company.

King, N. (1998), 'Template analysis', in G. Symon and C. Cassell (eds), *Qualitative Methods and Analysis in Organizational Research*, London: Sage, pp. 118–134.

Kolocotroni, V. and E. Mitsi (eds) (2008), *Women Writing Greece: Essays on Hellenism, Orientalism and Travel*, New York: Editions Rodopi.

Laderman, S. (2002), 'Shaping memory of the past: discourse in travel guidebooks for Vietnam', *Mass Communication and Society*, **5** (1), 87–110.

Larsen, J. (2006), 'Picturing Bornholm: producing and consuming a tourist place through picturing practices', *Scandinavian Journal of Hospitality and Tourism*, **6** (2), 75–94.

Leung, D., R. Law and H. Lee (2011), 'The perceived destination image of Hong Kong on Ctrip.com', *International Journal of Tourism Research*, **13** (2), 124–140.

Lew, A.A. (1992), 'Place representation in tourist guidebooks: an example from Singapore', *Singapore Journal of Tropical Geography*, **12** (2), 124–137.

Littrell, M.A., L.F. Anderson and P.J. Brown (1993), 'What makes a craft souvenir authentic?', *Annals of Tourism Research*, **20**, 197–215.

McBurney, D.H. and T.L. White (2010), *Research Methods*, Belmont, CA: Cengage.

Meethan, K. (2008), 'Remaking time and space: the internet, digital archives and genealogy', in D.J. Timothy and J.K. Guelke (eds), *Geography and Genealogy: Locating Personal Pasts*, Aldershot, UK: Ashgate, pp. 99–112.

Metro-Roland, M. (2009), 'Interpreting meaning: an application of Peircean semiotics to tourism', *Tourism Geographies*, **11** (2), 270–279.

Milne, J.G. (1898), *A History of Egypt under Roman Rule*, London: Methuen.

Morgan, K.L., S.L. Larkin and C.M. Adams (2011), 'Empirical analysis of media versus environmental impacts on park attendance', *Tourism Management*, **32** (4), 852–859.

Murphy, P., M.P. Pritchard and B. Smith (2000), 'The destination product and its impact on traveller perceptions', *Tourism Management*, **21**, 43–52.

Neuendorf, K.A. (2002), *The Content Analysis Guidebook*, Thousand Oaks, CA: Sage.

Nittel, J. (2001), *Wondrous Magic: Images of the Orient in the 18th and 19th Centuries' British Women Travel Writing*, Berlin: Galda Wilch Verlag.

Özdemir, G. (2010), 'Photographs in brochures as the representations of induced image in the marketing of destinations: a case study of Istanbul', in P.M. Burns, J.M. Lester and L. Bibbings (eds), *Tourism and Visual Culture, Volume 2: Methods and Cases*, Wallingford, UK: CAB International, pp. 169–180.

Paris, C.M. (2011), 'Understanding the statusphere and blogosphere: an analysis of virtual backpacker spaces', in R. Law, M. Fuchs and F. Ricci (eds), *Information and Communication Technologies in Tourism, 2011*, Vienna: Springer, pp. 443–456.

Pudliner, B.A. (2007), 'Alternative literature and tourist experience: travel and tourist weblogs, *Journal of Tourism and Cultural Change*, **5** (1), 46–59.

Ratzel, F. (1896), 'The territorial growth of states', *Scottish Geographical Magazine*, **12**, 351–361.

Richards, P.L. (2008), 'Knitting the Transatlantic bond: one woman's letters to America, 1860–1910', in D.J. Timothy and J.K. Guelke (eds), *Geography and Genealogy: Locating Personal Pasts*, Aldershot, UK: Ashgate, pp. 81–97.

Riches, J.K. (2000), *The Bible: A Very Short Introduction*, Oxford: Oxford University Press.

Shenhav-Keller, S. (1993), 'The Israeli souvenir: its text and context', *Annals of Tourism Research*, **20**, 182–196.

Squire, S.J. (1995), 'In the steps of 'genteel ladies': women tourists in the Canadian Rockies, 1885–1939', *Canadian Geographer*, **39** (1), 2–15.

Stokowski, P.A. (2011), 'The smile index: symbolizing people and place in Colorado's casino gaming towns', *Tourism Geographies*, **13** (1), 21–44.

Sui, D.Z. (2008), 'The Wikification of GIS and its consequences: or Angelina Jolie's new tattoo and the future of GIS', *Computers, Environment and Urban Systems*, **32**, 1–5.

Tang, L., R. Scherer and A.M. Morrison (2011), 'Web site-based destination images: a comparison of Macau and Hong Kong', *Journal of China Tourism Research*, **7** (1), 2–19.

Timothy, D.J. (2005), *Shopping Tourism, Retailing and Leisure*, Bristol, UK: Channel View.

Timothy, D.J. (2011), *Cultural Heritage and Tourism: An Introduction*, Bristol, UK: Channel View.

Timothy, D.J. and D.L. Groves (2001), 'Webcam images as potential data sources for tourism research', *Tourism Geographies*, **3** (4), 394–404.

Timothy, D.J. and V.B. Teye (2004), 'American children of the African diaspora: journeys to the motherland', in T. Coles and D.J. Timothy (eds), *Tourism, Diasporas and Space*, London: Routledge, pp. 111–123.

Towner, J. (1984), 'The Grand Tour: sources and a methodology for an historical study of tourism', *Tourism Management*, **5** (3), 215–222.

Towner, J. (1985), 'The grand tour: a key phase in the history of tourism', *Annals of Tourism Research*, **12** (3), 297–333.

Towner, J. (1988), 'Approaches to tourism history', *Annals of Tourism Research*, **15** (1), 47–62.

Towner, J. (1995), 'What is tourism's history?', *Tourism Management*, **16** (5), 339–343.

Towner, J. (1996), *An Historical Geography of Recreation and Tourism in the Western World, 1540–1940*, Chichester, UK: Wiley.

Turner, A. (2006), *Introduction to Neogeography*, New York: O'Reilly.

Vespestad, M.K. (2010), 'Promoting Norway abroad: a content analysis of photographic messages of nature-based tourism experiences', *Tourism, Culture and Communication*, **10** (2), 159–174.

West, T. (2007), 'Dark tourism: a content analysis of popular media regarding motivations to travel to Ground Zero', Master of Science Thesis, Arizona State University.

Williams, R.C. (2007), *The Historian's Toolbox: A Student's Guide to the Theory and Craft of History*, Armonk, NY: M.E. Sharpe.

Wise, N.A. (2011), 'Post-war tourism and the imaginative geographies of Bosnia and Herzegovina and Croatia', *European Journal of Tourism Research*, **4** (1), 5–24.

22 Community case study research
Dianne Dredge and Rob Hales

INTRODUCTION

Case studies are increasingly recognized as a valuable research strategy for the study of tourism (Xiao and Smith, 2006). Defined as 'an empirical inquiry that investigates a contemporary phenomenon within its real-life context', case study research is adopted by researchers seeking to describe, explore and/or explain complex and dynamic social systems (Yin, 2009, p. 13). Community case studies represent a particular subset of case study research. For the purpose of this chapter, a community case study in tourism focuses research attention on the way social processes within a community or multiple communities produce meanings about tourism and shape individual, organizational and institutional responses. This chapter explores and critically discusses community case studies in tourism and their application and value to tourism research and practice. The chapter concludes by identifying future directions and the need to address a number of issues if community case study research in tourism is to maximize its change-making potential.

THE NATURE OF TOURISM COMMUNITY CASE STUDIES

Defining Community

'Community' is a very difficult term to define and even the best attempts can be ambiguous. It is often taken for granted that community denotes a group of people who share some common features, i.e., they share the same ethnic background, are domiciled in proximity to each other, or they possess the same values. However, communities are far from homogeneous, which for many community case study researchers, is both a source of fascination and frustration. To illustrate, 'community' may be defined in a variety of ways including:

- *A spatially coherent group of people.* However, ambiguity emerges when the notion of scale is introduced, e.g., the local community and the global community.
- *A group of people sharing ethnic, cultural, professional or other characteristics.* However, that people share one or a number of common values and beliefs does not mean they are a homogenous community. People can share some common characteristics in one domain (e.g., ethnic background) and at the same time exhibit opposing values in another domain (e.g., adherence to cultural traditions, educational attainment or voting behaviour).
- *A group of people sharing of common beliefs, attitudes, interests, identities or other types of connections.* As in the above example, ambiguity emerges where some

people share common beliefs in one domain (e.g., attitudes to tourism) but vary in other ways (e.g., level of involvement in tourism).

In essence then, the term 'community' is inherently vague and dependent upon the context and the purpose for which it is defined. Individuals can belong to more than one community and communities can overlap and intersect depending upon the issues under investigation. However, good community case study research does not allow the problem of definition to get in the way. It accepts that community is socially constructed; the focus of the research is on the interactions between community members and this is often dynamic. Moreover, the concept of community is unbounded in that the researcher tends to determine the number of participants in the case by making value judgments about the minimum threshold needed to understand the social processes within that community. In this way community case studies are distinguished from other types of case studies that focus on objects such as particular policies or decisions.

CHARACTERISTICS OF COMMUNITY CASE STUDIES

Community case studies are empirical and context dependent, and cannot be abstracted from the situated interactions and practices of community members. They are also dependent upon the way in which 'community' is defined and by the particular theoretical explanations and frameworks that a researcher may choose to adopt. Notwithstanding this diversity, community case studies share a number of common characteristics:

- Tourism community case study research commonly seeks to describe, explore and/ or explain tourism or an aspect of tourism within the social context of a community or set of communities.
- Tourism community case study research focuses on the social interactions around an episode or event of some kind in a singe case or a multiple comparative case study setting.
- Tourism community case study research is undertaken *in situ*, exploring the phenomenon or a particular dimension of tourism in its natural setting.
- Tourism community case study research is undertaken over a period of time (e.g., a longitudinal case study).
- Tourism community case study research focuses on relationships between participants directly or indirectly involved in tourism or affected by it.
- Tourism community case studies draw from several data sources and employ multiple methods. Processes of triangulation and crystallization are often used in generating understandings.
- Tourism community study research commonly (but not always) includes learning and reflection on the part of the researcher, and these understandings may be shared with community members (Swanborn, 2010; Yin, 2009, 2011).

These characteristics find their origins in rich historical debates about the character, role and value of social sciences research in general. This background is now discussed.

BACKGROUND TO COMMUNITY CASE STUDY RESEARCH

Situating Social Research

The epistemological, ontological and methodological shifts occurring within the social sciences from the mid-twentieth century have had significant implications for case study research (Flyvbjerg, 2001; Gerring, 2007). At the risk of oversimplifying the discursive twists and turns taking place over the course of the twentieth century, the dominance of positivism in the early part of the century provided overwhelming support for rational scientific methods characterized by systematic data collection, analysis and the production of universal 'truths'. In this environment, case studies were often criticized as being less scientific, less reliable and therefore less useful, than scientific approaches (Flyvbjerg, 2006). However, as questions started to emerge about the rational and objective assumptions on which the scientific method was based, criticisms of positivism began to emerge. By the middle of the last century, the idea that there were overarching universal truths and cause-and-effect relationships that could explain the social world was increasingly questioned. Understanding the dynamics of social processes, as opposed to hypothesis testing and prediction, became an important imperative in social research. As a result, case study research, as an approach to uncover complex social phenomenon *in situ*, became increasingly accepted.

Underpinning this shift was the increasing recognition of the social situatedness of research. In the *Postmodern Condition: A Report on Knowledge*, Lyotard (1979) argued that all science was a form of story-telling, an interpretation based on the particular choices and preferences of the researcher who is situated within a particular research context. No single truth existed. Multiple realities could co-exist, which in turn opened up opportunities for researchers to take different but nevertheless legitimate approaches in researching the social world. This led to significant fault lines between natural and social science research communities across the world. Even within the social sciences, there were divisions between those comfortable devising hypotheses and emulating the scientific method, and those seeking to explore and investigate social phenomenon from a range of emerging postmodern perspectives.

These divisions played out over the last decades of the twentieth century, sometimes in bitter and subversive ways as evidenced by the Science Wars (Flyvbjerg, 2001; Segerstrale, 2000). By the end of the twentieth century however, the battlelines had softened and researchers had become more tolerant of the contributions of various research approaches and methods. An intellectualization of research methods was taking place. Researchers began to focus greater attention on the way the philosophical positioning of the researcher intersected with and influenced the choice of research approach and methods. These choices would inevitably influence findings, so the emphasis shifted from choosing the 'right' methods to explaining the values, position and influence of the researcher in the research process. For example, research commissioned by an event organizer with the aim of establishing the impacts of an event on a local community will likely yield very different results when compared to an ethnographer who also examines the community impacts of the same event. Being clear about these influences allows readers to better assess the value of the research and its findings in context and to compare against their own experiences and knowledge (May and Perry, 2011).

Tourism, as a complex multidisciplinary field of research, has benefited greatly from a breaking down of these methodological divisions. As Jamal and Hollinshead (2001) note, the very nature of tourism, and the inter- and multi-disciplinary influences upon it, implies that it is not a distinct social practice; research questions cannot be easily isolated nor simply aligned with quantitative or qualitative methodologies. Further, they argue, the drive for 'scientific' research that seeks out 'the truth' only limits fuller understandings of the situatedness of tourism as a dynamic phenomenon. These authors call for a dialogue that includes and values 'multiple approaches, theories, practices, methods, techniques that can assist those of us in tourism studies to do justice to the research topic and research questions we formulate and pursue' (p. 78). Against this background, community case studies in tourism have evolved considerably.

COMMUNITY CASE STUDIES AS MESSY RESEARCH

Previously, researchers under pressure to publish were bounded by the expectations and protocols of their disciplinary-based research communities and the academic tribes to which they belonged (Becher and Trowler, 2001; Tribe, 2010; Trowler, 1988). In those disciplines where case studies were less recognized, researchers often found themselves trying to create the illusion of a rational scientific approach, when in fact their research was much more organic and creative, drawing fluidly and simultaneously from a variety of theoretical and practical understandings. It was not until the latter part of the twentieth century that this began to change and social research came to be viewed as complex, messy and dynamic (Law, 2004).

In the case of tourism research, scientific approaches were inadequate in understanding complex problems, and calls were made for an extended range of approaches and methods. Law (2004) argued that, in trying to describe and analyse things in a coherent way, the social sciences had made a mess of trying to make sense of things that are inevitably messy, diffuse and complex. The methods, rules and frameworks derived from different social science disciplines have helped to produce the reality that we understand, but the weaknesses and flaws in these frameworks may also have produced 'black spots' in our understanding (Dredge et al., 2011). Law called upon researchers to explore other realities and understandings by drawing upon the rich hinterland of pre-existing social and material realities to bundle and reassemble it in different ways.

These views have been increasingly supported by those seeking a post-disciplinary tourism research agenda; an approach that adopts a creative and flexible approach to investigating problems and that embodies greater scholarly tolerance for different views and methods (Coles et al., 2006; Etchner and Jamal, 1997; Hollinshead and Jamal, 2007). These ideological shifts have stimulated an 'up-shifting' in empirical, contextualized research such as community case studies (Seidman and Alexander, 2001).

AIMS, VALUES AND PRIVILEGING PERSPECTIVES

In this context, there has been significant debate, refinement and development of the case study as a legitimate research approach (Gerring, 2007; Swanborn, 2010;

VanWynsberghe and Khan, 2007; Yin, 2009, 2011). Yin (2009) defines various types of case studies based on a 2 × 3 matrix wherein case studies can either be single or multiple case studies and can be focused on description, exploration or explanation. Yin's matrix is useful in thinking about case study design, and can help a researcher make decisions about the end goal of the research in terms of whether they are seeking to describe, explore or explain their case. However, as discussed above, the values, identity and positioning of researchers can privilege certain perspectives and influence findings (Mills et al., 2010).

Within the research process researchers also communicate, share information and influence the community and other audiences so Yin's idea that a case study describes, explores or explains needs to be revisited. Noted anthropologist Clifford Geertz captures this conundrum, arguing that 'finding somewhere to stand in a text that is supposed to be at one and the same time an intimate view and a cool assessment is almost as much of a challenge as gaining the view and making the assessment in the first place' (Geertz, 1988, p. 10). This in turn raises questions about whether case studies can be categorized as simply descriptive, exploratory or explanatory where the researcher is separate to and independent of research problem, the end goal of the research and the community. In other words, Yin's categorizations do not adequately capture the relationships and change that both the community and the researcher experience in many community case study research processes. Inter-subjective communication between the researcher and community members can be transformative (Reis, 2011). This then becomes a point of departure from Yin's typology because transformative community case studies go well beyond description, exploration and explanation to incorporate values-driven action.

RESEARCHER REFLEXIVITY AND POLITICAL ACTION

Inter-subjective communication refers to the process of communication and exchange between researchers and community members wherein all participants are reflecting and building intercultural understandings, and in the process, they are being transformed (Prus, 1997). There is a blurring of boundaries between researcher and community, between insider and outsider, and between theory and practice (Alvesson and Sköldberg, 2009; Chiseri-Strater, 1996). This dynamic process generates understandings that are not inert 'facts' but can become triggers for action and further reflection. In an evocative example, Noy (2004) explores how the identity of the backpacking community is constituted through narrative performance of adventure stories. Encouraging a conversational story-telling approach, Noy interviews Israeli backpackers. The backpackers tell stories of their adventure travels interwoven with expressions of self-change, personal growth and reflection. In the process, it was noted that the narratives were often told in an excited tone and there was an expectation by the performer of the narrative that the researcher shared mutual involvement in the story. Indeed, Noy notes that his own response to one of the narratives was that he not only felt witness to the tourist attraction being described but the experience of the story evoked his own touristic self-change.

This example draws attention to the culture of research production and the way research is produced, knowledge is exchanged and actions are identified and implemented (May and Perry, 2011). In the past, the traditional approach of producing research that was presented as an end product (i.e., a research paper, a consulting report, etc.) perpetuated a divide between research and practice. Researchers sought not to intervene or take purposive action, merely to present 'facts'. More recently, growing emphasis on researcher reflexivity, or the extent to which researchers recognize their roles and take purposive action to shape the outcomes, has led to optimism that research can make a difference to the problems that communities are experiencing.

We argue that researchers undertaking community case study research can adopt a position along a continuum of political action. At one end of the continuum is a phronetic approach (as described by Flyvbjerg, 2001) which places the researcher in a value-neutral position with respect to the community, but who is still politically embedded in the case study. In this approach the mere choice of the community/case/phenomenon under study is a political act because engagement by the researcher helps in achieving the (political) aspirations of the community. Moreover, the researcher still has personal perspectives and knowledge that will infiltrate their communications and behaviours making a truly apolitical stance impossible. Nevertheless, in this process the researcher seeks to understand all perspectives, promotes multi-perspective understandings of the issues within the community, and resists attempts by certain community members to legitimise particular stakeholder interests (Dredge, 2011). This approach to the community case study has been variously described by social scientists as phronetic case study research (Flyvbjerg, 2001; Maguire, 1997) and spiral case study research (Mills et al., 2010) wherein the researcher is reflexively constructing meanings about the case, sharing those meanings with community case study participants.

At the other end of the continuum, the researcher's position is more direct and overt in its political intent. The researcher chooses a case and actively engages in research openly sharing and pursuing the aspirations of the community they engage with. The approach sees the researcher embedding themselves within the case and siding with the community along with the sometimes disparate pursuit of their aspirations. This approach also entails the researcher either communicating the 'findings' of case study research in the public sphere or iteratively feeding their findings back into the community. In both instances the values that help align the action of the researcher are similar to the community. This approach can be described as the academic activist approach (Higgins-Desboilles, 2010; Maxey, 1999).

The position of the researcher somewhere along this continuum will influence the way the case study research evolves, the manner in which information exchange and knowledge production takes place, and the role and influence of the researcher in the process. In both approaches community case study research incorporates elements of participatory action research, ethnography and quasi-experimental research designs. They require that the researcher reflect upon and make decisions about such things as:

● The type and level of political action desirable and appropriate from both the researcher's and the community's perspective.
● The desired level of involvement by the researcher (e.g., from low involvement to highly overt political action) in the community case study.
● The level and characteristics of power that the researcher has and to what advantage this power can be used (or abused) to legitimize certain interests and outcomes.

- The level of personal and professional alignment the researcher has to the community over short, medium and long terms.

COMMUNITY CASE STUDIES IN TOURISM

Research, Practice and Ethical Action

Through application of theoretical frameworks, concepts and models, communication and reflection, community case studies in tourism bring together theory and practice. Moreover, this dialogic conversation between theory and practice can induce actions by both researchers and community members that unleash tourism's world-making capacity. Both Tribe (2004) and Jamal (2004) have argued for closer alignment between tourism knowledge generated by research and practical action. Tribe (2002) builds upon Schon's (1983) reflective practitioner, arguing for a 'knowing–in–tourism–ethical-action' wherein 'reflection and action are integrated where people act for the good of tourism societies' (p. 322). Jamal (2004) argues that Tribe's argumentation does not go far enough, and that, while action is good, further examination of the ethics underpinning research is needed. Building upon Tribe's work, and drawing from classical philosophy of Aristotle, Jamal argues that researchers must address what Aristotle called the 'good life' – a research life characterized by acting virtuously for the good of the community.

These authors provide important justifications for valuing practical, engaged community research that facilitates ethical action. Adding to this, we advocate that the dialogic sense-making that takes place in community case studies when researchers and community members engage in communication and reflection results in Mode 2 knowledge production (i.e., context and problem driven inquiry wherein both the researcher and the researched contribute to the production of knowledge) (Nowotny, 2003). This sense-making and ethical action approach can result in the researcher defining the problem and researching in consultation with the community (rather than independently of it). Unanticipated insights, derived through the co-production of local knowledge, can help to generate solutions and joint actions.

Bodorkós and Pataki (2009), for example, adopted a participatory action research approach to 'learn about the possibilities for bottom-up regional sustainability planning in a planning culture dominated by top-down institutional arrangements' in economically disadvantaged regions in Hungary. Ecotourism emerged as a possible action identified by stakeholders. Reflecting on the value of this community-based research the authors observed that it involved a different problem-structuring process:

> [It] takes a lot of time and effort; indeed, the mutual learning process is time-consuming. Researchers are necessarily required to spend a great deal of time listening to the local inhabitants, striving to become familiar with their priorities, problems, and visions. As compared to one-shot research processes typically applied in mainstream research, community-based research can create a better learning environment through providing more flexibility and being more responsive to local ideas. (p. 1130)

TOURISM COMMUNITY CASE STUDY DESIGN

The post-disciplinary tourism research agenda with its attendant creative and flexible approach to investigating problems has meant that methodology and techniques in research have become more diverse (Tribe, 2004). Not surprisingly, community case study design, data collection and analysis can appear messy. In what follows, three frames of philosophical traditions in social research are used to distil the diversity found in case study design, data collection and analysis in tourism studies. The data collection methods and analysis used in community case studies are invariably guided by these traditions, and will be discussed later in the chapter.

The first is the *postpositivist approach*. In this approach it is possible to generate hypotheses and test them within the case because within the case there are particular units which can be discovered and delineated by the researcher (Ragin, 1993). Reality is out there and it is the role of the researcher to discover these things and test for their existence. The researcher is thus positioned as separate from 'data' and the community under study. A problem with this approach is that the aspect of tourism being examined and tested is quite often conflated with the entirety of the case (VanWynsberghe and Khan, 2007). To illustrate, noting that networks have become a fashionable topic in the tourism literature, Costa et al. (2008) undertake a study exploring the benefits of networks and partnerhips characteristics in sport and adventure tourism companies in Portugal. In this example, the research problem is extracted from literature and defined independently of the community under study. The findings relate to one aspect of the community (i.e., the contribution of networks and partnerships to innovation) and support the view that small-and medium-sized enterprises contribute to innovation and economic development. However, and not diminishing the contributions of the study, the process of identifying the research problem and approach were undertaken within an academic context and whether or not the networks' contribution to innovation is important to the community is not relevant. There is also a tendency to generalize the characteristics of the networks with the community of sport and adventure tourism companies more generally.

In essence then, postpositivist approaches focus on understanding cause and effect, and there is an emphasis on establishing a high level of internal validity (i.e., the extent to which cause and effect can be confidently explained). The degree of emphasis on external validity (i.e., the extent to which the case study is generalizable across other cases) in the postpositivist approach is dependent on the purpose of the case study. For example, in research examining residents' attitudes towards cruise tourism in Canada's Arctic, Stewart et al. (2011) develop a resident attitude typology from the literature that is then tested in two communities. Local knowledge obtained from semi-structured interviews provided input into a grounded approach whereby results and theory were generated inductively and where data collection and analysis took place concurrently. This iterative process was useful in improving the study's internal validity, i.e., the extent to which the researchers were confident their results were representative of local community attitudes. External validity was addressed in part by comparing the results obtained in the two communities studied. It was also addressed through theoretical generalization (see Hyde, 2008) whereby the cases were compared with the findings of other cases reported in the literature. Whilst some similarities in community attitudes were noted, geographic factors influence the type, duration and regularity of encounters thus making generalizations across communities difficult.

The second approach that can be adopted in community case studies is a *critical theory approach*. It is not the purpose here to describe critical theory in detail, but to note that the underpinning tenet is that there is a history and social ordering that has led to contradictions in power, culture, race, ethnicity and gender. Transformation towards a better or more just world is the aim, although critical research is often chided for falling short of bringing about change and action (Bianchi, 2009). Critical theory approaches to case studies tend to define the unit of analysis as the phenomenon under study, although issues of power, influence and public interest are often central to such studies (VanWynsberghe and Khan, 2007). For example, Dredge (2010) shows how contrasting notions of public interest emerge and are given meaning by various stakeholders in an episode of community resistance over a proposed cruise ship terminal project. Here, the 'unit of analysis' is public interest. She illustrates how the state's historically embedded, top-down attitudes about public interest clash with locally driven bottom-up ideas of civil democratic society. Similarly, in another community case study, Dredge and Whitford (2011) examine how governance arrangements serve to (dis)empower different public spheres that emerge as a result of community resistance in the staging of a major event. So, whilst the unit of analysis can be diverse, these critical community case studies usually seek to highlight contradictions that lead to injustice, inequity and marginalization.

Researchers adopting a critical theory approach also strive for high levels of internal validity because the 'truthfulness' of the research process is important in any attempt to change the world. In tourism studies for example, this has been achieved through approaches that embed the researcher in the community, where barriers between the researched and the researcher dissolve and genuine community interaction is adopted. To illustrate, in a study by Matarrita-Cascante (2010) in Costa Rica 67 informants were interviewed and participant observation was undertaken to better understand tourism's impact on two communities' quality of life and well-being. Community interaction was the unit of analysis, with the research finding communication, participation, communion and tolerance were important factors in developing community-based tourism. External validity was relatively less important because the emphasis was not on generalizability across different communities but rather on the power of example. In this case study, Matarrita-Cascante (2010) illustrates the importance of interaction in purposive community-led tourism and additional case studies were recommended as a way of extending the external validity of these claims.

The third approach is the *interpretivist approach*. In this approach the focus of the community case study is to offer a story like rendering of a problem or issue through an in-depth description of everyday life and the real world. The interpretivist tradition acknowledges multiple entry points into any given reality and that social constructs can play a powerful role in tourism and travel. The unit of analysis is usually separated from the case through rich 'description and attempt to understand the conditions under which the concept, relationship, or event got the way it is' (VanWynsberghe and Khan, 2007, p. 90). For example, Tucker (2007) undertakes a study of women's increasing involvement in tourism work in Göreme in central Turkey. She explores the separation of gender in

Turkish village society and changing notions of power, control, honour and shame in an ethnographic study spanning 10 years. In doing so, she seeks to explore the entanglements that women are subject to in taking work outside the home, and in the process she highlights changing attitudes towards and impacts of tourism.

Explorations of different communities of travellers are well represented in the literature, also demonstrating this interpretivist approach (e.g., Jennings, 2005; Noy, 2004; Reis, 2011). Wilson and Little (2008) explore the characteristics of solo female travellers, focusing on how fear is perceived and experienced. Internal validity is not as important in this approach as the other two approaches because rich description and the power of example are emphasized, and the existence of multiple realities means that no two stories are the same. As a result, external validity (generalizability) is also not as important with the authors observing 'further research agendas which encompass such perspectives would broaden – and continue to problematize – our understanding of the complexities of women's "geography of fear"' (Wilson and Little, 2008, p. 183).

DATA COLLECTION AND ANALYSIS

A range of techniques can be employed in the data collection and analysis of community case studies. The choice of philosophical tradition is an important part of the research decision-making process and guides the type of data collection techniques employed. Data collection can include contextual data, primary data from the community itself and secondary data that is related to the community. A range of methods can be employed and may include historical archival analysis, grounded theory, ethnography, textual analysis, content analysis, media analysis and hermeneutics research to name a few. The 'how to' of these methods can be found in many standard texts on research methods (e.g., Jennings, 2010).

The nature of community case studies and the need for researchers to gain an in-depth knowledge of the phenomenon invariably means that the researcher becomes, to some extent, part of the case. In this sense, the choices made about processes of data collection and analysis are also dependent upon researchers' positionality, identity and belonging, since these aspects both open up or constrain opportunities for data gathering. Therefore, how data gathering is undertaken will differ depending on a range of factors including the:

- Characteristics of researchers' engagement with the community under study (e.g., number and diversity of participants, length of time spent in the community, etc.);
- Decisions about who defines the research problems and how they are defined (e.g., by the researcher, by the community, or in collaboration);
- Construction and application of data collection tools (e.g., surveys and interviews);
- Role and availability of secondary sources and archival materials to assist with crystallization;
- Power relationships between researchers and community case study participants;

- Power relationships between researchers and institutions that may influence the research and/or community (e.g., researchers' current and future institutional affiliations, direct and indirect clients of the research, etc.).

Ellis et al. (2011) offer a range of techniques for how the researcher can be reflexively embedded in the data gathering exercise and they draw attention to how these choices shape analysis. Reflexive techniques relevant to tourism community case study research include: narrative ethnography; reflexive didactic interviews; co-constructed narrative interviews; layered accounts using traditional data collection and analysis techniques with reflection and indigenous ethnography. A detailed exploration of these techniques is outside the scope of this chapter so, for further information on the 'how to' of these methods, see Ellis et al. (2011).

Adding a further challenge, discussions of triangulation and crystallization prompt researchers to consider more closely how data is analysed and findings are presented. Triangulation is much discussed in the literature as a strategy that combines multiple methods of data collection and analysis to improve internal validity, to produce more rigorous research outcomes and improve confidence in the findings (e.g., Bryman and Burgess, 1994; Oppermann, 2000). More recently, others argue that reaching a single point of understanding, metaphorically captured at the centre of a rigid two dimensional triangle, is not consistent with the postmodern social constructionist turn (Taylor and Trujillo, 2009). Rather, a crystal is a more appropriate metaphor from which multiple points of view are reflected and refracted:

> Crystallization combines multiple forms if analysis and multiple genres of representation into a coherent text or series of related texts, building a rich and openly partial account of a phenomenon that problematizes its own construction, highlights researchers' vulnerabilities and positionality, makes claims about socially constructed meanings, and reveals the indeterminacy of knowledge claims even as it makes them. (Ellingson, 2009, p. 4)

Yet despite the increasing discussion of crystallization in the broader methods literature, in the tourism literature the term is employed with little explanation, and its application remains locked within the researcher's 'black box'. Further examination of the concept and its application would be useful.

ADVANTAGES AND LIMITATIONS OF COMMUNITY CASE STUDIES IN TOURISM

Advantages of Community Case Study Research

A key value of community case studies lies in their capacity to contribute to human learning and the development of intellectual, social, cultural and political capital. Bourdieu (1977) and Dreyfus and Dreyfus (1986) explain that there is a developmental leap between rule-bound knowledge and the fluid and dynamic performance of knowledge demonstrated by experts. Reaching the world that world-making tourism professionals inhabit requires the development of, and fluency in, a range of knowledges that can be called upon dynamically to describe, explore, analyse, communicate and formulate actions. Flyvbjerg (2006, p. 222) argues that embedded case studies empower readers to develop the reflective and fluid knowledge of experts:

> Common to all experts . . . is that they operate on the basis of intimate knowledge of several thousand concrete cases in their areas of expertise. Context-dependent knowledge and expertise and knowledge are at the very heart of expert activity. Such knowledge and expertise also lie at the center of the case study as a research and teaching method . . . If people were exclusively trained in context-independent knowledge and rules . . . they would remain at the beginner's level in the learning process.

The development of expert knowledge that directly contributes to the 'world-making' potential of tourism is an important advantage of community case study research. Tourism has been described as 'world-making'[1] in the sense that it has a creative and transformative role in the making of people and places and in the production of meanings, values and understandings about the past, present and future (Hollinshead et al., 2009). Where well managed within an integrated and sustainable approach, tourism can give meaning to places and people, add value to cultural and environmental resources, and promote peace and understanding. It can increase cultural awareness and tolerance; address poverty, empower communities and contribute to improving economic and social well-being (e.g., Higgins-Desboilles, 2006, 2008; Sharpley, 2009; United Nations World Tourism Organization, 2010). Tourism community case studies can facilitate this world-making activity in a number of ways.

First, community case study research builds deeper understandings of the complex social world in which tourism takes place. Theerapappisit (2011) demonstrates this world-making capacity in a community case study examining the participation of ethnic communities in tourism planning in parts of the Mekong Region. The author examines stories told by local residents about the problems and benefits of participating in tourism, observing that 'these different ways of storytelling can bring about a much greater understanding of local contexts and traditional ways of life' (p. 220). The case study contributes to world-making by highlighting factors that inhibit and disempower ethnic minorities that have been marginalized within tourism development dialogues, and suggests that Buddhist ethics may serve as a developmental code of conduct to bring disparate groups together.

Second, tourism community case studies can contribute to world-making by interrogating the local implications of the grand narratives such as sustainable development, globalization, public management and participative democracy. In a seminal study in the late 1990s, Jamal and Getz (2000) describe the challenges of defining sustainable tourism in the context of community roundtables where individuals and agencies had very different ideas and understandings about the purpose of such an exercise. In the process the authors were also sensitized to the particular issues and interpretations held by local actors, highlighting that the global narrative of sustainable development is interpreted differently through the prism of one's own values and that addressing the challenge of collaboration is paramount in moving sustainability debates forward.

Powerful examples of how community case studies contribute to knowledge production are also found in studies of indigeneity and tourism. Scherrer and Doonan (2011) set out to integrate Aboriginal and western knowledge in a system to capture, translate and represent the intangible cultural impacts of tourism. The objective was to develop a 'holistic and ontologically appropriate evaluation toolkit' to assess cultural change (p. 275). However, it soon became clear that the domination of Western thought within the research process systematically marginalized Indigenous concepts and values, such as access to land, making it difficult to develop standards and indicators. Fundamental questions of power, control and the right and meaning of access to Indigenous lands were at stake which may not have been uncovered without the deeply engaged community case study approach that was adopted. The world-making contribution of this community case study was to highlight a fundamental disconnect between Indigenous values and institutionalized management approaches.

Third, community case studies can contribute to world-making by challenging hidden, and often unquestioned, assumptions; they can also prompt people and institutions to think and reflect on the broader conditions and social constructs that shape their engagement in and responses to tourism (Considine, 2005; Swan, 2008). Grybovych et al. (2011), for example, explore the how planners and policy makers helped to address sustainable tourism through actively engaging the community in a rezoning application in Ucluelet, British Columbia. One of the authors (Mazzoni) had strong connections with the community as a local resident and as the municipal planner. In the late 1990s, Ucluelet was a community with a stagnant economy, a decreasing tax base and at the mercy of 'fly-by-night and high risk developers' (p. 81). The chapter tells the story of the rezoning process of 800 acres of rainforest to permit a range of urban, recreation and tourism uses and details the struggle to manage community resistance, and to engage and negotiate acceptable outcomes. The long-term legacy and world-making contribution of this community case study was to develop a stronger consultation framework that embraced the multi-vocality of the community.

Fourth, community case studies can contribute to world-making by interrogating controversies and conundrums, inconsistencies and contradictions, i.e., local versus global; residents versus tourists; top-down versus bottom-up; and corporate versus community. Deeply engaged community case studies can contribute to the reframing of problems that can in turn generate alternative solutions. In this way, community case studies align with a movement that has become known as the Academy of Hope, which seeks to disrupt the dominating discourses of neoliberalism and globalization (Pritchard et al., 2011; Ren et al., 2010; Tribe, 2010). The Academy of Hope advocates for hopeful tourism inquiry, and positions research as a conduit to generate transformative models for human development. It strongly advocates humanist values including social justice, empowerment, equality and tolerance; it is value-driven, highly contextualized and change-oriented.

To illustrate, Richards et al. (2010) explore impediments experienced by travellers with a disability to participate in tourism. In this study the authors co-create knowledge about the tourist experience using accounts of both sighted and visually impaired tourists. In doing so they challenge an 'unsympathetic, unaccommodating sighted world' that, through their decision making, inhibits equity and enjoyment of the tourism experience. In this paper, the authors clearly identify they are engaging in world-making through advocacy scholarship and they seek to address these deeply embedded inequities.

Fifth, community case study research can also contribute to world-making by raising questions about the strengths and weaknesses of literature and by promoting engaged, critical reflection on theory. Pegas and Stronza (2010) employed an embedded ethnographic approach to investigate the use of ecotourism as a tool to protect sea turtles in the coastal community of Praia Do Forte, Brazil. They found that sea turtle harvesting that had put the conservation of the species at risk was the result of a complex interplay of social, economic and cultural factors. The use of ecotourism to generate employment and produce economic diversity had contributed to the community changing its attitudes towards sea turtles. However, incidents of illegal harvesting still occurred. In this research the universalizing discourse that positions ecotourism as contributing to environmental conservation was interrogated and a fuller understanding of social, economic, cultural, demographic influences of ecotourism relevant to this community were presented. The link between tourism, community development and environmental conservation was found to be not as simple as it is often portrayed in the literature.

LIMITATIONS OF CASE STUDIES

Case studies, as a form of empirical, context-dependent research, have received strong criticism over the years (Xiao and Smith, 2006). Community case studies, which are strongly value-driven and characterized by deep research-community entanglements, have been responsible for much of this criticism because they challenge long established research standards inspired by positivism and scientific rationality. As a result, community case studies have been criticized as being less scientific because they employ multiple methods; they can be quite organic in their approach to data collection and they rely of concepts such as triangulation and crystallization which cannot be explained independently of the researcher or outside the co-production of knowledge that takes place with the community.

Reis (2011) grapples with these potential limitations in a case study of hunters and trampers on Steward Island, New Zealand. Adopting a critical interpretivist perspective and reflexive and creative methodologies, Reis reflects that she could not separate herself from the 'fieldwork': 'there is no field out there to be "entered" and then "left"' (p. 16); nor was she able to isolate herself and her life experiences from the research in order to discover 'facts'. The evolution of her understanding was non-linear: 'my project changed dramatically, and negotiating that understanding with others became a major process in my research' (p. 16). In this example, Reis acknowledges these tensions but instead of framing them as limitations, they became liberating opportunities to explore alternate ways of understanding herself and the tramping community she identified with.

A second criticism is that case studies cannot be easily generalized and their findings applied to other cases. However, in a world where we recognize the multiple interests within communities and the multi-vocality of individuals themselves, external validity and reliability are less important and developing fuller understandings about how the world works at the community level is becoming more important (Xiao and Smith, 2006).

A third criticism of community case studies is that they are not useful in explaining cause and effect relationships and are therefore less useful in identifying solutions and actions (see Flyvbjerg, 2006). This criticism is again derived from a positivist worldview and does not take into account the complexity, multiplicity and constant change that characterizes tourism in a social world. It is simply not possible to isolate all variables and test the strength of relationships between them. Rather, the aim should be to provide plausible context-dependent explanations of phenomenon that in turn may be used to grow critical, creative thinking, deeper understandings of complex communities and contribute to Mode 2 knowledge production.

DeBerry-Spence (2010) illustrates this in an examination of the MASAZI Visitor and Welcome Centre, Ghana, a not-for-profit social venture, the aim of which is to support micro-businesses that preserve and promote Ghanaian arts and culture. Everything in this market space is negotiated and there exist complex dynamic relationships between administrators, vendors, customers and tour operators. In this case study the author explores the third space, a space where scholarship and practice blend 'in the making of both theory and practice' (p. 608). Working over time in the market, DeBerry-Spence observes that nothing is clear cut; processes of negotiation and acts of resistance abound and not everyone experiences these interactions in the same way. Binary positions of cause and consequence are not able to be isolated.

Fourth, case studies have also been criticized because they contain bias and tend to confirm researchers' preconceived ideas. This criticism is underpinned by an apparent expectation that researchers are objective, a myth we have previously acknowledged as misleading. All research, including that framed by scientific rationality, is subject to researcher and institutional entanglements that make it impossible to be objective. In the case studies discussed above, Reis (2011) and DeBerry-Spence (2010) celebrate these entanglements and argue that these research experiences have brought transcendental change in the way these researchers engage with and position themselves in the research. DeBerry-Spence argues that scholarship and advocacy do not have to be mutually exclusive and that awareness and change can happen from researchers actively engaging in embedded case studies of communities.

The above criticisms of case study research are derived from tensions between researchers that adhere to notions of objectivity and rationality and those that embrace value-laden postmodern, multicultural, transdisciplinary research. The former tend to be rule bound and seek 'truth' through research which interrogates cause and effect, while the latter seek a shift towards responsible, ethical, value-based social science research, to pursue knowledge that directly contributes to creating a more just and sustainable world (Pritchard et al., 2011). Xiao and Smith (2006) conclude that the perception of case studies as atheoretical, area-specific, one time and not following methodological procedures was unfair and not justified:

> . . . the majority of these instances [i.e. case studies] have followed scientific research procedures with sound analytic techniques. A substantial proportion of work relied on longitudinal and/ or triangulated observations for the published report. Some have come up with moderate to extensive discussions in the literature or theoretical contexts. (Xiao and Smith, 2006, p. 747)

FURTHER DEVELOPMENT OF THE COMMUNITY CASE STUDY APPROACH

In the development of this chapter it has become increasingly clear that, while case study research in tourism is relatively well developed, community case study research has not

Table 22.1   Factors to consider in tourism community case studies

Factor	Explanation
Definition of community	Dynamically defined dependent upon the context, the problem and the way the research unfolds *in situ* (i.e., the researcher will make decisions about the definition of the community in the field)
Researcher's position in relation to the community	Researcher has a relationship with the community; 'embeddedness' of the researcher is located on a continuum from casual to deeply connected
Approach	Includes postpositivist, constructivist and interpretivist approaches
Methods	Multiple methods including ethnography, interviews, participant observation, focus groups, archival research, grounded theory, media analysis, hermeneutics
Knowledge production	On a continuum from researcher generated knowledge to co-creating knowledge derived from reflexive engagement with communities
Reflexivity	On a continuum of political activism from phronetic (value neutral) to political activism depending upon values-based and change-making action of the researcher

received sufficient critical discussion. It is useful to make a distinction between case studies focused on objects such as policies or decisions, and case studies that focus on the social processes in communities that shape and give meaning to tourism. More importantly however, this distinction and further development of the community case study research method is warranted if researchers are to enhance the world-making capacity of tourism. By virtue of the entanglements that researchers develop before, during and after the community case study research process, there are opportunities for change and innovation to occur. Little attention has been placed on the role and ethical responsibilities of researchers in undertaking community case study research, which needs to be addressed in future work.

It has also become apparent that researchers seeking to undertake community case studies are motivated by a set of personal and professional values, are influenced by institutional factors, and are required to make a number of choices in framing their research (Thomas, 2010). Drawing from the discussion contained in this chapter, we identify in Table 22.1 those factors that need to be considered and justified by researchers in framing their community case studies in tourism.

The consideration of the factors in Table 22.1, and the choices and trade-offs required, are made through the prism of a researcher's ethical position, their work conditions, institutional values and other influences. While the idea of undertaking community case studies and acting virtuously for the good of society is certainly a position to strive for, it remains a difficult proposition in the current research environments of many western countries (Peck, 2001). Emphasis on performance indicators, such as publications and citations, rather than on the world-making contributions of research means that the value of community case study research needs to be vigorously and continuously argued. Furthermore, as the development of the ideas in this chapter took hold, it became increasingly evident that we were touching upon deep tensions in ontological politics and that, as researchers *and* practitioners, we were deeply entangled in these tensions. Our two perspectives are given below in the closing of this chapter.

REFLECTIONS

I (Dianne) remain convinced that a deep critical approach to studying tourism *in situ* reveals understandings and insights into globalization, neoliberalism, extra-local rule systems and new public management that are not revealed by adopting scientific methods. Through this approach I have becoming increasingly aware that the problems and gaps in tourism literature are not necessarily of interest nor are the findings directly or immediately useful to industry, policy makers and communities. Moreover the timelines required for deeply engaged community case study research sit uneasily against the needs of industry and government for quick results to specific predetermined (and usually narrow) questions. As a result the long-term benefits of community case studies, co-production of knowledge and reflexive action remain, to some extent, unproven benefits.

Specific case studies I have undertaken include community resistance to a proposed development of a cruise ship terminal and an international car rally, and the development and operation of local interest networks in a number of destinations in Australia. These embedded case studies have allowed me to develop both context specific expertise and theoretical understandings about a range of interconnected themes including intergovernmental relations, networks, participative democracy, knowledge production and public interest in tourism. However, my capacity to take or facilitate good actions based on reflection and communication is often limited by the temporal nature of the research task, which is often subject to ethical approval timelines, contractual obligations (if it is consulting-based research) and institutional demands for timely academic outputs.

There is also an uneasy tension in community case study research that seeks to locate itself at that end of the continuum that is embedded, reflexive and change-oriented, and the scientific rationality expected by many industry and government clients. Not only is the community case study research more organic and less able to be stage-managed by industry or government clients (one may argue that the community is the 'real' client), but the action and change orientation of community case study research does not provide industry and government decision makers with the opportunity to 'implement' recommendations and move through a 'rational' policy cycle.

Moving beyond these ontological tensions in the way consulting-based research is framed as a rational scientific exercise, and the organic process of a community case study approach, requires long-term commitment from researchers, their universities, government and other clients (Dredge and Hales, 2012). Embedded research takes time, long-term commitment and confidence in researchers, in the institutions they work for, in communities and government. Not surprisingly, the idea of a researcher-in-residence embedded within and working with communities seems a long way off.

When I (Rob) engage in community case studies in tourism, I face problems in deciding how to act as a 'researcher' and the meaning and consequences of those actions. As previously described in this chapter the positionality of the researcher can be placed on a continuum between value free to academic activist and, whilst there can be some guidance on the factors to consider in community case study research, 'what to do' is not laid down in a formula to guide research action in each context.

How to position myself in any case is inevitably determined by my actions within a case and quite often I am drawn to a particular side (or not) through considering the factors in Table 22.1; by considering who in the community I engage with, the approach that best suits the purpose of the research and for whom the knowledge is produced and for what effect. How I am 'drawn' can be best understood as follows.

Previously in this chapter the concept of virtue ethics (Jamal, 2004) was offered as a guide to a research life characterized by acting virtuously for the good of the community. It was noted that there was a lack of adoption of this ethical approach in community case study research. With the risk of oversimplification, this may be attributed to the inherent problems of 'what is good' and 'who is community' and 'how the researcher decides' such notions. A way I have overcome this problem was to use a normative guide similar to the moral philosophy of Kant's categorical imperative (Jamal and Menzel, 2009) as this allows personal decisions of the academic to be guided and justified by 'universal rights' such as international human rights or sustainability principles. In my experience such guides help with how to act virtuously in tourism community case studies.

For example, I was recently engaged in a consultancy which was to provide advice to government on the Indigenous consent to a potential World Heritage nomination. Because of the political issues in engagement with the community (i.e., key representative groups did not want to participate), this meant that the recommendations were partially completed. Additionally, after the consultancy was completed the research publication based on the project targeted this issue, among others, and used the United Nations Declaration on the Rights of Indigenous Peoples (United Nations, 2007) to justify the argument for improvements in community engagement. At the same time, I knew that the project was based on a government consultancy and had issues of confidentiality. In order to deal with issues of confidentiality the publication of the paper was delayed to respect the political processes that the consultancy had addressed. Thus, this type of research is very time consuming and does not sit easily under the 'publish or perish' paradigm in current university performance regimes.

In sum, we both agree that the positionality of the researcher can be envisaged along a continuum and that the choice of action by the researcher is a highly contextual and complex decision. We both agree that community case studies using progressive purposeful approaches have the potential for significant emancipatory impact on the community irrespective of the philosophical tradition and researcher reflexivity adopted in the community case study approach. However, community case study research is time consuming, physically exhausting and presents various challenges for project management and negotiating academic workload. Despite these challenges the potential for community learning is enormous and further reflection on the value of community case study research offers the possibility of undertaking research that can make a difference to people and communities.

NOTE

1. Tourism is not the only profession that can make a claim to 'world-making'. A range of other professions have 'world-making' potential, including nursing, medicine and engineering.

REFERENCES

Alvesson, M. and K. Sköldberg (2009), *Reflexive Methodology: New Vistas for Qualitative Research*, 2nd edition, London and Thousand Oaks, CA: Sage.

Arendt, H. (1958), *The Human Condition*, Chicago, IL: University of Chicago Press (reprinted 1998).

Becher, T. and P.R. Trowler (2001), *Academic Tribes and Territories: Intellectual Enquiry and the Culture of Disciplines*, Buckingham, UK and Philadelphia: Open University Press and The Society for Research into Higher Education.

Bianchi, R.V. (2009), 'The "critical turn" in tourism studies: a radical critique', *Tourism Geographies*, **11** (4), 484–504.

Bodorkós, B. and G. Pataki (2009), 'Linking academic and local knowledge: community-based research and service learning for sustainable rural development in Hungary', *Journal of Cleaner Production*, **17** (12), 1123–1131.

Bourdieu, P. (1977), *Outline of a Theory of Practice*, Cambridge: Cambridge University Press.

Bryman, A. and R.G. Burgess (1994), *Analysing Qualitative Data*, New York: Routledge.

Chiseri-Strater, E. (1996), 'Turning in upon ourselves: positionality, subjectivity and reflexivity in case study and ethnographic research', in P. Mortensen and G. Kirsch (eds), *Ethics and Representation in Qualitative Studies of Literacy*, Urbana, IL: National Council of Teachers of English, pp. 115–131.

Coles, T., C.M. Hall and D.T. Duval (2006), 'Tourism and post-discplinary enquiry', *Current Issues in Tourism*, **9** (4/5), 293–319.

Considine, M. (2005), *Making Public Policy*, Cambridge: Polity Press.

Costa, C., Z. Breda, R. Costa and J. Miguéns (2008), 'The benefits of networks for small and medium sized tourism enterprises', in N. Scott, R. Baggio and C. Cooper (eds), *Networks Analysis and Tourism: From Theory to Practice*, Clevedon, Bristol: Channel View Publications, pp. 96–130.

DeBerry-Spence, B. (2010), 'Making theory and practice in subsistence markets: an analytic autoethnography of MASAZI in Accra, Ghana', *Journal of Business Research*, **63** (6), 608–616.

Dredge, D. (2010), 'Place change and tourism development conflict: evaluating public interest', *Tourism Management*, **31** (1), 104–112.

Dredge, D. (2011), 'Phronetic Tourism Planning Research: reflections on critically engaged tourism planning research and practice', IV Critical Tourism Studies Conference: Tourism Futures: Creative and Critical Action, Cardiff: Welsh Centre for Tourism Research.

Dredge, D. and R. Hales (2012), 'Implications of the New Age of public management in higher education tourism research', paper presented at the Council of Australasian Tourism and Hospitality Educators Conference, Melbourne, 6–9 February.

Dredge, D. and M. Whitford (2011), 'Event tourism governance and the public sphere', *Journal of Sustainable Tourism*, **19** (4/5), 479–499.

Dredge, D., J. Jenkins and M. Whitford (2011), 'Stories of practice', in D. Dredge, J. Jenkins and M. Whitford (eds), *Stories of Practice: Tourism Planning and Policy*, Surrey, UK: Ashgate.

Dreyfus, H. and S. Dreyfus (1986), *Mind Over Machine: The Power of Human Intuition and Expertise in the Area of the Computer*, New York: Free Press.

Ellingson, L.L. (2009), *Engaging Crystallization in Qualitative Research: An Introduction*, Thousand Oaks, CA: Sage.

Ellis, C., T. Adams and A. Bochner (2011), 'Autoethnography: an overview', *Forum: Qualitative Social Research*, **12** (1), article 10.

Etchner, C. and T.B. Jamal (1997), 'The disciplinary dilemma of tourism studies', *Annals of Tourism Research*, **24**, 868–883.

Flyvbjerg, B. (2001), *Making Social Science Matter: Why Social Inquiry Fails and How it Can Succeed Again*, Cambridge: Cambridge University Press.

Flyvbjerg, B. (2004), 'Phronetic plannning research: theoretical and methodological reflections', *Planning Theory and Practice*, **5** (3), 283–306.

Flyvbjerg, B. (2006), 'Five misunderstandings about case study research', *Qualitative Inquiry*, **12** (2), 219–245.

Geertz, C. (1988), *Works and Lives: The Anthrolologist as Author*, Standford, CA: Standford University Press.

Gerring, J. (2007), *Case Study Research: Principles and Practices*, Cambridge: Cambridge University Press.

Grybovych, O., D. Hafermann and F. Mazzoni (2011), 'Tourism planning, community engagement and policy innovation in Ucluelet, British Columbia', in D. Dredge and J. Jenkins (eds) *Stories of Practice: Tourism Policy and Planning*, Farnham & Burlington: Ashgate, pp. 79–104.

Higgins-Desboilles, F. (2006), 'More than an "industry": the forgotten power of tourism as a social force', *Tourism Management*, **27**, 1192–1208.

Higgins-Desboilles, F. (2008), 'Justice tourism and alternative globalisation', *Journal of Sustainable Tourism*, **16** (3), 345–364.

Higgins-Desboilles, F. (2010), 'In the eye of the beholder? Tourism and the activist academic', in P.M. Burns, C.A. Palmer and J.M. Lester (eds), *Tourism and Visual Culture Volume 1: Theories and Concepts*, Wallingford: CABI, pp. 98–106.

Hollinshead, K. and T. Jamal (2007), 'Tourism and "the third ear": further propsects for qualtitative inquiry', *Tourism Analysis*, **12**, 85–129.

Hollinshead, K., I. Ateljevic and N. Ali (2009), 'Worldmaking agency: worldmaking authority. The sovereign constitutive role of tourism. *Tourism Geographies*, **11** (4), 427–443.

Hyde, K. (2008), 'Independent traveler decision-making', in A. Woodside (ed.), *Advances in Culture, Tourism and Hospitality Research, Volume 2*, Bingley, UK: Emerald, pp. 43–152.

Jamal, T. (2004), 'Virtue ethics and sustainable tourism pedagogy: phronesis, principles and practice', *Journal of Sustainable Tourism*, **12** (6), 530–545.

Jamal, T. and D. Getz (2000), 'Community roundtables for tourism related conflicts: the dialectics of consensus and process structures', in B. Bramwell and B. Lane (eds), *Tourism Collaboration and Parternships: Politics, Practice and Sustainability*, Clevedon, UK: Channel View Press, pp. 159–182S.

Jamal, T. and K. Hollinshead (2001), 'Tourism and the forbidden zone: the underserved power of qualitative inquiry', *Tourism Management*, **22**, 66–82.

Jamal, T. and C. Menzel (2009), 'Good actions in tourism', in J. Tribe (ed.), *Philosophical Issues in Tourism*, Bristol, UK: Channel View Publications, pp. 227–243.

Jennings, G. (2005), 'Caught in the irons: one of the lived experiences of long-term ocean cruising women', *Tourism Review International*, **9** (2), 177–193.

Jennings, G. (2010), *Tourism Research*, Brisbane, Australia: John Wiley & Sons.

Law, J. (2004), *After Method: Mess in Social Science Research*, Abingdon, UK: Routledge.

Lyotard, J.F. (1979), *The Postmodern Condition: A Report on Knowledge*, Minneapolis, MN: University of Minnesota.

Maguire, S. (1997), 'Business ethics: a compromise between politics and virtue', *Journal of Business Ethics*, **16** (12/13), 1411–1418.

Matarrita-Cascante, D. (2010), 'Beyond growth: reaching tourism-led development', *Annals of Tourism Research*, **37** (4), 1141–1163.

Maxey, I. (1999), 'Beyond boundaries: activism, academic, reflexivity and research', *Area*, **31** (3), 199–208.

May, T. and B. Perry (2011), *Social Research and Reflexivity: Content, Consequence and Context*, Thousand Oaks, CA: Sage.

Mills, A., G. Durepos and E. Wiebe (2010), *Encyclopedia of Case Study Research Volume 2*, Thousand Oaks, CA: Sage.

Nowotny, H. (2003), 'The potential of transdisciplinarity', *Interdiscipline*, available at http://www.helga-nowotny.eu/downloads/helga_nowotny_b59.pdf.

Noy, C. (2004), 'Performing identity: touristic narratives of self-change', *Text and Performance Quarterly*, **24** (2), 115–138.

Oppermann, M. (2000), 'Triangulation: a methodological discussion', *International Journal of Tourism Research*, **2**, 141–146.

Peck, J. (2001), 'Neoliberalizing states: thin policies/hard outcomes', *Progress in Human Geography*, **25** (3), 445–455.

Pegas, F. and A. Stronza (2010), 'Ecotourism and sea turtle harvesting in a fishing village of Bahia, Brazil', *Conservation and Society*, **8** (1), 15.

Pritchard, A., N. Morgan and I. Ateljevic (2011), 'Hopeful tourism: a new transformative perspective', *Annals of Tourism Research*, **38** (3), 941–963.

Prus, R. (1997), *Subcultural Mosaics and Intersubjective Realities: An Ethnographic Research Agenda for Pragmatising the Social Sciences*, Albany, NY: State University of New York University Press.

Ragin, C. (1993), 'Introduction to qualitative comparative analysis', in T. Janoski and A. Hicks (eds), *The Comparative Political Economy of the Welfare State*, New York: Cambridge University Press, pp. 299–319.

Reis, A. (2011), 'Bringing my creative self to the fore: accounts of a reflexive research endeavour', *Creative Approaches to Research*, **1** (1), 2–18.

Ren, C., A. Pritchard and N. Morgan (2010), 'Constructing tourism research: a critical inquiry', *Annals of Tourism Research*, **37** (4), 885–904.

Richards, V., A. Pritchard and N. Morgan (2010), '(Re)Envisioning tourism and visual impairment', *Annals of Tourism Research*, **37** (4), 1097–1116.

Sandercock, L. (2003), 'Out of the closet: the importance of stories and storytelling in planning practice', *Planning Theory and Practice*, **4** (1), 11–28.

Scherrer, P. and K. Doonan (2011), 'Capturing intangible culural impacts of tourism on Aboriginal land in Australia's Kimberley Region', *Tourism Recreation Research*, **36** (3), 271–280.

Schon, D. (1983), *The Reflective Practitioner*, New York: Basic Books.

Segerstrale, U. (2000), *Beyond the Science Wars: The Missing Discourse about Science and Society*, New York: State University of New York Press.

Seidman, S. and J.A. Alexander (2001), *The New Social Theory Reader*, New York and London: Routledge.

Sharpley, R. (2009), *Tourism Development and the Environment: Beyond Sustainability*, London: Earthscan.

Stewart, E.J., J. Dawson and D. Draper (2011), 'Cruise tourism and residents in Arctic Canada: development of a resident attitude typology', *Journal of Hospitality and Tourism Management*, **18** (1), 95–106.

Swan, E. (2008), 'Let's not get too personal: critical reflection, reflexivity and the confessional turn', *Journal of European Industrial Training*, **32** (5), 385–399.

Swanborn, J. (2010), *Case Study Research: What, Why and How?* Thousand Oaks, CA: Sage.

Taylor, B.C. and N. Trujillo (2009), 'Qualitative methods', in F.M. Jablin & L.L. Putnam (eds.), *The New Handbook of Organizational Communication: Advances in Theory, Research and Methods*, Thousand Oaks, CA: Sage, pp. 161–193.

Theerapappisit, P. (2011), 'The Mekong tourism dilemma: converging forces, contesting values', *Stories of Practice: Tourism Planning and Policy*, Surrey, UK: Ashgate, pp. 199–226.

Thomas, R. (2010), 'Academics as policy-makers: (not) researching tourism and events policy formation from the inside', *Current Issues in Tourism*, **14** (6), 493–506.

Tribe, J. (2002), 'The philosophic practitioner', *Annals of Tourism Research*, **29** (2), 228–257.

Tribe, J. (2004), 'Knowing about tourism: epistemological issues', in J. Phillimore and L. Goodson (eds), *Qualitative Research in Tourism: Ontologies, Epistemologies and Methodologies*, London and New York: Routledge, pp. 46–62.

Tribe, J. (2010), 'Tribes, territories and networks in the tourism academy', *Annals of Tourism Research*, **37** (1), 7–33.

Trowler, P.R. (1988), *Academics Responding to Change: New Higher Education Frameworks and Academic Cultures*, Buckingham, UK: The Society for Research into Higher Education & Open University Press.

Tucker, H. (2007), 'Undoing shame: tourism and women's work in Turkey', *Journal of Tourism & Cultural Change*, **5** (2), 87–105.

United Nations (2007), *The UN Declaration on the Rights of Indigenous Peoples*, New York: United Nations, available at www.un.org/esa/socdev/unpfii/en/drip.html.

United Nations World Tourism Organization (2010), *Tourism and the Millennium Development Goals*, Madrid: World Tourism Organization, available at http://www.unwto.org/tourism&mdgsezine/.

VanWynsberghe, R. and S. Khan (2007), 'Redefining case study', *International Journal of Qualitative Methods*, **6** (2), Article 6, available at http://www.ualberta.ca/~iiqm/backissues/6_2/vanwynsberghe.htm.

Wilson, E. and D.E. Little (2008), 'The solo female travel experience: exploring the "geography of women's fear"', *Current Issues in Tourism*, **11** (2), 167–186.

Xiao, H. and S.L.J. Smith (2006), 'Case studies in tourism research: a state-of-the-art analysis', *Tourism Management*, **27** (5), 738–749.

Yin, R. (2009), *Case Study Research: Design and Methods*, 4th edition, Thousand Oaks, CA: Sage Publications.

Yin, R.K. (2011), *Applications of Case Study Research*, Thousand Oaks, CA: Sage.

PART III

MIXED METHODS

In Chapter 23, Svetlana Stepchenkova discusses **Content analysis**, a research tool focused on the actual content and internal features of media. Content analysis is used to determine the presence of certain words, concepts, themes, phrases, characters, or sentences within texts or sets of texts and to quantify this presence in an objective manner. Researchers quantify and analyse the presence, meanings and relationships of such words and concepts, then make inferences about the messages within the texts, the writer(s), the audience, and even the culture and time of which these are a part.

Although initially limited to studies that examined texts for the frequency of the occurrence of identified terms (word counts), by the mid-1950s researchers were already starting to consider the need for more sophisticated methods of analysis, focusing on concepts rather than simply words, and on semantic relationships rather than just presence (de Sola Pool 1959). While both traditions still continue today, content analysis now is also utilized to explore mental models, and their linguistic, affective, cognitive, social, cultural and historical significance. Due to the fact that it can be applied to examine *any* piece of writing or occurrence of recorded communication, content analysis is currently used in a large range of fields, ranging from marketing and media studies, to literature and rhetoric, ethnography and cultural studies, gender and age issues, sociology and political science, psychology and cognitive science, and many other fields of inquiry. Additionally, content analysis reflects a close relationship with socio- and psycholinguistics, and is playing an integral role in the development of artificial intelligence. Uses include identifying international differences in communication content, detecting the existence of propaganda, Identifying the intentions, focus or communication trends of an individual, group or institution, describing attitudinal and behavioural responses to communications; and revealing psychological or emotional state of persons or groups.

In Chapter 24, Ulrike Gretzel and Heather Kennedy-Eden discuss **Meta-analyses**. The main benefits of meta-analyses are the more objective appraisal of evidence than in narrative reviews, the greater transparency which makes meta-analyses replicable, the potential to resolve uncertainty and disagreement in existing research, the ability to analyse the effects of research designs/study conceptualizations, as well as the opportunity to generate important research questions for future research.

Quantitative meta-analysis is a methodology that involves the statistical integration of research findings from separate studies It is a form of systematic review that uses statistical techniques to derive quantitative estimates of the magnitude of statistical effects and their associated precision. For quantitative meta-analysis to work, the findings in the individual studies need to be conceptually comparable (i.e., they must deal with the same constructs) and configured in similar statistical form. The advantages of quantitative meta-analysis in comparison to narrative reviews lies in the explicit structure imposed on the summary of research findings, the ability to code both magnitude and direction of effects, the opportunity to relate study characteristics to effect sizes, and the ability to synthesize a large number of studies resulting in estimates with greater statistical power.

Qualitative meta-analysis follows the same basic principles established for quantitative meta-analysis in terms of comprehensiveness and systematic approaches but applies qualitative research methods to the analysis of the studies included in the research synthesis exercise. Consequently, it is interpretive rather than aggregative. Qualitative meta-analysis does not aim at hypothesis testing. Rather, its main contributions lie in building of more abstract theories (meta-theory), theory explication and development of new theory. It requires assessing the qualitative research methodology as well as the influence of paradigmatic parameters and theoretical assumptions that guided the researchers. At the same time, it also needs to critically reflect on these issues in terms of how they affected the meta-analysis itself. Challenges faced by qualitative meta-analysis involve the loss of contextual information that is seen as essential to qualitative interpretation, which might lead to more descriptive rather than interpretive approaches implemented in the meta-analysis.

The authors note that the growing maturity of tourism as a field has spurred some meta-analyses. The technique has been successfully applied to a variety of research themes in tourism for which significant bodies of research exist and for which a synthesis and/or critical evaluation of approaches was necessary to achieve theoretical or methodological advancement. Quantitative meta-analyses have addressed income multipliers, tourism demand, service quality, service recovery paradox, tourism advertising and website evaluation. Examples of qualitative meta-analyses that aim specifically at theory explication and theory building include analysis of the different theoretical models used to explain travel decision-making processes, the ways in which the problem of peak oil has been conceptualized in tourism research as well as the literature on tourism and the environment.

The robustness of properly derived meta-analysis results makes them especially suitable for informing policy decisions and establishing practical guidelines. Like any kind of research, meta-analysis depends on the quality of the data and the rigor applied in the coding and analysis stages, and a thorough understanding of the statistical assumptions made.

In Chapter 25, Ehsan Ahmed discusses **Network analysis**. A *social network* is a social structure made up of individuals (or organizations) called 'nodes', which are tied (connected) by one or more specific types of interdependency, such as friendship, kinship, common interest, financial exchange, dislike, sexual relationships, or relationships of beliefs, knowledge or prestige. Nodes are the individual actors within the networks, and ties are the relationships between the actors. In its simplest form, a social network is a map of specified ties between the nodes being studied. The notion of connectedness or dependency therefore implies existence of an aggregated structure of relationships that extends beyond the conventional view of relationships between two objects in isolation. Studies on networks aim to capture these aggregated views of relationships and offer analytical insights to understand the role of relationships on the objects embedded within these relationships. Network analysis can generally be thought of as coming from two different but complementary perspectives: the view from the individual element embedded in a set of relationships (actor level) and the view from an aggregated form of analysis (network level).

The origins of network theory and practice may be found in research conducted in the late 1950s and 1960s on social behaviour and exchange, the social psychology of groups, exchange and power, operational research in local government and inter-organizational and exchange analysis.

The tourism industry may be regarded as an amalgamation of a wide range of suppliers clustering together to provide experiences of value to the tourist. By using the concepts of network and corresponding analytical tools, a network analyst can conceptualize, visualize and analyse these linkages and relationships between several tourism elements. A tourism network can be understood as a set of formal and informal (social) relationships that shape collaborative actions between government, the tourism industry and the general public. Tourism networks are often loosely articulated groups of independent suppliers linked to deliver an overall tourism experience. The multifaceted connections of the tourism firm with its suppliers, customers, surrounding community, and/or environment can be of various levels (e.g., local, regional, global), forms (e.g., informal, formal) and interest (e.g., economic, philanthropic). A tourism firm has connections not only with its suppliers and customers but also with its surrounding community and extended environment.

Ahmed distinguishes four different types of network research to provide the context for his discussion of its application to tourism. These are: the impact of actor(s) on other actor(s), the impact of individual actors on a network, the impact of a network on individual actors, and whole network or network-level interaction. The more that is known about the relationships between the various stakeholders in the tourism industry – collaboration, alliance, partnership, business clusters and similar other concepts – the better will be our understanding of the required strategies to maintain competitive advantage at the various levels from the firm to the destination.

REFERENCE

Pool, I de S. (1959), *Trends in Content Analysis*, Oxford: Illinois Press.

23 Content analysis
Svetlana Stepchenkova

NATURE OF CONTENT ANALYSIS AND ITS EVOLUTION

Content analysis was famously defined by Harold Lasswell as the technique that "aims at describing, with optimum objectivity, precision, and generality, what is said on a given subject in a given place at a given time" (Lasswell et al., 1952, p. 34). More recently, Weber (1990, p. 9) defined content analysis as "a research method that uses a set of procedures to make valid inferences from text." While these definitions emphasize textual materials as objects of content analysis, other scholars consider the method applicable to a broader range of content. According to Cartwright (1953, p. 424), the term refers "to the objective, systematic, and quantitative description of any symbolic behavior." In a similar definition Berelson (1952, p. 18) states that "content analysis is a research technique for the objective, systematic, and quantitative description of the manifest content of communication." Shapiro and Markoff (1997, p. 14) comparatively analysed various definitions of the term along several dimensions and suggested their own "minimal definition": content analysis is "any methodological measurement applied to text (or other symbolic material) for social science purposes." Content analysis examines data for patterns and structures, singles out the key features, develops categories, and aggregates them into perceptible constructs in order to seize meaning of communications (Gray and Densten, 1998); thus, the process involves the systematic reduction of the content flow, whether textual or otherwise symbolic. Content analysis is capable of capturing a richer sense of concepts within the data due to its qualitative basis and, at the same time, can be subjected to quantitative data analysis techniques (Insch and Moore, 1997).

Arguably, the first content analysis study was conducted in the eighteenth century in Sweden. It compared a popular set of 90 religious hymns of unknown authorship (*The Songs of Zion*) with an orthodox set from established songbooks by counting occurrences of selected religious symbols. No difference between the two sets of hymns was found, and the claim that *The Songs of Zion* were "contagious" was dismissed (Krippendorff, 2004). At the beginning of the twentieth century, with the growth in newspapers circulation numbers, the technique termed "quantitative newspaper analysis" emerged. Early studies employed mostly subject-matter categories such as domestic affairs, politics, crime, and sports to classify news content; for example, Mathews (1910) was concerned with the question of whether newspapers were devoted to coverage of religious, scientific, and literary affairs of the day, i.e., "real" news, or had shifted their attention in favor of sports, gossip, and scandals. The interest in studying public opinion, spurred by various social and political problems of the Great Depression era, the emergence of radio as a new communication channel, and increasing public acceptance of methodological advancements from social and behavioral sciences, led to formulation of the theoretical and methodological foundations of the content analysis technique in the 1930–1940s (Krippendorff, 2004). The topics of inquiry in those days ranged from presentation of

African Americans in news media (Simpson, 1934) to comparative analysis of US and US former enemies' history textbooks (Walworth, 1938) to studies of nationalism in children's books (Martin, 1936) to investigation of values expressed in Boy Scouts and Hitler Youth literature (Lewin, 1947).

Between the 1930s and 1950s, content analysis was propelled by the work of Harold Lasswell and his associates through studies of mass communication and, especially, one of its aspects – propaganda. During World War II, the US government organized groups of researchers charged with the responsibilities to content analyse enemy newspapers, radio broadcasts, leaders' speeches, propaganda films, etc. The Lasswell group adopted a view of reality as a symbolic environment of words, images, and their meanings, which surrounds human beings from their early existence. These symbols, though frozen at any given moment, exhibit changes if studied over longer periods of time. These changes are indicative of changes in reality: predominant ideologies in society, preoccupation with certain issues, and other political and social matters (Lasswell et al., 1952). During this period, the group contributed to development of content analysis methodology by addressing the issues of sampling, reliability and validity of content categories, as well as measurement problems (Krippendorff, 2004).

From the early to mid-twentieth century, the number of content analysis studies progressed very quickly. During the first two decades the average annual number of content analysis studies was 2.5, in the 1920s, 1930s, and 1940s increasing to 13.3, 22.8, and 43.3, respectively (Holsti, 1969, p. 20). During the 1950s, the average annual number almost reached 100. Survey of 1719 titles published between 1900–58 revealed that four out of five papers reported empirical studies while only 14.2 percent of all titles were concerned with methodological issues (Barcus, 1959). By discipline, sociology–anthropology, general communication, and political science accounted for 27.7 percent, 25.9 percent, and 21.5 percent of all titles, respectively. The most popular areas of inquiry were "the studies of social values, propaganda analyses, journalistic studies, media inventories, and psychological–psychoanalytic research"; collectively they accounted for 60 percent of all empirical content analysis studies (Holsti, 1969, p. 21). In 1955, the Allerton House conference at the University of Illinois was called to discuss the state of the method, share the developments across various fields of social science, and, at the same time, stipulate and address the methodological problems of the day. The scholarly legacy of the conference is the volume *Trends in Content Analysis* (Pool, 1959).

Another significant multidisciplinary gathering occurred at the University of Pennsylvania in 1967, and is known as the Annenberg conference. Within a decade after the Allerton House, research in linguistics and cognitive processes produced new theories relevant to content analysis. Furthermore, Stone and his colleagues (Stone et al., 1966) created The General Inquirer, the first language processing software which operated on mainframe IBM computers that supported the PL/1 programming language. The computer-based techniques allowed for the first time processing of huge amounts of complex data, routinization of time-consuming operations, as well as transformation of the data using programing languages. The aforementioned advances in theory and technology required rigorous explication of some previously intuitive techniques and procedures (Gerbner et al., 1969). The resulting volume, *The Analysis of Communication Content* (Gerbner et al., 1969) was mostly concerned with text analysis; however, two notable exceptions dealt with analysis of music (Brook, 1969) and visual records (Ekman et al., 1969).

The period of 1970–95 has been characterized as the routinization of the technique (Stone, 1997). Content analysis projects, which previously were contained in academic spheres, extended to the business environment where private companies made content analysis their specialization (e.g., the Gallop Organization). However, it was felt that by the late 1990s, the number of studies employing content analysis had changed from a flood (following the Annenberg conference) to a trickle (Shapiro, 1997). Computers were still expensive and not user-friendly. Some scholars continued with manual approaches, feeling that perfect reliability obtained in computer-assisted analyses often came at the expense of validity. During this time, social sciences shifted away from grand theories towards more practical, grounded approaches (Stone, 1997). However, emergence of Web 2.0 applications in the early 2000s brought new steam to the field, as technical capabilities, theoretical foundations, empirical knowledge, and practical need converged. A whole new research area of online behavior opened up, not only generating interest from social scientists but making content analysis relevant to a multitude of businesses all wanting to harness the power of social networks and user-generated content.

BACKGROUND AND TYPES OF PROBLEMS THAT CONTENT ANALYSIS IS DESIGNED TO HANDLE

In a number of situations, content analysis is a suitable research method. The technique should be considered when the analyst cannot obtain the data directly from human subjects – due to time, space, or financial constraints – and is limited to the documentary evidence only. Establishing authorship of unsigned works (Miles and Selvin, 1966) is an example of such analysis. Content analysis can also be used on free-elicitation survey responses for enrichment and triangulation purposes, in parallel with other techniques (Echtner and Ritchie, 1993). The technique is preferable in situations – most notably in psychology and psychiatry – when the subject's own language, with all its complexities and nuances, is crucial to the investigation (Mahl, 1959). Finally, the technique is helpful in studies of general media, movies, literature, and online forms of communication, where due to massive volumes all relevant data can rarely be examined by the researcher. With the proper methodological steps taken to ensure representativeness and suitability of the sample for the analysis, findings obtained from the sample can be inferred to the larger universe of the textual materials (Holsti, 1969).

There are two general classes of epistemologies employed for content analysis in social sciences: qualitative and quantitative. The former term refers to non-statistical and exploratory methods, which involve inductive reasoning, while the latter term refers to methods that are capable of providing statistical inferences from text populations (Berg, 1995). A central idea of quantitative content analysis is that "many words of text can be classified into much fewer content categories" (Weber, 1990, p. 7). George (1959) and later Shoemaker and Reese (1996, p. 32) argued that the process of reducing large volumes of text to quantitative data "does not provide a complete picture of meaning and contextual codes, since texts may contain many other forms of emphasis besides sheer repetition." Newbold et al. (2002, p. 80) agreed that "there is no simple relationship between media texts and their impact, and it would be too simplistic to base decisions in this regard on mere figures obtained from a statistical content analysis." Quantitative content analysis does not always account for source credibility, political or social context of messages being examined, and audience characteristics (Macnamara, 2003). However, despite its limitations, quantitative content analysis has long been employed in social studies due to its clear methodological reasoning based on the assumption that the most frequent theme in the text is the most important, as well as the ability to incorporate such scientific methods as "a priori design, reliability, validity, generalizability, replicability, and hypothesis testing" (Neuendorf, 2002, p. 10).

From a philosophical perspective, the quantitative tradition is based on the positivist premise that "there is something like an objective reality (social facts) 'out there' that can be observed, measured, analyzed and thus understood" (Newbold et al., 2002, p. 59); thus, decontextualization of the textual material and selection of the outsider variables for analysis of social phenomena are the main issues in quantitative paradigm. In contrast, the qualitative epistemologies share the view that reality is a social and cultural creation, which can only be interpreted, approximated but not fully apprehended; thus in qualitative tradition the focus is on complexity, context, and detail (Denzin and Lincoln, 1994). Qualitative tradition heavily relies on researcher's reading of content and includes such approaches as rhetorical, narrative, semiotic, and discourse analyses to textual data that cannot easily be summarized (Neuendorf, 2002).

Because it must consider multiple interpretational perspectives, the qualitative approach is time consuming and rarely involves large samples. It has been also pointed out that in qualitative data analysis causality cannot be established without high levels of subjectivity (Mehmetoglu and Dann, 2003), and qualitative studies have also been criticized as "impossible to do with scientific reliability" (Macnamara, 2003, p. 6). The complete separation of the two traditions, however, is not always possible, given the diversity of approaches and wide range of content analysis applications. Modern media scholars tend to view qualitative and quantitative content analysis as complementary and parts of a continuum of methods that can be applied to capture meaning and impacts of texts (Curran, 2002; Newbold et al., 2002).

Two dimensions of quantitative content analysis, interpretational and structural, became a basis for a 2×3 taxonomy suggested by Roberts (2000). On the structural dimension of Robert's taxonomy there are thematic, semantic, and network text analyses. The thematic approach is rooted in contingency analysis and involves counting themes belonging to a certain theoretical construct within the text blocks. In the semantic text analysis, textual data are broken into semantic units, for example, subject–action–object triplets. Every semantic unit is associated with a certain numerical sequence, which reflects the a priori established codes of themes (Franzosi, 1997). Lastly, in the network analysis text blocks are represented as networks of interrelated themes, and theme linkages are measured by specially generated variables (Kleinnijenhuis et al., 1997). The interpretational dimension reflects the perspective from which the data is interpreted, i.e., that of the speaker's or the researcher's. Perspective is considered representational if texts are used to identify the speaker's intended meaning. If the researcher's perspective is dominant, texts are interpreted in terms of researcher's theory and the analysis becomes instrumental. However, Roberts (2000) acknowledged that in many instances text analysis involves both perspectives. It is representational when words for thematic categories are coded based on their face value, yet the researcher might use the data on these themes to interpret the text instrumentally. Any quantitative text analysis produces a numerical matrix suitable for further statistical analysis. What is considered a classic, textbook content analysis is an instrumental–thematic method applied to the textual material; the following is a brief description of the method.

Textual Population and Sampling

A major research consideration in content analysis is defining a population of textual materials suitable to answer a particular research question. Textual population is usually a set of messages or documents, e.g., all newspaper editorials for a given year or all online hotel reviews for a particular period of time. It may, however, be a population of people who in the process of the study produce messages that are to be analysed. Sampling procedure "may involve as many as three steps: selecting sources of communication, sampling documents, and sampling within documents" (Holsti, 1969, p. 130). When all sources in the population or all sampling units are considered equally informative, non-probability samples should be avoided whenever possible (Neuendorf, 2002). When sources are unequally informative or differ in influence, circulation, or format, content analysts' concern is that "the selected texts are relevant to the research question and help to answer it fairly. Texts must be sampled in view of what they mean, the interpretation they enable, and the information they contain" (Krippendorff, 2004, p. 113).

Relevance, or purposive, sampling often focuses on "prestige" press because it is felt to represent most adequately the views of political elites, and, therefore, is considered "more influential" than local papers (Lacy et al., 1991). Danielson and Lasorsa (1997) used only two papers – *New York Times* and *Los Angeles Times* – in their study of political and social changes in American society. Some studies selected sources on the basis of the largest circulation: for example, Kayser (1953) made a comparative study of major daily newspapers of 15 countries for a 7-day period. For sampling within the sources, sampling guidelines are available from experimental studies: e.g., Mintz (1949) compared four methods of sampling newspaper headlines in *Pravda* for the entire month. The results revealed that every-fifth-day samples and odd-day samples did not differ significantly from the figures for the entire month, but weekly samples were inferior. Research by Riffe and associates (e.g., Riffe et al., 1993; Riffe et al., 1996a; Riffe et al., 1996b) provide the most comprehensive guidelines with regard to optimal sampling procedure and sample size for news media.

Units of Content

Most researchers recognize three main unit types in content analysis: sampling units, recording units, and context units (Neuendorf, 2002). Sampling units – e.g., newspaper articles, books, or websites – provide a basis for identifying textual population and selecting a sample for content analysis. The size of the sampling unit should be adequate to represent the phenomenon under investigation.

To obtain a numerical matrix for statistical analysis, the researcher must designate the textual unit for coding called the recording unit; this is one of the most fundamental decisions in the content analysis project (Weber, 1990). Holsti (1969, p. 116) defines recording unit as "the specific segment of content that is characterized by placing it in a given category." In some cases, recording units can coincide with the sampling units (e.g., Stepchenkova and Eales, 2011) but never exceed them. The smallest recording units are words or symbols; they were used, for example, in studies on readability (Flesch, 1948) and authorship detection (Miles and Selvin, 1966). Theme, which is understood as a single assertion about some subject matter, was widely used in research on propaganda (Holsti, 1969), values (Namenwirth, 1973), and attitudes (Osgood et al., 1957). Coding themes "by hand" is time consuming: the coder often needs to reduce the sentence into its component themes, i.e., recording units, before these recording units can be placed into established categories. This process is a source of error and can seriously reduce reliability in content analysis. Sentences, paragraphs, and entire documents are usually difficult to classify into a single category, which is a main reason why these recording units are rarely utilized.

Often, the meaning of a recording unit is seen more clearly from a surrounding context; therefore, a context unit has to be identified as well. For example, a researcher may be required when he meets a word "democracy" to search an entire sentence or a paragraph in order to find out what attitude toward democracy is exhibited by the source of content (Geller et al., 1942). In addition, a reporting unit is the element for which findings are reported (Neuendorf, 2002). In most social science investigations, the individual person is both the unit of data collection and the reporting unit. In content analysis research, however, units of data collection and reporting can differ: while sampling unit can be an article or a story, the reporting unit can be a month, a quarter, or a year.

Categories

In the often-quoted words of Berelson (1952, p. 147), "[c]ontent analysis stands or falls by its categories. Particular studies have been productive to the extent that the categories were clearly formulated and well adapted to the problem and to the content." There are common principles that researchers should follow while developing categories: they should be exhaustive (i.e., there should be a category for every relevant item in the text), mutually exclusive (i.e., no recording unit should be placed in more than a single category), and independent (i.e., assignment of any recording unit into a single category does not affect classification of other data units) (Holsti, 1969, p. 95). Weber (1990) particularly stresses the requirement of mutual exclusiveness and the statistical consequences of its disregard. The number of categories and the complexity of the coding scheme vary significantly among the studies, depending mostly on the level of detail that the analyst aims to provide. The classification system involves painstaking description and detailing of developed categories, as well as explication of coding rules for assigning numerical values to recording units.

There are two main traditions in the quantitative content analysis research: substitution model and correlational model. In the substitution tradition, text is analysed with a priori established categories, which are understood as "a group of words with similar meaning and/or connotations" (Weber, 1983, p. 140). For example, words "ice", "frost", "snowflakes", and "winter" all represent the same idea of cold, thus, can be united under one category, that of "cold". Various categories are organized into dictionaries used for making necessary substitutions in the text and obtaining category frequency counts.

When frequencies are organized in a matrix, correlations between categories can be calculated. In contrast, the correlational model discerns categories from the text itself. In this tradition categories are "groups of words with different meaning or connotations that taken together refer to some theme or issue" (Weber, 1983, p. 140). These themes, or categories, are extracted by a means of factor analysis or other multidimensional scaling technique from the matrix of word co-variations (Iker, 1974). One can follow the debate on comparative merits and disadvantages of the two approaches in Muskens (1985), Weber (1983, 1986).

Reliability and Validity

Among three types of reliability – stability, reproducibility, and accuracy (Krippendorff, 2004) – the issue of reproducibility, or inter-coder reliability, traditionally gets more attention than the other two reliability types (Shapiro, 1997). Unless an objective instrument such as a computer is used for coding, the analysts must rely upon pooled judgments of coders. Inter-coder reliability is a function of coders' skill, insight, and experience, clarity of categories and coding rules, as well as the degree of ambiguity in the data. Inter-coder reliability reflects the degree of shared understanding of the two coders. Since the nature of the data is usually beyond the investigator's control, opportunities for enhancing reliability are most often limited to improving coders, categories, or both. Experimental studies have demonstrated that training of coders conducted prior to the coding procedure can significantly increase inter-coder agreement (e.g., Kaplan and Goldsen, 1965). Defining an acceptable level of reliability in content analysis is a problem for which there is no single solution. Useful guidelines are given in Krippendorff (2004).

In contrast to reliability, validity cannot be asserted or declared through repeated trials. Validity is the extent to which research design on the whole and measurement procedure in particular lead to inferences about the concept under investigation. Adequate sampling and reliability of coding are necessary but not sufficient conditions for validity. Computer-assisted content analysis, though perfectly reliable, can be invalid if conceptually inappropriate words, symbols, or categories are specified for counting. Content analysts are always confronted with the choice what to prefer: more interesting and less reliable text interpretations or highly reliable or somewhat superficial text analyses.

APPLICATION OF CONTENT ANALYSIS TO TOURISM

Tourism marketing and management involves communication of ideas and images; thus, studies on destination image, tourism promotion, and, most recently, customer experiences and satisfaction with tourism and hospitality services are areas of applicability of the content analysis technique in tourism-related contexts. Tourism researchers employ sorting and categorization techniques to identify the frequencies of certain concepts, words, or people in textual and pictorial materials and treat the most frequent ones as variables, or dimensions, of the theoretical construct under study (Echtner, 2002). Scholars often utilize the technique at preliminary stages of the research, for questionnaire development (e.g., Baloglu and McCleary, 1999; Poria et al., 2006) or within Echtner and Ritchie's (1993) destination image measurement framework that involves analysis of both survey-based and free-elicitation responses (e.g., Murphy, 1999; O'Leary and Deegan, 2003; Rezende-Parker et al., 2003).

In a number of tourism studies, however, the technique has stood on its own. Within the "push–pull" framework, Dann (1977) used tourists' open-ended responses to investigate tourist motivations. Tapachai and Waryszak (2000) examined destination images of Thailand and the United States as a response to stimuli descriptions. Echtner (2002) analysed 115 brochures from 12 developing world countries and showed how myths around the destinations are created by stereotyping and emphasizing certain attractions, actors, and situations. Bandyopadhyay and Morais (2005) compared the representations of India in the brochures produced by the Indian government and American tourism media; the approach revealed the differences in two representations as they dealt with the colonial nature of international tourism and the postcolonial stage of India's nationalism. Stepchenkova and Eales (2011) analysed media messages about Russia in the prestige UK press and quantified them based on volume of the material, frequency of certain topics and themes, as well as favorability of coverage. The developed quantitative series were put in an econometric model of UK arrivals to Russia as variables accounting for the qualitative factor of Russia's destination image.

Advances in computer-assisted text analysis (CATA) software has made data handling easier for analysts, allowing for larger samples, and providing ways for data visualization. Andsager and Drzewiecka (2002) examined responses of college students to guidebook image stimuli with VBPro (Miller, 1993); the obtained matrix was cluster analysed to determine relationships between most frequent words to describe destinations. To investigate images of Australian cities and construct the perceptual maps, Ryan and Cave (2005) used data from qualitative interviews; the analysis was aided by CATPAC (Woelfel, 1998) and TextSmart software. Xiao and Mair (2006) analysed articles about China published in major English newspapers with the Nudist Nvivo program; the authors concluded that contrasting perceptions emerged in destination representational dynamics. Govers et al. (2007a) looked at images of seven destinations using online survey responses; the results produced with CATPAC were a three-dimensional visualization of image similarities and differences. Stepchenkova and Morrison (2008) derived stereotypical and affective images of Russia from open-ended survey responses and compared favorability of affective images for the US visitors and non-visitors combining two CATA packages. With the internet becoming a prominent means of destination marketing, several studies focused on destination websites as a promotional tool (Govers and Go, 2005; Stepchenkova and Morrison, 2006; Choi et al., 2007), while Govers et al. (2007b) used the data from online communities at three prominent travel websites to measured images of Middle Eastern destinations.

In the internet era, travelers themselves can serve as both image formation agents and information sources. Travel blogs and virtual communities generate accessible, credible, and readily available information able to influence travel behavior and purchase decisions (Litvin et al., 2008). A comprehensive survey of the still emerging field of travel blogs has been given recently by Banyai and Glover (2011). Besides interest in demographic profile of the bloggers, researchers have mostly focused on projected destination image and identity creation (Banyai, 2010; Enoch and Grossman, 2010; Karlsson, 2006; Law and Cheung, 2010; Schmallegger and Carson, 2009), monitoring visitors attitudes and experiences (Carson, 2008; Pan et al., 2007; Wenger, 2008), as well as visited locations, activities, and tourism products (Carson, 2008). In the context of online communities, Arsal et al. (2010) studied the influence of comments and advice provided by residents about a destination on travel-related decisions of potential visitors.

Customer experiences and satisfaction with tourism and hospitality services related online is an emerging topic of research because of its high practical relevance. Content analysis has been applied to comments from hotel distribution websites to investigate helpfulness of online hotel reviews (Black and Kelley, 2009), as well as commendations and concerns that travelers express when rating hotels (Stringam and Gerdes, 2010). Studies of hotel complaints with user-generated data has extended to examining sources of satisfaction and dissatisfaction with hotels (Lu and Stepchenkova, 2012; O'Connor, 2010), customer motives for complaining (Lee and Hu, 2004; Sparks and Browning, 2010), consistency of complaints with the expected level of service and room rates (Jeong and Jeon, 2008), and cultural aspects of the complaints (Au et al., 2010). Using comments from online restaurant guides, Pantelidis (2010) compared customer comments made in times of economic plenty and times of recession.

Studies that employed content analysis may not necessarily cite the technique as their research method; however, by applying principles of categorization and systematic data reduction to the textual data they adhered to Shapiro's and Markoff's (1997) "minimal definition". Crotts et al. (2009) studied guest satisfaction and competitive position of the hotels by drawing inferences on rationale, opinion, details and feelings, as well as repeat purchase intent of the visitors; the authors identified their technique as stance-shift analysis, which is a form of quantitative content analysis (Mason and Davis, 2007). Inversini et al. (2010) studied how the online reputation of London, UK, transpired through travel blogs; the authors classified reputation drivers into seven categorical dimensions (e.g., products and services, society, or environment) citing the Destination Online Reputation analysis as their methodological approach. Dwivedi (2009) used consumer queries posted on travel message boards to investigate the image of India, defining the technique as netnography (Kozinets, 2006). The technique included a quantitative component of data reduction, summarizing the wealth of textual data into six most highly discussed attributes such as natural resources, culture, or history and art.

All of the abovementioned studies use textual data as the primary source. Imagery analysis is less developed in comparison to the analysis of texts (for examples in tourism research, see MacKay and Couldwell, 2004; MacKay and Fesenmaier, 1997), and content analysis techniques used on texts are not automatically transferable to studying imagery. To illustrate, Tussyadiah and Fesenmaier (2009) collected 120 video clips about New York City from YouTube to investigate the roles that new media play as mediators of tourist experiences. Following a method proposed by Rose (2001), the researchers iteratively decomposed the visual material into sets of sequences, scenes, shots, and frames to quantitatively code visual data.

ADVANTAGES AND LIMITATIONS OF CONTENT ANALYSIS CONCEPTUALLY AND FOR POLICY FORMULATION

Content analysis is an unobtrusive research methodology that typically does not involve human subjects and can effectively utilize vast amounts of material already available on the 'information superhighway'. The technique has a rich history and very broad application area. From the perspective of usefulness of the technique to the tourism industry – for example, destination marketing organizations (DMOs) – content analysis is suitable for comparing communications about a destination and examining international differences in content. Auditing communication content in the target markets against the stated promotional objectives could help DMOs evaluate the effectiveness of the effort. Content analysis would allow maintaining the consistent brand and staying up to date on how the destination transpires in both general media and user-generated textual universe. As a research technique, content analysis is also suitable for description of attitudinal and behavioral responses of individual and organizational customers and stakeholders towards destination initiatives. Monitoring the responses of the potential travelers following destination promotional campaigns would allow adjustment of messages and correction of the communication flows. Since content analysis can reflect cultural patterns of groups, institutions, or societies, it can also be used for examining competition. The technique is relevant for making known the focus of individual or societal attention, as well as shifts in consumer preferences.

Obviously, the technique cannot be everything for everyone; it has its limitations. Readers are reminded that content analysis where the speaker's intentions and motives are the purpose of investigation, i.e., representational content analysis, requires higher interpretation levels and can be a source of increased error. Coding representational communication into content categories assumes, in the words of Pool (1959, p. 4) that "what an author says is what he means", which, as critics point out, overemphasizes manifest content of communication and leaves out latent message. The issue of "manifest versus latent content" has drawn a great deal of attention in the course of the technique development; however, not all documents are rich in latent meaning, and the importance of the latent content may be overestimated sometimes (Duriau and Reger, 2004). Moreover, manifest content can yield valid inferences despite the strategies of the source if what is said is beyond the voluntary control of the source (Osgood, 1959; Roberts, 2000). Echtner's (2002) investigation of the brochures produced by 12 developing world countries' DMOs is a good example; the analysis revealed that the brochures content promoted some unflattering stereotypes towards the countries, which was unlikely to be the intended DMOs strategy. From a more technical perspective, content analysis projects are large in scope and can be very time consuming which to a certain point can be remedied by using CATA packages; however, computer-assisted analysis clearly requires some amount of training.

FURTHER DEVELOPMENTS AND APPLICATIONS OF CONTENT ANALYSIS IN TOURISM RESEARCH

Stone (1997) made several predictions about the development of content analysis, which so far have proved remarkably accurate. We have been witnessing increased interest in content analysis studies, primarily due to nonparallel availability of texts on the 'information superhighway' combined with the rising processing power of computers and developments in CATA programs. Social scientists have been making significant contributions to explaining personal and organizational behavior in an ever-changing social environment that now increasingly involves human–computer interaction. Analysts have shifted their interest from the top-bottom grand theories approaches towards smaller scale bottom-up projects; well-founded valid inferences are produced with computers helping the investigators better situate thematic content analyses. Practical convenience and cost/benefit considerations have been guiding the division of labor between human coders and machines. Finally, over the past decade much of the thematic text analysis has been very practically oriented, as evidenced by the growing number of business, hospitality, and tourism content analysis applications.

CATA programs have routinely been used in content analysis research. Overall, quantitatively oriented software generally supports automatic coding of text using dictionaries, while qualitatively oriented programs better carry out operations associated with theme identification and category coding (Alexa and Zuell, 2000; Lowe, n.d.). Programs from the quantitative group typically include word frequency analysis, category frequency counts, key-word-in-context (KWIC) function, cluster analysis, and visualization, which Lowe (n.d) called "basic handful". Popping (1997) further divided quantitative software into six groups by its orientations towards thematic, semantic, or network content analysis, as well as being more suitable for representational or instrumental interpretation of texts. Programs with a qualitative focus are more of "an electronic version of the set of marginal notes, cross-references and notepad jottings that a researcher will generate when analyzing a set of texts by hand" (Lowe, n.d., para 1). There is also a group of programs – the development environments – that assists in construction of dictionaries and grammars and is oriented towards a specific application area, e.g., linguistics.

However, despite all developments in computer-assisted text processing, Mehmetoglu and Dann (2003), as well as Stepchenkova and Mills (2010), point out a relatively low acceptance of CATA in tourism research, with selection being confined to just a few CATA packages. The adoption of CATA is slowed down by insufficient functionality of any given CATA product in certain areas; at the same time, functional possibilities offered by various software programs are not used to their full advantage (Alexa and Zuell, 2000). This is due, at least partially, to an enormously wide range of possible content analysis applications, which makes it impractical to create a program which can support all conceivable operations for all types of content analysis. Studies that use CATA in tourism research often give very cursory justification for selection of a CATA package, and descriptions of the "technicalities" of the analyses are largely missing. To assist researchers, articles that would recommend a particular CATA package for certain types of content analysis, like the one by Mehmetologlu and Dann (2003), are highly welcomed.

Automated content analysis promises unparalleled opportunities for social scientists; however, many developments are still needed. Comparability of results from various content analysis projects and, thus, accumulation of comparable records are highly dependent on the usage of standardized categories. The two best-known dictionaries – Harvard IV Psychological Dictionaries (Dunphy et al., 1974) and the Lasswell Value Dictionary (Lasswell and Namenwirth, 1968) were created specifically for that purpose. However, with the focus shifted towards more grounded, bottom-top approaches, these dictionaries have been used much less often. Take, for example, the issues of attitudinal analysis and standardized categories in studies of customer opinions, experiences, and complaints. Content analysis of attitudes is a long-standing tradition; in studies of attitudes, the number of favorable and unfavorable characteristics attributed to a symbol or idea is often viewed as an indicator of the attitudes held by the writers, the readers, or their common culture toward that symbol or idea. Attitude objects are valued, "liked" or "disliked" in degrees ranging from positive to neutral to negative (Osgood et al., 1957, p. 189). Thus, in studies involving customers' opinions or complaints, classification of text on the positive–negative dimension, with subsequent hypothesis testing, would enrich the analysis beyond traditional category counting (for an example, see Lu and Stepchenkova, 2012). However, it is more difficult for individual researchers to create dictionaries for measuring positive–negative sentiments than for counting categories of themes.

Presently, several areas of tourism and hospitality inquiry are well-defined, with certain topics being recurrent. Coupled with the fact that the one-time procedure of dictionary development often significantly offsets time gains obtained as a result of CATA processing, it would make sense to create standardized dictionaries for certain content analysis applications – e.g., hotel reviews on various consumer websites – which would be easily expandable if needed. An efficient and user-friendly CATA package with a built-in attitudinal measure will further foster the tourism and hospitality research. Integration of the two types of dictionaries – with the standardized categories and favorability analysis – would bring CATA analysis even closer to being "automated". However, researchers are warned against "push-button" content analysis (Deacon, 2007). As Neuendorf (2002) rightfully noted, no content analysis can be completely automated, the role of researcher on any stage of the project, whether it is design, data collection, analysis, or interpretation – is the decisive factor of success.

REFERENCES

Alexa, M. and C. Zuell (2000), 'Text analysis software. Commonalities, differences and limitations: the results of a review', *Quality and Quantity*, **34**, 299–321.

Andsager, J.L. and J.A. Drzewiecka (2002), 'Desirability of differences in destinations', *Annals of Tourism Research*, **29** (2), 401–421.

Arsal, I., K.M. Woosnam, E.D. Baldwin and S.J. Backman (2010), 'Residents as travel destination information providers: an online community perspective', *Journal of Travel Research*, **49** (4), 400–413.

Au, N., R. Law and D. Buhalis (2010), 'The impact of culture on e-complaints: evidence from Chinese consumers in hospitality organizations', Information and Communication Technologies in Tourism 2010 Proceedings of the International Conference. Lugano, Switzerland, pp. 285–296.

Baloglu, S. and K.W. McCleary (1999), 'A model of destination image formation', *Annals of Tourism Research*, **26** (4), 868–897.

Bandyopadhyay, R. and D. Morais (2005), 'Representative dissonance: India's Self and Western Image', *Annals of Tourism Research*, **32** (4), 1006–1021.

Banyai, M. (2010), 'Dracula's image in tourism: Western bloggers versus tour guides', *European Journal of Tourism Research*, **3** (1), 5–22.

Banyai, M. and T.D. Glover (2011), 'Evaluating research methods on travel blogs', *Journal of Travel Research*, DOI:101177/0047287511410323.

Barcus, F.E. (1959), 'Communications content: analysis of research, 1900–1958', PhD thesis, University of Illinois.

Berelson, B. (1952), *Content Analysis in Communication Research*, Glencoe, IL: Free Press.

Berg, B.L. (1995), *Qualitative Research Methods for the Social Sciences*, Boston, MA: Bacon and Allyn.

Black, H. and S.W. Kelley (2009), 'A storytelling perspective on online customer reviews reporting service failure and recovery', *Journal of Travel and Tourism Marketing*, **26** (2), 169–179.

Brook, B.S. (1969), 'Style and content analysis in music: the simplified "plaine and easie code"', in G. Gerbner, O.R. Holsti, K. Krippendorf, W.J. Paisley and P.J. Stone (eds), *The Analysis of Communication Content*, New York: Wiley, pp. 287–296.

Carson, D. (2008), 'The "blogosphere" as a market research tool for tourism destinations: a case study of Australia's Northern Territory', *Journal of Vacation Marketing*, **14**, 111–119.

Cartwright, D. (1953), 'Analysis of qualitative material', in L.F. and D. Katz (eds), *Research Methods in the Behavioral Sciences*, Niles, IL: Dryden, pp. 421–470.

Choi, S., X.Y. Lehto and A.M. Morrison (2007), 'Destination image representation on the web: content analysis of Macau travel related websites', *Tourism Management*, **28** (1), 118–129.

Crotts, J.C., P.R. Mason and B. Davis (2009), 'Measuring guest satisfaction and competitive position in the hospitality and tourism industry', *Journal of Travel Research*, **48** (2), 139–151.

Curran, J. (2002), *Media and Power*, London: Routledge.

Danielson, W.A. and D.L. Lasorsa (1997), 'Perceptions of social change: 100 years of front-page content on *The New York Times* and *The Los Angeles Times*', in C.W. Roberts (ed.), *Text Analysis for the Social Sciences: Methods For Drawing Statistical Inferences from Texts and Transcripts*, Mahwah, NJ: Lawrence Erlbaum Associates, pp. 103–116.

Dann, G. (1977), 'Anomie, ego-enhancement and tourism', *Annals of Tourism Research*, **4** (4) 184–194.

Deacon, D. (2007), 'Yesterday's papers and today's technology digital newspaper archives and "push button" content analysis', *European Journal of Communication*, **22**, 5–25.

Denzin, N.K. and Y.S. Lincoln (1994), 'Introduction: entering the field of qualitative research', in N.K. Denzin and Y.S. Lincoln (eds), *Handbook of Qualitative Research*, Thousand Oaks, CA: Sage, pp. 1–17.

Dunphy, D.C., C.G. Bullard and E.E.M. Crossing (1974), 'Validation of the *General Inquirer Harvard IV Dictionary*', Pisa Conference on Content Analysis, Pisa, Italy.

Duriau, V.J. and R.K. Reger (2004), 'Choice of text analysis software in organization research: insight from a multi-dimensional scaling (MDS) analysis', 7th International Conference on the Textual Data Statistical Analysis, Louvain-la-Neuve, Belgium, pp. 382–389.

Dwivedi, M. (2009), 'Online destination image of India', *International Journal of Contemporary Hospitality Management*, **21** (2), 226–232.

Echtner, C.M. (2002), 'The content of Third World tourism marketing: a 4A approach', *International Journal of Tourism Research*, **4**, 413–434.

Echtner, C.M. and J.R.B. Ritchie (1993), 'The measurement of destination image: an empirical assessment', *Journal of Travel Research*, **31** (4), 3–13.

Ekman, E.M., W.V. Friesen and T.G. Taussig (1969), 'VID-R and SCAN: tools and methods for the automatic analysis of visual records', in G. Gerbner, O.R. Holsti, K.Krippendorf, W.J. Paisley and P.J. Stone (eds), *The Analysis of Communication Content*, New York: Wiley, pp. 297–312.

Enoch, Y. and M.L. Grossman (2010), 'Blogs of Israeli and Danish backpackers to India', *Annals of Tourism Research*, **37** (2), 520–536.

Flesch, R. (1948), 'A new readability yardstick', *Journal of Applied Psychology*, **32**, 221–233.

Franzosi, R. (1997), 'Labor unrest in the Italian service sector: an application of semantic grammars', in C.W. Roberts (eds), *Text Analysis for Social Sciences: Methods for Drawing Statistical Inferences from Texts and Transcripts*, Mahwah, NJ: Lawrence Earlbaum Associates, pp. 131–145.

Geller, A., D. Kaplan and H.D. Lasswell (1942), 'An experimental comparison of four ways of coding editorial content', *Journalism Quarterly*, **19**, 362–370.

George, A. (1959), 'Quantitative and qualitative approaches to content analysis', in A. Raftery (ed.), *Sociological Methodology*, Oxford: Basil Blackwell, pp. 135–144.

Gerbner, G., O.R. Holsti, K. Krippendorf, W.J. Paisley and P.J. Stone (1969), *The Analysis of Communication Content: Developments in Scientific Theories and Techniques*, New York: Wiley.

Govers, R. and F.M. Go (2005), 'Projected destination image online: website content analysis of pictures and text', *Information Technology & Tourism*, **7** (2), 73–89.

Govers, R., F.M. Go and K. Kumar (2007a), 'Promoting tourism destination image', *Journal of Travel Research*, **46** (1), 15–23.

Govers, R., F.M. Go and K. Kumar (2007b), 'Virtual destination image a new measurement approach', *Annals of Tourism Research*, **34** (4), 977–997.

Gray, J.H. and I.L. Densten (1998), 'Integrating quantitative and qualitative analysis using latent and manifest variables', *Quality & Quantity*, **32**, 419–431.

Holsti, O.R. (1969), *Content Analysis for the Social Sciences and Humanities*, Reading, MA: Addison-Wesley.

Iker, H.P. (1974), 'An historical note on the use of word-frequency contiguities in content analysis', *Computers and the Humanities*, **8**, 93–98.

Insch, G.S. and J.E. Moore (1997), 'Content analysis in leadership research: examples, procedures, and suggestions for future use', *Leadership Quarterly*, **8** (1), 1–25.

Inversini, A., E. Marchiori, C. Dedekind and L. Cantoni (2010), 'Applying a conceptual framework to analyze online reputation of tourism destinations', in Information and Communication Technologies in Tourism 2010 Proceedings of the International Conference, Lugano, Switzerland, pp. 321–332.

Jeong, M. and M. Jeon (2008), 'Customer reviews of hotel experiences through consumer generated media (CGM)', *Journal of Hospitality Marketing & Management*, **17** (1), 121–138.

Kaplan, A. and J.M. Goldsen (1965), 'The reliability of content analysis categories', in H.D. Lasswell, N. Leites and associates (eds), *Language of Politics: Studies in Quantitative Semantics*, Cambridge, MA: MIT Press, pp. 83–112.

Karlsson, L. (2006), 'The diary weblog and the travelling tales of diasporic tourists', *Journal of Intercultural Studies*, **27** (3), 299–312.

Kayser, J. (1953), *One Week's News: Comparative Study of Seventeen Major Dailies for a Seven-day Period*, Paris: Paul Dupont, for UNESCO.

Kleinnijenhuis, J., J.A. de Ridder and E.M. Rietberg (1997), 'Reasoning in economic discourse: an application of the network approach to the Dutch press', in C.W. Roberts (ed.), *Text Analysis for the Social Sciences: Methods for Drawing Statistical Inferences from Texts and Transcripts*, Mahwah, NJ: Lawrence Erlbaum Associates, pp. 191–207.

Kozinets, R.V. (2006), 'Netnography 2.0.', in R.W. Belk (ed.), *Handbook of Qualitative Methods in Marketing*, Cheltenham, UK and Northampton, MA, USA: Edward Elgar, pp. 129–143.

Krippendorff, K. (2004), *Content Analysis: An Introduction to its Methodology*, Thousand Oaks, CA: Sage Publications.

Lacy, S.R., F.G. Fico and A.F. Simon (1991), 'Fairness and balance in the prestige press', *Journalism Quarterly*, **68**, 363–370.

Lasswell, H.D., D. Lerner and I. de S. Pool (1952), *The Comparative Study of Symbols*, Stanford, CA: Stanford University Press.

Lasswell, H.D. and J.Z. Namenwirth (1968), *The Lasswell Value Dictionary. Vol. 1–3*, New Haven, CT: Yale University.

Law, R. and S. Cheung (2010), 'The perceived destination image of Hong Kong as revealed in the travel blogs of Mainland Chinese Tourists', *International Journal of Hospitality and Tourism Administration*, **11** (4), 303–327.

Lee, C.C. and C. Hu (2004), 'Analyzing hotel customers' e-complaints from an Internet complaint forum', *Journal of Travel & Tourism Marketing*, **17** (2), 167–181.

Lewin, H.S. (1947), 'Hitler youth and the Boys Scounts of America: a comparison of aims', *Human Relations*, **1**, 206–227.

Litvin, S.W., R.E. Goldsmith and B. Pan (2008), 'Electronic word-of-mouth in hospitality and tourism management', *Tourism Management*, **29**, 458–468.

Lowe, W. (n.d.), 'Software for content analysis: a review', vol. 1, 2008, available at http://www.ou.edu/cls/online/lstd5913/pdf/rev.pdf.

Lu, W. and S. Stepchenkova (2012), 'Ecotourism experiences reported online: classification of satisfaction attributes', *Tourism Management*, **33** (3), 702–712.

MacKay, K.J. and C.M. Couldwell (2004), 'Using visitor-employed photography to investigate destination image', *Journal of Travel Research*, **42** (4), 390–396.

MacKay, K.J. and D.R. Fesenmaier (1997), 'Pictorial element of destination in image formation', *Annals of Tourism Research*, **24**, 537–565.

Macnamara, J.R. (2003), 'Media content analysis: its uses, benefits and best practice methodology', vol. 2008.

Mahl, G.F. (1959), 'Exploring emotional states by content analysis', in I.d.S. Pool (ed.), *Trends in Content Analysis*, Urbana, IL: University of Illinois Press, pp. 89–130.

Martin, H. (1936), 'Nationalism and children's literature', *Library Quarterly*, **6**, 405–418.

Mason, P.R. and B. Davis (2007), 'More than the words: using stance-shift analysis to identify critical opinions and attitudes in online focus groups', *Journal of Advertising Research*, **47** (4), 496–506.

Mathews, B.C. (1910), 'A study of a New York daily', in *Independent*, **68**, 82–86.

Mehmetoglu, M. and G.M.S. Dann (2003), 'ATLAS/ti and content/semiotic analysis in tourism research', *Tourism Analysis*, **8**, 1–13.

Miles, J. and H.C. Selvin (1966), 'A factor analysis of the vocabulary of poetry in the seventeenth century', in J. Leed (ed.), *The Computer and Literary Style*, Kent, OH: Kent State University Press.

Miller, M.M. (1993), *User's Guide to VBPro: A Program for Qualitative and Quantitative Analysis of Verbatim Text*, Knoxville TN: University of Tennessee.

Mintz, A. (1949), 'The feasibility of the use of samples in content analysis', in H.D. Lasswell, N. Leites, R. Fadner, J.M. Goldsen, A. Gray, I.L. Janis, A. Kaplan, D. Kaplan, A. Mintz, I.d.S. Pool and S. Yakobson (eds), *The Language of Politics: Studies in Quantitative Semantics*, New York: George Stewart, pp. 127–152.

Murphy, L. (1999), 'Australia's image as a holiday destination: perceptions of back-packers visitors', *Journal of Travel and Tourism Marketing*, **8** (3), 21–45.

Muskens, G. (1985), 'Mathematical analysis of content', *Quality & Quantity*, **19**, 99–103.

Namenwirth, J.Z. (1973), 'The wheels of time and the interdependence of value change', *Journal of Interdisciplinary History*, 3, 649–683.

Neuendorf, K.A. (2002), *The Content Analysis Guidebook*, Thousand Oak, CA: Sage.

Newbold, C., O. Boyd-Barrett and H. Van Den Bulck (2002), *The Media Book*, London: Arnold (Hodder Headline).

O'Connor, P. (2010), 'Managing a hotel image on TripAdvisor', *Journal of Hospitality Marketing & Management*, 19 (7), 754–772.

O'Leary, S. and J. Deegan (2005), 'Ireland's image as a tourism destination in France: attribute importance and performance', *Journal of Travel Research*, 43 (3), 247–256.

Osgood, C.E. (1959), 'The representational model and relevant research methods', in I.d.S. Pool (ed.), *Trends in Content Analysis*, Champaign, IL: University of Illinois Press, pp. 33–88.

Osgood, C.E., G.J. Suci and P.H. Tannenbaum (1957), *The Measurement of Meaning*, Champaign, IL: University of Illinois Press.

Pan, B., T. MacLaurin and J.C. Crotts (2007), 'Travel blogs and the implications for destination marketing', *Journal of Travel Research*, 46 (1), 35–45.

Pantelidis, I.S. (2010), 'Electronic meal experience: a content analysis of online restaurant comments', *Cornell Hospitality Quarterly*, 51 (4), 483–491.

Pool, I. de S. (ed.) (1959), *Trends in Content Analysis*, Champaign, IL: University of Illinois Press.

Popping, R. (1997), 'Computer programs for the analysis of texts and transcripts', in C.W. Roberts (ed.), *Text Analysis for the Social Sciences: Methods for Drawing Statistical Inferences from Texts and Transcripts* Mahwah, NJ: Lawrence Erlbaum, pp. 79–100.

Poria, Y., A. Reichel and A. Biran (2006), 'Heritage site perceptions and motivations to visit', *Journal of Travel Research*, 44 (3), 318–326.

Rezende-Parker, A.M., A.M. Morrison and J.A. Ismail (2003), 'Dazed or confused? An exploratory study of the image of Brazil as a travel destination', *Journal of Vacation Marketing*, 9 (3), 243–259.

Riffe, D., C.F. Aust and S.R. Lacy (1993), 'The effectiveness of random, consecutive day and constructed week samplings in newspaper content analysis', *Journalism Quarterly*, 70, 133–139.

Riffe, D., S.R. Lacy and M.W. Drager (1996a), 'Sample size in content analysis of weekly news magazines', *Journalism and Mass Communication Quarterly*, 73, 635–644.

Riffe, D., S.R. Lacy, J. Nagovan and L. Burkum (1996b), 'The effectiveness of simple and stratified random sampling in broadcast news content analysis', *Journalism and Mass Communication Quarterly*, 73, 159–168.

Roberts, C.W. (2000), 'A conceptual framework for quantitative text analysis', *Quality and Quantity*, 34, 259–274.

Rose, G. (2001), *Visual Methodologies*, London: Sage.

Ryan, C. and J. Cave (2005), 'Structuring destination image: a qualitative approach', *Journal of Travel Research*, 44 (2), 143–150.

Schmallegger, D. and D. Carson (2009), 'Destination image projection on consumer-generated content websites: a case study of the Flinders Ranges', *Information Technology & Tourism*, 11, 111–127.

Shapiro, G. (1997), 'The future of coders: human judgments in a world of sophisticated software', in C.W. Roberts (ed.), *Text Analysis for the Social Sciences: Methods of Drawing Statistical Inferences from Texts and Transcripts*, Mahwah, NJ: Lawrence Erlbaum, pp. 225–238.

Shapiro, G. and J. Markoff (1997), 'A matter of definition', in C.W. Roberts (ed.), *Text Analysis for the Social Sciences: Methods for Drawing Statistical Inferences from Texts and Transcripts*, Mahwah, NJ: Lawrence Erlbaum Associates, pp. 9–31.

Shoemaker, P. and S. Reese (1996), *Mediating the Message: Theories of Influences on Mass Media Content*, White Plains, NY: Longman.

Simpson, G.E. (1934), *The Negro in the Philadelphia Press*, Philadelphia, PA: University of Pennsylvania.

Sparks, B. and V. Browning (2010), 'Complaining in cyberspace: the motives and forms of hotel guests' complaints online', *Journal of Hospitality Marketing & Management*, 19 (7), 797–818.

Stepchenkova, S. and J. Eales (2011), 'Destination image as quantified media messages: the effect of news on tourism demand', *Journal of Travel Research*, 50 (2), 198–212.

Stepchenkova, S. and J.E. Mills (2010), 'Destination image: a meta-analysis of 2000–2007 research', *Journal of Hospitality Marketing and Management*, 19 (6), 575–609.

Stepchenkova, S. and A.M. Morrison (2006), 'The destination image of Russia: from the online induced perspective', *Tourism Management*, 27 (5), 943–956.

Stepchenkova, S. and A.M. Morrison (2008), 'Revisiting Echtner and Ritchie: Russia's destination image among American pleasure travelers', *Tourism Management*, 29 (3), 548–560.

Stone, P.J. (1997), 'Thematic text analysis', in C.W. Roberts (ed.), *Text Analysis for the Social Sciences: Methods for Drawing Statistical Inferences from Texts and Transcripts*, Mahwah, NJ: Lawrence Erlbaum Associates, pp. 35–54.

Stone, P.J., D.C. Dunphy, M.S. Smith and D.M. Ogilvie (1966), *The General Inquirer: A Computer Approach to Content Analysis*, Cambridge, MA: M.I.T. Press.
Stringam, B.B. and Jr. J. Gerdes (2010), 'An analysis of word-of-mouth ratings and guest comments of online hotel distribution sites', *Journal of Hospitality Marketing & Management*, **19** (7), 773–796.
Tapachai, N. and R. Waryszak (2000), 'An examination of the role of beneficial image in tourist destination selection', *Journal of Travel Research*, **39** (1), 37–44.
Tussyadiah, I.P. and D.R. Fesenmaier (2009), 'Mediating tourist experiences: access to places via shared videos', *Annals of Tourism Research*, **36** (1), 24–40.
Walworth, A. (1938), *School Histories at War: A Study of the Treatment of Our Wars in the Secondary School History Books of the United States and in Those of its Former Enemies*, Cambridge, MA: Harvard University Press.
Weber, R.P. (1983), 'Measurement models of content analysis', *Quality and Quantity*, **17**, 127–149.
Weber, R.P. (1986), 'Correlational models of content: reply to Muskens', *Quality & Quantity*, **20** (2/3), 273–275.
Weber, R.P. (1990), *Basic Content Analysis*, Newbury Park, CA: Sage.
Wenger, A. (2008), 'Analysis of travel bloggers' characteristics and their communication about Austria as a tourism destination', *Journal of Vacation Marketing*, **14**, 169–176.
Woelfel, J. (1998), *CATPAC: User's Guide*, New York: RAH Press.
Xiao, H. and H.L. Mair (2006), '"A Paradox of Images": representation of China as a tourist destination', *Journal of Travel & Tourism Marketing*, **20** (2), 1–14.

24 Meta-analyses of tourism research
Ulrike Gretzel and Heather Kennedy-Eden

INTRODUCTION

As the name suggests, meta-analysis is a research method that involves the analysis of analyses. It aims at assessing "a field of study beyond one particular study" (Timulak, 2009, p. 591) by aggregating research findings from a number of existing empirical research studies. It is a relatively new methodology, especially in the social sciences, that is still under development and also controversial in some respect because of the potential biases it can introduce and the risk of comparing things that are not comparable. With the growing maturity of tourism as a field of inquiry one can expect that the integration of research findings provided through meta-analyses will grow in importance. A chapter dealing with meta-analysis in a tourism research methods book is therefore warranted. However, rather than replicating what others have already written, this chapter only provides brief summaries of the general issues and procedures and focuses attention on the applicability of meta-analyses to solving research problems in tourism and the specific challenges faced when conducting a meta-analysis related to tourism research. Examples of published meta-analytic research in tourism are presented to illustrate the processes involved and to demonstrate the benefits for knowledge advancement in tourism.

IMPORTANCE OF META-ANALYSIS AS A FORM OF RESEARCH SYNTHESIS

Science is a cumulative endeavour that requires the integration of research related to the same phenomena (Cooper et al., 2009). This ensures that a 'constant re-invention of the wheel' can be avoided and that knowledge is actually advanced. Research integration is typically achieved through reviews of existing research. Based on their goal, approach, coverage and perspective used one can distinguish broadly between two types of reviews: narrative reviews and systematic reviews (Figure 24.1). Narrative reviews are summaries or assessments that can be written from a neutral perspective or from an argumentative point of view. They are inherently subjective as the selection of what research is summarized is not systematic and the criteria that led to the inclusion of a piece of research in the summary are typically not made explicit. These reviews also do not have to be comprehensive but rather identify the most important/relevant research. In summary, they are selective and not guided by formal rules (Egger and Smith, 1997). Looking at the goal and format of narrative reviews, two types emerge: the typical literature review included in a publication or grant proposal and the review article. They differ mainly in scope, with the literature review being more selective and more focused, but also in their role: A review article critically evaluates more broadly what is known in a particular field

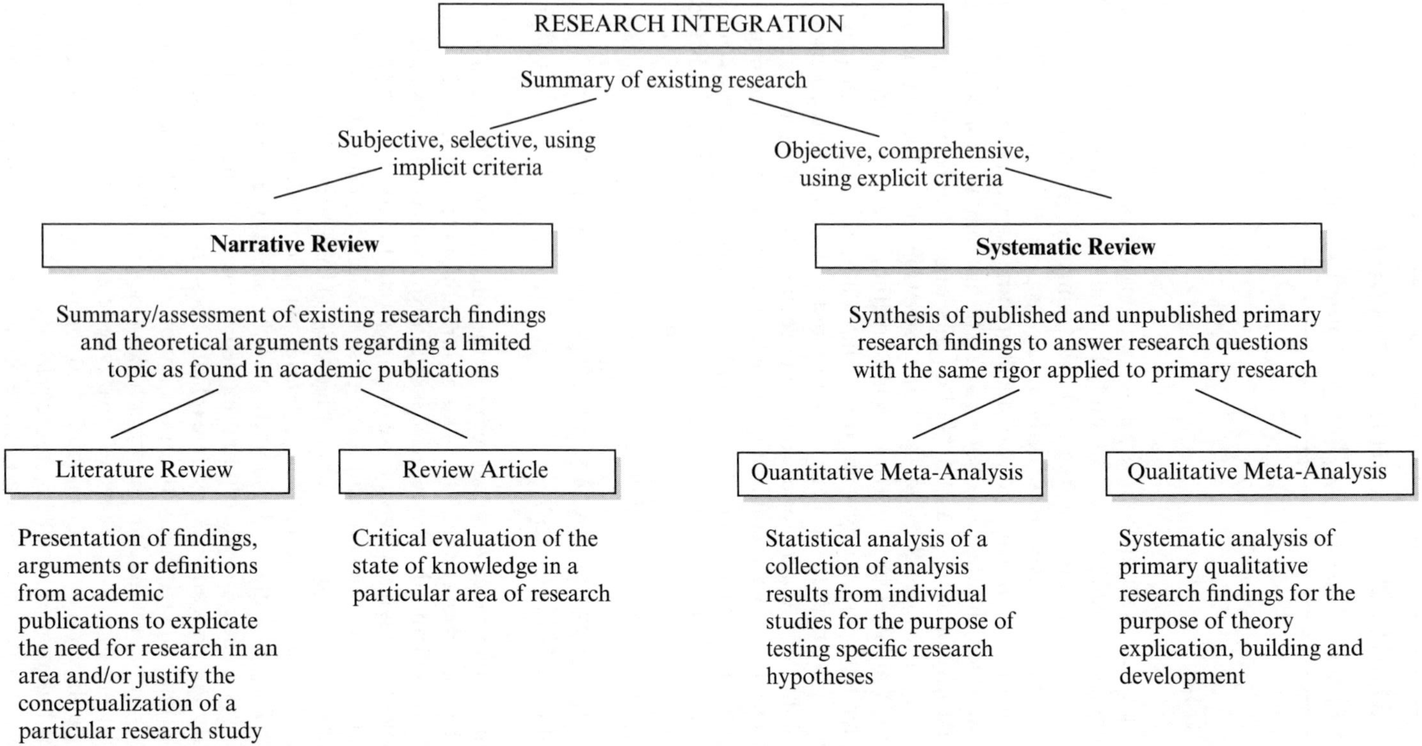

RESEARCH INTEGRATION

Summary of existing research

Subjective, selective, using implicit criteria

Objective, comprehensive, using explicit criteria

Narrative Review

Systematic Review

Summary/assessment of existing research findings and theoretical arguments regarding a limited topic as found in academic publications

Synthesis of published and unpublished primary research findings to answer research questions with the same rigor applied to primary research

Literature Review

Review Article

Quantitative Meta-Analysis

Qualitative Meta-Analysis

Presentation of findings, arguments or definitions from academic publications to explicate the need for research in an area and/or justify the conceptualization of a particular research study

Critical evaluation of the state of knowledge in a particular area of research

Statistical analysis of a collection of analysis results from individual studies for the purpose of testing specific research hypotheses

Systematic analysis of primary qualitative research findings for the purpose of theory explication, building and development

Figure 24.1   Research review typology

of research so that knowledge/research gaps can be identified. A literature review positions an empirical research study within an existing body of literature.

In contrast, systematic reviews focus on the synthesis of primary research rather than descriptive summaries or critiques, ideally including both published and unpublished studies and with the goal of being as exhaustive as possible in the inclusion and meticulous in the execution (Clarke, 2011). Systematic reviews are needed when there is 'a substantive question, several primary studies – perhaps with disparate findings – and substantial uncertainty' (Hemingway and Brereton, 2009, p. 3). Egger and Smith (1997) describe systematic reviews as types of reviews that have been prepared with strategies in place to avoid bias. Consequently, systematic means that clear criteria for the inclusion or exclusion of research in the systematic review are established and made explicit. Meta-analysis is a possible component of a systematic review aiming at a comprehensive description of a phenomenon beyond one particular study, usually also assessing the influence of the method of investigation on the research findings. As such it allows for cumulating knowledge across studies by aggregating outcome measures and correcting errors and biases in research findings as well as overcoming research artefacts that occur in all individual empirical studies (Woodside and Dubelaar, 2003). Meta-analysis is therefore only applicable to empirical research (Lipsey and Wilson, 2001). Of course, a meta-analysis is only as good as the quality of the primary research it includes, making it important to carefully judge studies before they are included. The typical steps involved in a meta-analysis are:

1. Definition of a research question
2. Identification of existing research studies
3. Assessment of the studies
4. Combining of the results of the primary research studies through coding and analysis
5. Interpretation of the findings.

According to Egger and Smith (1997), the main benefits of meta-analyses are the more objective appraisal of evidence than in narrative reviews, the greater transparency which makes meta-analyses replicable, the potential to resolve uncertainty and disagreement in existing research, the ability to analyse the effects of research designs/study conceptualizations, as well as the opportunity to generate important research questions for future research. Imminent challenges for meta-analyses are the issue of comparability of studies (the apples and orange problem) and the bias that can be introduced by focusing only on published studies as certain types of studies with certain types of findings have a higher likelihood of being published (file drawer problem) (Lipsey and Wilson, 2001).

Meta-analysis has been applied to various research questions in a variety of disciplines and research areas. This chapter provides an overview from the perspective of tourism research and cannot possibly discuss all aspects relevant to actually conducting meta-analyses. Thus, it is not a systematic review of meta-analysis articles and books but rather a selective narrative review to provide interested readers with an introduction. Detailed information about the specific steps and challenges related to meta-analysis can be found in the literature (for instance, Berman and Parker, 2002; Borenstein et al., 2009; Briggs, 2005; Charlton, 1996; Chatzisarantis and Stoica, 2009; Cooper et al., 2009;

Delahaye et al., 1991; Dickersin and Berlin, 1992; Lipsey, 2007; Lipsey and Wilson, 2001; Montori et al., 2003; Paterson et al., 2001; Rosenfeld, 2004; Rosenthal and DiMatteo, 2001; Rothstein et al., 2006; Schmidt, 2008; Shelby and Vaske, 2008; Uttl et al., 2008; Wheatley, 2001). Meta-analysis as a method of research synthesis can be either qualitative or quantitative in nature. Although the main principles are the same across quantitative and qualitative meta-analyses, there are specific steps and also challenges unique to the chosen research approach. Therefore, the following sections will discuss them separately. However, qualitative and quantitative meta-analyses can be combined to result in mixed-methods systematic reviews (Harden, 2010).

QUANTITATIVE META-ANALYSIS

Quantitative meta-analysis is a methodology that involves the statistical integration of research findings from separate studies (Egger and Smith, 1997). Rosenfeld (2004) defines it as a form of systematic review that uses statistical techniques to derive quantitative estimates of the magnitude of statistical effects and their associated precision. For quantitative meta-analysis to work, the findings in the individual studies need to be conceptually comparable (i.e., they must deal with the same constructs) and configured in similar statistical form. To facilitate comparisons across studies, quantitative meta-analysis uses a statistic that describes the strength and magnitude of an effect, the so-called effect size. This effect size is usually standardized to account for differences in sample sizes across the studies. The standardized effect sizes are treated as data and subjected to various forms of analysis.

The practical steps involved in conducting quantitative meta-analyses are explained in detail in Higgins and Green (2011), a free handbook available online, as well as in Lipsey and Wilson (2001). In general, the quantitative meta-analysis starts with the problem identification and formulation of research hypotheses. These hypotheses cover the main effects as well as moderating effects of research design characteristics. Then, studies to be included in the meta-analysis are gathered based on criteria determined by the research question(s), the so-called inclusion criteria (Berkeljon and Baldwin, 2009). These studies are then subjected to a review and eliminated if they have characteristics that exclude them from further analysis, the so-called exclusion criteria. Inclusion/exclusion criteria can relate to characteristics of study participants, a specific study design, the presence of certain outcome variables, publication language, etc. It is common practice to report not only the databases searched but also the search terms and the number of studies included/excluded at each stage of the process.

Once the sample of studies is determined, information from the studies is extracted in the form of codes, thus requiring a coding manual to explicitly describe the coding procedures and facilitate inter-rater reliability. The most important variable coded is the effect size. There are many types of effect sizes that can be selected and the choice usually depends on the kind of data that is reported in the published primary studies and whether one wants to investigate one-variable relationships (e.g., the proportion of travellers using social media to plan trips) or two-variable relationships (e.g., pre-post test contrasts, group contrasts, association between variables). Even more complex is the formulation of multi-variate problems (Jackson et al., 2011). Common effect size measures are proportions, arithmetic means, the Pearson product moment correlation coefficient, and odds ratios. Sampling error is smaller for effect sizes estimated from large samples than for those estimated from small samples; thus, effect sizes are usually weighted by their precision, with the weight typically being the inverse of the squared standard error (inverse variance weight). Formulas for calculating various effect size types as well as a very useful effect size decision tree to choose the correct measure are included in Lipsey and Wilson (2001). As mentioned above, multivariate effects are difficult to deal with but recent advances in meta-analysis statistics offer ways in which multivariate meta-analyses can be accomplished (see Jackson et al., 2011, for details). Variables related to the research methodology are also encoded.

The process continues with the analysis of the data in a way similar to primary research. Analysis often starts with the elimination of outliers that could influence the results and typically continues with the transformation of effect size measures into more convenient forms for analysis. However, the interpretation of results might require transformations back to more interpretable statistics. Further, specific standards against which results can be gauged are used to guide the interpretation. Again, Lipsey and Wilson's (2001) practical guide has specific information for transforming and interpreting the various effect size options. The regular analysis is typically followed by a sensitivity analysis that explores whether decisions made in the process affect the results substantially (Berkeljon and Baldwin, 2009). The findings can then be interpreted and questions for future research as well as practical implications can be derived.

Lipsey and Wilson (2001) describe the advantages of quantitative meta-analysis in comparison to narrative reviews as lying in the explicit structure imposed on the summary of research findings, the ability to code both magnitude and direction of effects, the opportunity to relate study characteristics to effect sizes, and the ability to synthesize a large number of studies resulting in estimates with greater statistical power. Berkeljon and Baldwin (2009) emphasize the unique suitability of meta-analysis for answering questions of generalizability due to its ability to aggregate findings of studies conducted in different settings and on different samples. The robustness of properly derived meta-analysis results also makes them especially suitable for informing policy decisions and establishing practical guidelines.

While the comparability issue and file drawer problem apply to all meta-analyses, they are of course especially problematic for quantitative meta-analyses that statistically integrate findings. If known, differences in research design and measurement need to be coded so that their effects can be analysed. To deal with the file drawer problem, which causes studies with greater and statistically significant effects to be more likely included because they have a greater likelihood of being published, efforts have to be undertaken to uncover unpublished studies. One can also calculate the number of non-significant or unavailable studies that would be necessary to change the cumulative effect size to a nonsignificant value (fail-safe N, see Lipsey and Wilson, 2001). Selection biases can also result from studies having to be excluded because of incomplete reporting. Another issue can be the inclusion of a large portion of studies produced by or in collaboration with a single author (Banas and Rains, 2010). In this case, comparisons of effect sizes of studies involving this author and of those which do not can help with identifying such bias. Multivariate meta-analysis has a number of limitations mostly due to estimation difficulties because of a lack of information, additional assumptions being required, the complexity of its interpretation, and the potential exaggeration of publication biases (Jackson et al., 2010).

Like any kind of research, meta-analysis depends on the quality of the data and the rigour applied in the coding and analysis stages, and a thorough understanding of the statistical assumptions made. However, it involves aggregation of data and, thus, also aggregation of potential biases, which can be very problematic. Consequently, quantitative meta-analysis require utmost care and what Lipsey and Wilson (2001) call a fish bowl approach that renders decision processes, criteria, data and analysis and interpretation procedures explicit.

QUALITATIVE META-ANALYSIS

Timulak (2009) defines qualitative meta-analysis as 'rigorous secondary qualitative analysis of primary qualitative findings' (p. 591). It therefore follows the same basic principles established for quantitative meta-analysis in terms of comprehensiveness and systematic approaches but applies qualitative research methods to the analysis of the studies included in the research synthesis exercise. Consequently, it is interpretive rather than aggregative (Paterson et al., 2001). In accordance with the general goals of qualitative research, qualitative meta-analysis does not aim at hypothesis testing. Rather, its main contributions lie in (1) building of more abstract theories (meta-theory); (2) theory explication; and (3) development of new theory (Schreiber et al., 1997). To reach these aims requires assessing the qualitative research methodology as well as the influence of paradigmatic parameters and theoretical assumptions that guided the researchers (Becken, 2011). At the same time, it also needs to critically reflect on these issues in terms of how they affected the meta-analysis itself. Therefore, it is important 'that the epistemology of a given qualitative meta-analysis and its embedding in a particular theoretical framework is reflected by the researchers throughout the analysis and commented on in a published account of it' (Timulak, 2009, p. 593).

Challenges faced by qualitative meta-analysis involve the loss of contextual information that is seen as essential to qualitative interpretation, which might lead to more descriptive rather than interpretive approaches implemented in the meta-analysis. Timulak (2009) also stresses that building on an existing body of knowledge can limit the openness to new discoveries in meta-analysis as it increases the tension between formulating a theory and assessing an existing theory.

While the overall steps involved in qualitative meta-analysis are similar to those for quantitative analysis, there are some important differences that require highlighting. First, while qualitative research also starts with the formulation of research questions, these are more global than the specific hypotheses to be tested in quantitative efforts and can actually change in the process if discoveries warrant reformulation or adding of new questions. Second, the collection of studies is also critical but comparability is an even greater issue for qualitative studies. In addition, it has to be decided whether quantitative studies should be considered or not. Further, while quantitative methods can easily deal with and actually often require large data sets, there are limits to the number of studies that can be qualitatively analysed by a researcher. Theoretical sampling and saturation can be used as guiding principles to deal with study selection issues. Evaluations of the quality of studies to be included in the analysis are again more difficult in the qualitative realm and need to focus on appraising studies based on their relevance to the research question as well as the credibility of the research procedure, sampling, data analysis and interpretation.

While quantitative meta-analysts can often calculate measures based on descriptive data included in the publications (e.g., means and standard deviations) or can even get access to raw data sets, it is very difficult for qualitative meta-analysts to obtain raw data. Therefore, special care needs to be given to making sure that original meanings and contextual information are understood and appropriately coded. As far as the analysis of the data is concerned, various qualitative methods approaches can be applied (Thorne et al., 2004). An important step unique to qualitative meta-analysis involves conducting credibility checks. According to Timulak (2009), these can involve (1) auditing (an auditor checks all steps in the meta-analysis to identify if alternative approaches and conceptualizations would have been possible); (2) independent analysts (researchers conduct the entire analysis or parts of it independently and later try to reach a consensus); (3) triangulation (use of additional, including quantitative data to complement the original analysis); (4) validation by the primary researchers (similar to validation by participants in primary studies); and (5) representativeness to the sample (checking how representative the findings are of the overall sample of studies included in the analysis).

The growing number of qualitative studies in tourism will likely encourage a greater number of qualitative meta-analyses. It is important to note that rigor and making assumptions and decisions explicit are criteria as important for qualitative meta-analyses as they are for quantitative ones but are probably even harder to communicate.

ROLE OF META-ANALYSES IN TOURISM

Tourism is a relatively young and small field of scientific inquiry. It is also a field that encompasses a large array of topics studied from various disciplinary backgrounds and with a multitude of methodologies. Experimental laboratory studies, which hold external conditions constant and often involve standardized procedures, are common practice in many disciplines but are rare in tourism research. In addition, tourism is an applied field with an extensive number of studies being conducted by the industry or by research consultants. Further, there are many institutions around the world who grant research-based master degrees in tourism that involve small individual studies rather than the work of research groups and are usually not published. All this leads to rather small numbers of scientific publications focusing on one topic using comparable methodologies. At the same time, it also results in a large number of publications in the form of master theses, industry reports, etc. This grey literature is often only promoted and available within institutional boundaries and therefore usually not open to meta-analytic inspection.

Challenges to meta-analyses in tourism are further rooted in the way scientific journals related to tourism operate. There is a very small number of top journals in tourism and a very large number (a longtail) of lower level journals. The top journal editors have only recently started to demand rigorous reporting of measurement items, descriptive statistics, correlation matrices and other information needed to judge and compare studies.

For older publications, reporting procedures were not standardized and, thus, critical measures necessary for quantitative meta-analyses are often not readily available. This is still very much the case for lower level journals.

In addition, although replication is a pillar of scientific research, replication is not rewarded in scientific journals. Journal editors and reviewers look for innovation and often do not recognize the merit of replication to challenge or further develop existing measures and methodologies. While this is true for many areas, it is particularly true for tourism. Rigorous testing and re-testing of measures as is common in psychology, for instance, does not occur in the tourism field. The file drawer problem is also a relevant one for tourism, with studies that resulted in insignificant findings not being published in tourism journals. Moreover, there is a general emphasis on citing only the most recent publications in an area, often neglecting original works and the historical development of theoretical positions.

Despite all this, the growing maturity of tourism as a field has spurred interest in reviews of the literature and of existing research related to specific topic areas. While most of these reviews have to date been narrative reviews, there are also some attempts of systematic reviews, at least as far as the identification and collection of materials to be reviewed is concerned. Ever better search technologies promise progress as far as the identification of grey literature is concerned and the above-mentioned efforts to make reporting in tourism-related scientific publications more complete will hopefully pave the way for opportunities to conduct meta-analyses in the future. Better search opportunities and greater access to publications also raises the awareness of research streams and of contradictory findings. This is very important for tourism as tourism-related research is published in a wide array of journals spanning many disciplines.

The importance of meta-analyses for the advancement of the field is especially high in tourism, where generalizability of results is a challenge because of the complexity and diversity of tourism settings. Due to the lesser degree of standardization in research methodologies, there is also a great need to inspect the effects of certain research designs and even seemingly unimportant details such as identifying the sponsor of the research (see Woodside and Dubelaar, 2003) on research outcomes. Weed (2006) presents a discussion of research synthesis for tourism research highlighting various application areas. That meta-analysis in tourism is not only possible but can indeed drive theory development, can shed light on contradictory findings and can lead to advancements in methodologies is explicated in the studies presented in the next section.

APPLICATIONS OF META-ANALYSES IN TOURISM

One of the research topics that has received great attention in tourism by academic and industry researchers is the one of income multipliers. It therefore lends itself well to meta-analysis. Baaijens et al. (1998), for example, looked at the question of why different researchers find different multiplier values for different regions and specifically wanted to understand the impact of using different estimation methods (standard input–output model versus Archer's ad hoc method). Their sample consisted of 11 multiplier values from a set of nine studies selected based on (1) source of study; (2) year of the data collection; (3) method of research; (4) reported multiplier values; (5) features of the economy;

(6) features of tourism; (7) features of the environment; and (8) tourism policy. The small sample size limited the kinds of analyses that could be performed but, nevertheless, the results suggest that regional tourism policies and the regional external environment of the destination influence multiplier values. As such, the study provides important directions for future research but also policy making in tourism.

Meta-analyses have also been conducted in the area of tourism demand. Brons et al. (2002) meta-analysed 37 studies on air transport passengers. They used transfer distance, fare class and geographic location to explain the variance among price elasticity estimates and employed research method, time horizon used and period of data collection as moderator variables. They found that long-run elasticities are higher in absolute value, that business class passengers are less sensitive to price, and that European passengers are not more price sensitive than their US and Australian counterparts. Crouch has published several meta-analytic studies on tourism demand (Crouch, 1992, 1994, 1995, 1996). Crouch (1995), for instance, meta-analysed 80 studies of international tourism demand and found that demand elasticities vary regionally in terms of both origin and destination, suggesting that international tourism demand coefficients depend on the pair of countries (origin and destination) of interest. Lim (1999) meta-analysed 70 studies of international tourism demand to test the hypothesis that international travel is positively related to income in the country of origin and negatively related to both transportation costs and relative tourism prices. The hypothesized relationships were confirmed for income and tourism prices but were inconclusive for the transportation cost variable.

Service quality is also a topic that has been studied widely in tourism and hospitality research. Lynn and McCall (2000) conducted a meta-analysis that linked service quality to tipping behaviour. They included both published (seven) and unpublished (six) studies in their sample and were thus able to look at the effect based on 2547 dining parties at 20 different restaurants. They selected the restaurant as the unit of analysis rather than the study and tip as a percentage of bill size was used as the dependent variable, which was linked to service quality evaluations. Coefficient r was selected as the effect size measure. The findings suggest that there is a small but reliable and positive relationship between service evaluations and tip sizes while patronage frequency is neither a strong nor consistent confound of the service-tipping relationship. De Matos et al. (2007) conducted a meta-analysis of the service recovery paradox (a situation in which a customer's post-failure satisfaction is higher than the pre-failure satisfaction) to resolve the mixed results that appeared in existing studies. Their sample included 21 studies with 24 observations in hotels, restaurants and other settings. The meta-analysis used the correlation coefficient as the effect size and found that there is a significant and positive service recovery effect on satisfaction but not on repurchase intention, word of mouth and corporate image. The research design (cross-sectional versus longitudinal), subjects (student versus nonstudent) and service category (hotel, restaurant, other) significantly moderated the effect on satisfaction.

There is also an abundance of conversion studies in tourism research, especially outside the academic literature. Woodside and Dubelaar (2003) conducted a quantitative meta-analysis of 32 published tourism-advertising studies to test whether the identification of the sponsor influenced the response rate (H1) and the estimated conversion rate (H2). They found support for both hypotheses, concluding that response rates are lower and conversion rate estimates are higher for studies that identify the sponsoring brand.

Website evaluation research has also been subjected to meta-analysis by tourism researchers. Park and Gretzel (2007) meta-analysed 153 academic papers related to e-satisfaction, e-loyalty and e-service quality. The theoretical dimensions of website quality mentioned in these papers were extracted from the text of these papers and then sorted into categories until nine categories that could no longer be consolidated emerged. More recently, Law et al. (2010) and Ip et al. (2011) conducted systematic reviews of the website evaluation literature relevant to tourism and hospitality extracting and categorizing the methodologies employed in tourism website evaluation efforts.

Bloom et al.'s (2009) study of vacation effects on health and well-being is a qualitative meta-analysis that illustrates very well the importance of reporting details of the inclusion and exclusion processes that lead up to the final sample selection. The research questions investigated were whether empirical evidence could be found for an improvement of health and well-being due to a vacation, how long such an effect lasts and whether specific vacation activities/experiences influence it. A systematic literature search was carried out in two bibliographical databases: PsychInfo and Medline. No publication year limits were set and the final search date was 15 June 2008. The following search terms were used within the fields 'title' or 'keywords':

- Vacation or holiday (1702 hits)
- Well-being or health or quality of life or satisfaction OR stress or burnout or recovery or sleep or mood or affect (829 536 hits)

The combination of these two searches resulted in 125 hits. The first selection round eliminated non-English papers (minus 22), and dissertations, short communications, letters, non-empirical and/or non-peer reviewed papers (minus 38), leading to 65 remaining papers. In the second round, papers not dealing with healthy, working samples (minus 14), studies not dealing with vacation effects (minus 35), and studies not including both a pre-test and a post-test (minus 5) were excluded, resulting in 11 remaining papers. Finally, a third round led to the exclusion of 4 more papers. In two cases, papers were written by the same authors, based on the same sample with the second paper not offering extra information. A third paper was excluded because it investigated outcome variables in spouses instead of vacationers themselves. The fourth paper was excluded because it did not fit the definition of vacation as a voluntary period off work. The entire process resulted in a final selection of seven studies. These studies indicate that vacations have a weak positive effect on well-being that unfortunately does not seem to last long.

Examples of qualitative meta-analyses that aim specifically at theory explication and theory building can also be found in the tourism literature. Sirakaya and Woodside (2005), for instance, analyse different theoretical models used to explain travel decision-making processes. Similarly, Becken (2011) looks at the ways in which the problem of peak oil has been conceptualized in tourism research while Jennings (2006) critically analyses the literature on tourism and the environment. Weed (2009), on the other hand, conducts a meta-review of reviews on sports tourism to illustrate how unsystematic narrative reviews are. Due to their comprehensiveness and systematic identification of research studies, the reviews by Li et al. (2005) and Song and Li (2008) of tourism forecasting research can also be seen as examples of systematic reviews although they mostly list and describe rather than synthesize existing approaches.

These examples show that despite the specific challenges that meta-analysis faces in tourism, it has been successfully applied to a variety of research themes in tourism for which significant bodies of research exist and for which a synthesis and/or critical evaluation of approaches was necessary to achieve theoretical or methodological advancement. These meta-analyses also illustrate the importance of research synthesis in tourism, not only from a theoretical perspective but also from a practical point of view, which is very important for an applied field like tourism.

CONCLUSION

Meta-analyses are rigourous research endeavours that seek to overcome the limitations of individual studies by producing robust and generalizable findings or higher level/ better conceptualized/more comprehensive theories. Like all research, they have limitations that need to be carefully considered. Potential biases need to be understood and if possible eliminated or explicitly taken into account as part of the analysis. If done well, they can make significant contributions to a field of scientific inquiry, including tourism.

Meta-analyses have been applied to tourism-specific research problems but the opportunities are far from being exhausted. Further, tourism has so far not contributed to the development of meta-analysis as a research methodology, which is unfortunate. This is probably partly due to a lack of awareness of the benefits of meta-analyses and their applicability beyond standardized experimental studies such as clinical trials. Further, some of the reviews found in the tourism realm are systematic and explicit in the data collection process but not in other areas of the research. There is certainly some confusion as to what a meta-analysis is and what it is not. The tourism-related examples presented in this chapter clearly illustrate the need for systematic reviews in tourism and will hopefully inspire the readers to formulate meta-analytic research questions and collect and analyse the necessary data following the recommended steps and reporting procedures.

REFERENCES

Baaijens, S.R., P. Nijkamp and K. Van Montfort (1998), 'Explanatory meta-analysis for the comparison and transfer of regional tourist income multipliers', *Regional Studies*, **32** (9), 839–849.
Banas, J.A. and S.A. Rains (2010), 'A meta-analysis of research on inoculation theory', *Communication Monographs*, **77** (3), 281–311.
Becken, S. (2011), 'A critical review of tourism and oil', *Annals of Tourism Research*, **38** (2), 359–379.
Berkeljon, A. and S.A. Baldwin (2009), 'An introduction to meta-analysis for psychotherapy outcome research', *Psychotherapy Research*, **19** (4–5), 511–518.
Berman, N.G. and R.A. Parker (2002), 'Meta-analysis: neither quick nor easy', *BMC Medical Research Methodology*, **2** (10), available at http://www.biomedcentral.com/1471-2288/2/10.
Bloom, J.d., M. Kompier, S. Geurts, C.d. Weerth, T. Taris and S. Sonnentag (2009), 'Do we recover from vacation? Meta-analysis of vacation effects on health and well-being', *Journal of Occupational Health*, **51** (1), 13–25.
Borenstein, M., L.V. Hedges, J.P.T. Higgins and H.R. Rothstein (2009), *Introduction to Meta-Analysis*, West Sussex, UK: John Wiley & Sons.
Briggs, D.C. (2005), 'Meta-analysis: a case study', *Evaluation Review*, **29** (2), 87–127.
Brons, M., E. Pels, P. Nijkamp and P. Rietveld (2002), 'Price elasticities of demand for passenger air travel: a meta-analysis', *Journal of Air Transport Management*, **8** (3), 165–175.

Charlton, B.G. (1996), 'The uses and abuses of meta-analysis', *Family Practice*, **13** (4), 397–401.
Chatzisarantis, N.L.D. and A. Stoica (2009), 'A primer on the understanding of meta-analysis', *Psychology of Sport and Exercise*, **10** (5), 498–501.
Clarke, J. (2011), 'What is a systematic review?', *Evidence-Based Nursing*, **14** (3), 64.
Cooper, H., L.V. Hedges and J.C. Valentine (eds) (2009), *The Handbook of Research Synthesis and Meta-Analysis*, 2nd edition, New York: Russell Sage Foundation.
Crouch, G.I. (1992), 'Effect of income and price on international tourism', *Annals of Tourism Research*, **19** (4), 643–664.
Crouch, G.I. (1994), 'Demand elasticities for short-haul versus long-haul tourism', *Journal of Travel Research*, **33** (2), 2–7.
Crouch, G.I. (1995), 'A meta-analysis of tourism demand', *Annals of Tourism Research*, **22** (1), 103–118.
Crouch, G.I. (1996), 'Demand elasticities in international marketing: a meta-analytical application to tourism', *Journal of Business Research*, **36** (2), 117–136.
Delahaye, F., G. Landrivon, R. Ecochard and C. Colin (1991), 'Meta-analysis', *Health Policy*, **19** (2–3), 185–196.
De Matos, C.A., J.L. Henrique and C.A.V. Rossi (2007), 'Service recovery paradox: a meta-analysis', *Journal of Service Research*, **10** (1), 60–77.
Dickersin, K. and J.A. Berlin (1992), 'Meta-analysis: state-of-the-science', *Epidemiologic Reviews*, **14** (1), 154–176.
Egger, M. and G.D. Smith (1997), 'Meta-analysis: potentials and promise', *BMJ*, **315**, 1371–1374.
Harden, A. (2010), 'Mixed-methods systematic reviews: integrating quantitative and qualitative findings', National Center for the Dissemination of Disability Research Technical Brief No. 25, available at http://www.ncddr.org/kt/products/focus/focus25/Focus25.pdf.
Hemingway, P. and N. Brereton (2009),'What is a systematic review?', available at http://www.medicine.ox.ac.uk/bandolier/painres/download/whatis/Syst-review.pdf.
Higgins, J.P.T. and S. Green (eds) (2011), *Cochrane Handbook for Systematic Reviews of Interventions* Version 5.1.0 [updated March 2011], The Cochrane Collaboration, available at www.cochrane-handbook.org.
Ip, C., R. Law and H.A. Lee (2011), 'A review of website evaluation studies in the tourism and hospitality fields from 1996 to 2009', *International Journal of Tourism Research*, **13** (3), 234–265.
Jackson, D., R. Riley and I.R. White (2011), 'Multivariate meta-analysis: potential and promise', *Statistics in Medicine*, doi: 10.1002/sim.4172.
Jennings, G. (2006), 'A meta-analysis of current research in tourism and environment', in G. Jennings and N.P. Nickerson (eds), *Quality Tourism Experiences*, Oxford: Elsevier Butterworth-Heinemann Publications, pp. 174–183.
Law, R., S. Qi and D. Buhalis (2010), 'Progress in tourism management: a review of website evaluation in tourism research', *Tourism Management*, **31** (3), 297–313.
Li, G., H. Song and S.F. Witt (2005), 'Recent developments in econometric modeling and forecasting', *Journal of Travel Research*, **44**, 82–99.
Lim, C. (1999), 'A meta-analytic review of international tourism demand', *Journal of Travel Research*, **37** (3), 273–284.
Lipsey, M.W. (2007), 'Unjustified inferences about meta-analysis', *Journal of Experimental Criminology*, **3** (3), 271–279.
Lipsey, M.W. and D.B. Wilson (2001), *Practical Meta-Analysis* (Vol. 49), Thousand Oaks, CA: Sage Publications.
Lynn, M. and M. McCall (2000), 'Gratitude and gratuity: a meta-analysis of research on the service-tipping relationship', *Journal of Socio-Economics*, **29** (2), 203–214.
Montori, V.M., Swiontkowski, M.F. and D.J. Cook (2003), 'Methodologic issues in systematic reviews and meta-analyses', *Clinical Orthopaedics and Related Research*, **413**, 43–54.
Park, Y. and U. Gretzel (2007), 'Success factors for destination marketing web sites: a qualitative meta-analysis', *Journal of Travel Research*, **46** (1), 46–63.
Paterson, B.L., S.E. Thorne, C. Canam and C. Jillings (2001), *Meta-Study of Qualitative Health Research*, Thousand Oaks, CA: Sage.
Rosenfeld, R.M. (2004), 'Meta-analysis', *Outcomes Research in Otorhinolaryngology*, **66** (4), 186–195.
Rosenthal, R. and M.R. DiMatteo (2001), 'Meta-analysis: recent developments in quantitative methods for literature reviews', *Annual Review of Psychology*, **52** (1), 59–82.
Rothstein, H.R., A.J. Sutton and M. Borenstein (2006), *Publication Bias in Meta-Analysis: Prevention, Assessment and Adjustments*, West Sussex, UK: John Wiley & Sons.
Schmidt, F. (2008), 'Meta-analysis: a constantly evolving research integration tool', *Organizational Research Methods*, **11** (1), 96–113.
Schreiber, R., D. Crooks and P.N. Stern (1997), 'Qualitative meta-analysis', in J.M. Morse (ed.), *Completing a Qualitative Project: Details and Dialogue*, Thousand Oaks, CA: Sage, pp. 311–326.

Shelby, L.B. and J. J. Vaske (2008), 'Understanding meta-analysis: a review of the methodological literature', *Leisure Sciences: An Interdisciplinary Journal*, **30** (2), 96–110.

Sirakaya, E. and A.G. Woodside (2005), 'Building and testing theories of decision making by travellers', *Tourism Management*, **26** (6), 815–832.

Song, H. and G. Li (2008), 'Tourism demand modelling and forecasting: a review of recent research', *Tourism Management*, **29** (2), 203–220.

Thorne, S., L. Jensen, M.H. Kearney, G. Noblit and M. Sandelowski (2004), 'Qualitative metasynthesis: reflection on methodological orientation and ideological agenda', *Qualitative Health Research*, **14**, 1342–1365.

Timulak, L. (2009), 'Meta-analysis of qualitative studies: a tool for reviewing qualitative research findings in psychotherapy', *Psychotherapy Research*, **19** (4–5), 591–600.

Uttl, B., B. Odegard, K. Kisinger and M. Henry (2008), 'Meta-analysis of meta-analysis: transparency matters', *Canadian Journal of Experimental Psychology*, **62** (4), 298.

Weed, M. (2006), 'Undiscovered public knowledge: the potential of research synthesis approaches in tourism research', *Current Issues in Tourism*, **9** (3), 256–268.

Weed, M. (2009), 'Progress in sports tourism research? A meta-review and exploration of futures', *Tourism Management*, **30** (5), 615–628.

Wheatley, K. (2001), 'Understanding meta-analysis', *Evidence-based Oncology*, **2** (3), 116–122.

Woodside, A.G. and C. Dubelaar (2003), 'Increasing quality in measuring advertising effectiveness: a meta-analysis of question framing in conversion studies', *Journal of Advertising Research*, **43** (1), 78–85.

25 Network analysis
Ehsan Ahmed

INTRODUCTION

We live in a social world, where, to some extent, every social object (living and non-living) is connected with, or dependent on others. In principle, the span of this generalized connectedness or dependency is without limit, can integrate multiple forms and objects, and can span over several attributes (e.g., age, race, species) and contents such as friendship, kinship, resource, information and so on. A tourism firm, for instance, has connections not only with its suppliers and customers but also with its surrounding community and extended environment. Moreover, the multifaceted connections of the tourism firm with its suppliers, customers, surrounding community, and/or environment can be of various levels (e.g., local, regional, global), forms (e.g., informal, formal) and interest (e.g., economic, philanthropic) (Scott, 2000). The notion of connectedness or dependency therefore implies existence of an aggregated structure of infinite relationships that extends beyond the conventional view of relationships between two objects in isolation. Studies on networks aim to capture these aggregated views of relationships and offer analytical insights to understand the role of relationships on the objects embedded within these relationships.

The importance of collaboration, alliance, partnership, business clusters and similar other concepts to better understand aggregated tourism relationships have been frequently noted by a number of writers in the tourism literature. Nevertheless, to date, little has been undertaken to examine these widely discussed tourism topics through the lens of network analysis. On the contrary, numerous business studies in the wider field of discipline identify the importance of networks studies on strategic alliances and collaborative relationships for businesses (Borgatti and Foster, 2003; Lemmetyinen, 2009). Arguably, there are plausible opportunities for tourism researchers to incorporate network analytical approaches into network studies. This chapter informs these opportunities and aims to outline a prospective research avenue for the tourism researchers and practitioners working or willing to work with tourism networks. It attempts to present what work has been done to study tourism networks, pointing out some of the differences and commonalities and then discussing where future research might best be headed. In so doing, the subsequent sections of this chapter are arranged as follows:

First, the chapter discusses the fundamental nature of network analysis techniques and its evaluation. Second, the chapter provides the background and types of problem that network analysis is designed to handle. This explicates the fundamental concept of tourism relationships within a network context. In this section the author also presents a four-fold typology of network research to classify empirical approaches to study tourism networks. Third, a review process of the modest literature on tourism networks is provided. Utilizing the four-fold typology and literature review, the chapter discusses the applications of network analysis to tourism, including the discussion of empirical works that have used the techniques and findings. Fourth, advantages and limitations of network analysis are pointed out. Finally, the chapter offers a discussion concerning what future directions might be taken by tourism researchers hoping to expand this important, but understudied, field of tourism research.

NATURE OF NETWORK ANALYSIS AND ITS EVALUATION

Fundamentally, a network can be described as a set of items, called *nodes*, with connections between them called *edges* (Newman, 2003). Using this concept, network analysis, in general, identifies relevant nodes, focuses on the connections between the nodes and seeks to model the nature, pattern and implications of the connections between the nodes (Scott, 2000; Wasserman and Faust, 1994). Transferring to tourism theories and practices, tourism elements (e.g., employees, tourism firms, stakeholders, etc.) can be presented by nodes (or actors). Corresponding relationships (e.g., monetary transaction, communication, membership, acquaintanceship, etc.) between the tourism elements can be presented by edges (or links). In this way, tourism nodes and corresponding edges can be aggregated to form a network of relationships (tourism network) and thus be employed to analyse relational properties of the tourism elements embedded within the tourism network. Figure 25.1 depicts a small example tourism network comprising five tourism related organizations (A, B, C, D, and E) and seven corresponding links. In the network, for example, actor A has direct links with actors B, C, and E but does not have any direct link with actor D. Again, as we can see in Figure 25.1, actor A has only outgoing ties with actor B, C, and E and actor D has both outgoing and incoming ties with actor E. Built around this common or core concept, network analysis can be utilized to investigate and analyse the nature and pattern of links between and/or among the tourism elements (A, B, C, D, and E) involved in different types of relationships. In a real-life tourism perspective, thus actor A may be a holiday resort; actor B is a tour operator, and actor C has spa and retreat facilities receiving special package deals from the resort (actor A) to attract potential visitors. The tour operator (actor B) uses the information and attributes of the spa and retreat facilities in its promotional materials. Actor E is the local tourism association where both A and C are members. Actor D is the regional tourism organization (RTO) that looks after the overall tourism development of the region, and in turn charges a membership fee from the local tourism association.

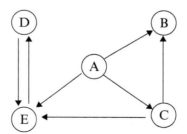

Figure 25.1   A small network with five tourism organizations (nodes) and seven corresponding links (edges)

In this way a network can represent an infinite number of tourism elements (actors) and a wide range of relationships between the tourism elements embedded in the network.

The concept of a network, at a very rudimentary stage, was a metaphor for the complex interactions among people in a social setting. The origins of network theory and practice may be found in research conducted in the late 1950s and 1960s on "social behaviour and exchange" (Homans, 1958, 1974), the social psychology of groups (Thibaut and Kelly, 1959), "exchange and power" (Blau, 1964), "operational research in local government" (Ward, 1964) and "inter-organizational and exchange analysis" (Levin and White, 1961; Miller, 1958; Reid, 1964). From the mid-1980s onwards network analysis and theory began to attract the attention of growing numbers of economists, planners, sociologists, geographers, psychologists, and politicians.

In sociology, the birthplace of network analysis, a network is defined as a specific type of relation (ties) linking a defined sets of persons, objects or events, and the sets of persons, objects or events on which a network is defined are called actors or nodes (Mitchell, 1969). Thus, from a sociological perspective, a network consists of a set of nodes (usually individuals), and ties representing some relationship between the nodes. Typically, a social network analyst would seek to model these relationships to depict the structure of a group or the individual members belong to the group (Wasserman and Faust, 1994). Today, there are many definitions of a network but, as pointed out by Jarillo (1988, p. 31), many have been developed by applying this basic definition to new areas such as the study of business organizations, internet blogs, tourism destinations, sexually transmitted diseases, terrorist attacks, academic publications, world wide web, or even to some extent biological systems or ecosystems.

Network concepts and theories in tourism studies date back only few years, as it became increasingly recognized that relationships between enterprises can stimulate inter-organizational learning and knowledge exchange, resulting in qualitative and/or quantitative benefits to businesses, communities and destinations (Morrison et al., 2004, p. 2). A tourism network can be understood as a set of formal and informal (social) relationships that shape collaborative actions between government, the tourism industry and the general public (Atkinson and Coleman, 1992; Dredge, 2006b). Scott et al. (2008) have described tourism networks as loosely articulated groups of independent suppliers linked to deliver an overall tourism experience.

BACKGROUND AND TYPES OF PROBLEMS THAT NETWORK ANALYSIS IS DESIGNED TO HANDLE

To date, a wide range of concepts and theories are available to study networks, with many more to be expected in the future. Typically, the majority of these approaches are crystallized around three interrelated network contexts. These are: (1) actors of relationships, (2) content/s of relationships, and (3) form/s (nature and pattern) of relationships.

Actors of relationships refers to any entity that forms or has the ability to form connections or linkages with other actors. This addresses "who" such as individual, group, organization, or to some extent non-human elements (e.g., natural environment, seasonality, etc.) having linkages or relationship with others. *Content of relationships* refers to the subjective type of relation represented in the connection between actors (e.g., friend-

Table 25.1   Typology of network research

Independent Variable or Input Focus	Dependent Variable or Outcome Focus	
	Actor	Network
Actor variable	Impact of actors on other actors through dyadic (one to one) interactions	Impact of individual actors on a network
Network variable	Impact of a network on individual actors	Whole network or network-level interactions

Source: Adapted from Provan et al. (2007).

ship, information and knowledge, power and authority, etc.). This addresses "what is the purpose of connection between the actors?" Finally, *form (nature and pattern) of relationships* refers to the relational properties (e.g., presence, strength, direction, density, etc.) of the connections between actors. This addresses "how the connections are taking place between and/or among actors of a network?"

Although, these three contextual grounds are customary and reflect simple mechanisms, they are not easy to define empirically in a tourism context. A tourism destination network, for example, comprises of a large number of tourism elements (actors) directly and indirectly related to tourism. These large numbers of tourism elements are again embedded in a myriad of relationships (links) with other elements within and outside the destination and can include several types of content, attributes, and forms of relationships (e.g., information exchange, economic dependency, friendship, memberships, etc.). Therefore, in a practical sense, the actors and their relationships within a tourism context can be anything from a list of infinite possibilities. This leads to the question: is there any specific research approach to study tourism networks, or alternatively, what are the empirical bases for studying tourism networks?

Most scholars who study the topic would agree that no single grand theory of networks exists (Faulkner and De Rond, 2000; Galaskiewicz, 2007; Kilduff and Tsai, 2003; Monge and Contractor, 2003). However, theorizing about networks can generally be thought of as coming from two different but complementary perspectives: the view from the individual element embedded in a set of relationships (actor level) and the view from an aggregated form of analysis (network level). Wasserman and Galaskiewicz (1994) also make this distinction, referring to a micro-level versus a macro-level network focus. Kilduff and Tsai (2003) and Marsden (1990) refer to the important distinction between a focus on the egocentric network versus the whole network. Building on these perspectives, Provan et al. (2007) categorized the research on networks along two dimensions: the independent variable or input focus being utilized for the study (actor variables or network variables) and the dependent variable or outcome focus adopted by the researcher (actor or network outcome). Using these dimensions, they also demonstrated the possibility of four different types of network research. These are: (1) impact of actor/s on other actor/s, (2) impact of individual actors on a network, (3) impact of a network on individual actors, and (4) whole network or network-level interaction (see Table 25.1).

Utilizing the aforementioned typology, this chapter reviews tourism research on networking.

APPLICATION OF NETWORK ANALYSIS TO TOURISM

A Review of the Empirical Literature on Tourism Networks

In an effort to identify recent empirical work done on tourism networks, the author undertook an extensive review of the literature. First, a search for web content utilizing snow-ball techniques was conducted using 'Google Scholar'. Consistent with the broad range of definitions of networks in the tourism literature, the search terms included *tourism networks*, *tourism collaboration*, *tourism relationship*, and *tourism alliances*. Web content found was reviewed and a corresponding list of references and citations were used to identify subsequent empirical works focusing on tourism networks. This process continued until most of the publications identified were already included in the list. For the sake and ease of access, only journal articles were recruited. Sources such as chapters or books were excluded due to accessibility and/ or length of treatment. The author also limited the search to the 10-year period from 2001 to 2011 because most of the empirical work on tourism networks has been done in recent years and because the study of networks is still relatively new in the tourism discipline.

After the initial search, the author culled through the abstracts of the selected articles. Often, the abstracts provided ample information about the methods and unit of analysis. Based on a reading of these abstracts, it was possible to eliminate the articles that were not based on empirical data. Initially, full-length journal articles typical of published research in a tourism networks and relationships were identified for examination. Notably, some of the articles often talked of a tourism network, but did not study the network itself, thus ignoring the basic network theoretical insight that actors and actor-to-actor relationships are likely to be influenced by the aggregated set of relationships (Mitchell, 1969). For example, many articles address computer networks, system designs, websites, and technological applications, and many dealt with the neural network paradigm. In similar perspective, many articles used the words "alliance", "relationships", "collaboration", "partnerships", and "networks" but predominantly focused on dyadic relationship limited to only two actors in isolation. Interestingly, in many instances, the term "*network*" is used in everyday speech without precision as a definition of a particular phenomenon. The concept of a network has "blurry edges" such as in its usage as part of a network ideology that advocates egalitarian, open communities (Wellman and Berkowitz, 1988, p. 81) or confusion with the term networking in a tourism context. This problem of definition of the term "network" is not confined to tourism research and applies also to network studies in the wider management literature. This wide usage has led to a diverse literature where the term network analysis is used as a metaphor, homology, paradigm or method (Wellman, 1988) in different contexts. In this chapter the definition of network used is "a complex set of inter-relationships in a social system" (Mitchell, 1969) and articles that did not focus on aggregated view of actor/s, contents, and forms of relationships were eliminated from the consideration list.

Table 25.2 *Search-summary of empirical tourism-network articles obtained from academic journals, 2001 to July, 2011*

Year	No. of empirical articles reviewed	Perceived Typology					Type of analysis	
		A	B	C	D	Mixed	Descriptive	Analytic
2001	4	1	–	–	2	1	4(1+0+0+2+1)	–
2002	1	–	–	–	1	–	1(0+0+0+1+0)	–
2003	1	–	–	–	1	–	1(0+0+0+1+0)	–
2004	2	–	–	–	1	1	2(0+0+0+1+1)	–
2005	4	1	–	–	3	–	3(1+0+0+2+0)	1(0+0+0+1+0)
2006	9	2		2	4	1	7(2+0+2+2+1)	2(0+0+0+2+0)
2007	7	1	1	–	4	1	6(1+1+0+3+1)	1(0+0+0+1+0)
2008	7	1	–	–	6	–	5(1+0+0+4+0)	2(0+0+0+2+0)
2009	16	4	2	1	8	1	12(4+2+1+4+1)	4(0+0+0+4+0)
2010	18	5	1	2	9	1	12(5+1+1+5+0)	6(0+0+1+4+1)
2011 (as of June)	4	1	1	–	2	–	1(0+1+0+0+0)	3(1+0+0+2+0)
Total	73	16	5	5	41	6	54	19

A major limitation of the search process is the language barrier of the author. Many articles on tourism networks are published in languages other than English, but were not included in the final list. Once relevant articles and potentially relevant articles were identified, the author went on to read the complete articles to make sure that each fit the requirements of the search.

Each article that fulfilled the requirement of focusing on tourism networks was then indexed. A summary was produced for the search result which list year, number of articles per year, typology, and types of analysis (Table 25.2). The final list of reviewed journal articles includes 73 empirical tourism network studies. All studies included in the review involve some type of data collection and analysis. Although the review was thorough, I make no claims that it is exhaustive and, despite my best efforts, I may well have unintentionally omitted a small number of tourism network studies from the review.

Search Findings

The article summary in Table 25.2 provides identifiable markers for comparisons of the research being conducted in tourism network studies. Several distinct themes emerged in the empirical research articles reviewed from tourism network literature. For one thing, most of these studies focus on the two extreme perspectives of network research approaches: actor level (typology A) and network level (typology D) (57 out of 73). There is a noticeable paucity of research approaches to examine the impact of individual actor/s on the whole network (typology B) and vice versa (typology C). Another clear finding is that there is an emerging popularity of network studies in recent times, indicated by the number of article published in the years 2009 (16) and 2010 (18) in comparison to the number of articles published in the previous years. Moreover, the sole dominance of the descriptive approach to study tourism networks in the early works is diminishing and an emergence of analytical and quantitative research approach can be noticed in the most recent articles.

What follows is an attempt to present the selected empirical works by utilizing the network research typology depicted in Table 25.1. In so doing, all the selected articles are organized in four types of network research approaches. There are 16 articles in category A, 5 articles in category B, 5 articles in category C, and 41 articles in category D. It is also important to note here that, many of the selected articles successfully focused on more than one typology (e.g., A and D, or A to B to D). Moreover, some of the studies largely fall under the grey area between the actor-level and network-level boundary line of the four typologies. Articles of these types are classified under a new category and named as mixed typology. There are six articles identified in the mixed typology.

Typology A: Impact of Actor/s on Other Actor/s

In this type of network research, researchers often utilize characteristics and attributes of individual actors to explain their relationships with other actors. Actor-level attributes such as trust, economic condition, nature of business, legal structure, etc. help to explain the nature of an actor's involvement with others. These views, often referred to as ego-centric, are concerned with trying to explain how involvement of an individual actor in a network affects its actions and outcomes. Network research of this category in tourism is predominantly descriptive in nature where several possible dyadic (actor-to-actor) relationships such as alliances, partnerships, social nominations are taken into account and analysed. Information collected from the actors in general covers a wide range of actor-attribute information along with relational data. The majority of the empirical works, identified as typology A, utilize in-depth interview and thick description supported by theoretical review and secondary information. The data analysis approach used highlights actor-level information and theoretical frameworks to explain how complex web of relations and shared concern of the tourism actors contemplates specific tourism phenomena of interest. The analysis helps the researcher to answer several relational questions that include: (1) the impact of dyadic or network ties on organizational performance, (2) which types of links are most or least beneficial to individual network members, (3) which network positions might be most or least influential, and (4) how the position of organizations in a network might shift over time in response to changes within and outside the network (Provan et al., 2007). Identified examples of this type in the tourism network context are as follows.

Tyler and Dinan (2001) investigate the role of interested groups (umbrella groups, professional groups, trade groups, decision makers, and public sector representatives) in England's emerging tourism policy network within the context of a theoretical discussion on public policy analysis, policy styles, and policy networks. Saxena (2005) investigated the patterns of interaction and communication of the actors to highlight how a complex web of relations provides relational capital for different actors to enable greater learning and co-operation, accommodate shared concerns about the local environment, and collectively sell of the destination. His empirical works rest on 45 semi-structured interviews comprising tourism managers in three case study areas – Castleton, Bakewell, and Tideswell in the Peak District National Park (PDNP). Nash (2006) implements network analysis to identify tourism issues in peripheral locations (North Scotland) and develops an empirical model representing the aggregated views of all respondents from each study region. Sheehan et al. (2007) discuss urban tourism promotion and explored the relationships between the DMO, charged with crafting and executing destination promotion, and its two most powerful stakeholders – the city (or urban government) and hotels (or accommodation sector). Tinsley and Lynch (2007) studies small tourism business relations within a rural tourism destination and their contribution to destination development. Wilkinson and March (2009) discuss the managerial application of network research in tourism. Based on interview data from the tourism managers they offer a method for investigating and conceptualizing network relationships between firms in the Australian wine region of the Hunter Valley. Lemmetyinen and Go (2009) propose that local tourism businesses must develop new key capabilities in order to face future global competition. Their study uses case methodology and in-depth interviews to examine organizational realities as a product of the subjective enactments or social constructions of individual actors through the perceptions of two coordinators. The case-analysis findings identify the coordination of cooperative activities in tourism business networks as a prerequisite for enhancing the value-creation process, and building the brand-identity process across the network. Fyrberg and Jüriado (2009) extended the understanding of tourism networks within the service-dominant logic. Their work uses empirical data from a travel industry network incorporating in-depth interviews and a survey of approximately 100 meetings professionals. They found that the network approach provides a deeper understanding of how actors integrate with one another and how this interaction leads to co-created outcomes that can be translated into value. Based on the narrative accounts of 22 actors in a strategic network of organizations promoting cruise tourism in the Baltic Sea region, Lemmetyinen (2009) analyses the extent of coordination of cooperation within the tourism industry. The study reveals different forms of coordination which enhance network development. Furthermore, it pinpoints the need for coordinated activities on the different levels and dimensions of cooperation. Tribe (2010) extends network study in a different but interesting tourism network context. His article critically analyses the territories and tribes of tourism studies focusing on the culture and practices of the academics working in the tourism discipline. Here, in his article, actor–network theory is deployed to link relevant objects (living and non-living) and reveal academic networks by interviewing tourism academics. Presenza and Cipollina (2010) examine 354 hospitality firms acting in Molise Region (Italy). Each operator in their study was asked through an interview to judge the importance of collaborating with other stakeholders to enhance the effectiveness of their management and marketing activities. Their study suggests that public stakeholders are more important for both management and marketing activities than those in the private sector. Wegner et al. (2010) report on in-depth interviews that explores a number of different types of partnerships involved in tourism and protected areas with the aim of providing recommendations to policy makers regarding how successful partnerships operate. Seven key themes for policy recommendations and potential implication emerge in their study. Based on a semi-structured interviews among 21 small accommodation operations around the city of Perth (Western Australia), including self-contained, bed and breakfast, and farm-stay businesses, Alonso (2010) examined the importance of relationships among the small hospitality operations. The study by Weidenfeld et al. (2010) in Cornwall, England, is based on in-depth interviews with tourist attraction managers and key informants, complemented by a survey of 435 tourists. Their study provides insights into the relationship between the nature of the tourism product, spatial clustering and tourism behavior. Zach and Racherla (2011) explore the determinants of perceived value derived from inter-organizational collaborations in a tourism destination. Examining the tourism organizations operating within Elkhart County, Indiana, they propose a theoretical model of perceived value, drawing upon the rich stream of literature related to strategic collaborations and inter-organizational networks. Their result suggests that a significant positive value of collaboration is achieved from dyadic relationships. Importantly, the results suggest that the positive effect achieved from one-to-one partnerships decreases once an organization collaborates with several other organizations.

Typology B: Impact of Individual Actor/s on a Network

In this type of research, analysts utilize actor-level phenomena to explain how individual actors and their actions might affect outcomes at the network level, such as network structures, stability, and effectiveness. Here, the key focus is the aggregated outcomes at the network level rather than for the individual actors that comprise the network.

In tourism, this approach is most likely to be found in the studies of tourism networks led by destination management organizations (DMO), larger organizations, entrepreneurs, or local tourism authorities such as government, local community, or policy makers. Here, the driving tourism organizations' actions are likely to affect the entire network through policy development within a destination network. Examples identified in the literature review include work by Henriksen and Halkier (2009), Lemmetyinen and Go (2010b), Wray (2009), Ziene and Hazel (2007).

Ziene and Hazel (2007) investigate destination networks by focusing on multiple ownership, or portfolio entrepreneurship, when more than one small or micro business within a specific destination is owned by the same entrepreneur. By investigating supply side and demand side of two destinations, the authors conclude that multiple ownership create webs of power which significantly impact on the business structure and operation of tourism destinations. Wray (2009) demonstrates how concepts derived from the policy community, policy network and issues management theories can be used to understand the roles, activities and interactions of government, corporate and pressure group stakeholders engaged in tourism policy, planning, and management in destination contexts. The application of this approach is demonstrated through a case analysis of the tourism policy and planning system that underpins the destination system of Byron Bay, a significant domestic and international destination on the East Coast of Australia. Henriksen and Halkier (2009) examine the process of policy change from local promotions towards regional tourism policies. Adopting an institution perspective, and based on in-depth case study, the authors conclude that the issue of localism has been effectively addressed by establishing and operating as a network-based body where individual stakeholders are mutually dependent on the specific capacities of their partners, a consensual style of decision making is prevailing, and a division of labor has been established that engages local actors in destination-wide tasks while at the same time enabling them to maintain close links with small tourism businesses in their area. Lemmetyinen and Go (2010b) investigate the role of a regional DMO in coordinating cooperation and enhancing the value creation process in three tourism regions and finds that by taking active roles in the project the DMO is able to enhance the value creation process through integrated marketing efficiency.

Typology C: Impact of a Network on Individual Actors

In this type of network research, researchers focus at the level of the network and try to understand the impact of network-level structures and behavior on individual actors. Here, the fundamental assumption is that actor/s are embedded in a myriad of social relationships, and it is impossible to understand their behavior without understanding the relational context in which they function (Granovetter, 1985). In this type of network research, the outcome or behavior of an actor is explained through structural attributes that incorporate the interaction among the different network members (Burt, 1987).

A common theme found in tourism literature is the impact of network involvement on organizational development, learning, or innovation. Identified examples in the tourism literature include work by Erkuş-Öztürk (2010), Kelliher et al. (2009), Mackellar (2006), Reinl and Kelliher (2010), Stokes (2006).

Stokes (2006) examines the inter-organizational network that influences the event tourism strategy of public-sector development agencies in Australia. A qualitative methodology of convergent interviews, followed by multiple case research across six Australian states and territories, was employed where networks of events agencies that impact on their strategy processes for events tourism are the core focus. In a single case study of regional festival in New South Wales, Australia, Mackellar (2006) demonstrates the links between interactive network and innovation. The research demonstrates innovation for individual organizations or business clusters as an effect of the event networks. Kelliher et al. (2009) examine the Tourism Learning Network (TLN), a small firm learning network model within the Fáilte Ireland (Irish tourism development agency). Their findings suggest that the approaches underlying TLN facilitate the development of organizational capabilities and result in active and substantial TLN involvement among participating tourism enterprises. Erkuş-Öztürk (2010) explores the role of local, global, and associational networking, as well as company size, in the contribution of tourism companies to the level of their creativeness. The study reveals that the level of creativeness of a company is influenced by its level of networking at both global and local levels, as well as its "institutional thickness". Based on the research findings carried out on another TLN, Reinl and Kelliher (2010) proposes a framework of cooperative learning. Their research findings offer insight into how network structures, support and interrelationships leverages organizational resources and may facilitate learning process completion in the micro-firm environment.

Typology D: Whole Network or Network-level Interaction

The majority of the works identified by the author falls under this category of tourism network research. Researchers using this approach choose to study the impact of multi-level actions and structures on network level outcomes. Typically, these structural issues are aggregated across the entire network to understand the outcome at the network level.

Several distinct themes emerge in the empirical tourism network articles. Apart from few exceptions (e.g., Zach et al., 2008), the majority of the whole network studies in tourism focus at tourism destination(s). Specific geographic location is defined as the tourism context of the whole network and corresponding tourism elements within the geographic boundary are considered as the actors of the network. Here, examination of the whole destination network(s) aims to facilitate an understanding of how a multilateral web of relationships operates within and influences a tourism region or destination. In concert, by using a whole network approach, several interesting tourism themes are discussed and examined in the tourism literature. For example, Baggio et al. (2010b), Beaumonta and Dredge (2009), Cooper et al. (2009), Gibson et al. (2005), Nordin and Svensson (2007), Pavlovich (2002), Shih (2005), Tinsley and Lynch (2007), Wesley and Pforr (2010) discuss destination characteristics and governance; Camprubí et al. (2008) and Lemmetyinen and Go (2010a) talk about destination image and branding; Baggio and Cooper (2010), Baggio et al. (2010b), McLeod et al. (2010), Miguéns and Corfu (2008), Pavlovich (2002), Scott et al. (2008) and Xiao et al. (2011) explore transfer of information and knowledge management; Novelli et al. (2006), Petrou, et al. (2007) and Romeiro and Costa (2010) discuss product development and innovation; Baggio and Corigliano (2009), Bhat and Milne (2008), Braun (2003) focus on ICT diffusion and use; Dredge (2006b) and Pforr (2006) highlight tourism policy networks; Baggio (2006), Baggio et al. (2010a), da Fontoura Costa and Baggio (2009) and Mariussen et al. (2010) discuss the complexity approach by utilizing web network data in tourism context; Fadeeva (2004), Halme (2001), Hede and Stokes (2009), Pavlovich (2001) and Timur and Getz (2008) examine sustainable tourism development; Anderson (2009), Brás et al. (2010), Hede and Stokes (2009), Moscardo et al. (2009) focus on special interest tourism and tourism events; and Baggio (2007, 2011), Beesley (2005) and Erkuş-Öztürk (2009) examine tourism collaboration and cooperation.

A clear finding is that the identified empirical works on the whole network can be classified into two distinct contextual grounds: (1) single network study, and (2) multiple network study. In a single network study the network analysis is restricted to a single network. Network analyses of this nature are again found in the literature examining a single network based on static and/or longitudinal relational data. The research outcome of the former approach (i.e., single network and static relational data) explores the existing relationships within a single network and can help our understanding of the nature and pattern of network relationships at a specific point of time. Prominent examples include the work by Shih (2005) who tested a sample of drive tourists for 16 destinations in Nantou, Taiwan. Travelers visiting sequence to these 16 destinations were the network links between destinations. A number of recommendations were made regarding the location and type of tourist facilities to be offered and promoted based on the concurrent network analysis. In a similar fashion Zach et al. (2008) collected empirical data from travelers who visited a regional destination in the United States. The traveling sequence of the sample visitors were used as the link between several places in the regional destination and then analysed with respect to its network structure. In another study of this type, Baggio (2006) examined and analysed the network structure of the community of websites belonging to Italian travel agencies. Bhat and Milne (2008), examined the network effects on destination website development in New Zealand. The major part of their study is based on the semi-structured interview of a network consisting of 35 CEOs or management of the organizations involved in the website development. Baggio and Cooper (2010) used a case study on Elba, Italy to illustrate the effect of network typology on information diffusion. A static structural characterization of the network formed by destination stakeholders was derived from the stakeholder interviews and website link analysis. Some other prominent examples of this type (single network and static relational data) are the works by Miguéns and Corfu (2008), Baggio (2011), Baggio and Corigliano (2009), Baggio et al. (2010a, b), Brás et al. (2010), Camprubí et al. (2008), Cooper et al. (2009), da Fontoura Costa and Baggio (2009), Lemmetyinen and Go (2010a), Mariussen et al. (2010), Romeiro and Costa (2010), Sainaghi and Baggio (2011).

The latter approach (i.e., single network and longitudinal relational data) collects relational data over a time period and can help to understand such issues as how networks evolve, how they are governed, and, ultimately, how collective outcomes might be generated (Fyrberg and Jüriado, 2009). Prominent examples include the work by Pavlovich (2001, 2003) who examined tourism destination evolution and transformation of the Waitomo Caves, New Zealand. Lisa Beesley (2005) conducted a 3-year qualitative study of a collaborative tourism research project in Hawaii, United States. Dredge (2006b) investigated the relationships between local government and industry to critically discuss the role of networks. Her study rests on a case study of the local tourism networks in Lake Macquarie over the period of 1970–2000. Using the Smith Beach coastal tourism, Western Australia, and residential development as a case study, Wesley and Pforr (2010) examined the nature of coastal tourism governance. Some other examples of this type (single network and longitudinal relational data) are the works by Gibson et al.(2005), Hede and Stokes (2009), Nordin and Svensson (2007), Novelli et al. (2006) and Pforr (2006).

In contrast to single network approaches, multiple network studies are comparative in nature. Network properties of the whole network are aggregated across an entire network and then compared with those of other similar networks. Prominent examples include work by Halme (2001) who studied six tourism networks in four European countries to investigate learning towards sustainable development in multi-stakeholder public–private networks; Pavlovich (2002) who explored tourism network structure in the UK, Italy, and Egypt; Petrou et al. (2007) who focused on the role of business networks using illustrative examples and findings from the case-study regions in the UK, Spain, and Greece; Scott et al. (2008) examined the structural properties of inter-organizational networks within destinations. Their paper outlined four Australian case studies that demonstrate the utility of network analysis. Erkuş-Öztürk (2009) examined the role of cluster types and firm size in designing the level of network relations among 12 geographic clusters of Antalya located at the Southern part of Turkey. Beaumonta and Dredge (2009) investigated how different tourism governance networks operate and the effects of this governance on local tourism policy. Three local tourism networks from Queensland, Australia, were examined in their study. These are (1) council-led network governance structure, (2) a participant-led community network governance structure, and (3) a local tourism organization (LTO)-led industry network governance structure. Some other examples of this type (multiple networks) are the works by Anderson (2009),

Fadeeva (2004), McLeod et al. (2010), Moscardo et al. (2009), Timur and Getz (2008), Tinsley and Lynch (2007).

Mixed Typology

At times the network researcher may be interested to examine several levels of network input and outcome. For example, relational data can be collected at a dyadic level (relationship between two actors) and analysis can proceed at the network level through aggregating the relationships between the dyads. In this way it is possible to utilize the same network data to examine various range of network outcomes (e.g., dyads, triads, clusters, whole networks). Network analysis is therefore not strictly confined within the four typologies presented in Table 25.1. Rather, a network analyst has the flexibility to amalgamate more than one typology, switch from one typology to another, and/or explore a wide range of network input variables and outcomes. Many of the works found in the literature review undertake permutations and combinations of the actor-level and network level dimensions. Prominent examples include work by Tinsley and Lynch (2001) who examined a small tourism business network and its contribution to destination development on the West Coast of Scotland. In their study, relational data were first collected from the small tourism businesses through in-depth interview (typology A). Information obtained was used to analyse networking between small tourism businesses and its contribution to destination development (typology D). Beesley (2004) examined knowledge-based networks. She explored the emergent pattern of knowledge not only within individual, group, organizational, and inter-organizational levels of learning, but also among them. Dredge (2006a) focused on the theoretical and practical implications of local tourism policy networks on collaborative planning. She examined the structures and social interactions between several clusters relevant to destination management policy and practice of Redland Shire located to the southeast of Brisbane, Australia. Data were collected to understand collaborative planning at the individual organizational level and sub-network level of a tourism destination. Sorensen (2007) examined the local and non-local social networks and innovation in tourism. Relational and attribute data were collected from individual tourism firms by interviewing key personnel. The analysis, conducted both at the organizational level and network level (local and non-local), has enhanced our understanding of different types of social network geography and their innovation benefit. Andersson and Ekman (2009) conducted a web-based survey with present members of ambassador (tourist) networks of five Swedish cities and towns. Their study indentified four main dimensions of networks and, on this basis, outlined a typology of four main categories of tourist networks. How individual influences their networks and subsequently how the networks influences other networks as a place branding tool is the major focus of this study. Pyo (2010) examined a tourism chain performance comprises of four attractions in Icheon City, located an hour's drive southeast from Seoul, in the Republic of Korea. Network efficiency of the four attraction areas is measured by collecting preference data from the tourist and strategic information from the attraction managers. Analysis was undertaken both at the individual level and tourism chain level.

ADVANTAGES AND LIMITATIONS OF NETWORK ANALYSIS CONCEPTUALLY AND FOR POLICY FORMULATION

The notion of networks seems to be relevant in industry analysis and is gaining popularity in tourism research as it has the ability to mimic and analyse the aggregated nature of relationships between various tourism stakeholders. In particular, from a structural point of view, tourism industry can be seen as ensembles of elements of many different sorts, many of which are connected by some kind of relationship (Leiper, 1989). As many authors have noted (e.g., Leiper, 2000; Pavlovich, 2001, 2003; Scott et al., 2008), these relationships within the tourism industry are numerous, diversified in nature, and can be regarded as an assemblage of elements with many aggregated structures forming a unitary whole. In a similar perspective, Wilkinson and March (2009), Crotts et al. (1998), and Smith (1988) have described the tourism industry as an amalgamation of a wide range of suppliers clustering together to provide experiences of value to the tourist. By using the concepts of network and corresponding analytical tools, a network analyst can conceptualize, visualize and analyse these linkages and relationships between several tourism elements (Scott et al., 2008). For instance, relational mapping, one of the fundamental network analytical tools, can provide a graphical representation of multifaceted relationships between several tourism elements. Theoretical frameworks of this nature have the ability to inform a wide range of relational forms such as who is connected to whom, number and direction of connections, most or least connected elements, existence of sub-group or cluster (Iacobucci, 1996). This information can be used to improve connectivity by intervening to mend broken or indirect links, or reconfiguring the aggregated relationships to be more efficient. Here, the diagnostics can aid several tourism phenomena such as collaboration and innovation (Cooper and Hall, 2008), information and knowledge management (Baggio and Cooper, 2010; Cooper 2006), policy and planning (Dredge, 2006b; Pforr, 2004, 2006), destination governance (Pavlovich, 2001, 2003), sustainable development (Halme, 2001).

Although there is a wide range of possibilities for utilizing network analysis in tourism studies, the network literature is far less extensive than many others in the wider literature on tourism research. Indeed, the broadest conclusion that can be drawn from the literature review of this chapter is that there is simply not very much of it. Numerous business studies discuss the importance of networks, strategic alliances and collaborative relationships for businesses. Despite such a rich body of knowledge, however, such discussion appears to have fallen short of incorporating network analysis in tourism research in a serious way. In fact, tourism studies exploring these dimensions are few and far between. What follows is a discussion of what the author believes as the primary limitation and methodological issues that must be overcome if significant progress is to be made on the topic.

As noted earlier, network analysis depends on relational rather than attribute data. Here, the presence and nature of relationships between actors is the focus, rather than the characteristics of each individual actor. Because of this focus on relationships, the techniques used to analyse networks differ substantially from conventional survey research methods and require supplementary knowledge and skills. Suppose we are studying economic ties among several tourism stakeholders within a destination. For example, an accommodation provider has been selected to be in our sample. When we ask the accommodation provider, he/she identifies strong economic ties with seven stake-holders. We need to track down each of those seven stakeholders and ask them about their economic ties, as well. The seven stakeholders are in our sample because the accommodation provider is (and vice versa), so the "sample elements" are no longer "independent". This means that actors are usually not sampled independently in network studies, as in many other kinds of studies (most typically, surveys). If one actor happens to be selected, then we must also include all other actors to whom our sample has (or could have) ties. As a result, network approaches tend to study whole populations by means of census, rather than by sample.

Another limitation of the network analysis can be pointed out as the boundary specification issue, i.e., the managerial and theoretical perspectives to distinguish whom to consider and whom not to consider within a network (Laumann et al. 1989). This is a challenging issue for any network studies both in tourism and non-tourism contexts. For example, a tourist attraction of any destination is connected to a wide range of support organizations that are directly and indirectly related to tourism. Here, the relationship between the attraction and the local tourism organization (LTO) is explicit and easily identifiable. They may have a formal membership program, belong to the same industry, work with similar types of customer product and value, share resources and knowledge, or may even organize promotions and events together. On the contrary, the relationship between the very same attraction and any other non-tourism organization such as road transport authority or fire service of that destination is significant but hard to relate in a tourism perspective. Similarly, two attractions within the same destination may compete with one another and may not have direct or identifiable relationship in between. However, they might influence one another through the invisible string of competition. Therefore, a network study may involve any number of actors, elements and type of relationships from a list of infinite possibilities. Nevertheless, in a practical sense, it is not possible to consider every element and all possible types of relational content. The network researcher has to stop somewhere in the recruitment process and must draw a boundary line to define the size of the network. The problem may also arise if the researcher is too stringent on the boundary issue. Strict boundary specification may cause omission of pertinent elements of the network. For example, membership network of local tourism authority may exclude non-tourism organizations (e.g., local chambers of commerce, SMEs, donor agencies, public hospitals, etc.) having significant contributions to the overall tourism outcome of the destination. Such strict delineation process may create confusion and can lead to misleading results (Albert & Barabási, 2002; Newman, 2003). Fortunately, several boundary specification approaches have been suggested in the wider literature of network studies. Every approach has its own set of advantages and disadvantages. Interested readers may wish to review Laumann et al. (1989), Marsden (1990), and Newman (2003) for further reading.

Another limitation of the network study is the time, cost and difficulties to access network data. As discussed before, collecting network data is not a random process as actors of the network members are not independent unit of analysis. Therefore, in many instances, network researchers have to seek information from the respondents that are difficult to access or not willing to participate in the research. For example, an external event management firm may organize a single annual event in a destination and works with a large number of local tourism stakeholders during the event. Realizing the economic benefit of the event, a large number of actors (stakeholders) may indicate a relationship with the event management firm. In this case, the network researcher is required to include the event management firm within the destination network and may even have to find the event management firm, or in extreme case, have to wait for the event to take place in the next year! Again, depending on the characteristics of the tourism context, the network researcher may have to include more than one network and multiple tourism elements ranging from individual actor perspectives to a large number of aggregated relationships. For example, a simple tourism network study may include 50 actors (accommodation, transportation, attractions, etc.), five relational contents (acquaintanceship, money, information, etc.), and on an average ten relationships per actor. Studying this network means a total of 2500 ($50 \times 5 \times 10$) data points for analysis. Trying to conduct a longitudinal study with this simple network of 50, the researcher will add 2500 additional data points (or more) for every cycle of data collection, a daunting task. In addition to network data, if the network researcher is also interested in collecting actors attribute data and if there are ten attributes per actor, this will add another 500 (50×10) data points for the analysis. Dealing with this large number of data is difficult and at times network researchers are bound to compromise valuable actor to actor relational data due to resource and time constraints.

Finally, networks are defined by their actors and the connections among them. Here, the individual connections between two actors are aggregated to form the network. In other words, connections between the actors are the fundamental building blocks of a network. However, there may be many connections between two actors in a network. For example, tourism stakeholders exchange personnel, money, information, and form groups and alliances. Relations among two destinations may be characterized by numerous forms of culture, economic, and political exchange. However, if we consider how the relation between two actors may influence their behavior or provide each with opportunity and constraint, it may well be the case that not all of these ties matter. Among many of the possible relational contents, it is always difficult to identify the most appropriate or a single element of connection that can provide reasonable research validity and reliability for all the network actors. For instance, within a set of tourism stakeholders, the monetary relationship between an accommodation provider and transportation provider may be more significant than the information ties, and exchange of employees may not come into consideration as these two types of organizations usually require different type of human expertise. Whereas, the relationships between an accommodation provider and destination organization within the same network – the information ties are more meaningful than the monetary ties as they predominantly exchange information and knowledge. A reasonable solution to this problem may be to construct several layers of network containing one type of relationship in each layer (multilevel networking). Again, in such case, the problem is to decide how many network layers are appropriate to measure relationships across a set of actors and how these layers are going to overlap with one another. Moreover, a single relational attribute (e.g., money, information) may contain several sub-level measures such as strength of relations, direction of relations, frequency of relations, and so on. Therefore, despite the core element of network analysis, it is always difficult to define relationship(s) as it contains a wide range of hidden issues such as form, measures, type, reliability, and validity.

FUTURE DEVELOPMENT AND APPLICATION OF NETWORK ANALYSIS IN TOURISM RESEARCH

It is useful to build on what we know and do not know to highlight those areas where future researchers might most productively focus their efforts in tourism network analysis. Consistent with the themes of the literature review, we can identify two broad areas of tourism network research in the future: (1) network properties and processes and (2) network development and evolution.

Network Properties and Process

Fundamentally, network analysis can be seen as a process that is used to collect and analyse relational data. In network research, the presence and nature of relationships among the actors is the focus (Knoke and Kuklinski, 1991) and the behavior of actors is seen as a function of their relationship within a network (Mizruchi and Marquis, 2006). In essence and as noted earlier, any network research is based on three contextual grounds: (1) actor(s) of the network, (2) content of relationship, and (3) form of relationships. Even though these three contextual grounds are the ingredients of any fundamental network research setting, tourism network research, in many instances, has tended to neglect these issues. Complete research design, defining and validating actors, contents and forms of relationship, is sparse in the literature reviewed. As a consequence, there is a relative dearth of work on empirically informed explanation of the network settings used to examine tourism issues. It is therefore suggested that a systematic research design to study tourism networks is essential and should be further explored, developed, and utilized.

Network analysis seeks to model the structure of relationships, focusing in particular on the nature and pattern of relationships between network elements (Wasserman and Faust, 1994). Based on this fundamental concept, the utility and implication of network structure is widely discussed in the tourism network literature. Indeed, it is clear from the literature that structural analysis on tourism networks has the ability to inform a wide range of tourism issues and research agenda such as policy development and implementation, knowledge management, destination governance (for a review, see Scott et al., 2008). Nonetheless, what is less clear is how to capture the nature and pattern of relationships in quantitative terms that mimics the effects of relationships in tourism. Using thick description in network analysis is manageable in case of small networks (e.g., network of less than 25 to 40 actors). However, with a larger network (e.g., more than 100 actors), it becomes increasingly difficult to manage. For example, let us compare two networks having 5 and 50 actors, respectively. The network with 5 actors can have a maximum of $20 \, (5 \times (5 - 1))$ possible links. In contrast, the larger network with 50 members can have a maximum of $2450 \, (50 \times (50 - 1))$ links. Similarly, a network with 100 actors can have a maximum of $9900 \, (100 \times (100 - 1))$ links, and a network with 1000 actors can have a maximum of $999\,000 \, (1000 \times (1000 - 1))$ links, and so on. Scary – but very few of the tourism networks in reality have less than 100 actors!

Many of the recent works on tourism networks have attempted to employ quantitative approaches and there is an emerging trend to utilize quantitative analysis to understand tourism networks. For example, in the literature review, 14 of the 18 quantitative studies using network analysis in tourism have appeared since 2008 (see Table 25.2). This is a welcome change. However, despite the strong methodological foundation, the majority of the quantitative approaches reviewed have paid very little or no attention to descriptive network analysis. Although there is hardly any serious alternative to quantitative methods for studying large-scale networks, additional insights into the structure and content of relationships, their development over time, the initial conditions at the formation stage of the network, and changing contexts could be gained by the additional use of qualitative methodologies such as narrative interviews, case study and participant observation. Nevertheless, from the literature review, it can be argued that there is a generalized tendency of the tourism network researcher to utilize only one of the approaches rather than using both. Quantitative and qualitative approaches in network studies might complement each other and can deliver a number of important insights which can be used to analyse tourism networks in the future.

Tourism outcomes can be conceptualized as aggregated activities of several individual stakeholders directly and indirectly related to the tourism industry. On this perspective, network study is an ideal research avenue for tourism research as it has the ability to represent and analyse the aggregated view of links and connections. Indeed, the concepts and techniques of network analysis can be used as a metaphor to represent the tourism industry both theoretically and practically. For example, any tourism stakeholder can be represented by a node and several forms and types of relationships of that stakeholder with others can be represented by links. The total combination of the nodes and links then can be represented by a network and analysed by using network tools and techniques. However, compared to the wider network literature, to date, a small portion of the network tools and techniques is discussed and utilized in the tourism network research. Despite all we know at this point regarding certain aspects of tourism network research, there are many perspectives that have not been adequately addressed in tourism network studies. Some important but under addressed research avenues for future tourism network research can be stated as:

1. Overlapping and cross examining actors' relational data (e.g., friendship, monetary, information, power, influence, etc.) and attribute data (e.g., occupation, age, size, economic condition, etc.).
2. Integrating, overlapping and cross examining multiple content of relationships such as friendship, money and resource exchange, information and knowledge sharing, flow of tourists, etc.
3. Examining correlation between several content and form of relationship such as how the presence of one relationship (e.g., friendship) influences the presence (or absence) of another relationship (e.g., information exchange).
4. Utilization of valued and directional data. For example, relationships can be measured in ordinal scale starting from very strong relationship to very weak relationship or no relationship; a relationship can also be directional by indicating who reports to (or does not report) to whom, etc.
5. Examining affiliation network effects such as how the choices of individual tourism actors to join a specific group, community, and/or activity may affect the choices of the individual actors.

Finally, the literature review of this chapter indicates that the influence of an individual organization on the whole network (e.g., influence of the state tourism organization on a specific tourism region) and vice versa (e.g., influence of the accommodation association on a small bed and breakfast hotel) are rarely examined and discussed in the tourism literature (see Table 25.2, 10 out of 73). The author believes that it is a potential ground of future network research in tourism.

Network Development and Evolution

A major theme for future research direction is that of network development and evolution. Although there has been considerable discussion on tourism network development (e.g., destination governance by Pavlovich (2003, 2008), evolution of tourism policy networks by Dredge (2006b), Pforr (2004, 2006), there has been scant discussion on the process of tourism network development, such as how network structures evolve over time and how or if these multilateral relationships are managed. The studies of tourism network development, evolution and governance, have suggested a number of directions for the study of networks: How do networks evolve from early birth to maturity and beyond? Does evolution occur in predictable ways, either in specific evolutionary stages or based on environmental conditions and internal pressures and changes? Are there critical pre-network activities (e.g., presence of a strong relationship between the early stakeholders) and structures that predict successful network evolution? Do networks continually shift and evolve in significant ways, or does network stability emerge at some point as an important factor for explaining network success? How does geography and climate change influence the evolution of network? To what extent can a whole network be stable (or dynamic) despite significant changes at the cluster or actor level or adoption of technology? What, then, is the impact of network structural characteristics on its development?

One of the main ways in which all forms of network research have changed during recent years is that longitudinal research has become much more prevalent, opening the way to in-depth consideration of network development (Provan et al., 2007). However, there is only a limited amount of such studies found in the literature review (Pavlovich, 2001, 2003, 2008; Dredge 2006a, b). Moreover, the majority of the longitudinal studies in tourism networks are limited to a single network. Whereas, longitudinal studies with multiple (more than one networks among the same group of actors) network approach is yet an untouched research avenue in tourism network research.

CONCLUSION

The chapter has provided an overview of studies of tourism networks, reviewing those empirical studies carried out during the past 10 years. In contrast to the abundant tourism research, especially with a focus on tourism collaboration, cooperation, alliance, and inter-organizational relationships, network research is still of a manageable size for a review chapter like this. On the more critical side, research on tourism networks has, so far, left many important questions unanswered. Apart from giving an overview of empirical studies of tourism networks, another aim of this chapter has been to raise such important questions, especially in regard to network properties and processes, network development and evolution, and network methodology in tourism.

Despite all the efforts the author has made to present a complete review of tourism network research, the study has clear limitations. Admittedly, the search procedure used was somewhat subjective, so that some studies that might be considered to be important in the topic area may not have been included. The search process was narrowly focused but serves to point out the relative dearth of empirical literature on the topic. Nevertheless, the limited set of empirical works were investigated in a way that should provide useful insights for future researchers choosing to focus on tourism networks or to include this important analytical approach in even more in-depth network implications.

REFERENCES

Albert, R. and A.L. Barabási (2002), 'Statistical mechanics of complex networks', *Review of Modern Physics*, **74**, 47–97.
Alonso, A.D. (2010), 'Importance of relationships among small accommodation operations around the city of Perth', *Tourism and Hospitality Research*, **10**, 14–24.
Anderson, W. (2009), 'Promoting ecotourism through networks: case studies in the Balearic Islands', *Journal of Ecotourism*, **8**, 51–69.
Andersson, M. and P. Ekman (2009), 'Ambassador networks and place branding', *Journal of Place Management and Development*, **2**, 41–51.
Atkinson, M.M. and W.D. Coleman (1992), 'Policy networks, policy communities and the problems of governance', *Governance*, **5**, 154–180.
Baggio, R. (2006), 'Complex systems, information technologies and tourism:a network point of view', *Information Technology and Tourism*, **8**, 15–29.
Baggio, R. (2007), 'The web graph of a tourism system', *Physica A*, **379**, 727–734.
Baggio, R. (2011), 'Collaboration and cooperation in a tourism destination: a network science approach', *Current Issues in Tourism*, **14**, 183–189.
Baggio, R. and M. Antonioli Corigliano (2009), 'On the importance of hyperlinks: a network science approach', *Information and Communication Technologies in Tourism*, 2009, 309–318.
Baggio, R. and C. Cooper (2010), 'Knowledge transfer in a tourims destination: the effect of a network structure', *The Service Industries Journal*, **30**, 1757–1772.
Baggio, R., N. Scott and C. Cooper (2010a), 'Improving tourism destination governance: a complexity science approach', *Tourism Review*, **65**, 51–60.
Baggio, R., N. Scott and C. Cooper (2010b), 'Network science: a review focused on tourism', *Annals of Tourism Research*, **37**, 802–827.
Beaumonta, N. and D. Dredge (2009), 'Local tourism governance: a comparison of three network approaches', *Journal of Sustainable Tourism*, **18**, 7–28.
Beesley, L. (2004), 'Multi-level complexity in the management of knowledge networks', *Journal of Knowledge Management*, **8**, 71–100.
Beesley, L. (2005), 'The management of emotion in collaborative tourism research settings', *Tourism Management*, **26**, 261–275.
Bhat, S.S. and S. Milne (2008), 'Network effects on cooperation in destination website development', *Tourism Management*, 1131–1140.
Blau, P.M. (1964), *Exchange and Power in Social Life*, New York: Wiley.
Borgatti, S.P. and P.C. Foster (2003), 'The network paradigm in organisational research: a review and typology', *Jounrnal of Management*, **29**, 991–1013.
Brás, J.M., C. Costa, D. Buhalis, N. Scott and E. Laws (2010), 'Network analysis and wine routes: the case of the Bairrada Wine Route', *Service Industries Journal*, **30**, 1621–1641.
Braun, P. (2003), 'Regional tourism networks: the nexus between ICT diffusion and change in Australia', *Information Technology and Tourism*, **6**, 231–243.
Burt, R.S. (1987), 'Social contagion and innovation: cohesion versus structural equivalence', *American Journal of Sociology*, **92**, 1287–1335.
Camprubí, R., J. Guia and J. Comas (2008), 'Destination networks and induced tourism image', *Tourism Review*, **63**, 47–58.

Cooper, C. (2006), 'Knowledge management and tourism', *Annals of Tourism Research*, **33**, 47–64.

Cooper, C. and M. Hall (2008), *Contemporary Tourism: An International Approach*, Amsterdam: Elsevier.

Cooper, C., N. Scott and R. Baggio (2009), 'Network position and perception of destination stakeholder importance', *Anatolia*, **20**, 33–45.

Crotts, J., A. Aziz and A. Rashid (1998), 'Antecedents of supplier's commitment to wholesale buyers in the international travel trade', *Tourism Management*, **19**, 127–134.

da Fontoura Costa, L. and R. Baggio (2009), 'The web of connections between tourism companies: structure and dynamics', *Physica A: Statistical Mechanics and its Applications*, **388**, 4286–4296.

Dredge, D. (2006a), 'Networks, conflict and collaborative communities', *Journal of Sustainable Tourism*, **14**, 562–581.

Dredge, D. (2006b), 'Policy networks and the local organisation of tourism', *Tourism Management*, **27**, 269–280.

Erkuş-Öztürk, H. (2009), 'The role of cluster types and firm size in designing the level of network relations: the experience of the Antalya tourism region', *Tourism Management*, **30**, 589–597.

Erkuş-Öztürk, H. (2010), 'The significance of networking and company size in the level of creativeness of tourism companies: Antalya case', *European Planning Studies*, **18**, 1247–1266.

Fadeeva, Z. (2004), 'Translation of sustainability ideas in tourism networks: some roles of cross-sectoral networks in change towards sustainable development', *Journal of Cleaner Production*, **13**, 175–189.

Faulkner, D.O. and M. De Rond (2000), 'Perspectives on cooperative strategy', *Cooperative Strategy: Economic, Business, and Organizational Issues*, **1**.

Fyrberg, A. and R. Jüriado (2009), 'What about interaction? Networks and brands as integrators within service-dominant logic', *Journal of Service Management*, **20**, 420–432.

Galaskiewicz, J. (2007), 'Has a network theory of organizational behaviour lived up to its promises?', *Management and Organization Review*, **3**, 1–18.

Gibson, L., P.A. Lynch and A. Morrison (2005), 'The local destination tourism network: development issues', *Tourism Planning & Development*, **2**, 87–99.

Granovetter, M. (1985), 'Economic action and social structure: the problem of embeddedness', *American Journal of Sociology*, **91**, 481–510.

Halme, M. (2001), 'Learning for sustainable development in tourism networks', *Business Strategy and the Environment*, **10**, 100–114.

Hede, A.-M. and R. Stokes (2009), 'Network analysis of tourism events: an approach to improve marketing practices for sustainable tourism', *Journal of Travel & Tourism Marketing*, **26**, 656–669.

Henriksen, P.F. and H. Halkier (2009), 'From local promotion towards regional tourism policies: knowledge processes and actor networks in North Jutland, Denmark', *European Planning Studies*, **17**, 1445–1462.

Homans, G.C. (1958), 'Social behaviour as exchange', *American Journal of Sociology*, **63**, 597–606.

Homans, G.C. (1974), *Theories and Paradigms in Contemporary Sociology*, Itasca, IL: F.E. Peacock Publishers.

Iacobucci, D. (1996), *Networks in Marketing*, Thousand Oaks, CA: Sage Publications.

Jarillo, J.C. (1988), 'On strategic networks', *Strategic Management Journal*, **9**, 31–41.

Kelliher, F., A. Foley and A. Frampton (2009), 'Facilitating small firm learning networks in the Irish tourism sector', *Tourism and Hospitality Research*, **9**, 80–95.

Kilduff, M. and W. Tsai (2003), *Social Networks and Organisations*, London: Sage Publications.

Knoke, D. and J.H. Kuklinski (1991), 'Network analysis: basic concepts', in G. Thompson, J. Frances, R. Levacic and J. Mitchel (eds), *Markets, Hierarchies and Networks*, Lodon: Sage Publications, pp. 173–182.

Laumann, E.O., P.V. Marsden and D. Prensky (1989), 'The boundary specification problem in network analysis', in L.C. Freeman, D.R. White and K.A. Romney (eds), *Research Methods in Social Network Analysis*, Fairfax, VA: George Mason University Press.

Leiper, N. (1989), 'Tourism and tourism system', Vol. Occasional Paper No. 1, Palmerston North Massey University.

Leiper, N. (2000), 'An emerging discipline', *Annals of Tourism Research*, **27**, 805–809.

Lemmetyinen, A. (2009), 'The coordination of cooperation in strategic business networks: the Cruise Baltic Case', *Scandinavian Journal of Hospitality and Tourism*, **9**, 366–386.

Lemmetyinen, A. and F.M. Go (2009), 'The key capabilities required for managing tourism business networks', *Tourism Management*, **30**, 31–40.

Lemmetyinen, A. and F.M. Go (2010a), 'Building a brand identity in a network of Cruise Baltic's destinations: a multi-authoring approach', *Journal of Brand Management*, **17**, 519–531.

Lemmetyinen, A. and F.M. Go (2010b), 'The role of the DMO in creating value in EU-funded tourism projects', *Scandinavian Journal of Hospitality and Tourism*, **10**, 129–152.

Levin, S. and P.E. White (1961), 'Exchange as a conceptual framework for the study of interorganisational relationships', *Administrative Science Quarterly*, **5**, 583–601.

Mackellar, J. (2006), 'An integrated view of innovation emerging from a regional festival', *International Journal of Event Management Research*, **2**, 37–48.

Mariussen, A., R. Daniele, D. Bowie, N. Scott and E. Laws (2010), 'Unintended consequences in the evolution of affiliate marketing networks: a complexity approach', *Service Industries Journal*, **30**, 1707–1722.

Marsden, P.V. (1990), 'Network data and measurement', *Annual Review of Sociology*, **16**, 435–463.

McLeod, M.T., D.R. Vaughan and J. Edwards (2010), 'Knowledge networks in the tourism sector of the Bournemouth, Poole, and Christchurch conurbation: preliminary analysis', *The Service Industries Journal*, **30**, 1651–1667.

Miguéns, J. and A. Corfu (2008), 'e-Destination structure: a network analysis approach', *Information and Communication Technologies in Tourism 2008*, 580–591.

Miller, W.B. (1958), 'Inter-institutional conflict as a major impediment to delinquency prevention', *Human Organisation*, **17**, 20–23.

Mitchell, J.C. (1969), 'The concept and use of social networks', in J.C. Mitchell (ed.), *Social Network in Urban Situations*, Manchester: University of Manchester Press, pp. 1–50.

Mizruchi, M.S. and C. Marquis (2006), 'Egocentric, sociometric, or dyadic? Indentifying the appropriate level of analysis in the study of organisational networks', *Social Networks*, **28**, 187–208.

Monge, P.R. and N.S. Contractor (2003), *Theories of Communication Networks*, Oxford: Oxford University Press.

Morrison, A., P. Lynch and N. Johns (2004), 'International tourism network', *International Journal of Contemporary Hospitality Management*, **16**, 197–202.

Moscardo, G., B. McCarthy, L. Murphy and P. Pearce (2009), 'The importance of networks in special interest tourism: case studies of music tourism in Australia', *International Journal of Tourism Policy*, **2**, 5–23.

Nash, R. (2006), 'Casual network methodology: tourism research application', *Annals of Tourism Research*, **33**, 918–938.

Newman, M.E.J. (2003), 'The structure and function of complex networks', *SIAM Review*, **45**, 167–256.

Nordin, S. and B. Svensson (2007), 'Innovative destination governance: the Swedish ski resort of Are', *The International Journal of Entrepreneurship and Innovation*, **8**, 53–66.

Novelli, M., B. Schmitz and T. Spencer (2006), 'Networks, clusters and innovation in tourism: a UK experience', *Tourism Management*, **27**, 1141–1152.

Pavlovich, K. (2001), 'The twin landscapes of Waitomo: tourism network and sustainability through the landscape group', *Journal of Sustainable Tourism*, **9**, 491–504.

Pavlovich, K. (2002), 'Pyramids, pubs, and pizzas: an interpretation of tourism network structures', *Tourism Culture and Communication*, **4**, 41–48.

Pavlovich, K. (2003), 'The evoluation and transformation of a tourism destination network: the Waitomo Cave, New Zealand', *Toursim Management*, **2**, 203–216.

Pavlovich, K. (2008), 'Network governance and connectivity: a case study', in N. Scott, R. Baggio and C. Cooper (eds), *Network Analysis and Tourism – From Theory to Practice*, England: Channel View Publication.

Petrou, A., E.F. Pantziou, E. Dimara and D. Skuras (2007), 'Resources and activities complementarities: the role of business networks in the provision of integrated rural tourism', *Tourism Geographies*, **9**, 421–440.

Pforr, C. (2004), 'The "makers and shapers" of tourism policy in the Northern Territory of Australia: a policy network analysis of actors and their relational constellations', *Journal of Hospitality and Tourism Research*, **9**, 134–151.

Pforr, C. (2006), 'Tourism policy in the making an Australian network study', *Annals of Tourism Research*, **33**, 87–108.

Presenza, A. and M. Cipollina (2010) , 'Analysing tourism stakeholders networks', *Tourism Review*, **65**, 17–30.

Provan, K.G., A. Fish and J. Sydow (2007), 'Interorganisational networks at the network level: a review of the empirical literature on whole networks', *Journal of Management*, **33**, 479–516.

Pyo, S. (2010), 'Measuring tourism chain performance', *The Service Industries Journal*, **30**, 1669–1682.

Reid, W. (1964), 'Interagency coordination in delinquency prevention and control', *Social Service Review*, **38**, 418–428.

Reinl, L. and F. Kelliher (2010), 'Cooperative micro-firm strategies leveraging resources through learning networks', *Entrepreneurship and Innovation*, **11**, 141–150.

Romeiro, P. and C. Costa (2010), 'The potential of management networks in the innovation and competitiveness of rural tourism: a case study on the Valle del Jerte (Spain)', *Current Issues in Tourism*, **13**, 75–91.

Sainaghi, R. and R. Baggio (2011), 'Complex and chaotic tourism systems: towards a quantitative approach', *International Journal of Contemporary Hospitality Management*, **23**, 7–7.

Saxena, G. (2005), 'Relationships, networks and the learning regions: case evidence from the Peak District National Park', *Tourism Management*, **26** (2), 277–289.

Scott, J. (2000), *Social Network Analysis – a Handbook (2nd edn)*, London: Sage Publications.

Scott, N., C. Cooper and R. Baggio (2008), 'Destination networks: four Australian cases', *Annals of Tourism Research*, **35**, 169–188.

Sheehan, L., J.R.B. Ritchie and S. Hudson (2007), 'The destination promotion triad: understanding asymmetric stakeholder interdependencies among the city, hotels, and DMO', *Journal of Travel Research*, **46**, 64–74.

Shih, H.-Y. (2005), 'Network characteristics of drive tourism destinations: an application of network analysis in tourism', *Tourism Management*, **27**, 1029–1039.

Smith, S.L.J. (1988), 'Defining tourism a supply-side view', *Annals of Tourism Research*, **15**, 179–190.

Sorensen, F. (2007), 'The geographies of social networks and innovation in tourism', *Tourism Geographies*, **9**, 22–48.

Stokes, R. (2006), 'Network-based strategy making for events tourism', *European Journal of Marketing*, **40**, 682–695.

Thibaut, J. and H.H. Kelly (1959), *The Social Psychology of Groups*, New York: John Wiley.

Timur, S. and D. Getz (2008), 'A network perspective on managing stakeholders for sustainable urban tourism', *International Journal of Contemporary Hospitality Management*, **20**, 445–461.

Tinsley, R. and P. Lynch (2001), 'Small tourism business networks and destination development', *International Journal of Hospitality Management*, **20**, 367–378.

Tinsley, R. and P.A. Lynch (2007), 'Small business networking and tourism destination development: a comparative perspective', *The International Journal of Entrepreneurship and Innovation*, **8**, 15–27.

Tribe, J. (2010), 'Tribes, territories and networks in the tourism academy', *Annals of Tourism Research*, **37**, 7–33.

Tyler, D. and C. Dinan (2001), 'The role of interested groups in England's emerging tourism policy network', *Current Issues in Tourism*, **4**, 210–252.

Ward, R.A. (1964), *Operational Research in Local Government*, London: Allen and Unwin.

Wasserman, S. and K. Faust (1994), *Social Network Analysis*, New York: Cambridge University Press.

Wasserman, S. and J. Galaskiewicz (1994), *Advances in Social Network Analysis: Research in the Social and Behavioral Sciences*, Thousand Oaks, CA: Sage Publications, Inc.

Wegner, A., D. Lee and B. Weiler (2010), 'Important "ingredients" for successful tourism/protected area partnerships: partners' policy recommendations', *The Service Industries Journal*, **30**, 1643–1650.

Weidenfeld, A., R.W. Butler and A.M. Williams (2010), 'Clustering and compatibility between tourism attractions', *International Journal of Tourism Research*, **12**, 1–16.

Wellman, B. (1988), 'Structural analysis: from method and metaphor to theory and substance', in B. Wellman and S.D. Berkowitz (eds), *Social Structures: A Network Approach*, Cambridge: Cambridge University Press.

Wellman, B. and S.D. Berkowitz (1988), *Social Structures: A Network Approach*. Cambridge: Cambridge University Press.

Wesley, A. and C. Pforr (2010), 'The governance of coastal tourism: unravelling the layers of complexity at Smiths Beach, Western Australia', *Journal of Sustainable Tourism*, **18**, 773–792.

Wilkinson, I. and R. March (2009), 'Conceptual tools for evaluating tourism partnership', *Tourism Management*, **30**, 455–462.

Wray, M. (2009), 'Policy communities, networks and issue cycles in tourism destination systems', *Journal of Sustainable Tourism*, **17**, 673–690.

Xiao, H., M. Li and E.C.K. Lin (2011), 'Diffusion patterns and knowledge networks: an inductive analysis of intellectual connections in multidisciplinary tourism studies', *Journal of Travel & Tourism Marketing*, **28**, 405–422.

Zach, F. and P. Racherla (2011), 'Assessing the value of collaborations in tourism networks: a case study of Elkhart County, Indiana', *Journal of Travel & Tourism Marketing*, **28**, 97–110.

Zach, F., U. Gretzel and D.R. Fesenmaier (2008), 'Tourist activated networks: implications for dynamic packaging systems in tourism', *Information and Communication Technology in Tourism*, **6**, 198–208.

Ziene, M. and T. Hazel (2007), 'Webs of power: multiple ownership in tourism destinations', *Current Issues in Tourism*, **10**, 279–295.

Index